# The Struggle for the European Constitution

The European Union (EU) Constitution was one of the most important developments in the history of the EU, aiming to make the EU more transparent, relevant and accountable to the citizens of its member states. Current anxieties over the pace and direction of EU integration place this comprehensive study at the forefront of the EU governance debate.

O'Neill goes far beyond a simple account of the EU Constitution, focusing also on the response to the current crisis of confidence between the Union and its citizens and how those in power have responded to the challenge.

Making a substantial contribution to the literature on the EU, the book's key discussion points include:

- the political crisis behind the Constitution
- the power politics at work in the negotiations
- how the Constitution affects EU policymaking
- the impact on the citizens of the EU.

This is essential reading for all those wishing to understand the background to one of the key areas within European politics.

**Michael O'Neill** is Jean Monnet Professor in EU Politics at Nottingham Trent University.

# Routledge Advances in European Politics

# The Struggle for the European Constitution

## A past and future history

**Michael O'Neill**

Routledge
Taylor & Francis Group

LONDON AND NEW YORK

First published 2009 by Routledge
2 Park Square, Milton Park, Abingdon, Oxon, OX14 4RN

Simultaneously published in the USA and Canada
by Routledge
711 Third Avenue, New York, NY 10017

*Routledge is an imprint of the Taylor & Francis Group*
© 2009 Michael O'Neill

Typeset in Times New Roman by
Bookcraft, Stroud, Gloucestershire

*British Library Cataloguing in Publication Data*
A catalogue record for this book is available from the British Library

*Library of Congress Cataloging-in-Publication Data*
O'Neill, Michael, 1946 Nov. 23-
The struggle for the European constitution: a past and future history /
Michael O'Neill.
    p. cm. – (Routledge advances in European politics)
    1. Constitutional law—European Union countries.
    2. European Union—Constitution. 3. Treaty Establishing
    a Constitution for Europe (2004)
    I. Title. II. Series.
KJE4445.O54 2008
342.2402—dc22                                    2008025175

ISBN10: 0-415-37800-1 (hbk)
ISBN10: 0-203-88602-X (ebk)

ISBN13: 978-0-415-37800-0 (hbk)
ISBN13: 978-0-203-88602-1 (ebk)

To the memory of my father, James O'Neill 1918–2004

The tragic events we have lived through ... have perhaps made us wiser. But men pass on and others take their place. We will not be able to hand on our personal experience. It will die with us. What we can hand on are institutions. ... Institutions, adequately structured, can accumulate and transmit the wisdom of successive generations.

Jean Monnet

# Contents

**PART 3**
**The politics of ratification**                                329

# Tables

# Acknowledgements

Many obligations are accumulated in the business of writing: the forbearance of friends and loved ones; the advice tendered by colleagues; the tolerance and support of editors; and so on. The period of gestation for the present book has been an unduly long one, though in some measure not entirely through this author's fault. The business of constitutionalising the European Union has proved to be protracted, and no less difficult an endeavour. What began as a Convention to review problematic governance and became in time an Intergovernmental Conference did indeed deliver a Constitutional Treaty signed up to by the EU's then 15 member states, and accepted by its soon-to-be additional member states. But in the time-honoured fashion of democratic politics a process that was launched partly with citizens in mind, to make the EU more 'user friendly', was in the end hoist with its own petard as those same citizens, or at least those in the member states where the 'man in the street' was asked for his opinion on these great matters, declined to endorse what was colloquially known by then as the 'European Constitution'.

What had begun for this writer as a seemingly straightforward narrative of ex post facto treaty making became an altogether more complicated and no less problematic discussion of why that historic outcome was knocked back by 'the people'. This turn of events delayed matters more than somewhat, and as the aftermath of this event turned into a period of 'reflection' by the Union's political leaders, always the first instinct of politicians when events do not turn out as expected and they know not what to do next, so the period for writing this book and no less the research required to accommodate these unanticipated events expanded beyond the original deadline. This in turn put additional pressure on all those relationships outlined above that envelop any researcher and shape the circumstances in which he works. And for that reason I ask indulgence from all concerned and hope that they will think the eventual outcome worth the wait.

I want to make special mention here of Cristina Rotar, who has been very supportive of me during these long months of research and writing, and whose assistance in the technical preparation of the manuscript has been invaluable. Many of the ideas discussed in the book have figured in seminar and conference presentations, notably in my continuing work as a visiting professor in the Faculty of European Studies at the Babes-Bolyai University in Cluj-Napoca, Romania, where I am particularly appreciative of the many kindnesses of Professor Nicolae

Paun; and in my work as a founder member of the Centre for Advanced European Studies and Research in the University of Novi Sad, Serbia, where Professor Fuada Stanković has been a most generous and stimulating host. I am grateful too to my good friend, Professor Reinhard Meyers, of the Institut Für Politik-wissenschaft in the West Fälische Universität Münster, who read an early draft of this book and made helpful and perceptive comments. Terry Hanstock of the Nottingham Trent University Boots Library has provided his customary outstanding support, finding for me elusive publications and chasing up obscure references. Nothing I asked of him was too much trouble, or if it was he did not complain. Without his help I would not have been able to complete this work. I must mention, too, a personal debt. My father, James O'Neill, passed away while this book was being written. He was always my steadfast support during the long apprenticeship years, supportive, gently encouraging and wise in his advice. To lose him was a blow, and I miss his sweet-natured presence in my life. But in a way this book will always be associated with his memory because of the timing of his passing. There are many other people, too, colleagues in Nottingham and further afield, whose comments, advice and encouragement have greatly contributed to the final outcome, not least those who reside in that city once aptly described by Joseph Conrad as a 'whited sepulchre, but otherwise known as Brussels. Needless to say, any remaining shortcomings are entirely the fault of the author.

# Prologue

In the decade or so since the Maastricht Treaty was enacted the European Union (EU) has faced unprecedented challenges. The scope of its governance has steadily increased, yet at the political level there is a growing public perception about democracy deficits, concern about the effectiveness of its institutions, the remoteness and disconnection between these same institutions and the citizens in whose name they function. And disquiet, too, about the complexity of its decision-making procedures. These are serious matters for the EU in as much as they call into question both the efficiency and legitimacy of EU governance. The political class can no longer rely on the implicit 'performance legitimacy', the notion that things somehow work well enough that once permitted political leaders and functionaries to shape Community agendas, to manage its affairs, making policy bargains beyond public scrutiny or censure, untroubled either by demands for greater accountability or by any concerted demand for popular involvement or participation in the Union's affairs.

These shortcomings became apparent throughout the 1990s, and more so after the sudden collapse of Soviet domination in Eastern/Central Europe prompted the EU to undertake an ambitious enlargement of its membership from 15 to 27 states and possibly more. European construction was always a project of mixed purposes. On the one hand, it was underpinned by idealism, a reaction to the horrors of rampant xenophobia in the continent that led to unspeakable horrors perpetrated in the name of nationalism, and culminating in the barbarism of the Second World War; and on the other hand, there was pragmatism rooted in the recognition of the limitations of the nation-state as the most reliable medium for post-war economic reconstruction as Europe's political leaders sought to restore Europe's structural fabric after unprecedented destruction.

Meanwhile, the public were not directly engaged with European construction. This was after all more a technocratic project than a democratic one, with people at large simply expected to support the endeavours of governments, in effect to be grateful for the material benefits that accrued from European co-operation as trade recovered, markets expanded, prosperity grew and political stability became the norm in the continent that had invented the idea of democracy but whose pre-war experience of politics had belied that progressive legacy. Public indifference to, indeed exclusion from, the process of Community building – and no doubt the two conditions are closely connected – has characterised the building of the post-war European project. Indeed, it was an unspoken assumption of many of the project's principal architects that such arcane, complicated and mostly technical matters were better left to those with the expertise to deal with them. If European construction has acquired public approval along the way, this is more by default than by design, a consequence of cumulate economic success and long years of peace in a continent where such benefits had been experienced unevenly and spasmodically during the turbulent decades of the nineteenth and early twentieth centuries.

The public's remoteness from the project to build a transnational Community is most clearly manifested in dismal turn-out figures in successive elections to the European Parliament, and in low levels of public knowledge as recorded in many opinion surveys about the Community's institutional procedures, the way European governance actually works. In recent years indifference to these matters has been overtaken by public disquiet, and even incipient hostility over what is being done by the politicians in their name. There is certainly widespread unease about the pace and the direction of European integration, a clamour for reform that those who manage affairs could hardly ignore. The most recent attempt to overhaul EU governance, indeed to supposedly constitutionalise the European project is in part a response to these anxieties. The reasons for this crisis of confidence between the Union and its citizens, and how and with what effect the political class has responded to it is the principal focus of this book.

Reform does not come easily to the EU. The nature of the Union's polity, its very contestedness as a project caught between intergovernmental and supranational preferences, the lack of a singular constitutional tradition amongst its member states or of a clear constitutional narrative as between its institutional actors and the member states about how EU governance should operate, and not least an ongoing dispute between its principal actors about the meaning of European integration, its final destination or *finalité*, all serve to add to the difficulties of enacting reform. The need to reconcile quite different views about the purpose of the European project, to balance the competing interests of the common institutions and the member states, offsetting differences between national interests, the policy priorities and preferences of the member states makes trade-offs and suboptimal bargains the normal way of things, with the maintenance of equilibrium between these competing forces more of a priority, and certainly easier to bring about, than a wholesale constitutional refit.

The uneven history of treaty reform since the founding treaties were signed in 1957 might indicate that the European Community/Union is structurally resistant to the degree of far-reaching reform required if it is to adjust to the immense challenges of enlargement and globalisation. Altogether new pressures, both within and beyond the boundaries of the Union, have overtaken, if not yet overwhelmed, a polity whose institutional architecture was designed more than half a century ago for the relatively modest purpose of building and regulating a common market of only six founder members. Successive and increasingly frequent intergovernmental conferences (IGCs) have failed to resolve abiding problems with the EC/EU's institutions, as challenges to the efficacy and latterly to the legitimacy of EU governance have arisen, both from within and further afield.

The usual reform procedure, setting up an intergovernmental conference to review the options as the governments of the member states see them, has proved to be inadequate for the task at hand: too narrow as to their personnel, the mostly governmental membership who preside over these exclusive events, and unrepresentative of the institutional interests and no less of the Union's cultural and social fabric. Those trade-offs, the sub-optimal bargains that are the usual outcome of such narrowly based and insular negotiations, were increasingly found wanting during the 1990s as a means for responding to pressing problems, the need to adjust – and expeditiously – to multiple challenges. Not least, because these forums avoided for the most part the most controversial issues, preferring instead to tinker with what have proved to be deep-seated problems with EU governance, above all avoiding reforms that would connect this polity with, and make it more responsive to the concerns and aspirations of its citizens.

Over time the Union's political class did respond to these shortcomings, or at least they showed greater willingness to face up to the fact that if a Union of 'only' 15 states was struggling to manage its affairs, how much more difficult it would be to ensure effective and, no less urgent in an age where democracy and rights have acquired added value, legitimate governance in an enlarged Union of 27 or more member states. The prospect of the unprecedented enlargement scheduled for 2004 significantly raised the profile of this polity problem, giving urgency not only to its design as governance but also to persistent deficits in democracy and legitimacy by which any polity claiming to be in touch with its people is measured. The public mood played its part, confirming a sense of disconnection between the political class, the EU's contemporary 'princes' and people at large. The decision of the Union's leaders at the Laeken European Council (December 2001) to launch a Convention on the Future of Europe to deliberate on these very matters, and prospectively to recommend measures for far-reaching constitutional reform, was the Union's timely response to what some commentators chose to see as nothing less than a crisis in public confidence.

A review of how these deliberations on constitutional change took place and their outcome reveals much about the limits and the prospects both for governance and for democratic politics at the European level. How the EU addressed, or rather has failed to address, some of the critical matters it faces at a time of prodigious change contributes much to our understanding of the complex dynamics of European integration, the singularity of its politics, the arcane nature and peculiarities of its governance. Not least, it reveals where power actually lies in this heterarchical and non-standard polity, the 'who governs' and how questions posed by political scientists as the ultimate gauge of power and democracy, and with what consequences for 'princes' and publics alike. In short, to review the processes for reforming this recondite polity tells us much about the distribution of public power in what is the most advanced example to date of transnational and multi-level governance in the international system. In an evolving world order where the Westphalian nation-state remains as the norm, the conventional model for governance, the workings of EU governance are to say the least novel, and reveal much to the student of political science about the nature and logics of governance in the global age. In this sense, the study of the EU polity is at the leading edge of research into questions first raised by Aristotle and his contemporaries in the Greek academy some three millennia ago. As such, the EU is a fascinating laboratory for students of contemporary governance.

This is a bold claim but hardly an exaggerated one. Even convinced advocates of the realist or neo-realist narratives of the 'great game' that is international politics now tend to concede that something is indeed underway in the fabric of contemporary governance, that things are changing, important shifts taking place in the architecture and the culture, the practice and the normative underpinnings of governance. The study of the struggle for a European Constitution, the processes, dilemmas and challenges posed by international change, the ever-more complex interface between domestic and international politics yields important insights, not merely into the way the EU works but also into the nature of modern statehood, and likewise the processes that are bringing about the transformation of its governance and politics.

## Part 1: why a European Constitution?

The study of Europe's recent attempt to write a constitution begins with a review of the historical, institutional and theoretical issues that inform this endeavour: the problematic nature of the EU polity, its experience thus far of implicit and incremental rather than explicit and wholesale constitutionalisation, the processes by which reform occurs, and the theoretic narratives that accompany and attempt to explain the endeavour. There is discussion, too, of the experience of constitutionalism elsewhere in order to suggest some benchmarks and useful comparators for enacting and possibly for predicting the likely outcomes for EU constitutionalism.

Chapter 1, 'A problematic polity', is a broad overview of the difficulties of effecting efficient decision-making in a polity based on different, indeed competing ideas about the very purpose and logics of European integration. These problems have been met to date with a less than purposive attempt at wholesale, never mind cogent constitutional reform. Even when severe pressures on the institutions and manifest problems with decision-making procedures instigated the latest endeavour to reform the EU polity, the outcome in the shape of the Constitutional Treaty was much less a radical conclusion to a purportedly constitutional overhaul than some commentators had anticipated, not least those with federalist inclinations who have long advocated a European Constitution.

In the event, it amounted to a less than comprehensive overhaul of EU governance than this constitutional lobby preferred, a modest outcome and one somewhat tamely described by some political leaders as merely a 'tidying up' of existing procedures. To a degree the insistence from some quarters that the outcome of the Convention's deliberations over some 18 months is more a treaty than a constitution clearly shows the constraints on far-reaching reform in this unique polity. There has long been, and there remains, resistance from some parts of European political opinion to the very idea of a constitution for what is, after all, still essentially a confederation of sovereign states. The idea of constitutionalising what these critics see as 'merely' an elaborate international regime has provoked a lively debate at every level, from politicians to the academy and the mass media. Yet the nomenclature of constitutionalism is, nevertheless, appropriate for describing the endeavour launched by the Laeken Council in 2001, when the EU's political leaders acknowledged (SN300/1/ 01 REV1 Annexe I) that the Union is indeed at a crossroads in its political development, and that as a consequence needs to become 'more democratic, more transparent and more efficient'.

Chapter 2, 'The idea of a European Constitution', reviews the theoretic debate about the relevance of constitutionalism for this singular polity. The European Court of Justice (ECJ) has long been a central actor in this process, and we discuss here the Court's important contribution to the implicit, or as some critics see it the covert, constitutionalisation of the European Union, precisely because its landmark judgements have challenged national discretion, redefining the meaning and calling into question the boundaries of national sovereignty. As a consequence, these judicial interventions have provoked a reaction from some national constitutional authorities, and from some member states. The term 'constitutionalism' has certainly acquired increased political resonance as a direct consequence of judicial intervention in what is clearly the realm of politics, even if the idea has hardly yet become common political currency outside the hermetic world of the EU's insiders, those who from the outset have set the pace and determined the trajectory of European integration. The interface between the judicial and political domains has nevertheless framed the EU's distinctive constitutional tradition, setting limits to, but also fuelling the aspiration in some quarters for a formal EU constitutional order.

For this very reason the EC/EU has thus far had a history of incremental constitutionalisation, what might almost be described as constitutionalisation by stealth, long before its political leaders launched their recent initiative to move beyond 'mere' treaty amendment and to attempt to make a European Constitution. The routine procedure for steering change has been a miscellany of conventional diplomacy and altogether more novel ways of transacting business between states that reflects the ambivalent nature of the European project. Periodic changes in the Community's treaty base, negotiations and bargaining between the member states in intergovernmental conferences to reform the founding treaties was supplemented by a more covert but no less deliberate process whereby the European Court of Justice sought to assume the role of judicial review, to operate as the Community's supreme court *de facto*.

The most recent phase of European constitutional endeavour that is the principal focus of this book is hardly then a unique experience, though it is in many ways markedly different from what has gone before. And it may turn out to be rather more of a defining moment than either the usual intergovernmental routine or the Court's covert constitutionalism, though the recent decision to revert to an IGC as a way out of the impasse on the Constitution does not offer any immediate prospect on that score. The future is always hard to predict, and more so where the

EU is concerned. Reflecting on the ultimate destiny of constitutional endeavour here, trying to evaluate its significance for the Union's constitutional development, indeed its eventual political destination, is precarious to say the least, in part because the impasse that settled on affairs in the aftermath of failed referendums in France and the Netherlands showed a distinct lack of leadership, a failure of political imagination on the part of the politicians.

It may be easier to assess the longer-term consequences of recent developments for the way the EU goes about its constitutional business once the dust raised by the unanticipated consequences of the 'no' votes in the ratification referendums in two leading and founder member states has settled, and the political class and public alike have had more time to reflect on the consequences, both the achievements and the shortcomings of the recent endeavour, than they allowed themselves before returning to their former ways of going about reform. At the time of writing these same leaders, or in some cases new occupants of high office but with much the same elitist instincts as their predecessors, have decided that the best way out of the crisis that arose over the Constitution is simply to rewind, to go back to the tried and tested formula, taking back matters exclusively into their own hands. In effect, to jettison the very idea of constitutionalising the Union. The IGC mandate agreed in Brussels in June 2007 means just that, as if reverting 'back to what we know best' will somehow resolve the deep-seated problems that came to light during these difficult months. The final conclusions of the German presidency boldly proclaimed that: 'The constitutional concept, which consisted in repealing all existing Treaties and replacing them with a single text called "Constitution", is abandoned.'

It may well be reassuring for politicians to argue this way, but the genie of popular disquiet once escaped from confinement as it did during the various ratification campaigns may not be so easy to recapture. The apparent determination of the politicians to push ahead with selective reforms, many of them included in the failed Constitution and in the same old way, without consulting a public disconcerted by the spectacle of remote governance may be at best a short-term solution. Whether this 'solution' will convince, let alone reassure a public sufficiently discomfited by remote politicians, as was apparent during many of the national ratification campaigns, remains to be seen. There are undoubtedly interesting times ahead for the European Union, and the final outcome of the endeavour to reform its governance is as hard to predict as it ever was. We shall return to this important question in the concluding chapters of this book.

What is beyond dispute is the fact that this latest stage in the EU's constitutional development has ignited a lively debate about the prospects for constitutionalising a polity that, even in the current stage of its development, and with institutions that reflect some of the functions traditionally associated with the nation-state, is far from being a state-like polity. Despite the *sui generis* quality of the EU polity, its 'in-between-ness' suspended as it is between competing ideas about the nature and purpose of governance, the abiding tension between intergovernmental and supranational preferences, the review of the historical development and the theoretical debates on constitutional politics in this same chapter does confirm the aptness of normative and structural ideas rooted in classical and comparative constitutional discourse, both theoretical and procedural and not least comparatively, by drawing on experience elsewhere, both for the more efficient organisation and for improving the legitimation of governance in the EU polity.

## Part 2: constitutionalising the European Union

The theoretic, normative and historical issues reviewed in Part 1 are the necessary precursor for understanding what was at stake when the Laeken Council undertook the historic commitment to embark on a formal constitutional endeavour. Laeken established a Convention on the Future of Europe precisely to address the Union's constitutional shortcomings and to review various options for reform. This was to be a deliberative arrangement, at least compared to the previous IGC procedure, and was modelled on the earlier Convention on the Charter of Fundamental Rights (1999–2000). The intention was to launch an inclusive debate on EU governance and policy. Chapter 3, 'Europe's Constitutional Convention', discusses how and why the Union embarked on this constitutional endeavour, and considers the political forces and circumstances that gave renewed momentum to a thoroughgoing overhaul of the EU's institutional arrangements, decision-making and policies. The Declaration of the Heads of Government and State issued at the Laeken European Council of 2001 agreed an agenda for constitutional reform and set out the Convention's tasks: improving the efficiency of governance by simplifying the arcane procedures accumulated from successive revisions of the treaty base, more effective decision-making and accountable governance and improving the Union's democratic life as a means of better connecting with citizens. This agenda is reviewed at Chapter 4, 'Agendas for change'.

The Convention on the Future of Europe is a new way of doing constitutional business in the Union, and there is much to be learned about the changing dynamics of EU politics from reviewing the Convention's procedures, how it went about its work. Chapter 5, 'The Convention at work' examines these organisational logics, the conduct and style of its deliberations, its internal alliances and ideological fault lines, the coalitions of large and small, new and established member states, and the ensuing tensions between the radical aspirations of some participants compared with a familiar reticence about bold reform of the principal participants, notably the leading member states. These political dynamics determined the outcomes of deliberations and shaped the compromises that ultimately produced the draft Constitutional Treaty, though this draft was itself subject to further modifications in the IGC that was convened to take the final decision on the EU Constitution.

The Convention addressed the critical institutional and policy issues that confront the EU, both currently and prospectively. It incorporated its conclusions about possible reforms into the final text of a Constitutional Treaty presented to the European Council at the Thessaloniki summit in July 2003. In the final analysis all political systems are about the distribution and use of organised power and their inter-institutional relations determine, in Harold Lasswell's pithy aphorism, the 'who gets what when and how' of politics. Institutional actors are the critical agents and agencies, their interactions are the opportunity structures with the political capital and capacity for determining resource allocations and for effecting policy outcomes. The question of where power actually lies in the EU has long been a matter for political debate by practitioners, and more recently for prescriptive conjecture by normative theorists drawn to the study of the EU by the challenge of explaining the shifting locus of public power.

This change in academic fashion signifies the growing importance of the EU, both for understanding the changing boundaries of governance – what has been described as the emergence of the post-national polity – and for the conduct of international affairs in a globalising world order. This was certainly one of the most critical matters considered by the Convention. And the issue of power distribution was sufficiently sensitive for the presidency to postpone its formal review, at least until the Convention had acquired enough momentum, sufficient good will and a head of steam, a reservoir of consensus from its successful deliberations on the less controversial issues. The crucial institutional issues were addressed only latterly, and with barely enough time to do them justice. In the event, discussion of what the EU actually does, the distribution of institutional power and competencies between the central institutions and the member states overshadowed the important matters of democracy and legitimacy deficits, lack of transparency and meaningful citizenship. So that the Convention barely considered the normative question of who *should* exercise power and why, the very questions that ought to figure in any constitutional endeavour worth the name.

The reform of the EU's institutions and decision-making procedure is reviewed in Chapter 6, 'Reforming the European institutions', with a view to determining how far the institutional arrangements proposed in the Constitutional Treaty might resolve or merely compound a familiar complaint from several quarters, that the EU is too narrowly based, a complex multi-level polity and one poorly connected to its citizens. And a polity that lacks either meaningful democracy or much by way of public legitimacy. The task of mapping power and defining the appropriate competencies of the respective institutional actors is by no means straightforward in a polity that combines both supranational and intergovernmental procedures. Indeed, relations between the domestic and the common institutions in what is now a multi-level polity makes for abiding tensions. These relations are more problematical in the EU than in a fully-fledged federal state, where the competencies attributed to the respective levels of governance are located in a hierarchic framework of power legitimised by a formal constitutional order. Resolving the competency issue, what has been described as the *Kompetenz-Kompetenz Katalog*, in essence determining the balance of power between the national, sub-national and the EU levels, the extent of national autonomy as defined by the provision for subsidiarity, is a leitmotif of the Union's constitutional history.

The allocation of competencies and the related issue of subsidiarity, and other matters such as the prospects for accelerated integration between those member states committed to co-operating more closely in some policy domains through the medium of enhanced co-operation, the EU's legal personality, the way it makes laws, are all matters that figured prominently at the Convention. The very complexity of EU governance has reinforced the perception amongst the wider public of remote and unduly complicated governance, a fact that persuaded the leaders meeting at Laeken to simplify decisional procedures. These issues, critical not only for more efficient decision-making in the enlarged Union but also for making those procedures more comprehensible to the citizens, are discussed at Chapter 7 'Simplifying EU governance'. Democracy, or the lack of it, has become a matter of concern in the EU, as it must be in any polity that places great store by input legitimacy. Closing the gap between the governors and the governed is as critical for ensuring that the EU fulfils its purposes as a polity, resolving the shortfall in legitimacy and closing its democracy deficits as is the reform of the institutions and decisional procedures.

Part of the answer to this predicament is to instil in citizens a deeper sense of attachment to a polity too often seen as out of touch with their concerns. The concept of EU citizenship was introduced in the Maastricht Treaty and was developed, albeit in limited fashion, in subsequent treaty revisions throughout the 1990s. The Convention revisited the citizenship issue and proposed some additional measures designed to foster the so-far notional sense of EU citizenship as an expression of, and some would say as a vehicle for cultivating, European political identity based on a sense of individual affiliation, membership and 'belonging' to the European polity. This was, as we shall see, hardly a priority for those insiders, the vested interests who dominated proceedings, whether in the Convention or in the IGC that followed it, or for that matter in what has happened since then.

The development of a European civic culture, the search for common values, the improvement of democratic life at the EU level, simplifying the Union's governance so that citizens might better understand and thus relate to its mission, or at least appreciate its considerable impact on their everyday lives, its role in their general well-being and welfare, are key to redressing the problem of disconnection that became apparent during the ratification campaigns on the Constitutional Treaty throughout the Union. The idea of a common citizenship has an important part to play in instilling a sense of a shared identity above and beyond the primary affiliation to the nation state. Yet in this critical matter the Convention failed to deliver much beyond platitudes and well-meaning rhetoric, and certainly nothing of sufficient substance to respond to growing public disquiet about the disconnection between the politicians and the people.

The academic debate on contemporary citizenship has two distinct themes: on one side is a rights-based narrative that confirms both the benefits and obligations of membership of a polity, defining citizenship in legalistic rather than in political terms. This is an unduly narrow perspective that lacks the ontological meaning of political membership, the connotations of identity that instil in citizens, both individually and collectively, a sense of personal membership, belonging and affective attachment, what might even be called in this context European solidarity. The Convention gave greater consideration by far to the legal definition of citizenship, incorporating the free-standing Charter of Fundamental Rights into the Treaty agreed in 2000, and though it reiterated the existing citizenship articles it hardly developed them to any great extent. On the crucial question of how to deepen affective European identity, both the Convention and the following IGC were largely silent.

There is a lively debate in some parts of European civil society, and no less in the academy, about the meaning of and the prospects for developing EU citizenship beyond the notional rights attributed to this novel status in the Maastricht Treaty. Competing narratives about how to realise transnational citizenship beyond mere rhetoric, or the normative prescriptions of scholars steeped in Kantian idealism, now figure in the debate in the academy about the reimagination of political community. Another contribution to the progressive discourse on citizenship maintains that there is a prospective European solidarity beyond exclusive primordial identity, one made possible by the cultural and to a degree the technological developments brought about by accelerating globalisation, allowing either an inclusive cosmopolitan identity, or as some commentators see it multiple and complementary layers of identity and overlapping political membership. Both of these progressive narratives about the prospects for refashioning political identity claim what their respective advocates see as socio-cultural foundations for post-national citizenship.

On the other side of the debate are those commentaries rooted in the classic realist tradition that remain sceptical about the prospects for transnational citizenship, regarding the very idea as merely fanciful, an unrealisable objective, and especially so in a European polity that purports to be democratic yet lacking demos. Critics on all sides of the citizenship/identity debate, whatever their normative preferences, tend to see the current development of EU citizenship as little more than notional, tokenism contrived by Europe's political class in response to public clamour against a remote political elite. Certainly, the issue of membership and identity is as relevant to the challenge of reforming the Union's problematic polity as is reforming its institutions, establishing an effective balance of power between them so as to ensure more efficient decision-making procedures.

Identity is only one aspect of citizenship. Fundamental rights are critical, too, for cementing a sense of loyalty, and thus of membership, in any polity that adheres to democratic norms. A culture of fundamental human and civil rights is, as in every case of successful polity-building, essential for securing public approval of governance, but also for instilling a sense of loyalty to and identity with the polity. The logics here are functional: commitment to a polity tends to deepen as citizens acknowledge its contribution to their personal welfare and security. The Constitutional Treaty did address the issue of fundamental rights with rather more alacrity than it did the question of citizenship *per se*, though these issues are connected, proposing to consolidate a corpus of political and social rights by incorporating the Charter of Fundamental Rights into the Treaty. The Constitutional Treaty also included some additional flanking measures designed to deepen the citizens' sense of personal security, measures for improving the monitoring of EU agencies and in some aspects of freedom, security and justice policy, for instance by enhancing judicial co-operation and facilitating legal integration, improving transnational police co-operation, and even by harmonising some aspects of the criminal law. These important matters for improving the citizen's sense of personal security in the face of some alarming trends in international criminality, and supposedly for bringing the Union closer to the citizens, are discussed at Chapter 8, 'A people's Europe: citizenship, rights and justice'. Whether these measures are enough to win hearts and minds, let alone to instil an ontologically meaningful, an affective sense of personal affiliation between the citizen and the European polity, not least by facilitating greater public participation in politics, is rather less certain.

Constitutional politics operates at different levels. Formal or legalistic discourse formulates and then enacts individual rights and defines institutional procedures. Socio-cultural processes, on the other hand, help to foster a sense of engagement in a shared enterprise, connecting people at every level in what they come to regard over time as a common endeavour, the habit-forming solidarity indispensable for building a stable political community. Of course, mapping power and allocating competencies, the very essence of a constitutional order, are important matters for any political community. Building strong institutions that embody domestic legitimacy and foster a sense of popular solidarity also has consequences beyond the primary political community confirming, or for that matter, where such bonds are weak or non-existent, diminishing its status as a reliable actor in the wider international system. Some constitutions address these matters rather better than others, and especially federal polities, which by their very nature are systems of multi-level governance, and necessarily include in their constitutional arrangements some consideration of how to manage external relations.

The EU is no exception here, and though it is not a state but rather a confederation of states it nevertheless aspires to collective influence beyond its borders. The European Union has long wrestled with the problem of how best to conduct its arrangements for effective external action. In part, this is a response to the eponymous Kissinger question raised by the then US Secretary of State, who wondered whom he should contact when he needed to 'speak to Europe'. This issue figured prominently in the recent constitutional endeavour. Willy Brandt's widely quoted observation, to the effect that the EU is an economic giant yet remains a political pygmy, is a matter of increasing concern to its political leaders, and especially so since the implosion of the communist system in Eastern and Central Europe as the end of the Cold War altered the balance of forces in the international system. The Convention and the IGC deliberated on these matters, and the Constitutional Treaty made some novel recommendations, such as the proposal for an EU foreign minister and diplomatic service. The Treaty likewise went further in the development of a European defence and security policy, and for ensuring the material capacity for its delivery, though without overcoming the reticence of many member states about deepening integration in a policy domain that is elemental to the very idea of national sovereignty. These issues are discussed at Chapter 9, 'The EU and the new international order'.

### Part 3: the politics of ratification

Some EU governments, not least those of some leading member states, might have preferred the Convention to do little beyond reviewing the issues without agreeing the details of a draft constitutional treaty. A comprehensive draft treaty would tie the hands of the governments in the following IGC. In the event, Giscard's effective management of the Convention, supported for the most part by the praesidium and ably abetted by the secretariat, saw it rise to his challenge 'to make history', to become 'founding fathers rather than founding failures'. The Convention adopted a draft Constitutional Treaty, albeit at the eleventh hour and subsequently delivered by Giscard to the heads of government and state assembled at the Thessaloniki European Council in July 2003. This was an achievement in its own right, but it was far from a conclusive settlement of some of the critical questions that figured in the Convention's deliberations, let alone an exercise in what might be called 'constitutional closure'.

The draft Constitutional Treaty was subject to further negotiations by the member states in the IGC that followed the Convention. The outcome was far from certain, for with the fate of the Treaty back in their own hands some member states decided to challenge some of its fundamental conclusions. More than merely quibbling over details, some governments tried to recover what they saw as ground lost in the Convention by unpicking key points. There was some renegotiation, though the fact that the Convention had managed to agree a full version of a treaty text did restrict governments' room for manoeuvre. The IGC debated some contentious issues for almost a year, and there was some repositioning on the so-called 'red-line' issues, mostly on policy matters regarded by the member states as essential national interests, but also on some aspects of the structure and powers of the principal institutions, such as the extent of qualified majority voting (QMV), voting weights in the Council and the distribution of Commission seats. In the event, and after some adjustments to the Convention's final text, the member states signed the final draft of the Constitutional Treaty on 29 October 2004 in the Sala Degli Orazi e Curazi, where the original Treaty of Rome had been signed. This supposedly final act in the drama of making a European Constitution is discussed at Chapter 10, 'The politics of ratification', and critically reviews the politics of the IGC and charts the Constitutional Treaty's troubled political aftermath, the ratification campaigns in the member states, including the new accession states who joined the Union in May 2004. In the end, what was assumed to be simply straightforward foundered in the face of mounting public antipathy to a deal done out of their sight and beyond their power to influence, resulting in a resounding 'no' vote in ratification referendums in France and the Netherlands and widespread concerns elsewhere. What many commentators have subsequently described as nothing less than a constitutional crisis brought the ratification process to an abrupt halt, giving rise to a period of prolonged uncertainty amongst the Union's leaders about what to do next, circumstances some way removed from what optimists had anticipated would be steady progress towards constitutional finality.

There was much discussion during this period of 'crisis' about 'what happens next', the fate of the Constitutional Treaty. The imbroglio that followed the referendum defeats provoked a lively debate about how – or indeed whether – the Union would easily recover from this set-back. The debate over constitutional finality assumed a significance barely anticipated when the political leaders met in Rome to sign the Constitutional Treaty. For a time the outcome of these events was difficult to predict, though some scenarios seemed rather more likely than others. There was little agreement amongst the pundits who closely follow these events about how the present impasse might be resolved. Some possible scenarios for the future of the European project are reviewed at Chapter 11, 'Crisis or "normal" politics?'. Past experience is a notoriously unreliable guide for predicting future outcomes in politics. The world is shaped more by contingency than by certainties, and as likely as not unanticipated consequences prevail over expected outcomes. Nevertheless it was hard not to anticipate that the EU's political leaders would try, and sooner rather than later, to retrieve the initiative lost after the referendums, and so it has proved. It was always likely after the shock of these defeats at the public's hands that the Constitutional Treaty, at least in its current format, was beyond saving. But it was just as certain that the governments would try to salvage those reforms in the Constitution deemed to be essential to more efficient decision-making, for coping with the pressures of unprecedented enlargement and the challenge of globalisation. This fact alone explains the persistence of the politicians in recovering ground lost after the referendums, though this was conveniently described by them as 'merely' revising the current treaties.

In the meantime, the politicians dealt with unprecedented crisis by taking time out for reflection, as they are wont to do whenever the European project finds itself in difficulties. Political leaders absorbed the political shock of the ratification setbacks, most of them coming to terms, however reluctantly, with the public's disquiet over the direction of European integration. Reform is now back on track, though shorn of any hint of a constitutional make-over. The 'princes' have reclaimed ownership of the business of making the rules, and, rhetoric about 'listening' and 'communication' notwithstanding, we are back now with the notions of permissive rather than active consensus where reform of governance is the issue. This response may not be enough, however, to quieten the public concerned about remote and mostly undemocratic governance. We may well wonder if the brief constitutional moment is indeed over, or whether the public's voice will be raised again in protest.

The evidence from public opinion surveys would suggest that it is as certain as anything can be in the recondite world of politics that the Union's political leaders will be required at some future time to revisit the issues of democracy, legitimacy and citizenship raised in the debate on the Constitutional Treaty but barely improved by it. They will return to these issues because they must, for they have little choice in the matter if the European Union is to resolve abiding democracy and legitimacy deficits. When they do they will do well to approach matters with greater humility, with a willingness to listen and to respond to these concerns than has been their wont so far. If they fail to do so the crisis over the Constitution may well become a crisis of 'Europe' *per se*.

The shorthand for public engagement of this kind is a constitutional conversation. On the face of it this prospect might seem to worldly-wise observers to be merely wishful thinking, misplaced idealism. A conversation between governors and citizens is part of the affective cement of democratic and constitutional politics, an implied contract that underpins every national polity, but this seems to be a remote prospect in the European polity. Remote it may be, but it is a requirement none the less of legitimate governance, here as in any polity that claims democratic credentials. The challenge of responding to the EU's democratic shortcomings is discussed at Chapter 12, 'Towards a constitutional conversation', which reviews the procedures and prospects for connecting 'princes' and people, considers how the Union's political class might initiate a meaningful a transnational conversation and indicates some mechanisms for establishing a Europe-wide public space.

The struggle for the European Constitution has been protracted and replete with difficulties. It certainly did not commence at Laeken, though the decision of that historic European Council to launch a formal constitutional endeavour was a signal moment in what had so far been an incremental and largely ad hoc process of treaty reform. Constitutional reform has been a persistent theme throughout the EC/EU's political development, though admittedly in times past it was more a subtle coda than a major harmony. The impact of enlargement and the challenges of globalisation that prompted the political leaders to contemplate a thorough overhaul of the Union's governance remain in play. A reprise of the EU's constitutional endeavour, in effect a future constitutional history, is the likely outcome of the persistent dilemmas that confront this problematic polity, though seemingly not quite yet. Constitutionalism in the full sense of that term will surely return to the Union's agenda, prompted by the abiding disconnection between governors and governed, those issues that relate to democracy and legitimacy deficits, and no less to meaningful citizenship. Those very issues that were marginalised by powerful political interests during the events that are the subject of this book.

**Part 1**

# Why a European Constitution?

# 1 A problematic polity

## In praise of Europe and yet ...

The progress made towards closer co-operation between Western Europe's nation-states begun in 1945 is a remarkable achievement measured against the continent's turbulent past. Reconciliation and reconstruction have banished warfare to Europe's geographical margins, common institutions are now in place to address problems of mutual concern, fostering a sense of shared purpose and endeavour previously unimaginable to all except idealists. There is much to celebrate in these developments. An extensive and well-organised single market whose institutions amount to a tier of transnational governance, a sophisticated monetary system that after an unsteady start is consolidating the euro as a major global currency, common procedures for managing foreign policy, initiatives to establish a European defence capability, all confirm progress undreamt of by Europe's long-suffering peoples at the end of the Second World War. To these achievements must be added the growing corpus of European case law and legislation covering many aspects of public policy, from macro-economic management, labour market regulation to the environment, social policy and higher education.

Optimism must be tempered nevertheless by caution, for these achievements are only a part of the story. There are distinct limits to the achievements of European construction. The European project has failed to engage, let alone to enthuse, the public at large, and its cumulate institutionalisation reflects far more the interests and aspirations of Europe's political, administrative and business elites than it does those of its citizens. This is due, in no small measure, to the model adopted in 1950 for rebuilding the European economy and social infrastructure. The Coal and Steel Community was a technocratic agency, chosen in preference to a more democratic federal design. Thereafter, the Community's decision-making procedures remained opaque to the ordinary citizen, its operations altogether too difficult for them to comprehend, let alone to access in order to influence public policy. This was primarily an economic Community, and one that barely met democratic standards. Over time what had started as a common market and regulatory regime has become a polity, but its arrangements lack either public accountability or democratic legitimacy as this is understood in liberal polities. And this despite accession criteria that make democratic norms and procedures a requirement for joining the club.

The legitimacy problem is inbuilt in the EU system, but became an issue only during the early 1990s, as public opinion grew restive about the pace and direction of European integration after the stormy passage of the Maastricht Treaty in some member states. The problem of what contemporary commentators call 'disconnection' between elites and citizens has not gone away and indeed has worsened, reflected in widespread public indifference to the intergovernmental deals that resulted in the treaties of Amsterdam and Nice. These political bargains may have satisfied the governments who negotiated them, but they barely signified with the people at large. The negative publicity surrounding the Commission's tribulations in 1999 after a Parliamentary report had levelled serious charges of incompetence and corruption merely served to confirm the Union's low public esteem. This much is to be expected from a polity that from the outset has combined divergent, indeed competing, political purposes. Political tension over the meaning and direction of European integration is hardly new; it has defined the project from the outset.

The founding bargain that established the Coal and Steel Community accommodated quite different ideas about integration, a balance between governments convinced of the need to work more closely together for broadly mutual ends, and supranational interests and agencies represented in the Community's institutions, for whom the project was an escalator towards a European federal polity. It suited both sides of this debate to play down ideological differences, to concentrate instead on making a bargain that suited their respective interests. As such, the European project has harboured an abiding ambiguity throughout about the meaning and trajectory of European integration. This compromise is most clearly reflected in the Community's institutional arrangements, almost a 'treaty-based federal arrangement in certain policy areas', though 'without having a formal, constitutionally based federation'.[1] On the one hand, the Community was designed to accommodate the interests of historic nation-states, though not to the exclusion of their common interests.[2] On the other hand, 'ever-closer Union' has its own momentum, and more than that its own prophets, who exhibit zealous faith as to its destiny, convinced that it will one day replace the nation-state with its own exclusive sense of identity, what amounts to a transEuropean patriotism, and a degree of cultural integration giving rise to common European values and mutual aspirations, and not least a sense of common purpose in a fast-changing world.

While ambiguity remains, and as some see it continues to sustain the project's broad appeal, there are signs nevertheless of a distinctive process of 'Europeanisation' under way. One consequence of European integration has been a fundamental shift in the European political order, reducing the primacy of the post-Westphalian nation-state and state system in the region's politics.[3] The coexistence in the Community's founding bargain of national interests and supranational aspirations has produced an 'in-between' politics, ambivalence about fundamental purposes that is not resolved one way or the other, but balances quite different preferences in the policy process. The member states pool elements of their sovereignty, participate in common institutions and abide by an agreed legal code in order to solve mutual problems, though this unprecedented co-operation is constrained by national policy preferences and lacks the affective cement of a shared political identity. At the same time, states are no longer the singular or exclusive actors they are in the classic realist paradigm of international relations. The impact of such co-operation has given momentum to 'Europeanisation', a blurring of once pristine boundaries between levels of governance, and with it a growing commonality of values, a common approach to some important aspects of public policy once the exclusive preserve of the nation-state.

The boundaries between domestic and international politics now have a porosity that has altered the dynamics of governance – though less so of politics – at both the domestic and international levels, irrevocably changing conventional policy-making strategies.[4] Government is much less the exclusive prerogative of state actors, with the EU 'slowly defining political arrangements, altering policy networks, triggering institutional change, reshaping the opportunity structures of member states and their major interests'.[5] Domestic interests that once relied solely on the state to represent their interests abroad engage directly in transnational policy networks. Contemporary governance is multi-tiered with the national, *meso* and supranational levels increasingly interdependent, each level 'sharing the responsibility for problem solving because neither [level] has adequate legal authority and policy instruments to tackle the challenges they face'.[6]

In the process formerly hermeneutic states have become 'hollowed out', with at least some elements of their sovereignty spilling over to transnational agencies, the impact of these transactions in turn spilling back into national affairs, reshaping contemporary governance.[7] This has been a cumulate and an incremental process, rather than the result of any formal constitutional bargain or defining moment constituting a European polity. As such, the institutional deficiencies that result from such a weakly connected, non-hierarchical governance architecture are plain to see, their consequences all too apparent in the Union's current predicament. This is a polity without paramount public power, lacking either a monopoly of legitimate coercion within its boundaries or the means to defend its collective interests abroad. Above all, it lacks the over-arching identity found even in culturally plural and institutionally federated states, the normative ballast of public legitimacy that underpins what is, in effect, an implicit contract between 'princes' and people ensuring popular approval for the exercise of power. Indeed, this is a polity without even an agreed territorial space, 'a political arena which is not fixed but in a constant state of construction'.[8]

Crisis is an over-used word in contemporary politics, but few close observers of the European scene now dispute the fact of growing public unease with a polity that touches the lives of its citizens to an unprecedented degree, yet one that remains beyond either the public's effective control or comprehension. Public concern is apparent on several fronts: a discernible lack of empathy between decision-makers and citizens, and widespread public indifference to and incomprehension about remote governance. This mood finds expression in popular disapprobation of the apparent misdemeanours of some office-holders in the principal institutions, a mood that now extends beyond mere malaise and is reflected in negative media coverage, adverse public responses to opinion pollsters and low levels of participation in European elections. At the heart of the problem is the construction of the EU polity itself, an institutional muddle designed at the outset as a compromise between quite different visions of the Europe project, and one that makes for problematic governance.

## Problematic governance

The EU is a multi-tiered polity whose institutional actors at various levels have quite different, indeed competing preferences about the purposes of their common endeavour.[9] For the national governments represented in the European Council and the Council of Ministers, the European project is essentially about promoting and defending national interests, though this does not in itself preclude deals between them, usually in response to external challenges: bargains that commit the member states to a remarkable degree of commonality in public policy.[10] The Union's common institutions tend to regard such collective action as the precursor of yet more supranational governance to come, activity with a potentially federal outcome and for some even the harbinger of a European state-in-the-making. What began as 'merely' a common market has certainly developed into complex governance,[11] governance that differs markedly 'from [that] of the European state as we have come to know it'.[12] However, the system's asymmetry, its loosely coupled institutions are a direct legacy of the founding bargain.[13] This is an inchoate rather than a hierarchical polity, one lacking a clear or undisputed locus for political authority, and one without an authoritative constitutional narrative, where 'many decisions get made betwixt and between the established mechanisms of democratic control as matters of executive or administrative discretion'.[14] The executive function, such as it is, is located in a supranational Commission, an institution lacking any demonstrable legitimacy other than the authority conferred by the treaties and the mandate to propose and supervise agreed common policy bestowed by the member states who appoint its president and College of commissioners. The Commission is ultimately accountable to the governments of the member states, yet it has considerable discretion in initiating policy.

What passes for legitimacy in this polity resides with an intergovernmental Council of Ministers, in fact several sectoral or functional councils meeting periodically, co-ordinated as far as possible by a rotating presidency. But this institution legislates neither with transparency nor with a democratic mandate worth the name. The European Parliament on the other hand is elected and it does have supranational aspirations, but even the recent acquisition of a significant co-legislative role through co-decision and its growing budgetary powers have not entirely redressed its limited capacity to shape the Union's policy agenda, let alone to embody what might be called the General Will, the authority conferred by the people to 'speak for Europe'. Above all, party politics here is loosely organised, remote from the electorate's affections, and its elections are widely seen even by those who participate in them as second-order contests deciding little of significance for their everyday lives, at best an opportunity to send a mid-term warning to their governments. And though legitimacy is assumed by its elected members, this is not legitimacy securely grounded in a European demos, for much more is required for a pan-European deliberative democracy than merely 'submerging a national democratic government into a larger and less democratic trans-national system'.[15]

The Court of Justice, too, falls some way short of the standard set by constitutional courts in democratic polities. While it lays claim to the role of final arbiter of the public interest as embodied in the judicial function, the fount of judicial (and ultimately of constitutional) review, a function that is the ballast of legitimate governance in national polities, in practice the Court falls short of the benchmark for classic judicial review. Its expansive legal order enjoys supremacy by means of the dual principles of direct effect and primacy over national law, but only in specific aspects of public policy, and even then without any independent means for enforcing its writ.

Measured against any conventional yardstick this is a muddled political architecture, and one that makes for complicated and hardly for efficient governance.[16] Competencies are shared between these diverse institutions, a mix of mutually dependent public and private actors who must make bargains in order to maximise their preferences and realise their policy objectives and political goals.[17] And in ways that deliver something less than optimal policy outcomes, and all too often result in costly 'decision traps' that exasperate special interests and baffle the citizens at large.[18] The Commission, the principal engine for initiating common policy, lacks any independent capacity for enacting agreed policy outcomes.[19] Whereas the Council of Ministers' legislative function lacks proper democratic accountability or the means for effective public scrutiny. Despite recent advances in its powers, the Parliament remains much less the cockpit of a robust deliberative democracy, a truly European democratic space holding the power-brokers properly accountable. The Court, meanwhile, depends on the goodwill of other agencies to enforce its judgements. It is an understatement to describe these arrangements as merely 'untidy'.[20] The lack of a constitutionally guaranteed separation of powers makes for disjointed governance, weak authority and opaque decision-making.

Some commentators see in these institutional deficiencies the roots of the Union's present legitimacy crisis.[21] The 'permissive consensus' that prevailed in the early years of the European project, whereby ministers in the Council unanimously and covertly made decisions, and assumed that the people at large accepted their right to do so, could no longer suffice as the basis for authoritative decision-making once the Union moved to decisions by qualified majority. Nor was 'performance legitimacy' – another convenient rationale for unaccountable EC decisions, whereby political elites are assumed to act in the best interests of the people – sustainable, given the extension of decision-making into areas of public policy central to citizens' everyday concerns. The legitimacy deficit and how to redress it has become over time the focus of a debate about reform, prompting acceptance in some quarters of the need for a European constitutional order.[22] Institutional arrangements have evolved, but not in ways that have deepened legitimacy or enhanced the Union's democratic credentials.

The democratic deficit is as apparent now as it was at the outset, indeed it is a matter for more serious concern, because the scope for policy-making has increased significantly since 1986, when the passage of the Single European Act launched the Single Market project.[23] The extension of policy domains, the geographical enlargement of the Community and, not least, the sheer scale of the challenges facing the EU in a fast-changing global order all make for heavy demands on governance constructed in more relaxed times and for less demanding purposes. Moreover, these arrangement too often deliver sub-optimal bargains that privilege special interests above those of citizens at large, whether as consumers, employees or the socially excluded.[24] Yet institutional reform has proved difficult to bring about. Even where it has occurred, it has been for the most part reactive, *ad hoc* and pragmatic adjustments made between the power-holders, incremental adaptations to the status quo, 'muddling through' rather than bold, imaginative or transformative change to address the formidable challenges that lie ahead.

The crisis that engulfed the Commission in 1999 when a parliamentary inquiry found evidence of defective public standards was some indication that these institutional shortcomings had finally caught up with the EU. The fall-out from this incident, together with the pressures from the policy challenges required for addressing accelerating globalisation and, not least, the prospect of impending EU enlargement to include ten new member states, the majority of them from East/Central Europe, all served to concentrate official minds on the question of reform. The impact of further enlargement on an already complex governance was of particular concern to would-be reformers as the debate on institutional shortcomings gathered pace, taking as their cue the Commission report submitted to the Lisbon Council (1992), which gave some hint that Brussels' insiders, too, were amenable to a major rethink about the direction of the European project.[25]

## Democracy deficits in the European Union

The EU's institutional shortcomings not only make for inefficient decision-making but also for serious democracy deficits.[26] Lack of effective channels for popular participation, exiguous accountability between decision-makers and citizens means the 'lack of any systematic normative and popular legitimisation of European political institutions'. This is as much a cultural as a structural problem, a grave 'constitutional deficit'[27] caused in no small measure by the lack of connectedness between those who manage EU affairs and the wider public, and 'the paucity of sustained debate' about the Union's 'overall shape and reach' amongst the Union's political and bureaucratic elites.[28] Accordingly, EU governance is seen by its citizens as remote, lacking the means for broader input into policy-making and agenda-setting,[29] a situation compounded by a serious shortfall in democratic accountability.[30] The abiding impression amongst the public at large is of a polity and a policy procedure remote from their everyday concerns, indeed one that is more a matter of 'the private management of public business'.[31] To date, European integration has been primarily managerial in orientation, more about technocrats and insider interests than about citizens. The transfer of decision-making in key areas of public policy from domestic governance with long-established procedures for both democratic participation and accountability, to supranational institutions 'whose performance, as assessed by the criteria of democratic legitimacy, is comparatively poorer in a number of respects', has done little to improve the Union's democratic fabric.[32]

The European Parliament, which supposedly represents the wider public interest, has exerted less effective scrutiny over executive action than have most national parliaments, though it is more than two decades since the Dooge Committee (1985) recommended more open and accountable Community governance.[33] Citizens have seemingly drawn their own conclusions about these shortcomings. Low levels of participation in European elections, the only opportunity for direct involvement by citizens, confirms widespread public indifference towards the Union, with increasing scepticism about its purposes. There are many reasons for low electoral turn-out, but there is evidence that citizens are less inclined to participate in elections they regard as inconsequential or meaningless.[34] Even those who do vote, do so as they would in a mid-term referendum on the performance of their respective national governments. As such, the one political institution designed to connect citizens to EU governance signally fails to do so.[35] This is no inconsequential matter even for a non-statal polity. An active and politicised public was indispensable for embedding a democratic culture in Europe's nation-states, instilling in turn a sense of individual membership and belonging to the body politic.[36] Why then should this requirement be any less relevant for a EU polity that likewise sets considerable store by democratic norms? The EU has failed to address this serious shortcoming in successive treaty reforms since the Single European Act. Indeed, the political class has largely avoided the democracy question, concentrating instead on institutional tinkering to ensure better performance in the technocratic quest to implement and regulate a single market, the launch of an ambitious monetary regime and action to improve the Union's international standing. A brief review of the European Union's institutional architecture confirms the extent of what is an endemic polity problem.

## Institutional deficiencies

### *The European Commission*

The Commission's ambition to become the Community's pivotal institution, in effect a government for 'Europe', remains unfulfilled in the face of resistance from most of the member states.[37] The 1965–6 crisis and the Luxembourg reforms that resolved it confirmed a confederal arrangement as the dominant model for EC/ EU governance, with governments determining the big issues, broadly setting the policy agenda. The Commission has had mixed fortunes in its pursuit of supranationalism, motivated by its goal of upgrading the common interest over narrow national interests. It undoubtedly gained respect at every level during the energetic Delors presidency, though the so-called 'Wise Men' did censure a presidency widely thought to be too preoccupied with its grand design for Europe and rather less concerned with public accountability.

The shock administered by the Danish electorate's rejection of the Maastricht Treaty in that country's first ratification referendum did produce renewed soul-searching, but the moment passed without any serious reform and familiar insouciance prevailed. Pascal Lamy, Jacques Delors's *chef de cabinet*, highlighted the extent of the problem, giving a revealing insight into an official mindset more attuned to benevolent despotism than to democracy, when he observed that: 'Europe was built in a St Simonian way from the beginning, this was Monnet's approach ... The people weren't ready for integration, so you had to get on without telling them too much about what was happening.' More recently, Lamy was minded to concede that 'St Simonianism is finished. It can't work when you have to face democratic public opinion.'[38] Meanwhile, contemporary critics continue to voice doubts about whether the familiar remoteness, even detachment from the world, of Brussels's technocrats has passed.

The blame for the disconnection between 'princes' and the public by no means lies entirely with the Commission. The member states are culpable too. After all, it is governments that determine the EU's policy agenda by means of the Council presidency and the Committee of Permanent Representatives (COREPER), as well as through interventions by influential national pressure groups, domestic policy experts and senior civil servants participating in, if not entirely monopolising, the processes of policy-formulation. Above all, it is governments rather than the supranational actors who take the big or 'historic' decisions that determine the pace and trajectory of European integration, though much of the *minutiae* of technical policy remains the province of the Commission, working with and through networks consisting of national and transnational special interests.[39] The tussle between national and wider loyalties, the frictions caused by governments jostling amongst themselves to secure coveted Commission policy portfolios, all serve to accentuate institutional incoherence, making for untidy governance at best, undermining a clear sense of purpose and mitigating transparent policy-making, and no less squandering political capital on negotiating narrowly sub-optimal policy bargains.

Council prerogatives are not the only evidence of abiding intergovernmentalism in the conduct of EU affairs. The Commission's supranational ethos is discernable, though conditional. On the one hand, the Commission is a 'propulsive elite' embodying the spirit of the European project, providing its principal 'motor'.[40] The Directorates-General, the Commission's policy agencies, recruit and socialise their personnel with supranational *esprit* and *élan*. The same might be said of individual commissioners who swear an oath to serve 'Europe'. But this is not the whole story, for the appointment of commissioners remains the prerogative of the member states, albeit subject to the European Parliament's approval. Moreover, commissioners import their own cabinets, mostly recruited from the home base, though this preference is changing. It is not misleading to say that 'intergovernmentalism starts in the (commissioners') cabinets. They are mini-Councils within the Commission.'[41] They certainly maintain close contact with their country of origin, though less as national tribunes and more as two-way communicators, sounding out domestic opinion, working to engineer consensus with Brussels, facilitating policy bargains that will not subsequently be held up in the Council. Secondment of national civil servants to Brussels is another firm bridge between the domestic and Community levels.[42]

The Commission is a political system in its own right but is not a singular, let alone a single-minded actor. A recent study points to serious deficiencies in this regard, noting the 'many political threats to (the Commission's) effective operation', not least 'the lack of co-ordination; the impact of ... temporary staff; discontent over personnel matters; unreliable communication and information flows; and the inadequate use of available resources'.[43] Factionalism always intrudes on professional bureaucracies and detracts from a coherent outlook on policy priorities, and the Commission is no exception. These internal turf wars preclude a common front against the Council. Even the collegiality of commissioners is exaggerated. Strong leadership does cement common purpose, but the most successful Commission presidency to date based its success less on collegial consensus and rather more on a single-minded leader and the supportive efforts of a core group of influential colleagues.[44] Human foible adds to organisational shortcomings. Commissioners and their cabinets strive to maximise the profile of their respective policy portfolios in the Brussels pecking order. The cabinet offices, too, are intrinsically political, further undermining collegiality, whereas further down the hierarchy the Directorates-General compete for resources and favourable 'policy windows' in an ever more congested policy timetable.

The Commission is hardly a supine and neither is it a secondary actor. The policy process makes this institution the focal point of an extensive web of policy networks, epistemic communities and advocacy coalitions that bring together government agencies, policy experts and domestic and transnational interests, facilitating alliances between key domestic and Europe-wide sectoral interests, and submitting sustainable policy proposals.[45] The EU could not maintain policy momentum without the Commission orchestrating these disparate actors, engaging with the Council machinery, liaising with vested interests, consulting with experts at every level, and by these means facilitating the co-operation required for putting together the policy bargains that keep the European show on the road.[46] Recent treaty reforms have confirmed the Commission's central role in this tangled weft of transnational policy-making, notably the introduction and expansion first of the co-operation and latterly the co-decision procedures. As does the extension of QMV in the Council, widening the range of 'winning coalitions' needed for the passage of policy, enhancing the Commission's leverage as a facilitator of policy bargains *vis-à-vis* other institutional actors. But it is not only as a mediator between competing interests that the Commission exerts influence over policy-framing and concocting policy bargains. There are opportunities, too, for the Commission to be a policy entrepreneur, to utilise its critical institutional resources – information, expertise, organisational know-how, an impressive network of contacts with all manner of sectoral interests – to orchestrate policy debates, enabling it to steer policy, at least in the first pillar, though even this falls some way short of the political leadership aspired to by Commission personnel in the early years, before Charles de Gaulle curbed Brussels's ambition to 'govern' Europe.[47]

The Commission's presence at the epicentre of policy formulation and policy-making brings its own problems for efficient and transparent policy-making. The obligation, for instance, to work with governments, especially in the COREPER nexus, in order to fashion broadly acceptable policy proposals that will pass the Council, as well as reliance on the member states to legislate, implement and monitor these policies, serves to encourage narrow bargains, those insider deals that reinforce the tendency in all bureaucracies for opacity. The preference for a dependable clientele, another familiar bureaucratic trait, and for making cosy deals whether with special interests or public agencies, obliges the Commission to concentrate on building sustainable policy packages rather than encouraging radical or innovative thinking about democracy deficits or bringing 'the people' on board, even if it was so inclined.[48] This is a system of decision-making that privileges special interests at the expense of the wider public interest. Resourceful and well-motivated special interests are more active in EU policy domains than are representatives of an inchoate, and as yet barely mobilised European civil society, with these 'insiders' more accustomed to lobbying governments, advising the Commission and accessing Parliament's committees. Organised interests exert considerable influence over policy outcomes, constraining the Commission's room for manoeuvre.[49] As one observer sees it: 'To expand [even] gradually the scope of Union competence without alienating national governments or powerful sectoral interests tests the Commission's legendary political skills to the utmost.'[50]

These organisational deficiencies are compounded by a climate of political uncertainty. The Commission's *raison d'être* at the outset was to set up and administer a common market, whatever the idealistic aspirations of its founders. The watchword here was negative rather than positive integration, the removal of obstacles and impediments to market-making. In the meantime, the pace of integration accelerated, its reach was extended, indeed over-extended for such a relatively small organisation, provoking reaction from member states and ultimately leaving the Commission altogether less sure about its role in a developing project whose member states are determined to retain control of its overall political direction. Even so, the Commission could perform better than it has. This is less a case of strategic slippage or mission drift – for governments have always steered the Community, set the broad agenda – than of abiding institutional deficiencies in the face of fast-changing circumstances. The Commission is nevertheless as complicit in this failure to respond to the demands of contemporary policy-making as are governments, because tardy about undertaking those administrative reforms it is empowered to make without reference to the Council, such as reorganising its departments, redistributing portfolios to respond better to changing tasks and not least communicating what Europe is all about to a wider audience and widening access to non-privileged actors.

The Commission's shortcomings are, in part, a consequence of the contestedness of the EU polity, with reticence on all sides about confronting institutional problems head-on in case a constitutional refit should disturb the delicate balance between institutional actors, requiring that the founding bargain be recast. And by so doing to risk reopening ideological warfare over the project's central purposes, a battle between the principal stakeholders over fundamentally different preferences for EU governance. Again, the fault here does not lie entirely with the Commission. Distinguished experts from Tindemans (Report on the European Union, 1976) to Spierenburg (Report on the Working of the European Institutions, 1979) have made recommendations for reform, but the member states have for the most part resisted them. The question of institutional reform came to the fore in successive IGCs during the 1990s as the Union enlarged its membership and extended its policy reach. But the really difficult questions were mostly postponed, precisely for the reasons outlined above, critical matters such as the number and allocation of commissioners, their distribution as between large and small countries, the role of commissioners' personal cabinets, the link between policy portfolio and DGs and whether and in what manner the Parliament should 'elect' commissioners and hold them to account.

In the end, narrow self-interest prevailed over the need to confront institutional deficiencies. The larger states, for instance, were reluctant to forgo the status and clout in Brussels of a second commissioner, and more recently the smaller states have defended the right to 'their' own seat in the Commission College because of the prestige that attaches to it. Similar reticence was evident over administrative appointments, with insistence on maintaining national quotas rather than appointment by merit of the 'most suitable candidates'. Governments cling tenaciously to their 'share' of appointments in the secretariats of every EU institution, and a European civil service based in classic Weberian fashion on a career service of the talents is accordingly discounted. When these issues were raised during the Amsterdam IGC most governments were reluctant to confront them.

### The Council of Ministers

The Council, too, has serious institutional shortcomings that stem directly from its intergovernmental ethos. The Council presidency operates as the principal mediator between competing national preferences as it seeks to manage a cogent policy agenda during six-monthly rotating terms.[51] The requirement for an effective presidency is compromise rather than resolute executive leadership, working to ensure consensus rather than provoking controversy by unilateral action. The Council's institutional culture is 'a shared culture ... in spite of the public and publicised pictures of tension and antagonistic posturing' that governments occasionally display for domestic consumption. Council politics is rooted in consensus, the management of differences, negotiated trade-offs that are invariably sub-optimal bargains made between competing policy preferences, and orchestrated by adept Council presidencies. The path to compromise here is smoothed by *engrenage*, as 'decision-makers in the Council, in spite of their national roots, become locked into the collective process, especially in areas of well-established and recurrent negotiation'.[52] In these circumstances, policy outcomes tend to be insider deals, with the various councils acting 'in certain ways as ... part of a collective system of decision-making', facilitating 'give and take' between the member states and between the institutional actors.[53] What Helen Wallace has described as entrenched 'co-operative modes' for transacting business.[54]

QMV is the real test of this consensus, in so far as it depends on a culture of sequential negotiation across a range of issues, trading short-term national advantage for future gains, replacing an adversarial outlook with one rooted in compromise. This rests, above all, on confidence that other actors will play the game when their turn comes to eschew their veto and compromise on national interests. The system works best where the principal actors share basic values about the distribution of power and resources in the Union, where there are no great disparities of wealth or other values between them. Successive enlargements since 1973 did not weaken the underlying consensus, but the impending eastern enlargement negotiated during the 1990s was bound to strain this cosy bargaining culture by bringing into the Union states with only limited experience of market economies, and unfamiliar with the trade-offs associated with consensual decision-making and consociational politics.

The newcomers were more likely to be suspicious, too, of what they saw as the privileges of the current members, and as such to become *demandeurs* for a redistribution of voting power. Whereas the larger states, for their part, were just as likely to resist any significant reweighting of votes that favoured small and demographically unrepresentative blocking minorities. The reluctance nowadays to push decisions in the Council to a formal vote, let alone to exercise a national veto, expands the optimal size for a winning coalition on many policy issues, in turn persuading those on the losing side of the need to make compromises. But respective voting weights are crucial to the outcome, with abiding differences of opinion about precise weightings as between the large and small states. The more QMV is applied to decisions, the more crucial the need to settle the deep differences over the allocation of votes, an issue the Union failed to resolve in successive IGCs. This issue became more controversial as the Union grew larger, and it was bound to figure in any major reform of this institution.

### *The European Council*

Summit meetings confirm the governments' control of the EU agenda, the headline issues, whether as crisis management or more usually as informal diplomacy around the dinner table or bilateral confessionals in quiet corners to smooth the way for policy deals in plenaries. To this extent, European Councils do what was intended when they were launched in 1974, providing a useful forum for member states to manage the affairs of a confederal polity.[55] Contact at close quarters does help to remove blockages, but even camaraderie or intimate and off-the-record statecraft is no guarantee of success. Again, the picture here is far from straightforward. The Commission makes an input into, and has considerable informal influence on, these intergovernmental deliberations. And though governments represent 'domestic' negotiating positions during these summits, they are influenced in their deliberations by the sense of a broader European interest.[56] Enlargement again threatens to reduce the sense of intimacy that is this institution's principal virtue. For this reason alone, and with an historic enlargement imminent, advocates of reform saw the need to review the Council's role.

### The European Parliament

Since its direct election in 1979 the European Parliament has acquired much greater influence over legislation and with it a degree of legitimacy, though it hardly compares with the role of national parliaments as the principal source of political legitimacy, let alone an effective watch-dog over those who perform executive functions. And neither does it exert the same degree of control over budgetary affairs. The 1970 treaty to amend budgetary provisions permits the Parliament to share with the Finance Council the prerogative of setting non-compulsory expenditure, but it continues to play only a nominal role in the critical matter of setting compulsory expenditure. Further reform of budgetary procedures in 1975 enhanced the Parliament's amendment powers: the right to reject a budget in its entirety, though without shifting control of the revenue–expenditure process from the Commission–Council nexus.

Parliament's limited influence on the EU policy process was confirmed by the reluctance of the member states to concede the proposal in the Vedel Report (1972) for a general right of co-legislation with the Council, though modest increments did bring about a gradual improvement in its legislative capacity. The European Court of Justice's landmark *Isoglucose* ruling (1980) finally enforced the Treaty requirement that the Council should not enact regulations without proper parliamentary consultation. The Court has also confirmed the Parliament's role in setting the medium-term financial perspective. Parliament's standing was further improved by the Single Act enacting the co-operation procedure, though this reform 'disappointed Parliament', in so far as it 'received only a limited right of rejection rather than a positive right of approval' of proposed legislation.[57] The Treaty on European Union (1993) redressed this matter by introducing co-decision, with the Amsterdam Treaty (1997) streamlining co-decision, with a substantial upgrading of the Parliament's legislative capacity, ensuring it has 'a very substantial legislative role [carrying it] a good part of the way towards achieving equality with the Council as far as legislation and accountability of the Commission are concerned'.[58] A development that has also enhanced its role in agenda-setting.[59]

There are limits nevertheless to this steady increase in parliamentary authority, not least the Parliament's limited control over the two executive institutions, notwithstanding its right since 1994 to subject incoming commissioners to confirmation hearings as required by the Treaty on European Union. The Commission's day-to-day operations are even more difficult to monitor, a familiar problem for democratic assemblies everywhere, but more so in an arrangement where institutional actors occupy different geographical locations, and one without any executive presence in the chamber except fleeting ministerial visits to report on progress, for instance the reports at the beginning and conclusion of presidency terms. The Commission is no more susceptible to democratic control than any other professional bureaucracy, regardless of a backlash after the debacle of 1999, when a report instigated by the Parliament led to the resignation of the Santer Commission.

Parliament remains handicapped then in its pursuit of greater democracy and accountability in EU governance, in part because the absence of European demos deprives it of an elective role in choosing those who govern the Union, thereby reducing its legitimacy, precluding any clear mandate for a central role in the Union's affairs. The lack, too, of meaningful party politics at the EU level confirms the Parliament's limited legitimacy. Europe's citizens resist the idea that this assembly represents the public interest or embodies the collective popular will, preferring that critical democratic function to remain with national parliaments.[60] Figures speak for themselves in this regard. Turn-out in European elections is consistently lower than for national elections: a Community average high of 63 per cent in 1979, down to a low of 56.5 per cent in 1994, and further depressed to 45.7 per cent in 2004, an all-time low. The development of pan-European party politics is further hindered by the primacy of regulatory politics, a preoccupation with technocratic governance that hardly mirrors the redistributive politics that shapes political competition in national politics. One recent study reported the telling fact that some 70 per cent of critical EU decisions are left entirely to the discretion of insiders during the all-important policy formulation stage, not least powerful and well-resourced interests.[61] Regulating and managing an internal market involves net gains and losses; it is distributive politics but not in quite the same way as national party politics. It is much more about regional disparities, changing market and employment prospects, effecting critical macro-economic and supply-side reforms.[62] Of course, these are issues with real potential for connecting with the traditional socio-economic and communal cleavages that continue to shape the mainstream national politics of left and right, but so far without quite the same resonance at the EU level for average voter.[63] The plain fact is, the Europeanisation of politics hardly mirrors the Europeanisation of public policy.[64] What passes then for politics at the European level, the narrow policy bargains that reflect the priorities of special interests and mostly privileged constituencies, fails to strike chords with EU citizens. This is not 'politics' as most Europeans understand it, and for the most part it fails to enthuse let alone to mobilise them.[65]

### The Court of Justice and Judicial Review

Aristotle first postulated the centrality of law in a 'just' state. The rule of law is fundamental for a democratic polity. A true republican polity is a *Rechtsstaat*, a 'state of law' where governance is bound by consistent principles and agreed procedures. The Swiss jurist Benjamin Constant acknowledged the virtue of the republican polity as a 'union ... under the empire of laws'.[66] The EU conforms more closely to this republican principle in its legal regime than it does in its political arrangements. But there are limits even here. The Union's legal order remains remote from ordinary citizens, in part because the remit of EU law is restricted to specific policy domains, and was designed so as not to impinge on those aspects of civil and criminal law citizens associate with personal security.

Community law is assimilated by national judiciaries according to the principles of 'undisputed supremacy', 'direct effect' and 'implied powers', in as much as the 'preservation of the Community character of the law' ensures 'that in all circumstances the law is the same as in all states of the Community',[67] with 'identical effects over the whole territory of the Community'.[68] The European courts operate as an agency of judicial review at every level, adjudicating the actions of citizens, corporate bodies, governments and their agents, and the EU institutions. This implies a Community rule of law, though its agency is usually indirect, another legacy of the founding bargain.[69] Introduced in 1963, 'direct effect' reverses 'the normal presumptions of public international law whereby international legal obligations are result-orientated *and addressed to states*, such that public international law typically allows the internal constitutional order of a state to determine the method and extent to which international obligations may, if at all, produce effects for individuals within the legal order of the state.'[70]

This legal base and the principle of direct effect clearly demarcates EU law from international law, ensuring that EU law has the status of domestic law. Nevertheless, there are significant differences with the domestic legal order of the member states. Enforcement depends on national legislatures incorporating directives, regulations, Court judgements and other legal norms into national law. This very process reduces citizens' awareness of what is in effect an expansive transnational legal order, the fact of their membership of an emergent European *Rechtsstaat*, restricting the public's sense of how far their rights and obligations in those areas where EU law applies rest on judicial authority beyond the nation-state. The same might be said of the European Court of Justice's practice of announcing its opinions collectively rather than individually, confirming an impression of detached judicial Olympians pursuing a supranational agenda, thereby weakening the perception of justice as a constitutional conversation between the Court and the wider community that characterises national judicial review. This sense of remoteness is made worse by the fact that judicial decisions are taken in secret, often by simple majority. Although this practice shields the Justices from political pressures, it weakens the legitimacy of the lawmakers, and confirms the public impression of this institution as being far removed from their everyday concerns.[71] How to better connect the EU legal system with the wider community, to establish a true *Rechtsstaat*, is a challenge the Union has so far singularly failed to address.[72]

## Rules of governance and boundaries of competence: the 'who does what' question

Constitutions determine the functions and relations of the respective authorities in a polity. Clearly, the EU's loose-coupled political order lacks the constitutional cogency of most of its member states, with successive treaties superimposed on preceding treaties, and with no definitive review so far of the respective boundaries of institutional competence. The competence issue has been addressed, but only in an *ad hoc* fashion, with the attempt during the 1990s to devise a formula for governance rooted in subsidiarity and acceptable to all sides of the ongoing debate between federalists and those who prefer that the Union remains a confederal polity. In fact, it might even be argued that the resort to subsidiarity was attractive to those on both sides of this debate precisely because it avoided the politically difficult challenge of embracing a definitive EU constitutional order. For by enshrining the concept of competing preferences for an EU polity, subsidiarity permitted both sides of a long-standing debate about the proper scope for EU governance to claim ascendancy for their respective position, rather than bringing matters to a head by clarifying the boundaries of competence between the EU level and the member states.

Subsidiarity was formally introduced in the Maastricht Treaty (1992) as a gauge for allocating decision-making competencies. Thereafter, it became apparent that if subsidiarity did address the 'who does what' question, it did so less as a constitutional principle and more as an interim solution to a persistent problem of multi-level governance. In fact, the Union has remained wary of embracing head-on a 'multi-level constitutionalism' appropriate to its complex system of tiered governance.[73] Subsidiarity has tended to operate as a constraint on actors at the Community level, ensuring that they resist commonality as the first reflex of policy-making.[74] The Amsterdam Protocol both confirmed and further refined the principle as follows: 'For any proposed Community legislation, the reasons on which it is based shall be stated with a view to justifying its compliance with the principles of subsidiarity and proportionality; the reasons for concluding that a Community objective can be better achieved by the Community must be substantiated by qualitative or, wherever possible, quantitative indicators.'[75] However, subsidiarity does not amount to a clear constitutional principle, but rather avoids any definitive resolution of the 'who governs' question. For intergovernmentalists subsidiarity confirms the primacy of national governments, even if this interpretation bears little resemblance to the more complex relations between the member states and the Union as determined by the treaties. Although Article 5 (2) of the Treaty of the European Community (TEC) confirmed that the Community may act 'only if and in so far as the objectives of the proposed action cannot be sufficiently achieved by the Member States and can therefore, by reason of the scale or effects of the proposed action, be better achieved by the Community', this article was not intended to unequivocally endorse the primacy of the member states, but rather to confirm when the Community might act, a reflection of the fact that the scope for legitimate action by the Union had considerably increased in several areas of public policy.

The Court was familiar with turf wars over competency as the use of the national veto increasingly fell into disuse and the scope for EU policy increased. In these circumstances, 'protecting such areas of exclusive national competence is accordingly awkward, at least once the naked political fact of veto power in Council as a means of halting unwelcome legislative ambition has been surrendered [and] under the influence of both the political and the judicial institutions of the European Community, national systems have become gradually subject to EC incursion in ever wider fields [and] there is no STOP! sign'.[76] The matter of demarcation is so politically sensitive that the Court, unlike a *bona fide* constitutional court, has been understandably reticent about resolving the matter, leaving this delicate issue to the member states. Subsidiarity is one attempt to find an answer to the competence question. The failure to settle this issue once and for all is a reflection, in part, of the Union's polity problem, the lack of a definitive constitutional order, a polity that rests on competing claims to political authority with the result that 'there simply is no nucleus of sovereignty that the member states can invoke, as such, against the Community'.[77] Consequently, 'subsidiarity may be treated as a PAUSE! sign – pause and consider whether the Community should act'.[78]

The case made by federalists for a European constitution has long maintained that a clearer demarcation of competencies would improve decision-making, removing the potential for such confusion and with it immobilisation, by ensuring greater clarity about who does what, both for key institutional actors and citizens alike, and as such defining the nature of political authority in the Union and enhancing its legitimacy. But this case was resisted throughout the Community's early years and beyond. The prevailing view was that the competence conundrum can never be resolved satisfactorily, indeed should not be so, that the Union's political novelty, what makes this unique polity work is precisely that it balances competing claims to authority. And that as such, it cannot be based on a definitive constitutional order that defines the relations of government and politics as they are authoritatively demarcated in a hierarchically ordered statal polity. Any attempt to resolve the ambiguity over who does what, the *Kompetenz-Kompetenz* or 'who governs' the Union question, by establishing a definitive constitutional order risks jeopardising, as these commentators see it, the very flexibility that allows this unique non-statal polity to function. From this perspective, a definitive constitutional order would threaten the fragile balance, impede the very flexibility which is the novelty of EU governance, the sharing of authority between the national institutional actors and Community institutions.[79]

Resistance to a formal constitutional order in part reflects persistent reticence about endorsing an implied federal agenda, not least because the competence issue figures prominently in the classic federalist narrative, where the critical question is always that of relations between the concurrent tiers or levels of governance, with sovereignty shared in an authoritative constitutional settlement between the federal and territorial polities. Those who resist the idea of a formal constitutional settlement for the Union do so precisely on these grounds, that it is not a state polity but rather a confederal arrangement balancing distinct national interests with mutual preferences. They maintain accordingly that codification is anathema to the sort of 'give and take' that has been the key to the Union's survival thus far, in as much as legal formalism implies rigidity, threatens deadlock, those periodic stand-offs between the particular institutions or levels of governance. And for that reason is more likely to bring about the constitutional crises that have fractured some historic federal states, and is even more likely to do so in a polity lacking the underlying cement of a shared identity, those affective bonds of affiliation and common identity that have enabled some federal polities (Canada and Belgium readily come to mind here) to amicably negotiate their way out of constitutional crisis. For those who espouse this pragmatic outlook, the advantages of constitutional flexibility far outweigh the virtues of adopting a formal constitutional order.[80]

The need for flexibility in such a socially, culturally and economically diverse Union would seem to preclude a formal constitutional order, and this has become the watchword for those who oppose a European Constitution. As with subsidiarity, the concept of flexibility appeals to both sides of the debate about EU governance. For federalists and quasi-federalists it promises deeper integration, an appropriate solution for those impatient to hasten the process of closer union, exasperated by what they see as deliberate stalling by Eurosceptical member states. In short, it suggests a way forward without waiting for the tardy member states to catch-up. Opponents of deeper integration on the other hand, those with reservations about a federal prospectus, a shared political endeavour with common policy objectives and an agreed timetable for their enactment, regard flexibility as a convenient excuse for self-exclusion, permitting them derogations, an excuse for not taking the inside track whilst still remaining a member state. As with subsidiarity, flexibility appeals as an *ad hoc* rather than as a formal constitutional principle precisely because of its pliancy, and it was amplified on those very grounds in the Amsterdam arrangements for the open method of co-ordination.[81]

These changes in the Amsterdam Treaty – further elaborated in the Nice Treaty – were especially timely with impending enlargement scheduled to include eight Central and Eastern European states, an outcome that promised (or threatened as some saw it) to bring unprecedented diversity to the Union, whether in terms of legal norms, administrative procedures or policy preferences. As a response to the challenges of European integration throughout the 1990s flexibility became a 'landmark feature of the EU's constitutional terrain'. The flexibility procedure permits member states to adopt policy commitments under Community competencies differentially according to domestic circumstances, promoting a 'managed and non-exclusionary deepening of collaborative endeavour by most, but not all, member states'.[82] Some commentators see these arrangements as a practical response to the familiar problem of reconciling differential EU policy preferences, a problem almost certain to loom larger after the latest enlargement. As with subsidiarity, the appeal and no less the qualified success of flexibility goes against the grain of a definitive EU constitutional order, challenges 'the dynamic nature of the process', the idea 'that constitutionalism has a necessary anchorage in *fixed* reference points'.[83]

Again, it seemed to be more an *ad hoc* response to circumstances than a cogent and considered solution to the competency conundrum. For even as its practical appeal became apparent as a remedy for coping with unprecedented diversity, a way of ensuring forward momentum if new – or for that matter existing – member states claiming special circumstances resisted deeper integration, flexibility seemed less than effective as a means for resolving the Union's competency question, a problem that needed to be confronted as the Union expanded both in size and in the scope of its policy domains. In these circumstances, the usual resort to ad hocery, muddling through, making pragmatic adjustments, seemed to be out of kilter with the times, given the sheer extent of the challenges facing EU governance. Instead, as the most extensive enlargement to date approached, the imperative for a more formal constitutional settlement of the competency question, a clearer demarcation of competencies, of who does what, gained momentum.[84]

The stand-off between those who advocate a formal constitutional settlement and those resistant to any such outcome was not immediately resolved but in typically protracted fashion as the EU avoided settlement of many of the critical governance issues in a succession of treaty revisions during the 1990s. Grudging consensus of sorts began to emerge on the idea that the EU needed to overhaul its institutional and decision-making processes in the face of mounting challenges, and urgently, so as to ensure more efficient decision-making and the better management of its affairs. In these circumstances, the idea of a European constitution became fashionable currency. The Constitutional Convention established by the Laeken European Council in 1999 was the Union's response to these challenges. The Convention's primary task was to address these institutional problems, to improve decision-making in order to respond to the challenges of a changing international order, and by these means supposedly to bring the Union closer to its citizens. How far it managed to meet these challenges is the subject of what follows.

## The case for constitutional reform

The brief review above of the Union's institution deficiencies points to serious shortcomings, whether the Union's governance is judged by the narrow performance or output criterion of efficient decision-making, or by the more testing input criterion applied to any polity with a democratic purpose, and required as such to reflect citizens' concerns and to respond to them. Reform is essential for enabling the EU to respond to pressing challenges: for instance, alleviating the impact of global economic forces and demographic shifts on national welfare systems and labour markets;[85] keeping the regional peace at a time of rising ethnic tensions and the politicisation of linguistic and cultural diversity;[86] responding to new budget priorities;[87] ameliorating the impact of exponential technological change; managing monetary union; and dealing with the consequences of an unprecedented enlargement. The extent of these challenges and their consequences for citizens, whether as workers, consumers, pensioners, students and so on, and in ways barely countenanced when the project was launched in the 1950s, persuaded some influential political actors that the Union needed nothing less than a constitutional overhaul.[88]

As Dinan sees it 'the likely size and diversity of such [an enlarged] Union make it imperative for the existing members to devise in advance a workable institutional system and a durable policy framework'.[89] Yet by the late 1990s the Union had failed to respond, preferring tinkering to wholesale reform, such that 'the institutional history of the European Commission [was] one of almost continuous adjustment – but not of radical restructuring or reform – in response to successive enlargements'.[90] What had been achieved thus far was much less a constitutional refit than 'a Europe of bits and pieces'.[91] Institutional reform is needed, but it is only part of the solution, for these formidable challenges cannot be met without engaging the public.[92] The Union has to address a serious democracy deficit, it requires legitimacy for its incursions into policy domains that impact directly on citizens.[93] When the Community was 'merely' a common market engaged in regulation and standard-setting this was less of a problem. But the EU is no longer just a regulatory regime, an organisation for managing commerce, and it exercises governance even if it is not a state.[94] As some see it, 'the scope of these [policy] measures is such that they increasingly impinge very directly on the concerns of the citizen [and] it is this situation that has caused some analysts to see the treaties as becoming *de facto* the constitution of the EU'. This affects, in turn, the way the Union changes its rules, for 'the treaties do embody constitutive decision', and for that reason 'one would expect a rather different negotiating process to be emerging, involving consultation and debate and some form of ratification by all those affected [for] in a democratic political system it is the constitutive decisions that most require popular involvement and sanction'.[95]

This became clearer as EU governance expanded as a consequence of the Single Market project launched in 1986. The familiar 'insider' culture of narrow intergovernmental bargains legitimised by vague claims to permissive consensus – implied rather than overt legitimacy – and concern about weak democratic credentials became matters for greater concern during the 1990s, giving rise to the idea of a constitutional refit, though as we shall see this has proved easier to prescribe than to deliver. There is more to engaging the public in constitutional politics, and not least at the transnational level, than elites proclaiming that they speak for 'the public interest'. More, certainly, to launching a democratic conversation about such matters than 'interactive' exchanges or structured dialogues with civil society through Commission web-sites, or tokenism on transparency by allowing the media to eavesdrop on the preliminary exchange of courtesies before European Councils go into secret conclave where the real business takes place. Critics increasingly made the case that the Union was seriously out of touch with its citizens, its functionaries beyond the people's effective influence.[96] One close observer saw the problem thus:

> As the saying goes: if it *is* broke, fix it. That means a long hard look at the European Union from the bottom up. Instead of a patchwork of treaties drawn up and amended over time, Europe is crying out for a full-blown constitutional settlement. No more backroom fudging, pretending that nothing profound is actually happening. It's time to debate this truly enormous project where it belongs: out in the open. My preference would be for the method adopted by the last people to dream of building a new society from a diverse, fractious continent. Like the first Americans, Europe needs a constitutional convention.[97]

This proved easier to recommend than to realise, as we shall see below. The problem here is as much about political culture as it is one of institutional complexity. The Union's politicians are simply not accustomed to thinking in terms of democratic constitutionalism, though the Union does have constitutional foundations, a range of legal sources on which to build a constitutional order.[98] One reason lies in the Community's origins as a bargain that relies on authority conferred by the member states. These states rather than European demos are the 'masters of the treaties'. Historically democracy comes before constitution-making, and the EU is not by any stretch of the imagination a democracy. As Dieter Grimm sees this problem, the mediating structures that are indispensable for democratic politics 'have hardly even been formed yet. There is no European-ised party system, just European groups in the Strasbourg parliament, and, apart from that, loose cooperation among pragmatically related parties'. As such, 'the European Union falls far short not just of ideal conceptions of a model democracy but even of the already deficient situation in member states'.[99]

The problem here is with the Union's constitutional design, and it will not be easily remedied. The EC/EU was designed with governments in mind and it continues to depend on governments rather than on citizens. Primary Community law goes back, not to a European people or demos but to the individual member states and it depends on them even for its enactment. Consequently, 'while nations give themselves a constitution, the European Union is given a constitution by third parties. The "masters of the treaties" are still the member states, who have not, as it were, been absorbed into the Union.'[100] Moreover, the integrative capacity of EU law, the 'coherence of purpose achieved by the Court of Justice', is frequently overstated, 'confusing the legal order as a constitutional order'.[101] The cultural impact of this legacy, in terms of its consequences for a full-fledged constitutional order, should not be underestimated, and no less the abiding 'perception of EU governments that it is only behind closed doors and with a limited number of actors with defined interests that the kind of package deals which characterise these constitutive decisions can conceivably be reached'.[102]

Governments and the other national agencies retain a firm hold on the Union's political process.[103] Indeed these very obstacles have reinforced the view in some quarters that a formal constitutional order is inappropriate for this transnational polity, precisely because it would resolve once and for all the abiding differences of this contested polity. According to this argument it is preferable to accept this contested political order, a design that balances quite different aspirations for the European project, rather than to 'freeze – or attempt to freeze – a historically specific set of social relations into some political structure which then limits and curtails future choices', and risks pushing things to breaking point.[104]

## Does the EU need constitutional ballast?

Although the EU is not a state, nor likely to become one, the contention that it does not need proper democratic procedures or means for legitimising the decisions taken in the name of its citizens has been criticised as misguided by academic theorists and political activists alike.[105] Yet the case for constitution-alising the Union has not been convincingly made, at least where it ought to be made, with the citizens. The political elite that embarked on a formal attempt to constitutionalise the EU polity failed to carry public opinion, as the outcome of referendums in two of the Community's founder states shows, though the case for a European Constitution is much the same as for any constitution in a polity claiming democratic credentials: to provide the body politic with a formal map of institutional power charting 'who does what, when and how' in a polity, the very same rationale for legitimate and accountable governance that has sustained constitutionalism everywhere during the age of democracy. The requirements developed over the past century or so for installing a legitimate and stable political order, the better to reconcile the competing demands of what Robert Dahl called the 'democratic dilemma', apply as much to this non-statal polity. The European Union is not a state but it is a polity, and one that bestows considerable political and economic power on its institutional actors. Moreover, it is increasingly involved in allocating values in key areas of public policy, disbursing resources, allocating collective goods and exercising the functions of governance, and for all of these reasons it should have proper constitutional ballast.[106] The EU is not a state polity but it does intrude into the everyday lives of its citizens. The problem, however, is that to date this polity has been constitutionalised only by default and mostly behind the scenes, and with output legitimacy taking precedence over input or polity legitimacy, when in fact both aspects of legitimacy are indispensable for a properly grounded and stable constitutional order.[107]

As a polity that subscribes to democratic norms as a condition of membership, the EU does require its own form of constitutional authority, if only to 'satisfy the general criteria that apply to the legitimation of any liberal democratic system'.[108] Legitimacy in the constitutional sense relates both to the regime *per se*, the particularities of the polity's institutions and procedures through which public power is exercised and to what officials and politicians do with such power, its outputs as public policy. Regime legitimacy is especially important for the EU as a non-statal polity and a regime type with few if any historical precedents to provide either normative or practical benchmarks for the rightful exercise of power.[109] Both forms of legitimation are essential for constitutionalising what is aptly described as *un objet politique non identifié*.

The critical question here is what sort of constitutional arrangements are appropriate for legitimising a non-state polity? Clearly, the EU is not a primary political community: it does not have first call on the loyalties of its citizens. The very fact that the Union consists of pre-existing historic polities – the member states – familiar to their citizens, who have invested them over time with primordial allegiance, is bound to influence the conduct and shape the outcome of the EU's constitutional endeavour. And, not least, it affects how both national governments and their citizens see this endeavour. The EU polity has other peculiarities too that have significant consequences for its constitutional order. With the partial exception of the ECJ, whose judgements have primacy and direct effect in those policy domains where European law applies, the Union's principal institutions are not politically sovereign within EU territory in any way that remotely corresponds to national political institutions. On the contrary, the available polling evidence on political affiliation and identity confirms that 'there is a widely and deeply-held sense in member state electorates that the central political institutions of the member states are (and should remain) the dominant and decisive force of allegiance and activity within the topography of the EU, and that, as far as the populations of these states are concerned, their polity's continuing membership of the

EU and its agreement with or acquiescence in its policy are at its discretion, and not to be taken for granted'.[110]

These circumstances are bound to determine the nature of the constitutional endeavour. The constitutionalisation of the Union should be based then on pragmatic desiderata as much as on any general appeal to common values, let alone to European demos or a meaningful sense of European identity. Social solidarity in this sense may eventually emerge, but if it does it will be as a consequence, an effect rather than a cause of shared constitutional endeavour that connects with popular concerns across the EU. In the meantime, if constitutionalism at the transnational level is to succeed, those who undertake the task have to find means for connecting citizens with the process.[111] Some commentators doubt whether the EU can rise to this challenge, let alone meet the objectives usually associated with historic constitutionalism, though historical precedents give some cause for optimism. Constitutions constructed in response to deep-seated political and cultural crises have on occasion more than fulfilled the expectations of their founders, though to be sure this has never before been attempted in a transnational polity. The challenge facing the Union here is certainly formidable, though this is no reason for its leaders to shirk the challenge as it confronts problems in critical aspects of public policy, problems that no one European state can reasonably be expected to resolve on its own. Moreover, this endeavour covers some important aspects of public policy that cannot be resolved without public support, including, *inter alia*: the reform of welfare arrangements under unprecedented strain; responding to the competitive challenge of globalisation; bringing some urgency to the debate about climate change and other threats to public health from nature; reinforcing regional security against the threat of international terrorism, cross-border crime and other potentially destabilising threats to security; and so on.

More is required for making an effective response to these challenges than 'mere' institutional tinkering. Citizens can, and more to the point should, be involved in what are by any gauge 'historic' issues. Legitimacy is indispensable political capital for addressing critical policy challenges in any polity, and no less so for the EU, for ensuring public support for difficult decisions, a means for deepening the citizens' sense of affiliation, instilling a sense of solidarity across borders as member states confront common problems and undertake common policies. This is less a matter of ideals, a sense of 'being European', than it is of practicalities, the search for solutions to mutual problems across borders, though the idea of transnational governance has always appealed to idealists. The fact is that the EU is not a state but nevertheless it does increasingly intrude on its citizens' lives in critical aspects of public policy. To meet these formidable policy challenges, and at the same time to ensure the public's support for making, and just as important for enforcing, policy decisions with distributive and redistributive consequences, it is essential that the Union carries citizens with it. This is why the constitutional endeavour remains a priority, notwithstanding the problems that have befallen the Constitutional Treaty. After all, it was the perceptible sense of disconnection with citizens that finally prompted political leaders to consider constitutionalising EU governance, to simplify decision-making and bring it closer to the people after a series of 'top-down' treaty reforms had signally failed to do so, let alone to settle the question of where authority lies in this inchoate and multi-level polity.

The Union's belated attempt at constitution-making has failed nevertheless to convince, and even more to connect with, citizens. Instead the political class has reverted to type, falling back on the familiar formula of top-down treaty reform, though it is a response that hardly addresses democracy and legitimacy deficits. How then should what is described as the disconnection problem be addressed? As Skach sees it, the key here is what she describes as constitutional realism, to acknowledge the limits of what is politically feasible in this unique multi-level polity, and above all not to over-reach. A European constitution cannot be the same as a national constitution. It will not, for instance, realise European demos, nor will it create a European society, nor even a framework for EU-wide democratic politics.[112] At the practical level, and by taking account of the limits of the Union's constitutional endeavour, it can nevertheless contribute to enhancing performance legitimacy in EU governance by improving policy-delivery, installing a simpler, altogether clearer framework for collective decision-making, defining procedures and clarifying the allocation of competences between the various tiers of multi-level and so far ravelled governance.[113]

These may seem modest goals compared with the ambitions of federalists for a fully-fledged European constitutional order. But the pay-off from even this modest prospectus, measured in the normative currency of legitimacy, should not be discounted over the longer term. Legitimacy as public trust in governance comes ultimately from performance as much as from merely abstract normative referents, what sociologists describe as political culture. Norms about 'good' governance are important, but they are dependent rather than independent variables, they come from citizens' experiences and do not exist a priori. What actually works matters, and just as important how citizens see it working matters as much as what idealists prescribe as 'good' constitutional principles. Over time, 'good' practice acquires procedural legitimacy, and in the process enhances regime legitimacy. This after all was how regime legitimacy became embedded in national polities, a cumulate and by no means an unproblematic process and one based in the early stages on effective performance. Performance is important for enhancing the legitimacy of the European polity with its citizens. For this reason alone, there is a case for making the sort of institutional reforms outlined in the Lisbon Treaty, though bargains made behind closed doors by political insiders are insufficient on their own to win hearts and minds on the ground.

Citizens everywhere in Europe are increasingly becoming perturbed by the prospect of international disorder, from criminality to terrorism, health scares to climate change, and from population movements to threats to financial stability posed by unregulated activity in cyberspace. These threats to public order are paradoxically an opportunity for the Union's political class to launch a transnational conversation, to seriously engage the public in an inclusive discussion about, an opportunity 'to co-ordinate society against these other, potentially negative and disintegrating mechanisms that are emerging as potential alternatives' to the long period of prosperity and peace that has prevailed in Europe since 1945.

Political leaders must explain better what the EU actually does, what it is about, what it contributes to citizens' well-being. Above all, they should learn to listen to the public's own concerns, hear what citizens, after all the Union's democratic stakeholders, have to say about their own preferences, priorities and aspirations for European public policy, giving the public a fuller and more realistic account of the balance of benefits and consequences for national discretion accruing from transnational co-operation, not least as a counterweight to 'the disintegrating, centrifugal mechanisms' that come from the widespread sense of dislocation or anomie resulting from globalisation.[114]

This may be some way removed from the altogether grander aspirations associated with the classic European constitutional tradition, but it is important none the less. Above all a constitutional order for Europe rooted in the public interest rather than the narrow and elite preoccupations will present people with real choices about their future governance, a solution to current legitimacy and democracy deficits, a way of connecting the Union with its citizens, finally replacing constitutionalism by stealth with a public *pouvoir constituant* and bringing the people into a democratic conversation about the Union's future direction. This is the only proper basis for European governance rooted in a liberal and democratic constitutional order.

## Constitutionalising *un objet politique non identifié*

The Union is not a state, nor is it remotely on the way to becoming one. Yet neither is it merely an international organisation or regulatory regime, but rather is something between a federal polity and a congress of nation states, in essence *un objet politique non identifié*, making the task of constitutionalising it that much more difficult. As defined by international law the EU is a union of independent sovereign states that derives its competencies and the authority of its institutions solely from its member states. It possesses no sovereignty on its own account other than those fragments of sovereignty invested in its institutions by the member states, and entirely at their own discretion, though even this may be repatriated should any one of them so decide. Any member state may freely secede from the Union without hindrance, other than losing the benefits of membership and undoubtedly squandering considerable political capital. The federalist quest to widen the base of the Union's political legitimacy by making 'the people' *per se* the final arbiters of its power has faltered precisely because there is not a European demos.

The arrangement whereby the member states both retain ultimate discretion over their sovereignty, whilst agreeing to invest a degree of national power in common institutions and policy-making procedures, is both the essence of the Union's unique political and legal status, and the root cause of difficulties in the search for a cogent constitutional order.[115] Tension between competing intergovernmental and supranational preferences was built into the Community's institutional architecture from the outset, a unique quality of ambiguity and inter-institutional balance identified by Robert Schuman as '*le supranational*', an arrangement for common decision-making in some aspects of public policy whereby 'the supranational is situated equidistant from, on the one hand, international individualism and, on the other, a federation of states subordinating themselves to a superstate'.[116]

The ambiguity of this arrangement has been broadly endorsed by Europe's political leaders, a bargain most recently defined by Jacques Chirac, when French president, as a 'United Europe of states'. Britain's Tony Blair has likewise referred to this unique arrangement as 'a Europe of free, independent sovereign nations who choose to pool that sovereignty in pursuit of their own interests and the common good, achieving together more than we achieve alone', confidently predicting that 'Europe will remain a unique combination of the intergovernmental and the supranational ... such a Europe can be a superpower, but not a superstate.'[117]

This dynamic balance between opposites, the juxtaposition in the institutions and decision-making procedures of competing preferences continues to drive the EC/EU polity. The tension between these competing ideas for transnational governance has never been resolved one way or the other, and indeed cannot be resolved without risking what would surely be a debilitating, possibly even a terminal crisis. To pursue a definitive settlement of these competing impulses for European integration, imposing constitutional finality on the Union in the manner of the classical constitutional narrative we are familiar with in the history of nation-building in Europe is to risk destabilising, and maybe even destroying, the delicate balance between the Union's supranational and intergovernmental preferences. And in the process, to jeopardise the future of what is, by any comparator for transnational governance, a remarkable political achievement. But at the same time, the Union carries in its institutional arrangements and organisational culture residual problems that urgently require reform, and not merely tinkering but wholesale change that might be described as constitutional make-over.

This is the predicament that confronts the Union's would-be constitution-makers. To acknowledge the scale of the task, however, is by no means to rule out a successful conclusion. The EU clearly requires far-reaching reform if it is to meet the challenges that face it. As always in this unique polity, the watchword must be caution; the requirement to balance competing preferences for common governance and not least about the ultimate ends of the European project is indispensable to the constitutional task in this polity. As one contemporary commentator sees this task: 'Europe, it would seem, is as ever at the very limits of experimental governance: a largely unforeseen integration dynamic giving rise to an ever-changing, and ever novel, climate of market "socialisation" and post-national polity building ... has clearly exposed the limits of "discipline-internal" constitutional thought ... within Europe [and] just as the foundations of social organisation have been radically overhauled, so too, must constitutional law engage in an identification of the rationalities which underlie its formal provisions; and furthermore, critically submit such bedrock conceptualisations to a test of their continued compatibility with "real world" conditions'. In short, 'Europe is an evolving and uncertain polity', and its constitutional design must accommodate these facts.[118]

Valéry Giscard d'Estaing, the president of the Convention charged with the task of reviewing the Union's constitutional options, was aware of these constraints, observing that 'Europe's answer to the "federation or confederation question" is the acknowledgement that the Union is a unique construct which borrows from both models.' As Giscard saw it, the Convention's task was not just to write *a* constitution, but one that would not try to resolve this constitutional conundrum one way or the other, rather 'formalising' the Union's structural and ideological ambiguity.[119] It was clear from the outset, that the very idea that a European Constitution could settle abiding tension between competing ideas about EU governance, reconciling once and for all the intergovernmental and supranational impulses, was never a serious option.[120] The Convention's task was in a way to decant new wine into old bottles, to find ways of reforming collective governance, more efficient ways of making decisions, to simplify procedures and to make them more transparent and no less democratic, to more clearly demarcate the boundaries between the domestic and EU levels. Above all, to accomplish all of this without altering the delicate balance between competing preferences for Europe embedded in the Union's existing institutional design. In effect, the Conventions' mandate was to draft 'a progressive constitution of legitimate institutions and powers at the European level, which are complementary to the national constitutions and designed to meet the challenges of an evolving global society'.[121]

This is no easy task, and one constitutional expert defined this considerable challenge as follows:

> Europe must not be built on an either/or model. ... the Union is not a state, is not on the road to becoming one and it should not take that road. Instead it sets up a system of governance in which its Member States have distinct but complementary roles to play. 'Multi-level governance' acts as a rather neat shorthand for describing the way in which Europe (and not only Europe) is the subject of many layers of intersecting legal and political authority, some territorially defined, others sectorally defined, not necessarily capable of subjection to a single, internally consistent rule of authority, yet working more or less successfully because of adaptation along the way and the vested interest of participants in avoiding conflict. [Multi-level governance requires then] multi-level constitutionalism, within which national and European level systems of governance interconnect. [A multi-level approach thus acknowledges] the importance of different levels of governance in dealing with the growth of trans-national economic activity [governance whose very novelty requires an entirely new constitutional narrative as] a reliable framework for the taking of collective action.[122]

European integration was always a response to the limits of the nation-state as the primary actor in international politics after the anarchy that led to two world wars in less than a generation. As globalisation has accelerated, the boundaries between national and international politics have become more porous, domestic and international realms more meshed, levels of governance more fused than ever before.[123] The European project has been defined by paradox from the start, the idea that by sharing power, pooling some elements of national sovereignty with near neighbours, small and medium-sized states increase their purchase on events, pursuing common interests in the international domain otherwise beyond their capacity to influence. Collective endeavour is certainly required if Europe's small and medium-sized states are to survive and prosper in the face of insidious global forces, to respond effectively to policy challenges of such scope and complexity that they can only be effectively tackled by transnational cooperation.

This in essence is what constitutionalising the EU is about, indeed it is what European integration has always been about. One member of the convention described the predicament that confronts the modern state as follows:

> states are both losing sovereignty and expanding it at the same time. By giving up power, they gain more power. By giving up absolute power, states gain relative power. ... Europe, the birthplace of the national state, is again at the cutting edge. Now it is seeking forms for the supranational authority of the post-nation state era. Supranational decision-making is being first implemented on a regional basis, with Europe leading the way in this regard. The European Union is the most ambitious and bold step. It expresses the most extensive format of shared sovereignty.[124]

But this is only one aspect of the constitutional project. For this arcane governance needs popular legitimacy as never before, otherwise it is in danger of alienating citizens more than they presently are, a fatal outcome for any polity that claims democratic credentials. How the EU has responded to this constitutional challenge is the focus of what follows: the way the principal actors, both governments and European institutions, perceived this constitutional task and how they went about it as would-be founding fathers.

# 2 The idea of a European Constitution

## Why constitutions?

Constitutionalism is as problematic as any concept in the political science lexicon. Liberal narratives define the art of constitution-making as a progressive endeavour, the formal act of constraining the exercise of power in a polity. Constitutions in this narrative are nothing less than a foundational moment, a new beginning, the 'symbolic proclamation of the creation of a new political community'. More than that, they have a social function, an expression 'of political leaders' benign attempts to enhance social integration in systemically divided polities'.[1] Some contemporary commentators are less than convinced about such claims, though there is at least a broad normative consensus that a virtuous outcome is precisely what the constitutional endeavour ought to be about.

In the liberal tradition, a constitution is a formal text that provides the authoritative framework for the exercise of political authority, a map of power relations that identifies the principal institutional arrangements and the procedures for government, outlining relations between the respective branches of government, and prescribing how disputes between agencies should be resolved. It sets limits to public power and allocates competences between the respective institutions of government.[2] Such functions are especially important for a system of multi-level governance. Public order requires a predictable and 'a stable standardised framework of social rules' for mediating the multiple boundary exchanges, associations and interaction between political actors at every level of governance and the body politic, so as 'to facilitate effective decision-making and social well-being'.[3]

Constitutions in democratic polities also confer a catalogue of fundamental rights and duties beyond the scope of ordinary law-making, ensuring citizens' civil liberties and determining their obligations to the polity.[4] A key aspect of the power-constraining function is to safeguard permanent minorities – usually defined in terms of ethnicity or some other cultural category – against the misuse of public power by the majority.[5] In effect, constitutions establish clear limits to political and public power, ensuring that citizens are defended against both public encroachment on or private infringement of their liberties. In democratic polities political order must be balanced by 'democratic legitimacy', or what has been described by some commentators as 'input-orientated authenticity'.[6] More recently, constitutions have also conferred social rights that ensure equitable access to basic welfare and to other public goods. Above all, a constitution sets out the rules for changing the rules, 'the terms by which power is divided or shared in the political system', and arrangements that may 'be altered only by extraordinary procedures'.[7]

In addition to defining the distribution of legitimate political authority, democratic constitutions also ensure the conditions for political stability. They are one means for safely negotiating potentially disruptive episodes of structural change that occur periodically even in well-founded polities.[8] The point of a constitution, as Lyn Dobson sees it, is to make the exercise of power both more accountable and more transparent. Transparency is as indispensable for a constitutional order as it is for any aspect of a democratic polity, and contributes to what John Stuart Mill celebrated as the necessary clash of opinions, in essence an ongoing conversation between all of the stakeholders in a polity about their common future. Openness about how power is distributed – and indeed constrained – and how the rules operate is required for citizens to better understand how public power is exercised in their name, that they might have 'full knowledge of the relevant circumstances pertaining to their decisions'.[9] As stakeholders, citizens rely on 'clarity, transparency, and publicity ... for the formal and material equality of [their] effectively exercisable civil and political liberties'. Citizens are undoubtedly hindered in the exercise of their rights, 'if they do not know what they are, nor how the polity that is the institutional mid-wife of their community is put together: how powers and competencies are distributed'.[10]

In essence a constitution establishes the ground rules for the civilised conduct of governance and politics, balancing the imperatives in any democratic polity for, on the one hand, individual rights, liberties and voluntarism that mean freedom under law; and on the other hand, the indispensable requirement for political order, predictable rules and procedures, itself an institutional framework essential for balancing competing interests and ensuring liberty. As one political scientist has defined this critical equation, clear rules are necessary for ensuring 'policy performance effectiveness' or 'output-orientated effectiveness'.[11] Balance here between order and freedom is essential for good governance, but it is harder to ensure than to prescribe. As such, it presents a challenge to constitutional design, a challenge notably described by Robert Dahl as the 'democratic dilemma'. The precise constitutional design for ensuring such equivalence is a daunting task for any polity. These are essential requirements for a liberal constitutional order, though there is no neat formula for ensuring balance, for circumstances vary according to the particularities of place, historical legacies, political culture and the norms of the polity.[12] Constitutions are more than merely inventories of formal rules, or an outline plan of institutional architecture. They are prescriptive in as much as they reflect the ideological preferences of their founders. To this extent constitutions enshrine what theorists call a *Grundnorm*, a legal doctrine 'embodying the fundamental goals of the social community to be organised'.[13]

A normative foundation in this sense performs two distinct, albeit related functions in a democratic polity. In the first place, it sets clear boundaries to the exercise of authoritative political power. In so far as power has both positive and negative potential, a constitution guarantees the former and constrains the latter. Above all, it ensures that power is exercised according to known rules that make clear 'the correspondence between the goals of the legal system and the organisation of public powers that have to implement them'.[14] These fundamental norms perform another important function: they make clear to the citizen their right to access governance, the means for their participation, legitimise the political opportunity structures that reinforce a sense of common membership, reinforcing the affective bonds that bind citizens more closely to the polity's common endeavours. In this sense, a democratic constitution has a cultural as much as a political or legal function. It confirms a shared sense of purpose between rulers and ruled and is an expression of common values.[15] A constitution is a matter then for the citizens who are bound by its rules, as much as it is for those elites and vested interests who negotiate its fabric and write it down. For a constitution is symbolic of what a democratic polity represents, 'the supreme affirmation of the primordial power of a people over themselves (as a collectivity), and over the space they occupy'.[16]

Constitutions are hardly a new phenomenon, though in the history of European governance formal contracts between governors and governed, the critical constitutional moment or *annus mirabilis* when the body politic gives its consent to an authoritative formula for future governance is an altogether more recent occurrence. A 'constitutional moment' in this particular sense tends to occur at a significant historic juncture, usually a break with the past, for instance after defeat in war, liberation from tyranny or during periods of post-revolutionary turmoil, whether in response to domestic deliberation or imposed by external power. Moreover, 'historic' moments tend to be cathartic, usually requiring a far-reaching rethink of, rather than merely tinkering with, governance.[17] Constitutionalism in democratic polities represents nothing less than an expression of the public's will to confront endemic problems, to reimagine the future, a moment when 'citizens rationally and dispositionally choose to bind themselves in respect of their contingent and occurrent possibilities'.[18]

This may be the general experience of classic constitution-making, but constitutionalism by no means always conforms to this template. Constitutional activity is not always dramatic, nor are its outcomes conclusive and may in a well-ordered and stable polity be rather more a matter of incremental adjustment to exigent circumstances, the 'quasi-constitutionalisation' of an already established constitutional order engaged in the periodic review of its rules and procedures. To date, EU constitutionalism has been of this variety.[19] Much less the cathartic 'constitutional moment' familiar to students of historic European state-building than the 'low intensity constitutionalism' aptly described by Maduro as 'an incremental and bottom-up constitutionalism [and not] the product of a constitutional moment but of a judicial and political step by step development often constructed by reference to national constitutional sources'.[20] The Union's experience since its foundation hardly matches this constitutional tradition, though some insistent voices called for a new start, for the Union to have its 'constitutional moment'.

## The European constitutional tradition

Constitution-making is an established political art in Europe, though until recently one restricted to state-building. Even here it has been mostly confined to the second half of the twentieth century as erstwhile dictatorships gave way to more enlightened regimes.[21] Wariness about 'constitutionalism' as new-fangled, and above all as unduly radical politics with unforeseen consequences for established regimes, was apparent in the response of the Habsburg Emperor Francis to the demand by his otherwise loyal Tyrolese subjects for a local constitution to better ensure their autonomy in Europe's most ethnically diverse state. Resisting the very idea as inimical to the mysteries of the 'natural order' of things, Emperor Francis duly reproached them, warning that 'the whole world has gone crazy, and abandoning its good old laws is searching for idealised constitutions [for] you have a constitution which you have received from your ancestors. You love it and I love it. I shall cherish and defend it and hand it down to my dependents.'[22]

This sanctimonious notion of an organic constitution is anathema to statesmen of a liberal or democratic disposition. As they see it, constitutionalism is progressive, or should be progressive, and for that reason confined until quite recently to established and mostly stable political communities, invariably states. Moreover, it is political activity only lately regarded as 'normal' in the continent's turbulent history of regime change. The movement to install a liberal and democratic constitutional order began in earnest in Europe only after the First World War had brought to an end the mostly authoritarian empires that had emerged in Europe at the close of the high Middle Ages, putting an end to free republics and independent city states. The process gained momentum in the aftermath of the Second World War, itself a direct response to the vacuum left by the collapse of tyrannical regimes in states where fragile democracy had been subverted by fascism.

A second wave of democratic constitution-making followed the voluntary transfer of power from European imperialism to successor states during the late 1940s and 1950s. A more recent phase has seen constitution-making in the postcommunist states of Eastern and Central Europe following the collapse of Soviet hegemony in 1989, and was about making or more usually remaking national constitutions the better to respond to contemporary challenges. The recent initiative to constitutionalise the EU stands squarely outside this cumulate tradition, a novel experience precisely because it seeks to formally constitutionalise a polity that is not a state, and a polity that is not only multi-ethnic but transnational in its construction. As such, this endeavour reminds some commentators of the historic precedent of building a federal polity on the American continent at the end of the eighteenth century, a comparator that has attracted much academic interest on both sides of the Atlantic, of which more later.[23]

Constitution-making in contemporary Europe shares one fundamental objective: to protect the freedom and rights of citizens by enshrining procedures in a supreme legal order that constrains central power. The primacy accorded to citizens' rights *vis-à-vis* government is a relatively recent, and even in Europe a quite rare phenomenon, only becoming significant in the years between the two world wars with the generalised incorporation into constitutional texts of formal declarations of rights, a natural reaction to growing executive power.[24] This emphasis on rights was in some measure a response to developments in mass politics, not least the consolidation of the party machine, firmer party discipline in parliaments, the rise of xenophobic mass movements and so on. The principle concern here was to protect political rights by embedding them in constitutional texts. The trend in Europe since 1945 has not merely been to expand the catalogue of rights available to citizens, but to change the normative and legal status of all rights, both 'old' and 'new'. The social and cultural change that followed the Second World War has lately given rise to demands for so-called 'third generation' rights, for instance social, gender-specific and environmental rights. Whereas before 1939, 'the constitution was still defined in continental Europe as the standard by which public power was defined, above all with respect to legislators whose actions give rise to law', post-war constitutions have come to be seen as the direct source of law, especially of those 'fundamental rights that directly empower (and bind) the citizens'.[25] It is a process formally rooted in the advocacy and interpolation of citizens' rights, with national constitutional courts entrenching and then protecting such fundamental rights.

In short, the European constitutional tradition has brought about over time the rights-based polity, setting out the institutional framework and affirming judicial benchmarks for 'good' practice to guide policy-makers and governance. Constitutionalism here is process more than it is 'end state', ongoing and organic change as much as a singular 'founding' moment. This organic quality has been influential in the development of the European Union's constitutional order, and the more so because for the first half century or so the EC/EU avoided the idea of a formal constitution to describe its legal and political arrangements, though a formal constitutional order for Europe has always appealed to federalists.

Constitutionalism is a natural response to defective government and it takes many forms. At the very least, it amounts to 'a clear conception of government and ministerial responsibility', standards of legitimacy, accountability, transparency in the exercise of public power. This is undoubtedly so in democratic states.[26] And though the EU is not a state and is unlikely to become one, these same standards apply to what is after all governance at the European level.[27] The idea of a European constitutional order was first raised by supporters of pan-European economic co-operation as long ago as the 1920s, a legacy of the intellectual opposition to the destructive clamour of nineteenth-century nationalism.[28] After the Locarno treaties (1925) had provided a more secure basis for Franco-German co-operation, Aristide Briand described these early, tentative arrangements as 'the draft of the constitution of a European family within the orbit of the League of nations ... the beginning of a magnificent work, the renewal of Europe'.[29] The International Economic Conference that convened at Geneva in 1927 used similar language, its chairman referring to the move towards 'an economic league of Nations whose long-term goal ... is the creation of a United States of Europe', and tellingly as the only political force capable of resisting the growing economic might of the USA.

This, however, was as far as it went. A project conceived by idealists, a pan-European constitutional order hardly appealed to most Europeans, and certainly not to those who wielded public power. The idea did survive the frenzy of the 1930s and the carnage of the 1940s, but though it emerged from the war years as part of the resistance movements' plans for a new Europe, an antidote as they saw it to the failure of nation-states to stem the tide of fascism, by the time of the Hague Congress in 1948 it was little more than an undercurrent of the debate about European reconstruction, and as remote from popular sentiments as ever. The notion of a political community as an accompaniment to the putative European Defence Community (EDC) hatched by Jean Monnet and René Pleven in 1950 led to what Monnet's biographer, François Duchêne, called 'desultory exchanges' about a 'constitutional conference to raise a political roof over the prospective Coal and Steel and Defence Communities', and Italy's prime minister, Alcide De Gasperi, had proposed that an EDC Assembly 'should prepare a draft European constitution for the governments to negotiate'. But in the event, the idea never flew.[30] In so far as a European polity was seriously considered, the idea appealed far more to intellectuals and idealists, and it has remained largely their preoccupation, an esoteric idea appropriately described as 'top down constitutionalism', paradoxically a discourse that even for federalists was 'rooted not in popular concerns about misuse of power', a process led 'by governments and states and not citizens'.[31]

Constitutionalism at the European level has found little support amongst either grassroots politicians or the general public, but it has always appealed to lawyers, who trade, after all, in the currency of fundamental rights. The European Court of Justice has long been the driving force behind a process that some have described as constitutionalism by stealth, embedding a rights-based European constitutional order that, on the basis of the primacy and direct effect of EC law, strongly influences the domestic legal order.[32] The idea of a rights-based European polity has in turn influenced the debate about a Europe-wide constitutional order.[33] As Weiler sees it, the development of even a limited EU constitutional order has been premised at least for some of its principal agents, notably the Justices in the Court, 'as if its founding instrument were not a Treaty governed by international law but, to use the language of the European Court of Justice, a constitutional charter governed by a form of constitutional law'.[34] European case law is a rich source of fundamental rights and applicable at every level of the Union, as is the European Convention on Human Rights (ECHR), to which all of the member states are signatories.

The fact that national constitutions ensure rights according to variable procedures seemingly precludes a uniform EU-wide basis for fundamental rights, though it does not quite work like that in practice. The national and EU constitutional orders are by no means parallel universes; they do connect and they do cross-fertilise. The consistent application of EC law, its very primacy and its direct effect, has facilitated, in practice if not in name, what amounts to a rights-based European constitutional order. The current treaty arrangements confirm as much, referring to 'fundamental rights as guaranteed by the European Convention on Human Rights and such as they result from the common constitutional traditions of the Member States'.[35] Incremental constitutionalism operates at the EU level, but it has been by no means without controversy. One major problem here is the translation of national constitutional norms and procedures from their familiar domestic context to the transnational level.[36] There is nevertheless the basis here for common constitutional endeavour beyond the nation-state, a medley of shared norms about 'appropriate' political, civil and related rights that provides the EU with an implied if not (or not yet) a formal constitutional order. Even so, the Union's constitutional arrangements remain complicated, defying straightforward classification in terms of the 'normal' experience of European constitutionalism. Not least because the Union is not a state: its constitutional order rests on national constitutional norms which may, and on occasion do, conflict with the norms of the European Court of Justice.

## Constitutionalism by stealth: the role of the European Court of Justice

European integration has dramatically changed the conduct and parameters of governance, within the member states as much as between them, reducing the scope for autonomous action, constraining sovereignty in some important areas of public policy that have traditionally defined nation-states as independent actors in the international system. This process has mostly come about intentionally, the consequence of formal revisions of the founding treaties. There are, however, unintended consequences from *ad hoc* revisions of the treaties, explication *de jure* in various rulings by the Court of Justice about the meaning of the treaties, what was supposedly intended by the Community's founders. Accordingly, the Court of Justice has made a momentous contribution to constitutionalising the Union. The Court's landmark rulings have significance beyond the substantive cases that give rise to them, putting in place an expansive legal order that confirms that Community as something more than a mere international organisation.[37]

This judicial process is intrusive, impacting on the separate national legal orders, and it has constitutional as much as 'merely' legal implications, at least in the narrow sense of that term. As one legal expert sees it, the logic of what we might call implied constitutionalism means that 'Community law takes precedence over national law in the Community sphere', so that 'in each of the member states, the Community is a source of new law whose provisions prevail over domestic norms of any level'. The supremacy of this new body of law 'liberates national judges who must apply it from their duty of absolute submission to national law, including national constitutional law, and, in effect, transforms them into Community judges'. And even more than that, 'the supremacy of Community law substantially modifies the formal subordination of governments to their respective Parliaments, whose principal consequence for the domestic legal order of member states is the supremacy of statutes over delegated legislation and executive orders', such that 'the supremacy of "derived" or secondary Community law, made by the representatives of national governments in the Council of Ministers, turns upside down this relationship'.[38]

The national courts have tended to incorporate EC law into domestic law as a normative benchmark, albeit with some significant exceptions, and by this means to extend the Union's supranational reach. This outcome is the more significant because, for the most part, it was not what the Community's founders intended. The Treaty of Rome did not formally specify that European law should be directly applied in national courts. Nor did it stipulate that Community law must prevail over national law in the event of any conflict between these respective legal orders. This development has been contingent, the result of circumstances rather than design, and it has created a 'constitutional deficit' with consequences at both the national and EU levels. These consequences are clear to see in a catalogue of landmark rulings. The important principle of the direct application of Community law in the national courts was established by the decision in *Van Gend en Loos*, a ruling that determined that the direct effect of Community law was actually implied by the founding Treaty.[39] The pertinent part of the ruling states that:

> The objective of the EC Treaty, which is to establish a common market, the functioning of which is of direct concern to interested parties in the Community, implies that this Treaty is more than an agreement which merely creates mutual obligations between the contracting states ... the Community constitutes a new legal order of international law for the benefit of which the states have limited their sovereign rights, albeit within limited fields, and the subjects of which comprise not only Member States but also their nationals. Independently of the legislation of the Member States, Community law therefore not only imposes obligations on individuals but is also intended to confer on them rights which become part of their legal heritage.[40]

The Court followed this with a second important principle, again one with important constitutional implications. The *Simmenthal* judgement established the primacy of European law, such that: 'every national court must, in a case within its jurisdiction, apply Community law in its entirety and protect rights which the latter confers on individuals and must accordingly set aside any provision of national law which may conflict with it, whether prior or subsequent to the Community's rule'[41] This was confirmed in *Factortame*, to the effect that: 'Community law must be interpreted (by national courts ruling in a case concerning Community law) as meaning that the sole obstacle which precludes it from granting interim relief is a rule of national law, must set aside that rule'[42] The judgment in *Internationale Handelsgesellschaft* went even further, giving Community law precedence, even in cases where national constitutionally protected rights are concerned.[43] This means in effect 'that Community treaties and law have both direct effect in the territory of the member states upon passage, and supremacy over domestic law – previous and subsequent – constitutional or statutory'. Moreover, the concept of supremacy here 'precludes any challenge to the constitutional validity of community treaties, even via control over the constitutionality of laws authorising their ratification or their incorporation into national law'.[44]

In the opinion of many legal experts this process of embedding EC/EU law in the national legal order amounts to nothing less than the indirect, and as some see it the covert, constitutionalising of the EU legal order, the Court acting in effect as a self-appointed *pouvoir constituant*.[45] The Court has acted as it was intended that it should, to protect the rights of the individual citizen, in the first instance in their capacity as economic citizens. However, the cumulate impact of the Court's decisions has been to extend judicial protection, and to expand individual rights for citizens *vis-à-vis* national authorities and Community institutions alike, beyond those relating solely to the functioning of a common market.[46] This, too, has had unanticipated consequences for the member states and the Union alike. As Weatherill sees it, the founding Treaty is 'constitutive of the system that is the EC legal order', and thereby 'establishes institutionally relatively sophisticated forms of lawmaking which reflect forms of representative democracy at both national and European level'.[47] As a consequence of an expansive interpretation of rights, a quasi- or informal constitutional order emerged, what has been described as 'thin' as opposed to 'thick' or formal constitutionalism.

The Court has pushed this interpretation of its role as far as possible, even going so far as to describe the Treaty as a 'constitutional charter'. This has become a (indeed *the*) working principle *de facto* of the Union's legal order, reflecting the Court's view that the exercise of public power in Community affairs at whatever level is subject to judicial review, whether or not this fact is explicitly acknowledged in the treaties. Significant here was the ruling in *Parti Ecologiste Les verts* v. *Parliament*, the Justices maintaining that the EC is 'a Community based on the rule of law, in as much as neither its Member States nor its institutions can avoid a review of the question whether the measures adopted by them are in conformity with the basic constitutional charter, the Treaty'.[48]

The mutually reinforcing doctrines of supremacy and direct effect, and landmark judgements based on these principles, have constitutionalised the Union, though covertly and without much by way of democratic procedure, let alone public participation. On the contrary, constitutionalism in this 'thin' sense is exclusively for judges. The prevailing view of the Justices, that Community Law should be applied in preference to national law even where it challenges a domestic legal norm, and broad acceptance of this interpretation by national authorities, has been the basis for the Union's incremental constitutional order.[49] This process confirms the marked difference between the Community's legal order and a system of public international law as established by treaty, although the substance of the Union's legal order hardly corresponds to the Court's extravagant claim to preside over a comprehensive rights-based constitutional order.[50] Legal rhetoric and for that matter judicial ambition, to say nothing of wishful thinking, continue to be way ahead of what is accepted practice here. Nevertheless, a rights-based jurisprudence that was initially intended merely for the adjudication of market-making rules has brought about the constitutionalisation of the Union's legal order, as critics see it incrementally and by stealth.[51]

So much so, that the European legal order seems to some commentators to resemble nothing less than the constitutional arrangements of a federal state, to the extent that as a general principle, 'national courts do accept by and large that EC law is capable of direct effect in national proceedings and by and large they do not contest that within the scope of its application EC law prevails over national law', though less so where matters of fundamental constitutional principle are at stake. We shall return to this important matter below. European law intrudes into national legal and administrative culture beyond anything that is implied by the terms of an orthodox international treaty arrangement. The claim is even made in some quarters that intrusion into national jurisdiction is the European Court's 'great genius and … what makes good the assertion that EC law is truly *sui generis*, occupying a space somewhere between the law of a (federal) State and the law of an international organisation and performing functions that are similar to those performed by legal rules in both types of system'.[52] It is this very 'in-between-ness' in legal matters that continues to give rise to lively debate about the constitutional implications of the EU legal order.

The matter is certainly controversial. One problem with this doctrine is the mismatch between the national and EU constitutional orders. The Court's notion of implied, what might be described as 'nested,' constitutional orders is built, as Llorente sees it, 'so to speak, "on air" with only the weakest basis in the member state constitutions'. Critics point out that this means, in effect, that the European Court has not taken cognisance 'of the particular nature, the wide differences of the respective national constitutions', when it made landmark judgements. And though the doctrine of supremacy does acknowledge that the founding treaties and their subsequent revisions do have firm constitutional grounding, judicial practice in every member state reaffirms distinctive national constitutional traditions. The Court for the most part has overlooked, or rather chosen to ignore, the consequences of this signal fact for embedding a definitive European constitutional order. Discrepancies between the European and national constitutional orders cannot be simply overlooked, and the Court has pushed its claim to be a constitutional *pouvoir* beyond what is politically permissible, even in a confederal union and certainly for one rooted in democratic norms. The European Court has sustained this position on the basis of federalist logics, that 'the relationship between the Community and the member states is not international in character [and by] viewing member states as the "black boxes" of classic international Law, whose internal legal problems have no effect on the obligations imposed by Community law'.[53]

Accommodating the member states' constitutions to the Community legal order in these circumstances has been mostly *ad hoc*, more a matter of national constitutional authorities amending national constitutions, the adoption of generic clauses or constitutional provisions in order to satisfy the different requirements of the respective authorities. One important requirement here, in what is clearly not a federal state, is to more clearly demarcate between the member states and the Union in terms of law and competencies, to iterate precisely which elements of national sovereignty, which domestic competencies in the field of public policy, are the legitimate concern of the Union, and by definition which are not. And by so doing, not only to formally acknowledge the limits of national sovereignty in order to accommodate the requirements of European integration, but, just as important in what is, after all, a confederal and not a federal polity, to underline the constraints on the process of legal (and by implication, constitutional) Europeanisation. For this process by no means implies the Europeanisation of domestic law, at least not for national authorities, but rather the opposite, with the accommodation of two quite distinct if overlapping legal orders amounting in effect to the nationalisation of Community law.

So far only two member states, France and Germany, have amended their national constitutions with the express purpose of giving their membership of the Union formal constitutional status, whilst simultaneously placing other barriers in the way of further constitutionalising the Union's political order. Instead of wholesale European constitutionalisation being driven forward by the Court operating as a *de facto* European Supreme Court, it is customary practice for national judiciaries rather than the ECJ to determine the extent of acceptable conformity between national norms, rules, laws and legislative acts and EU law and legislation. National legal authorities retain this important prerogative as it is customarily practised by the courts of most of the member states, in a way a kind of legal subsidiarity. This practice is most graphically illustrated by the outcome of the landmark decision of the German constitutional court of 12 October 1993 and discussed below.

The principles of direct effect and supremacy notwithstanding, judicial procedure nevertheless confirms the lack of a formal constitutional order as this applies to democratic polities, one that 'nests' the national within the European constitutional order. This is one reason why constitutionalism at the European level has not advanced much beyond *ad hoc*, incremental and, it has to be said, contested actions by the Court to enhance rights under the treaties. Moreover, this, too, is why federalists place altogether more faith in politics as the agent of a legitimate, formal and not least a democratic constitutional order than law-makers.[54] As they see it, judicial action can take the constitutional endeavour only so far, and 'little beyond a formal re-elaboration of the Treaties whose "constitutional" nature already has been reiterated often and emphatically by the European Court'.[55] Constitutionalism by default is not, according to this view, constitutionalism in any legitimate sense of the word. A formally constituted and publicly sanctioned constitutional order for the Union, one enacted by a *pouvoir* of democratically elected representatives of the Union's body politic rather than by unelected judges acting independently and, to say the least, at the very limits of their authority, is the *sine qua non* of a constitutional order for Europe, as for any democratic regime. Without these conditions in place, any 'proposed (European) constitution would still be ontologically distinct from member state constitutions, and would remain separated from them by more than just the quotation marks in which the word itself is frequently placed. More importantly, it is unlikely to provide a solution to the material problems facing the Community.'[56]

The issues raised here did not immediately signify, either with the Union's political or judicial authorities. The Court's landmark legal decisions were absorbed by national legal authorities, without much by way of objections. These issues were by no means uncontroversial but they were highly technical, and though they stirred concerns amongst national authorities, legal and political alike, they remained below the public's radar. One outcome of this process has been to install *de facto* 'a (European) constitution without constitutionalism', a quiet judicial revolution amounting to discreet constitutionalisation, what some critics have described since as 'judicial creep', unfolded on the back of arcane but no less significant legal decisions.[57] The process is perhaps best explained by the Community's preference for consensus in decision-making on technical matters.[58] The Court operated successfully above politics and without undue interference from national authorities in developing rights within its legal competence, but in the process stretched the definition of these competences and with it its constitutional authority. It carried out this role by playing down, and critics would say even disguising, the political significance of judgements, whilst claiming legitimacy from its undoubted reputation as both a credible and an effective agent of market-making, establishing a cogent legal base for economic integration, as conferred by the treaties.[59]

National judiciaries accepted the authority of ECJ decisions for a variety of reasons, both pragmatic and principled. The appeal of universal legal norms pertaining to economic transactions was hardly controversial in what is, after all, a common market. And there was the inducement, too, for national judges to exercise additional powers by reinforcing agreed European norms as agents of the Court.[60] In time, the 'quiet revolution' raised objections, as it must do in any regime adhering to democratic norms, as the Court's actions impinged on other, altogether more politically sensitive matters. The political significance of apparently 'technical' decisions became more apparent, and political objections were raised by both national legal and political authorities to the very idea of the Court imposing a European constitutional order by default.[61] One can quite see why; after all, the EU is not a federal state and the Court does not enjoy the constitutional status of a supreme court. Neither does it have the right to exercise judicial review, the prerogative of supreme courts in federal systems. The member states jealously defend their right to determine domestic constitutional norms, not least because there is no singular formula here. Each national constitutional order is the outcome of quite different histories, shaped by distinctive constitutional norms and separate procedures.[62]

In these circumstances, it has proved impossible to resolve once and for all the controversial issue of whether Community law is a legal, and by extension a constitutional, order, free-standing and wholly independent of the respective national orders. Both superior to the national legal order and, as such, 'an integral part of the legal systems of the Member States ... which their courts are bound to apply'.[63] In so far as EU law remains dependent for its authority and for its application on the national legal order, with each national system connecting with the Union's legal/constitutional order in accordance with its own distinctive procedures and normative codes, the Union's constitutional order is far from being embedded in that of the member states in the manner of federal law in a fully federal state.[64] The facts are plain to see here. National authorities, both legal and political, have always harboured, and sometimes famously expressed, doubts about the degree of constitutional discretion that might be legitimately exercised by the ECJ, claiming precedence over the ECJ as the legitimate guardians of their citizens' liberties and rights, and maintaining that Community law in these critical matters is merely a secondary authority.[65]

These reservations have been voiced by constitutional courts in the member states, institutions whose primary function is to safeguard national constitutional norms. And for that very reason these authorities are loath to relinquish this duty when confronted by the ECJ's claim to judicial supremacy in matters of constitutional law. Resistance to the Court's implied role here from national legal authorities has usually been expressed as normative deliberation rather than as concrete judicial review, the adjudication of specific cases, though there have been some notable landmarks rulings here that demarcate the boundaries of legal competence as these national legal authorities see it. By and large, however, neither side has forced the issue, preferring consensus to confrontation, though on occasions these boundaries have been tested, but never to the point of a constitutional showdown. On the contrary, the European Court of Justice has showed restraint here, aware no doubt of the tenuousness of its claim to be seen as the Union's ultimate constitutional authority, concerned not to push matters to a stand-off that would propel the Union into unprecedented crisis. On the one hand, the Court has upheld fundamental rights deriving from the ECHR and national constitutional norms and traditions alike. [66] But on the other hand, it has only contemplated striking down those acts that conflicted with either of these universal and national norms or standards.[67]

National constitutional authorities have on occasion resisted what they saw as undue interference by the Court in matters beyond its comptence.[68] The most notable challenges to the ECJ's role as the Union's self-appointed constitutional arbiter have come from the *Bundesverfassungsgericht*, the German Constitutional Court.[69] That court's *Solange* ruling, for instance, invalidated any Community law that compromised the fundamental rights of German citizens under the national constitution. This decision affirmed the Court's concern that Community law could conflict with national constitutional norms.[70] Although this sanction has not so far been utilised it draws a clear line, thereby demarcating what are seen as quite separate jurisdictions. Similar concern about the European Court's competence, in effect an objection to what was seen as 'backdoor constitutionalism' likewise informed the *Bundesverfassungsgericht* ruling (1993) on the Maastricht Treaty.[71] Concern about maintaining firm legal/constitutional boundaries has by no means been confined to the German authorities.[72] Resistance to the European Court of Justice's assumption of authoritative jurisdiction in constitutional matters has been expressed at various times by the constitutional courts of Denmark and Italy, no doubt silently cheered on by justices in other EU constitutional courts.[73] But this clash of norms and indeed of legal cultures has never quite come to a head. Restraint rather than outright confrontation has been the preferred strategy by both sides.

National constitutional authorities have avoided a showdown with the European Court, preferring to signal their concerns about intrusive supranational judicial

review in normative language rather than by concrete actions, no doubt anticipating that this would be sufficient deterrent to transgressing boundaries, rather
than risk a head-on challenge. Even the *Bundesverfassungsgericht* has preferred
to send warning shots to signal these boundaries rather than to challenge the Court
in a climactic showdown.[74] This conciliatory approach was signalled for instance
in the conciliatory tone of that court's *Solange II* ruling, compared with the patent
irritation of *Solange I*.[75] The overriding concern has been to avoid what could
easily escalate into a political crisis, with who knows what consequences. For
as Weatherill observes, 'once a threat is executed things may never be the same
again, both as between the (judicial) parties to the dispute and, by a process of
spill-over in application to other interested parties as well. The parties know this.
They want to avoid "deciding" big questions which probably cannot be decided
to the satisfaction of both parties. By declining to answer the question no one
overtly wins but no one loses either, and both parties maintain their own position to mutual advantage. In this sense, in fact, both win.'[76] A 'practical concord-
ance' exists then about the status of EC law, both at the national level and in the
European Court, which confirms the interdependence of these quite distinct legal
orders, reinforced in turn by awareness all round of just how much is at stake from
maintaining economic and political interdependence.

Interdependence between domestic and European legal orders was confirmed in
the European Court's *Internationale Handelsgesellschaft* judgement in December
1970. Reciprocity is precisely how the system does work: direct effect and
supremacy can only be effective so long as these two legal orders co-operate,
are sufficiently flexible about the interpretation and enforcement of respective
legal norms.[77] The system requires mutual tolerance and, more than that, creative
ambivalence about the interpretation and application of norms, the avoidance of
an unduly rigid constitutional code.[78] In effect, to survive at all the EU constitutional order depends on flexibility, and would be wrecked by any attempt to
impose too rigid a framework. Constitutionalism at the European level is necessarily rooted in ambiguity, focused 'on creating arenas for problem-solving (which
might involve problem-avoiding) within an overall system which emphasises the
necessary interconnection of national and European constitutional legal orders'.[79]
This arrangement works 'precisely because each participant can rest its consent to
involvement on different bases which may be constitutionally irreconcilable in a
purely formal sense but which do not cause any practical need to choose'.[80] Central
to this approach is avoidance of resolving definitively the crucial boundary question of which level of authority has ultimate supremacy, a situation that 'would be
problematic only if there was some attempt to find the "correct" answer – that is,
to adjudicate who is the winner and who the loser – the either/or question'.[81]

One might conclude from this that the EU has avoided constitutional crises
familiar in federal states elsewhere precisely because it has avoided such 'constitutional finality'. To resolve this question of constitutional competence once and
for all would undoubtedly threaten the delicate balance between the supranational and the intergovernmental domains, whereby '*both* sources of (constitutional) authority have complementary roles to play [and] the current constitutional

plurality pattern permits this'.[82] As Palermo sees it, the EU could not exist without the states that constitute it as a polity, but the contrary is equally true, the states likewise rely on the Union. The outcome is an interdependence that requires 'the establishment of common principles', and though these do not have quite the same effectiveness as common constitutional traditions (not least, because they are not immediately enforceable in the courts) they are nevertheless 'of great importance in shaping the relations between member states and the Union: something which is in between soft law and constitutional traditions common to the member states'. What this means in effect is that European integration has given rise to a thin rather than thick, an informal rather than a formal constitutionalism, 'a bundle of reciprocal influences that, in spite of not being directly justiciable by a court and thus not immediately binding, have enormous legal relevance'.[83]

This formula has worked well enough, but over time it has become strained, not least as common governance has intruded into some politically sensitive domains. As the EU expanded its policy domains the boundaries between the domestic and European legal and constitutional orders has given rise to legal challenges by the former, but also to a renewed debate about formalising the constitutional design, precisely to clarify who does what, and with what legal authority. Ambiguity has become an increasingly unreliable foundation for consistent, and no less for authoritative, governance, giving rise to calls in both theoretical debate and from practitioners alike for an appropriate post-national constitutional order to reflect changes in European governance on the ground.

## Tensions in the European constitutional order

The Court's normative preference has always been and remains implicitly federalist. This much is clear from those occasions when the Court overreached itself, provoking resistance from those concerned lest it push the boundaries of its jurisdiction beyond what was intended by the Community's founders, or for that matter enshrined *de jure* in the treaties.[84] The German constitutional court's ruling on the *Brunner* case (1994) rebutted the European Court's attempt to covertly constitutionalise the Community, and in the process to rewrite the German Federal Constitution by assuming a 'right' to rule on the applicability of EU law within the national realm.[85] And since most national constitutions incorporate a bill of rights, and the putative 'European constitution' did not do so until the Charter of Fundamental Human Rights was written with the intention of incorporating it into the Constitutional Treaty, it has remained the prerogative of national courts to review EC law in the matter of rights so as to ensure its conformity with national law.[86] This legal norm does not in itself resolve the matter of constitutional discretion. The European Court has always responded vigorously to what it sees as any challenge to its constitutional authority, seeking to convince national judiciaries that EU law does indeed encompass fundamental rights, by embracing in its jurisprudence all of the common norms and international standards on human rights contained within the corpus of treaties and conventions subscribed to by every member state. Such that, by what amounts to implied judicial consensus, 'these rights become EU rights and as such are subject to interpretation "within the structure and objectives of the community"'.[87]

The Court was able to pursue its mission to constitutionalise the EC/EU precisely because it operated above the political radar, by and large without those closely monitored political constraints that have always been exercised over the political institutions by governments and national political institutions, principally courts and parliaments. National courts, and for that matter national politicians, have generally been rather less vigilant where the Court is concerned. Consequently, the Court was able to stretch 'mere' case law to incrementally fashion its preoccupation with market-orientated rights into something approaching an informal or quasi-constitutional order.[88] Yet whenever the national constitutional order was confronted by the Court on constitutional matters, and especially on any matter where national constitutional norms and a putative rights-based EU constitutional order conflicted, it managed to see off the challenge.[89]

The Court's assumption a priori that it was the Union's supreme constitutional arbiter was always tenuous, more appealing to the Court than to either domestic legal or political authorities. More to the point, it hardly matched political realities, for though 'the Court's assertion of the supremacy of EC law implies a federal structure based on the hierarchical ordering of sovereign power, in which the particular interpretation and implementation of general formulations can be devolved down to subordinate bodies',[90] the fact is that the EU is a contested regime with a 'federal deficit', and one lacking a definitive, let alone an authoritative, constitutional doctrine.[91] The Justices simply assumed the Community to be 'a federal organisation of power, with certain aspects of state sovereignty definitively ceded to the Community'. Accordingly, EU measures were assumed to 'derive their validity solely from European law', and for that reason could not be challenged 'on the basis of conflict with national laws – even those of a constitutional status – "without the legal basis of the Community itself being called into question"'.[92]

Critics did not see things in quite the same way, and made much of significant differences between the national and EU legal orders that had already made for difficulties when national legal systems had to assimilate EU laws and directives, and there are also abiding differences in legal cultures.[93] The European Court has tended to interpret rights according to libertarian and economic preferences, mostly relating to norms appropriate to a free market; whereas national legal orders are steeped in normative referents and case law that favour a more progressive model of social rights.[94] There is accordingly a cultural disparity between the Court's view of constitutionalism rooted in libertarianism and that of national legal cultures with more collectivist preferences. The ECJ has, for instance, 'been relatively intolerant of minority language rights, regarding them not just as restrictions on the four freedoms that can increase transaction costs by, for example, requiring multilingual labelling, but also on freedom of expression, although they could be equally interpreted as defending this latter'.[95]

There have been other, equally significant discrepancies between the Court's normative benchmark and those of the member states. In *Grogan* (Case C-159/90 *SPUC (Ireland) Ltd* v. *Grogan* [1991] ECR I-4683) for example, 'the dilemma posed by the Irish Constitution's protection of the right to life of the unborn child was largely side-stepped, though the Court's definition of abortion as a "service" clearly poses problems for the Irish state's attempts to deny its citizens access to it'.[96] These are but two examples of the normative lacuna that exists between the judicial cultures of the European Court and those in most member states. Regardless then of an assumption of a European constitutional order rooted in an 'overlapping consensus on shared liberal democratic principles and the rule of law', it is clear from actual case law that 'substantial differences remain'. And these normative differences weaken significantly the Court's claim to be the Union's constitutional arbiter. This in turn makes 'the boot-strapping operation of the ECJ in creating a definitive European Constitution … a remarkable example of the self-validating nature of law'.[97]

In so far as the EU has a constitutional order *de facto* it is not, as we have seen above, a political contract made between polity and people, but a narrowly defined rights-based order made by judges.[98] It follows from this that if there is to be a EU constitutional order it cannot come about by stealth on the back of legal rulings handed down by unelected Justices, but only from the will of elected politicians, and ultimately with the express consent of the people.[99] For the Court to claim to be the *avant-courier* of a constitutional order on this basis challenges the very idea of democratic constitutionalism.

Democratic constitutionalism requires political consent more than it needs legal largesse, however well intentioned. Of course, law matters; it is the normative bedrock of every democratic constitutional order. But democratic constitutionalism is political or it is nothing. Constitutions in democratic polities are contractual arrangements between the stakeholders. These transactions must be a transparent, above all the outcome of a deliberative process giving rise to demonstrable legitimacy, acceptable to those required to submit to its procedures and rules.[100] Constitutionalism is a political bargain rather than merely a legal arrangement precisely because it involves making significant choices, and more often than not difficult choices. Not least about how to organise governance, the principles that inform authoritative rule-making and rule enforcement, determine the allocation of authoritative power and so on.[101] As such, constitution-making in any polity claiming democratic credentials is far too important to be left to unelected judges, however wise or benevolent they may be.

Constitution-making is more political art than legal science, although political science both as normative theory and as the residuum of institutional and comparative studies does provide would-be 'founding fathers' with the basic meta-theoretic and empirical material from which to construct the constitutional fabric. Above all, the art of constitution-making is a pragmatic as much as a theoretic endeavour. It depends on relating general principles and fundamental norms to the practical task of building a legitimate, and thus a sustainable political order. Constitutions, if they are to last, must be grounded in practical experience, with a sense of what is feasible, what will work. As Elazar sees it, 'constitutional documents cannot be treated in the abstract, divorced from the power systems of which they are a part and the political cultures from which they grew, and to which they must respond'.[102] Polity-building in contemporary Europe at whatever level 'must be seen not only as the summit', the formal framework, but also as process, 'the relations of contention and alignment at the intersection of elites, mass, local, national and supranational actors and institutions'.[103]

The public are as important here as those privileged insiders who make these critical bargains that underpin social order on their behalf. This is hardly a new idea, though the public voice has always been less audible in the process of making the European polity than it ought to be.[104] A constitutional Convention was to be the Union's answer to this constitutional deficit, a deliberative exercise that brought together not only government spokespersons but also representatives from politics and civil society. Whether the public at large were entirely convinced by this exercise in supposedly democratic constitution-making for the transnational European polity is, on the evidence of the subsequent ratification process, altogether less certain.

## Constitutionalism and democracy

Constitutionalisation and democratisation are complementary projects in any modern polity that subscribes to liberal norms, and the EU should be no exception.[105] So far, however, the EU is remote from its citizens, for the most part a technocratic and regulatory project and one driven largely by elites. Some commentators are unperturbed by the Union's failure to accommodate liberal constitutional norms or procedures, maintaining that the liberal variant of democracy is inappropriate here.[106] Representative democracy, as they see it, is difficult to reconcile with a confederal polity, one lacking demos and without the means for conducting, and in plain language, a meaningful conversation about policy preferences and the values that inform them, and one mediated by democratic agencies such as political parties, civil society or a Europe-wide mass media. Some critics of contemporary politics go even further, arguing that liberal institutions are devalued now even in the national polities that gave rise to them, overtaken by hyper-mobile capital and the powerful forces of globalisation which easily outmanoeuvre traditional representative institutions, the would-be watchdogs of the public interest. In this narrative, citizens cannot be said to consent in any meaningful sense to policies enacted in their name. Accordingly, these particular circumstances require an entirely new approach to democratic politics.[107]

The neo-republican narrative prescribes an open and inclusive politics, with altogether less emphasis on the passive or 'top-down' procedures of plebiscitary democracy, and requiring instead a civic culture based on active and politically alert citizens. The public interest here is determined neither by benevolent 'princes' nor through intermediation by elected representatives with those technocrats whose manage the policy process, but as the outcome of an inclusive and democratic conversation between governors and people. Citizens are the rightful as well as rights-bearing agents of political and social transformation, the only legitimate interlocutors of the public interest, and for that reason the best guarantors of a just and a democratic society.[108] This radical narrative sets an impossibly high standard for democratic governance in any polity, and especially so in the transnational

EU, as even some of its staunchest advocates acknowledge. There is no guarantee that even if citizens had greater opportunity to participate in their own governance they would do so. Many will prefer to invest scarce leisure time in the pursuit of private gratification rather than in public service. Yet for radical republicans this is a feasible model for democratic constitutionalism in the EU, 'a formal setting out of the rules in accessible form after an extensive public discussion or rather series of discussions among the multiple publics that constitute the population of the EU'. And a conversation that, as Kuper sees it, would 'go far to reverse the cynicism and disillusionment which is so widespread in relation to the European Union'.[109]

Advocates of democratic constitutionalism refute any suggestion that it is either far-fetched or unduly idealistic. It is feasible, they maintain, precisely because of the cultural shifts and technological innovations resulting from structural changes in the international system. The Union's very diversity, not least the lack of a singular political identity, enhances more than it limits democratic potential. Cultural pluralism, the fact of multiple and coexistent identities, and especially uniquely multi-level governance, makes for greater tolerance and receptiveness to accommodating differences. This, in turn, has its own potential for fostering a sense of common identity in Europe. Technological change, too, plays its part, with the potential to link by virtual means people otherwise separated by geographical distance through the broadcast media or in cyberspace. These cultural agencies give rise to a sense of solidarity, an awareness that in a turbulent and fast-moving world Europeans face similar problems.

Those who make this case do not discount difficulties in the way of political transformation, but neither do they dismiss the prospect out of hand. What is required for solidarity across borders, according to Kuper, is nothing less than 'a double conceptual disengagement: of citizens from nationality and ethnicity and of democratic constituency from territory defined nationally, and in some cases from being defined in territorial terms at all'. Citizens' rights and the obligations of EU membership 'must be separate from and not dependant on (prior) member-ship of some community where membership is defined in national or ethnic terms'. Neither outcome can be taken for granted, but there is some evidence that changes are underway in the processes of identity formation. Though individuals may and usually will invest affective commitment in their primordial identities, for Kuper 'the simple identification of the democratic constituency with the territory of the nation state and sub-order democratic communities with regional and local territo-rial divisions of that state [has become] increasingly unsatisfactory'.[110]

This narrative makes much of citizens' capacity for empathy with 'strangers' beyond the bounds of the primary political community, detects a growing sense of solidarity across historically defined borders, that what 'we' have in common is greater than what separates us. Habermas, amongst other writers in this vein, remains fairly sanguine about the prospects for what he describes as 'inter-subjec-tivity', meaning citizenship rooted in shared affinities shorn of nationalism or ethnicity, arguing that 'what unites a nation of citizens as opposed to a *Volksnation* is not some primordial sub-state but rather an inter-subjectivity shared context of possible understanding'.[111] Much is made, too, of the idea of European civil society, the prospects for engagement by citizen-based action groups, political organisations, NGOs, trade unions, church bodies, women's groups and the like in a shared political and constitutional conversation, and one that is conducted in a defined transnational public space. This is what Habermas means by a 'Europe-wide integrated public sphere', operating 'in the ambit of a common political culture: a civil society with interest associations: non-governmental organisations; citizens' movements; and naturally a party system appropriate to the European arena'.[112] The idea of a shared public space is critical for this radical model of transnational politics, and we shall return to the important question of agency, of how it might be realised, in Chapter 12.

There are some fairly large claims made by those who propose this case. Suffice it to say here that agency is the critical question, how to facilitate public participation in transnational politics. This is indeed a challenge, and one that requires more than wishful thinking for its solution, for this is no simple endeavour. David Held has acknowledged the scale of the task, noting that: 'The problem of democracy in our times is to specify how democracy can be secured in a series of *interconnected* power and authority centres. ... Democracy within a particular community and democratic relations between communities are interlocked, absolutely inseparable, and ... new organisational and binding mechanisms must be created if democracy is to survive and develop.'[113] This outcome is easier to prescribe, more difficult to realise. What is clear from the Union's recent constitutional endeavour is that the politicians have barely considered the prospect for citizen engagement, let alone tried to facilitate it. The usual response is to deny there is a problem with public engagement, or else to propose measures to improve communications, procedures for explaining to citizens what the Union is about.

Of course, public information is important, too; essential for engaging citizens in a conversation about their governance, a necessary but by no means a sufficient condition for a democratic constitutional order at the European level. After six years and more of constitutional deliberation in the EU the question we are left with is whether such a democratic conversation is possible. More even than that, we must consider how democratic constitutional change might come about in a Union still dominated by narrow vested interests, a polity whose privileged insiders and institutions remain, half a century after its foundation, both geographically remote from and procedurally unfamiliar to its citizens.

## Constitutional narratives

There has been vigorous debate about whether Europe needs a constitution. On one side are those who refute the very idea of a constitution for what is, after all, a non-statal polity. On the other side are those who see the European constitution as the indispensable foundation for a democratic polity, a charter no less for a people's Europe, and for some even for a state-in-the-making. A median position sees a constitution as a requirement for resolving long-standing disputes over institutional powers and competencies, settling once and for all 'who does what' in this complex multi-level polity.

## The case against a European Constitution

The sceptical narrative maintains that whatever 'Europe' is about, it is not about constitution-making. Constitutions, as those who take this position see it, regulate power and confer authority in sovereign states, providing an authoritative framework or map of the competencies and inter-relations of political institutions. As an international organisation and at most a confederation of nation-states, the EU is not in need of a formal constitutional order. More than that, the European Union cannot be constitutionalised precisely because it is not a state, and lacks those elemental qualities of statehood, not least demos and an affective sense of identity whereby citizens 'come to resemble each other', aspire 'to become one',[114] to be bound together by some 'minimal common cultural denominator'.[115] In short, Europeans are not a people already constituted as 'a collective entity by organic-cultural definition'.[116] This argument is a familiar one in the writings of intergovernmental theorists and in the pronouncements of politicians, determined as they are to resist the idea that the EC/EU is, or can ever be, anything other than a community of co-operating yet inalienably sovereign states. This narrative corresponds closely to the realist account of international politics, the long-standing claim that European integration is a process driven primarily by national preferences.[117] Far from making the nation state obsolescent, European integration is instead but one response to those challenges that confront nation-states in the global age.[118]

The case against a European constitution has been made by Dieter Grimm, amongst other political theorists. As Grimm sees it, the Union's political order does not rest, nor should it rest on formal constitutional principles as do Europe's democratic nation-states. These states are hierarchically structured, whereas the EU, as the brief review of the Union's political architecture in Chapter 1 makes clear, is a heterarchical design. Moreover, one lacking the socio-cultural attributes for transnational politics, not least a pan-European public space, a civil society and meaningful citizenship defined here as identity-based membership of a polity.[119] In liberal democracy citizens are the principal source of legitimacy for the rightful exercise of public authority,[120] and 'the deepest, most clearly engraved hallmark of citizenship in our democracies is that in citizens vests the power, by majority, to create binding norms'.[121] Legitimacy is thereby conferred on those who occupy public office by directly elected representative institutions, in effect by citizens constituted as a demos.

For Grimm and those who share his outlook, the crucial linkages between citizens and their governors, the special quality of solidarity rooted in a common history ensures that legitimacy can be realised only in the nation-state. The absence in the European polity of anything that remotely resembles a shared sense of identity, in effect European demos, is central to the case he makes against a European constitution. Demos is essential to constitutional authority and 'democracy does not exist in a vacuum', but instead 'is premised on the existence of a polity with members – the demos – by whom and for whom democratic discourse in its many variants takes place'. Authority and legitimacy conferred by a majority of citizens can exist, as Grimm sees it, only within effective boundaries defined by demos. And there can be no democracy without demos, an ontological sense of belonging to a clearly defined community.[122] Solidarity in this sense does not exist in the EU, for 'a demos, a people cannot ... be a bunch of strangers', and strangers to one another is precisely what EU citizens are.[123]

Of course, the nation-state is not the only meaningful fount of political identity. Territorial and sub-national political communities exist, and they are becoming increasingly important in European politics. The sense of affiliation to something beyond the nation-state is altogether more problematical, though it may come about in due course, rivalling nationalism in its capacity for instilling a sense of shared identity. For the time being, however, the nation-state remains the primary focus for political identity and for emotional attachment. And the persistence of national affiliation figures in the case made by Grimm and others against the prospects both for realising a European polity and for a European constitution.[124] Whatever the changes underway in the structure and logics of the international community, the consequences for the exercise of public power of rapidly accelerating globalisation, this narrative maintains that the 'obstinate' nation-state remains as the central actor of international politics.[125]

Much is made here of the absence of a European lingua franca, a vernacular medium for engaging the public in a conversation across borders about matters of common interest. Reference is often made in this debate to John Stuart Mill's observation in his *Considerations on Representative Government* (1861), to the effect that: 'Among people without fellow feelings, especially if they read and speak different languages, the united public opinion necessary to the working of representative government, cannot exist.'[126] Much is made, too, of the lack of a common civic space in which to debate public policy. Europe's many languages and its cultural diversity quite simply 'restrict participation in European opinion-forming and interest-mediation, and there is no "European" media, no "European" public', and consequently 'no "European" political discourse'.[127]

As such, 'Europe' is neither a people nor is it a nation, it has 'neither the subjective element (the sense of shared collective identity and loyalty), nor the objective conditions which could produce these (the kind of homogeneity of the organic national-cultural conditions on which people-hood depend such as a shared culture, a shared sense of history, a shared means of communication) exist'. For all these reasons, as Dobson observes, those 'long term peaceful relations with thickening economic and social intercourse' that are the legacy of 60 years of peace in Europe 'should not be confused with the bonds of people-hood and nationality forged by language, history, ethnicity and all the rest'.[128]

### The case for a European Constitution

The case made for a European Constitution inverts the sceptics' arguments. Those who support the idea of a European constitution base their case on the claim that far-reaching changes are indeed underway, and make much of the processes of 'Europeanisation', a nebulous concept that broadly includes the consequences of accelerating structural and cultural interdependence, a process, too, that is altering not only the dynamics of politics but also its normative framework. So much so, that the EU is acquiring state-like qualities, and for that very reason could and for some should be constitutionalised.[129] Indeed the EU needs a constitutional order in the full sense of that term in order to regulate its governance and to be consistent with the commitment to democratic norms it imposes on any would-be member state.[130]

This narrative reverses the case made by Grimm and others against a transnational constitution. It questions the capacity of the modern nation-state in the global age to perform its traditional functions, not least its primary obligation to defend citizens' interests and secure their welfare. Zielonka, for instance, sums up the present situation thus: 'Globalisation has eroded the capacity of any integrated political unit to maintain a discrete political, cultural, or economic space within its administrative boundary. Economic sovereignty in particular has been eroded by massive international labour and capital flows that constrain individual abilities of governments to defend the economic interests of their units [and] territorial defence along border lines has been made largely obsolete by modern weapons technology.' Furthermore, 'migration and other forms of cross-border movements are on the rise [and] normative models and cultural habits are spreading via satellite television and the internet in a largely uncontrolled manner'.[131]

For Jürgen Habermas, a leading exponent of a European constitutional order, these far-reaching structural changes and cultural shifts have undermined the capacity of nation-states to perform their basic functions, whether to ensure security against external threats, or to manage all manner of boundary-crossing problems, from climate change, pandemics and mass population movements, to international criminality or the economic consequences of global markets. Accordingly, Habermas seeks solutions to these multiple post-modern challenges beyond the customary locus of the nation-state, and he sees potential for a supranational and democratic European political order rooted in what he believes is an emergent transnational civil society.[132]

Those post-national thinkers who share his vision – for this narrative is more visionary than it is empirical – acknowledge the obvious constraints on realising a European politics where borders are discounted, not least those constraints imposed by prevailing political culture and political experience. Nevertheless, Habermas remains optimistic, and proposes building a European constitutional order on foundations put in place by the EU polity. However, his design for a European polity in these terms is quite conventional, state-like if not exactly a state and rooted in social democratic values, its politics shaped by familiar redistributive logics. This is a narrative of post-national governance that in effect seeks to reinvent the social democratic state at the transnational level, for Habermas cannot envisage solving the Union's 'deficit of collective action capacity, especially those distributive problems which follow in the wake of the enhanced steering power of trans-national capital and the EU's own "market-making" strategies of negative integration, without a regulatory wherewithal and legitimacy akin to that of a welfare state'. Moreover, this is a design for a post-national state that is 'federally organised and committed to the principle of subsidiarity'.[133]

Although this is a radical prospectus, it hardly breaks the mould of European politics as we have known it this past century or so. Central to the case for a

European polity is the claim that the modern nation-state is no longer capable of controlling the powerful forces driving globalisation.[134] The international system that emerged from the Peace of Westphalia (1648) was based on territorial states, the primary units of political organisation and public power, both for domestic governance and for conducting international relations.[135] The national and democratic revolutions of the late eighteenth and early nineteenth centuries consolidated the nation-state, and as democratisation gathered pace embedded the idea of nation-statehood as the fount of legitimate governance firmly in the political imagination. The liberal democratic state that emerged from this historical process is the normal form of governance in Europe, and for that matter elsewhere. Faced with rising demands from below, these states embraced redistributive policies, delivered by means of progressive taxation and welfare reforms. What this arrangement offered its citizens was security in exchange for patriotism, an implicit contract across the generations between 'princes' and people, and by and large a successful one.

As some critics see it this system has had it day, overtaken by events beyond its capacity to control or even to significantly influence. Times have changed, and with them the capability of the nation-state to effectively perform its traditional governance or security functions.[136] Accelerating globalisation has diminished the capacity for governments to manage economies, and together with demographic change has undermined national welfare systems. Interdependence is eroding the once-pristine division between domestic government and international relations, muddling the boundary between 'home' and 'abroad'. This, in turn, has prompted rethinking of former certainties about governance, giving rise to new ideas about the scope for autonomous action, whether at home or abroad. Or at least it has for some academic thinkers and political activists.

According to this narrative, there are new and by implication better ways of doing things. The EU figures prominently in this reimagination of governance, not least because it has long been in the forefront of finding new ways of managing cross-border transactions. The focus here is on commonality rather than on separateness, and on Europe *per se* rather than its nation-states as the appropriate location for problem-solving. As La Palombella sees it, the idea of 'the European "whole" is certainly conceivable, indeed visible in many perspectives', not least in 'active coexistence among different ethical-cultural positions … or again, as fair procedural control over a common space that would otherwise risk being exposed to arbitrary power or conflict'.[137]

Constitutionalism is essential in this narrative, the *idée force*, no less, for ensuring a new transnational regime has appropriate decisional norms and procedures for legitimate governance, with once-sovereign states increasingly pooling elements of their sovereignty, agreeing to undertake in common some critical aspects of governance and public policy previously the exclusive preserve of the nation-state: whether the disbursement of public goods, setting legal norms, raising revenue and allocating financial resources or even managing collective security.[138] And though the EU is not a state, this narrative does see the Union moving in that direction. According to Dobson, 'despite its being a perplexing hybrid sovereign [the EU] has many of the required features [of sovereignty]: one thinks immediately of qualified majority voting in the Council, direct election of a parliament (in a system of increasing legislative bicameralism), and the legal doctrines of supremacy and direct effect. In particular, the EU confers a direct citizenship, demonstrable formally as codified by Treaty and informally in practice'.[139]

This narrative makes much of the cultural impact of globalisation, sees new governance as a direct consequence of the incapacity of 'mere' nation-states 'at a loss to deal effectively with the domestic and international consequences of globalisation', unable to protect their citizens from insidious and even menacing forces. This process has potential, too, for reimagining political identity. Whether negatively, by reviving 'the burgeoning identity politics and xenophobia', those forces that redirect allegiance to territorial or ethnic/cultural communities below the level of the nation-state. Or more positively, by persuading citizens to think in inclusive terms about their membership of a broader political community.[140] Both of these responses challenge liberal nationalism, giving rise to new ideas about governance built 'on the ruins of the old ideologies', and both weaken citizens' loyalty to the nation-state.[141] Yet in this narrative the fragmentation of nation-states apparent in the rise of populist and territorial movements throughout Europe is no solution to the depredations of globalisation. A European state, on the other hand, that fosters a sense of inclusiveness has 'a lesser tendency to fall prey to the anarchic autonomy of state sovereignties', is a remedy for the supposedly 'failed' nation-state, presenting a 'broader vision and the single-mindedness' which might usefully be harnessed 'to the exercise of Europe's vast economic power', and might even 'be able to influence the global market'.[142]

Demos, the sense of being a people belonging to a political community, is not a prerequisite, *sensu stricto*, for embarking on effective transnational governance, but democracy certainly is. And so is collective endeavour, a sense of shared purpose, for confronting common challenges is in this narrative more likely to deepen the citizen's sense of membership in the emergent post-national polity because it offers a bulwark against the incubus of xenophobia.[143] This is where constitutionalism is indispensable for grounding an emergent transnational political process in appropriate normative ballast. A constitutional framework implies known and knowable rules, provides a clear map of power, enhances legitimacy, and this in turn may mobilise public opinion in a way that mere market-making or regulation cannot do, instilling in citizens the constitutional patriotism that replaces narrow nationalism as the ideological cement that sustains the transnational polity.

This amounts over time to nothing less than reimagining government and politics, a shift in political affinities 'promoted by the constitutional process [that] would lead to a European demos'.[144] The claim here is that constitutionalism can create conditions for demos, by deepening solidarity, the very reverse of the process of political identity formation as described by realist theorists and the like. Citizenship is central to this case, though it is not defined as merely formal rights and duties, nor as membership based on birth, blood or territorial residence,[145] but instead as inclusive membership of a transnational polity.[146] The very antithesis of the 'expressivist conceptualisation of an organicist ethno-cultural collectivity' that is the legacy of the Westphalian settlement.[147]

Some advocates of this case take a more advanced position, claiming that the EU is already a polity with state-like qualities, and is being transformed into a federal state.[148] They make much of the cumulate impact of 'Europeanisation',[149] of the resultant interconnectedness of multi-level governance.[150] And much, too, of a growing corpus of EU law directly applied and with precedence over domestic legal norms.[151] Law is an important driver here of political change. The Union's legal order closely approximates what von Bogdandy describes as a 'supranational federation'.[152] A process that by degrees gives considerable emphasis to 'the contribution of certain routinised institutional practices to the constitution of the *acquis*', which in turn has 'transformed understanding of the EU in legal-political terms'.[153] Moreover, this legal order is implicitly a constitutional order, albeit one that operates for the time being without a formal constitutional framework.[154] Why then resist the next and logical step, a constitutional settlement, the *sine qua non* of federalism? For Mancini only 'a European federal state capable of steering clear of the excesses and the abuses which have marked the history of its constituent units is ... conceivable'. More than that, he maintains, 'if – and this is the big if – the force of circumstances were to kindle the necessary political will, it could even be feasible'.[155]

A Constitution is essential then for grounding in appropriate norms the far-reaching and multiple (sociological, economic, political and cultural) transformations underway in contemporary Europe. Norms that make sense of but above all that legitimise governance during this transformative process. A constitution would give authority to novel structures and procedures of transnational governance. A European Constitution is vested here with much the same iconic status as the American Constitution, and it performs a similar function. This is radical thinking, yet paradoxically it is also a cautious if not quite a conservative response to contemporary challenges in Europe. It is radical in as much as it confronts the staid traditionalism of the 'no change, no constitution' narrative. Yet cautious in so far as some of its proponents hold to a familiar statal design for governance beyond the nation-state.[156] Critics point here to a lack of imagination in rethinking governance for a post-Westphalian European polity. What these same critics propose is something altogether different, a polity that reflects the novelty of post-national governance, and one framed in terms of a 'convincing alternative vocabulary [that expresses] the mixity, "betweenness" or liminality of the EU'.[157] Those who make this critique propose nothing less than a wholly exceptional constitutionalism for what they see is a post-national European polity.

### The case for constitutional exceptionalism

This narrative makes the case for constitutional exceptionalism, for a post-national constitutional order that is appropriate to the EU's unique power-sharing arrangements, a mix of intergovernmental and supranational dynamics.[158] Over time the EU has acquired extensive legal competencies, governance functions and policy domains that closely resemble those of states, though statehood is by no means the inevitable or even the likely outcome of its political development. Significant differences remain between statehood as it currently operates in the international system and EU multi-level governance, not least the constraints on the Union's capacity to directly (and legitimately) enforce its rules within the territory of its member states. Moreover, although the Union's policy competencies are impressive, they are conferred by the Treaty (Article 5.1), as confirmed by the Court.[159] And though the Union has own financial resources its budget remains modest in comparison with the fiscal resources available to its member states, and it lacks direct tax-raising powers to rectify this situation.

The Union's 'liminal' political status is the outcome of its distinctive political history, in part 'a response to the political and economic failings of Europe'. To attempt, however, as some would have it, to impose a statal model on the Union, 'to re-establish the traditional State, albeit at pan-European level' would be, as one eminent legal theorist sees it, 'to sell its ambitions short, while simultaneously disregarding its history'.[160] Constitutionalism has a part to play then, both in setting the ground rules and legitimising transnational governance for its citizens, though this is quite different from the constitutional order prescribed by those who see the Union as a state *manqué*. For Weatherill: 'Constitutionalism [in the EU] has come to represent a useful shorthand description of the transformation of a regime founded on an international Treaty into a complex organisation that does not – cannot – set aside its Treaty-based roots and yet has evolved into something that is significantly more constitutionally and institutionally sophisticated than an orthodox international organisation and in which the supervision of the relevant actors, at national and trans-national level, is achieved according to methods and standards that reflect the deep impact of policy-makers and policy-executors on the life of all European citizens.'[161]

If we follow this logic, EU constitutionalism is not about establishing a federal state but more about redressing persistent democracy and legitimacy deficits, by installing effective procedures for transparency and accountability in a polity that represents the most advanced example so far of transnational governance.[162] The priority here is greater clarity about governance, explaining the balance of institutional power and the allocation of competencies between the various tiers of governance, and not least simplifying decisional procedures.[163] But there is more to this constitutional endeavour than merely resolving the 'who does what and how' question, important though that is for any democratic polity. Legitimacy and democracy are at least as important to constitutional endeavour, and especially so for a polity that lacks demos. As Joseph Weiler sees it: 'Europe's constitutional architecture has never been validated by a process of constitutional adoption by a European constitutional demos and, hence, as a matter of both normative political principles and empirical social observation the European constitutional discipline does not enjoy the same kind of authority as may be found in federal states where their federalism is rooted in a hierarchy of normative authority or in a hierarchy of real power.'[164]

This is close to the case for an EU constitution proposed by Joschka Fischer, the German foreign minister, in his seminal speech 'From Confederacy to Federation: Thoughts on the Finality of European Integration' delivered in May 2000 at the Humboldt University, Berlin to commemorate the fiftieth anniversary of the Schuman Declaration. The Union's multi-level governance requires, as Fischer saw it, a constitutional formula that avoids the classical statal model. The European federal state (*Europäische Bundesstaat*) as an alternative to the nation-state is quite simply outmoded, 'an artificial construct which ignores the established realities of Europe'. In its place Fischer proposed a *Europäische Föderation*, a polity that reflects the essence of sophisticated confederalism. In this arrangement the nation-state 'will continue to exist and as the primary and constituent unit of a European level', and it will have in the reformed European polity 'a much larger role than the Laender have in Germany', for 'closer co-operation does not automatically lead to full integration, either by the pressure from the facts and the shortcomings of the "Monnet Method"'.[165] However, balancing respectively the interests, powers and competencies of the nation-state and the EU polity does require a new European constitutional order. A formal constitution would clarify these ravelled procedures and sometimes tense inter-institutional relations, making clear 'who does what and when', and, just as important for the citizen, 'why, giving the Union's multi-level governance a constitutional philosophy that is presently lacking.[166] In these circumstances, a constitutional treaty is nothing less than foundational, 'a deliberate political act to re-establish Europe'.[167]

Some critics accused Fischer of ignoring the fact that the Union already has a constitutional order, and if not formally constituted, no less the 'progressive constitutionalisation of the treaties effected by the European Court of Justice throughout the last four decades with the acquiescence, sometimes express through treaty amendments, sometimes implicit, of the States'. On this reading of events, Fischer had simply missed the point, ignoring the fact that 'upgrading the treaty into the current constitution of the Community has produced a constitution by default, a provisional legal fiction in want of something better, but one that is at the same time normatively warranted, workable and advantageous to most of the actors concerned'. For those who argue thus Europe already has its constitution, and it would be 'a redundant waste of energy to try to strike again deals and reach constitutional agreements that are already up and running'. Accordingly, 'any constitutional project for the future of Europe must take seriously its constitutional present, building on it, not negating it'.[168] How valid is this criticism?

As we saw in previous discussion, the Union's implicit 'constitutional' arrangements do closely proximate the experience of historic federal states, they 'are very much like similar sets of norms in most federal states', in so far as they aim to govern relations between the centre and territorial polities.[169] But the exceptionalism narrative regards even these developments as insufficient for legitimising post-national governance, and see this as unfinished business. There is still much to be done to make the Union ready for the tasks that face it, the coming challenges. Whilst accepting that the EU is no stranger to cumulate constitutionalism, Weiler for instance maintains that to simply and unreflectively adopt the classic federal design for the EU is no answer to problematic governance. A federalist design for a polity that is not a federal state, and moreover is unlikely ever to become one, is impracticable, and, further, is muddled thinking. In so far as federal constitutions 'allocate certain powers to federal institutions, and typically policies and laws emanating from the exercise of such powers are the supreme law of the land ... and in case of conflict they trump conflicting norms', the outcome of resorting to a federal design would be to impose a statist model. An arrangement wholly out of kilter with the Union's unique multi-level arrangements and post-national orientation, what he describes as 'the grand principle of supremacy', which 'is every bit as egregious as that which is found in the American federal constitution itself'.[170]

Federalism for Weiler is not an appropriate model for EU governance, not least because it goes against the grain of the Europe's cultural diversity. He is particularly wary of classic federalism's propensity for centralisation, of too much power gravitating to the political and administrative centre, thereby compromising the autonomy of territorial polities.[171] As he sees it, a quite different political dynamic operates in the EU. The Union is a multi-level arrangement that enables 'Europe to square a particular vicious circle: achieving a veritably high level of material integration comparable to that found only in fully-fledged federations, whilst maintaining at the same time – and in contrast with the experience of all such federations – powerful, some would argue strengthened, Member States'.[172]

The requirement for a careful distribution of political and institutional power, though important, is only part of the case for an altogether new design for European governance. Account must also be taken of the cultural differences between the EU and classical federal polities, differences that require an exceptional constitutional architecture. The case made by Weiler and others who share his reservations about adapting an inappropriate political design for entirely novel governance and politics requires nothing less than a new constitutional order to fit wholly new arrangements. As he sees it:

> Europe's constitutional principles, even if materially similar, are rooted in a framework which is altogether different. In federations ... the institutions of a federal state are situated in a constitutional framework which presupposes the existence of a 'constitutional demos', a single *pouvoir constituant* made of the citizens of the federation in whose sovereignty, as a constituent power, and by whose supreme authority the specific constitutional arrangement is rooted. Thus, although the federal constitution seeks to guarantee State rights and although both constitutional doctrine and historical reality will instruct us that the federation may have been a creature of the constituent units and their respective peoples, the formal sovereignty and authority of the people coming together as a constituent power is greater than any other expression of sovereignty within the polity and hence the supreme authority of the Constitution – including its federal principles.[173]

This situation hardly applies to the EU. The lack of European demos, the fundament of constitutional legitimacy even in the federal state, is quite simply missing in the European Union. But for Weiler this is more a strength than a weakness in this 'remarkable and unprecedented arrangement'.[174] Exclusive and narrow constitutional patriotism is, he maintains, inappropriate as the basis for solidarity in such a culturally diverse polity. The objective of political development here, the 'end state' so-called, cannot be statehood based primordial affiliation, what he describes as 'in-reaching' or organic identity. Even if a composite European identity could somehow be constructed from the various parts, it would be at best artificial, and for that reason fragile. And even if it succeeded in forging meaningful identity between Europeans, its exclusivity would be dysfunctional, harking back to narrow nationalism, the insularity that has in times past led to conflict with significant (or as some xenophobes would have it, insignificant) 'others'. This sort of solidarity would ultimately undermine the prospects, weaken the appeal of post-national solidarity rooted in, indeed celebrating cultural pluralism, by 'hindering outsiders from entrance', and in the process betraying 'the promises implied in the vision of a merely supranational, rather than statal, Europe'.[175]

Constitutionalism is essential then for legitimating EU governance, but the key for those who subscribe to exceptionalism lies not in enacting formal legal texts, embodying an over-arching *Grundnorm* in a constitutional contract, by repeating the classic but time-worn constitutional model that encapsulates 'fundamental values of the polity and … in turn, is said to be a reflection of our collective political identity as a people, as a nation, as a Community, as a Union'.[176] Rather the process should more precisely reflect, and more than that it should celebrate, the EU's cultural and social diversity, seeking appropriate procedures that will deepen popular affiliation, embedding a sense of shared endeavour amongst ordinary citizens in a multi-ethnic, culturally pluralist community of peoples, rather than the *unum e pluribus* paradigm of American experience.[177] Cultural pluralism is after all, as Zielonka maintains, 'a normal state of affairs' in the EU, and 'some would even argue that divergence … "pluralism" by another name … is Europe's greatest historical and cultural treasure'.[178] Above all, the EU constitutional process must be inclusive, not least because 'the boundary between … "us" and "them" is plenty deep and does not need a further deepening, which a European state would surely bring about'.[179]

From modest beginnings in the 1950s as a common market, European integration has developed as a polity, and in the process has confronted the challenge of accommodating deep diversity. A process that as Weiler sees it stands for nothing less than a 'remarkable expression' of constitutional tolerance. It is, he maintains, 'a remarkable instance of civic tolerance to accept to be bound by precepts articulated, not by "my people", but by a community of distinct political communities; a people, if you wish, of "others"'.[180] In this situation 'I compromise my self-determination in this fashion as an expression of this kind of internal-towards myself – and external-towards others – tolerance'.[181] Civic forbearance cannot be assured here if the constitutional order is constructed as merely a narrow bargain, a functional trade-off between competing national interests and one imposed from above. Furthermore, the very structure of the European polity, its deep cultural diversity precludes even a conventional federal design, for 'a neo-Westphalian European state could only work in a relatively homogeneous environment [for] Common laws and administrative regulations cannot cope well with a highly diversified environment, and consequently various complicating opt-outs and multi-speed arrangements are required'.[182]

The 'exceptionalism' narrative prescribes a constitutional order for the EU, but one that fits its unique arrangements. Constitutional norms that define membership (citizenship), that confer and adjudicate fundamental rights, that ensure democratic governance between levels (horizontally) and between different categories of actors (vertically) and facilitate public accountability are no less important for legitimising and stabilising governance in this non-statal and transnational polity than for the nation-state.[183] These political values and the procedures for delivering them may be rather more difficult to realise in a polity lacking demos, but they are no less important if the European polity is to properly connect with its citizens, and carry them with it as it navigates the uncharted waters of an emergent global order.[184] Indeed, the need here for a constitutional order is both urgent and long overdue. For Zielonka, 'democracy can hardly work in a complicated, if not impenetrable, system of multi-layered and multi-speed arrangements run by an ever-changing group of unidentified and unaccountable people. Similarly, affection and identity can hardly develop in a complex system of open-ended arrangements with fluid membership, variable purposes, and a net of cross-cutting functional frames of co-operation. Cultural identity and democracy require transparency, simplicity and a sense of belonging to a defined community, and these are difficult to acquire in a highly diverse and open-ended environment.'[185] In these circumstances the challenge to constitutionalise the European polity is a difficult one but by no means a hopeless task. Indeed, for those who subscribe to this narrative there are some encouraging signs. To meet rising expectations for democratic standards even in this inchoate post-national polity is feasible, if hardly easy, for the very logics and processes of contemporary social change have capacity for connecting people and for reducing spatial, social and cultural difference in ways that 'makes solidarity between strangers possible'. Not least, because the uniquely transnational European polity 'decouples citizenship and nationhood', an arrangement unprecedented in European history, though the Habsburg Empire in its response after 1848 to the liberal revolution came close to it.[186]

What to say then by way of conclusion in this brief review of competing cases for and against a European constitutional order? Constitutions are by no means the exclusive preserve of nation-states, and indeed they historically predate states.[187] But constitutionalism as applied to the multi-tiered and culturally heterogeneous EU polity is a particular challenge to political ingenuity, reflecting as it must do the European Union's unique political arrangements, its historical legacies and quite distinctive cultural fabric.[188] The case made for exceptionalism is correct in its claim that a European constitutional order simply cannot follow the historical pattern of state-building, because state-building, and no less federal state-building, is not what European integration is essentially about. The EU is not a state but rather a third-level or transnational polity. And a polity whose constitutional order is emerging from 'mutual contacts and influences', and one 'shaped by the reciprocal acceptance of the non-binding/binding nature of their respective behaviour'.[189] As Cata Becker sees it, 'EU constitutionalism can be thought of as shorthand for the way Community institutions, member States and sub-national peoples struggle to reach some sort of equilibrium between these three forces, each of which embodies such distinct visions of the meaning and limitations of union within Europe'.[190] In short, unique circumstances demand novel solutions, not merely a harking back to failed or inappropriate constitutional design. Yet there are still those who maintain that the American experience of federalism some two centuries ago is the appropriate path for Europe to follow in the twenty-first century.

## Historic comparators: is America a precedent?

The attempt since 1945 to construct a European political order has attracted comparison with the founding of the American Republic in 1787. The development of the European Union 'is seen as paralleling that of the United States of America. As if European integration were just like what happened in North America only 200 years later.' One participant in the EU's Constitutional Convention ruefully observed that 'the ghost of the Philadelphia Convention plagues European debate'.[191] This historic forerunner of continental union may be a useful lens on the challenge of constitution-making for a Union of pre-existing states, but it hardly bears a close resemblance to polity-building in the EU in the late twentieth century. The comparison between these two historic events is more notional than analogous, not least because, as Kiljunen points out, in North America 'the choice had to be made between a confederation and a federation', and though idealists suppose that 'Europe is now supposed to be at the same crossroads ... this is hardly the case'.[192]

These are two quite different historical circumstances, with little to connect them. The American states that met at Philadelphia were already a confederation of states with a common purpose, facing a singular threat to their independence. And because of this they were already convinced, from necessity if not from principle, of the practical case as much as the abstract virtue of nation-statehood. Moreover, national integration here was facilitated by a sense of shared identity, and for some participants even by a sense of manifest destiny. The EU lacks any such cultural or social cement, and it remains a confederation of national states. Whatever binds this unique polity together, or gives it a sense of common purpose, 'One Nation under God' it clearly is not. There is no similarity of circumstances, let alone of intention, between negotiating a federal compact amongst 13 small, agrarian former British colonies brought together by the urgent need to resist military threat and a trammelling of their fundamental liberties, each one sharing a common historical experience, a common language, legal traditions, political culture and the Protestant faith, and building a community of nation-states, the situation that currently pertains in the European Union.

The American experience of nation-building is no useful parallel, was certainly no template for Europe's constitution-makers meeting in their own Convention some two centuries after Philadelphia.[193] There are at best some interesting parallels between events more than two centuries apart. In both cases political leaders addressed the issue of intergovernmental relations, critical for any multi-level polity, and particularly the 'three major problems of balance ... in the division of power ... equality of member states, the relationship between a member state and the Union and the balance between union institutions'.[194] Both situations were concerned, too, with the appropriate locus of primary power: federalists in both conventions wanted hard power to reside with the centre, whereas advocates of states' rights resisted the claim that federal power would ensure better domestic governance, or even provide security against external threats. But this is as far as we can usefully take comparison. The EU is a confederation, but a much looser political arrangement than the American confederation that preceded the Republic, altogether more contested and lacking anything that approximates a common identity. It is a union of sovereign states, each with its own distinctive history.

These fundamental differences were remarked on by Giscard d'Estaing, who presided over Europe's Convention, in his Henry Kissinger Lecture delivered at the Library of Congress in Washington in February 2003. He observed on that occasion that Europeans are not a single people but rather 'a Europe of many nations'.[195] The Founding Treaties have acknowledged this incontrovertible fact from the outset, expressly referring to Europe's 'peoples'. Moreover, Article 1 of the first draft of the EU Constitutional Treaty acknowledged cultural diversity as an essential element of the Union's constitutional endeavour, maintaining that it is a Union of European states which, while retaining their national identities, closely co-ordinate their policies at the European level, and even 'administer certain common competencies on a federal basis'.[196] This allusion to federalism with regard to shared competencies proved too much for Britain, and indeed some other member states, and telling is the fact that the relevant Article was reworded in subsequent revisions to omit the 'f' word.

The founding fathers assembled at Philadelphia on 25 May 1787 had a quite different mandate: to draft a founding treaty for governing relations between 13 former British colonies. A decade after their successful war for independence from the imperial 'motherland' the representatives of these states determined to consolidate this remarkable political and military achievement, by establishing a constitutional framework for the stable management of future continental relations. This task was made less onerous than it might have been in so far as there was already broad agreement amongst them that effective governance implied common statehood, though there was no consensus about how to frame that objective. In the aftermath of their war for independence these states had negotiated a treaty of confederation, itself an indication of their determination to avoid unduly centralised authority.[197]

The challenges that followed independence, not least maintaining their independence from Britain, obliged these states to revisit the issue of their future governance, each state sending a representative to a Continental Convention in Philadelphia. However, that Convention was less than representative, either of the populations or of the range of socio-economic interests in these former colonies. Nor were its arrangements particularly transparent. Indeed, Philadelphia was a more exclusive affair even than the Convention that drafted the Constitutional Treaty. While both forums were quite aware that they faced important choices, there are considerable differences between them. The Philadelphia Convention negotiated in private and as state delegations, with each member exercising one

vote. The Union's Constitutional Convention deliberated rather more than it negotiated, and it did so in public, at least during its plenary sessions, with the media
shadowing its every move, and with all the documentation and other materials
placed in the public domain, readily available to a wider audience via the internet.
Above all, consensus was its guiding principle.

There are other and greater differences between the events at Philadelphia and
those in Brussels. For though Philadelphia's founding fathers did contemplate
merely revising the existing Articles of Confederation, in the end they established
a new federal state in North America. And while this same radical option did figure
in the deliberations in Brussels, encapsulated by what one of its more vociferous
participants described as asking *the* fundamental question – 'Are we a nation?'
– the response to this question was quite different in each case. The response of
the Philadelphia Convention was in the affirmative, though with varying degrees
of enthusiasm, an agreement to found a United States of America no less, 'a
single state, a federal state ... whose power would derive from the people, not the
member states. A union of people not of states.'[198] The response in Brussels some
two centuries later, on the other hand, was altogether more equivocal, much less
conclusive about what was at stake.

One indicator of the differences between these two quite distinct events is the
way both conventions approached the question of citizenship, the individual's
relationship with the polity. Philadelphia confirmed equality, both of citizens
and of member states, whereas Brussels hardly addressed the idea of the citizen
as a member of the polity, and endorsed the pre-eminence of states, expending
considerably more political energy on ensuring that voting weights in the Council
reflected demography. The idea of citizenship was central to deliberations at Philadelphia, with federalists such as James Madison pressing for a federal government and legislature as the political centre of a new nation, a Republic embedded
in popular legitimacy with political authority determined directly by popular vote.
The anti-federalists wanted a legislature or Congress to be indirectly nominated
by the legislatures of the states of the Union and they lost the argument to the
federalists. What is, in effect, the essence of European Union, the idea that sovereignty should reside with the individual states, lost out at Philadelphia to those
who preferred to relocate political authority in a new political centre.

For a time it seemed that Philadelphia might actually founder on this controversial issue, but a compromise was eventually reached that reconciled these seemingly incompatible concepts of political authority, one that combined states' rights
with the democratic principle of popular sovereignty. This compromise took the
form of a bicameral Congress, one house to represent the people at large, the other
the states on the principle of territorial equity regardless of size, with the consent
of both houses required to pass legislation. This same compromise was available,
at least in principle, to the *conventionnels* who gathered in Brussels. Except that
few of those present were under any illusion that writing a European constitution
was remotely a precursor to founding a European state. These latter-day founding
fathers settled instead for an altogether more modest outcome, preferring to give
the enlarged EU a more cogent institutional and legal base, and to resolve long-

standing argument about the proper allocation of policy competencies to the respective levels of governance.

There are considerable differences then between the political design and the political culture of federal and confederal polities. The European Convention did not follow its famous predecessor, and instead confirmed confederalism as the Union's political design. A confederation is, after all, 'a union of sovereign states … it is not a state in itself'.[199] The member states of a confederation, though they might agree to pool some aspects of their sovereignty, do not surrender it *in toto* to a federal centre, let alone in perpetuity, as the 13 American colonies did when they founded the United States of America. In a federal polity, 'the member states forfeit their sovereignty to the federation, which is based on the sovereignty of the people, not of the member states'.[200] The EU member states retain their sovereignty for determining both internal and external affairs, and they remain independent sovereign states. In effect, sovereignty 'pooled' rather than surrendered *per se* when EU member states undertake to abide by the Community method of decision-making, is restricted only to those competencies that member states agree to share in common. Even then, states may repatriate such powers on their own initiative, though presumably only after protracted negotiations and at the very least after signalling their intention to their partners in advance.

The opening Article of the EU Constitutional Treaty acknowledges as much, stating that the Union 'shall exercise on a Community basis the competences they (the member states) confer on it'.[201] Consequently, the Union and its institutions enjoy no authority other than that conditionally conferred by the member states. Member states in a confederation agree merely to undertake closer co-operation in agreed policy domains – and even then, with opt-outs and derogations available to them – to participate in shared endeavours and limited governance through common institutions. A process 'policed' by an overarching legal order, though one that applies to some but by no means all of these common pursuits. Not even the acquisition of some of the symbols of statehood, from citizenship to a common currency overseen by a European Central Bank, or a budget with 'own resources', a common foreign policy, an elected parliament or even the iconic trappings of a flag or an anthem, or for that matter a constitution, have anything like the same emotional resonance as these same symbols of common political purpose do in the United States of America.

These accoutrements do not in themselves transform the EU into a federal state, let alone make for a country called 'Europe'. There are fundamental differences, too, over the respective legal and constitutional bases, the founding acts of federal and confederal polities. Confederations are based on a treaty made between sovereign states under international law. This is a binding arrangement, in so far as the signatories undertake to respect their mutual obligations and to abide by agreed undertakings framed, more often than not in the EU's case, by legislation enshrined in law that has direct affect in the member states and that has supremacy over national law. But despite even this solemn and binding undertaking, nothing here remotely supplants the legal or normative primacy of the national constitutional order.

Philadelphia transformed a confederation of post-colonial states into a fully-fledged federal state, its central purpose was state-building and, by extension, nation-building. The Brussels Convention on the other hand was more concerned with revising the EU's existing treaty base, a wholly different constitutional project. Hirschl has put it rather more prosaically, observing that the European Convention was all about 'tidying up', the 'standardisation' and 'simplification' of a complex and muddled multi-level governance, with governments 'driven primarily by a quest for efficient solutions to complex co-ordination problems'.[202] This may well be to understate the significance of what was at stake at Brussels, but the differences between these two historic events are significant and should not be diminished by careless comparison. Federal arrangements may well offer a solution to the European Union's inordinately complicated governance, but this is by no means the same thing as equating transforming it with a fully-fledged federal state.

## Federalism: a constitutional model for Europe?

Constitutions are the *sine qua non* of federal polities, but there are many variants. Daniel Elazar, the eminent theorist of federalism, has identified no less than five basic constitutional models. The EU's constitutional arrangements do not correspond as such to any of these classic constitutional designs, but draw on more than one historic type.[203] Framework constitutions are a just that, a framework for the conduct of governance, mapping power and guaranteeing fundamental rights, a model whose classic expression is the American Constitution. This oldest and most iconic of modern democratic constitutions outlines the political architecture and lists the powers attributed to the principal institutions, and summarises their procedures and inter-relations. The Convention on the Future of Europe that devised the draft European Constitution tried to follow the framework model, in so far as it sought to define 'who does what' in the EU polity, to clarify the competencies of the respective actors and to incorporate the free-standing charter of fundamental rights. Yet somehow, the example of its famously parsimonious precursor got lost in translation!

The classic framework constitution makes a virtue of avoiding excessive detail, of not being too specific about prescribing institutional arrangements, or even about meticulously iterating citizens' rights. The American Constitution is certainly a model of parsimony, but the same can hardly be said of the cumbrous document that was the outcome of the Brussels Convention. One can quite see why the European Constitution was overlong on detail. Brevity in a constitutional text is only possible if there is abiding consensus on the values and principles that underpin the polity. And more than that, a sense of solidarity between constituent parts of the polity rooted in shared traditions, a common discourse about the means and ends of governance, an ongoing constitutional conversation conducted in the language of shared values.

The EU does not remotely meet these exacting conditions. Where there are abiding differences over the fundamental purposes of a polity, as there is in the EU, with almost every aspect of governance contested, and not least its very *raison d'être* as a polity, a detailed constitution is not so much preferable as unavoidable. This has certainly been Europe's experience of constitution-making since the late eighteenth century, with constitutions tending to cover every eventuality, even anticipating future challenges to the division of powers and the allocation of competencies.[204] The Constitutional Treaty certainly followed this baroque design, seeking to cover every aspect of governance and even policy, but *in extremis* and as a consequence it was unduly complicated, weighed down by an overelaborate description of governance procedures and a tedious catalogue of policy competencies.

In recent times, the debate has intensified over whether the Union's constitutional order is, or should be, a federal arrangement, notwithstanding broad acknowledgement by most commentators that the American experience of federalism is not a relevant comparator for constitution-making in the EU.[205] Federalism is still a referent in this debate, even though the EU is not a state, nor likely to become one in the foreseeable future. It is relevant nevertheless, precisely because the meaning of federalism itself has changed in response to cultural and structural shifts within the nation-state and at the international level. Changes that reflect both the immense challenges of managing globalisation, as well as significant normative shifts towards new forms of post-national politics as evidenced by anti-globalisation and anti-poverty campaigns, radical ecologism and the new politics of climate change.[206]

Few close observers of contemporary events would deny Llorente's claim 'that the EU has brought about a profound transformation of the State – a development that obliges us to rethink old categories and create new ones'. This explains, in part, why federalism is now back in vogue, a heuristic tool as much as a prescriptive one for redesigning governance, whether within Europe's nation-states or at the EU level itself. For what were once firmly rooted political communities are everywhere being challenged from below by the revival of ethnic and other forms of cultural identity, and from above by an insidious interdependence that is bringing about global regimes and institutions, a style of governance described by the academy as liberal institutionalism.[207]

Federalism is on the agenda now precisely because it seems to offer one solution to the challenge of reconciling the twin imperatives of living together in a continent facing multiple but also common challenges, whilst at the same time acknowledging persistent internal differences that give rise to challenges to once monolithic nation-states. Federalism, or more appropriately perhaps in these circumstances federalisation, processes for managing policy interdependencies by building international regimes and consolidating universal norms, is not necessarily about building a European state, but rather putting in place a system for sharing power between actors, both vertically and horizontally, at the different levels of contemporary governance, 'the combination of shared-rule for some purposes and regional self-rule for others within a single political system so that neither is subordinate to the other'.[208] This is no easy solution to current policy challenges, but it is one that requires a wholly new approach to constitutional politics. And it is an arrangement already familiar to students of international regimes, and nowadays one that is by no means confined to federal states. Moreover, it has an appeal nowadays that was lacking when the European project was launched immediately after the Second World War.

The EU is not a federal polity in the conventional sense, yet much of what passes for governance here 'is what has classically been known as federalism; that is to say, the combination of constitutional choice, design, and institution-building to accommodate both existing states and trans-state linkages by combining self-rule and shared rule'.[209] Rather like Molière's ingenuous *bourgeois gentilhomme* who spoke prose without realising it, those who debate the future of EU governance use a federalist lexicon without always acknowledging it as such. Federalism in this contemporary and non-statal sense is certainly useful as an indicative design, for first reimagining, then for remaking EU governance, not least because it is a process rather than an end-state. Or more to the point, it is not a process that must necessarily end in a state.[210] It does not have to end up as a European state, but by adopting it the classical European nation-state is irrevocably altered. As a constitutional endeavour it involves making 'a series of choices about matters such as the division of powers and relationships between levels of government', choices with 'implications for the future balance of powers between centre and units, between the national components of multinational states and between political actors in the form, for example, of elites, political parties and interest groups'.[211]

Choice is precisely what the Union's recent constitutional endeavour is all about, but choices are more difficult to carry with the public where there is no broad consensus about fundamental political principles. Building a European polity that accommodates competing preferences requires eclecticism in constitutional design, borrowing from quite different constitutional traditions. As Palermo describes this process, there can be 'no federal big bang', but instead only incremental adjustment, compromise between quite different preferences for European governance. It is a process whereby 'a continuous mutual influence [takes] place between these respective levels of constitutional experience'.[212]

This is of course where the European Constitution foundered, the preoccupation with narrow interests, reticence about constitutional innovation, the lack of an overarching constitutional philosophy. The would-be founding fathers in Brussels were hampered by reticence about undertaking a bold constitutional design. The European polity is necessarily eclectic, borrowing from quite different constitutional traditions, balancing competing ideas about governance. But this exercise need not be a recipe for political impasse so long as those who undertake it have a clear vision about the polity and willingness to think outside the box, 'designers [who] can borrow a mechanism here or there'. There must be clear thinking, too, as well as merely invention, for 'in the last analysis, these mechanisms must be integrated in a manner that is true to the spirit of the civil society for which the constitution is designed'.[213] This was precisely the challenge that faced the Union's would-be founding fathers, but as we shall see they rather lost sight of this need for vision, becoming immersed in the minutiae of procedures, the politics of side payments and usual sub-optimal bargains. In the end they delivered an encyclopaedia and not a constitution worthy of the name.

# Part 2

# Constitutionalising the European Union

# 3 Europe's Constitutional Convention

## Changing EU rules: the logics of intergovernmental bargains

The EU's procedures and rules are the preserve of its member states, with revisions of the treaties undertaken by government representatives in intergovernmental conferences (IGCs).[1] Although both the European Commission and the Parliament do influence the IGC agenda the member states dominate the process,[2] ensuring in turn that national preferences prevail over the putative 'common interest'.[3] Although the Commission aspires to be the principal interlocutor on treaty reform (Article 48 of the Treaty on European Union (TEU) permits the Commission to make proposals to any IGC) steering usually falls to the Council presidency, with the Commission's role 'reduced to a simple spectator'.[4] The Luxembourg presidency (1985) did allow the Commission an informal role in setting the agenda in the IGC that negotiated the Single European Act, and it likewise participated in the 1990–1 IGC that established Economic and Monetary Union. Jacques Delors presided over the committee that set the agenda, and in effect brokered the political deal that was eventually endorsed by the member states.[5] This was exceptional, however, and by no means the norm.

A less than convincing performance by the Commission during Santer's tenure hardly improved its claim to a greater role in reforming the treaties.[6] The crisis that enveloped the Commission (1999) made the member states even less favourably disposed to the Commission's ambition to give a lead in the 2000 IGC. The Commission had to settle for an advisory role, placing its technical expertise at the disposal of the Council secretariat and the presidency as these agencies worked on successive treaty drafts.[7] The European Parliament's role in IGCs is even more peripheral, its presidency acting merely as an observer, meeting occasionally with IGC delegations to the ministerial sessions and engaging in little more than an informal exchange of views. The Parliament may send observers to these ministerial deliberations, but without voting rights. It also contributes papers and opinions, though these carry little weight compared even with Commission recommendations.[8]

Governments dominate IGCs. Negotiators representing the member states review possible solutions, with the final decision left to the heads of state or government meeting in a special European Council.[9] This procedure served the

Union well enough, until the process of European integration gathered momentum after the 1984 Fontainebleau summit had paved the way for the Single European Market, relaunching 'Europe' after the doldrum years of the late 1970s and early 1980s. The pace of change noticeably quickened, four new treaties following in relatively quick succession, though they failed to resolve some of the outstanding governance issues. After Maastricht, the governance debate acquired a distinctly constitutional tone, reflecting the growing feeling even in government circles that more substantial changes were needed, both to resolve the institutional shortcomings, and just as important to better connect remote governance with the citizen. By no means all of the Union's principal actors were convinced about the need to broaden the debate on governance, especially the leading member states. Nevertheless, with the idea of a 'people's Europe' much in vogue now in Brussels concern about disconnection between the Union and its citizens – a concept first introduced in the Treaty of European Union – brought widespread acceptance of the need for 'a qualitatively different kind of Union altogether – a Union taking on some of the resonances of a single political community'.[10]

The limitations of the IGC method for any such undertaking were clear to see. Governments concentrate energy on their own preferences in these forums, and the prospect of blocking minorities and even outright deadlock makes positive sum negotiation the usual 'logic of exchange and bargaining', with the likely outcome a sub-optimal one.[11] Giscard d'Estaing acknowledged as much in his opening address as Convention president, when he described IGCs as 'an arena for diplomatic negotiations between member states in which each party sought legitimately to maximise its gains without regard for the overall picture'.[12] This invariably weakens the sense of common purpose, each player bringing their own distinctive preferences to the table,[13] quite aware that they are being judged by domestic audiences according to how effectively they defend the national interest.[14] The resulting bargains are almost always trade-offs 'specifically tailored to suit the particular requirements of states and groups of states', and as such are hardly the best way of reaching agreement on constitutional principles.[15] This explains in part why successive IGCs had failed to resolve politically sensitive issues such as the distribution of commissioners, Council decision-making arrangements – not least voting weights – and the extension of QMV to policy domains such as taxation and social policy, still regarded by many governments as essentially domestic matters.[16]

These limitations were plain to see at both the Amsterdam and Nice IGCs, with too many governments simply lacking any incentive to compromise on matters they regarded as fundamental national interests.[17] As one critic tersely observed, 'the stewards of the Union treated the Amsterdam IGC as if it were a meeting of the Council wrangling over price support for pork'.[18] The United Kingdom, for instance, resisted making any concessions on the harmonisation of taxation policy, whereas France declined accommodation on liberalising trade policy. The smaller member states followed suit, refusing to give up what they saw as their 'automatic right' to appoint a commissioner.[19] The inevitable result of these negotiating logics is that problematic issues are deferred, handed on to a subsequent IGC where the process starts over. The issues left over from Amsterdam were passed on to the Nice IGC,[20] resulting in 'an outpouring of bile' which poisoned relations thereafter.[21] The impasse in the Nice IGC, too, was as much about politics as it was about procedure, though the IGC method did play its part delaying agreement on pressing matters.[22] A situation made worse by a temporary hiatus in Franco-German relations that prevented either country giving its customary lead in these complicated negotiations.[23]

Other political complications played their part in preventing IGCs from delivering much needed reform, not least a growing division between the big and the small countries, a fault-line clearly visible in the Convention. The Nice IGC was characterised 'by a spectacularly bad tempered row between big and small member states' at the special European Council in Biarritz. Another tense encounter at Nice delivered 'a messy compromise' on the main issues: the size of the Commission, Council voting weights, QMV in the Council and the allocation of seats in the Parliament. It would hardly be an exaggeration to say that the Treaty of Nice 'was loathed by almost everyone who signed it'.[24] By the late 1990s then the IGC method was seen as a procedure least likely to resolve the outstanding matters left over from previous attempts to reform the founding treaties.[25] Even the British prime minister warned that 'we cannot do business like this in the future'.[26]

Impending enlargement merely added to the urgency of resolving these matters.[27] After their experience at Nice, most heads of government and state endorsed a Declaration on the Future of the Union (December 2000) calling 'for a deeper and wider debate' on the future of the Union, and setting 2004 as the deadline for another IGC to settle issues left over from previous IGCs.[28] A debate was launched about how best to tackle reform. Joschka Fischer, the German foreign minister, made a particularly important contribution with his speech at the Humboldt University (May 2000), urging what he called 'constitutional finality'.[29] Merely dabbling, he argued, was not enough to ensure the legitimacy and democracy still lacking after consecutive treaty reforms. Fischer called instead for bold and imaginative thinking about the future shape of EU governance. He proposed a non-centralised federation of nation-states, and one with one an altogether clearer demarcation of roles and competencies between member states and the Union. As Fischer saw it, this would reinforce the principle of subsidiarity, both facilitating common policy where the Union has competency to act, but also enhancing the role of domestic actors at the EU level, with the second chamber of a bicameral European parliament representing the views of national parliaments at the centre of the European policy process. There was no question here of turning the Union into a federal state. Each member state would retain its national identity and remain ultimately responsible to its national demos, just as the German constitutional court had decreed after the Maastricht Treaty. Neither was this merely tinkering. Fischer had in mind a radical overhaul of governance to ensure more efficient policy-making, and above all to ensure a more democratic polity 'capable of action, fully sovereign yet based on self-confident nation states'.[30]

This was bold thinking, not least from an accredited foreign minister, though not the sort of radical thinking likely to appeal to most governments. Few political leaders shared Fischer's concerns about the Union's constitutional deficit, and fewer still wanted any fundamental change of political arrangements. Chirac for instance, speaking during a visit to the Bundestag, preferred to endorse only Fischer's reference to a Europe based on its nation-states, 'the source of our identities and roots [and] the first reference points' of Europeans, though he did acknowledge the urgency of reform after the failure at Nice to resolve important institutional issues.[31] Prime Minister Blair, too, in a speech in Warsaw in early October 2000, spoke of a need to face up to some awkward issues. But he, too, made more of Fischer's proposal for enhancing the role of national parliaments in Union affairs than he did of the call to 'constitutionalise' the Union.[32] There was by now at least growing recognition, and not least from the leading member states, that something had to be done – and soon – to ensure the Union had support from its citizens. Some political leaders even endorsed the call from more radical voices to widen the process, to include representatives of political parties and civil society.[33]

There was no mention at this stage of a European constitution as such, but the clamour for change did concentrate official minds on the need to adapt the Union's governance for unprecedented challenges ahead, and not least enlargement.[34] The difficulties encountered during the Nice and Amsterdam IGCs persuaded many EU leaders that something more was needed than merely tidying up the muddled legacy by 'giving the treaties a wash and brush up'.[35] Public opinion played its part in changing official minds.[36] A sizeable 'no' vote in the Irish referendum on the Nice Treaty (June 2001), widespread public disquiet over the impact of Monetary Union on consumer prices, to say nothing of the costs of imposing the stringent financial discipline required by EMS membership for the provision of public goods and services, all registered with politicians. The fact, too, that the young, a constituency normally favourable to European integration, now saw 'Europe' as more about markets than about 'people' or 'peace', voicing their disaffection in disruptive and occasionally violent anti-globalisation protests at both the Gothenburg and Genoa G-7 meetings, added to the sense of urgency.[37] Some member states were rather more receptive than others to change, more in tune with the public's mood. The Belgian government, for instance, gave a firm lead, as smaller member states have done so often in the past at critical junctures in the development of the European project, making constitutional reform the central theme of its presidency in the second half of 2001.[38]

## A new approach to treaty reform

Consensus began to emerge on an agenda for necessary changes, though without any clear idea about how to take it forward. The post-Nice debate focused on four issues: clearer demarcation of competencies between the Union and the member states; simplification of the treaties to ensure citizens are better informed about what the Union does and how; the legal status of the Charter of Fundamental Rights; and clarification of the role of national parliaments in EU governance, one way of improving the links between the domestic and European levels of governance.[39] The Nice Council agreed to hold another IGC in 2004 to deal with these and other outstanding issues, and the Swedish and Belgian presidencies embarked on a round of consultations designed to ensure that the latest reform round would be more accessible than before, addressing the public's concerns rather than exclusively focusing on those of insiders.[40] At this stage some of these 'insiders' were less than convinced about abandoning a tried and tested formula that had always ensured that governments remained 'masters of the treaties'. The larger states in particular were wary about losing control over treaty reform, quite aware that federalists in the Union's supranational institutions – and a preference likely to be well represented in the Convention – would use the occasion to promote a radical agenda.[41] And though most governments came round to accepting the Convention in principle, they saw it nevertheless as more think-tank than *constituante* body, merely the precursor of the 'real' negotiations that would take place in the following IGC, the forum that as most governments saw it 'alone has the authority to change the treaties'.[42]

The more Eurosceptical member states thought the idea politically risky, an awkward precedent.[43] The governments of France, the United Kingdom, Sweden and Denmark were especially reticent about giving a platform to federalist voices.[44] These same governments accepted the Convention only after the Laeken Council had backed their demand that the final word on a constitutional treaty would remain with the member states in an intergovernmental conference. They insisted, too, on Convention members being selected not elected, pre-empting any suggestion that that they were members of a *constituante* assembly.[45] By degrees governments were reassured that this process could be managed to advantage.[46] The former Belgian prime minister, Jean-Luc Dehaene, appointed as one of the Convention's two vice-chairmen, spoke for many governments when he warned that 'crisis' beckoned unless the Union addressed the consequences of imminent enlargement.[47] Politicians, faced with the inevitable, made virtue out of necessity.[48] In keynote speeches, Finland's prime minister, Paavo Lipponen, and Jacques Chirac of France endorsed the idea of opening up the reform process, though both insisted that this was merely 'consultative'.[49] Even the British government became reconciled to the idea of a convention, reassured that the involvement of national parliamentarians would ensure a brake on the supranational preferences of federalists representing the Union's institutions.

The Belgian presidency took the lead, encouraged by Germany, Finland and Portugal.[50] Frustrated by what they saw as the hauteur of the 'big three' at Nice, some smaller member states pressed at this early stage for more transparent negotiations, seemingly a democratic reflex but no less a pragmatic one, a way to increase their own influence.[51] To this end, a group coalesced around Finnish Premier Lipponen.[52] Confident of support for a more inclusive procedure, Belgium's Prime Minister Verhofstadt issued a memorandum proposing a constitutional convention intended to be both more open and deliberative, a forum tasked with preparing the ground for a subsequent IGC.[53] His foreign minister, Louis Michel, made the same case strongly at the Laeken European Council.[54] This was a new approach to reforming EU governance, though some way short of more radical ideas circulating amongst MEPs and in the Commission. Ever since the European Parliament had drafted its 'treaty' on European Union in 1984,

MEPs in particular had acquired the habit of 'thinking about alternative treaties'.[55] The Parliament has long advocated more open and representative procedure for reforming the treaties, concerned that 'the institutional balance of current provisions (Article 48) favours governmental actors'.[56] The case for wider consultations was made in both the Tsatos and Mendez de Vigo Reports.[57] Since then MEPs have called for the treaties to be properly constitutionalised.[58] There are precedents for a more openly deliberative approach to treaty reform, such as the *ad hoc* Assembly convened in 1952–3 that openly debated the preparatory draft of a proposed treaty for a European Political Community. More recently, the rights convention opened the Union's covert reform procedure to wider participation, some optimists even maintaining that this was nothing less than 'a kind of constitutional coming-of-age for the EU polity, a recognition and affirmation of its hard-won maturity ... a significant symbolic discontinuity with the past'.[59] The Belgian presidency and those member states who supported its initiative wanted to go further than this convention, with its specialised personnel and limited remit, precluded after all from issuing any mandate for a subsequent IGC.[60] Even so, that convention was widely regarded as successful and the method appealed to MEPs precisely because more inclusive than any IGC, with membership drawn from parliaments both in Strasbourg and the member states, and with the inclusion of representatives from civil society.[61] Much was made of the proposed Convention's democratic credentials, one observer even claiming that the procedure would be nothing less than to move the EU 'towards a new combined constitutional method'.[62]

By the time the heads of government and state met at Laeken initial reservations had been set aside, and there was confident talk about the Convention laying the foundations for a European constitution.[63] There were still difficulties to be overcome, not least procedural matters, the all important matter of how decisions should be made. The Tampere Conclusions that established the procedures for the rights convention had defined its task as making 'final conclusions' so as to indicate a range of options, with 'consensus' the preferred outcome. The rights convention had also eschewed formal voting, and the Charter of Fundamental Rights was adopted without a vote, though its final draft did include a minority report from members who objected to the final conclusions.[64] This forerunner was the most likely model for the Union's constitutional convention.[65]

## Breakthrough at Laeken

The Laeken European Council in December 2001, chaired by the Belgian presidency, launched the Convention on the Future of Europe.[66] It was tasked with undertaking a thorough review of the Union's governance at a time when the Union stood 'at a crossroads, a defining moment in its existence'.[67] The Declaration on the Future of the European Union adopted by the Council on 15 December 2001 mandated the Convention to review issues essential for the Union's development.[68] The Convention was expected 'to think big (Constitution-building) and "out of the box" (no taboos)'.[69] The principal task was to more clearly demarcate the Union's competencies from those of the member states. And no less, to simplify the Union's complex constitutional order, its 'incredibly layered, incoherent and incomprehensible morass of treaties', given that four new treaties had been enacted in less than two decades (the Single European Act (1986), the Treaty of Maastricht (1992), the Treaty of Amsterdam (1986), and the Treaty of Nice (2000)). A body of treaty-based law that amounted to some 700 articles, 50 protocols and more than a thousand declarations totalling over 80,000 pages.[70]

This was the first time that 'the word "constitution" was mentioned in an official mandate for revision of the founding treaties'.[71] But the very fact that most of the Convention's personnel was drawn from governments and national parliaments, and even from EU institutions, was bound to constrain the exercise, limit its scope to mainly institutional or inter-institutional matters. And so it proved, for these constraints were apparent from the outset. Britain's Europe minister, Peter Hain, pointedly described the Convention's task as merely 'clarifying a tangled web of treaties which are unintelligible', and not remotely to establish 'some sort of framework for a super-state'.[72] There was no suggestion from any source that mattered that the Convention was in business to 'redesign the EU from scratch'.[73] The schedule, too, was exclusively in the hands of the European Council, who refused to countenance any extension of time available for the exercise.[74] Costs were to be shared between member states and the EU institutions. A budget of 10.5 million euros was allocated, with EU15, the candidate countries and the EU institutions each contributing resources 'in kind' valued at an additional 6.5 million euros, mostly in the form of seconded staff and meeting-room facilities. The big three EU institutions provided some 4 million euros in cash, the bulk of which (2.6 million euros) came from the Commission to cover the translation and interpretation of documentation into the 11 working languages, and for travel, accommodation and secretariat staffing costs.

Membership was decided by the so-called twin-track approach established by the previous convention, with *conventionnels* selected from both national and EU institutions, implying 'recognition of the dual source of legitimacy in the European Union', though the actual choice of personnel was left to those bodies.[75] Governments indirectly maintained control over proceedings by appointing Valéry Giscard d'Estaing as president (nominally a presiding officer, but in effect more than that) and 'one of their own', a former head of state and the man accredited with establishing the European Council, the principal forum for pursuing national interests at the epicentre of EU governance. As such, Giscard was hardly likely to be in favour of drastic changes let alone unduly radical ideas, but he was as concerned as most governments to reform cumbersome decisional procedures to meet changing times.[76] And so it proved, for it soon became apparent as proceedings got underway that the member states, and especially the larger ones, exerted considerable leverage, by means of regular bilateral consultations conducted by Giscard with the respective heads of government. Giscard orchestrated (his critics say manipulated) the Convention from the outset, and he proved to be a dependable ally of the leading member states, though he was not entirely dependent on them, and won some significant concessions from their representatives on key issues, by no means always to their liking. The interim drafts of what became the Constitutional Treaty bore his firm imprint. Indeed these were mostly written in his own hand and they reflected his cautious approach.[77] Although the final draft of the Constitutional Treaty did make some significant changes to EU governance, essential if the Convention was to conclude its business, these were changes that the member states could live with.

Not everything was quite so stage-managed. Despite agreement at Laeken on the need for a fundamental review of EU governance, exactly what the Convention would submit to the European Council remained far from settled until the latter stages. Laeken had considered two possible outcomes. Most member states preferred the Convention to review possible options, but with the initiative for the final decision about a constitutional treaty remaining with governments in an IGC, in effect business as usual. An altogether more ambitious option discussed at Laeken was for the Convention to deliver a fully-fledged draft constitutional treaty, assuming that it could reach a consensus, by no means a foregone conclusion. Many governments expected and some hoped it would fail this test. But as the Convention went about its business it soon became apparent – in no small measure as a result of Giscard's determination – that *conventionnels* for the most part preferred the latter and more ambitious option, attracted by Giscard's appeal to them to 'make history'. Once this fact registered, governments began to take the Convention altogether more seriously than some of them had initially been inclined to do. France and the United Kingdom had already decided not to take any chances, dispatching senior ministers as their official representatives from the start. Other governments followed suit, bolstering their official representation by parachuting in higher-ranking personnel to make their case and above all to defend their interests.[78]

## Launching the Convention

The inaugural session of the Convention on the Future of Europe met on 28 February 2002. In his opening address in the plenary hall of the European Parliament building in Brussels Giscard deliberately emphasised the historic challenge of transforming the EU into a credible actor in international politics. One, as he saw it, that was 'respected and listened to, not only as the economic power it already is, but as a political power which will talk on equal terms to the greatest powers on our planet, either existing or future, and will have the means to act to affirm its values, ensure its security and play an active role in international peacekeeping'.[79] The prize awaiting the *conventionnels*, as Giscard saw it, was nothing less than a place in history. He reminded them that their forum would be the first occasion since the Messina Conference (1955) to undertake a thorough review of the European institutions, and he appealed for consensus, because it was obvious that unanimity was simply out of the question.[80] Of course, this was wishful thinking. Things are never quite that straightforward in the EU. Too many *conventionnels* preferred to represent only their own institution, or their own country, and this in turn gave rise to turf wars across the range of issues.[81] But with an altogether bigger picture in mind, Giscard resisted the very idea of institutional or national partisanship, deliberately coining the neutral term *conventionnel* to describe the membership of a forum that, in his view, would rise above such narrow preoccupations.

The Convention's task as he saw it was nothing less than to write a constitution, albeit one 'which takes the legal form of a treaty since in contrast to a national constitution, the powers conferred on the Union derive from the States which conclude the Treaty'.[82] This idea was well received by *conventionnels* from the start, an early indication that they were quite prepared, as Giscard put it, to be 'founders rather than failures'.[83] Some *conventionnels* even claimed *constituante* status for the Convention, in effect an independent mandate for making a European constitution in much the same way as its historic predecessor in Philadelphia, though the member states had expressly denied it any such role.[84] Giscard reminded them that they sat neither as a parliament nor a constituent assembly in the same way as their famous predecessors, but as a deliberative forum consisting of 'a group of men and women meeting for the sole purpose of preparing a joint proposal [which] if it succeeds will "light up the future"'.[85] Above all, he expected members to rise above narrow partisanship, prepared to be bold and imaginative and to be infused by what he liked to call the 'Convention spirit', a 'collaborative attitude aimed at finding common ground and avoiding a tight defence of national and/or institutional interests'.[86] To this end he imposed flexible seating arrangements, and permitted members to make 'within reason' unscheduled *ad hoc* interventions during proceedings.[87] Certainly Giscard was no visionary. He assumed that *conventionnels*, for the most part 'experienced politicians used to fighting their corner' and above all 'used also to making deals', would find practical solutions to the questions under consideration.[88]

Of course, *conventionnels* from some 40 separate national and European institutions were bound to differ on every issue, and the Convention was a far more fragmented body than any IGC.[89] The fact that many *conventionnels* belonged to several political groups simultaneously – for instance to political parties and governments, to national and EU institutions, or to particular pressure groups – was nevertheless advantageous in so far as it facilitated networking and helped to ensure political deals on some of the more controversial issues. On the downside, the Convention lasted some 18 months, and this meant periodic changes in personnel as *conventionnels* with elected mandates, some of them members of national governments, had to face the capricious cycle of elections, cabinet reshuffles and personal resignations. This took its toll of Giscard's fabled 'convention spirit', hindering both continuity and collegiality. But in the end, the Convention rose to the challenge and these difficulties were more than offset by willingness to give and take. Above all, as the Convention got to work, there was widespread acceptance that squabbling and intransigence would undermine both their credibility and their capacity to reach an outcome that governments would have to take seriously.[90]

## Membership

One hundred and five *conventionnels* participated in the Convention: 56 national parliamentarians, 28 government representatives, 16 MEPs, 2 commissioners, and the three-man presidency team, with alternates appointed to shadow each full-time *conventionnel*. The European Parliament was particularly well represented, with some governments (Greece, Luxembourg and Spain) deciding to appoint MEPs as their national representatives. Significantly, government representatives were in the minority. In addition, there were observers from the Committee of the Regions, the Economic and Social Committee, the European Social Partners and the Office of the European Ombudsman. Although more broadly based than its predecessor and broadly representative of the Union's national make-up (see Table 3.1) the Convention's membership was hardly demographically representative of European society.

*Conventionnels* were, for the most part, drawn from the professional and political classes (see Table 3.2), and pro-integration voices were more in evidence than Eurosceptics. Women were seriously underrepresented, with 17 female *conventionnels* (16.35 per cent) and 23 alternates, and only 2 women in the Presidium's team of 12. Only one female *conventionnel*, the British MP Gisela Stuart, was appointed to chair a working group. This was barely an improvement on the unbalanced composition of the rights convention, where women were a mere 15 per cent of the total membership. Giscard's facile remark, to the effect that '*elles compensent cette situation d'infériorité numerique par la fort personnalité de beaucoup d'entre elles*', did little to improve matters.[91] Even fewer *conventionnels* were appointed to represent Europe's

*Table 3.1* Convention membership by nationality

| Member states | Presidency | European Commission | MEPs | Government representatives | National MPs | All | Observers |
|---|---|---|---|---|---|---|---|
| Austria | – | – | 1 (2) | 1 (1) | 2 (2) | 4 (5) | 1 |
| Belgium | 1 | – | 1 (0) | 1 (1) | 2 (2) | 5 (3) | 3 |
| Denmark | – | – | 1 (2) | 1 (1) | 2 (2) | 4 (5) | – |
| Finland | – | – | 0 (2) | 1 (1) | 2 (2) | 3 (5) | 2 |
| France | 1 | 1 | 2 (2) | 1 (1) | 2 (2) | 7 (5) | 2 |
| Germany | – | – | 3 (1) | 1 (1) | 2 (2) | 6 (4) | 2 |
| Greece | – | – | 0 (0) | 1 (1) | 2 (2) | 3 (3) | – |
| Ireland | – | (1) | 0 (1) | 1 (1) | 2 (2) | 3 (5) | – |
| Italy | 1 | (1) | 2 (1) | 1 (1) | 2 (2) | 6 (5) | 2 |
| Luxembourg | – | – | 0 (0) | 1 (1) | 2 (2) | 3 (3) | – |
| Netherlands | – | – | 1 (0) | 1 (1) | 2 (2) | 4 (3) | – |
| Portugal | – | 1 | 1 (2) | 1 (1) | 2 (2) | 5 (5) | 1 |
| Spain | – | – | 1 (1) | 1 (1) | 2 (2) | 4 (4) | – |
| Sweden | – | – | 0 (0) | 1 (1) | 2 (2) | 3 (3) | – |
| UK | – | – | 3 (2) | 1 (1) | 2 (2) | 6 (5) | – |
| *Subtotal* | 3 | 2 (2) | 16 (16) | 15 (15) | 30 (30) | 66 (63) | 13 |
| All candidate countries | – | – | – | 1 (1) | 2 (2) | 3 (3) | – |
| *Subtotal* | – | – | – | 13 (13) | 26 (26) | 39 (39) | – |
| Total | 3 | 2 (2) | 16 (16) | 28 (28) | 56 (56) | 105 (102) | 13 |

Note: figures in parentheses denote alternative or 'shadow' members of the Convention

ethnic or cultural minorities, or the wider network of European social movements and NGOs. The socially excluded were inadequately represented, too, those organisations that speak for the old, the disabled, the poor and legally resident nationals of non-EU countries living and working in the EU, contributing to the Union's prosperity yet denied both EU citizenship or access to the legal and social protection available to citizens. This narrow social base does raise serious questions about the Convention's claim to embody public legitimacy, and goes some way to explaining why the draft Constitution failed to resonate with the public.[92]

### (i) Community institutions

#### The Commission

The Commission's main aim is to promote European integration, and it regarded the Convention as a historic opportunity. Although the Commission had only two representatives, Antonio Vitorino, the commissioner for justice and home affairs, and Michel Barnier, the commissioner for institutional affairs, their influence was disproportionate to their number. Vitorino had participated in the earlier rights convention, and Barnier had played a significant role in the Nice IGC.[93] The commissioners and their support staff were particularly well informed about first-pillar procedure and policy, but also on many matters pertaining to the Justice and Home Affairs pillar, about which Commissioner Vitorino spoke with great authority, not least the consequences of incorporating the Charter on Fundamental Rights into the Treaty, giving it the status of a 'legal watchdog'.[94] The

*Table 3.2* The professional status of government representatives

|  |  | Member states |  | Candidate countries |
| --- | --- | --- | --- | --- |
| Deputy Prime Minister | 2 | Italy, Sweden | – | – |
| Deputy Minister for Foreign/European Affairs | 6 | Belgium, France, Germany, Ireland, Spain, United Kingdom | 8 | Bulgaria, Hungary, Latvia, Lithuania, Poland, Romania, Slovakia, Turkey |
| MEP | 2 | Luxembourg, Greece | – | – |
| Former senior statesman | 4 | Austria, Denmark, Netherlands, Portugal | 2 | Cyprus, Estonia |
| Academic/adviser | 1 | Finland | 1 | Malta |
| Senior civil servant | – | – | 2 | Czech Republic, Slovenia |

Replacements over the duration in the representation of: Czech Republic; France; Germany; Hungary; Ireland; Netherlands; Portugal; Slovakia; Spain; Turkey

Commission's influence was enhanced by putting its formidable administrative expertise at the disposal of the Convention's fledgling secretariat, ensuring it a greater degree of informal influence than had been the case in the earlier convention, and considerably more than in its role as 'an unwelcome guest' in the two preceding IGCs.[95] The Commission was able to draw on its considerable experience of IGCs, its fabled 'institutional memory' giving it a distinct advantage over most of the national representatives, at least on key technical and procedural matters. At the Amsterdam and Nice IGCs, for example, it had organised a task force of officials to support its official representatives.

The appointment of commissioners as chairs of two of the praesidium's 10 working groups – the main forums for generating ideas that would find their way into the final proposals – gave them a significant role in shaping the agenda and influencing the plenaries. Their offices issued briefing papers and background notes to *conventionnels* in support of the Commission's agenda. Yet the Commission's influence was tempered by internal wrangling that squandered valuable political capital.[96] By early 2003 its influence was 'significantly impaired by its inconsistent positions and internal disagreements' on some of the critical issues.[97] One incident in particular shows the extent of the problem here. Commission President Prodi insisted on presenting his own version of a draft constitution, the so-called Penelope document drawn up by a small group of Commission insiders, notwithstanding the objections of his fellow commissioners.

This personal manifesto was leaked to the media, quite possibly at Prodi's instigation, and certainly timed to coincide with the publication of the Commission's own official paper: a maverick act that made for confusion and, worse, resentment within the College, earning Giscard's disdain and compromising Barnier and Vitorino. The best that can be said about this incident is that the Penelope document did make a thorough technical appraisal of many of the key issues, and was actually a more sophisticated document than the Commission's official submission. And, for that reason, it remained 'on the table', a useful referent throughout the subsequent deliberations. Worse was to follow after Prodi gave his personal endorsement to *conventionnels*, mostly from the smaller member states, who demanded what they saw as their 'right' to retain one commissioner for each member state. This fragile coalition eventually collapsed after the defection of the Benelux countries, the result in part of internal differences but also of pressure from the larger member states. This confirmed the impression of a Commission both accident-prone and out of touch, and reinforced the secretariat's 'unchallenged monopoly of initiative'.[98]

The Commission's commitment to constitutional reform was patent, though its ambition exceeded its influence on events. The Commission's formal submission, a paper entitled *A Project for the European Union* lacked cogent proposals on key issues.[99] The subsequent Commission paper, *Peace, Freedom, Solidarity*, did at least address the critical institutional issues, making the case for better inter-institutional balance, but again it undermined its own position by making its usual claim for increased powers. In what was broadly a federalist agenda, the Commission made a bold play for the right of initiative in all legislative areas other than military matters, including economic and foreign policy and police co-operation, and proposed its own direct election by the Parliament; the extension of the Community method and co-decision to all areas of EU law-making, replacing unanimity with QMV in Council decision-making, though on the revised basis of a dual formula of states and population; and an end to the budgetary distinction between compulsory and non-compulsory expenditure.[100] The Commission also opposed a permanent Council presidency, backing the demand of the smaller member states for parity of membership, in effect the continuation of rotation. And though the Commission endorsed the proposal for an EU foreign minister, it preferred that the new office should report to both the Commission and the Council.[101]

The Commission was playing for high stakes here, as it always does where treaty reform is the issue, seeing a European Constitution as a charter to establish 'the world's first true supranational democracy'.[102] A European Constitution would be the foundation, as the Commission saw it, for the 'development of the European model of society', and no less of a political system 'whose vocation is to exercise the responsibilities of a world power'.[103] But it failed to make its case where it mattered most, provoking a hostile reaction from the leading member states. It fared little better even with the smaller member states, who might have been expected to see the Commission as an ally against the 'big three'. The prevailing impression, certainly amongst leading member states who are after all the EU's power-brokers on the critical issues, was of an institution if not quite in disarray at least lacking effective leadership and pursuing barely disguised self-interest.[104]

*The European Parliament*

Sixteen *conventionnels* were MEPs, selected to reflect the Parliament's current party balance. The Parliament has played a more marginal role in IGCs even than the Commission, framing opinions or taking votes on some issues, yet denied any real influence, not least because it could not attend meetings. Although it was not even invited to submit formal proposals, it did win the minor concession of 'observer status' in the 2000 IGC. The Convention brought the Parliament more fully into the picture, though MEPs were outnumbered by representatives from both national parliaments and governments. What they lacked in numbers, however, they made up for in enthusiasm and experience. They brought to the Convention sound knowledge (certainly compared with most national *conventionnels*) of how 'Europe' actually works. MEPs are well versed in the procedures of transnational politics, quite 'used to working as a collective – usually together with the Commission and against the Council'.[105] MEPs tend to better understand the arcane legal matters and the procedures that frame EU business, and with the Convention meeting in Brussels they were on home turf, giving them ready access to alternative information resources from the Parliament's secretariat and supplemented by the Commission. They took advantage, too, of their links with European civil society networks, and in some cases of their connections with national parliaments. This gave them a distinct advantage over *conventionnels* whose institutional bases were far removed from Brussels, altogether less familiar with the way the EU works. Even so, this increased workload took its toll of their time and energy.

The way EU political parties work also made co-ordination difficult. The Parliament's political groups monitored proceedings closely and the various parliamentary committees regularly issued reports, but this merely added to information overload as MEPs were 'bombarded with instructions and exhortations often of a contradictory nature'.[106] Party and other differences notwithstanding, MEPs did try to put their institutional stamp on proceedings, and there was a measure of agreement beyond party or ideological divisions about what they wanted from a constitutional treaty: for instance, more co-decision, an elective role *vis-à-vis* the Commission president, and greater budgetary powers. There was evidence, too, of effective teamwork. For though it was the praesidium's practice after reaching agreement on an issue not to revisit it, the two MEPs on the praesidium tended to continue liaising with their colleagues in the plenary body to press for the reopening of some issues, though on the crucial issues this hardly made much difference when confronted by government representatives.

### (ii) National MPs

The largest single group of *conventionnels* was the members of national parliaments, exceeding the representatives from all of the EU institutions by a ratio of 4:1. If this numerical imbalance was intended to ensure the primacy of the domestic over the supranational interest, the Convention's political dynamics brought about a rather different outcome. Numerical preponderance was no guarantee of influence, and was more than offset by this group's lack of a 'common culture', detracting from its 'capability to act as a single body'.[107] National parliamentarians also lacked the detailed knowledge of EU procedures and experience of actually working inside the Union's institutional nexus, inside knowledge available to MEPs or for that matter to commissioners. The fact that seven MEPs had participated in the rights convention, and thus had knowledge of how conventions actually work, as had three of their alternates, was experience they used to good effect. MEPs proved adept, too, at using the praesidium, and especially their membership of the various working groups, to shape the agenda. By and large, MEPs brought energy and commitment to proceedings, qualities noticeably lacking in many national representatives.

It soon became apparent from proceedings that there was more tension than common purpose between the two groups of parliamentarians. To a degree this is a reflection of the design of EU governance. Many national parliamentarians resent their exclusion from Union decision-making, or see Strasbourg flourishing 'at the expense of national parliaments', some choosing to believe that MEPs are somehow 'instinctively unwilling to share power with or otherwise strengthen its national counterparts'.[108] For these reasons relations between national and European parliamentarians are by no means always cordial, notwithstanding a mutual commitment to representative democracy. Contacts tend to be minimal and, even when they do occur, competitive. And so it proved in the Convention, where nationality, rather than any 'natural' ideological affinity or party affiliation, was a stronger bond between elected representatives than empathy. This served to unite 'national parliament and national government delegates ... in pursuit of a perceived national interest or preference', with national parliamentarians regardless of party affiliation frequently endorsing their own governments' positions.[109]

### (iii) The member states

The member states were directly represented in the Convention, as they had been in the earlier rights convention. Some MEPs wanted *conventionnels* to be recruited exclusively from the ranks of parliamentarians, but the leading member states resisted this, not least because it would invest the Convention with legitimacy reminiscent of a *constituante* assembly. Governments were determined to have the last word on any new treaty, and regarded the Convention as merely advisory, a forum for debate.

As personal envoys of their heads of governments the national representatives were influential participants. Some of them were, or had been, EU insiders and as such were knowledgeable both about procedure and substantive issues. The Spanish and Greek presidencies that coincided with the Convention were represented by current or former MEPs, and the Danish representative had previously served as a commissioner. There were marked differences, however, between governments regarding appointments. Some governments, realising what was at stake, sent senior personnel from the start, whereas others were convinced that the exercise was less crucial, though even these slow-starters eventually appointed more senior representatives.[110] Although the Convention outwardly conformed to the principle of equal representation between states regardless of demographic size or membership status (for instance, as between EU15 or the candidate countries), things did not quite work that way in practice. The views of the smaller EU15 member states did not signify as much as those of the 'big three'. And though impending enlargement was a principal reason for the constitutional endeavour in the first place, and the candidate countries were determined their views should be heard as much as those of more established member states, parity of esteem did not translate into parity of influence. This fact contributed to the eventual fall-out over voting weights that delayed agreement on the final version of the Constitutional Treaty in the IGC.

National governments were determined to seize the initiative, and they did so, though some more than others. This is hardly surprising, the member states see themselves after all as the 'masters of the treaties', and the political resources available to the larger member states ensures their primacy in the business of treaty reform. As soon as these governments realised that the Convention was determined to deliver a full-blown treaty, they not only took the proceedings more seriously, lobbying hard for their preferences, but some participants tried to pull rank on the critical matters of power and policy. The impression from proceedings, both in plenaries and praesidium, is of governments forming alliances to push their own preferences. The long-standing alliance between France and Germany was particularly important in this respect, their joint paper proving highly influential in shaping discussion and determining the outcome on the key institutional questions. After some horse-trading this agenda was accepted in the main by other key players, notably the United Kingdom and Spain. Nevertheless, there were differences between governments, as there always are over treaty reform, the main fault-line being that between the larger states determined to push their preferences for a more effective executive capacity, and small states concerned to resist *directoire* domination of the proceedings. Significantly, the presidency tended to defer to the 'big three' on these critical issues. Giscard was especially receptive to representations from these leading national ministers, to whom, as one observer saw it, 'he showed due deference'.[111] This much was predictable, after all Giscard had been chosen to preside over the Convention precisely because leading governments saw in him as reliable advocate of their interests, a safe pair of hands. Nor did he disappoint them, for this patrician 'made no secret of his affection for the European Council (his own creation) and respect for national leaders'.

### *(iv) The regions*

The regions have acquired significance in the EU governance that reflects their role in what many commentators now describe as a multi-level polity. This is a concept of European integration rooted less in the currency of power politics, of *juste retour* and competing national interests, but instead in the complicated and multiple networking of cross-border transactions and transnational co-operation. Europe as a common endeavour confronting by means of institutional interdependence what David Mitrany once disparaged as 'the tyranny of nation state boundaries'.[112] There are limits, however, to the regions' influence, and they fared badly at the Convention. The Committee of the Regions, the one European institution that might reasonably claim to speak on behalf of regional interests, was given merely observer status. The Committee of the Regions in its Liège Declaration did make the case for a greater role for regions in a new constitutional settlement, receiving petitions of support from various EU regions. The Committee requested that those territorial governments (from Spain's autonomous communities to German *Länder*) already exercising legislative competencies should nominate observers to the Convention, with the right to a more direct involvement in proceedings related to their interests. France and to a lesser degree Spain objected to even this modest proposal, and the regional voice of the regions was much weaker than it deserved to be.[113]

This reflects the modest status of the regions in the Union's current political arrangements, the fact that they are still barely mobilised to put their case on the key issues. Representatives from national institutions dominated the Convention, as Table 3.1 shows, making it difficult for regional interests to build the sort of transnational and inter-institutional coalitions necessary for exerting real influence.[114] Those member states better disposed towards regionalism in their national constitutions, not least three of the EU's federal states, lacked either the incentive (Germany) or the political clout (Belgium and Austria) to make the case for the regions. Germany, the one federal state that might conceivably have made a difference, put pragmatism before principle, deferring in this matter to member states (France and the United Kingdom) with more centralist traditions.

## (v) Political parties

Party affiliation was not used explicitly as a criterion for selecting *conventionnels*, but in the circumstances it was unavoidable. Making a European constitution is after all a political endeavour, and representatives from all of the principal European political parties colonised the Convention, whether as government or national parliamentary representatives, or as commissioners and MEPs. The left–right axis was the principal ideological cleavage in the Convention (see Table 3.3), with the European Parliament's principal party groups, and particularly the socialist PES, the Christian-democrat PPE-ED, and the liberal ELDR dominating, though by no means entirely monopolising proceedings in both the plenary sessions and the praesidium.

The party 'families' conducted informal bargaining on a wide range of issues, holding regular meetings that brought together party affiliates from various institutional bases, and facilitating co-operation between MEPs and national parliamentarians, giving structure to otherwise inchoate networks. Notable here were

*Table 3.3* Composition of the Convention by party political affiliation

|  | Presidency | European Commission | MEPs | Government representatives | National MPs | Total |
|---|---|---|---|---|---|---|
| PES | 1 | 1 | 5 (31.25 %) | 3 (20%) | 13 (43.33%) | 23 (34.84%) |
| EPP | 2 | 1 | 6 (37.5%) | 4 (26.66%) | 11 (36.66%) | 24 (36.35%) |
| ELDR | – | – | 1 (6.25%) | 3 (20%) | 4 (13.33%) | 8 (12.12%) |
| UEN | – | – | 1 (6.25%) | 2 (13.33%) | 1 (3.34%) | 4 (6.06%) |
| GRN | – | – | 1 (6.25%) | 1 (6.67%) | – | 2 (3.03%) |
| GUE/NGL | – | – | 1 (6.25%) | – | – | 1 (1.52%) |
| EDD | – | – | 1 (6.25%) | – | – | 1 (1.52%) |
| FPÖ | – | – | – | | 1 (3.34%) | 1 (1.52%) |
| N/A (EPP) | – | – | – | 1 (6.67%) | – | 1 (1.52%) |
| N/A (PES) | – | – | – | 1 (6.67%) | – | 1 (1.52%) |
| Total | 3 | 2 | 16 (100%) | 15 (100%) | 30 (100%) | 66 (100%) |

Source: Adapted from CEPS data, December 2002.

Notes
EDD – European Democrats group
ELDR – Alliance of Liberals and Democrats for Europe, known since 2004 as ALDE
EPP – European People's Party
FPÖ – Austrian Freedom Party
GUE/NGL – Confederal Group of European United Left and Nordic Green Left
GRN – greens
PES – Party of European Socialists
UEN – Union for Europe of the Nations Group
N/A = no formal party attachment and showing the party affiliation of the heads of states.

the 'informal dining clubs of movers and shakers which enabled ideas to flow, policies to crystallise and consensus to form', facilitating the bargains that eventually resulted in a draft treaty.[115] The party caucuses brought together parliamentarians from both the national and EU party groups, including government representatives of the same ideological disposition, meeting in groups known as *composantes* before each plenary session to review the issues of the moment. The party groups issued regular interim reports or position statements, though differences of interest and even of ideology within these fraternal party organisations made reaching agreement difficult. Too many of the position papers issued by these groups were vague, lacking either clarity or focus, or both.

The PSE was more active than the other parties in mediating intra-party differences.[116] It eventually issued a manifesto, *Priorities for Europe*, based on discussions during its Birmingham meeting in August 2002. However, narrow political considerations prevented agreement on some common principles.[117] The party's leading thinkers on constitutional matters were marginalised, as was the case too in the PPE-ED. In fact, the PPE was altogether more reticent about radically reforming EU governance. Only after direct intervention by the Italian prime minister, Silvio Berlusconi, who called for action on the Constitution, did the party belatedly issue a manifesto authored by two leading Christian democrats, Wilfred Martens and Wolfgang Schauble, and launched at a PPE congress in Lisbon in October 2002.[118] If the two principal party groups were hesitant about recommending constitutional reforms, the smallest of the three main party families, the liberal ELDR, contributed some novel thinking on these same questions, though their radical tenor was in no whit matched by political clout, and few of these ideas found their way into the draft Constitution.[119]

What does this say about the capacity for political parties – after all agencies that on home ground throughout the democratic world have transformative potential – for operating effectively as change agents at the transnational level? The pattern of party competition in Europe's domestic politics is shaped by long-established social and ideological cleavages. The most significant cleavage, the left–right axis, confirms that socio-economic interests are the primary indicators of party choice and the determinants by and large of headline party policy. This cleavage has been transposed from national to European parliamentary politics, yet it lacks at that level quite the same salience for shaping party politics or public policy. A more recent cleavage, and one much less firmly established in European politics at any level, is the clash of ideas about the meaning and purpose of European integration. Europhiles broadly accept that 'Europeanisation', the interdependence of domestic and EU policy-making, has potential as a source for political allegiance and party competition, though they may differ over its political significance or institutional consequences. Europhobes, however, resist this trend, seeing only conventional redistributive ideas and national interests as the forces that shape politics, and indeed should shape politics within and beyond the nation state.[120]

The debate about 'Europe' raises passions, but not enough so far to be the basis of a meaningful ideological or party cleavage at the European level. 'Europe' is an important issue in its own right, and one that was bound to surface in the

Convention, though it was by no means as prominent in deliberations on policy, competencies or institutional reform as some commentators had anticipated. In the ensuing debates about how the EU should respond to the challenges of globalisation, international competitiveness and the European social model, even *conventionnnels* who belonged to pro-Europe parties tended to adopt a narrowly national outlook, or one shaped by more familiar left–right preferences, rather than lining up on either side of a 'more' or 'less' 'Europe' divide.

The 'Europe' issue had less salience with the public than with politicians precisely because it cuts across the class and regional cleavages that continue to shape party competition on the ground. 'Europe' divides parties and party families rather more than it unites them, and this was as true in the Convention as it is in national politics. Herbert Kitschelt, writing in the mid-1990s, was unconvinced about the potential for a firm 'Europe cleavage' replacing redistributive politics as the basis for party competition at any level of European politics, at least for the foreseeable future. In no small part, he argued, because 'much of European legislation is of a highly technical nature', and as such has ' few broad redistributive implications'.[121] Nothing that happened in the Convention contradicts this conclusion. *Conventionnels* from Europe's mainstream parties did not fundamentally challenge the ideological foundations or the cultural base of European party politics, though there were some notable interventions. A relatively small if voluble federalist lobby tried hard, as it always does on such occasions, to challenge the conventional outlook, but its impact was marginal on the outcome, let alone on public opinion at large, the steady 'Europeanisation' of public policy notwithstanding.[122]

More important than new thinking about Europe was the imperative for parliamentarians of every political stripe not to appear to an attentive national media to be selling short the national interest. The Convention's day-to-day work confirmed as much. In the 'fraternal' caucuses, those groups that organise what passes for party politics at the European level, national allegiances as much as ideology determined responses to the various issues. Many *conventionnels* were more concerned to mobilise behind what they saw as national interests, in the process making alliances that cut across and thus undermined the already scant cohesion of the European 'parties'. National representatives, regardless of party affiliation, held joint meetings and even lined up on the same side on some of the key issues.[123]

### (vi) A role for civil society?

Civil society actors are excluded from IGC negotiations but were given limited representation in the Convention.[124] The reason here was supposedly to enhance the Convention's credibility with society at large.[125] But things did not quite work like that in practice. Although *conventionnels* were expected to engage the public, to take the issues out to the people, this hardly happened in practice. Some 207 separate NGOs and related organisations took part in this consultation exercise, but they were by no means representative of European civil society, and there were also some notable omissions. Organisations representing some of Europe's most marginalised social groups such as asylum seekers or immigrants were entirely excluded, and there was only a very limited participation from civil society organisations in the accession countries, and for some reason no participation whatsoever by any representative from Portuguese civil society.[126] Even this selective engagement with civil society was 'heavily tilted towards organisations from inside the Brussels ring road'. The entire process was tellingly described by one Commission official as a 'gallant failure' because, though well disposed to the usual 'insider' lobbies, it simply failed 'to get through to the general public'.[127] Moreover, this failure prompted calls in some quarters for a more genuinely deliberative EU public space.[128]

Disconnection between politicians and public meant that debate was 'restricted to the familiar audiences', the usual political and administrative interests, as well as organised and especially corporate lobbies.[129] This much was clear from the agenda, the key issues being much the same as for any IGC: namely, the distribution of institutional power and demarcating competencies as between the Union and the member states, and policy issues such a security, foreign policy, economic governance and the like. Post-modern and post-material issues, identity politics, citizenship and improving democratic life – all of them issues that might appeal to civil society, and especially to disaffected youth – were discounted. Even where there was contact with civil society actors it was contact with favoured clientele. At Giscard's instigation, representatives of European NGOs and European youth organisations were encouraged to make direct representations to the Convention. But these were by no means independent, let alone militant voices, and participants were selected from client groups, many of them in receipt of Commission largesse and as such disposed to make only 'reasonable' demands, with their input mostly limited to written submissions.[130] The principal arena here was the Forum, a network of organisations connected to civil society through contact groups, and entitled to regular information about the proceedings.[131] They were certainly no match for those powerful insider lobbies with direct links to the Union's principal institutional and national actors.

The way the Convention was organised also contributed to lessening the impact of more radical voices. The working groups, the main conduit for circulating ideas, held only a limited number of open hearings, with participation confined for the most part to privileged 'insiders', whether politicians or officials. And though working groups were supposed to be open to the general public, they were in fact largely inaccessible, because they met in the Council building in Brussels where entry required an official pass. The same complaint was made about plenaries, widely criticised for the way civil society representatives were selected, and amounting as some critics saw it to 'a gathering of the Commission's payroll of funded lobby groups, the usual suspects saying the usual things'.[132] Of those selected to speak on behalf of the public interest in the Youth Forum, too many were self-appointed or too closely linked with Commission-sponsored networks. Others were merely remote from the grassroots, and for the most part had closed minds, too 'practiced in the clichés, jargon and fixed ideas of the parties that sent them'.[133] In their own way, these supposedly 'public' voices were as much a part of a self-selected and some would say a self-serving political elite as most other *conventionnels*. The praesidium controlled the arrangements for meetings with representatives from civil society, the timing and agenda, and even which target groups or NGOs were to be invited. The fact, too, that participants were limited to five-minute presentations made a mockery of genuine debate.[134] Much the same could be said of the structured dialogue conducted by vice-president Dehaene and other presidium members with the assorted networks and groups that represent civil society, organised by the Economic and Social Council (ECOSOC), which had observer status in the Convention. One spokesperson for civil society duly complained that Forum issues were neither of their choosing nor reflected their priorities, with the agenda imposed from above. These are familiar criticisms, and show that the lessons that should have been learned from the rights convention went unheeded.

The 'dialogue' with civil society was hardly that, and neither did it involve actual contacts but in part was conducted virtually through the medium of the internet, with some 160 organisations participating. National Forums were also organised within the member states and the candidate countries to supplement this experiment with cyberspace democracy, as well as special meetings with the observers from the Economic and Social Committee, the Committee of the Regions, the social partners and various European NGOs.[135] These disparate activities culminated (June 2002) in a 'hearing' for representatives of civil society, preceded by preparatory meetings organised into eight contact groups, each one chaired by the praesidium. On the face of it considerable activity, though the evidence from the Forum is rather less convincing, achieving 'little on the score of harnessing broad social support', and though undoubtedly well intentioned it was engagement of 'a rather perfunctory character', failing 'to reach much beyond the established European political in-ground'.[136]

Much has been written about the role of the electronic media in facilitating participation in contemporary politics. Some commentators are dismissive, seeing these media as merely cosmetic, more placebo than participation and lacking substance, little more than tokenism at a time when there is a serious decline in the public's engagement with mainstream politics. Yet other commentators see real potential in new technologies for opening a transnational public space. The Forum website was intended to generate debate about the Constitution, but in fact did little to improve public access through its webpages and 'chat sites', beyond a minority of dedicated subscribers. What is fashionably called 'blogging' seems to have little appeal for the wider public, and these sites were mostly colonised by vested interests, the usual *habitués* of the Brussels scene. Some Convention members did take part in public debates, and others addressed academic conferences or wrote for the press about the momentous choices facing the Union. Yet overall there was little serious effort by the principals to inform, let alone to educate, the public on the key issues. The few occasions where such initiatives did occur seemed more like exercises in news management and media manipulation than effective public education.[137]

The public tend to rely on the media for their information about politics, and the media gave scant treatment to the issues, offering sketchy and usually partisan coverage.[138] A survey conducted in April 2002 reported that only 28 per cent of

EU citizens were actually aware of the Convention,[139] a fact confirmed by a *Eurobarometer* survey.[140] Closa's distinction between merely 'passive' and 'active' popular participation is pertinent here.[141] The passive citizen may have access to information on significant issues, the usual way of things in the limited plebiscitary democracy that is the norm in modern liberal polities. But it is only by means of 'active' engagement, using information to help form opinions and indeed to act on them by participating in public affairs, that citizens can really influence public policy. This matter was bound to be problematic for the Convention's legitimacy. The consequences for the EU of public disaffection had been acknowledged at the Laeken Council. One way of better connecting citizens with transnational governance discussed during the Convention's early stages was for a simplified constitutional text, to separate the treaty into two distinct parts as an aid to understanding what the Union is, how it works and what it does. It would comprise a first part outlining the Union's architecture, the institutions, describing their interactions and competencies. The more technical second part would be designed not so much with the public in mind but rather as specialised guidance for institutional actors and policy practitioners, and would list complicated decision-making procedures and policy domains.[142] This idea was fairly promising, but was lost sight of as the Convention got underway. The objective of simplification, making the whole enterprise more accessible to citizens, became submerged in the usual deals and trade-offs between vested interests. By the time the final draft of the treaty text was published it was an unwieldy, not to say an encyclopaedic document, some 400 pages of arcane 'Eurospeak' wholly beyond the public's comprehension. In any event, connecting with 'the people' requires more than merely revising the treaty base. Altogether more and better information, greater all-round transparency is indispensable, though by no means a sufficient condition for reducing the gulf between politicians and people.

The Convention rather lost sight of early good intentions, and its proceedings mostly passed the citizens by. Opinion poll data confirm this, showing what Scott has called an 'attention deficit', with the Convention the least recognised EU institution after the Committee of the Regions.[143] This polling evidence also shows widespread public mistrust of the Convention process itself. *Eurobarometer* polls at the time reveal that whereas support for a European constitution remained fairly constant in the three surveys conducted between autumn 2001 and autumn 2002 (63 per cent to 67 per cent, with only 9–10 per cent against the idea), the same polls indicate that public knowledge of the actual proposals being discussed in the Convention was a mere 28 per cent, with only some 35–39 per cent of respondents attaching any significance to and only 25–29 per cent expressing any trust in the proceedings.[144] The failure to 'connect', to explain the Constitution, and in plain and accessible language, encouraged popular misconceptions, many of which surfaced during the referendum campaigns in France and the Netherlands that eventually sank the Constitution.[145] Well before these fateful events, one prescient voice predicted that: 'If the output [of the Convention] is seen to be a European constitution produced by an elite it may have an entirely contrary impact on legitimacy, and the development of the European political space, to that intended.' To avoid this outcome required *conventionnels* to reach 'beyond organised civil society to the wider public', something they signally failed to do.[146] The rest, as the saying goes, is history.[147]

### (vii) The candidate countries

The candidates for the latest and largest enlargement so far, scheduled for May 2004, had as much interest in the Convention's outcome as the EU15 states. The Convention was an opportunity to demonstrate commitment to European integration, as well as to influence the agenda. And an opportunity, too, for making useful contacts, to construct strategic alliances, developing good working relations both with influential member states and the Union's institutional actors. Things did not work out quite like that in practice. For one thing, the mood was soured by what the newcomers regarded as discrimination, not least by the denial of their full participation in the praesidium. The accession countries were further hindered by a failure to provide them with full translations either of working documents or even of the official record of proceedings. The casual hint that EU15 national parliamentary representatives might reallocate one of their own praesidium representatives to the candidate countries simply failed to materialise, with political parties from the candidate countries excluded from the key EPP–ED and PES meetings convened to decide praesidium representation.

The candidate countries signalled their exasperation at what was clearly their second-class status, but the situation was only partially rectified when the Secretariat eventually permitted a representative from Slovenia, Alojz Peterle, to attend the praesidium, though only as a 'permanent guest' and without full membership rights.[148] The Secretariat made other modest concessions, for instance by recruiting some of its staffers from the accession states and allowing any speaker from a candidate country to supply translations in the Convention's working languages, though this had to be funded from the newcomers' own meagre administrative resources. The restrictions on candidate countries were apparent, too, in the rules on procedure, which expressly stated that the newcomers could not impede consensus between EU15 representatives. This 'clubbishness' confirmed the newcomers' sense of discounted status, and what they saw as the intention 'to distribute gains between current members'.[149] Nevertheless, the accession countries worked energetically within these constraints to make their respective points on the issues of importance to them, quite aware that whatever decisions were reached would impact on them as surely as on EU15.

## Movers and makers

### The president

The procedure for selecting the Convention president did not follow the precedent of the rights convention. The leading governments canvassed their preferred candidates so as to ensure political advantage. Laeken had decided to 'elect' a president and vice-president from a short list of only two preferred candidates: Wim

Kok, the former Dutch prime minister, and the former president of France, Valéry Giscard d'Estaing, with Antonio Guterres and Giuliano Amato briefly considered as possible outsiders. The preferences of the smaller member states hardly signified here, thanks in part to poor organisation but mainly because they lacked political heft.[150] Even before Laeken, Chirac was canvassing his own candidate, with support from Germany and Austria. The only concession to political balance, secured by Dutch pressure after their own candidature stalled, was the appointment of two vice-presidents, one each from Italy (Amato) and Belgium (Jean-Luc Dehaene), both of whom asserted their independence from Giscard.[151]

The decision to appoint a French patrician, a former president of his country and with strong intergovernmental preferences, was by no means unanimous, but it was carried nevertheless. Giscard's appointment reveals something of the current state of EU politics. The bigger member states saw him as 'one of their own', a former national leader and for that very reason a 'safe pair of hands', because more likely to be well disposed towards the Council than to the Commission. And more inclined, too, towards the interests of the larger member states, the key after all to any agreement.[152] Giscard did not disappoint, showing his *directoire* preferences from the start by opposing Prodi's supranational ambitions as expressed in the so-called Penelope document. Philip Norman has described this Olympian figure as follows: 'He was, after all, the man who had invented the European Council and he made no secret of his view that President Prodi's vision of the Commission forming the "government" of the Union was based on a misunderstanding of history.'[153] Meeting with the European Parliament's constitutional affairs committee in October 2001, Giscard conceded that 'the Union's founding fathers had indeed envisaged that the Commission would develop into a European government', the seat of 'the future European executive'. But he insisted that such fanciful notions were now outdated, changed, and irrevocably so, by the emergence of the European Council, his own singular contribution to EU governance.[154] What Giscard was looking for from the Convention was not a federal Europe and certainly not a proto-European state, but rather more modest reforms in accordance with his confederalist disposition: a stable Council presidency and a markedly more limited role for the Commission.

Giscard's credibility was compromised to a degree by unseemly controversy over his demands for remuneration, a salary equivalent to that of the EU Commission President, as well as generous personal and office expenses. By comparison, Roman Herzog, the chair of the rights convention, had received only expenses. And though Giscard eventually bowed to pressure on the salary issue, settling instead for generous expenses, some critics felt that at some 1,000 euros per day these were still excessive. This unseemly wrangle undoubtedly dented his reputation, if not quite his authority.[155] There were doubts about his independence, a propensity as some saw it to defer to the 'big three' on the grounds that, after all, they represented a majority of the Union's population and dominated the Union's institutions.[156] The Laeken Declaration required that the Convention president report on progress to the European Council, an arrangement the Spanish presidency described as confirming the office's 'synergic relationship' with the Council.[157]

To see Giscard's role as merely that of neutral interlocutor, however, is to under-estimate both his ambition and his capacity to exert influence on the proceedings. He showed consummate diplomatic skill throughout, drawing on his reputation as a statesman of international repute to direct proceedings in accordance with his own preferences, taking advantage of 'his duty to report as an instrument for … voicing his (own) views' on the key issues.[158] His didacticism invariably attracted criticism from *conventionnels* concerned about a proprietary interpretation of his presidential role.[159] His habit of imposing his own singular interpretation of what occurred, whether in the praesidium or in the plenaries, was particularly disconcerting to his critics.[160] One praesidium member compared his imperious manner unfavourably with the altogether more conciliatory style of his two vice-presidents, notably Dehaene. Observing Giscard at close quarters, one praesidium member, Gisela Stuart, was convinced that his hauteur and particularly his insist-ence on French as the praesidium's working language did much to undermine the Convention's reputation as a democratic forum:

> It was only in the final months of the Convention that simultaneous transla-tion was provided for presidium meetings and we could be accompanied by an assistant to give legal advice. Even then, texts would arrive late and only in French. Whenever the president expressed his irritation at my inability to conduct legal negotiations in French, I offered to switch to German. He never took me up on it. Some members of the secretariat showed particular irritation with my insistence that documents be produced in English. On one occasion, a redraft of articles dealing with defence mysteriously arrived just before midnight. They were written in French and … verbal reassurances were given that this was little more than a 'linguistically better draft of the earlier English version'. The draft was discarded when some of us spotted that references to NATO had mysteriously disappeared. Sometimes wordings would be agreed in the presidium without being translated into the official texts circulated to the rest of the 200-strong convention. … Consensus was achieved amongst those deemed to matter, who made it plain that the rest of us would not be allowed to wreck the fragile agreement struck.[161]

On numerous occasions, Giscard expressed opinions antithetical to those of a majority of *conventionnels*, whose collective views he was, after all, supposed to represent.[162] He was particularly hostile to the federalist aspirations of some *conventionnels*, utterly opposed, for instance, to their proposal to rename the Union so as to reflect their preferences, and instead pursued his own controversial proposal for a Congress of the Peoples of Europe, a body consisting of national parliamentarians and MEPs, and with the task of reviewing the state of the Union.[163] There were many such examples of Giscard's conceited and occasionally over-bearing manner. In the crucial debate on the third pillar, for instance, the official summary noted that 'a large majority [of *conventionnels*] … argued in favour of full "communitarisation" of current third pillar issues'.[164] Giscard's account of these discussions, however, focused on his own preference for an entirely pragmatic approach to policy, and discounted anything remotely resembling a federal design.[165] Accordingly, in one plenary he confronted those *conventionnels* who wanted to limit the blocking power of national parliaments on EU legislation, pointedly 'inviting' the chairman of the appropriate working group to consider enhancing the role of national parliaments in the European policy process.

Giscard certainly proved adept at using the role afforded to him to maximum effect, directing (critics said manipulating) the Convention's agenda for his own purposes, by limiting genuinely deliberative exchanges, playing off one group against another and ensuring – in so far as this was possible in such a diverse body – that ensuing compromises would reflect his own preferences.[166] And he did this adroitly, some observers judging the eventual draft Constitution to be nothing less than the translation of 'his own agenda into the Convention agenda', with Giscard 'behaving as an omniscient interpreter of public opinion and public wishes'.[167] Critics attributed his assertiveness to arrogance or egotism, or both, a preoccupation with his place in history. Certainly, he did little to dispel this impression, and on one occasion even likened his own role to that of one of the founding fathers of the American Constitution, observing that: 'I tried to play a little bit the role that Jefferson played, which was to instil leading ideas into the system. Jefferson was a man who wrote and produced elements that consolidated the Constitution.'[168]

This is an exaggerated reading of these events. There is no doubt that Giscard cared greatly about the future of the European project, and his natural hauteur did not preclude his wish for consensus on much-needed reforms. Even if that meant going on occasion against the grain of his own strong preferences, making concessions to ensure the resolution of otherwise difficult issues. In truth, Giscard was less an autocrat than a consummate 'fixer'. And though he had a clear idea about his role, using to the utmost his prerogative to steer the agenda, he realised early on that there could be no presidential *domaine réservé*. His eye may have been firmly fixed on making 'history', but if history was indeed to be made he knew that it required consensus to do so, with carefully crafted compromises, not least on the big and controversial constitutional questions. He worked assiduously to this end, most especially during the critical end-game in April 2003.[169] In the crucial negotiations that preceded the publication of the draft treaty Giscard was the linchpin of the ensuing agreement, one that was achieved in the end not by diktat but by listening, cajoling, reassuring the various actors – and not least the governments' representatives – about the need for compromise. As one observer saw it, 'Giscard had no blue print for reforming the Union [but] he had a compass and he knew how to change course as circumstances dictated'.[170]

The judgement of history on Giscard's stewardship will undoubtedly be mixed, but the overall impression he left on his contemporaries was of a shrewd diplomat, a smart political operator. A man prepared to take risks, to trim in order to resolve obstacles to a deal, though on the available evidence as much on his own terms as possible. In the end, he proved to be less the 'hide-bound traditionalist' portrayed by his staunchest critics, and much more the arch-pragmatist, convinced that the Union required 'drastic surgery if it was to adapt to the demands, the requirements of governance in an enlarged Union'.[171] There was even some palpable relief amongst *conventionnels* of all political persuasions that his bold steward-ship had somehow 'spared them the onerous task of compromising on those last controversial bits' of the draft treaty, precisely because he had 'shouldered the job of devising them alone'. In the end, it was Giscard's supreme achievement that seemingly elusive consensus was finally achieved, that the Constitutional Treaty was acclaimed on all sides and without recourse to a vote.[172] Giscard lacked the modesty of his famous predecessor, Jean Monnet, but he shared with him a clear vision of what he wanted from an historic process and something of the political arts of persuasion needed to realise it.

### The praesidium

The praesidium was intended to be the Convention's principal agency, tasked at Laeken with providing direction, setting the agenda, managing the working parties, establishing links with civil society and not least with collating the work of the legal experts seconded from the EU institutions. It was responsible, too, for responding to the plenaries, by devising draft articles in response to their proposed amendments – no less than 3,000 between February and May 2003 – and incorpo-rating these proposals into a cogent draft treaty. The praesidium was in effect the Convention's bureau and comprised the president and two vice-presidents, nine Convention members representing the governments, including those occupying the Council presidency during the Convention (Spain, Greece and Denmark) and two representatives from the national parliaments (Gisela Stuart, a British Labour MP, and John Bruton, the former Irish prime minister), the European Parliament (Mendez de Vigo of the European People's Party and the German Social Democrat Klaus Hansch, representing the PES) and the Commission. A thirteenth member was added in April when Alojz Peterle representing the Slovenian government joined, initially as a guest member to speak on behalf of the accession countries, but after intense lobbying by them eventually accepted as a full member. The praesidium's critical role in shaping the Constitution persuaded the member states to select, for the most part, representatives with considerable experience of EU politics, usually political heavyweights who were either Brussels or Strasbourg 'insiders'. Spain, for instance, was represented by Ana Palacio, chair of the Euro-pean Parliament's human rights and justice and home affairs committee, and soon promoted as Spain's foreign minister. Denmark chose Hening Christophersen, a former finance and foreign minister and previously a Commission vice-president, whereas Greece selected George Katiforis MEP.

An executive or steering group should represent the balance of interested parties, but not be so unwieldy as to be ineffective, and there were soon doubts about the praesidium on this score. There was also concern about possible bias, some *conventionnels* seeing the praesidium as unduly favourable to the three larger member states. In fact, the wider Community interest was well represented, 10 of the 12 praesidium members being nominated by the European institutions, or otherwise sitting as *ex officio* representatives of the European Council. The secretariat, too, was staffed by functionaries drawn from the Council's general secretariat and staff seconded from the Commission and the European Parliament. If there was any imbalance here it was regional rather than institutional, with the southern European countries well represented, but the small countries of northern and central Europe 'all but shut out'.[173]

The praesidium was nevertheless slow to get off the mark, and when it did begin work its cohesion was undermined by divisions between a majority of members committed to a more integrationist, and for some even a federalist, agenda and a minority of confirmed intergovernmentalists. Even so, strong representation from the European institutions did not translate into a preponderant supranationalist bias, though it did dictate the tactics of some governments. Alarmed by more strident radical voices in the praesidium some government representatives resorted to Fabian tactics, biding their time and waiting for the periodic plenary sessions, where national parliamentarians were well represented, to recover ground they considered 'lost' in the praesidium. Politicking inevitably delayed matters, prolonging the original timetable, but it also strengthened Giscard's hand as mediator.[174]

Expectations at the outset that the praesidium would operate collegially as a single working group proved impossible to realise because there was no agreement on the critical issues. In the circumstances it was left to the presidency/secretary-general to mediate between the various factions and competing proposals.[175] This in turn permitted Giscard to operate *divide et impera* tactics on some of the key issues, with praesidium members effectively 'cut out of the loop and presented with a *fait accompli*'.[176] Giscard used divisions within the praesidium to steer his own course, taking the lead in drafting the key articles, even though members 'sometimes complained that the articles in question bore no relation to the work of the Convention so far'.[177] The decision to forgo formal voting and to base recommendations on a consensus seemingly 'expected to emerge in some mystical fashion'[178] also reinforced his role as 'the authoritative interpreter of the common will of the Convention'.[179]

The praesidium only began to get into its stride towards the latter stages, when it increased both the regularity and the duration of its meetings. It eventually devised a procedure for minimising internal differences: in the first instance by securing agreement on the less problematic issues, before tackling more contentious difficult issues such as the Council presidency, the composition of the Commission and so on. But this was by no means plain sailing, for even supposedly non-controversial issues required much debate and extensive bargaining before anything remotely resembling agreement emerged. This, in turn, reduced the time available for discussing the difficult institutional issues, postponing them to an impossibly short time-frame right at the end of proceedings that left barely two months for resolving the most complex and, needless to say, controversial issues. The obvious solution was to extend the Convention, but that request was refused by member states anxious to regain their hold over the constitutional agenda at the earliest opportunity, a fact made patently clear when Giscard broached the matter at the Athens Council. The heads of governments held firm to their original deadline for submitting a draft constitutional treaty, the Thessaloniki Council scheduled for 20 June 2003.

The original intention that the praesidium would steer the Convention was overtaken by circumstances, a culmination of internal divisions and a determined presidency assisted by a well-organised secretariat. Lack of agreement hampered the praesidium's capacity for leadership.[180] And while it was the praesidium that formally issued a version of the treaty, in October 2002, a draft that served as the template for subsequent discussions on details, the 'meat' that was eventually grafted on to these bare bones was in fact the work of the presidency/secretariat team. Confronted with a praesidium too often divided against itself Giscard seized the initiative and steered the agenda according to its own lights. He was ably abetted by his head of secretariat, Sir John Kerr, and two assistants. Giscard worked with Kerr (mostly at his home near Paris) on the 15 critical draft articles relating to the institutions. And though this brought protestations from praesidium members who objected to their own exclusion from the drafting process, with accusations of bad faith, a blatant repudiation of due procedure and even a 'betrayal' of the Convention itself, Giscard pressed on regardless, convinced that agreed procedures – debate, working group input on details, followed by further debate – would simply not settle the crucial institutional issues within the remaining time-frame.

The fiction of teamwork was of course maintained throughout, but mainly as cover for bruised egos. Giscard's announcement to the special European Council in Athens in April 2003 of firm proposals on the questions discussed at Nice and subsequently at Laeken, though formally attributed to the praesidium and based on the conclusions of the working groups, were much more the work of the presidency team. The praesidium was given due credit for addressing the issues raised in the Laeken mandate, not least the proposals for a single EU legal personality; a single treaty base; a new institutional architecture; and progress towards establishing an area of freedom, security and justice. But truth to tell, the praesidium followed rather more than it led the deliberative process.[181] Altogether more reactive than proactive, responding to rather than shaping the preferences of altogether more resolute, and above all better-organised actors.

## *The working groups*

The rights convention did not appoint working groups, but the Constitutional Convention utilised them as an indispensable source of expertise.[182] These supposedly independent groups actually took their cue from Giscard, who in turn took his lead from the Council in what amounted to a process of 'forward linkage' between the Convention and the IGC. Giscard's overriding concern here was politics as the art of the possible, in effect 'to reach settlements that had a chance of gaining acceptance in the IGC'.[183] The groups' remit was predictable enough, closely following the Laeken mandate, though suitably amended during the course of discussions to reflect current circumstances. Again, the presidency took the lead, controlling the groups' activities, with Giscard imposing chairs selected from the praesidium, despite protests on grounds of underrepresentation by *conventionnels* from some smaller EU15 countries, notably Denmark, Finland, Austria and Luxembourg.

Five working groups were established in May 2002 to deal with constitutional issues, including subsidiarity; the charter of fundamental rights; the EU's legal personality; the distribution of EU competencies; the role of national parliaments; and with another reviewing the important issue of economic governance and financial co-operation. No working party was planned at this stage on the all-important institutional questions. This, too, was Giscard's decision, with institutional questions seen by him as a matter of concern for every *conventionnel* and therefore to be discussed only in the plenary sessions. A further four groups were subsequently established: three of them covering key policy issues, freedom, internal security and justice; EU external relations; and defence, with the final group addressing the need for the enlarged Union to simplify its legislative procedures. All working groups were required to report by the year's end.

Against his own inclination Giscard was eventually persuaded to launch a working group to review Social Europe, although he did resist setting up groups on regional and local government, and especially the demand from some quarters for a group to cover the sensitive issue of the European institutions, though a think-tank was established on the European Court of Justice. The performance of the working groups was variable, some operating more effectively than others, exerting greater or lesser influence in their particular domain depending on the qualities and commitment of their various members. The working groups that reviewed the Union's single legal personality, the role of national parliaments in monitoring subsidiarity, the inclusion of the Fundamental Rights Charter in the treaty, tidying up the EU's legal instruments and applying QMV to some decisions relating to internal security, asylum and immigration were all widely regarded as notable successes. Others were less successful, for instance the working groups on foreign and security policy, economic governance and tax and social policies. The specific mandates for the working groups are detailed in Table 3.4.

Each working group consisted of some 30 *conventionnels* chaired by a praesidium member, though meetings were open to all *conventionnels*. Membership arrangements were fairly flexible, with no particular selection criteria: any *conventionnel* or alternate could contribute to the work of any group. On balance, these arrangements worked well enough. The working groups gave substance to discussions, bringing valuable expertise to bear on the review of the critical issues, thereby enabling *conventionnels* 'to discuss the nitty gritty of the business in detail'.[184] But flexibility had its drawbacks. *Ad hoc* recruitment to working groups meant that membership was on occasions unbalanced, unrepresentative of the wider Convention let alone of the Union's body politic. The defence working group, for instance, drew more than one quarter of its members from the neutral and non-aligned countries, and as such was hardly representative of EU-wide opinion on this important issue.[185] On the other hand, the working groups sought to avoid debilitating factionalism, seeing collegiality as a better guarantee of being heard and more of their recommendations receiving serious consideration in praesidium and plenary alike.[186]

Relatively relaxed and informal meetings helped in turn to facilitate creative thinking and to foster a sense of common endeavour. The informal atmosphere dissuaded participants from hiding behind prepared statements, or resorting to

*Table 3.4* Mandates of working groups

| Subject | Chairperson | Report: reference/ publication date |
|---|---|---|
| Subsidiarity | Inigo Mendez de Vigo | CONV 286/02 23 September 2002 |
| Charter of Fundamental Rights; EU membership of the ECHR; its incorporation into the Treaty | Antonio Vitorino | CONV 354/02 22 October 2002 |
| EU's legal personality and the simplification of the treaties | Giuliano Amato | CONV 305/02 1 October 2002 |
| Role of national parliaments in EU governance | Gisela Stuart | CONV 353/02 22 October 2002 |
| Complementary competences or areas where the EU would support actions at national/regional level | Henning Christophersen | CONV 375/02 4 November 2002 |
| Economic governance; increased cooperation in economic/financial matters after the introduction of the euro; Social Europe | Klaus Hansch | CONV 357/02 21 October 2002 |
| External relations – to include ways to improve policy consistency, the role of community methods, the role of the high representative and improving the EU's external representation | Jean-Luc Dehaene | CONV 459/02 19 December 2002 |
| Defence: tasks, capabilities, improving decision-making, enhanced co-operation, improving arms procurement and R&D | Michel Barnier | CONV 461/02 16 December 2002 |
| Simplification of legislative procedures; extension of QMV / co-decision; simplification of the budget procedure; clarification of legal instruments | Giuliano Amato | CONV 424/02 29 November 2002 |
| Freedom, security, justice – including improved instruments; judicial cooperation on criminal matters; treaty definitions of asylum/ immigration policy | John Bruton | CONV 426/02 2 December 2002 |
| Social Europe – including reform of EU competencies and reduced unanimity | George Katiforis | CONV 516/1/03 4 February 2003 |

dogma, encouraging speakers to both explain and justify their position on key issues, after all the essence of deliberative democracy. Each working group tended to focus on specific issues, and interventions were not constrained by the three-minute rule that applied in the plenaries, though tight deadlines did limit their capacity for really imaginative thinking.[187] These working arrangements did help foster consensus, though this on its own was no guarantee of agreement when the most controversial issues were raised, either in the praesidium or the plenaries.[188] And the fact that the most difficult questions relating to institutional matters were postponed until last, and not broached in a dedicated working group but left to the plenary, meant that when they did come up for discussion there was none of the usual groundwork to take the edge off raw politics.

### The secretariat

Secretariats perform important functions in the conduct of EU affairs. The Council secretariat has been a significant actor in successive IGCs, working on the basis of a European Council mandate though exerting considerable independent influence in a 'behind-the-scenes role that offers many opportunities to translate its bargaining resources into influence over outcomes',[189] including the preparation of most of the draft legal texts and policy documents.[190] The Council's secretariat had used its pivotal position to good effect in the rights convention, assisting the praesidium in drafting the Charter. The political stakes were altogether higher in the Constitutional Convention and the Council secretariat was subsumed within a more amorphous secretariat; in effect, reduced to being part of a team of officials recruited from the secretariats of the Commission, the European Parliament and seconded national officials.[191] This 'lack of a clear institutional identity, in contrast to the clear pro-integrative and pro-Council bias of the Council Secretariat', curbed the combined secretariat's appetite for playing politics, and ensured that it functioned more as a neutral body, albeit one with considerable influence on outcomes.

Giscard appointed Sir John Kerr, former head of the British foreign office, to head the secretariat, with a noted Giscardian loyalist, Pierre de Boissieau, as his deputy. A secretariat managed by this distinguished and astute former diplomat was bound to be aware of, and probably sympathetic to the preferences of the principal member states. The 15-member secretariat was hand-picked by Giscard and Kerr, 'a blend of talents ... lawyers, diplomats, administrators and academics' drawn from 10 different EU nationalities. Experts from the principal EU institutions were included, too, though significantly 'enthusiastic federalists were kept at bay'.[192] Kerr forged a cohesive and effective team, using twice-weekly strategy meetings to discuss successive versions of the draft papers that shaped the Convention's deliberations in the early months. In the process, secretariat staff 'learned to work with one another, creating a team spirit that paid off as the pressure of work mounted', with the result that 'the secretariat became the powerhouse of the Convention'.[193] He employed similar teamwork during the crucial drafting stages, with 'brainstorming' sessions that made the most of the individual qualities of secretariat staffers, allocating the most appropriate candidates to the various working groups.

The secretariat was the Convention's nerve-centre and it deftly managed the agenda from the outset, ensuring that a fragmented praesidium had at least an organisational core, that both its working parties and the plenaries were supplied with appropriate information.[194] The secretariat likewise arranged plenaries so as to cover the issues identified in the Laeken mandate, each one allocated to one of the working groups. The secretariat drafted articles on the basis of the praesidium's texts – though it was in fact the instigator of much that occurred in praesidium meetings – summarising discussions in both the praesidium and plenaries, excising contradictory drafts or duplication, and responding to the best-supported plenary amendments to the draft articles. Not a circular process as such, but one very much orchestrated by agencies at the presidency's personal disposal. The secretariat's virtual monopoly of legal expertise gave it significant influence, both at the negotiation and drafting stages. To that extent, it was able 'to subtly skew outcomes' in the drafting stage by 'distilling the numerous submissions, amendments, and reports from the plenary and working groups into a final Constitutional Treaty'.[195]

Giscard was the principal beneficiary of this convoluted procedure. The secretariat ensured that he had both the organisational resources and the expertise at his disposal to exert influence on outcomes throughout the various stages of deliberation, and not least at the critical drafting stage. The president's success in steering the drafting procedure is a testament to Kerr's experience and above all to his diplomatic skill, for the presidency's command over affairs was hardly anticipated at the outset. The secretariat should have been no match for the Commission's cumulate know-how or experience, even if its authority was by now somewhat tarnished. The Commission has, after all, significant 'informational advantages *vis-à-vis* most other actors in both IGC and convention methods in most issue areas'. And in light of the Commission's role in the Union's legislative and executive processes, this did provide the Commission 'with detailed insights into the substantive workings of the EU Treaties that are not possessed by any other actor', a fact that 'is especially evident in policy areas that are at the core of the Community'. For instance, the Commission's capacity for processing information is generally 'matched only by the foreign ministries of the largest Member States', except in the classic intergovernmental domain of the Common Foreign and Security Policy (CFSP).[196] This considerable inside-knowledge of how things actually work should have given the Commission the edge over the secretariat, both in negotiating and sustaining effective coalitions between the representatives from the EU institutions, but things did not work quite like that in practice. Nor was the Commission without allies, whether current MEPs or former MEPs such as George Katiforis (Greece) and Ana Palacio (Spain), both sitting as government representatives of member states well disposed to European integration, or the former commissioner, Henning Christophersen, and the representatives of the small member states, who tend to regard the Commission as their natural ally against the larger countries with *directoire* predilections.

The general expectation was that the Commission or even MEPs were much better placed than secretariat parvenus to steer deliberations, especially on first-pillar matters. Both of these institutions 'have expertise and deep knowledge of EU affairs; they have material resources (background documents, staff, etc.); and both may more easily behave as a cohesive group'.[197] On the face of it the Commission has considerable political resources at its disposal, not least its 'direct personal knowledge and shared experience' of EU governance – what is sometimes called 'institutional memory' – enabling it to facilitate networks, those inter-personal and frequently informal means by which the Commission and MEPs might have been expected to impose an 'EU ethos' on events. But things were not quite so clear-cut in practice. For one thing, the Commission failed to make the most of these considerable resources, and in the process it failed to live up to its reputation as the 'motor' of European integration. No one was more surprised by this outcome than Kerr himself. Aware of the Commission's considerable reputation, he expressed surprise at 'the detached, disengaged and distant stance' the Commission adopted towards the Convention.[198] Although both commissioners on the praesidium did make significant contributions, the Commission seemed curiously detached from affairs, and apart from his monumentally ill-timed intervention discussed above even the Commission president failed to leave his mark on events.

The Commission simply failed to punch its political weight in the Convention. It was undoubtedly undermined by internal divisions, differences over strategy as much as over constitutional objectives. These shortcomings are explained only in part, however, by the below-par performance of individual commissioners. The Commission's failure here is a mark of deeper shifts in EU politics. Times have indeed changed, and the Commission now is in a weaker position *vis-à-vis* the other EU institutions compared with its predecessors in the 1980s and 1990s. What some now describe as the Commission's 'heroic phase' under Delors's dynamic leadership, boldly steering the Single Market programme, though admittedly a project well suited to its technocratic instincts and rationale, is long gone. The EU nowadays is a different political creature, both larger and more diverse, its citizens much less inclined to accept remote and unelected leadership, and indeed with many of them, prompted by the media, much less indifferent now and some even hostile to Brussels's seemingly insatiable appetite for yet 'more Europe'. The Convention confirmed this trend, and the public's reaction to it even more so. The mood that prevails today throughout the European Union is much less favourable to direction from Brussels, with growing support for flexible integration and for 'soft' policy rather than hard law as the preferred policy instrument. The secretariat for its part carried none of this baggage. Indeed, part of its appeal to other participants, one reason for its success in guiding the Convention, was precisely that it was task-specific, recruited solely to manage the Convention's affairs without the drag of entrenched institutional legacies to distract it from that singular purpose.

# 4    Agendas for change

## Agenda setting

The Convention's agenda was outlined by the Laeken Council in a document whose very title – *Europe at the Crossroads* – implied a sense of urgency, the need 'to reverse out of this (present) dead end' to meet contemporary global challenges by reforming EU governance.[1] Reform was seen as essential for responding to public disquiet, and not least to prepare for impending enlargement, though the Convention was not tied to a specific agenda but had 'a relatively open mandate'.[2] Laeken identified some classic constitutional themes that were bound to figure in the Convention's work. Every constitutional polity requires a definitive statement of the values and guiding principles that define its mission and purpose. This is bound to be problematic in a polity that lacks identity and consists of pre-existing states, each with its own history and demos. There was certainly no Laeken mandate for resolving the EU's normative ambiguities, its 'in-between' status, those tensions inherent in a transnational polity that must balance the supranational aspirations of some of its stakeholders with the abiding national preferences of its member states. There was awareness nevertheless amongst *conventionnels* about the need to more clearly demarcate the boundaries between the national and EU domains.[3]

Another critical aspect for any constitutional endeavour is to codify institutional power and attribute competencies more clearly, a task that is especially complicated in the EU in view of its multi-level institutional architecture and mixed governance. Again, the Laeken mandate was imprecise here, making a commitment on the one hand to both rationalise and simplify these inordinately complicated institutional arrangements so as to make them more comprehensible to the citizens. And by this means to improve the citizens' access to information and to deal with democracy and legitimacy deficits.[4] The Union's procedures are arcane and cluttered even for 'insiders', let alone those less familiar with its workings, and as things stand EU citizens are very much 'outsiders' in this sense. As Dobson sees this problem, the 'three streams down which politics flow in the EU are inadequately integrated [and] do not facilitate purposive citizen activity because the opportunity structures and access/veto points available are mostly informal and indirect'.[5]

Greater clarity and public awareness about what governance institutions do is an essential prerequisite for legitimacy in any polity, central to the task of constitutionalising contemporary governance, and no less so for the EU.[6] The very complexity of EU governance has undoubtedly contributed to the public's growing indifference or worse to a polity characterised by its critics as one with 'an especially grotesque disparity between the tiny elite of citizens "in the know" and the rest who, being thereby made recipients of others' political agency, suffer the imposition of an effective inequality'.[7] In these circumstances bringing the citizen closer to EU governance by putting in place 'mediating institutions that might enlighten citizens' was a critical concern of the Convention. A constitution was seen by many as essential to this endeavour, for 'if citizens do not understand the overall political shape of things they will be shorn of vital links needed to engage in the means-ends reasoning to fulfil (the polity's) purposes'.[8] This was one view of the Convention's purpose, though as we shall see there were other, quite different expectations.

### (i) Responding to Enlargement

The timetable for the Union's most extensive enlargement so far agreed at Copenhagen in 1993 envisaged a so-called 'big-bang' accession, a first wave of 10 new member states joining in 2004, with at least 2 more to follow. No one involved in negotiating this historic enlargement had any doubt about its likely impact on the Union's structure and operations. Not least the fact, as Hughes observed, that 'the political balances – and bargains – across different policy and institutional areas will change', considerably expanding 'the range and variety of alliance and coalition formation', and with much greater uncertainty about future political dynamics by 'impacting negatively on effective and coherent decision-making'.[9] Significant, too, is the fact that this enlargement shifts the Union's geographical axis if not yet its political or economic centre of gravity further east, with all manner of consequences for the way the Union conducts its business and for its policies.

The 2004 enlargement would bring in states with quite different experiences and priorities from the existing members. Clearly, the relative poverty of the newcomers was bound to give greater urgency to redistributive politics, intensifying the struggle over budgetary resources, leading in turn to greater competition over the structural and cohesion policies, and on related economic issues such as deregulation, trade liberalisation and social dumping. And not least, enlargement will exacerbate conflict over the common agricultural policy, still the largest recipient of budgetary resources. There is much at stake here for new and existing members alike, and these considerations were a major incentive to overhaul the Union's decisional procedures. On one side, the existing member states had interests to protect, and on the other the accession countries had their own reasons for supporting reform, quite aware that without a significant shift in the balance of institutional power they were in danger of merely replacing one form of hegemony based in Moscow with another in Brussels.[10] The first enlargement wave would increase the number of smaller member states from 10 to 19, altering the balance between the large and small member states. The newly enlarged Union is a community of mostly small states. There are more small than populous states in EU27 (20 of 27), with only Poland amongst the newcomers (and Romania, which joined in the second mini-wave in 2007) qualifying as a 'big' (i.e. populous) state. At the same time, the proportion of the Union's population residing in the larger states remains at about two-thirds of the total. These demographics were bound to be a matter of concern for both EU15 and candidate states alike, though from quite different standpoints.

One obvious way that enlargement impacts on governance is Council voting weights, critical for the distribution of power between the member states. The larger member states were concerned about the impact of the voting weights formula agreed at Nice (December 2000) for their capacity to put together either a winning coalition or blocking minorities on future policy. Without some adjustment to decision-making procedures, voting weights and institutional arrangements, the small states would wield a degree of influence out of proportion to their demographic weight and, as the larger states saw it, out of line with their international political clout and economic standing. Nice increased the voting weight of the larger countries, raising the threshold required for a qualified majority vote, a change that lessened the influence of the small countries but without necessarily improving the prospects for the larger states to secure an agreement in the Council. More than that, it increased the scope for blocking decisions in the Council. The new arrangements introduced three criteria for securing a Council majority: a QMV threshold of 74 per cent of the total votes cast, a majority of member states and a minimum of 62 per cent of the EU's population. This procedure was criticised in some quarters, both for reducing the relative simplicity of Council votes and, directly linked with that, for reducing transparency. Critics had suggested an alternative system based on a simple double majority voting system: a dual majority of population and of countries, an arrangement that accommodates the interests of the larger states, but one that 'also has the considerable advantage of transparency and simplicity'.[11]

Another critical issue affected by enlargement was whether and how far to extend qualified majority voting (QMV) in order to expedite policy decisions in a much-expanded Union. Without more QMV, the EU policy process was threatened with gridlock should member states decide to veto policy proposals they saw as detrimental to national interests. This in turn raised concerns about democracy deficits. For these reasons the QMV formula agreed at Nice prompted serious questions about the Union's legislative process, with some critics calling for more co-decision. These issues were central to the debate about more effective and accountable governance. The larger states preferred to centralise the conduct of EU business to ensure their own influence would prevail.[12] Though agreeing to a review of these issues in the Convention, the leading member states worked assiduously to avoid being outflanked, concerned above all to maintain their political advantage.[13] In order to achieve this end they largely excluded the accession countries, denying them fair representation in the Convention, but above all by pushing hard for a strong executive presidency at the centre of EU governance, in accordance with the position taken by the Council secretariat at the Barcelona and Seville summits.

Although the budget and structural policy were not strictly part of the Convention's mandate, EU social and economic policy was bound to be discussed in any review of EU policy. Tension in EU15 between net contributors and the recipients of structural and cohesion funds had long been significant for the Union's political dynamics, and this tension would be exacerbated after enlargement by a three-way division between the richer member states and both the former beneficiaries of structural assistance and the new accession countries, who expect – a matter for them of fairness as much as naked self-interest – that a greater share of limited budgetary resources should be allocated to the poorest member states solely on the basis of need. Accordingly, the post-enlargement EU faces 'a new north-south-east triangle which will expand the traditional dynamics of the budget debates', ensuring a 'fundamental split between net contributors and net recipients, particularly the current cohesion four, and the new net recipients of Central and eastern Europe – who may not find ways to make common cause with the current net recipients'.[14] This matter was certain to be raised at the Convention.

Finally, enlargement would have implications for the Union's foreign and security dimension, its capacity to play a significant role in the emerging post-Cold War international order. The collapse of Soviet hegemony in Eastern and Central Europe may well have realised the prospect for peace and reconciliation between two formerly antagonistic 'Europes'. At the same time, the very fact of enlargement has brought the Union into direct contact with altogether new threats, with some of the newcomers facing difficult neighbours and for that very reason expected to contribute to EU-wide security. The collapse of Soviet hegemony has not, as some commentators foolishly predicted, brought about 'the end of history' – which they took to be the end of ideological tensions, and with it emergent global consensus on the ends as much as the means of politics – but instead has raised all manner of new demons, whether civil disorder from revived ethnic populism suspended for long decades in the permafrost of communism, or else by unleashing mass migration, unprecedented levels of cross-border crime or security threats from 'failed' or 'rogue' states in the enlarged Union's new and volatile neighbourhood.

### (ii) The competency question and the subsidiarity/proportionality debate

Subsidiarity was widely supported in the Convention, though most *convention-nels* saw this less as an expression of states' rights, a defence of pure intergovernmentalism, and rather more as a corollary of multi-level governance. There were marked differences, however, about precisely how to deal with subsidiarity. Some *conventionnels* preferred a simplified expression of the principle, listing and demarcating competencies as between the Union's institutions and the member states in order to show citizens more clearly 'who does what' as a requirement of more efficient, and no less of more accountable governance. Yet other voices inside the Convention and indeed beyond it were reticent about listing competencies, concerned that defining 'who does what and at which level' of European governance risked imposing a straitjacket that would be unduly restrictive, 'potentially limiting future integration'. And perhaps even provoking turf wars that would make compromise even more difficult to achieve than it presently is.[15]

A clear definition of policy instruments is particularly relevant for a polity where competencies are shared between the domestic and the European levels. An indeterminate allocation of competencies not only detracts from effective policy-making but also undermines transparency and weakens accountability, adding to the polity's legitimacy deficit. These issues were discussed as part of the Lisbon process (March 2000), which advocated more open policy co-ordination, and 'soft' rather than 'hard' strategies for ensuring greater commonality of labour-market and related policies, including the use of bench-marking, peer pressure and agreed common policy guidelines. But enlargement was more likely to increase the risk of such disparities of performance and compliance, making more difficult an approximation of common policy standards. There were other problems to be considered, too, in this debate about competencies, not least the abiding tension in the Union's governance between intergovernmental and supranational preferences. Some member states wanted some policy competencies repatriated from the Union, in part because they anticipated that governments would wield less influence as a consequence of reduced voting weights, the loss of a commissioner and especially with a full-time Council presidency removing the opportunity for each member state to take its turn in shaping the Union's agenda. On the other side of the argument, federalists were bound to argue for even more policy competencies to be relocated from the member states to the Union, including the co-ordination of economic policy, foreign/security policy and home affairs. This stand-off is hardly new it has been at the centre of the debate about European integration from the start and as such was bound to figure on the Convention's agenda.

### (iii) Rationalising the EU's institutional architecture: executive capacity and political leadership

Efficient decision-making and effective political leadership in an enlarged Union of 27 and more member states was central to the constitutional endeavour. It became apparent almost as soon as the Convention began discussing the issue that there was no agreement on how to improve on executive capacity. The rotation of the Council presidency was seen by its critics as a particular problem here, 'a source of instability and discontinuity', not least because the presidency's workload and duties had expanded to such a degree 'that one can hardly expect a government to take them up besides its normal tasks'.[16] As the larger member states saw it, especially France, the United Kingdom and Spain, a short-term presidency limits the scope for resolving complicated and protracted issues, though defenders of rotation disagree that it limits executive capacity, except in the matter of external representation.[17] A permanent presidency would improve the management of external affairs, for the current troika arrangement is both cumbrous and unreliable, sharing responsibility between past, present and forthcoming presidency countries and resulting in a 'sometimes-undignified representation of the Union abroad by three Heads of State, plus the High representative'.[18]

Calls for reform here are hardly new. The Council secretariat, reflecting the views of the leading member states, had proposed changes to the presidency and the General Council in a paper submitted to the Barcelona European Council, along with a recommendation to elect the Council and procedural changes designed to improve the running of European Council meetings. The paper also proposed a reduction in the number of Council formations, reforming the General Affairs Council by restricting the size of delegations, increasing QMV in the functional councils and using the Council only as a decision-maker of last resort when the functional councils are deadlocked. These same issues were discussed at the Seville Council (June 2002) and they would be revisited at the Convention.

There was by now widespread support from the larger member states for an executive president to chair the European Council, to give leadership on EU foreign and defence policies and to represent the Union further afield. The British foreign secretary, Jack Straw, had already endorsed similar proposals[19] and that country's Europe minister, Peter Hain, likewise supported a French proposal for a full-time presidency to run concurrently with the Commission term.[20] The most significant move here was the Franco-German proposal (published in January 2003) for a permanent EU presidency to be tasked with providing strategic direction, ensuring both continuity and policy co-ordination, representing the EU 'abroad', and chairing four annual EU summits. What was not clear at this early stage, however, was what the implications might be of such an office for the High Representative for the Common Foreign and Security Policy.

These proposals for concentrating executive power in a full-time post were bound to be controversial. For one thing, they highlighted the long-standing struggle in the EC/EU over the locus of institutional power, and for that matter over the very meaning of European integration, with the big member states firmly committed to a confederalist model of governance. These confederalists likewise preferred 'one of their own', a former head of government, to occupy such a leadership role, and to use the office to limit the Commission's role in agenda-setting, ensuring that the Council retain ultimate authority in sensitive policy domains such as CFSP, EMU and police and judicial co-operation. But the idea was bound to attract criticism, not least from federalists. For some critics, this proposal seemed to conflict with the Laeken objective of simplification, making for less rather than more coherence and co-ordination of policy-making. One problem here was how to ensure effective liaison between the two presidencies, not least because under current arrangements the Commission does exercises a degree of executive power. This prompted one commentator to observe that the likely consequence of this proposed reform might be the very opposite of what was intended from a full-time Council presidency, in effect 'a very weak President [and] not the new strong leader intended by the larger countries'.[21]

There were more principled objections, too. Finland, for example, objected to a reform that threatened to undermine the Commission's role, a view that found an echo in the Convention, where the German MEP Elmer Brok criticised the concept of a full-time presidency as an unpalatable choice between Monnet and Metternich.[22] The Commission, for its part, weighed in on the issue, predictably proposing an increase its own capacity in some key policy domains, for instance in macro-economic policy, foreign relations and home affairs. There were further objections from those opposed to concentrated executive power, not least those smaller states concerned about a loss of political status should they relinquish their periodic occupancy of the Council presidency.

This issue was more than a straightforward battle about power. Where institutional power resides in a polity is a critical matter for any constitutional endeavour, but in this particular polity this is not zero-sum conflict over 'who does what or how', but more a matter of striking a balance between efficient decision-making at the centre and national interests, an abiding predicament for EU actors at every level. Many of the smaller states openly acknowledged this dilemma. Aware on the one hand of the need for policy continuity and for an effective response to crises in a fast-changing global order, they conceded that short-tenure presidencies were certainly inefficient, or at least ineffectual. On the other hand, these same actors remained wary about undermining the authority of the Union's institutions, and indeed about any changes that might enhance the already disproportionate influence of the larger countries. Concern to avoid so-called *directoire* dominance did increase support in the Convention for the idea of a shared or 'team' presidency, in effect a revised version of the troika arrangement, to be headed by a current head of state rather than a full-time appointee, and operating in a steering capacity to ensure consistent and co-ordinated leadership, though lacking the authority of the executive-style presidency advocated by the big three.

The principal objection to a full-time presidency as proposed by the leading member states is the perceived loss of power and influence by smaller states, though in a Union of 27 or more member states each would occupy the presidency only once every 15 years or so under rotation. Even so, the issue was symbolic as much as practical. Loss of authority, however fleeting the prospect of running the show, was certainly a major concern for these states. They remained unimpressed by the counter-argument that infrequent occupancy of the presidency under rotation in an enlarged Union would undoubtedly mean a loss of institutional memory, the cumulate know-how 'on tap', as it were, and the expertise to run a presidency. How to ensure these same states a degree of influence was critical for a successful outcome here, and this gave rise to a lively discussion of compromise measures, for instance sharing out the technical council chairs so as to ensure that every member state, even the smallest, would retain some capacity for directing EU affairs.

The accountability, and ultimately the legitimacy, of a full-time president also featured in this debate. The main issue here was how to demarcate the role and remit of an executive Council presidency from its Commission counterpart, especially where both offices are appointed by the heads of government and state, the result of trade-offs between vested interests rather than of open elections. Again, this issue brought to the fore the confrontation between federalists and confederalists. The former preferred a Council president to be accountable to the Union *per se*, whether indirectly elected by the European Parliament or directly by the citizens from a list of candidates proposed by the Parliament's principal party groups, rather than being in the gift of power-brokers in the leading member states. Election in whatever form is the surest way of ensuring legitimacy, and the best guarantee of 'strong, visible and unified leadership'.[23] Larger states predictably resisted the very idea of election. The balance of powers, and no less the respective claims to authority between these offices, also figured in this debate. Co-existent full-time Council and Commission presidencies would require special selection rules to avoid accentuating not just the endemic rivalry between the two institutions, but also between smaller and the larger member states. It was inconceivable that the incumbents of both offices should come from either a large or from a small country, though the spoils of office would need to be shared between the *directoire* states and the rest: but how to do it? Formulating a procedure was bound to be controversial, and should the Convention fail to resolve the matter the decision would almost certainly fall to the European Council, hardly a democratic solution and one that would do little to assuage public concern about democracy deficits.

A clash of authority between Commission and Council presidencies was a likely outcome of these proposed reforms. One solution was to merge the two executive offices into a 'super' or 'double-hat' presidency, supposedly removing, or at least reducing, institutional friction, and by overcoming administrative duality meeting other objectives identified at Laeken, such as improving the Union's executive capacity, ensuring more efficient decision-making and not least simplifying governance.[24] Dual presidencies would however mean overlapping competencies and invariably ravelled governance. There were other objections, too, from vested interests who favoured retaining duality regardless of the consequences. It was clear from the outset that these questions were at the very core of the drive to refashion EU governance for the tasks ahead, but they were controversial, and the Convention was wary of tackling them.

There was certainly no suggestion in these discussions that an executive president would reduce the scope of the Commission, let alone replace it as the principal source of strategic direction in EU policy-making; or indeed subvert that institution's primacy in the detailed drafting of proposed first-pillar legislation. One argument here maintained that an executive presidency is a solution to the Union's lack of strategic dynamism, a way of equipping it to meet regional and international challenges, and to compensate, too, for the Commission's recent failures even in its own domain to effectively frame the Union's policy agenda. Certainly, there was no plot afoot to subvert the Commission's conventional role as the driver of some important aspects of European integration. On the contrary, those who wanted to change the way the EU manages its affairs maintained that a permanent executive president would continue to depend on the Commission's considerable resources, to harness its unparalleled expertise and experience, not least because a new executive office would be shorn of the administrative support currently provided by domestic civil services for rotating national presidencies. But there was a great deal at stake here, and the Convention approached the issue with due caution.

### (iv) Rationalising the EU's institutional architecture: the Commission

Two competing ideas about EU governance figured in Convention discussions, each giving rise to quite different proposals for institutional reform. On one side intergovernmentalists, by and large though not exclusively government representatives from the larger member states and from national parliaments, sought to increase the Council's powers, and were reticent about if not exactly hostile to the Commission's claim for an enhanced executive role. On the other side of the argument, advocates of more supranationalism, mainly but not only commissioners or MEPs and supported by many of the smaller member states, maintained that a strong and independent Commission is the most reliable bulwark against *directoire*. This is a familiar stand-off, yet both sides had a mutual interest in avoiding what they saw as a worst-case scenario, an ineffective European Council president and a weak Commission.

The Commission, for many the embodiment of the European project, has lost much of its early lustre. Despite the prodigious contribution of the Delors-led Commission in the mid-1980s to relaunching the European project, the so-called *relance européenne*, the institution had lost influence throughout the 1990s, overshadowed by both the Council of Ministers and on the headline issues by the European Council. Commentators were more likely now to allude to the fact that the Commission 'looks increasingly weak, with an absence of strategic leadership or strategic framework', and noted the tendency for 'the current Commission to fragment into separate, relatively unco-ordinated policy domains, with varying degrees of political control by individual commissioners over those policy domains and with a serious absence of genuine collegiality'.[25] The Commission's problems with legitimacy and organisational efficiency had worsened during the Prodi presidency. Critics now saw an institution that was 'weak, undemocratic and in some respects out of control'. Prodi's tenure had resulted in 'a damaging absence of strategic leadership and direction', leaving a 'vacuum at the centre'. The organisational cogency that characterised the Delors presidency had given way, as these critics saw it, 'to 20 fiefs', with 'the Commission now lacking the political clout to deal with national governments and to control its own bureaucrats.'[26] At the very least, this was by now an institution badly weakened by 'debilitating internal turf wars over policy and a widespread culture of pettifogging squabbles over personal advancement that served to obstruct the commissioners' policy programmes'.[27]

To some extent, this decline was contingent, a direct consequence of losing a dynamic incumbent. But there were structural reasons, too, for the Commission's waning influence. Not least, the determination of governments, and the big three in particular, to put their own interests before the common good, resisting what they saw as the Commission's incursion on to their turf.[28] The Commission itself was by no means averse to reform, alerted to its own shortcomings by the crisis that precipitated the resignation of the Santer Commission (1999). In fact, the Commission had been prompted by those events to propose its own reforms. However, observers were less than convinced by these proposals, seeing the White Paper on Governance (2001) as little more than self-exculpation, a thinly veiled bid by the Commission to enhance its regulatory powers, rather than to embrace real change through greater transparency and public accountability. The Commission's initiatives to broaden policy consultation, for the most part *ad hoc* arrangements, bilateral discussions conducted within a narrow circle of favoured 'insiders' likewise failed to impress its critics.

The Commission had tried for instance to widen consultation. Draft consultation standards, published in June 2002, proposed to expand both the number of, and the type of parties to, any consultation, and to include representatives of the general public. This attempt to improve transparency of the inordinately specialised and arcane comitology procedure, with the Commission submitting draft implementing regulations to committees of experts from the member states, was reminiscent of the American 'notice and comment' model of administrative law that requires proposed regulations be first submitted for public comment. But these arrangements fell some way short of the more exacting requirements of the American procedure. The scheme required that any branch of the Commission proposing a draft regulation should announce a consultation process through a common internet 'access point', and then allow six weeks for public comments before any draft is presented to the college of commissioners for endorsement.

The explanatory memorandum that accompanies a Commission final draft regulation to the Council and Parliament must also include full details of consultation, with an explanation of how the public's concerns are to be accommodated. This was better than nothing, and in its way progress of sorts, permitting those previously excluded from the Brussels policy loop, including the mass media, to become better informed about proposed policy, 'to see for the first time the framework of the debate from the same perspective as the Commission staff', and allowing officials 'to see the tapestry of the policy debate as a whole', so they might 'better anticipate objections and how to accommodate them'. This reform did require the key policy actors, the Commission, the Council and the Parliament, in principle to 'address more precisely the diversity of interests represented on any given policy issue and defend difficult policy choices'.[29] Even so, it was not enough to convince the Commission's strongest critics. Many felt that this procedure would hardly redress the Union's legitimacy shortfall, in so far as organisations and no less individual citizens remained 'largely dependent on second-hand information from Brussels intermediaries of various kinds – consultants, associations, the informal EU advisory committees (including the Economic and Social Committee) and so on'. And that as such, this would make it 'difficult for even those in Brussels to have a sense of the whole or a detailed, nuanced understanding of the substance of an ongoing policy debate'.[30]

The Convention revisited this issue, even contemplating a European 'public space', in effect procedures for conducting meaningful dialogue with civil society, including a weekly online question-time and a more active role for national MPs in questioning the Commission and Council presidencies. Better linkages between 'Brussels' and the national political systems is certainly one way of improving the public's awareness of what the EU is about, a means for reducing public indifference to the EU. Moreover, such linkages are necessary 'precisely because the EU is not a state with directly equivalent political structures to those of individual member states, which results in problems of legitimacy and comprehensibility'. For that reason alone, it is important 'for all those involved in EU political developments and institutions to ensure that the structures that do exist are as open, accessible and engaged with the wider public as possible'.[31] More and better information and improved communications, though important, are only part of the solution to the Union's legitimacy deficit. Just as important for deepening the citizen's sense of attachment to the European polity are measures that increase public access to the pre-policy debates that allow wider participation in the discussion of policy choices, and the Commission is the linchpin here.

The Convention raised these questions as part of its general review of the institutions. The size of the Commission was a particular concern, in so far as it relates to its efficiency in an enlarged Union. The size, and no less the composition, of the Commission College is directly linked to that institution's claim to embody the essence of transnational integration, and as some see it to be nothing less than the Community's 'conscience', the ultimate guardian of the treaties. The Commission has always made much of its claim to embody the common European interest, to be the *interlocuteur valable* for both transnational interests and for those of every member state regardless of demographic size, and especially those with limited political heft. This is the institution's claim to political legitimacy, albeit indirect legitimacy in an institution lacking the formal authority conferred on elected governments. Legitimacy is of course indispensable for governance at any level, but legitimacy shared between competing political institutions as it is in this multi-level polity is a recipe for confusion. As such, the Convention tried to resolve the problem by more clearly demarcating 'who does what'. And this gave rise in turn to consideration of the Commission's own presidency arrangements, not least the controversial issue of whether and how to 'elect' the Commission president: either directly in an EU-wide election, or indirectly through an electoral college such as the European Parliament. Or even, as one contributor the Convention's deliberations proposed, to elect individual commissioners.[32] The case for direct election has been made, and persuasively, by Hoffmann as follows:

Having a European Parliament elect the Commission President would be highly beneficial to the European political process. It would make the President accountable to a political body which is directly involved in European politics and which has the expertise to do so. It would mean that European citizens elect a European Parliament which is then responsible for electing the head of the executive. This is in line with the long political tradition of parliamentary democracy in Europe. It is a system which works and which people understand. It would bring a face to the European Parliament election campaign and stimulate public debate and media interest. It would allow European parties to develop further and use their institutional capacity and infrastructure to fight a European wide campaign on European policy issues, an element which has hitherto been missing in European elections. The EU needs a political system which is efficient whilst being accountable, legitimate and democratic. Having the Commission President elected by the European Parliament is a first, yet crucial step to achieve exactly this.[33]

The case being made here may be plausible, but it is altogether easier to put the normative case for election as a means for enhancing the Commission legitimacy than it is to implement in practice. There are numerous procedures for doing so, all of them with distinct drawbacks. The most frequently cited procedures for electing commissioners is directly by the Union's citizens, or indirectly, with Parliament acting as an electoral college and choosing from a list agreed by the European Council, or with the European Parliament deciding, preferably by a free vote so as to reduce the pressure to vote for a party affiliate, and concentrating instead on European issues rather than on narrow partisan preferences. Whether such procedures are democratic in the proper sense of the term depends on the election procedure. This raises another question: whether the procedures of liberal democracy are appropriate for an institution that is primarily a policy-proposing rather than a legislative body. And one whose business is more about technocratic and especially regulatory issues than either distributive or ideological politics. Democratic election might be better confined to the EU's legislative institution, and even then it is by no means easy to find an appropriate 'one size fits all' electoral procedure.

The Convention reviewed the various options. Some *conventionnels* preferred the European Parliament to indirectly elect the Commission president for a five-year term, to run concurrently with its own term, the party federations each selecting their own candidate for the office and campaigning on a joint manifesto. Twin elections would, or so it was claimed, give greater prominence to Europe-wide issues, instead of the domestic referendums that European elections presently are. The claim here is that the importance of the office would somehow impress voters with the civic duty of making a considered choice, and by raising public interest in the contest increase electoral turn-out. But would it work quite like that in practice? After all, the case for direct election is premised on assumptions about transnational political behaviour that are by no means proven. At the practical level, too, this procedure raises as many questions about legitimacy as it resolves.

Some *conventionnels* went even further, recommending the direct election of the entire Commission College. However, this procedure did not appeal to most governments, reluctant as they are extend the Parliament's elective function beyond its present right to approve the member states' nominee for president, to endorse or otherwise individual commissioners or after due procedure to sack the entire college. For to do so would increase Parliament's leverage on the Commission, reinforcing accountability and no less improving the Commission's democratic legitimacy *vis-à-vis* the Council. Federalists have long advocated the Commission's direct election, although various procedures are canvassed. The Convention did consider the proposal for an electoral college consisting of the lower houses of national parliaments, each one with a votes tally equivalent to their allocation of seats in the European Parliament. In this system, the national parliaments would vote for candidates for the Commission presidency, national votes being turned into electoral college votes. This arrangement would, it was argued, enhance the idea of a genuinely trans-European politics by introducing the left–right cleavage at the level of the Union. It would also supposedly encourage the public's interest in politics at the European level.[34]

However, even some federalists challenged this 'solution' as being unduly idealistic and ultimately unworkable. In part, because it would not significantly democratise EU politics, and might even have the very opposite effect. In view of the extent of executive control over national legislatures, an electoral college would merely place the decision as to presidency candidates firmly in the hands of national governments. Furthermore, national parliamentarians would more likely choose a candidate closest to their own party affiliation, rather than one best suited to steering the Commission. There are other objections to this procedure. Neither the structure nor the *modus operandi* of the European Parliament is appropriate to classic parliamentary adversarialism, because it 'does not have a permanent majority coalition and [its] party structures are not all pervasive'.[35] As such, under these arrangements the Commission president would be wholly detached from his electors, and this would merely increase the office's remoteness, its non-account-ability to the people at large.

For these reasons, federalists have insisted that only direct election can remove such distortions of democracy, electing the president from nominees of the Euro-pean parties after a Europe-wide election campaign. As Hoffmann sees it, this would both enhance the office's legitimacy and, by focusing on genuinely Euro-pean issues, be more 'likely to increase public interest in, and media focus on, the European political process in general and the European Parliament election more specifically'.[36] A Commission president directly elected by whatever means would undoubtedly strengthen the democratic linkages between two institutions, both of them key actors in co-decision, ensuring the Commission's due account-ability to Parliament, an improvement on present arrangements. As things pres-ently stand, 'people feel they cannot influence what is happening in Brussels', and a European election which gives the Parliament a mandate to elect the Commis-sion president would transfer 'more accountability to the EU institutional order and also more power back to the European citizens'.[37] This may well be so, but it was not remotely acceptable to the larger member states, and for that reason it made little headway at the Convention. Politics usually trumps principle when they meet head on, and so it proved on this issue. Procedures for the Commis-sion's democratic election remain a remote prospect. The lack of demos is the root of the problem, the absence of the cultural and sociological preconditions for democracy at the European level.[38]

Reforms that enhance the Commission's democratic credentials are useful as a counterweight to the Council's legislative powers even where, as in the co-decision procedure, there is a tendency for the Council to react to Commission proposals less on their merits as policy than from political expediency, too often fudging hard choices by concocting package deals and making 'side payments' that reflect narrow coalitions of national self-interest rather than the wider European interest. Co-decision is, nevertheless, a distinct improvement on previous legislative proce-dures, and it provides safeguards of sorts for all the Union's principal institutional actors. It is a procedure that ensures a balance of inputs into the policy process and facilitates conciliation should deadlock occur. Balance between competing actors is one thing, after all this is how the Union works. But the member states resist anything that might politicise the Commission, and this was exactly what happened at the Convention. Those who wanted these democratic reforms denied the claims of opponents that this would compromise the Commission's independence, even claiming that anyway 'politicisation is another word for democracy [and] without democratic legitimacy, how can the Commission retain the right to put forward legislative proposals and to defend the common interest?'[39]

Governments were not remotely convinced by claims here of merely good intentions. And even if they had been persuaded that such reform was an improvement on previous arrangements there was still a problem with procedure. For a workable electoral procedure is made unduly complicated by the Union's democratic deficits, its institutional complexity, the lack of any clear institutional hierarchy and not least by the abiding contestedness, the long-standing ideological dispute over what European integration is about. This makes it difficult for citizens to see any clear causal connection between the act of voting and the exercise of legitimate authority. As Hoffmann sees this problem:

> One of the major problems of the European political and institutional order is that it is too complicated. Voting procedures are generally a matter of advanced mathematics, and ordinary legislative procedures are more complicated than constitutional amendments in most liberal democracies. Qualified majority, conciliation committees, unanimity, consensus, vote allocations in the council, majority of states and majority of people: all these different factors and expressions mean nothing to most European citizens.[40]

The case for improving Commission efficiency was no less controversial. Some *conventionnels*, and some governments, too, preferred to reduce the number of commissioners, on the grounds that less means more, a familiar argument about an optimal-sized executive. The idea here is that a smaller College of no more than a dozen or so commissioners 'would provide genuine collective leadership and better co-ordination among departments', ensuring 'greater communication and co-ordination of strategic planning across the three institutions'.[41] Some have even claimed that a reduced College would remove the vestigial intergovernmentalism from this supranational institution, safeguarding EU policy-setting from undue interference by governments by breaking the direct link between the college and national representation as of right. Linked to this reform is the idea of changing the make-up of commissioners' cabinets, by requiring that they consist, unlike most present cabinets, of a greater mix of nationalities. Whether these changes would markedly improve European policy-making is debatable. There was a clear difference on this issue between the larger member states who favoured change, and the smaller ones who saw it as yet another attempt by the big three to dominate EU affairs.

### (v) Simplifying EU decision-making arrangements

Proposals for an executive presidency and a reformed Commission were in part a response to the Laeken objective of simplifying complicated decision-making arrangements. The emphasis here was on rationalisation, continuity and efficiency, as for instance in the proposal to reduce to 10 the number of functional councils, with the member states selecting their chairs for a term of 30 months rather than the present 6, and by QMV so as to ensure greater consensus. What the present arrangements do confirm is that not every minister of an incumbent presidency has either the aptitude or resources for managing their policy domain, a problem likely to increase in the enlarged Union.[42] Accordingly, it was proposed that the special-ised Council chairs should also sit collectively as a steering or executive group to provide greater continuity and cogency of policy, with ministers in charge who had 'proven qualities of consensus-building', and who likewise would have 'gained the respect of their colleagues because of their knowledge of the dossier', in marked contrast to the present personnel lottery. Political leadership would come from a full-time Council president, in post for no less than 30 months and possibly for 5 years.[43] Chairs would, moreover, be designated *ad personam*, so that personnel changes in national governments would not automatically mean a vacated chair would pass to a minister's domestic successor. Chairs would, however, retain the right to vacate their post should any tension arise between the incumbent's role as neutral arbiter of the various national interests and his/her preferences. By this arrangement, specialised and long-term chairs would release the Council presi-dency from the onerous task of managing the entire policy process, supposedly ensuring a more coherent and a continuous executive function, because enabling the presidency to focus on agenda-setting and headline issues.

This reform was suggested so as to complement the proposals tabled for reforming the Commission, and was intended to 'produce two remarkably similar looking cross-portfolio executive bodies'.[44] It became clear, however, during discussions that there were problems with this 'solution' to inchoate governance. One obvious draw-back would be the opposite of what was intended. Not better co-ordination of policy but confusion, the fact that quite different national policy styles would be in play in the management of the various portfolios. Another problem was whether diver-gent national interests can indeed be aggregated, let alone reconciled by the Council secretariat in its co-ordinating capacity, or even by a Council president seconding his own official representative to the respective chairperson's offices. There was the problem, too, of how to balance representation, to ensure parity between those member states represented on the executive Council and those excluded.

Co-ordination was a critical matter, too, for Council–Commission relations. Reforming the Union's principal institutions was bound to foment misunder-standing at the very least, and more likely than not conflict, though few insiders doubted that the Commission would be the net loser. From the Commission's standpoint the proposed changes looked like a bid to reduce its role in shaping the Union's policy agenda, a distinct and deliberate threat to its already reduced power base, and even to supplant it as the engine-house of common policy. For this very reason the Commission had little good to say about a proposal that threat-ened its own power base, preferring to avoid the issue, making the case instead for expanding its own role in the policy-making process.[45] As we shall see below (Chapters 6 and 7), much of the Convention's energy was directed at resolving these important institutional matters.

### (vi) Improving democratic life in the Union

Efficiency was one concern that was raised at Laeken, but so too was lack of transparency and public scrutiny of EU procedures.[46] The EU has never been unduly concerned about democracy. Michel Barnier, one of the Commission's representatives on the Convention, was candid in his admission that 'until now we have built Europe for the people but without them'.[47] The Community's ethos from the outset was predominantly a technocratic one, and thereafter its specialised and principally regulatory policy domains have hampered popular participation and even effective public scrutiny. The fact, too, that the EU's most powerful political institutional actors, the Council of Ministers, the European Council and the Commission, are appointed, or at best indirectly rather than directly elected merely serves to worsen these democracy deficits.

This was much less of a problem when the public were mostly indifferent to the work of the EU institutions, affording political and administrative elites considerable discretion. However, what was called 'permissive consensus' has long since disappeared, replaced now by perceptible public disquiet about the management of affairs. The long-standing reliance on performance or output legitimacy, based as this once was on respect for technocratic expertise and regulatory efficiency, the ability of the principal institutional actors to respond effectively to largely arcane and specialised technical issues, is no longer a reliable base for public support, let alone for due legitimacy.[48] As the Union has increased the scope of its policy domains and extended the reach of its legal competences, what is now widely regarded as a legitimacy deficit must needs be addressed. This much was already clear to the politicians who assembled at Laeken.

Transparency and better communication between policy-makers and the public, finding ways of ensuring the citizens' voice is heard, are critical benchmarks of good governance, in the EU as it is in any democratic polity. The quality of democratic life does not depend only on institutional procedures, but requires a culture of transparency; even more, normative shifts that facilitate a 'dynamic and participative democratic system'.[49] This is easier to prescribe than it is to realise in any polity, but especially so in the EU. The European Council, widely regarded as 'the apex' of Council machinery, the EU's supreme political authority where political leaders meet and debate political direction, has resisted transparency, preferring to work out of sight of the public. The very nature of the institution makes for a culture of deals and side payments, with 'last-minute bargaining over details', and the public interest very much an afterthought.[50]

The same institutional dynamics reduce the scope for transparency and public accountability of the Union's principal executive/legislative institutions, the Council of Ministers and the Commission. The Council comprises both specialised and 'ordinary' sectoral councils – notably the General Affairs Council, that of EU foreign ministers – and the member states take turns at managing the Union's affairs, an exacting task that makes heavy demands on both the political capital and diplomatic ingenuity of even the best-resourced countries. The Council of Ministers does have formal democratic legitimacy, in so far as it consists of members of democratically elected governments. Hence, the assertion of the then British foreign secretary, Jack Straw, that the Council is the more democratic of the EU's two executive institutions on the grounds that it is the only institution that consists of politicians who are formally accountable to domestic electorates. But the Council *per se* is not elected, and neither is it representative of any recognisable public constituency, let alone accountable to the EU electorate when it acts in its legislative capacity. At best, national parliaments hold only their own ministers to account for their actions in the Council, and even this scrutiny is exercised less than rigorously in many member states.

This lack of accountability is compounded by the fact that many key issues are settled by the specialised councils, often through trade-offs and insider deals that preclude either accountability or transparency.[51] Council decisions made in conclave commit governments to collective action, even if a national minister has opposed a proposed measure on grounds of national interest unless he/she exercises a veto, a rare occurrence these days. Furthermore, these binding decisions are too often entered into before national parliaments have had an opportunity to express a considered view, or to otherwise call their minister to account. This has serious implications for parliamentary democracy as it is practised in every member state. The only directly elected EU institution, the European Parliament, does little to reduce these democracy deficits, in part because it is still a secondary actor, its role 'still reflecting a lower degree of parliamentary representation and majority decision-making in the European political process than [do parliaments] in national democracies'.[52] Thus far the Parliament has failed to convince its severest critics about its positive contribution to Europe's democratic life. Indeed, the institution experiences considerable problems with legitimacy as a result of its 'lack of visibility', and the lack, too, of 'knowledge and awareness among EU citizens' of what it does. A fact that is exemplified time and again by the persistently low turn-out of voters in European elections.[53]

These circumstances point to serious shortcomings in democracy at the European level. One familiar response to this complaint is simply to deny a problem exists, to claim that since the EU is not a state the question of democracy or its absence is irrelevant. Those who argue thus maintain that citizens' interests are adequately represented in EU councils by national ministers who are responsible to domestic parliaments for their actions, and ultimately to their electorates through the usual national democratic procedures. A parallel argument makes the case that because the EU is essentially an intergovernmental organisation, concerned primarily with highly specialised technical matters, it simply does not – nor should it – lend itself to public scrutiny in the same way as domestic political institutions. These arguments, needless to say, are challenged as complacent and misplaced by critics concerned about the seemingly relentless expansion in both the scope and reach of EU governance. The technocratic alibi, namely that EU governance is principally concerned with functional policy outputs for which public legitimacy is not overtly required, no longer applies to governance in a Union whose collective actions now extend into the most politically sensitive domains of public policy. As one critic sees it, 'the argument that citizens are *only* interested in efficiency, in "delivery", is an argument that at best abandons the attempt ... to improve democracy and at worst is fundamentally anti-democratic'.[54] But merely to acknowledge that there is a democracy problem is not the same thing by any means as finding workable solutions.

To a degree, the problem here is normative as much as it is 'merely' procedural. The majoritarian model of European liberal democracy can hardly be accommodated to the EU polity, precisely because the Union is not a state and lacks demos. Nor is it even a transnational public space capable of sustaining a meaningful conversation with its citizens about policy priorities, or at least not yet. Rather, the EU is a confederation of sovereign nation states, each with elected governments legitimised by multiple demoi. And legitimacy is bound to be problematic in a confederal and multi-level polity lacking common identity and demos. For one thing, governments bring to their common dealings in the Council quite separate claims to legitimacy, each rooted in their own particular domestic constitutional procedures. But this default position is no answer to those critics for whom governance at every level requires due legitimacy and proper democratic ballast. According to this viewpoint, direct democracy is indispensable for the Union, in so far as it authoritatively allocates values, making and imposing decisions with important redistributive consequences. Again, it is far easier to prescribe appropriate political norms than it is to embody them in feasible procedures.

Giscard, by no means an instinctive democrat, was quite aware of these problems. Indeed, he raised the legitimacy issue during the Convention's April 2000 plenary meeting, acknowledging that the very remoteness of the Union's institutions, their lack of connectivity with citizens' everyday concerns was indeed a problem. Predictably for a former French president, he thought the matter was best left to the national, or even to the sub-national levels of governance. As he saw it, the Convention should devote the limited time available to it to reviewing ways of making the Union's institutions more visible to citizens.[55] To say the least this was complacent, and it failed to convince a majority of *conventionnels*. Critics in the Convention continued to make the case that nothing less than decisive action was required, 'not only to make the EU more comprehensible but also more transparent, more representative and more participative – with the last two of these characteristics in many ways the most challenging'.[56] But as we shall see, radical and democratic solutions were not especially high on the agenda of most of the member states, more concerned as they are with power than with democracy.[57]

### (vii) The EU as an international actor

The world is a much less predictable, indeed is a more dangerous place nowadays than it was during the bipolar era of the Cold War, the years immediately after 1945 that determined the shape and trajectory of European integration. The view of some critics that the EU has failed to make its mark in international politics compared to its achievements as a trading power is an unpalatable truth, and one of some concern to its current leaders. There is every incentive in a globalising world to improve the Union's capacity for influence, not least where international affairs are dominated as never before by the American hyper-power seemingly

bent – at least during the George Bush (junior) Administration – on strident unilateralism. The quest for equilibrium in the emergent international system, sharing
the considerable burdens and confronting the challenges of global management
requires, as many Europeans see it, the capacity for the EU to play its part. Not as
Washington's client, but rather as an alternative pole of influence in the conduct
of liberal internationalism. But how to do it? The case for a European foreign and
security policy is by no means uncontroversial. Pan-Europeanism vies with Atlanticism, and with all manner of hybrid positions in between. These issues figured
rather more prominently in the Convention than was intended even when Laeken
set the agenda because of the diplomatic fall-out from the Iraq war.

These issues loomed large in discussions of the Union's role and capacity as
an international actor. Events unforeseen at Laeken played their part in making
this debate much less one about theoretical options, as it has so often been in
the past, and more a matter of deciding between some difficult alternatives. The
issue of European participation in the interim force operating against the Taliban
in Afghanistan after the horrendous events of September 11 2001 had convinced
some member states to try to confine the Union's role in international policing to
a limited contribution to crisis-management operations. The impact of the direct
attack on the USA had far-reaching consequences, not least in Europe, where it
served to reinforce the view, widely shared by all shades of mainstream political
opinion other than out-and-out Eurosceptics that the EU must actively contribute
to stabilising the new international order, both within Europe and out of region.
The sheer impact of global terrorism on domestic security, policing and home
affairs policy after these awful events was bound to increase the salience of the
Union's international role. But the issue was far from straightforward. There was
a deep division between the member states, as there has been since the start of
the European project about how to conduct international policy at this level. On
one hand, the French minister, Louis Michel, sought, as French statesmen have
been wont since Charles de Gaulle put his imprimatur on his country's external
policy, to establish a firmer regional base for European security. Whereas some
other EU states, notably though not exclusively the United Kingdom, prefer to
lock regional security into the Atlantic Alliance. The outbreak of armed hostilities
in Iraq during the Convention ensured that this long-established fault-line would
become a central theme of this debate.

The political fall-out from Iraq confirmed just how far the EU has yet to travel
if it is to become an independent, let alone an effective global actor, a fact readily
seized upon for his own partisan ends by Donald Rumsfeld, the US secretary of
state for defense, when he made much of the schism between what he called 'old'
and 'new' Europe. The growing rift between Europe and the USA nevertheless
confirmed the urgency of reviewing the Union's role, its capacity to operate more
effectively as an international actor: whether in responding to the threat of rogue
states, to climate change in the aftermath of the Kyoto Climate Convention, the
challenges of environmental management, as well as energy policy, trade issues,
the establishment, rules and remit of the international criminal court and so on. A
case has been made for the Union to adopt a multilateral approach to managing the

global commons through international forums, pursuing multilateral solutions to security issues. Yet this case is challenged by those who make much of the failure so far to offer a convincing or consistent response.

The prospects for a convincing European voice in international affairs is even more problematic after the latest enlargement, with more diverse interests in EU councils representing mind-sets shaped by historical and political experiences different from those of EU15, states with quite different perspectives on security and external policy. Enlargement has confirmed the continuing discrepancy between the EU's role as a formidable economic actor and its relative lack of credibility in international diplomacy. Yet the very fact of enlargement has raised the stakes here, and more than that has added 'to the pressure to become at least a stronger regional power'.[58] For there is no escaping the fact that current 'political and economic needs and pressures' demand 'a well-managed set of economic, political and security relations across the new EU borders – in a way that should be, though may not be, complementary to the enlargement and development of NATO's relations with countries beyond the EU'.[59]

The onset of the conflict in Iraq made this a matter of even greater moment, but the issue had already been signalled at Laeken in the following terms: 'Does Europe not, now that it is finally unified, have a leading role to play in a new world order, that of a power able to play a stabilising role worldwide and to point the way ahead for many countries and peoples?'[60] The Convention's task here was not merely to deliberate on an appropriate institutional framework for managing EU foreign and security policy, but also to consider the connection between external and internal policy. And in particular, the legal bases of the Union's international policies, from trade, aid and development policy, to setting technical standards, environment policy and climate management, human rights, justice and home affairs policy, as well as structural and cohesion policy and even social exclusion. The launch of the Euro-zone, too, has reinforced the case for more weighty EU representation in global regulatory and financial regimes such as the World Bank, G8 and the IMF, those agencies tasked with managing the international economic order. All of this had underlined the centrality of international policy in the conduct of EU policy *per se*. Few *conventionnels* doubted that international issues were part of their remit, but there were deep differences over precisely how to meet the broad objective of improving the Union's international capacity. These took the familiar form of a stand-off between those who preferred either a supranational or an intergovernmental remedy.

The Convention reviewed proposals for improving the co-ordination of external policy, not least how to balance foreign and security policy. As things stand, the Commission has much greater influence in matters of trade, aid and development policy; whereas the Council, though now required to liaise with the Parliament, retains control of the CFSP. As with so many other aspects of policy, 'the Council and the Commission have varying roles and powers both across and within policy areas which impact negatively on coherent, integrated and effective policy-making'.[61] Central to this issue was whether to simplify the Union's legal base by merging the EU's supranational Community pillar with the intergovernmental second CFSP pillar established by the Maastricht Treaty. The Commission, and understandably so in view of its supranational preferences and its aspirations for closer political union, preferred to merge the three post-Maastricht pillars, seeing this as a prerequisite for deeper integration.[62] Accordingly, the then trade commissioner, Pascal Lamy, called on the EU to make the governance of globalisation an urgent priority. Lamy advocated an extension of Commission competence to cover all aspects of trade policy, giving Brussels authority to speak (and negotiate) on the Community's behalf in matters relating to the international management of globalisation. This bold view was endorsed, in turn, by some *convention-nels*.[63] There was bound to be resistance, however, and it came from a predictable quarter. Although national representatives did support an extension of Union competencies in these critical policy domains, they countered the supranational case, arguing instead that the member states should retain ultimate authority over these matters, a position endorsed by Giscard himself.

These are issues of principle as much as matters of procedure, and for that very reason they were never going to be resolved simply by enacting institutional reforms, though some of the institutional changes reviewed and eventually adopted by the Convention are especially relevant to this vexed question. For instance, the proposal for reforming the General Affairs Council, establishing a more specialised Foreign Affairs Council, was undoubtedly influenced by the quest to improve co-ordination between member states' foreign policy. As one commentator saw it: 'A more focused, separate and consistent Council could contribute to moving forward in terms of much greater attention to priority setting and establishment of clear strategic frameworks in foreign policy.'[64]

Likewise the merger of the High Representative (representing the Council) with that of the Commissioner for External Relations, was another proposal intended to improve coherence and ensure greater consistency in the conduct of external policy. Although it supported merger, the Commission preferred that the combined office and the prerogative for initiating policy be vested exclusively in its own offices.[65] Much the same organisational logics were applied to the proposal from some quarters to extend QMV to foreign policy, though not at this stage to the complementary fields of security and defence policy. The significant changes wrought by the Treaty of Amsterdam notwithstanding, QMV was expressly excluded from CFSP, though the case for it was indeed argued, and will continue to be made as the stakes of globalisation are raised and the common dangers facing Europe increase.

All of these critical issues figured in Convention deliberations and were essential to its task of designing a European constitutional order appropriate to meeting current challenges. This much was new and its impact on policy should not be underestimated. Nevertheless the Convention's deliberations, though wider in scope by far than those of any previous IGC, were shaped much less by the imperative to constitutionalise the European political order in the classic sense of that term than by the selective preferences and singular interests of the leading member states: whether directly through their representatives in the Convention, or more generally by the continuing impact of these states on prevailing ideas about the purposes and meaning of European integration. Before we examine in more detail how the Convention approached these important matters, it is useful in light of this fact to review these sometimes competing, often complementary national preferences.

## Negotiating dynamics and national preferences

### *(i) The Franco-German alliance, British pragmatism and* directoire

The Franco-German alliance is both long-standing and influential, and has exerted considerable influence on the pace and direction of European integration from the outset. France has long been the principal driver of this alliance, though there are signs that Franco-German co-operation is undergoing a subtle shift, becoming a more equal but also a more conditional partnership. This was apparent in the Convention, with palpable tension between Paris and Berlin, or rather between Schroeder and Chirac, on some issues, thereby strengthening London's hand. Nevertheless, France and Germany did work closely from the start to push their own ideas, presenting a series of bilateral proposals, and most notably a joint paper on the EU's institutional architecture (January 2003).

However, these two countries no longer exert quite the same leadership they once did. For one thing, the impact of successive enlargements has altered the Union's political dynamics, making it more difficult for them to dominate affairs as in times past.[66] The latest enlargement is bound to further reduce even their combined influence. Some basic facts help to explain why this is so. France and Germany together now account for barely one third of EU27 population, and something less than half of total GDP. Political dynamics are as important here as demography, in that enlargement increases the available coalitional options, preventing any attempt by these close allies to impose leadership on smaller countries increasingly resistant nowadays to attempts by the 'Kaisers' of Berlin and Paris 'to promote their own interests and dominate the EU'. To claim leadership in these circumstances is to invite rebuff, and more than that to weaken the cement that binds the Union, for 'the more France and Germany create the impression that they are attempting to jointly dominate the EU, the more reluctant others will become to invest more power to these [European] institutions'.[67] There are no longer any automatic leaders in the EU. Any state seeking even a modicum of influence must adjust to this fact, though neither France nor Germany is easily reconciled to this situation. Even Prime Minster Blair, though aware of these post-enlargement logics, assumed a *directoire* demeanour, with his personal representatives in the Convention operating as part of a self-assured, and as many other participants saw it a self-serving, triumvirate seeking to impose its own agenda.

Events, as much as the familiar reflex to make alliances determined the responses of the principal players. The Iraq crisis was bound to impact on the delicate political relations between the three leading member states. The diplomatic fall-out surfaced on all manner of issues beyond foreign policy and security co-operation, and a fault-line opened up between Germany and particularly France on one side, and the United Kingdom over the direction of EU foreign policy, and likewise on security policy. This became apparent when Britain's official representative, Peter Hain, confirmed his government's confederal approach on this issue, preferring to abrogate the management of the common foreign policy to the Council and to reaffirm the unanimity procedure; whereas his German counterpart, Peter Glotz, called for a greater role for the EU *per se*. Yet these same states had mutual interests, too, and in the end commonality of purpose as much as their disagreement over the war or even ideological differences over the meaning of 'Europe' saw them make common cause on many of the critical issues.

Relations between 'the big three' can only work on the basis of compromise, making mutual adjustments between their respective preferences. And there were some notable examples of this during the Convention. The most significant German concession to *directoire* – more a strategic calculation designed to paper over the deep differences between France's confederal preference and Germany's quasi-federalist instincts – was Joschka Fischer's reluctant acquiescence to a much reduced role for the Commission presidency, accommodating France's preference for a full-time Council presidency.[68] Fischer had initially opposed this, preferring the Council to give genuine leadership, to adopt a pan-European perspective instead of merely acting as the creature of governments. As he saw it, the creation of this new power centre 'could be considered a setback to achieving substantial improvements towards a more accountable and democratically legitimate structure of European policy-making'.[69] But in the end, and leaned on by his senior coalition partner and Chancellor Gerhard Schroeder, Fischer was 'persuaded' to set aside his principled objections in favour of the pragmatic approach favoured by Paris and London.

The differences between the big three over the Commission's size were also resolved by a timely compromise, albeit one couched in convenient rhetoric about the 'virtues' of democratic legitimacy, the supposedly democratic deficit that would ensue from reducing the number of commissioners, whilst at the same time strengthening the Commission's executive capacities, notably in economic policy. France on grounds of efficiency preferred to reduce the overall size of the College and persuaded Germany to revisit the agreement at Nice giving one commissioner to each member state. Another compromise settled the equally sensitive matter of Council voting weights, this time in Germany's favour. On this issue, it was France's turn to show reluctance about unstitching the deal made at Nice, though Germany had been the clear loser from it. France agreed to a review of the Nice formula and accepted Germany's preference for extending co-decision, in exchange for Germany backing France's preference for an enhanced role for national parliaments, and the so-called 'early warning' system on Commission proposals recommended by the working group on subsidiarity. The German and French governments were in agreement, too, about the need to sharpen the Union's international profile by appointing a foreign minister, a post to be nominated by the Council though approved by the Commission president, and for this office to be supported by an EU diplomatic service. France was receptive to Germany's preference for CFSP decisions – other than those pertaining to defence/military issues – to be subject to QMV, but the United Kingdom's objections put paid to any procedural change here.

On occasion, London muscled in on this cosy and long-standing alliance, not least by backing French efforts to bring Germany behind the strictly confederal executive Council presidency, and to support the proposal for an EU foreign minister. Britain had its own reservations about this proposed new office and gave its backing only on condition it remained an instrument of the member states, in effect of the leading states, since they would provide the bulk of its diplomatic resources and of the military hardware and other resources required for any common actions.[70] The British government also backed France on curbing Commission ambitions, without blocking that institution's capacity for policing compliance with agreed policy, or confirming its role as initiator of 'first-pillar' policy, albeit 'within the strategic priorities set by the European Council'.[71] Otherwise, London sought to limit the Commission's discretion and autonomy in the policy process, to transform it into a kind of secretariat whose main purpose is to serve the European Council.[72] It made common cause here with Paris, both governments resisting election of the Commission president on the grounds that this would enhance the legitimacy of the office, making for greater tension between the Council and Commission. And though initially insistent on the Nice arrangements on voting weights and on reducing the Commission, the United Kingdom eventually agreed to changes in both areas, opposing neither the double-majority voting rule for the Council nor a smaller Commission. But it traded these concessions for reciprocal support for its own so-called 'red lines', the maintenance of national vetoes in some crucial policy domains.

The United Kingdom did clash with the Franco-German concordat over its determination to resist extending QMV, and even though it was eventually persuaded to accept some increase here it insisted that any change in the Nice votes formula should not improve the capacity of smaller states to veto policy, and should likewise permit the larger states to more easily build blocking minorities. Britain resisted pressure, as it always does, to relinquish unanimity in key policy domains, notably taxation, social policy and foreign policy, and objected to the *passerelle* clause (in Article 1-25 of the draft Constitutional Treaty) that would permit QMV by a unanimous vote in the European Council. This doggedness was easier to carry off precisely because France and Germany had their own and by no means identical sticking-points.[73] In effect, the big three made their bargains in the same way as in any IGC, by trading their respective preferences for an all-round package deal.[74] And there was more to unite than divide them, not least a determination to reform the common institutions and to sharpen decisional procedures whilst resisting demands for more supranationalism other than making token concessions, whether from the parliament or the Commission.[75]

These trade-offs between the national preferences of the big three shed some light on the Convention's political dynamics. For these bargains showed just how much the big three have in common, as well as some abiding differences of interest, outlook and aspirations between them and smaller states, of which more below. One can see why this fault-line exists and why is likely to persist. Any suggestion of convenient deals made between the so-called *directoire* was bound to cause resentment amongst the 'others', whatever the actual merits of the case, a fact confirmed by the fall-out between the bigger and smaller member states that had already marred the Biarritz European Council in autumn 2000. The conceit, as some saw it, of the *directoire* was not just a momentary irritation, the outcome of Convention bargaining and deal-making but something that is built into the very fabric and is part of the dynamics of the enlarged Union. What many saw as *hauteur* by France and Germany, and the United Kingdom, too, though Blair sought to make common cause with the newcomers as possible allies on Iraq and other policy issues, was especially irksome to the smaller states. As it was to *conventionnels* from the European Parliament, an all too familiar *amour propre*, a concerted attempt to impose narrow national preferences at the expense of a fairer distribution of influence when it comes to determining what is in Europe's best interest.

British governments tend to take a pragmatic approach to European integration, and the Blair governments were no exception.[76] Despite the prime minister's promise when he assumed office in 1997 to 'put Britain at the heart of Europe', a rash commitment as things turned out, he reverted to type soon enough when faced with pressure from Eurosceptics at home and by unpalatable events abroad. By the time the Convention met Downing Street was exhibiting familiar reticence about 'Europe'. The unresolved issue of when, or even whether, Britain would hold a referendum on joining the single currency had already caused friction with the other EU states, not least France and Germany, underlining the gulf between easy rhetoric and real politics. And this caution about Europe carried over to London's response to the prospects for a European Constitution.

Nor was reticence over the Convention confined to the 'usual suspects' on the Eurosceptical right or amongst tabloid editorial writers. Even some notable pro-Europeans were wary of wholesale constitutional change, unsure as one prominent commentator observed 'whether the constitutional blueprint approach is the most appropriate one (for taking forward the big policy issues currently on the EU agenda)'. Helen Wallace voiced reservations, warning that 'it is not obvious that grand designs make for best institutional practice across the particular core policy areas that seem to be in most urgent need of development'.[77] The government certainly had its own deep reservations about the 'constitutional' project from the start and it showed. Although favourable to reforming the treaties, adapting the Union's governance the better to respond to formidable policy challenges, the government was as reluctant as any of its predecessors about anything remotely resembling a federalist agenda, or what might be construed as such by a malevolent media. The British government was careful in these circumstances not to become isolated from its partners, to be outmanoeuvred by the long-established Franco-German alliance, and whenever possible it made common cause with them.

The big three had much in common, then, and this became the basis for agreement on the major institutional and policy issues. Nevertheless, all was far from plain sailing, for each country brought to the negotiations a quite different outlook, the legacies of their respective pasts, on 'Europe'. German history has determined that country's almost idealised and so far mostly unconditional support for European integration[78] Though there is some evidence nowadays of 'a growing [German] scepticism *vis à vis* the European integration process'.[79] This historical baggage – or burden, as many Germans see it – was quite apparent in the contributions of German *conventionnels*, for instance their support for a raft of quite radical proposals for democratising the institutions, making its decision-makers more accountable, and strengthening the linkages between the Commission (both the presidency and the college) and the citizens via an elective mechanism, including the Parliament's right to vote for or to impeach the Commission president. But Germany's official position on Europe has begun to shift in response to a public that now has more reservations about European integration, whether expressed as concern about the euro or resistance to shouldering disproportionately the financial and other burdens of further enlargement.

The defence of national interests has become almost respectable again, encouraging politicians to be more critical of at least some aspects of the EU. There were some indications of this during the Convention. Germany's political elite is still broadly enthusiastic about the European project but not at any cost; despite being better disposed to reform, including greater transparency, accountability and democracy in Council proceedings, Berlin was quite aware of limits imposed by public opinion. For this reason, it was especially wary about extending QMV to the domestically sensitive issue of immigration policy.[80] French politicians, for their part, whether of the left or the right, are hardly sentimental about 'Europe', carrying little of the emotive baggage and none of the guilt of their near-neighbours. For the French political elite, the EC/EU has always been first and foremost a vehicle for pursuing the national interest, an instrument for domestic policy objectives and not least for solving the historical 'German problem'. This pragmatic outlook was much in evidence in contributions from French *conventionnels*, whatever their party-political base, and particularly so in proposals from Paris for developing the Common Foreign and Security Policy.

In the event, all three big member states achieved their principal objectives. France, for instance, secured the full-time Council presidency and the EU foreign minister it wanted, whereas the United Kingdom obtained executive reform, though not a 'double-hat' Council–Commission presidency, a say for national parliaments in EU policy-making and made sure, too, that the foreign minister would primarily be an agent of the Council despite having a seat in the Commission. Furthermore, London successfully defended its so-called 'red lines', resisting expansion of EU competencies or extension of QMV into sensitive policy areas such as taxation and the security/foreign domains, as well as reinforcing the broadly liberal approach to the management of economic policy. Germany secured an increase in QMV, if not in all the policy areas it preferred, and a favourable revision of Council voting weights.

Some important differences of interest and emphasis remained, however, between the Paris–Berlin axis and London. The British government was constrained, as it always is, by the endemic Euroscepticism of domestic opinion, primed by a media mostly hostile to all things 'European'. The fact that the British government made significantly more amendments to the presidency's first draft of the treaty articles than any other government is testament to these constraints. Yet, overall, there was rather more agreement than conflict between the big three, and especially so on the critical governance issues. This spirit of co-operation did not extend, however, to their relations with the other member states, many of them concerned by what they saw as a fault-line between the big and small countries. London's role was crucial in bridging this divide, for the smaller states are quite used to Franco-German hauteur. An assurance from Prime Minister Blair that the British government had no wrecking agenda, and that while it would not block necessary reforms it understood the concerns of smaller countries, was not, however, entirely convincing. Anxiety to dispel suspicion that London was hostile to the interests of the smaller countries did not prevent the government's official representative supporting reforms designed to privilege the role of the larger member states.

The outcome of these bargains says much about the dynamics of EU politics. The claim is often made that 'only when the most influential politicians in Europe put European interests first, as they did when the Community was set up, will truly satisfactory long-term solutions be reached'.[81] This might be so in an ideal world, but in the real world of politics national interests – or what is computed by statesmen as national interests – prevail, and the EU is no exception. The key players regarded the Convention as a forum for pursuing their own preferences, and to this extent it merely reflected the overriding reality of EU politics.

### (ii) The small countries stake their claim: or 'vainly resisting directoire'

The latest enlargement has made the disparities in demographic size and economic power between the Union's largest and smaller states even greater than they were in EU15. Only 7 member states out of a total membership of 27 are demographically large states, and only 2 of these (Poland and Romania) are from the new intake. Yet these large states account for 80.2 per cent (378 million) of the EU's total population of some 482 million, and some 77 per cent of its GDP. The group of 8 medium-sized states, with populations of between 8 and 16 million, contribute 85 million (19 per cent) of the total EU population and 17 per cent of GDP. The smaller states, with populations of between 5 million and 400,000, account for a further 30.5 million of the Union's population and a mere 7 per cent of GDP.

This discrepancy between large and small states makes EU27 markedly different from the European Community of the 1950s. The six founder states were more evenly divided, with three big and three medium or small states. The present balance differs, too, from EU15 which consisted five big, six medium-sized and four small member states. Changing demography has impacted on the Union's political dynamics. A Union where the majority of member states have populations below 10 million has ensured an 'enhanced insistence among the medium and small countries on equality of states' rights'.[82]

One of the Convention's tasks was to address such disparities of power and influence, to find ways of managing increasing diversity so as to ensure a manageable balance of power between the member states, and between them and the common institutions. The abiding impression of many of the smaller and especially new member states is one of disappointment and even resentment about the Convention's failure to redress the apparent manipulation of events by the big three in their own interests. This imbalance of power was apparent from the outset, yet the way the Convention went about its business seemed to confirm collusion between the *directoire* and the presidency, with Giscard consistently refusing 'to incorporate the proposals of the smaller countries or to come up with a compromise solution until some changes occurred in the final stages'. Giscard even admitted as much, observing 'that one should not naturally assume that the [member] states are equal'.[83]

Of course, this situation did not go unchallenged. A group of 16 of the smaller member states from both EU15 and the accession countries, calling themselves 'Friends of the Community Method' (FCM), tried to increase their bargaining position by co-ordinating their responses to proposals from the big three. This *ad hoc* group met for instance on the occasion of the Athens European Council (April 2003) to show solidarity, signalling their objection to what they saw as being taken for granted. They published a position paper, *Reforming the Institutions: Principles and Premises*, endorsing the Community method and criticising the big three for pursuing their own narrow preferences, and they emphasised parity as a first principle of Union membership, translated as a seat for every member state in the European Council, in COREPER and in the Commission.[84] The group's riposte that they represented a majority of EU member states was met, however, by the claim from the 'big three' that 'they nonetheless represented a minority of the EU's population'.[85]

Opposition here had little more than nuisance value and FCM unity eventually unravelled. These states had their own distinct views on many of key issues, and not least on the situation in Iraq, differences that undermined the group's unity. The Netherlands, for instance, a leading light in the FCM at the outset, eventually distanced itself from the group's generally pro-integration position in response to rising Euroscepticism at home. Belgium, another prominent participant, eventually broke ranks over the Council presidency issue. There was in fact no consensus amongst the smaller states about the critical institutional issues, for instance whether or indeed how to reform the Council, some small states preferring a strong and therefore a permanent Council, others wanting a shift in the balance of institutional power towards the Commission and the Parliament.[86] The status quo was their best chance of redressing *directoire* domination, though the Belgian representative objected to the 'inefficiency' of rotation, making much the same case for a permanent presidency as the big three. Concern with national prestige and retaining some leverage over the Union's agenda persuaded most of these smaller states to support retention of a commissioner for every member state, and for the same reason to back that institution's autonomy.[87] But there were differences amongst the smaller states even on these issues. Despite general support for electing the Commission president there was no consensus on procedure. Some member states, however (Austria, Greece, Belgium, the Netherlands, and from the candidate countries Bulgaria and the Czech Republic) preferred indirect election by the Parliament. Greece's representative, supported by Slovakia's representative, proposed that the Parliament's political groups should nominate candidates on a party political basis. Whereas Ireland and Denmark wanted a different type of electoral college and Malta suggested a congress of national parliamentarians. Another group (Sweden, Portugal, Finland and Estonia) preferred the status quo, leaving the matter of 'election' to governments, though with the European Parliament having the right to endorse their choice.

These issues had already featured at Nice, where the smaller member states had resisted a proposal to streamline the Commission. These states were hardly persuaded by the case made by the big three for rotation of commissioners as a fair solution, for as they saw it 'a small state without a nominee commissioner is never in the same position as a large state without a nominee', in as much as 'in an enlarged Union of twenty-seven or more states, a small state will have less influence and will be less able to obtain special treatment, and agreements will be harder to reach, even by qualified majority'.[88] Most of the smaller states likewise placed considerable reliance on the Commission president's strategic role, and above all on retaining the Community method as the best guarantee of receiving a fair hearing, for proper recognition of their own interests in the policy process. The subversion as they saw it by leading member states of the Commission's policy-making and agenda-setting functions, undermining that institution's mediation role that enables every member state to contribute to policy setting in the first pillar, were all matters that exercised representatives of the smaller member states. The Commission is for these states both a resource and an ally, and indispensable when they assume the presidency.[89] As such the small states had far more to lose from any reduction in the Commission's powers. As Temple Lang sees this situation:

> It ought to be clearly understood ... that smaller States have much more to gain than to lose from the Commission enforcing for example EU rules on State aid [for] if Member States indulge in unrestrained competition to subsidise their domestic industries, France and Germany can afford to pay larger subsidies for longer than small States. It is therefore quite clearly in small States' interests to strengthen the Commission, and not to allow pique or irritation to weaken policy in this respect. Small states would not be better off, in a Union of twenty-five or thirty States, with a weak Commission. Small states need the Commission to apply the rules on State aids strictly in the ten new Member States, too. ... The interests of small States call for a Commission which is respected by other Member States, and whose policy-proposals will be taken seriously and whose decisions will be respected and carried out.[90]

These issues were critical for the Union's institutional balance of power and they became a source of considerable political friction in the Convention between the *directoire* and the small states. On the face of it this looked to be an ideological stand-off over competing ideas about the meaning and purposes of EU governance, a struggle between arch-confederalists and those states claiming to be Monnet's heirs. In effect, 'a "battle" between supporters of the community method and supporters of the intergovernmental method', a principled defence of the European idea against those who continued to pursue national advantage.[91] The facts do not, however, support such a neat interpretation of events. The motivation for states that defended the Community method against *directoire realpolitik* was shaped just as much by the pragmatism they so disparaged in their opponents, by self-interest as much as idealism about the purposes of European governance. The struggle in the Convention between the smaller states and the big three was less a climactic struggle for the 'soul' of European integration, pure principle versus unalloyed self-interest, than a skirmish over relative power that translated into familiar national interests. The big states, as we shall, see prevailed on most of these critical arguments, not because they had the 'better' case but precisely because they were more powerful, better organised, more determined and above all because they had far more to lose.

### (iii) Members or guests? The role of the accession countries

The accession countries shared many of the concerns of the small EU15 states about avoiding a constitutional settlement that would confirm their second-class status as EU members. The newcomers were even more disadvantaged in making their case by the refusal of EU15 to allow them proper representation in the Convention. Nor were these countries unduly idealistic about the European project, accepting the fact that the EU was realistically the 'only game in town' and seeing their membership as more a matter of political and economic necessity than of historic destiny to 'rejoin' Europe. The EU seen from the east is a vital political resource for responding to the demands of political and economic transition, a source both of material assistance in adjusting to the discipline of a market economy and also indispensable political capital for stabilising otherwise brittle democracy.

The special circumstances pertaining to the accession countries from Eastern and Central Europe, their recent history as former satellites of Moscow, was bound to shape their responses, not only to the issues discussed at the Convention but also to EU membership *per se*. The experience of Soviet hegemony has made for 'very different identities and visions of the future of Europe'.[92] And not least, understandable wariness about compromising hard-won independence, subsuming new-found identity as free nation-states within a Union dominated by larger states. The newcomers for all these reasons were understandably circumspect about joining a community of states whose political centre and cultural core is situated half a continent away in what is a very different 'Europe' from the one they have recently escaped, yet one led nevertheless by states with similar imperious instincts to those of Moscow.

The 'new Europeans' are naturally wary about being manipulated, or at least of being taken for granted. This much became apparent during the Convention in the responses of some EU15 states to the Iraq crisis. Telling here was the disdain with which Jacques Chirac treated the decision of those accession states that backed the Anglo-American coalition to contribute to the military force being assembled to overthrow Saddam Hussein's regime in Baghdad. Seven EU and accession states (Poland, Hungary, the Czech Republic, together with Portugal, Denmark, Italy and the United Kingdom) endorsed the Allied position in an open letter initiated by the Spanish premier, José María Aznar. This letter was published on 30 January 2003, but without informing beforehand either France or Germany, the Union's leading opponents of a pre-emptive war or, as diplomatic courtesy required, the Greek presidency. This missive was followed by another joint letter of support for the Allies signed by the so-called 'Vilnius Ten' – Slovakia, Slovenia, Lithuania, Estonia, Latvia, Romania, Bulgaria, Croatia, Macedonia and Albania. Chirac condemned both actions at the extraordinary meeting of the European Council on 28 February, openly castigating the accession states for 'behaving like children'.[93] Such hauteur brought resentment, not least because it seemed to reinforce these states' impression of second-class status, a fact that merely made them even more determined to resist what their politicians and publics alike saw as condescension, or even bullying.

None of this was entirely unanticipated, for the experience of the accession countries throughout protracted accession negotiations had left them with few illusions about where power actually lies in the EU, or in whose interests it is usually employed. Concern to improve their modest diplomatic status, and not least to counter the impression of fickle domestic electorates, of being merely supplicants, explains to an extent their preference for a strong Commission. Likewise their support for the Community method, long regarded as 'a reliable defence against the dominance of the larger more established member states whose instincts are to ignore, to over-ride, to take the interests and preferences of the smaller states for granted'.[94] Nevertheless the fall-out over Iraq hardly improved their impression of the Union, seemingly confirming that despite cutting loose from Moscow they still moved in the shadow of bigger players, the penumbra cast by *directoire*. This lack of diplomatic clout did little to reinforce an already faint voice in the Convention, with their representatives feeling very much like outsiders, adopting a low profile on the critical issues and barely contributing to the important debates in case they offended potential allies amongst EU15.

There were few exceptions to this generally subdued approach, though some newcomers did raise an occasionally critical voice. Latvia's Rihards Piks, for example, expressed concern during discussion on security policy about the creation of a Eurodefence-zone that 'might differentiate between those EU member states that are part of the defence Union and those that remain outside it [and] that would not foster co-operation, mutual trust and solidarity among member states, and would lead de facto to the creation of a two-tier membership of the EU'.[95] The Polish foreign minister, Cimoszewicz, similarly raised mild objections to what he saw as the limited role for the newcomers in framing CFSP proposals, pointing with studied irony to the patent mismatch between the dominance of some member states in their preference for developing CFSP under the leadership of a 'directorate', in stark contrast to the principle of partnership between member states. He pointedly observed that 'some recent statements could be interpreted as expressions of an underlying belief that "all states are equal, but some states are more equal than others" [and] this is certainly far from helpful'.[96]

Otherwise, the newcomers barely signalled their arrival on the EU stage. For the most part they were marginalised in the Convention, a fact that played badly with domestic audiences already concerned about the impact of joining this Western club, both on vulnerable national economies and no less on their capacity for remaining as independent states. For these states, the Convention was an object-lesson in what they could expect from membership of a less than equitable Union.

# 5   The Convention at work

## Procedures

The Convention on Fundamental Rights had operated without precise procedural rules, an oversight that undoubtedly complicated its organisation and delayed the outcome. These lessons were duly registered. Although Laeken did not determine actual procedures for the Convention it did confirm that there would be procedures.[1] Laeken prescribed two options for the Convention: either to present the European Council with a list of proposals for further consideration in an IGC; or to write a draft constitutional treaty. However, the political leaders did not anticipate the subsequent IGC being bound by either of these outcomes. Legitimacy is a critical resource for constitution-making and the Convention fared better in this regard than some governments, wary about having a constitution foisted on them, might have preferred. The fact that the Convention was a representative forum did confer a degree of authority that governments could hardly ignore. At the very least, it increased the pressure on governments to take note of, 'to listen carefully to dominant and more resonant interests within the Convention itself'.[2] The sheer novelty of the exercise enhanced the Convention's credentials as a forum for constitutional deliberation. The wide-ranging membership brought a reflexivity to proceedings rare in EU forums, notwithstanding the presence and preferences of the leading member states throughout the proceedings.[3] Discussion was remarkably candid, with evidence throughout of a thorough review of the issues, and a determination to resist pressure to fall in behind the 'big three'.

The agenda was shaped by the leading member states, though unlike IGCs not exclusively by them. The conduct of business, too, was quite different from IGC diplomacy. Many *conventionnels*, especially those not directly affiliated to governments, maintained autonomy from the principals, whether governments or the European institutions.[4] And though this was not always apparent from the way it conducted its business, the Convention did at least try to make its own distinctive response to the questions raised at Laeken. As the Convention got to work it soon became clear that this was no surrogate IGC, though awareness by the leading governments of what was at stake ensured that the governments would have the most influential voice.[5] Indeed, on occasions the foreign policy establishments of the leading member states saw fit to remind the Convention of its purely advisory role, and that IGCs after all are the legitimate location for negotiating (rather than for deliberating on) treaty reform. Some governments expressed barely disguised impatience with what they saw as the presumptiveness of some *conventionnels* to 'speak for Europe' as if harbingers of a European Constitution. This friction simmered throughout the proceedings, taking its toll on them as we shall see. Yet many *conventionnels* maintained commendable independence, investing considerable energy and enterprise in responding to momentous and immensely complicated issues.[6] Regardless of the fate of the Constitutional Treaty governments will in future surely find it difficult not to repeat the exercise of on-the-record and candid discussion of issues.

The praesidium, and especially the presidency/secretariat team, took the lead in managing the agenda, including drafting proposals for discussion in the plenaries. The presidency was the fulcrum here, strategically situated so as to liaise with the representatives of the member states, the EU institutions and all shades of opinion in the Convention. And on that basis to broker compromises on the critical issues. Giscard brought his distinctive style to the proceedings, his own way of brokering deals. Even more than that, he was determined to impose an agenda, in so far as this was possible, and at the very least to be proactive rather than merely reactive.[7] His patrician persona exuded both confidence and authority, based on his considerable knowledge of the issues, a 'well honed personal perspective of what could be achieved'. Above all, he exhibited a 'a keen sense of timing', a way of stage-managing affairs to ensure that all the key issues would be tackled, and with the best chance of them being resolved.[8]

More mundane reasons, too, explain his success in harnessing the Convention to his own ends. The presidency team had the distinct advantage of being small in number, with the president having the exclusive prerogative of summarising the critical discussions. Even if *conventionnels* had been inclined to challenge Giscard over his handling of key issues, there were too many differences amongst them to successfully carry it off. They faced other handicaps too: insufficient time to assimilate the plethora of official documentation, and too many of them with insufficient knowledge of how the EU actually works. *Conventionnels* tended to rely instead on the presidency's 'backbone' briefings, summaries and background papers as their primary source of information.[9] All of this strengthened Giscard's hand and enhanced his authority overall. The only real resistance to Giscard's leadership, and even then barely effective, came from a group of some 16 MEPs who wanted radical changes in EU governance, though in the end were too divided over their own priorities to have an impact.[10]

The rules of procedure when they were eventually published confirmed the praesidium as power-broker, with the exclusive right to determine the agenda order, and with the president permitted to use his considerable personal authority to resolve deadlocks and broker compromises.[11] Some *conventionnels* criticised this top-down approach, claiming that it compromised the Convention's democratic credentials, but to no avail.[12] The presidency ran the show from the start, vetting the agenda, determining the composition of the working groups, providing the documentation – working papers and background briefings – though usually only after due consultation on technical matters with Commission officials. The technical assistance provided by the secretariat operating directly under the president's aegis shaped plenary discussions, and as such largely determined its outcomes.

Much was made before the Convention met and thereafter about its democratic credentials, following the precedent of the rights convention.[13] But in fact, this Convention had much less discretion than its forerunner.[14] Nevertheless, its proceedings were more accessible and certainly more transparent than any IGC, with plenaries held in public and on the record, all documents and plenary records available for public scrutiny and without restriction on the Convention's website. Plenaries were broadcast on the EU's EBS satellite channel, and, as the Laeken Declaration had required, all important documents were translated into each of the EU's 11 languages. Moreover, contributions from the floor were permitted in any language and published in all of the languages in which they were submitted.

This was quite different from the way IGCs go about their business. But there were limits, too, to the deliberative ideal. Transparency, for instance, did not extend to all praesidium meetings, where much of substance was not merely discussed but actually settled. Neither did it extend to the important business transacted by the presidency or by the secretariat. And whereas working group documents were published online, it was left to the discretion of group chairs to decide whether to open their sessions to a wider audience.[15] Furthermore, the accession countries were for the most part excluded from making any real contribution to proceedings, though they petitioned for parity with EU15. The fact that the presidium did permit summary notes of the plenary sessions to be translated by the national representatives was hardly compensation.[16] Neither was the belated concession to allow representatives from the candidate countries to address plenaries in their native tongue, a practice first used in the rights convention, where it was seen as one way of facilitating access for NGOs.[17]

Although the Convention was more accessible than an IGC, it was hardly a model of the deliberative democracy anticipated by some *conventionnels*.[18] Government representatives working in the praesidium and through the presidency largely ran the show, building strategic intergovernmental coalitions on the key issues, much as they do in IGCs.[19] The sheer range and complexity of the issues and the time constraints imposed on individual interventions in plenaries was hardly conducive to reflexive discourse, let alone to the free play of ideas.[20] This was some way removed from the Laeken commitment to a '"broadly based" conversation'.[21] Moreover, proceedings were stage-managed. Debate was hardly spontaneous, and the recommendations that came from it tended to reflect the presidium's proposals, themselves shaped in the main by Giscard's team, and based more often than not on the documents circulated amongst *conventionnels* by the secretariat. As for the style of these proceedings, *conventionnels* too often resorted to reading out 'prefabricated statements without any reference to previous contributions from their colleagues'.[22]

Plenaries usually followed the same pattern, a discussion of position papers submitted by the secretariat, followed by a more detailed review of available options in the working parties, with a further plenary session to consider their report. Plenaries were infrequent, and when they did occur, handicapped by their unwieldy size; by and large they proved to be incapable of translating their undoubted 'enthusiasm for the [constitutional] task' into effective influence.[23] The presidency directed, or as critics saw it manipulated, plenary sessions, deciding how much time to allow for discussion, who was called to speak and in what order and responding in person to interventions from the floor. The praesidium's procedural revision (March 2002) did little to allay concern about such manipulation.[24] The plenary of February 2003 that discussed the praesidium's first 16 draft treaty articles illustrates these procedural shortcomings. The praesidium published its draft articles, with written comments and amendments tabled from every side. However, the very range of these proposals, their technical complexity, and not least the limited time-frame for discussing them, merely served to inflate the presidency's influence. The praesidium was formally charged with steering the agenda, but its sessions were conducted *in camera*, and even when minutes were posted on the Convention website they were 'not particularly illuminating'.[25]

Divisions on all the really important and even on lesser issues precluded the collegiality that might have made it a rival to Giscard. For that reason, the praesidium simply failed to give an independent lead, and resorted to issuing bland summaries lacking the sort of inspiration that might appeal directly to *conventionnels*. For their part, *conventionnels* were required to signal interventions one week in advance by means of a 'blue card' system, and were limited to only one minute, hardly conducive to meaningful debate, let alone to forensic scrutiny. And though plenaries did meet more frequently as the Council-imposed deadline for submitting a draft treaty approached, they nevertheless remained inchoate affairs. Too often, 'the real work [was] done behind closed doors, in the praesidium', leaving the plenary merely 'to acclaim the result'.[26]

The presidency was the key player throughout. Giscard avoided outright diktat, permitting *conventionnels* to request the praesidium to add matters of their own choosing as additional points to the agenda, one way of heading off rebellion from the floor. *Conventionnels* were more successful on the informal level, lobbying members of the working groups, where there were real debates about EU governance, and with informative contributions from government offices, the political parties, academia, think-tanks, special interest groups and even from representatives of civil society. Some of these exchanges were 'on the record', but for the most part it was *ad hoc* and informal activity, an unscripted and mostly unrecorded trade in ideas that relied as much on interpersonal dynamics as it did on the intellectual cogency or persuasiveness of the case *per se*.[27] Some *conventionnels* also used informal contacts with praesidium members to get their views across, hoping that these might somehow reach Giscard.[28] Informality was a useful political resource for fostering what Giscard chose to call 'the Convention spirit'. The avoidance of formal plenary votes contributed to this *esprit*, but in reality it strengthened Giscard's hand more than it facilitated democratic deliberation, for subsequent interpretations of what was said were very much based on Giscard's own reading of these exchanges.

## The 'convention spirit'

Consensus is the preferred way of reaching decisions in a deliberative forum, though consensus is conveniently imprecise, as much a matter of interpretation as concrete fact. And though Giscard made much of what he described as the 'Convention spirit', many *conventionnels* believed this to be mostly rhetoric, a convenient cover for his own strong convictions about what a European Constitution should or indeed could be, the very single-mindedness that drove him to impose his own preferences.[29] Giscard set out his own vision from the start, reminding *conventionnels* in his inaugural address that they were not participating on their own account but as representatives of their institutions. Not, however, as delegates mandated to follow a party or institutional line, but charged instead with thinking about what was 'best for Europe'. To this end, he eschewed unnecessary protocol that might cramp deliberative style, preferring to tackle the issues head-on, with the presidency seeking to reconcile contentious views, to foster the fabled 'Convention spirit'.[30] Note-taking was forbidden in the interests of candid debate, as was formal voting, for the same reason, so as to minimise adversarialism and facilitate compromise. The praesidium voted only as a last resort, most notably at the very end of the Convention, when impasse threatened the ultimate prize of a draft treaty. On the face of it, what seemed to be genuinely deliberative endeavour was in reality something quite different. By leading from the front, rallying the *conventionnels* behind the idea of being constitutional founders, Giscard set the tone for what was to follow.[31] He certainly operated on the assumption that *conventionnels* mostly shared his broad mission to reach agreement on a constitutional treaty, rather than merely handing on to the IGC a wish list of *ad hoc* reforms. From the outset he wanted nothing less than an agreement that would 'open the way towards a Constitution for Europe', to deliver a *fait accompli* that Europe's political leaders would find difficult to unravel in the IGC.[32] He manipulated the agenda to that end.[33] A loosely drafted so-called 'non-paper' issued from vice-president Amato's office in June 2002 confirmed the objective as a 'Foundational Treaty'.[34] Giscard convinced the presidium that, though an ambitious goal, it was achievable.[35] The presidium fell in behind this objective,[36] as did the Commission, another key actor.[37]

Momentum grew behind the idea of a fully-fledged Constitution as *conventionnels* bought into Giscard's argument that this was the best, indeed the only way to bring influence to bear on the governments at the forthcoming IGC.[38] A group of *conventionnels* and alternates formally proposed a motion calling on the Convention to prepare a Constitutional Treaty, requesting the Commission to prepare a text for discussion at the plenary scheduled for October 2002, to be based on proposals from both *conventionnels* and from leading academics.[39] Giscard's role here was significant. His gravitas and self-assurance, the authority invested in his office by the governments who had appointed him, together with his considerable skill as a political 'fixer', confirmed his undoubted leadership, though he was far from being 'fully in control of the political dynamics of either the praesidium or of the convention as a whole'.[40]

Nevertheless, Giscard did give a powerful lead throughout, showing himself capable of settling differences between quarrelsome parties, a role that suited his patrician style. Giscard is hardly a natural democrat, neither is he modest. Indeed, he was motivated at least as much by a personal ambition to 'make history' as by any conviction about the virtues of deliberative democracy. He simply assumed that his intention to be a founding father of a constitutionalised EU was shared by at least most of the parties represented at the Convention, and certainly by all those that mattered.[41] It was clear from the outset that he was pushing his own agenda, and that 'consensus' as he understood the term 'stood for "mainstream opinion" ... as interpreted by the praesidium', but in fact by the president himself.[42] Telling here is the observation of a leading journalist who covered the Convention, who writes that Giscard, 'after an animated [plenary] debate ... uttered the two words "*Je constat*", which roughly translates as "I determine that ..." before announcing there was indeed a consensus. He declared the rules accepted and the squabbling subsided.'[43] And while he did not have an entirely free hand he did have powerful allies, and this determined his strategy, ensuring that throughout the proceedings he would be better informed about, altogether more sympathetic to the preferences of the leading member states than he was to those of smaller states, or those of the supranational institutions.

Dominance over proceedings is of course hardly diktat, and Giscard was obliged to trim and compromise in order to keep things on track, and even to maintain his overall authority. Timely concessions were required to realise the ultimate prize, a fully-fledged constitutional treaty, and this was by no means a guaranteed outcome at the outset.[44] Considerable political resources notwithstanding, he failed to carry some of his own proposals. Neither the praesidium nor the plenaries were entirely compliant. There were some politicians of note to be reckoned with, both in the praesidium and in the plenaries, not least MEPs and government representatives who persistently lobbied on critical policy and institutional issues in a way that the presidency could hardly ignore. The presidency had to be on its mettle throughout, ready to make its case, and in the process to concede some ground in both the praesidium and the plenaries, though this was more the exception than the rule. He was obliged, for instance, to accept the widely supported demand for a working group on social issues, and even to include a proposal from federalists to merge the EU's three pillars, thereby weakening the firm boundaries between the supranational and intergovernmental domains. And he was required, too, to abandon his own idea to rename the EU, as he was his idea of holding a joint congress of MEPs and national MPs.[45] These compromises notwithstanding, an objective assessment of Giscard's role would confirm his considerable personal influence and his command of proceedings. There is widespread acknowledgement from those closest to events that he made good use of the authority invested in his office 'to push the agenda and ambitions of the Convention ... beyond some governments' comfort zones'.[46]

Giscard was the Convention's pre-eminent figure, and he had few reservations about using his position, manipulating the agenda to accommodate his own view of what was required for a constitution that would be taken seriously rather than something to be overridden or dismantled by the following IGC. The clearest example of his tactical savvy came with his decision to postpone discussion of the critical institutional issues so as to prevent the Convention becoming 'bogged down in a political confrontation between ... two grand designs' for the EU, designs that have shadowed the project from the beginning. Whether his gamble paid off here is debatable. On one side are those who shared his view that delay on these issues was essential for building trust and goodwill on less controversial issues, before tackling the big issues.[47] But some critics have pointed out that as a direct consequence of this delay these important and politically awkward 'constitutional' issues were squeezed into an impossibly limited time-frame right at the end of proceedings, and as such unduly rushed. The general view, however, of those closest to events is that, in the end, his single-mindedness did pay dividends. Assisted by two politically astute deputies, Giscard ensured that the Convention did deliver a draft treaty, and within the allotted time-limit. In the end, a majority of *conventionnels* were prepared to accept his challenge 'to be remembered among the "founding fathers"'.[48]

## Political dynamics

Matters are rather more straightforward in IGCs. There are fewer participants for one thing, so the fault-lines are both less and more clear-cut, with fewer constituencies to be accommodated. Negotiations are also rather easier to stage because participants sit around one conference table, whereas *conventionnels* were both more numerous and came from a wider range of institutional locations.[49] The Nice IGC, for example, had divided along only two cleavages: on the one side, participants who preferred to strengthen the Union's institutions, ranged against those who defended the status quo; and another discernible, if less ideologically charged, division between the larger and smaller member states.[50] The fundamental rights convention, too, had been more straightforward, with a much narrower range of participants because focused on the particular issue of the content and legal status of the Charter on fundamental rights.[51]

The Convention had none of these organisational advantages. Its agenda was more eclectic, and multiple constituencies made for shifting coalitions on the various issues.[52] The logics of multilateral bargaining are invariably complicated. Even with careful preparation and good intelligence participants lack full knowledge of other actors' motivations and preferences. As game theory illustrates, an added complication is that participants in international forums are adept at concealing their true preferences, disguising their minimal demands so as to improve their bargaining position, the point at which they will 'settle'.[53] Indeed, the 'game' here is far from being a rational exercise, with some actors not even clear about their own preferences, 'and the situation changes unpredictably with the dynamics of the negotiations where written and oral proposals are floated around the table by all the participants at frequent intervals'.[54] This same commentator has described EU negotiating logics as follows: 'Treaty reform negotiations are often, despite extensive preparations at both the national and EU-level, poorly defined negotiating situations, with national representatives possessing incomplete knowledge of their own preferences and those of other actors, and details of the multitude of complex issues on the agenda.'[55]

This was precisely the problem in the Convention. The praesidium received some 1,087 proposed amendments to the first 16 draft articles, which meant that few if any *conventionnels* at any stage had 'a fully synoptic view of the state-of-play'.[56] In these circumstances it is difficult for participants to identify in advance feasible compromises from amongst the multiple, competing and amended bargaining positions, and working out possible trade-offs between them is invariably time-consuming. This is routine fare in EU negotiations, with actors locked into a permanent game with no exits, and where their expectation is not to settle for less than critical domestic audiences expect from them.

The variety of opinions and the range of institutional interests represented in the Convention actually strengthened Giscard's hand, enabling him to mediate between competing interests, playing off one against another, to steer a course that suited his own preferences, ably abetted by the 'flexible and hard working' secretariat which was far 'better organised than the presidium'.[57] He was assisted in the task of securing a compromise by representatives from the national parliaments, by far the largest single group in the plenaries. The expectation that these national parliamentarians would simply back their national interest proved to be unfounded. Many of them did display a commendable independence of mind, some even resisting political pressure from their governments and party leaders at home, or from the domestic media, to support particular national preferences. But there were limits to their autonomy. In fact, most of them behaved much like ministers do in IGCs, displaying a more combative nationalism when talking for domestic consumption to their own media, whilst being more flexible in actual negotiations.[58] Significant presence by governments in the Convention was bound to impact on the way things worked. Governments were much better represented there compared to the rights convention, with two government vice-presidents, three first-rank ministers, three junior ministers and one senior official, bolstered by two MEPs, a lawyer and three academics who represented their governments.

At the outset, some governments saw the Convention as merely a talking shop, and were content to hold fire until the 'real' negotiations began in the IGC. When they realised, however, that the Convention was actually determined to write a Constitution they changed tack. Those governments that had not already done so, appointed representatives with greater seniority, authorised to speak (and negotiate) on behalf of their national interest. Greece, Latvia and Slovenia for instance raised the seniority of their representation, and Spain even promoted one of its senior *conventionnels*, Ana Palacio, to the post of foreign minister. Germany drafted in Foreign Minister Joschka Fischer, and France appointed Foreign Minister Dominique de Villepin. For the most part, the member states made their representation count, with timely interventions at every stage, cultivating the presidency in order to get their own ideas on to the agenda. Chirac, in a speech delivered on the occasion of the fortieth anniversary of the Elysée Treaty of Franco-German reconciliation made clear that the leading governments were intent on pressing their own agenda.[59] Germany followed suit, Fischer informing a plenary session that 'anything that is not settled within the Convention will not be settled elsewhere'.[60] Aware that this was no mere side-show, governments raised their diplomatic game soon enough.[61]

As governments began to take the Convention more seriously, so *conventionnels* representing national parliaments became resolved not to let the side down. As one observer saw it: 'There is no doubt that Convention members did actually represent their countries. Preparation for Convention meetings did not take place in a vacuum; there was careful consultation at home.' This much was made clear when the really critical issues came to the fore, so that 'the further the Convention progressed, the more clearly the national dimension began to emerge in the performances of the members'. In the early stages interventions were recorded merely as submissions by individuals. But once politically sensitive issues were broached, interventions by official national representatives were attributed as such.[62] This marked a shift in Convention logics from a deliberative forum to an arena for negotiating between national preferences, and one confirmed by the promotion of Ana Palacio to the position of foreign minister. Even before her preferment she saw the Convention in much the same way as her prime minister, José María Aznar. And though denying any mandated instructions from Madrid, she did confirm that Aznar had communicated to her his preferences on security, freedom and justice policy, as well as on 'the maintenance of the *acquis communautaire*, the completion of the single market and the need to raise the Union's profile in the world'. This candid admission was hardly exceptional, for all of the senior ministers who represented their governments in the Convention spoke up for their national interests, and most brought with them motivated and capable national officials to help them make their case.[63]

In these circumstances, the Convention looked much less like a deliberative forum and more a surrogate IGC.[64] There was of course wide-ranging debate, much of it on the record, but this in itself did not amount to anything remotely resembling a democratic conversation about Europe's future governance.[65] It was mostly inward-directed discussion, entirely remote from the wider audience beyond Brussels. The dominant voices here as much as in any IGC were those of powerful vested interests, with the public's voice barely heard, if at all.[66] As one commentator sees it, it is 'hard to justify [the Convention] as a democratic innovation' precisely because its affairs were steered throughout by a small coterie of vested interests, orchestrated by a presidency and secretariat more favourable to governments than to other interests.[67] The most convincing proof of this is in the choice of language used in these 'constitutional' debates, and eventually in the Constitutional Treaty itself, a lexicon that was 'still very close to that of the existing treaties'.[68] In the view of Clive Archer, 'the rather technical nature of the new draft, especially with its threefold structure and its still very legalistic language', simply failed to reach the audience beyond the Convention.[69]

## Making the constitution: pre-drafting phases

The Convention's work occurred in distinct phases. It began with a 'listening phase' to review the range of issues facing the EU at the beginning of the new century. This was followed by a 'study' phase to address the particular questions identified at Laeken, and on that basis to establish a framework for drafting a constitutional treaty. The 'listening' phase occupied the opening four months, providing an opportunity as Giscard saw it for the Convention to find its own distinctive working style. It focused on general issues relating to the Union's future, more concerned with procedural than with substantive matters.[70] The first question before the Convention – 'What do you expect from the European Union?' – reviewed the Union's role in a changing international order, its capacity to be a credible and effective international actor. The plenary session that convened on 15–16 April 2002 discussed these issues and reached some general, though by no means unanimous conclusions about how to implement a more effective common external policy. Subsequent plenaries in late April and May 2002 addressed the matter of EU competencies, of who should do what and at what level of EU governance.

Giscard had considerable presence in the plenaries, whether directly or through his team, notwithstanding complaints from some *conventionnels*, notably MEPs keen to tackle the critical institutional issues and concerned that the listening phrase was taking up valuable time that should be used instead to discuss 'real' constitutional issues. But Giscard held firm, convinced that a gradual induction was indispensable for a successful outcome. By no means were all *conventionnels* aware of the EU's complexities, so that dealing with less controversial issues first was one way, as he saw it, of flattening the learning curve, a useful opportunity for national parliamentarians and other *conventionnels* outside the EU loop to acquire familiarity with its arcane rules and complicated procedures. Building confidence was part of his plan, and it paid dividends. Over time a sense of common purpose did emerge. Discussions at every level were 'more focused and interactive' as *conventionnels* learned how to operate more effectively, 'whether in one-off coalitions to present documents to the Convention, and writing open letters to the chairman, or caucusing before or around the meetings of the Convention in longer run groups'.[71]

By sheer force of personality Giscard instilled a climate which encouraged *conventionnels* to seek agreement, even on the most contentious issues. Amongst the issues discussed at this stage were the following: the need for a more effective external policy; concerted action on cross-border crime; better co-ordination of macro-economic policies; and clearer demarcation of subsidiarity. The routine that emerged did much to foster co-operation, a commitment from most *conventionnels* to making things work. Reassured thus that the Convention could indeed rise to the challenge of drafting a complete version of a constitutional treaty, Giscard confidently launched the second, or working phase establishing specialised working groups to deliberate more specific and controversial issues. There was nevertheless a price to be paid for this carefully managed procedure, for it considerably reduced the time available for dealing with the important institutional questions to barely 4 out of the 16 months available. And as the months passed the timetable became log-jammed, with too many important issues crammed into a limited timeframe, compromising in turn the deliberative tone by increasing the praesidium's (in effect, the presidency's) leverage, its scope for stage-managing outcomes.[72]

The Convention embarked on the 'study phase' in July 2002 after the praesidium had launched the first of the working groups.[73] These groups were essential for the praesidium's work on drafting an outline constitutional treaty, a task aptly described by vice-president Giuliano Amato as setting 'the building blocks for the final product'.[74] But in fact it was Giscard rather than the other praesidium members who directed these proceedings. He imposed his own agenda on the working groups and their role was a secondary one. In fact, by the time Giscard published what was in effect his own first version of draft articles on 28 October 2002 only two of the working groups (on subsidiarity and the EU's legal personality) had actually submitted their own reports. The way the presidency handled the agenda suggests collusion between the key players as the important issues began to come to the fore. There was a marked contrast, for instance, between 'the excellent and lengthy documents' the secretariat produced for the early plenaries, and the more abbreviated papers it presented for the all-important January (2003) review of institutional questions.[75] Even the praesidium's role was downgraded somewhat by the sheer force of Giscard's personality, his determination to steer the process, to lead from the front. The secretariat's detailed position papers on institutional issues were not even discussed by the praesidium as the Convention moved to discuss simplifying the legislative process, foreign policy, freedom, and security and justice policy, followed (February 2003) by the much less controversial social and regional issues. Significant, too, as the more politically sensitive agenda items came to the fore is the fact that the provision of information came less from the secretariat – required by its mandate to serve the entire Convention – and more from sources with a vested interest in the outcome, especially from the diplomatic offices of the leading member states. The most notable intervention by far here was the Franco-German position paper that proposed, amongst other things, twin presidencies, making a signal contribution to the debate that in the absence of any clear steer from other Convention sources framed all subsequent discussion.[76]

After the 'listening' and 'study' phases, countless words, much rhetoric and hundreds of written amendments the drafting process began, culminating in a first substantive version of most, though not quite all of the draft treaty articles. But this occurred only at the end of May 2003, leaving an almost impossibly tight time-frame of barely two weeks for further debate, if the Convention was to meet the final deadline of presenting a draft treaty to the Thessaloniki summit scheduled for 20 June 2003.[77] This outcome was a direct consequence of the presidency's decision to retain control of these most politically awkward issues, in close consultation with representatives of the leading member states. Postponement until almost the end of proceedings meant that these politically sensitive issues were dealt with in unseemly haste, and this resulted in sloppy drafting of some of these most critical articles. Worse even than that, the drafting procedure lacked proper transparency, too much of this over-hasty bargaining taking place 'behind closed doors and in corridors'.[78]

## The drafting process

The drafting process was divided into distinct stages, each one directed by the praesidium/presidency. John Kerr and his secretariat team, in close consultation with Giscard, began by drafting a paper outlining the important 'constitutional' questions: the institutions, decision-making procedures, the principles and goals of the Union and citizenship rights. These tentative proposals reflected Giscard's caution, and as some critics saw it his conservative instincts, a reticence that was reinforced by Kerr's circumspection, the natural reflex of any career civil servant. Giscard made no secret of his preference for a full-fledged constitutional treaty, a single text but in two parts: one addressing constitutional issues, the other dealing with EU policies. In the event, pressure from governments ensured that the Constitutional Treaty would also include an unwieldy, almost encyclopaedic catalogue of policy competencies, as well as the Charter of Fundamental Rights as a separate Part II. It was clear from the tone of Giscard's public utterances and press statements that, regardless of his admiration for the Community method, Monnet's singular legacy, he was determined to resist any significant increase in supranationalism.[79] Giscard's preference throughout was for 'a union of nation states', though one with closely co-ordinated policies, and some common competencies organised on quasi-federal lines.[80]

### Giscard's 'skeleton': the preliminary draft, October 2002

The presidency's imprimatur was apparent in the preliminary three-part draft of the Constitution presented to the October 2002 plenary on institutions and policies. This so-called skeletal draft was, in some degree, a response to pressure from praesidium members to move things on from merely talking, and to actually begin drafting a European constitution. And though only a skeletal draft, it did confirm to *conventionnels* and governments alike that the Convention was finally in the business of constitution-making, even if this draft made clear that the objective was not a constitution *per se* but rather a constitutional treaty.[81] Both of these terms carry a distinctive and quite different meaning, reflecting long-standing differences about the purposes and not least the ultimate destination of European political union. Giscard was determined from the start to resist the federalist ambitions of some *conventionnels*, those who saw 'a constitution' as a landmark on the road to a European state.[82] In his introduction to the preliminary draft, Giscard was careful to describe the endeavour as a 'Draft Treaty establishing a Constitution for Europe', though 'the words "Constitution for Europe" [were] printed bigger and in bold'. Draft Article 1 referred accordingly to the administration of 'certain common competencies on a federal basis'. This sent a clear signal that all that was implied here was pooling some limited aspects of national sovereignty.[83] There could be no doubt from this intervention about Giscard's intentions regarding the present, or indeed the future state of this European Union. The draft confirmed that any action by the Union 'must be carried out in accordance with the provisions of the treaty, within the limits of the competencies conferred by the treaty', and that 'any competence not conferred by the Constitution rests with the member states'.[84] Giscard's 'skeleton', with the subsequent addition of a fourth part incorporating the Charter of fundamental rights became the basis for all subsequent drafts.

The closest the preliminary draft came to provoking controversy was on the issue of the Union's legal status, the current 'anomaly' whereby the three European communities (the EC, EURATOM and the former ECSC) each has a separate legal personality. The pillarised structure adopted at Maastricht had merely consolidated the problem, and though the issue was reviewed at Amsterdam it was not resolved there. Laeken had picked up the challenge, and proposed a review of the distinction between Union and Community, the pillarised structure adopted at Maastricht, on the grounds that this would make for more efficient governance, would simplify EU procedures, streamline decision-making and ensure a clearer delineation of competencies with the Union becoming a 'subject of international law'. The idea here was to provide an altogether firmer legal basis for the EU to conduct its international relations, permitting the Union to sign international treaties and endorse international conventions, to be accountable before international courts of law and permitted to join international organisations.[85] The working group on legal personality proposed a singular legal status in its report of October 2002, though it was left to the praesidium to settle the precise political and legal implications, with some governments alerted to a possible encroachment by the Union on their traditional foreign policy preogatives.[86] These issues were eventually resolved, but with governments more than ordinary *conventionnels* taking the lead in discussions.

The draft was on altogether firmer ground when it addressed the relatively 'soft' issues of common values and objectives, what the Union stands for and what it 'means' to its citizens. The question of values did subsequently become a matter for dispute, but at this stage few *conventionnels* demurred from the blandishments in draft Article 2 that iterated what 'Europeans' have in common: *inter alia*, respect for human dignity, rights, democracy, the rule of law and so on. Article 3 likewise listed standards for 'good governance' as these apply to any international regime: the protection of common values and the independence of the Union; the promotion of economic and social cohesion; strengthening the internal market and economic and monetary union; promoting high employment and social protection; environmental protection; facilitating technological and scientific development; setting up an area of liberty, security and justice; developing a common foreign and security/defence policies. These 'appropriate values', supposedly common to all Europeans, were never intended by Giscard to be anything more than benchmarks for EU membership, a normative gauge for mutual endeavour, and certainly not the indispensable requirements for constitutional patriotism, let alone for common European identity or demos.[87]

### *Putting flesh on bare bones: the praesidium's draft articles, January–February 2003*

The praesidium's steering group began early in 2003 to draft more detailed articles, using Giscard's draft as a template. By 16 February 2003 articles were in place on the Union's political character, its values and legal personality, its competencies and the rights of its citizens. Further draft articles were to follow – on the Union's finances, its democratic life, EU membership and relations with neighbouring states, ratification, legal continuity with previous treaties, and the geographical scope of the constitution – and confirmed by the plenary sessions prior to Easter 2003. This was mostly routine fare, with the contentious institutional questions and the matter of foreign and defence policy postponed until almost the last minute, precisely because they were controversial. But by this stage it was the leading governments who were calling the tune, and it was a tune most *conventionnels* had hardly anticipated at the outset. Until the Athens European Council (16 April 2003), *conventionnels* had assumed that Part I of the final draft would comprise the main constitutional provisions, Part II would contain policies and legal bases, and Part III would cover the general provisions.

After the Athens Council refused to extend the Convention's term this schedule was revised by Giscard's team. When Part I of the first complete draft was published on 26 May 2003 it contained the constitutional text, but the Charter of Fundamental Rights was now incorporated as an entirely new Part II, with the policies and legal bases renumbered as Part III, and the general provisions becoming a new Part IV. The process of bargaining and trade-offs that usually characterises EU treaty politics turned the Constitution into a convoluted and cumbrous document that was bound to baffle citizens, but just as much many of the national parliamentarians who would have to ratify it. Giscard's original plan for a streamlined two-part constitutional treaty had grown like Topsy into an unwieldy four-part treaty and this even before the really problematic institutional issue had been broached.

### The revised draft, May 2003

The Convention was almost a year into its work before these controversial institutional questions were seriously discussed, giving the leading member states time to position themselves, and not least to seize the initiative. And they were both motivated and well-placed to do so. France and Germany moved first, issuing a joint position paper in January 2003. Giscard responded with his own proposals for the institutions.[88] The European Council's refusal at Athens to extend the Convention's tenure prompted Giscard to take unilateral action, drafting the key articles himself with only the assistance of a small team of secretariat officials. This provoked *conventionnels* from smaller states to complain that he was acting at the behest of the *directoire*. The fact he got away with it shows just how deeply fractured was the Convention, and no less so the praesidium. This much became clear at the praesidium meeting on 22 May, where Spain's representative objected to Giscard's proposal to reopen the agreement reached at Nice on Council voting weights, seeing this as clear evidence that Giscard was giving primacy to the preferences of the big three. With this particular grievance out in the open all sorts of similar complaints surfaced, and not merely from the smaller states. The United Kingdom's praesidium representative, for instance, questioned some of the other changes agreed at Nice, including the distribution of seats in the European Parliament, and introduced the even more controversial question of whether smaller states should be deprived of their own commissioner.[89] Another contentious issue was security and foreign policy, its salience considerably heightened by the Iraq crisis. A group led by France and Germany determined to use this crisis to push for the inclusion of 'enhanced co-operation' in Part III of the draft treaty, a move intended to facilitate closer regional integration in security policy. This provoked in turn a predictably hostile reaction from some member states and candidate countries determined to resist a policy development likely to undermine NATO.[90]

The pattern here was plain to see: the more important the issue, the greater the prospect for controversy, the harder it was to be to close a deal. Mistrust was rife and even the reopening of those deals already closed became a distinct possibility. Agreements so carefully negotiated suddenly threatened to unravel, with praesidium members questioning Giscard's conduct at their 22–23 April meeting.[91] That meeting was crucial, for it threatened to derail the Convention, though in the event Giscard held his nerve, came into his own as an interlocutor, and was able to reconcile disparate views in a compromise final draft.[92] He was by now the pre-eminent figure, a presence felt at every level of proceedings, informal as much as formal, the linchpin of any outcome, not least because the praesidium was unable to overcome its own divisions, and simply failed to rise to the occasion by making common cause and presenting its own clear and unequivocal proposals. Assisted by the secretariat, Giscard had secured by this critical stage a 'virtual monopoly over the power of proposal'.[93] After a praesidium session lasting three days (21–24 May 2003), members agreed to Giscard's proposed revisions to Part I of the draft on institutional reforms, though it held out on the most contentious issues of voting weights and the distribution of parliamentary seats, not least because the governments themselves were so deeply divided on these issues.[94]

On the rather less controversial matter of external policy Giscard's deputy, Jean-Luc Dehaene, tried for a compromise by making some fairly radical proposals. These were based on the working groups' recommendations, and they took account of views expressed by *conventionnels* rather than merely accommodating the preferences of the big three.[95] Even so, it was a compromise the big three could live with. These proposals did endorse closer co-operation in foreign policy but did not weaken the principle of national self determination, proposing to increase 'the pressure on recalcitrant nations to work towards [external] policies that can be supported by all the states of the Union', whilst acknowledging the right of 'nation states, large and small' to '"walk away" from common foreign policy positions if they wish'.[96] The equally contentious matter of co-decision was settled by an agreement to extend the procedure to some 30 new policy areas, a modest extension most governments could live with. What was clear by this stage was that Giscard was actively engaged in orchestrating a trade-off between the leading member states on the most contentious issues, as with his decision to remove the word 'federal' from the Treaty, a concession to British sensibilities.[97]

The eventual outcome was a compromise, but compromise was what the endeavour was mostly all about. The presidency team worked hard for its success, though Giscard had powerful allies amongst the larger member states just as determined as he was to resist a radical agenda. He led from the front from the start, warning *conventionnels* of the risks of failure, pushing them to adopt flexible working arrangements. Just when momentum seemed to be flagging, energies dissipated by endless squabbling over detail and principles, and with the deadline looming, he called for renewed effort, demanding more frequent attendance, imposing additional *ad hoc* and interactive plenaries to settle outstanding issues. Informality was the key here and he used it to good effect, so as to overcome rooted objections, bypassing the formal plenaries which by now had become mostly 'lacklustre affairs'.[98] One close observer describes a lively nexus of 'informal cross cutting dining clubs of movers and shakers' that enabled 'ideas to flow, policies to crystallise and consensus to form'.[99] Again it was Giscard who was central to the process, organising and orchestrating *ad hoc* meetings between the political families, utilising these networks of 'contact groups that had sprung up in the Convention over the previous fifteen months, turning the corridors and bar near the plenary hall into hot beds of gossip and speculation'.[100]

Information was an essential resource in this process, with the secretariat manipulating communications, releasing or holding back documents as it saw fit so as to create a climate in which even the most partisan *conventionnels* 'would eventually settle for a compromise'.[101] The presidency set up small 'consensus-broking' groups to resolve the most difficult issues, with Giscard's team much in evidence as interlocutors and facilitators, reporting back to the praesidium on both points of progress and on sticking-points alike.[102] Giscard realised that *conventionnels* representing national parliamentarians, and especially the praesidium's government representatives, each concerned in their own way about loss of national sovereignty, were key to a successful outcome. Accordingly, he assigned his two vice-presidents to liaise with these constituencies: Dehaene with the parliamentarians and Amato with the government representatives. Above all, Giscard appealed directly to *conventionnels*, not least to their sense of history, issuing an almost irresistible challenge to them that 'if they want to be founding fathers, they will have to move. Otherwise, they will be founding failures.'[103]

The Commission, for its part, was largely a bystander during these events, evidence of its much diminished authority, hardly measuring up to Prodi's early boast that the Commission would make 'a full and enthusiastic contribution' to the proceedings, by 'drawing on all of its own experience and its expertise', to say nothing of his absurd promise of 'ice cream and fireworks for everybody'.[104] In reality, the Commission was mostly out of step with the principal constituencies, and too 'publicly identified with policies diametrically opposed to those of the praesidium'. In these circumstances, Prodi could hardly be expected to be an alternative mediator, let alone put himself forward as a rival to Giscard. The failure to carry its preference for one commissioner per member state was a measure of the Commission's reduced standing.[105] Even the Benelux countries, normally staunch in their support of the Commission as a kind of tribune for the rights of the smaller states, eventually endorsed the praesidium's proposal for a smaller college.[106] With the support of the big three member states, Giscard secured a timely compromise here, acknowledging the small states' claim to equal representation by proposing they retain 'their' commissioner for the duration of the Commission beginning its term in 2004. This was much less a victory for the smaller states than it seemed at the time, and a 'defeat' that the big three again could live with. Otherwise Giscard held firm to his original draft articles, especially in the critical areas of taxation and foreign policy, where he resisted demands from federalists for greater encroachment by the Union into domestic governance by replacing the unanimity procedure in these policy domains with QMV.

By spring 2003 Giscard felt sufficiently confident about the outcome to put a revised text of Part I of the draft constitutional treaty before the Convention

(26 May) for discussion.[107] A second catalogue of proposed articles, including the Charter on Fundamental Rights, was published as Part II, with Part III consisting of a catalogue of policies and their legal bases and the general and final provisions.[108] A final volume, Part IV, consisting of protocols and supplementary material[109] and incorporating an explanatory commentary and overview was published on 27 May.[110] This was in all but name the final draft Constitutional Treaty, and contained most of the proposals that had featured in earlier discussions, with the relatively minor adjustments described above. Agreement was nevertheless delayed by continuing dispute over the institutions, and by the emotive issue of the wording of the preamble, the part of any constitution that outlines what the European polity stands for.

The prospect of the Convention failing at the final hurdle was enough to concentrate the minds of all but the most recalcitrant *conventionnels*. Even those determined to hold out for concessions on their main sticking-points allowed themselves to be persuaded by Joschka Fischer's timely warning to the plenary session that the historic opportunity of making a European Constitution was slipping away, that those governments looking for a convenient excuse to denigrate the Convention as a failed experiment, to set aside its conclusions, would seize on impasse as their best hope.[111] The message made its mark and the final draft was agreed, albeit only at the eleventh hour, endorsed by the plenary on 30–31 May, only days before the concluding session. After two further days of frenetic discussions on the outstanding details of agreement personally supervised by Giscard and his team, he was able to triumphantly announce the fact of a draft Constitutional Treaty.

### Making history: the final draft treaty, June 2003

Giscard tabled the final version of a draft Constitutional Treaty on 12 June, and representatives from the main party families and the Convention's various groups, 'an extraordinary coalition of conventionnels representing governments, parliaments and the Commission, from left, right and centre of the political spectrum endorsed the text and the work of the Convention'. As one observer described the scene, a 'palpable sense of satisfaction suffused the plenary hall of the European Parliament building in Brussels as Convention members outbid each other to hail their achievements with statements that contrived to be sincere'.[112] It was a close call but by any standards a remarkable achievement, though hardly the historic breakthrough in the way the EU goes about its constitutional business that some *conventionnels* had anticipated at the outset. Nor was it entirely unanimous. A group of seven die-hard Eurosceptics who condemned the draft treaty as nothing less than a Trojan horse for federalism issued a minority report criticising it as a wholly inadequate response to Laeken's promise to make the EU more democratic, code in this Eurosceptical narrative for failing to bring about a European polity sufficiently responsive to the interests of governments, and one unaccountable to national electorates.

What they proposed instead was a 'Europe of Democracies', a wholly intergovernmental design.[113] But the draft treaty was hardly federalism *manqué*, whatever its detractors might say of it, but rather a typical EU fudge. The usual trade-off between competing ideas about European governance, the by now familiar bargain made between competing designs for European governance, a typical fusion of state-centric and federalist preferences, a balance of intergovernmental and supranational logics that has been the way of EC/EU treaties from the start.[114] To that extent, it followed a formula first utilised in the Treaty of Paris and repeated as a *sine qua non* of successful European treaty-making ever since, a treaty 'with which everyone could live'.[115] This much is patent from the wording of the final draft. The draft text acknowledged as fact that EU governance 'is rooted in dualities', and in no way sought to disturb this delicate balance of forces, but instead 'sets out to reconcile' them, to anchor this compromise more firmly in a new constitutional settlement. To that extent, the EU remains, in essence, what it has been from the beginning, 'a Union of states and citizens, a Union of the federal and intergovernmental where states both pool sovereignty and co-operate on policies'.[116] What emerged from the Convention then was very much business as usual, though in a somewhat tidier format.[117]

Not that this precluded hyperbole to mark the occasion, plaudits fittingly led by Joschka Fischer, who could claim to have launched the process with his Humboldt speech. Fischer described the Convention's achievement as nothing less than a bold step towards Europe's emergence as a global force, no doubt an oblique sideswipe at American neo-cons ever contemptuous of European 'pretensions' to be a political as much as an economic force in world affairs. In the circumstances, Fischer might be forgiven his proud boast that the Convention had 'demonstrated that, differences notwithstanding, there is not an old and a new Europe but a Europe of citizens and states, a Europe of freedom, a Europe of justice and a Europe of democracy: our Europe!'[118] Even *conventionnels* who had earlier expressed reservations about what might be achieved were overtaken by the sense of occasion. Ana Palacio, the foreign minister of a country that had resolutely objected to the revision of the Nice formula on Council voting weights and would soon return to the issue, praised the process, if not quite its outcome, as 'a legal revolution without precedent', and one that has finally put 'an end to nineteenth century diplomacy where we signed such things behind closed doors'.[119]

Whether this is so is debatable, but this was not the moment for carping. More than anyone Giscard was entitled to savour the occasion, and he was hardly averse to indulging in *amour propre*, referring in his concluding remarks to an epic journey, a constitutional odyssey no less, that has 'piloted our vessel, sometimes through the mists, sometimes through the waves [but] the important thing is our ship has reached port'.[120] And who could deny him his moment, for there was much to be pleased about, the Convention's efforts were prodigious. Over some 16 months and after 26 plenary sessions, *conventionnels* had made 1,850 individual interventions, contributed 386 written inputs to these plenaries and 773 to the various working groups, and some 6,000 further proposals for amendments. The 50 praesidium meetings had laboured tirelessly to iron out the many differences, both of detail and principle, as they produced by degrees the draft articles, all of them requiring debate, compromise and synthesis. The presidency and the secretariat orchestrated this outcome with consummate diplomatic skill, and with determination to see the job through, though with some subterfuge and not a little political cunning.

Giscard was able to present the outcome of these considerable efforts, a draft Constitutional Treaty, on schedule to the Thessaloniki Council on 20 June 2003, with the clear recommendation that it be used as the basis for IGC negotiations. On that occasion, he reminded the assembled heads of government and state that 'the closer you stick to our text, which has been discussed at great length, the lighter will be your task'.[121] There was still some outstanding business to be settled, the Convention reconvening early in July to deal with some 1,687 further amendments tabled to the articles in Part III of the draft treaty, again with a wholly inadequate time-frame for thorough debate. Some important issues were even revisited at this late stage, for instance the sensitive a matter of QMV on foreign and security policy and social and fiscal policy, but these matters were not as such reopened. The final version of the draft treaty was handed on to the Italian presidency (18 July 2003) prior to the start of the IGC.[122]

The venture was by any standards a remarkable achievement, marking a shift in the way the EU goes about its constitutional business. And for optimists its conclusions amounted at the very least to 'a significant improvement on what currently exists', and possibly 'a harbinger of better governance'.[123] Critics, however, maintained that it had missed the key target set at Laeken, failing to bring the Union closer to the citizen.[124] At almost 400 pages the Constitutional Treaty matched the world's longest constitution (India's), and was some 10 times longer than the American Constitution. It was hardly the cogent, accessible 'shirt pocket' guide anticipated by Giscard at the start, and moreover was written in 'inelegant and ungainly' Euro-speak that simply failed to resonate with the public imagination, and hardly matched the vision 'of a spanking new constitutional treaty that many want'.[125]

These are pertinent criticisms, but by no means the full story. The Convention did at least show another way of conducting the business of European treaty reform, broadening participation, however modestly, to include other members of the Union's political class, and conducting its business on the record and in the public domain, though again hardly matching the truly deliberative procedure anticipated at Laeken. For that reason alone, the Convention set a benchmark by which all future constitutional revision will be measured. But in the event, it flattered to deceive. The impasse that overtook the Constitutional Treaty has recently seen the Union's political leaders revert to type, meeting in conclave and reclaiming their prerogative as 'masters of the treaties'. This has led to a new treaty, but whether the public will acquiesce in this return to the old way of doing things remains to be seen. Criticism of the Constitution will not be so easily set aside. It may well be that the real legacy of the Convention on the Future of Europe is not so much the Constitutional Treaty, or its pale imitation the Lisbon Treaty, but rather an expectation from deep within the Union's body politic that in future the important governance questions are a matter not just for the 'princes' but must somehow 'involve the people'.[126]

# 6 Reforming the European institutions

## Towards constitutional finality?

The EU's institutional architecture is uniquely hybrid, combining both intergovernmental and supranational aspects, a legacy of the founding bargain which had sought to reconcile quite different views of European integration within the Community's institutional architecture. The prospect of an enlargement, whereby six states would account for some three-quarters of the population, was bound to complicate these institutional arrangements. As Hughes sees it, 'until now the EU has managed successfully, despite occasional tensions, to reach an institutional and organisational balance that took account of both sovereignty and size'. Whereas an enlarged EU of 27 states was bound to raise 'serious challenges as to how to re-engineer that balance'.[1] Negotiations on these matters stalled after tense exchanges at the Biarritz and Nice European Councils, and subsequently at the Seville Council in June 2002.[2] Yet the issue remained on the table. Reforming the institutions so as to improve their capacity for efficient decision-making was one of the objectives agreed at Laeken; indispensable if the EU is to adjust to a historic enlargement.

The fruit of this endeavour was the draft Constitutional Treaty, seen by those who negotiated it as a landmark in the development of a European constitutional order. By no means the founding or 'constitutional moment' dreamt of by federalists, it was nevertheless a positive step towards resolving some of the governance issues 'left over' from previous attempts to reform the treaties. The Constitutional Treaty did achieve some of the Laeken objectives, including simplification of EU governance and even a modest improvement in democracy.[3] These reforms were timely yet hardly designed to make EU governance more accessible or accountable to its citizens. On that score, a constitutional settlement that brings about clearer demarcation of institutional power remains as elusive as ever. What Henry Kissinger once called 'creative ambiguity' has characterised EU governance from the start, caught as it is between the pursuit of common purpose on the one hand and the enduring interests of the member states on the other. The key to reform in this 'mixed' polity is to avoid upsetting the unique 'institutional quadrilateral, by giving one institution considerably more (or less) powers than any of the others'.[4]

As soon as the Convention began to consider institutional matters, it became apparent that any dramatic overhaul of the institutional architecture simply lacked political support where it mattered. The politically sensitive nature of the issue persuaded Giscard to delay discussion of the distribution of institutional power, with the exception of the proposal for a European foreign minister and consideration of a legislative council. No papers relating to these matters were put before the praesidium, other than secretariat working papers broadly outlining various options.[5] Taking their cue from Giscard, and on the basis of advice from Sir John Kerr, the secretary-general, the praesidium declined even to set up a working group on the institutions, leaving these matters to subsequent plenary sessions. The first of these plenary meeting took place only in January 2003, almost a year after the Convention began its work. Meanwhile, discussion on these crucial issues was mostly informal, taking place 'in corridors and behind closed doors', confined to 'the periphery of the Convention sessions for the whole of 2002'.[6] And even when these issues did eventually come to the fore, the presidency stage-managed the discussion, determined to impose an agenda that reflected the preferences of the leading member states. Once these issues came up for consideration, the big three member states with Giscard's implicit support pulled rank, preferring to settle matters amongst themselves outside the Convention's formal framework, a matter 'not so much [of] the IGC happening within the Convention but the IGC happening in parallel on the outside'.[7]

The Convention has been criticised in some quarters for failing to deliver the constitutional make-over anticipated in the Laeken Declaration. One critic has complained thus:

> The original good intentions have been lost along the route. The final document is more than 300 pages long and written in legalese. It is repetitive, turgid and often utterly incomprehensible. The most intelligible part – the Charter of Fundamental Rights – is misleading. Clauses have been attached to ensure that it only applies to EU laws, not to national laws. It's all 'Alice in Wonderland' … in not a single area does the constitution return power to member states. In fact it centralises power in around 30 different areas of policy. Far from being a broad-brush document establishing basic principles, it delves into the minutiae of policy areas that are the domain of the nation state.[8]

This is damning criticism, but criticism rooted in a fundamental misconception about what is possible in European constitutional politics. Rewriting the European treaties as a single text, though indispensable for consolidating and no less for simplifying the Union's constitutional order, is hardly the same as Joschka Fischer's opening call for constitutional *finalité*. To resolve once and for all the competing preferences for governance and institutional power is simply impracticable in this contested polity. Indeed, many political pundits are doubtful about whether the EU can ever be constitutionalised in the usual meaning of the term.[9] And the demand made here to revert to the status quo ante, to repatriate powers back to the member states or, indeed, the opposite reflex for a federal union, are equally unrealistic. After all, this is a polity that not only balances quite different ideas about the purposes of European integration, but one that also lacks any clear idea as to its eventual geographical reach.[10]

The Constitution has been criticised from every side of the political spectrum: federalists expressed disappointment at a timid exercise in tidying the treaties, whereas Eurosceptics saw insidious supranationalism eroding ancient sovereignties; the left regarded it as a neo-liberal charter that puts markets before people, whilst conservatives found fault with excessive regulation. Where the EU is concerned the truth is always somewhere in between such extreme and too often ideologically contrived viewpoints. The Convention was never intended nor could it remotely aspire to be Europe's Philadelphia, a *constituante* assembly presiding over the founding moment of a European federal polity. The Convention was rather more about adapting institutions and revising decision-making procedures than it was about historic transformation. An attempt to 'improve the existing settlement but without disturbing the *acquis*', not least because the *acquis* symbolises 'both a remarkable historical achievement and hard fought bargains amongst the states'. And for that very reason, as Clive Church has observed, 'it is very hard to move away from it without destabilising the whole venture'. After all, the EU 'has had fifty years of *acquis* not just the eleven that the Americans had had'.[11]

This was not a fresh start, nor was it intended to be so by the governments who agreed to a constitutional refit at Laeken, but instead a thoroughgoing revision of governance and policy in an established polity facing mounting challenges. Seen from this minimalist perspective, the Constitutional Treaty was more success than failure, though as we shall see its failures were significant ones. In the estimation of one legal expert, there is good reason 'for treating that [constitutional outcome] not as a failure but rather as a positive development', in as much as any attempt to define the latest Treaty 'as a potential end-destination, at which core constitutional questions will be "settled", is at odds with the historical evolution of the Union'. And, by the same token, 'neglectful of a network of complex but largely inter-related devices for meeting in a more sophisticated fashion the perceived weaknesses of the Union than would be achieved through the adoption of a formal constitution and, ultimately, fundamentally incompatible with how it *should* be seen, as a Non-State actor which causes profound adaptation in the structures of the States that are members of it'.[12]

This pragmatic view of constitutional purpose prevailed, and with good reason, for it reflects political realities, the limits and constraints under which this multilevel polity operates. The Constitutional Treaty sought to balance these competing preferences for EU governance, and this in no whit diminishes its achievements, not least for improving decision-making. Whether the same can be said for communicating this sense of necessary reform to the citizen – and in a way they could grasp – is a different matter, and one that we shall return to later.

## Executive power: the presidency

Appropriately enough for a polity that combines intergovernmental with supranational logics, executive power in the EC/EU does not reside in one institution but is shared between the principal institutional actors: the Commission, the European Council, the General Affairs Council and latterly the High Representative responsible for managing the CFSP. This makes for complex governance at best, and at worst for confusion, in as much as the Union lacks government in the usual sense of the term. Consequently, 'it is neither apparent who carries out what function or who holds which competencies nor whom these different executives are accountable to'.[13] One of the Convention's main tasks was to more clearly map these power relations. To define the locus of executive power was central to this task, and debate here focused on three distinct, though related themes: the role and powers of the Council and Commission presidencies; the remit of their authority, notably whether and by what procedures incumbents are 'elected' to office; and the role and competencies of a proposed EU foreign minister, an office designed to enhance the Union's authority in international politics.

The issue of executive competence, and especially the rotation of the presidency, the office that manages day-to-day affairs of the Council of Ministers and organises both ministerial and summit meetings, was high on the Convention's agenda. Much is made by critics of the rotating presidency's lack of co-ordination, not least on the critical matter of external representation. The troika system, though revised in the Amsterdam Treaty, increases more than it resolves the sense of muddle over the Union's role in international affairs. Some take the view that a more permanent executive office would give clearer direction to the CFSP, by providing an institutional focal point for the Union's growing international presence in as much as 'the EU loses diplomatic clout when its agenda changes every six months, as a new group of officials takes over and starts promoting another country's own pet projects'. This problem was first remarked on by Henry Kissinger, when, as US secretary of state, he pondered 'who' he should contact who could speak authoritatively 'for Europe' on the big international issues. The problem with these executive arrangements is precisely that 'the EU sends mixed messages because several people claim to speak for it', requiring it 'to send a three-person delegation around the world to represent the presidency, the Commission and the High Representative for foreign policy'.[14] This predicament is a hardly new, but its impact and consequences have worsened as global challenges have raised the costs of failing to respond effectively to events.

A closely related issue was the impression, especially in the foreign and diplomatic services of the larger member states, that the EU loses credibility as an international actor when one of the smaller member states occupies the presidency. The diplomatic resources required to undertake the exhaustive round of consultative visits to every member state before the biannual European Councils, let alone to perform the extensive range of consultative and mediating functions for a presidency tests to the limits the diplomatic resources of even the best-equipped member states. Critics frequently make the point, too, that however well-organised or energetic a presidency is, important international actors and global agencies are much less inclined to take the EU seriously when a smaller country is directing its affairs. Yet these states are reluctant to relinquish their turn at the helm, to forgo the prestige and influence that goes with the role. These concerns have reinforced the case made in some quarters for a full-time and permanent Council president. The problem here, as with so many other issues discussed in the Convention, is that while interested parties want changes, others see advantage in the status quo. The rotating presidency appeals to smaller countries as an opportunity periodically to be centre-stage, directing affairs, and above all it is an embodiment of the principle of parity of membership.

There was disagreement, too, on the related question of whether to retain the twin presidencies of Council and Commission. On one side were those who complained of overlapping functions and debilitating turf wars getting in the way of a purposeful and clear-sighted response to critical domestic and international issues; and on the other side those who were unconvinced that adopting a permanent Council presidency would, on its own, resolve these shortcomings, and might even bring different problems. Complementary presidencies are one thing, but as these critics saw it, 'two high-profile Presidents' would do little to remove muddle and might instead merely institutionalise 'confusion, overlap and rivalry' at the centre of the Union's political architecture.[15] One solution to this conundrum is the so-called 'double-hat' presidency, combining the two presidencies in one person. It has been claimed for this solution that it 'has the advantage both of giving a single clear presence on the international stage and of limiting and inhibiting institutional rivalry while promoting co-ordination [for] under the current institutional system, it would be difficult for the Commission President to be the EU's international presence, even if the rotating presidency gave up that role, since CFSP remains predominantly intergovernmental'. The 'double hat' would supposedly resolve this problem 'without creating a problematic two-President EU'.[16]

The Convention discussed a proposal from two *conventionnels*, Andrew Duff and Lamberto Dini, for a combined or 'double-hatted' Commission/Council President, to be elected by qualified majority in the Council and endorsed by Parliament, and simply to be known as the 'Union President'. An office exercising authority over all of the Union's executive functions, and with the president and the commissioners chairing a smaller number of executive councils.[17] When the Convention eventually got around to this issue the smaller countries were quite aware that a powerful coalition of the big member states, supported by Giscard himself, had made the outcome of separate presidencies all but inevitable. They directed their efforts instead to curbing the powers of a full-time council presidency. The Benelux states, for instance, proposed that the Commission president should chair the General Affairs Council, and there was growing support in the plenary for a Commission role in the preparation of the new multi-annual framework agenda. The Commission, too, for its own reasons supported rotation, a system that in its view could be improved by 'sensible' reform, for instance by sharing the more onerous administrative tasks between the member states, thereby allowing the Council presidency to focus on 'core tasks'.

A single presidency would certainly simplify governance, and possibly even make it more comprehensible to the citizen. But this reform would be far from straightforward, precisely because it requires accommodating quite different ideas about the meaning and purpose of European integration within the same office. And though the case for 'double-hatting' was made in functional terms (in essence the need to improve efficiency and to ensure greater transparency of decision-making by avoiding the blurring of competencies that invariably occurs when two separate offices share functions) this was a thinly veiled attempt to advance the federalist cause. Or at least, this was how it was perceived by government representatives, and this explains why it failed. Events played their part, too. The Iraq crisis reinforced Giscard's predilection for firm executive direction at the centre of EU governance, with a permanent Council presidency in his view as the best means for making a coherent EU response – or at least for minimising discord – on external policy. Giscard's role was critical here, shaping the Convention's response to this issue. His hands-on approach and determination to steer proceedings was apparent on this issue perhaps more than most. He was careful to resist pressure in the plenaries from representatives of the smaller states pushing hard to retain rotation. The conclusions he presented to the January 2003 plenary for a president to be elected by the European Council for a two-and-a-half-year renewable term framed subsequent discussion, and eventually found its way into the Constitutional Treaty (Article 1-22). In the event, high politics determined the fate of this 'milliner's tale', with the larger, more influential countries (the United Kingdom, France and Spain) making clear that they subscribed to the 'separate hats' option, and with Germany brought on-side in January 2003, when that country subscribed to the two presidencies model in the joint position paper with France on the institutions.[18] The presidency question impinges, too, on the working of both the Council of Ministers and the European Council, and is discussed in the following section.

These issues were raised fairly early in the Convention's proceedings, and especially by the leading member states. Britain's foreign secretary, Jack Straw, confirmed his government's preference for a permanent Council presidency.[19] Tony Blair likewise endorsed the idea of a full-time Council chair with supporting team presidencies to obviate the problems of rotation and the lack of executive permanence.[20] The British government followed this by circulating a discussion paper early in 2003 with concrete proposals for a reformed presidency, an office to be tasked with a long list of executive functions: *inter alia*, preparing and managing European Council meetings; co-operating with the Commission in preparing the EU's multi-annual strategic agenda, as well as chairing the General Affairs Council; administering the sectoral Councils; superintending the work of the High Representative, and co-ordinating deliberations on foreign policy in the European Council; representing the Council in inter-institutional meetings with the Commission and the Parliament, not least in joint initiatives on international financial affairs, immigration and counter-terrorism; supervising EU relations with the other international actors, participating in crisis management and attending G8 summits.[21]

A full-time presidency was endorsed in principle by the French president, Jacques Chirac.[22] A similar proposal came from Spanish premier, José María Aznar, based on Spain's recent experience of running the presidency.[23] All three large member states, supported by Sweden, Denmark, Spain, and by Poland from the accession countries, gave their backing to a permanent presidency. It was a formidable coalition, made more so when France and Germany presented their own proposal, in a joint paper that eventually became the basis for discussion, for an executive president to be elected by qualified majority in the European Council, and tasked with chairing both its summit meetings and those of the General Affairs Council, as well as 'representing' the Union in international affairs. In this arrangement, the Commission president would be 'elected' by qualified majority in the Parliament, and endorsed subsequently by a qualified majority in the European Council. The joint paper described by the British government's official spokesman at the Convention, Peter Hain, as 'a breakthrough' also proposed a European foreign minister answerable to the Council, but with a base in the Commission, in effect combining in a single office the roles of the current High Representative, Javier Solana, and that of the then commissioner for external affairs, Chris Patten.[24] These proposals were designed to enhance member states' steering capacity, in as much as a long-tenure Council presidency would supposedly ensure greater strategic direction, enhancing policy co-ordination and continuity and not least better represent the EU 'abroad'.[25]

Although the 'big three' lined up behind this proposal they faced opposition, for this issue goes to the very heart of the debate about where power should reside in the Union. Many *conventionnels*, especially those from smaller countries, objected to a full-time presidency, seeing it as an attempt by the big states to hijack the Union's political agenda for their own narrow purposes. They preferred either to retain rotation, or for a combined or 'double-hatted' EU president to be located in the Commission, a preference reinforced by their hunch that a full-time president of the European Council would almost certainly be selected from candidates proposed by the bigger member state, and in any event would be their political captive. Some opposed it on principle because it would further entrench confederalism, seeing it as a move deliberately intended to weaken the Commission, the long-standing institutional champion of smaller states' interests. A joint memorandum from the Benelux countries said as much, firmly rebutting what it saw as *directoire* self-interest.[26]

After much debate the twin presidency survived, and with the Council president designated as a full-time appointment in the gift of the heads of government and state. This outcome has to be counted as failure to answer critics' concerns about a lack of accountability and democratic practice at the very heart of the Union's governance. Although in this arrangement the Council president is responsible, both for giving the Council strategic direction and as the EU's representative in the international arena, this is accountability only to a narrow constituency. As such it hardly satisfies the Laeken commitment to improve the Union's democratic life, the criticism levelled in the Convention by those who were as convinced about the need for greater executive accountability and transparency in the Union as they were about more effective policy management. Some critics saw this outcome as nothing less than an opportunity squandered, claiming that 'vital steps forward on the legislative side have been matched with steps backward on the executive', and as such 'a typical European muddle' and no less 'a disappointing outcome for those looking for a real democratic breakthrough'.[27] Those who argued thus saw the maintenance of dual presidencies as 'a weak and inadequate outcome' of the drive for reform.[28]

Other *conventionnels*, however, preferred to be cautious on the matter of reforming the institutions, and took the contrary view that sharing executive power in contradistinction to the usual separation of powers that prevails in most democratic national polities better reflects the Union's unique inter-institutional balance, and indeed the ideological balance between intergovernmental and supranational preferences that has characterised Community governance from the outset. Those who took this view saw the Convention's compromise here as the sensible outcome of what Paul Craig describes as 'the lessons of history', the fact that any institutional arrangement must be acceptable to the member states. For the plain fact is that the Union's principal institutions do 'represent different interests, with the consequence that it is acceptable in principle for executive power to be shared by a body representing state interests, and a body representing the Community interest, each of which is legitimised in different ways'.[29]

This principle has been built into the very fabric of EU governance, but problematic here is how the powers and competencies of these offices should be demarcated, and indeed whether or how far these are co-equal and commensurate offices. The proposal from some quarters was that the Council president should not be permitted to hold national office during his/her term, though not explicitly precluding the incumbent from concurrently holding another EU office. This was a 'loophole' that would make it possible 'for the Presidencies of the Commission and the European Council to be held by one person', leaving open the possibility, political circumstances permitting, of a 'super president' of the Union.[30] Whether the heads of government would ever allow this outcome is questionable, at least on current form. The final version of the Constitutional Treaty did at least offer some guidance as to the allocation of competencies between these two executive offices. These changes and indeed many other institutional reforms reviewed in this and in the following chapter have found their way into the latest Reform Treaty signed in Lisbon in December 2007. While the Commission would draft the annual and multi-annual programme, the Council president had responsibility for preparing the Council's work, for strategic direction and for chairing meetings. However, the Legislative and General Affairs Council would be chaired, not by the new Council president but according to the rotation principle, with all the attendant problems for continuity and co-ordination.

This complicated arrangement was a response to some of the concerns expressed by the smaller member states led by Belgium, determined both to curb the discretion available to the new Council presidency and to ensure a greater role for the Commission than was seemingly countenanced by the big member states. Yet such overlapping arrangements remain problematic, for they run the risk of fuelling institutional rivalry and are likely to make for 'considerable conflict over policy and strategy development, with the Commission emphasising its right of initiative while the Council presidency emphasises his/her control of strategy'.[31] In effect, this arrangement threatens greater confusion over the hierarchy of authority between these executive functions, and even potential strife over 'who does what'. As such, it fails to meet another key Laeken objective, that of clarifying the distribution of inter-institutional power.[32]

There are two potential – some would say likely – pressure-points stemming from these proposed arrangements: on the one hand, conflict between the Council and Commission presidents; and on the other hand confusion over the functions of the new EU foreign minister. The French government's representative in the Convention proposed that this problem could be avoided by 'double-hatting' the Council/Commission foreign policy offices, with the High Representative occupying a role in both institutions, though with the Council having primacy. The Convention settled in the end for this hybrid arrangement, a 'half-state, half-intergovernmental construction' with executive power shared between the Commission and the Council, but it should be said 'with the Laeken objectives of more democracy and greater simplicity in EU governance as its principal casualties'. Accordingly, the Constitutional Treaty 'provides the EU with two full-time presidencies, each located in Brussels', and as such bound to compete over their respective powers and authority, neither of which would, in the view of one commentator, 'be properly legitimate'.[33]

The broad responsibility for steering policy resides with the European Council, though the drafting of detailed annual or multi-annual agendas is usually carried out by the Commission and presented to the Council and the Parliament. To redefine this as a joint responsibility, as the British and some other governments preferred, is a recipe, however, for both rivalry and confusion. Trying to reconcile two separate draft agendas produced by two secretariats is problematical, to say the least. And if the Commission College has approved a draft agenda, how then would the Commission president negotiate, let alone agree a definitive version with the Council President? These proposed arrangements made for greater muddle than clarity, risking 'considerable conflict over policy and strategy development, with the Commission emphasising its right of initiative while the Council president emphasises his/her control of strategy'. In the circumstances, the temptation might well be for both offices to test the boundaries of their respective authority, rather than seeking to build consensus, with the reformed Council president preferring 'to engage in serious inter-institutional turf-fighting with the Commission in particular, in an attempt to try to limit and restrict the title and nature of the job'.[34]

Clearly, more questions were raised by this proposed reform than are resolved by it. How, for instance, would the powers and authority of the two presidents be delimited? Would they be co-equal, or would the new European Council president have the final word?[35] The change from a rotating Council presidency – essentially, a part-time position – to a semi-permanent, full-time executive post when it comes, as it will as a consequence of the Treaty initialled in Lisbon (October 2007), is bound to have a profound impact on the workings of EU governance. Though quite how this will work out in practice is by no means clear. On the contrary, the scope for overlap and confusion over precise functions is endemic in the arrangement. For instance, the proposal that the Council president shall prepare the Council's work and effect continuity, 'in co-operation with the president of the Commission and on the basis of the work of the General Affairs Council',[36] whereas under the tasks designated for the Council of Ministers it is the General

Affairs Council's responsibility 'in liaison with the Commission [to] prepare and ensure follow-up to meetings of the European Council', is surely a recipe for organisational disarray.[37] There is a question mark, too, over whether and how far the European Council president will be able to supplement or alter the Commission's draft strategic programme. Or whether this office might instead take the lead in co-ordination and follow-up work. As always in institutional matters, the formal rules matter much less than exigency, the impact of the unforeseen, of events as they unfold, and not least the interplay, ambitions and abilities of the personalities who occupy these crucial roles.

There is scope for confusion, too, over the management of external policy, with doubts expressed in some quarters about how far the new arrangements proposed in the Constitutional Treaty and carried over to the latest Lisbon Treaty would meet the anxieties of some member states for better representation of the Union's views and interests in international forums. Both the Constitutional Treaty and the new security strategy proposed by Javier Solana, the High Representative for CFSP, at the Thessaloniki summit emphasised the importance of a co-ordinated approach to external relations as between the respective offices. Few experts are convinced that this proposed arrangement, likewise carried over into the Lisbon Treaty, will work without a hitch. The wording used in the Constitutional Treaty is hardly reassuring on this score, to the effect that: 'The President of the European Council shall, at his or her level and in that capacity, ensure the external representation of the Union on issues concerning its common foreign and security policy, without prejudice to the powers of the Union Minister for Foreign Affairs.'[38] This, to say the least, is ambiguous. On the one hand, it might be construed as giving primary responsibility for the conduct of the Union's foreign policy to the presidency, though this was not the interpretation, let alone the intention of most EU governments. There is uncertainty, too, about the precise authority of the new-style Council president in his relations with the wider international community.

What is not disputed by critics and supporters alike of this imminent reform is that the new office will exert considerable power and authority, notwithstanding the manner of its appointment. Apart from defining the Union's broad strategic priorities, the office will 'make "the essential choices"' about closer co-operation, and monitor the threats and challenges that confront the Union. As well as deciding the composition of the Council, the presidency will also exercise 'a significant constitutional power through "enabling clauses"'.[39] This may well be so, but the general impression is that the office would function more as an interlocutor, brokering deals and reconciling differences between member states over external policy, in so far as this is possible. As such, the Council president would represent the Union in matters pertaining to common security and foreign policy 'without prejudice to the responsibility of the Union's Minister for Foreign Affairs'. The Commission would retain its present role in managing external representation, except for the Common Foreign and Security Policy. Whereas the new EU foreign minister (an office discussed below, and again at Chapter 9) would 'conduct the Union's common foreign and security policy'. And, wearing his institutional hat as a vice-president of the Commission, would also have responsibility for 'handling external relations and for coordinating other aspects of the Union's external common action'.[40]

What could be clearer than this! It remains to be seen whether such a Byzantine arrangement, and one to be installed in the pending reforms of institutional arrangements, can deliver an orderly or effective outcome. Common sense suggests otherwise. The Constitutional Treaty did anticipate a possible solution, by not precluding eventual merger of the two presidencies, whether organised along the lines of the so-called 'double-hatted' model, or as a single executive presidency as prescribed in the proposal by MEPs Duff and Dini.[41] In the meantime, in its attempt to secure a compromise on this delicate matter of attributing executive authority, the Constitutional Treaty and its successor merely perpetuates abiding conflict between two competing ideologies of European integration.

Conflict might be anticipated, too, on the equally critical matter of determining the Union's strategic direction. Under present arrangements the Council presidency co-ordinates the agendas of the various Council meetings and prepares for EU summits. The civil services of the respective presidency countries are assisted in this planning function by both the Council and the Commission secretariats, the latter acting as an indispensable liaison in view of the fact that EU summits frequently make formal requests to the Commission for policy and for other initiatives. The end of rotation will foreclose on this valuable national administrative resource, thereby increasing the administrative burden on the two European secretariats. And no doubt encouraging demands, too, for an expansion of the Council bureaucracy, as well as sharpening institutional rivalry.[42] It is reasonable to assume, however, that a permanent Council presidency will generate its own, not inconsiderable organisational resources, principally located in its secretariat. Institutional logics as well as past experience point to gradual institutional adjustment, a sort of inter-institutional pragmatism that has over time helped the Union's governance adjust to changing times. Institutions do have capacity for creative adaptation to systemic and to exogenous challenges, and the Union's institutions are by no means exceptional in this regard. The Union's history shows many examples of institutions developing in this way, 'often outside the strict letter of the Treaties, as a response to pressures or concerns relating to institutional balance of power within the Community as a whole'.[43] More doubtful, however, is whether a change that confirms the Council presidency's status, in effect as 'first amongst equals', and alters the balance of power between the Commission and the Council can ensure effective co-operation between the two institutions. These arrangements will surely give rise to confusion over policy co-ordination and implementation. The case for a full-time Council presidency is based on the need for effective agenda-setting and for steering, efficient policy-making and, not least, for consensus between the policy actors. Without such consensus, even a full-time presidency will not enhance the Union's international standing.[44]

Tension between the two presidency offices will likely continue under the latest arrangements. A Council president appointed by the heads of government would probably have a weaker claim to authority than an elected Commission president whose status is comparable, in some degree, to that of the elected heads of government sitting in the European Council – one reason why the member states refused to countenance direct election. But this in itself will not preclude continuing tension, or even occasional conflict between the respective offices. In a Union where commonality of interest remains elusive, with considerable differences of interests between the member states on important policy issues, 'it is highly unlikely that the heads of state and government will manage to appoint a person [to the Council presidency] that will be able to exercise a sufficient influence over them and speak for the EU in the international arena', let alone someone who will possess the legitimacy and authority in international diplomacy of democratically elected national leaders.[45] Politics, however, overrode 'mere' logics here, as it does in so many aspects of EU governance, and the leading member states were unconvinced by this argument, putting their weight behind an executive Council presidency. And this is not the only source of strain. One 'solution' to the problems anticipated from dualism has its own consequences for the conflicts of interest between smaller and larger member states. The Convention proposed to reassure the smaller states by balancing appointments to these executive offices, the larger states certain to monopolise the Council presidency but the smaller ones compensated by heading the Commission. This arrangement, should it be adopted, might well meet the need for balance, but it is just as likely to institutionalise tension both between the two offices and between the larger and smaller states.

There are other potential sources of conflict, or at least cause for confusion in these arrangements. The end of presidency rotation raises for instance questions about how the compensatory rotation of chairs envisaged for the Council of Ministers would co-ordinate their work, one council with another and of either with the new council president. The British government amongst others wanted the Council president to head a co-ordinating committee. In the event, the Constitutional Treaty allocated this task to the Legislative and General Affairs Council. These issues were not unresolved in the draft Constitution and they will surely be revisited in light of pending reforms. The potential for conflict here and the failure to find satisfactory procedures for resolving disputes is a shortcoming subsequently confirmed by the 2003/4 IGC. The only provision made for adjudication was unduly vague, in effect that the Court of Justice 'shall ensure that in the interpretation and application of the Constitution the law is observed' (Article 1-29), although 'one has to search in Part III where Articles 360 to 381 specify all the types of legal disputes in which the Court has jurisdiction'.[46] Doubts remain about the Court's objectivity as a legal adjudicator, with suspicion in some quarters that it might be more inclined in view of its long-standing federalist preference to favour appellants from the Commission or the Parliament who support deeper European integration, rather than the Council or any particular member state. There is lack of clarity, too, about another procedure for ensuring the accountability of the powerful actors, the use of a censure motion against the Commission (Article 3-340).

The debate over 'who does what' confirms, then, rooted difference over the exercise of executive power in the Union. On one side are those who maintain that clarity of purpose, institutional efficiency and closer political integration require a single locus for political power. From this perspective, bifurcating executive power is certainly a recipe for confusion. On the other side, however, is the view that the EU is custom-built for complex power-sharing, combining as it does in its institutional architecture quite different, even competing ideas about transnational governance. As such, executive power has 'always been divided de facto between the Commission and the European Council [and though] this may not be neat ... it is how the Union has worked for the last thirty years at least'. Those who take this line do not see these arrangements as necessarily leading to impasse, for it has not so far prevented forward momentum, nor precluded the two executive institutions working 'symbiotically in developing the Union's agenda'.[47]

From this perspective, to combine these quite separate institutions within one executive office would be to ignore significant differences of function between the two presidencies, and indeed to overlook deep-seated and competing aspirations for the European project. The Council speaks unequivocally for the member states, even though its work has contributed to upgrading the common or European interest, whereas the Commission for its part represents the broader Community interest, though its college is nominated by the member states. Neither of these quite different institutional arrangements has prevented inter-institutional co-operation taking European integration forward.

The Convention revisited these familiar arguments, and concluded that the sheer difficulty of accommodating such fundamental differences did preclude a combined executive presidency. The larger member states in particular resisted an arrangement whereby the Commission president would chair Council proceedings, and the smaller states and representatives of the Union's common institutions likewise refused to consider significantly reducing the Commission's autonomy *vis-à-vis* the Council. Executive dualism survived this familiar stand-off, sustained in part by past performance but above all because it was the least divisive, even if was by no means the most efficient option.[48] Yet efficiency was a key aspect of the Laeken mandate, and some *conventionnels* made the case for a permanent executive president primarily on these grounds. Whether the case for efficiency is quite so clear-cut is, however, debatable.

The case for a combined executive on efficiency grounds alone may well be exaggerated. On the face of it, the short duration of rotated presidencies, some of them with limited organisational resources or modest ambitions for their term, seems to present an easy target for reformers. Yet there is no guarantee that a full-time presidency will necessarily ensure greater continuity of EU business, except perhaps in the important field of foreign affairs or possibly the work of the General Affairs Council. Concern to facilitate continuity, entirely understandable in a polity faced with significant policy challenges, is one thing. But it must be seen in context, and not least from a historical perspective that points to a less than conclusive outcome. The case for efficiency is by no means as clear-cut, then, as some would have it. Some commentators question the likely benefits from a full-time president, not least for providing more effective Council leadership. One observer wonders, for instance, how far a permanent Council president would 'interact with the other council formations to ensure that in future an important policy is not neglected as was the case with the decisions on justice and home affairs agreed at the Tampere European Council in Autumn 1999'.[49] The only direct control exercised by the European Council over the other councils in these arrangements is deciding their formation and the precise rotation arrangements for their presidencies, after 'taking into account European political and geographical balance and the diversity of the member states'.[50]

The absence so far of what might be called institutional cogency has by no means prevented significant achievements, important bargains made as sub-optimal deals between actors with quite different preferences, and facilitated by energetic and purposeful Council presidencies. As Hughes sees it pragmatism, even realpolitik, is never far from the surface in EU affairs, for though 'each new presidency can at best add or emphasise one or two items on the EU's agenda in its six months, possibly at best adding five per cent to the overall rolling agenda', the mere fact of the rotating presidency 'has not impeded major political developments'.[51] The European project could never have got off the ground, let alone progressed as far as it has done on the basis of idealism alone. The presidency arrangements, though hostage to unpredictable events and subject to structural constraints that limit its scope for taking the initiative have seen some strikingly successful policy initiatives and projects, not least the development of the single market and the launch of the European Central Bank and Economic and Monetary Union. These debates about institutions and how to improve their functioning will continue in practice as much as in theory with the impending changes to the Union's executive arrangements following Lisbon.

Finally in this overview of executive functions, we must consider how the Constitution accommodated the Laeken objectives of improved democracy and greater accountability in EU governance. There was little in the final draft of the Constitutional Treaty to indicate any convincing response to the growing public perception of a democracy shortfall in EU governance, nor much to suggest greater accountability of executive power. The proposals in the Franco-German paper, and those, too, of the British government, did propose an appointment procedure for the presidency but this was hardly radical, involving selection from a short list of candidates agreed by the member states with the Parliament subsequently approving their choice. This procedure is firmly in line with these actors' confirmed intergovernmental preferences, and in effect is more selection than election. Federalist voices predictably advocated an open election procedure, but in view of the powerful forces ranged against them this altogether more radical case was defeated. Under the agreed procedure, the Council president would be appointed, almost certainly after a typical behind-the-scenes deal between the leading member states.

The same arrangement will apply under the latest reforms, and this will surely compromise the legitimacy of the office, with any incumbent quite possibly wielding less authority than his predecessors appointed by rotation. For under these arrangements, a current head of government chairs the European Council as an elected head of government or state, whereas an appointed president will not have quite the same degree of authority.[52] The Commission president would be appointed by a similar process, again a far from transparent, let alone a democratic procedure. It seems likely that a permanent Council presidency appointed by these means will carry the stigma of dependence on those leaders who select him, lacking any independent base for authority, and just as important lacking the capacity for exercising political initiative. In short, there is the risk that this office will lack political credibility because it lacks demonstrable legitimacy, though much will depend on the drive and personal credentials of incumbents.[53]

## The European Council

The European Council remains a controversial actor, without a legal base in the founding treaties, a largely *ad hoc* arrangement and in the strictest sense not a Community institution though its existence was acknowledged in the Single European Act. The Council was incorporated into the Community's political architecture, a response to the pressures of a mutable global order and the need for political leaders to meet regularly so as to better deal with headline issues and determine strategy. Summit meeting of EC heads of state and government had been proposed by General de Gaulle as early as 1960 in the abortive Fouchet proposals. However, this attempt to bypass, and as some saw it to subvert, the Community institutions, or even to hijack its political leadership by locating the EC's governance in Paris rather than Brussels, was resisted by the other member states determined to avoid weakening the nascent European institutions. There were occasional if infrequent summits thereafter, but it was only in 1973, in the aftermath of the first enlargement that the then French president, Valéry Giscard d'Estaing, supported by the West German chancellor, Willy Brandt, proposed holding regular summits. The European Council was the outcome, though not intended to be a Community institution *per se* but rather to remain outside the Community's orbit, to be independent of and indeed elevated above the Commission, and designed to give political leadership, a firm steer on problematic issues as and when required.

The European Council has consolidated its position as the Union's political epicentre, so that 'in reality, [it] has become the political guiding light of the Union and all the significant steps of integration have stemmed from its proposals'.[54] It is the Council that determines, for instance, the Union's common position on the big or 'historic' decisions.[55] It is likewise the locus of the bargains and trade-offs that must be made just to keep the EU show on the road, taking due account of and trying to balance the member states' competing preferences. Summits are invaluable opportunities for 'member states to promote their objectives together', and this uniquely collegial and relatively informal body (political leaders are restricted in the number of officials they may take into even formal Council sessions) is the one forum that gives the Union both political authority and even indirect legitimacy.[56] The plain fact is 'that nothing of major importance happens within the EU without its approval. It has a major say in setting the legislative agenda, in setting the Union's priorities, in deciding on the pace and direction of change within the Union, whether this be in relation to the timing of monetary union, or enlargement.'[57]

Informality has been indispensable for the Council's successful operation from the start, but successive enlargements have reduced informality, making it more difficult to manage negotiations or to bring them to a successful conclusion. The latest enlargement to 27 member states, and with more members likely to follow, has made even more urgent the task of reforming the European Council. The current rules on rotation mean that each member state will occupy the presidency only once every 13 years, and less frequently if there is any further enlargement. This, in turn, will diminish 'institutional memory', the availability of senior staff in government service with experience of running a previous national presidency, as well as compounding the difficulties of ensuring reliable communications between the presidency and the other member states.

The Laeken agenda identified this as a central issue for the Convention. The Seville Council (June 2002) had already proposed some changes designed to improve the Council's operation, though without any agreement between the member states as the Convention began its work.[58] Reform was bound to feature on the Convention's agenda for other reasons, too. The European Council has been roundly criticised from several quarters, whether as a forum for dealing with increasingly complex decision-making or as one for resolving the Union's abiding policy problems. The agendas of its brief summits are frequently overcrowded, sometimes burdened with quite mundane matters that reflect the particular preferences of the incumbent presidency more than they do wider concerns, or else cluttered with issues that previous incumbents have failed to resolve. Summits may also be hijacked or otherwise overwhelmed by a sudden crisis. Moreover, despite their relative informality summits are hardly a politics-free zone. Some of them have an air of staged adversarialism conducted *in camera*, though once participants are outside the conference room and facing the full glare of media scrutiny on camera, too, with statesmen becoming politicians again and inclined to strike postures, playing up to domestic audiences. The drawbacks here are patent. As one critic sees the problem: 'It is a monumental waste of prime ministerial and presidential time to spend days haggling over minor issues, so that each has some small victory to present to the electorate on returning home.' Nor is it an efficient procedure, for too often 'the result is low-quality decisions, because the heads of government are prone to grandstanding and cannot necessarily follow all the details of the issues they are discussing'.[59]

The changes proposed for the European Council confirm the intergovernmental tenor of EU governance. The Constitutional Treaty acknowledged, and for the first time, that the European Council is an institution of the Union (Article 1-19.1) and tasked with providing the Union 'with the necessary impetus for developments'. Furthermore, that it 'shall define the general political direction and priorities thereof', though excluding the legislative function (Article 1-21.1). Wessels judges this to be an 'understatement of its institutional capacity', because it conceals the part played by heads of government as the principal EU actors.[60] The Constitutional Treaty also reaffirmed the European Council's role, both for setting the broad agenda and issuing policy guidelines (Article 3-258 and Article 3-295) and for convening IGCs (Article 4-443.3). Again, Wessels concludes that 'while it is not explicitly mentioned in the specific treaty article, it is expected that the heads of government will continue taking final decisions on any treaty revision'.[61] The inclusion in the Constitutional Treaty of so-called 'bridging clauses' or *passerelles* would permit the heads of government to adopt a European decision by a qualified majority vote in place of the unanimity rule (Article 1-40.7), or to change a 'special' into an 'ordinary legislative procedure' (Article 3-210.3), whilst permitting national politicians to veto such proposals (Article 4-444.3). The European Council might also make a decision on some institutional matters, for instance the distribution of seats in the Parliament (Article 1-20.2)) or the configurations (Article 1-24) and the presidency of the Council (Article 1-24.7).

The European Council also retains authority to propose candidates for the Commission presidency (Article 1-27.1 and 2), to appoint the president of the European Central Bank (Article 3-382.2) and to elect its own standing president (Article 1-22.1). The procedure for electing the full-time president of the European Council has been reviewed above. Acting in co-responsibility with the Commission president and the European Parliament, the Council would participate in appointing the Union's foreign minister (Article 1-28.1). Finally, the Constitutional Treaty confirmed the European Council as the final arbiter in the event of appeals in some circumstances by member states against draft legislative proposals. These are all powers that confirm the Union's intergovernmental ethos, with the heads of government permitted to interfere in Council business 'whenever they feel that there is an important issue at stake'.[62] The president 'will serve as the "face" and "voice" of the European Council ... watching over the other EU institutions – especially the Council, the Foreign Minister and the Commission'.[63]

These changes are incorporated into the Lisbon Treaty Some commentators see scope here for purposive, if not quite for the firm leadership usually implied by executive office, with incumbents at least 'emancipated from the mandates of national governments', and in a way that over time 'might then lead to some kind of a federal-style leadership'. Whether this is reminiscent of Hallstein's claim in his prime to be the president of the Community before de Gaulle put paid to any such ambition is doubtful.[64] Of course, one can never entirely rule out any eventuality in this unpredictable polity, though on current evidence this seems to be a fanciful, more than a realistic prospect for the Union's future governance.

## The Council of Ministers

The greater part of the limited time available for discussing institutional questions was devoted to the presidency question, such that the important matter of reforming the Council of Ministers was almost neglected. The Council of Ministers, the principal forum for the member states to meet and pursue their national interests, is hardly a model of institutional efficiency. Problems of complexity and overlap, and the scope for competition between the various councils thanks in part to overlap of their respective policy domains, have increased as the functional councils have multiplied to accommodate the expansion of EU competencies. The Seville Council (June 2002) addressed this issue and proposed a reduction in the number of councils from 16 to 9. Another proposal discussed there was to separate general affairs from external relations, the latter including development policy, external trade relations and what currently passes for EU security policy. However, differences between the larger and smaller member states prevented agreement on the Spanish presidency's proposal for reforming the cumbrous General Affairs Council (now renamed as the General Affairs and External Relations Council) so as to enable it to better manage EU business.

When the Convention eventually got around to discussing this matter it reviewed various measures for improving efficiency and transparency, again with the Franco-German partnership leading the debate. The Seville proposal to separate the Council into two quite distinct entities remained on the Union's agenda, as did a proposal to reform the management structure and chairing arrangements of the respective councils, with an Executive Council comprising the present General Council, the Council for Foreign and Security Policy, the Economic and Finance Council and the Council for Justice and Home Affairs. The General Council would be chaired by the Council President and the Council for Foreign and Security Affairs by the Union's foreign minister. A Legislative Council would be responsible for processing legislation, though it was less than clear in the Franco-German proposal who would chair its proceedings, the joint paper hinting at rotation between the member states. Of course, efficiency is important, but there was nothing in these proposals to redress the lack of democratic accountability in Council procedures. Nor for that matter anything to remedy confusion over its functions resulting from the various councils operating in both a legislative and in an executive capacity.

The Convention considered several proposals, including a team presidency to operate below the permanent president of the European Council, with a term of up to four years and with biannual rotation as between the various sectoral chairs. The advantage here of permitting the smaller countries a degree of power is outweighed, however, by the lack of continuity in a crucial office, and with the additional drawback of merely increasing confusion in already complex executive arrangements. For in effect, this would mean installing a second 'college' alongside the Commission, further complicating agenda-setting and undermining co-ordination. There was discussion, too, of arrangements for chairing the various council configurations, much of it linked with the parallel debate about the powers of the new council presidency. The Convention considered a mixed system: permanent chairs for the General Affairs and the External Affairs Councils, with rotating chairs for the sectoral councils. But again, this proposal would do little to improve executive co-ordination. Furthermore, the lack of a clear distinction between the legislative Council and executive Council formations would blur the separation of powers in the EU, preventing an 'enhanced synergy between the Commission and executive Council formations in fulfilling executive tasks', and depriving the Union 'of the capacity for strategic agenda-setting and co-ordination across different policy domains'.[65]

The proposal to fuse two quite distinct functions within the General Affairs Council, one concerned with the general management function – reviewing policy, co-ordinating the work of the other councils and preparing and co-ordinating European Council meetings – the other, in conjunction with the Parliament, concerned with enacting legislation under the expanded co-decision procedure, was not set aside by the IGC as some predicted it would be. Meanwhile, the member states would continue to have one representative on the Council of Ministers, depending on the issue under review. Again, this is hardly an improvement on the current arrangements, and has been described by one commentator impatient for reform as 'a botched compromise that can satisfy no-one'. For by 'combining legislative and executive functions it runs counter to one of the Convention's principal objectives: simplification'.[66]

The various Council chairs, except the Foreign Affairs Council, which would have responsibility for managing EU foreign and security policy chaired by the new European foreign minister, would under these arrangements rotate annually between the member states. However, no decision was taken in the Convention about how rotation would operate in practice, these arrangements being left to the European Council after taking due account of political and geographical balance. This arrangement, should it be adopted, will require group rather than singular chairs and team presidencies drawn from several countries. It is anticipated by some critics that these reorganised councils might well prefer, on grounds of continuity, a term in excess of one year. But the matter was not settled and as such leaves more questions unanswered than it resolves, not least whether the chair of the General Affairs Council or the council presidency would assume the critical function of co-ordinating the Council team.

More significant in terms of the Laeken objective of improved transparency and accountability was the proposal to open up the Council's legislative role to greater public scrutiny. A majority of *conventionnels* favoured open legislative sessions, the surest guarantee of transparency. There was support, too, for a separate legislative council whose ministerial members would have authority to legislate in all areas of EU policy, with participation by the sectoral ministers as required. The Convention came round to the view that democratic norms, as these pertain to EU governance, should facilitate proper scrutiny by parliamentary institutions at every level, both of the Union's executive institutions and of member states' implementation of European legislation. But the proposed reforms hardly matched this aspiration. The Convention recommended more open Councils, an extension of the arrangement for public opening and concluding sessions of Council meetings already agreed at Seville. The matter of transparency naturally attracted rather less interest from government representatives than it did from other *conventionnels*, and this modest reform bears their influence, for it is little more than cosmetic. Even if it is eventually enacted the prospect of the sectoral councils or even of a separate legislative Council becoming properly transparent remains remote.

Council decision-making procedure was bound to be a controversial issue, with the prospect of decisional gridlock in an EU of 27 and more member states. Laeken had proposed restricting unanimity in Council decisions and extending QMV, and this set the scene for discussions in the Convention. QMV was to be the normal decisional procedure (Article 1-23.3), one way of improving decision-making, removing the temptation under unanimity for awkward member states to make deals on otherwise unrelated issues, so as to extract maximum concessions for their own national interests. The prospects for blocking are bound to increase in an enlarged EU, adding to the problem of sub-optimality, and what Scharpf has described as the 'decision-traps' endemic in the way the EU goes about its business.[67]

Some experts take the view, admittedly based on incomplete evidence from the voting behaviour of some EU15 member states on the services directive, on action to curb restrictive access to labour markets, and based, too, on the behaviour of the newcomers on VAT exemptions, that without implementing the sort of voting reform contained in the Constitutional Treaty, 'negotiations on important dossiers may become more difficult in the future'.[68] This, it should be said, is more under-statement than hyperbole. Post-enlargement voting behaviour in the Council so far indicates that while there has been less blocking than some anticipated, in part because actual votes are infrequent, the prevailing culture is one of making accommodations between competing preferences, with member states seeking outcomes that incorporate one another's national interests as the norm. Yet enlargement has taken its toll of former familiarity. Decisional dynamics had markedly changed in EU25/27, making 'consensus-building more time-consuming', so this would be a timely reform.[69]

The working group on simplification chaired by Giuliano Amato recom-mended QMV as the general procedure for deciding business, and the Convention followed suit and proposed an increase in QMV, most notably in Justice and Home Affairs, where there is a growing sense of urgency about facilitating more effec-tive decisions in politically sensitive matters relating to asylum policy and judicial co-operation for combating cross-border crime and terrorism. A contentious point that subsequently resurfaced in the IGC is whether any outvoted member state can, as of right, refer such matters back to the European Council, where unanimity would apply to the final decision. And there was likewise no firm agreement on the equally contentious issue of whether governments should retain their veto on such politically delicate matters as taxation and commercial policy. Conse-quently, though the Constitutional Treaty did indeed extend QMV, resistance from some governments prevented its application to key policy domains such as foreign and security policy, social policy and taxation, and also for determining 'own resources' and the multi-annual framework, all of which remain by default subject to unanimity. The European Council would, however, be empowered in this reform to authorise the Council to use the QMV procedure.[70]

The rules on majority voting are critical because something like 80 per cent of Council decisions are currently subject to QMV, and are binding even on those states that vote against them in the Council. And though in practice most policy decisions are reached by means of elaborate compromises and by trade offs, with barely 10 per cent of decisions actually voted on, changes in procedure did make the matter of 'safeguards' even more important. The issue of safeguards is important because, notwithstanding that the Council operates by consensus, the evidence 'points to the fact that voting in the Council has not been unusual in the years since 1999 when voting results began to be published'.[71] Concern about the extended use of QMV in sensitive domestic policies gave rise for instance to the so-called 'emergency brake' procedure which permits any member state to resist majority decisions whenever 'fundamental aspects' of its national social security or criminal justice systems are at stake.

Even more contentious than QMV *per se* is the formula for allocating council voting weights. This is a familiar problem in federal and confederal polities where the requirement, in what are invariably asymmetrical political arrangements based either on demography or territorial size, is to ensure an equitable balance of power between the larger and smaller territorial polities. And, likewise, to ensure fair representation in decision-making procedures for both the constituent polities (in the EU's case, the nation states) and in terms of population. This problem is a particularly difficult one to resolve in the EU where there are large population disparities between the member states. A comparison between the respective demographic patterns of the EU and of the founding states of the USA, where this problem of balanced representation in a confederal polity first surfaced, serves to illustrate the problem in relation to allocating voting weights.

The data in Table 6.1 show that the EU is a more asymmetrical polity than the USA was at its founding when it adopted a federal constitution. The 2004–7 Enlargement has increased these demographic disparities. As such, the strict application of the normal principle of democratic representation – one vote per citizen – whether for the allocation of parliamentary seats or for calculating voting weights in the Council, would mean unduly skewing the composition of the Union's only directly elected institution, as well as further complicating the Council's decision-making procedure, and in the process distorting the principle of 'fair' representation. There is of course no objective formula for making such calculations. Any calculus is invariably imprecise and must balance competing claims to representation. Decisions are bound to be 'the subject of continuous power politics and insider trading', and with the perceived 'losers' more than likely to condemn the eventual outcomes.[72] The Convention settled for a compromise here, a solution that took into account both population and territoriality in calculating seat allocations in the Parliament and voting weights in the Council of Ministers.

In part, the logics of QMV guarantees balance of sorts, ensuring that a bloc of large states acting in concert cannot pursue their collective interests at the expense of the smaller states, and similarly a coalition of small states cannot hold up legis-

*Table 6.1* Relative size of member states in the USA and the EU

| EU (2003) | Share of total population | USA (1787) |
|---|---|---|
| 10 | Below 5% | 4 |
| – | 5–10% | 6 |
| 1 | 10–15% | 2 |
| 4 | Above 15% | 1 |
| 15 | Total number of states | 13 |

Source: K. Kiljunen, *The European Constitution in the Making* (Brussels, 2004), p. 122.

lation on their own. The voting weights formula then in operation was agreed at the time of the Eftan enlargement in 1995, with 65 votes required for a qualified majority and 26 votes representing a blocking minority, a formula that reflects a delicate political calculus, as of course it is bound to do. A qualified majority required a majority (eight) of the member states representing a minimum of 71 per cent of EU population. This ensured that a minority of member states or a coalition representing a minority of the Union's population was precluded from defying the will of the majority of member states/population. The actual percentages and the number of states in the QMV formula has changed over time, but the ratios in use are those agreed by the founders of the Community institutions. Thus, small states have fewer votes than large states, but more votes in proportion to population. The large states each have the same number of votes, regardless of differences in population.

The Nice Council had revised this formula, and supposedly settled the issue for the foreseeable future by introducing a demographic quotient into the equation. These changes became effective from November 2004 under the terms of the Accession Treaty, and gave the larger states an increased voting weight with the majority threshold increased, but with the whole procedure becoming even more complicated with the addition of two new majority thresholds: 50 per cent of membership (countries) and 62 per cent of total EU population. The problem of reconciling Germany's large population weight (some 80 million after reunification in 1990) with the concern expressed by some other member states about that country's potential for dominating decision-making was seemingly resolved by offering Berlin compensations for a lower weighting than it was entitled to based on demography. In what amounted to typical EU fudging, Germany settled for a reduced voting weight relative to population in exchange for additional seats in the European Parliament.

In a further attempt to assuage Germany's concerns, a clause was inserted into the Nice Treaty stipulating that a member state could block a qualified majority decision if it was endorsed by states representing less than 62 per cent of the Union's population. The voting weights of all the other small member and accession states were adjusted accordingly, but without reference to the demographic quota, and at the expense of the accession states that at this juncture were unable to make their case in the European Council. France, however, would not accept any formula that reduced its influence *vis-à-vis* Germany, and so the United Kingdom and Italy, both with populations in excess of 60 million, had to receive the same voting weight. Spain, too, considered itself to be a big player and demanded an equivalent voting weight, duly receiving 27 weighted votes, a mere two votes less than Germany though it had only half of that country's population. And what had been granted to Spain could not reasonably be denied to Poland, the largest of the accession countries.

A direct consequence of this formula is that the three largest member states can always block a proposal if Germany is in the blocking coalition. This is the most negative consequence of the Nice formula: that since a QMV decision requires a majority of member states, the large states acquired increased power to block decisions if not to pass them, an arrangement one commentator has deemed to be, 'incredibly, tantamount to a triple majority', in that 'a legislative decision by the Council requires a qualified majority of votes, a majority of member states and 62 per cent of the population'.[73] This compromise merely serves to increase the complexity of EU decision-making, with the consequence that: 'From 2005, a decision by QMV in a Union of 25 would thus have to go through the following hoops [and] it would need at least 232 votes in the Council from a total of 321: a pass rate of 72.27 per cent. It would have to be approved by a majority of member states, if it was based on a proposal of the Commission – otherwise the threshold would be two thirds. It could then be blocked by the 62 per cent population rule.'[74]

Those more concerned about improving representative democracy than with mere political convenience found the Nice deal difficult to defend, either in terms of equity or transparency, or for that matter of simplicity in an enlarged EU. On these grounds, some *conventionnels* made the case for a simple double majority voting system, with a requirement that a 'majority' must include 60 per cent of the Union's population. This arrangement had the appeal for its proponents both of simplicity and greater transparency, and it also encompassed the twin precepts of legitimacy appropriate to a classic federal order, namely territoriality (representing the member states) and demographic weight (representing population). But this formula was resisted by some of the larger states reluctant to unpick the painstaking compromise on voting weights reached at Nice. In order to streamline an inordinately complex formula, the Convention's working group on simplification proposed the double majority voting system (a dual majority of a majority of member states representing a majority of the Union's population), although not the double majority variant initially proposed at the Nice IGC before calculations of national self-interest came to the fore.

In the event, the Convention settled on this simplified QMV procedure, replacing the convoluted Nice arrangement, though only after making concessions to address the concerns of the larger member states. As it presently operates, QMV requires a minimum of 62 votes out of 87 to secure the passage of a legislative proposal. To meet the twin objectives of simplification and transparency the Convention eventually arrived at a formula with two quite distinct thresholds, requiring a majority of both population (after deliberation, the Convention settled for a three-fifths or 60 per cent requirement) and countries (a minimum of one half of EU member states). In the revised procedure, the vote of each member state would consist of two distinct elements: population share and membership share (one twenty-seventh of EU 27). This formula met the objections of the big four to voting weight changes and the Constitutional Treaty made provision for the Nice/Accession Treaty rules to be replaced in 2009, by which time the EU would have 27 members.

The new voting rules would also improve the chances of securing a majority, making it easier for the EU to pass legislation – statistically as easy in EU27 as in EU6 – though these rules alter the distribution of power as between different categories of member state. The critical change here (Article 1-25.1) relates to the percentage of member states and of the EU population required for a winning coalition, whereas the Nice formula actually made it more difficult to build a winning coalition. In most cases this is 55 per cent of the members of the Council, comprising at least 15 of them, and 65 per cent respectively of EU population. This changes the formula initially agreed by the Convention, whereby a qualified majority would consist of a majority of states (13 of 25) representing three-fifths of the population (60 per cent), and makes it slightly more difficult to pass Council decisions, though easier than under the present rules. In some politically sensitive policy domains such as foreign and security policy, justice and home affairs, or monetary policy, when the Council is not acting on a proposal from the Commission or from the Union's foreign minister, and where the policy initiative remains with the Council, the member states or even the European Central Bank rather than with the Commission, the qualified majority threshold rises to 72 per cent of the Council members, comprising at least 65 per cent of the population of the Union (Article 1-25.2). The details of these various thresholds are listed below.

The revised votes formula was a political bargain designed to persuade Poland and Spain, the two states holding out for the deal made at Nice, to cease their opposition to the proposed change. A blocking minority must now consist of at least four countries, giving the medium-sized states rather more leverage *vis-à-vis* the three larger states. A further measure to assuage concern about blocking procedures is that, in the event of determined opposition to a proposed measure from a group of states slightly smaller than the required blocking minority, the Council may work to ensure compromise. These arrangements will apply until 2014, though the Council, by QMV, may extend it. Although this was intended to avoid impasse on an issue that threatened to wreck the Constitutional Treaty, some commentators and even some Brussels insiders see it as a retrograde step. One determined more by political exigencies than by concern for procedural efficiency, and an attempt to appease narrow national interests that threaten to delay agreement on the Treaty. As these revised rules apply in EU27, of 134 million possible coalitions only some 2 per cent will meet the Nice Treaty's QMV criterion. Experts calculate that it will be easier to secure a winning coalition under this procedure, 'since 21.9 per cent of all coalitions meet the new QMV rules'. One principal reason for this is that 'the highest majority threshold is lowered to 60 per cent from 72 per cent, and 40 per cent of the power is concentrated in the hands of just four nations'.[75] At the same time, making legislation easier to expedite also enhances the power of the Commission and the European Parliament as power-brokers.[76]

Enlargement was the main reason for changing procedure on voting weights. The demographic size as much as the number of the new accession countries was the critical factor here: three of the six founding members are large states, but of the EU27 states only six are large or medium-sized states, a matter of some concern to those member states seeking to maintain their ascendancy in EU affairs. The revision of QMV weights in the Constitutional Treaty represented a marked shift in voting power in favour of the larger states, and even a modest gain for the smaller member states. There was predictable resistance from the principal 'losers' to unpicking the Nice deal, the medium-sized countries, notably Spain and Poland, but also from France, whose objections were rather more about politics than demography. This issue was in fact one of the most controversial aspects of the entire constitutional endeavour, as became clear from the impasse on this issue in the IGC.

A study by Baldwin and Widgren has anticipated the likely impact of these new voting arrangements on the distribution of power in the Council, measured in terms of the capacity to cash in voting strength so as to make or break a winning coalition in the Council of Ministers. By using a computer program (the Banzhaf index) to calculate the likelihood of any given member state's weighted vote being critical to a given winning coalition on a random issue – whether under the Nice rules, or those proposed in the Constitution – these scholars confirm that the real winners under the new arrangements are the four big member states, Germany, the United Kingdom, France and Italy. Indeed, Germany's share of voting power rises by some 65 per cent, from 8 per cent under the Nice rules to 13 per cent in the new proposals. If this formula is adopted, the biggest five member states will increase their voting power from 31 per cent to 40 per cent, whereas 17 medium-sized and smaller member states whose population is between 3 and 40 millions will actually lose out.[77]

This fact goes some way to explain why the bigger states, not least France, dropped their initial objections to changing voting weights. These same researchers explain this outcome as follows: the Nice rules take account only of weighted votes, with the big countries having more votes than the smaller ones though far fewer votes than would accrue if the population-proportionality criterion is applied, as it is under the revised voting rules. In EU27 the Nice voting rules allow for 2.7 million winning coalitions, only 23 of which fail on the other two criteria. In short, the proposed arrangement for dual weighting (population share and membership share) 'shifts voting weights in two opposing directions. Under the population weighting, Germany's share rises to 17 per cent, but under the new scheme's membership weighting, Germany's vote share falls to 1/27th.' In effect, the new voting weights are an average of these two criteria, but with the population factor counting for much more than the membership share, whereas for the smallest member states the population size counts for much less than the membership share. And 'because power shares must sum to 100 per cent, the in-between nations lose [in as much as] they only see mild differences between their weighted-vote under Nice and their population and membership shares under the draft Constitution'.[78] It was for this very reason that Poland and Spain, two states in the medium population range, objected strenuously to the abandoning of the Nice formula.

The specific arrangements for QMV are summarised in the Constitutional Treaty as follows:

- QMV in relation to enhanced co-operation (Chapter III, Article 1-44.3) confirms the above procedural change. In this case, a blocking minority is designated as the 'minimum number of Council members representing more than 35 per cent of the participating Member States, plus one member, failing which the qualified majority shall be deemed attained'. The same formula applies to those instances where the Council is not acting on a proposal, either from the Commission or from the foreign minister.

- QMV with regard to decisions taken by the Parliament to suspend certain rights resulting from EU membership now requires a qualified majority of at least 72 per cent of the members of the Council, representing the participating member states, and comprising at least 65 per cent of the population of these states (Article 1-59.5). This likewise revises the figure of a two-thirds majority of votes cast, representing the majority of EU members in the initial draft treaty. The final version of the Treaty also added the provision that, following a decision to suspend voting rights in the institutions, or to do so on the recommendation of the Commission, the Council should act by a qualified majority representing at least 55 per cent of the members of the Council representing the participating member states, and comprising at least 65 per cent of the population of these states. A blocking minority in this case would consist of at least the minimum of Council members representing more than 35 per cent of the population of the participating member states, plus one member; failing which, a qualified majority is deemed to be attained.
- QMV with regard to agreements reached with any state seeking a voluntary withdrawal from the Union was designated in the final Treaty draft as at least 72 per cent of the Council members representing the participating states in the decision, and comprising at least 65 per cent of the population of these states (Article 1-60.4). No QMV figures were stipulated in relation to this matter in the initial draft of the Constitution.
- QMV in relation to common economic policy was redefined (Article 3-179.4 – ex article 99 TEC and Article 3-76.7 – ex article 104 TEC) as at least 55 per cent of the Council comprising at least 65 per cent of the population of the participating states. And a blocking minority was now defined as including states representing more than 35 per cent of EU population of the participating member states, plus one member.
- QMV in provisions specific to members of the Euro-zone (Article 3 194 new), and transitional arrangements for states acceding to the euro (Article 3-197 – ex Article 122.1 and 122.3–5 TEC) are defined as at least 55 per cent of the Council comprising at least 65 per cent of the population of the participating states. And a blocking minority was now defined as including states representing more than 35 per cent of EU population of the participating member states, plus one member.
- QMV with regard to the Council adopting a European decision confirming structured co-operation on military capabilities in relation to common foreign and security policy after consultation with the Union foreign minister, would require a qualified majority of at least 55 per cent of the members of the Council representing the participating Member States comprising at least 65 per cent of the population of these states. A blocking minority must include at least the minimum number of Council members representing more than 35 per cent of EU population of the participating member states, plus one member. The same voting rules would apply (Article 3-312.4 new) to the suspension from structured cooperation of any member state that no longer meets the criteria, or is no longer able to meet the commitments for participation. All other decisions

and recommendations by the Council pertaining to structured co-operation, other than those referred to above, would be agreed by unanimity amongst the participating member states.

## The Commission

Reforming the Commission and not least reducing the number of commissioners was the main theme of discussions on this institution, though by no means the only one. The fact that each member state currently retains a commissioner not only confirms the notion of nationality in what is supposedly a supranational office, but also makes overall policy co-ordination more difficult. The Commission's traditional role as 'defender' and 'upgrader' of the Community interest seemed likely to be undermined by an unprecedented enlargement that increases both the range and disparity of member states' interests. And it was no less likely to curb the Commission's appetite for bold initiatives of the sort that have served the Union so well in the past. Moreover, some Brussels-watchers felt that such an absence of leadership might well encourage member states to take advantage of flexible co-operation arrangements, to opt for common intergovernmental initiatives outside the treaty framework, with 'the danger ... that it could set in motion its own disintegration dynamic', so that 'in such a context it would become less efficient and effective and would thus lose legitimacy for lack of convincing "output" [and] a slow erosion of the capacity to act'.[79] These are important issues, and the Convention was bound to consider them in its review of the Commission's role and purpose in a much enlarged Union.

The Commission is a hybrid institution. On the one hand it undertakes administrative, policy-framing and managerial functions appropriate to any bureaucracy. On the other hand, the College of commissioners performs distinctly political functions usually associated with executive governance: for instance, launching major policy initiatives, evaluating ongoing policy, implementing and monitoring EU rules and regulations, as well as representing the wider European interest in its relations with the Council of Ministers and the European Council, in effect the Union's confederal institutions. These are important tasks, but the Commission undertakes them on the basis of only flimsy legitimacy, with much less accountability for its actions than is desirable in a polity that subscribes to democratic norms. Concern over the Union's legitimacy and democracy deficits meant that the Convention was bound to consider this issue, and how to make the Commission more accountable for the exercise of its considerable powers. The Commission was quite aware, too, of this need to improve its public image, with many MEPs demanding a marked improvement in the institution's performance.[80]

These criticisms are hardly new, and they reflect long-standing concern about the status of an institution that defies classification in the conventional lexicon of governance. Critics, especially those in the member states, have long censured the Commission for overreaching itself, critical of it for harbouring inappropriate aspirations to steer the European project, and no less wary about its supranational mission. The Commission is seen here as being inappropriately situated for its role as outlined in the founding treaties, a secretariat or international civil service operating on behalf of the member states, albeit a bureau with some considerable discretion for influencing policy, and in some specialised policy areas even autonomy. Of late, however, new criticisms have surfaced, with the Commission reproached for lackadaisical procedures, organisational ineptitude that in 1999 culminated in the enforced resignation of the Santer Commission. There are other, less exigent but nevertheless problematic issues facing an institution that, as some critics see it, has outgrown its role as the Community's *modus vivendi* and guardian of the treaties. Some, for instance, see the Commission's role in enforcing agreed rules as a task more appropriate to the Court of Justice, while other critical voices point to a College grown unwieldy as a consequence of successive enlargements, and thus incapacitated in the performance of its essential task of ensuring a relevant and cogent policy agenda in those areas for which it retains this important responsibility.[81]

The same complaint is made about the Commission's contribution to the Union's democracy deficit. The presidency arrangements hardly confirm democratic norms, appointed as this office is by the member states after behind-the-scenes horse-trading in the European Council, with the prospective candidate nominated by qualified majority vote and only subsequently 'approved' by a simple majority vote in the Parliament. The proposal to 'elect' the Commission president figured in the Franco-German drive for institutional reform. And although Berlin's motives here did reflect noble intentions, not least to balance the considerable power vested in the new office of the Council presidency with a degree of countervailing legitimacy in the Union's principal supranational office, French motives were altogether more self-seeking, involving a trade-off between a limited form of 'election' for the president and securing Germany's acquiescence to its plans for better co-ordination of the Union's foreign policy.[82]

The case for greater democracy in the Commission's affairs was a more pressing matter for the Convention. Concern to redress weak legitimacy and improve democracy are familiar themes of the federalist narrative, the idea that some form of elective democracy is the surest way of instilling in citizens a sense of personal affiliation to the European polity, an antidote to endemic apathy revealed in poor voter turn-out at European elections. One solution to these democracy and legitimacy deficits that found ready support in the Convention was to install a procedure to indirectly elect, and for some even to directly elect its president. The Convention considered various elective procedures, though without reaching agreement. Government representatives were bound to be wary about ceding the power of appointment over such an important office, and in the end the best that *conventionnels* could come up with was a proposal that the European Council would select the president from an 'approved' list of candidates. Radical voices rightly see this arrangement as 'election' in only the loosest sense of the term, a weak procedure at best 'and not a large step forward from the current position, given that it allows the European Council to have the key role of nominating one single candidate upon which the European Parliament can vote'. For it is by no means certain that the Council will 'simply fall into line and nominate the candidate of the party with the largest number of votes'.[83]

There is a view that sees scope here for imbuing this important office with a legitimacy that has so far eluded it. As Kiljunen sees it, 'for the first time, the presidency of the Commission will become a political appointment', and this 'is a major step [for] the president will no longer be appointed on the basis of competence and nationality alone, but also on the basis of consultation with European parties represented in the European Parliament'.[84] But is it likely that this limited elective procedure will resolve the legitimacy deficit? For the successful candidate would owe his/her office to a narrow and unrepresentative constituency, a privileged electoral college. The legitimacy of the presidency is hardly likely to be enhanced by any procedure whereby the Council retains the definitive say in which candidate the Parliament is required to confirm, rather than to actually choose one on its own initiative.

In the end, none of these proposals survived debate. The idea of election raised familiar objections. Democracy is less attractive to political elites than it is to citizens, especially those who are active in civil society. For one thing, it raises the spectre of populism in minds rather more disposed to authority than to democracy. Governments were concerned here that an elected Commission might become unduly politicised, falling under the influence of one or other of the Parliament's party groups, and as such under pressure to surrender its independence in what would be *de facto* a parliamentary system of governance. Predictably, most governments took the view that the elective principle was inappropriate for an institution that presently functions, not in a legislative capacity but as a secretariat. Some went even further, making the case that election in the usual sense would compromise its administrative functions, ensuring that 'the Commission would not be able to exercise some of its strongly apolitical tasks of a purely administrative body (e.g. competition policy) ... because it would depend more on the political composition of the European Parliament than nowadays and hence be more vulnerable to the possible motion of censure'.[85]

Formal censure is, of course, an important aspect of accountability for any public office, and it did figure in the Convention's discussions. Again, however, the need to balance quite different points of view on this issue meant that the outcome fell some considerable way short of the customary benchmarks for democratic procedure. There has always been tension in the College between commissioners' individual stewardship over their designated policy portfolio, the collegial principle and the president's discretionary leadership. These are quite different, indeed competing functions and by no means easy to reconcile. The Constitutional Treaty settled for the relatively safe option of reinforcing the president's authority at the expense of the College, permitting the president to dismiss individual commissioners should circumstances warrant such drastic intervention. Yet the Constitutional Treaty did not remotely entertain the bold step of installing democratic responsibility in the management of Commission affairs, by allowing Parliament to censure the president by means of a vote of 'no confidence'. Instead, it maintained the limited provision whereby Parliament may censure only the entire College.

Some *conventionnels* made more radical proposals from the floor, notably for the democratic election of the president or even of the entire College at the same time as the European elections, with each party group in the Parliament nominating its leader as a presidential candidate, by using the primary and second round procedures familiar as in some national presidential elections that allow for a run-off between the two candidates with the largest votes in the first round. More cautious voices prevailed, however. Doubts were expressed, for instance, about whether Parliament would choose candidate(s) of sufficient stature, and there was no clear agreement about 'appropriate safeguards' for a nomination procedure. The case for direct election assumed a democratic dividend, that a presidency or College election would boost turn-out in European elections, somehow making transnational politics more relevant for citizens, and not least enhancing the salience of Europe-wide issues at the polls. As one commentator saw it, elections would enhance the legitimacy 'not only of the European Parliament but of the Union as a whole [for] the European Union is in need of a more active and aware public'. As Hoffmann sees it, 'giving voters more responsibility by linking the European Parliament elections to the Commission President nomination would do exactly that'.[86] Moreover, as an elected office holder the Commission president would undoubtedly have more influence in the European Council, where presently he 'is the only non-elected leader'.[87]

The Convention also considered giving Parliament the right to elect the Commission College, a marked improvement on its present role of merely approving a president's College in its entirety. There was a proposal, too, for permitting Parliament to approve or otherwise individual commissioners, so as to 'increase the political authority of the individual Commissioners and of the College as a whole', as well as to improve 'the accountability of the Commission to the Parliament and ensure that not too much political power was concentrated in the hands of the Commission President'.[88] But these radical ideas failed to win support where it mattered, and Giscard used the situation to canvass his own more modest proposal, with the European Council keeping its prerogative to choose the Commission. His case for the status quo was the same as that made by the leading member states, namely the need to avoid empowering or unduly politicising the Commission. As such, the elective principle remains largely meaningless in EU governance except at the margins, and lacks proper procedures for public participation in deciding who holds high executive office.

Once again, politics trumped principle. Resistance from three of the largest member states, with Giscard's complicity, put paid to any idea of the Parliament electing the Commission president. The Commission president was to be 'elected' after a fashion, but by a procedure that looks, as one critic put it, 'curiously unlike most other democratic elections', and in fact is rather more reminiscent of elections in the former Soviet Union![89] The European Council, 'taking account' but no more than that, of the outcome of the European Parliamentary elections, would select its own preferred candidate for the Commission presidency, forwarding a single name to the Parliament for endorsement. In the event of the preferred candidate failing to secure the requisite votes, the European Council would then put forward another candidate. However, a single candidate for this important office proposed to the Parliament by the European Council on a 'take it or leave it' basis is hardly a meaningful democratic exercise. And neither will it ensure a truly representative candidate, for in effect Parliament is invited merely to endorse the choice of political leaders. The patent lack of legitimacy of any candidate 'elected' by these means would detract from the authority of the Commission, and no less diminish the incumbent's authority when it comes to allocating portfolios amongst the other commissioners, for these same proposals (Article 1-27.2) also give the Commission President greater influence over the selection of the College.

Some MEPs interpreted this flawed procedure nevertheless as Parliament's right to nominate candidates for the office during European election campaigns, but neither Giscard nor most governments saw it in this light. When the issue was raised in the Convention the representatives of Austria, Greece, Belgium, the Netherlands, and amongst the candidate countries Bulgaria and the Czech Republic, proposed an elective role for the Parliament. The Greek representative supported by Slovakia even proposed a compromise, to the effect that the European political parties in the Parliament should nominate candidates. But this was opposed by Sweden, Portugal, Finland and Estonia. Meanwhile, Ireland and Denmark proposed an electoral college as a compromise, one tasked with choosing between candidates. Whereas Malta proposed that this elective function should be exercised by a congress of national parliamentarians, with voting weighted according to a demographic quotient. The leading countries resolutely opposed any change in procedure, and they prevailed. This issue highlights the residual ideological differences over where power should reside in the Union.

Opponents of the elective principle maintain that the EU is simply not a suitable case for representative democracy as this applies in the European nation-state. They point to the absence of a thriving party politics that is indispensable for representative democracy, and to the lack of a European public space in which these transnational parties might operate as a bridge between policy-makers and citizens. More significant even than these deficiencies is the absence of European demos, the shared political identity essential for sustaining common endeavour amongst citizens and the indispensable socio-cultural foundation for democratic politics. These are familiar objections to a democratic EU polity in the classic sense, and voiced as such by government representatives in the Convention. Direct election by Parliament would certainly place the Commission under the control of the majority party group, or a coalition of parliamentary parties, though a more democratic electoral procedure – for instance, one requiring a two-thirds or three-quarters threshold of MEPs for electing the Commission – would broaden the political base of successful candidates, and do much to redress this institution's persistent democracy deficit.

Legitimacy and accountability are also problematic issues for this remote institution. Objections from powerful vested interests notwithstanding, the case for increasing Commission accountability by introducing some form of elective procedure to replace 'mere' appointment is convincing. Closer political linkages between the Commission and the Parliament are more likely to improve democracy than the Commission relying on the European Council for what is at best second-hand authority. The Council after all represents member states' interests, and for it to remain as the Commission president's exclusive 'elector' hardly improves that office's legitimacy. As things stand the electorate is too removed from EU governance. Establishing an elective linkage between these two 'Community' institutions would not mean the Commission's outright dependence on Parliament, for both institutions represent quite distinct interests and different constituencies. The Commission represents the common or European interest, Parliament the people. These are complementary but by no means identical constituencies, and each has its own distinctive 'European' agenda. For Hoffman, 'linking them together through the election of the Commission President by the European Parliament would strengthen both institutions because the powers of the European Parliament (and the stakes during its elections) would be increased'. To elect the Commission president in a way that avoids 'appointment' by a cabal of political leaders would, or so proponents see it, 'be to open up a genuine political space at the European level'. Those who object to election on the grounds that it will politicise the office simply miss the point, for it 'it needs to be recognised that democratisation and politicisation are two elements of the same thing'.[90] Commentators who see this objection less as principled concern to ensure independence and non-partisanship than as thinly veiled vested interests are closer to the mark. After all, the Commission is already politicised, 'the reality is that ... the current Commission could be characterised as a grand coalition between Social Democrats and Christian Democrats'.[91]

It is difficult to deny that the Commission is a creature of politics in the most basic sense of the word in as much as it allocates scarce resources. Better, then, to acknowledge that fact, Craig asserts, for it 'to be out in the open so that voters can directly or indirectly make their considered choices'.[92] Indeed, politicisation may be no bad thing, and anyway may be unavoidable, a fact of life in Brussels. The only possible threat to the Commission's professional integrity would be if the election of its president became unduly politicised, for instance with the Parliament's political groups nominating competing candidates standing on ideological programmes. These concerns surfaced during the Convention. Accordingly, the final version of the Constitutional Treaty makes no mention of precisely how a new Commission should be 'selected', almost certainly a deliberate omission. What it did say is that the president-designate, the foreign minister and the other members of the college 'shall be subject as a body to a vote of approval by the European Parliament'. How these offices are to be filled in the first place confirms the prevalence of governments over democratic forces. The Treaty merely states (Article 1-27.2) that these individuals 'shall be selected, on the basis of the suggestion made by Member States, in accordance with the criteria set out in Article 1-26.4 and 6 second subparagraph'. This is a much less clear-cut description of the selection procedure than appeared in the initial draft of the Treaty. And it neither materially alters the basis of the commissioners' mandate, nor does it compromise their independence. It does confirm, however, that the member states control the process of who they select as their representatives.

With the 2004 enlargement set to increase the size of the College, the Convention addressed the equally controversial matter of organisational efficiency. The Commission had already launched an ambitious reform agenda in the Governance White Paper, a response in part to the debacle of 1999.[93] The view on every side of this debate was that 'collective leadership, effective policy co-ordination, and effective and democratic use of the Commission's right of initiative, will be increasingly difficult if the Commission keeps to the current system of having one commissioner per member state'. But there agreement ceased. There were those who wanted to retain national commissioners for every member state, whatever the impact on collegiality or efficiency. And on the other side of the argument were those who preferred a smaller College, indispensable, as they saw it, for efficiency, and for some (federalists, but not exclusively so) breaking the link between a Commission presence and the defence of the national interest so as to ensure 'a genuinely pan-European view free of national influence'.[94] From this perspective, a more compact College would better reflect the institution's European outlook, representing the Community interest by disconnecting commissioners from their national bases, a linkage that still causes some incumbents to be particularly receptive to domestic interests. These same logics persuaded would-be reformers to propose widening recruitment to commissioners' cabinets, to include a greater mix of nationalities, avoiding the current bias in favour of national recruitment, thus encouraging a more pan-European outlook at the centre of policy-making.

These ideas are hardly new, and nor were they confined to federalist opinion. The Protocol on Enlargement attached to the Nice Treaty had anticipated changes, breaking 'the link between the number of Member States and the number of Commissioners', declaring that when the number of member states reached 27 the number of commissioners would be fewer than the number of member states, though without specifying an upper limit.[95] The large member states had put their considerable political weight behind this change, prepared to forgo one of the two Commission seats allocated to them since the days of the High Authority of the Coal and Steel Community as a *quid pro quo* for greater efficiency, some governments seeing a smaller College as one way of sharpening political control of the Commission's complex administrative structures.

By no means every government subscribed to this view. Many of the smaller states and the candidate countries, too, anticipating much reduced influence if they gave up 'their' national Commission seat, challenged the Nice compromise. They argued for parity of representation on the grounds that membership of this focal institution not only ensures influence at the centre, but also offers less well-resourced member states their best apprenticeship in EU procedures, invaluable experience of how 'Brussels' actually works. When it became apparent that the fight to retain symbolic parity had been lost in the Convention the small states determined to continue the fight, subsequently reopening the issue in the IGC, though without avail, except to secure an interim delay in implementation.

In light of this controversy, the fact that Giscard lined up with those who would reform the Commission was crucial to the outcome. His position here was close to that of the leading governments, that efficiency was the surest way of restoring the Commission's credibility, and of providing effective and strategic leadership at the centre, convinced that collegiality would be more easily maintained in a smaller college. He expressed doubt as to whether, under present arrangements, there would be enough 'real' commission portfolios to go round after enlargement. Nevertheless, he was under no illusion that this reform would be easy to deliver, for it raises as many problems as it resolves. Compromise was required to carry it off, and this deal centred on adopting some form of rotation. Former Commission President Jacques Santer had proposed rotation of Commission portfolios as between every member state. This would mean the exclusion periodically of one or more of the larger states, threatening, as some saw it, to further impair the college's leadership capacity and potentially its legitimacy. More to the point, it was by no means certain that the large member states would readily accept policy proposals – and especially in controversial policy domains – from any Commission in which they were not represented. The larger states, naturally enough in light of their own interests, preferred a two-tiered arrangement consisting of senior and junior, voting and non-voting commissioners, with their own participation in the first rank guaranteed and with rotation confined to the smaller states.[96]

Selective rotation was defended on the somewhat dubious grounds that all member states enjoy *de facto* legal equality, a semantic point but hardly a reassuring one for those states required to surrender their permanent seat, and in effect it amounted, as one critic has observed, to little more than 'a comfort blanket', in that 'advisors, with no votes in the Commission, and no clear role, and no right to be involved in all the work of the Commission, are clearly no substitutes for commissioners'.[97] Those who opposed a tiered Commission countered that the Commission is already a hierarchical arrangement, with the allocation of Commission portfolios ensuring commissioners of variable political weight and influence; and that a Commission consisting of voting and non-voting members would merely compound this inequity, be more likely to unbalance the Commission in that the non-voting incumbents would tend to be second-rate and certainly second-class candidates who might feel absolved from any responsibility for the decisions of their voting colleagues.

As the Convention reviewed these options it became clear that the larger member states laid claim to a commissioner in perpetuity, a reflection both of their political power based on demographic weight and, as some of them saw it in more basic terms, their higher budgetary contributions. The figures are incontrovertible, though whether wealth should ensure disproportionate power is questionable. After the 2004 enlargement the six most populous states, each with populations of more than 40 million, represent some 74 per cent of the Union's population, with the three largest accounting for some 35–40 per cent of the total. A Commission without any representation from the largest member states could certainly be challenged as not adequately reflecting the interests and concerns of these leading countries, thereby undermining the institution's legitimacy overall. Giscard made precisely this point, observing that a Commission lacking a voting commissioner from one or more of the Union's political heavyweights for a period of five years would not only have reduced its legitimacy but diminished its authority.[98] Yet this argument can be stood on its head, and it was by representatives from the smaller states, supported not least by the Commission. As they saw it, basing the claim to political influence merely on population size is problematical on two counts.

On the one hand, it reinforces confederalism, and by the same token diminishes the idea of a common European interest in what is after all the Union's primary supranational institution. And in so far as this claim to special treatment reinforces *directoire*, it consolidates a damaging fault-line in the Union's political fabric. Once it became apparent that the small countries were indeed losing the argument for what they saw as 'fair rotation', they reverted to the default position, defending their right to retain a national commissioner. To a degree resistance paid off, securing a delay in the implementation of what most commentators see as the inevitable downsizing of the Commission.

The accession countries were in the same camp on this issue as the smaller EU15 states. They too demanded one commissioner per member state, concerned that a streamlined Commission would be too easily manipulated or checked by the big member states. The accession countries had been mere bystanders during the Nice IGC that had first broached this matter, and barely influential during the Convention. However, they raised their game after becoming full member states, putting their collective political weight behind the demand from the admittedly few EU15 member states who wanted this issue revisited in the IGC. The Commission endorsed their demand, President Prodi informing the European Parliament in September 2003 that 'no people of the Union deserves to be represented by a second-class commissioner'.[99]

In the event, their campaign brought only a modest return, a College reduced to 15, to include the president and the foreign minister, with every member state represented by means of equal rotation, though after the Commission that assumed office in 2004 has completed its term in 2009. The Constitutional Treaty stipulated (Article 1-26.6) that succeeding Commissions 'shall consist of a number of Members, including its President and the Union Minister for Foreign Affairs, corresponding to two thirds of the number of Member States, unless the European Council, acting unanimously, decides to alter this figure'.[102] Contrary to Giscard's advice, the Convention inserted a proposal from a coalition of 16 small/medium-sized member states in the final round of negotiations for a two-tier college with equal rotation from 2014, but in the meantime retaining one commissioner per member state, though this compromise did not find its way into the final draft. Commissioners would be selected (Article 1-26) according to the strict rotation criterion agreed in the Nice Treaty,[101] with the Commission College reflecting 'the demographic and geographical range of all the Member States'.[100] Much was made of the need to give the newcomers time to 'play themselves in', to find their way around a still unfamiliar Euro-land, using the experience of their admittedly temporary commissioners to learn the ropes, to facilitate alliances with the bigger players that will stand them in better stead for maximising influence by means of established networks when they do eventually surrender 'their own' commissioners. This was the 'solution' preferred by the big three, but it was resisted by the smaller countries and the accession countries alike, seeing themselves as the principal losers. The issue threatened deadlock and it was only resolved by another 'typical' fudge, a compromise that was more 'damage limitation' than it was well–considered, let alone principled reform. Time constraints, the fact that the appointment of a new Commission term was imminent, played a part in ensuring agreement.

This meant 25 commissioners in the first instance, one per member state during the first critical stage of the latest enlargement, although Romanian and Bulgarian accession (2007) triggered the Nice Protocol on Enlargement, which requires that on reaching a threshold of 27 member states the Union must reduce the Commission college, to less than the number of member states, 'corresponding to two thirds of the number of Member States', at the discretion of the European Council but without specifying the exact number of commissioners. The final draft of the Treaty included a clause that reaffirmed the 'equality' of each member state (Article 1-5.1), though it is doubtful whether this in itself will be sufficient to assuage resentment amongst 'the others' over losing permanent representation in the Commission College. This arrangement confirms that it is governments that determine important institutional matters, in particular the larger states and especially the big three. The foreign ministers, meeting in Naples in November 2003, confirmed this deal, agreeing even before the Constitutional Treaty was finalised to revert to one commissioner per member state with parity of voting rights, though with rotation to be applied subsequently by agreement.

One further concession to bruised sensibilities was the provision in the final version of the Constitutional Treaty that confirmed the requirement for any future downsized Commission to take due account of the views of those member states that do not have their own commissioner when conducting its business. The final piece of this bargain was a compensatory mechanism raising the minimum number of MEPs for any member state, from four to six in the case of Luxembourg and pro rata for other small states in proportion to their population, thereby increasing the total membership of the Parliament from 736 to 750 (Article 1-20.2). There is nevertheless no equivalence between gaining MEPs and losing a commissioner. The prospect was discussed too – an inducement to embrace this controversial institutional reform – that if the reduced Commission should seem not to work as expected the system of representation *ex post facto* might be restored by the European Council was permitted, though this default decision would require unanimity.

This reform survives in the Lisbon Treaty, and it will almost certainly generate political friction once it is implemented. Stubborn resistance by the perceived 'losers' from this deal with their concern about diminished status will surely lead to political wrangling, not least over the number of, and no less the powers exercised by commissioners. Whatever compromise is reached on this, it will almost certainly be too many commissioners for the effective management of business, and too few for those losing direct representation. This matter will not easily be resolved and will likely weaken the Commission, to say nothing of stirring up inter-institutional rivalry, hardly 'the most productive way to build a new transparent and efficient and democratic Union'.[103] More than that, a tiered Commission, with voting and non-voting members, runs the risk of imbalance and, worse, the prospect of non-represented member states absolving themselves from responsibility for Commission decisions.

One possible solution to the problem of Commission representation discussed in the Convention was for a tiered College of voting and non-voting members, another example of putative compromise between quite different preferences for allocating institutional power, and one that invites obvious criticism. One *conventionnel* described it as 'the most pathetic of all possible solutions', maintaining that 'if the Convention can be said to have failed at anything, it was in the composition of the Commission [for] what purpose would be served by Commissioners who have no vote and no operative responsibility? They would be eunuchs … More than that they would be a Fifth Column in the Commission.' In these circumstances, Kiljunen continues, 'the only task left to the non-voting Commissioners would be to safeguard their national interests [and] that would demolish the common European approach and spirit that should inform the Commission's work'.[104] The role of the non-voting commissioners is, to say the least, vague. How, for instance, would rotation be organised as between the voting and non-voting members of the college, and what would be the geographical basis for rotation? Rotation between the two tiers risks institutionalising geographical, and for that matter other divisions, with the same countries always belonging to these respective groups.

Moreover, rotation as applied to the upper-tier might prove especially difficult in the case of the president and the foreign affairs minister, in view of their distinctive roles and special appointment procedures. An obvious criticism of these proposed arrangements was that the simplification of governance prescribed at Laeken as a key to greater legitimacy is hardly likely to follow from them. These procedures are less a convincing attempt to reform a key institution than they are 'an unhappy compromise … between those who wanted a small Commission, seeing this as potentially more effective and providing stronger collective leadership (and thus control over the administration) … and those who wanted to retain a large commission with every member state having a commissioner'.[105]

The case was frequently made during the Convention that 'whatever compromise might ultimately be devised, it is quite patent that it is simply impossible to design a Commission of ten to fifteen members' that will reflect the regional, let alone the particular national diversity of the Union's member states.[106] This may be so, but the Constitutional Treaty provided insufficient detail about these critical matters to settle the argument either way. Too much was left to chance in these arrangements, and as with any institutional reform what is intended and how things actually work out in practice may not coincide. There is certainly no clear indication as to how selection of these roles might operate in practice, let alone how 'a Commission of ten or even fifteen commissioners could "reflect satisfactorily" twenty-seven or more member States'.[107] Clarification of these important matters was postponed, precisely because they are so controversial, the principals content merely to have made a deal in principle. The Council has the task of deciding, and unanimously, the precise arrangements in due course. We can reasonably surmise that the outcome of arrangement will be contingent depending as these matters invariably do on institutional dynamics.

Other changes, too, confirm the prevalence of confederal preferences where institutional design is the issue. The Committee of Permanent Representatives, a bastion of intergovernmental influence and bargaining in Brussels, and one expressly intended from the outset to constrain the Commission's prerogative for proposing policy, is specifically mentioned in the Treaty (Article 1-24.5), and in a way that confirms intergovernmental predilections. The initial draft of the Constitutional Treaty made no mention of this 'watchdog' of member states' interests, settling instead on a vague formula that merely referred to the function of the legislative and General Affairs Council for ensuring consistency in the work of the Council of Ministers. Some governments were determined, however, to bolster COREPER's role and the final version of the draft treaty omitted an earlier draft's reference to the Council in its General Affairs capacity being required to liaise with the Commission in preparing and following up European Council meetings, a direct outcome of member states' lobbying during the IGC.

An explicit reference to COREPER as a medium for policy-making was inserted in the final draft. None of these revisions, however, significantly alters, let alone reduces the Commission's role in pillar-one policy-making. It would retain for instance the exclusive right to propose legislation in those policy domains where it has always exercised this prerogative, and it even acquired additional power of initiative in criminal justice and police co-operation, and in drafting the budget through the submission of initiatives for the annual budget and the multi-annual financial framework. There was the prospect, too, of the Commission expanding its direct influence in another important intergovernmental policy domain with the new European foreign minister designated as a Commission vice-president, though required to work closely with the Council and with no autonomy over EU foreign and security policy. But neither did the Commission noticeably expand its role *vis-à-vis* the confederal institutions in other increasingly important policy domains beyond its central role in the governance of the single market.

We have reviewed the distribution of power in the Union's executive institutions, and in this important matter the Constitutional Treaty made some important recommendations that would markedly improve the efficiency, though hardly the democratic nature of decision-making. Laeken had raised other concerns, too, mandating the Convention to simplify governance and to make decision-making more transparent to the citizen, with a view to improving legitimacy. These matters relate to democratic life in the Union, a question that is central to any serious constitutional endeavour, though one that has not so far featured over-much in the European treaties. The democracy question, as we have seen, figured in the debate on procedures for policy-making, though for the most part incidentally. In a polity that subscribes at least formally to liberal democratic norms, and no less one that requires commitment to such values as a condition of membership the quest for improving the quality of EU democracy must be measured, and in no small part, against the standards of the Union's own parliamentary procedures.

## The quest to improve the quality of democratic life

What passed for legitimacy in the Community's early years was based rather more on performance criteria than on democratic credentials *per se*.[108] Not even the direct election of the European Parliament since 1979 has done much to improve the legitimacy of the Community's decision-making, and arguably even less to deepen popular affiliation with what is widely perceived to be remote politics and non-accountable governance. Indeed, the European Parliament has its own problem with legitimacy, confirmed by its poor turn-out figures in successive European elections. The weak sense of public affiliation to the EU polity is connected, and in no small measure, to the widespread perception of democracy deficits.

This became a matter of some concern for politicians during the 1990s, as the pace of integration accelerated, and public opinion showed signs of disapprobation with 'Europe'. So much so, that improving democratic life in the Union figured on the Laeken agenda. The reason for this had rather more to do with pragmatism than with principle, a need to better connect with citizens who, despite widespread support for the broad aims of the European project 'do not always see a connection between these goals and the Union's everyday action'. In these circumstances, the Convention was mandated to find ways of bringing the Union closer to its citizens, by making it 'more democratic, more transparent and more efficient'.[109] Transparency was one obvious solution for a polity where 'deals are all too often cut out of their sight', and yet where the public 'want better democratic scrutiny'.[110] In the event, the Convention failed this test, more so than it did the challenge of reforming the institutions and decision-making procedures. Cynics might claim that the reason for this is fairly obvious, that democracy matters less than power, at least to those who would wield power in the institutions.

To a degree, this is valid criticism, but it is by no means the whole picture. There are other factors to be considered here. The Convention did not avoid the democracy question, making specific proposals for a separate title in the Constitutional Treaty on 'the democratic life of the Union'. The response here was hardly sufficient for dealing with the problem. The fact that limited time was made available to discuss democracy, or more to the point the lack of it, confirmed that this was hardly a priority for politicians. Giscard preferred to keep the issue off the main agenda, seeing here an issue that could mobilise federalists. But there was more to avoiding the issue than Giscard's own prejudices. There are considerable difficulties in promoting collective action across borders, and there is no greater challenge facing the EU than facilitating popular participation and establishing meaningful transnational democracy. The Convention concentrated on matters that could be resolved, such as measures designed to improve accountability. The expert committee on Commission mismanagement (1999) had concluded that 'a culture of irregularities and irresponsibility' is more likely to develop wherever proper accountability procedures are lacking.[111]

The Convention responded to the challenge. Lack of transparency, what to many seems to be a culture of indifference to norms and values appropriate to public accountability, is endemic in the European institutions as it is in any bureaucratised governance, whether in the Union's long-established or its more recent bureaus such as Europol, Eurojust and the Office of the High Representative for foreign affairs. Disconcerting, too, was the fact that effective public scrutiny did not apply to the European Central Bank. The multi-level design of the Union's political architecture raises particular problems in this regard, and it is a serious hindrance to a culture of democracy. This is no one's fault in particular, but rather a consequence of a unique institutional design with 'built-in ambiguities', the logics of a polity that tries to balance supranational with state-centric preferences which unavoidably reinforce tensions 'between and within institutions'.[112]

In these circumstances, opening up the Union's decisional processes to public scrutiny is only part of the solution, though transparency is indispensable for robust democracy. More controversially for a polity that privileges institutional actors as stakeholders rather than citizens is that democracy is measured by citizens' participation in governance. And though the Convention did discuss more effective scrutiny of administrators and decision-makers, it had little to say about how to improve public participation in EU politics, whether through the medium of political parties, the European Ombudsman or by contributions from civil society. In one revealing intervention about how to engage the public in public affairs beyond the nation states, Vice-president Dehaene admitted that even 'the availability of information does not automatically entail a higher degree of [public] interest'.[113] The official response to this critical matter was disappointing, and in no whit 'remedied by a constitution which is restricted to offering a framework to be filled this way and that by political actors', those insiders who have managed affairs from the start.[114]

The failure to engage with the public at large is not a problem that should entirely be blamed on actors at the European level. It is as much the fault of national politicians. National political parties are after all the core of the European party families, and it is one of their functions to engage with their own electorates on European policy, 'to make the interactions of voters, parties, parliament and government work at the European level as satisfactorily as it does at the national level'.[115] That national parties have mostly failed to do so is apparent from the way that European issues are discounted in national politics, trivialised as a simple, and too often a simplistic calculus of 'the' national interest. Suffice it to say here that the task of raising public awareness of the complex nature of 'European' issues, explaining how they intersect with domestic policy, is by no means an easy one. This has rather less to do with confronting public perceptions – and all too often prejudices – about 'Europe' *per se*, bringing home to ordinary citizens the fundamental changes that have occurred over recent decades in the structures of government, even if domestic parties were prepared to explain the growing interdependence of national and EU-level governances. It has just as much to do with cultural shifts in the way people see politics.

People are less tribal nowadays in their politics, disinclined to trust authority, less disposed to believe what politicians tell them, and with good reason. In modern mass societies party politics is everywhere discounted, and at the European level is bound to face greater obstacles even than on home turf, hardly a reliable agency then for connecting people at the grassroots to remote European governance. This is in part a problem of scale, but not entirely so. Certainly, there is nothing that remotely resembles a Europe-wide political culture, let alone European demos. National electorates have quite different preferences about public policy, and no less about European integration. And the problem as always is one of agency, for the representative model of liberal democracy that connects citizens to the national body politic does not easily translate to the European level. All manner of procedural and cultural obstacles stand in the way of realising a popular transnational politics, in effect a meaningful democratic conversation within a public space. For one thing, party politics as it is conducted at the EU level, though it reflects to a degree the enduring pattern of socio-economic cleavages that shape domestic party competition, does not do so to anything like the same extent. Parliamentary procedure at Strasbourg, where MEPs lack a significant elective function and where no executive resides, militates against robust adversarial politics, giving rise instead to coalitional or consociational politics, more often than not non-ideological co-operation between the two main party blocs, the PES and the EPP –ED. This is inter-party and intra-party politics more reminiscent of the American Congress than of parliamentary politics in the European tradition, for it is based, by and large, on collaborative arrangements and deal-making that does little to enhance the quality of democratic life, let alone to sharpen the public's sense of being included in a European conversation on the momentous policy issues. And it likewise does much to confirm the public's less than favourable impression of an insular elite mostly out of touch with their own lives and everyday concerns.

The root of the problem here is the Union's remoteness from the citizen, a structural circumstance as much as geographical condition. Citizens lack any meaningful sense of connection, let alone engagement with 'the system', failing to see the relevance for their lives of what occurs at this distant level. There is no sense of the EU as a public space in which to conduct a democratic conversation about public policy. This situation owes something to the persistent lack of communication between governors and governed, but not only that. The proposal in the Constitutional Treaty for a Legislative and General Affairs Council might just make a difference in this respect, by facilitating 'a vital, democratic and long-overdue opening up of EU legislation'. There is potential in this arrangement for improving media reporting, and thereby for enhancing 'domestic understanding of European politics and European power – television footage of ministers voting in Council', by making clear 'where EU legislation comes from'. But critics were nevertheless disappointed that 'the Council continues to combine legislative and executive functions'.[116] Yet more co-decision, a procedure that markedly increases the Parliament's legislative capacity, will also improve democracy, as will the onset of citizens' initiatives. The 'yellow card' system designed to give national parliaments greater oversight of subsidiarity should bring domestic and EU-level politics closer than they presently are. These proposed reforms are an improvement on current arrangements, but they hardly get to the root of the problem, not exactly an afterthought but for the most part limited reforms that do little to bring people closer to governance.

The same might be said of the proposals for monitoring EU agencies and institutions, permitting national parliaments a role in supervising Europol and Eurojust and giving the Ombudsman the right to follow up complaints about EU institutions/agencies. These, too, are an advance on current arrangements, but mostly cosmetic change. The inclusion of the Ombudsman's mandate under the title of 'the democratic life of the Union' is a case in point. The office is indispensable for ensuring democratic accountability. Yet despite dedicated work by Jakob Söderman, its first office-holder (and his successor, Nikiforos Diamondouros, who took up post in April 2003), the Ombudsman's biannual reports indicate that the office is spending too much time addressing administrative complaints from within the administrative machine than it is operating as an effective mechanism for redressing citizens' grievances. One such recent report observed that, even where the office does pursue maladministration cases on behalf of citizens, 'the low rate of acceptance and implementation of the Ombudsman's draft recommendations by the institutions is regrettable'.[117]

Whether these changes would significantly improve accountability is questionable, for these proposals seemed to be reactive than part of a cogent scheme for addressing democracy and legitimacy deficits. As one critic has put it: 'In marked contrast to most of the work of the Convention, the title on democracy appears to lack any structural philosophy. It is a mixed bag, bringing together some abstract principles and some specific provisions that might just as well be placed elsewhere in the treaty.'[118] What was missing from the Convention's deliberations here was a thoroughgoing review of the challenges confronting transnational democracy, whether as process but just as much as normative commitment to new ways of doing politics in Europe. The Constitutional Treaty did make reference to the principles of political equality and to democratic participation, but this was more as an afterthought than as a necessary condition of the Union's evolving constitutional order.

The matter was not treated as seriously as it should have been, and though the Convention did endorse the principle of democratic legitimacy, the idea that no European legislation should be adopted without Parliament's approval, it omitted to review in any significant detail what that principle actually means in relation to the other common institutions. As we have seen above, the 'election' of the Commission president hardly conforms to basic democratic standards, and the new Council president will be appointed by a qualified majority decision and in secret rather than by an open procedure. And though formally accountable to the Council, this office is only required to 'report' to the European Parliament. For all of these reasons, 'the legitimacy of the new European Council president will be very weak [and] given that the post is likely to be filled by a former prime minister, appointed behind closed doors, it seems unlikely that this new post will have adequate credibility with his or her peers, let alone with foreign leaders'.[119]

Close observers of these powerful executive institutions have pointed out that while accountability does not in itself require that these offices be subject to parliamentary scrutiny as comparable institutions are in national polities, their significance for the policy process is such that there is a 'need to have [their] powers ... properly ring-fenced by law', in ways that 'would bind them to public disclosure of their activities and give the European Parliament the powers necessary to scrutinise them if it finds reason to do so'. For that very reason, the 'principles of effective participation and accountability' should have informed the Constitution's otherwise feeble efforts to improve the democratic life of the Union 'with the vision and focus it so far lacks'.[120] This is damning criticism, and another critic similarly observed that: 'As it stands, the draft [Constitutional] treaty represents a weak and inadequate step in the accountability of the executive powers of the Commission', as well as providing 'an inadequate step in the political strengthening of the president and commissioners relative to the officials in the bureaucracy'.[121] We might conclude from this that the proposal of the Seville Council to permit public scrutiny of the opening and conclusion of the Council meeting amounted to little more than tokenism, that what followed in the Convention and IGC was a wholly inadequate response to rising public disquiet about remote governance. The most that can be said about these proposed reforms is that the Legislative and General Affairs Council, though far from being a second legislative chamber, and with considerable and non-accountable power accruing to unelected officials in its various working groups, 'is, nevertheless, a significant move in the right direction'.[122]

The problem here is cultural as much as it is political. *Conventionnels* were less inclined on the basis of what they understood to be 'normal' democratic procedures from their experience of national politics to contemplate anything as seemingly fanciful as transnational democracy. But practical politics did play a part in the outcome. Those *conventionnels* who mattered most – and by no means just the representatives of governments – were reluctant to sanction reforms that threatened either their institutional power base or their national interests. The Convention was more preoccupied with the big institutional questions, the allocation of powers and competencies, and complex inter-relations between principals than with improving democracy or facilitating a transnational political culture that would encourage citizens to more effectively monitor governance at the European level. This much was clear from the praesidium's decision not to appoint a specialised working group on democracy, for undoubtedly such a group would have recommended 'much more powerful and thoughtful proposals on democracy'.[123]

A significant case in point is election procedure. Laeken had considered changing the Union's electoral procedure so as to make European elections more relevant to citizens. The issue here was whether to conduct European elections on a transnational basis, a uniform election procedure, to establish an EU-wide constituency, one way supposedly of deepening public interest in European issues and thereby of instilling a so far elusive sense of individual membership of the European polity. Or whether instead to maintain the status quo, holding these elections according to national arrangements, thereby confirming their second-order status, the fact that they mean little more to citizens than a mid-term referendum, an opportunity to register a protest or otherwise on the state of domestic politics.

The Amsterdam Treaty had already permitted Parliament to make arrangements for holding elections 'in accordance with principles common to all member states'.[124] And though Parliament drafted an electoral act on that basis, the sheer difficulty of harmonising diverse national election arrangements left considerable scope for variation in procedure. The working group on simplification took up this challenge, recommending a further protocol on a uniform election procedure. However, resistance from some governments and national party establishments to a reform that, as they saw it, might weaken the affective bond between domestic electorates and the national polity persuaded the Convention to drop the proposal.

The same working group had rather more success with measures to enhance the Parliament's legitimacy, for instance by making co-decision the normal legislative procedure. Further, albeit modest improvements to democratic procedures included enhancing Parliament's 'elective' function, though not in ways preferred by some *conventionnels*. As we have seen above, the Commission president would be 'elected' by the majority of MEPs (Article 1-27.1) rather than merely approved by the Parliament, though only from a list comprising one candidate, a name decided upon after the usual closeted trade-off between members of the European Council. If Parliament should object to this candidate, the political leaders would submit an alternative name within the month. The assumption here is that the Council will merely 'take note' of Parliament's preferences, though only practice can establish precedent, and political dynamics on the ground have a habit of defying formal rules, or even of undermining expectations about how these rules will actually work in practice. The Parliament may yet surprise its critics on this matter, and even this limited change may in time have far-reaching consequences for EU democracy. The Commission, too, would be directly and collectively accountable in this sense to the Parliament. Of course, it has always been accountable after a fashion, but the fall-out from the 1999 crisis revealed that the Parliament's hand was weaker here than many MEPs and others with democratic proclivities might prefer.[125] These proposed reforms, too, were mostly token gestures. When it comes to facing up to the challenges of democratising the Union, the Constitutional Treaty simply failed to deliver.

The Convention's failure to deal with the long-standing issue of Parliament's geographical location is another example of lack of concern about that institution's credibility with its electorate. Nothing is more symptomatic of Parliament's seeming disregard for wasted time and squandered resources than the absurd spectacle of the frequent shuffling of personnel and papers between multiple sites, while the locus of power remains in Brussels. The Constitutional Treaty did, nevertheless, improve the European Parliament's role in EU decision-making, reinforcing its status as co-legislator, confirming the equivalence between the Council and the Parliament (ex Article 251 – retitled as Article 3-396) in jointly enacting legislation (Article 1-20.1), though with the Commission retaining its role of formally initiating policy (Article 1-26.2). With co-decision designated as the 'ordinary legislative procedure' (Article 1-34) for European Laws and Framework Laws (Article 1-34), the legislative procedure is now very much an inter-institutional relationship, and for that reason much less predictable as to its outcome than in the days when the only relation that really mattered was that between Commission and Council. The Constitutional Treaty extended the ordinary legislative procedure to a further 47 cases, and also to new policy domains in the increasingly important area of justice and home affairs and trade policy. Wolfgang Wessels calculated accordingly that 'the [legislative] cases in which the European Parliament is not involved will decrease, if the Treaty is ratified, from 47 per cent (Nice) to 26 per cent (TCE)'.[126] Of course, the Treaty was not ratified, but these new rules will apply under the Lisbon Treaty.

The Treaty also increased the Parliament's budgetary powers (Article 3-404). The present division of the budget into compulsory and non-compulsory expenditure was rescinded and Parliament has the final word on budget expenditure, though its approval is not required for any decision relating to 'own resources', and is confined merely to consultation (Article 1-54.3). The Council of Ministers retains control of the multi-annual financial framework which determines the all-important revenue side of the budget. As for the Parliament's constitutional role, the Constitutional Treaty accorded it a clear role in initiating and preparing for IGCs (Article 4-443), although, significantly, ultimate control over this process of constitutional review was to remain with the IGC (Article 4-443.2), and as such with the member governments in the European Council.

A transnational democratic order, what is often described as a European public space, remains an unlikely prospect on the basis of such limited reforms. One may wonder, too, whether deeply ingrained habits about the exercise of public power, the customary reflexes of the political class determined to impose its own narrow preferences and not least to maintain a firm hold on institutional power might not prevail over tenuous democratic aspirations. Circumstances are hardly favourable to change here. The EU does lack the cultural cement of shared identity, the sociological fabric that underpins a sense of political community, the social solidarity necessary for any meaningful conversation between Europe's historic peoples. What passes for 'European' politics is still for the most part activity between governments and other elite agencies, whether trading national preferences or sectoral actors pursuing common interests across borders, and in both cases making bargains below the public's radar and mostly out of sight of electorates.

This much was apparent, even before the crisis that followed the 2005 referendums derailed the Constitution and put on hold even these notional changes. How far these important issues are discounted by the politicians was made clear when the Brussels European Council (June 2004) considered the next incumbent of the Commission presidency. Meeting at a time when there was little reason to doubt that the Constitutional Treaty would not be ratified in due course, the Union's leaders blithely set aside the unresolved issues of legitimacy or democracy deficits, and indulged instead in their usual power play, wrangling over preferred candidates in a way that would not have been out of place in a medieval enclave called to fill the vacant papacy. And this regardless of the fact that the European elections had taken place only in the week prior to this summit, elections that had shown widespread disquiet with the Union.[127]

## Allocation of MEPs

The European Parliament does possess democratic credentials, but not even the onset of direct elections in 1979 has compensated for the continuing inequitable representation of the EU electorate. A system of degressive representation means that MEPs from the smaller countries represent far smaller electorates than do those from the larger countries. The most striking result from this arrangement is that although the larger states have the majority of the seats they nevertheless have fewer in proportion to their population size. As a consequence, the vote of a citizen from the smallest state, Luxembourg, has greater weight than that of a citizen of the largest member state, Germany. This unsatisfactory situation had been under review prior to the Convention. Even before the Nice IGC, Parliament had proposed a formula whereby the proportional allocation of MEPs would be adjusted after any future enlargement so that every member state would receive a minimum of four seats, and with a ceiling of 700 MEPs.

The Convention did not significantly alter the allocation of parliamentary seats, which had been increased over time to reflect successive enlargements, most recently at the Nice IGC in order to accommodate the latest enlargement, with the total seats increased from 626 to 732. The problem of increasing Parliament's size to accommodate new accession countries was signalled in evidence to the Convention from the Parliament's General Secretariat, to the effect that even 30 additional MEPs would be beyond the capacity of the Parliament's present facilities, both in Strasbourg and Brussels. The Parliament's then president, Pat Cox, observed that: 'We have reached the limits of what is possible. The Parliament must not become something akin to the Chinese People's Assembly, choked by numbers and nothing more than a rubber-stamp.'[128]

The Constitutional Treaty formally recognised the Union as a representative democracy based on the equality of its citizens, and this did mean revising the over-representation of smaller states in a 'degressively proportional way'. Reallocating seats so as to better reflect the balance of population gained support amongst those member states that were losers under the current rules, and the issue was revisited in the IGC. The demand made by some member states for fairer representation persuaded the Italian presidency that oversaw the first stage of the IGC to propose a modest change in the minimum number of MEPs for each country from four to five, and to raise the total complement of MEPs above 736, so that Germany – demographically the largest EU country by some way – would not lose any of its current quota of 99 members. This target required in turn a reduction in the seats allocation for the other EU15 member states. Some of the 'mini' and 'micro' member states (Cyprus, Malta, Luxembourg and Estonia) wanted this floor raised to six, a position openly endorsed by Britain and some other member states.[129] The accession of 10 new member states complicated the bargaining process, as did the uncertainty at the time over when Romania and Bulgaria would join the Union.

The eventual outcome was another example of EU fudge, with a reallocation of the parliamentary seats allotted to the second-wave entrants, though only temporarily. It was agreed that in the event that these two second-wave entrants acceded to EU membership before the 2009 parliamentary elections (which they did, in 2007), the Nice seats formula (with a limit of 732) would remain in place for the 2009 elections, but only temporarily and with a further reallocation amongst existing member states thereafter. The minimum threshold would now be 6 seats, with an upper limit of 96 – thus reducing Germany's pro rata membership, a generous concession by Chancellor Schroeder, who wanted a successful constitutional outcome. The total number of MEPs would not exceed 750, compared with the figure of 736 in the initial draft text (Article 1-20.2). This issue got dragged into the deal to recalculate Council voting weights. The figure of 750 takes account of the accession of Romania, Bulgaria, and prospectively of Croatia. The Constitutional Treaty did not determine the actual distribution of seats between the member states but it did permit the European Council, on a proposal from Parliament, to allocate seats in advance of the 2009 elections. These are significant changes, but they do not as such redress disproportionality, and neither do they deal with even more critical questions about Parliament's functions, its contribution to the Union's democratic life, the remoteness of MEPs from real power in many important policy domains, its capacity for influencing and properly scrutinising the executive (particularly the Council) and so on.

## Democratising EU governance: the role of national parliaments

Democracy has proved to be elusive at the European level, in part because of objections from some quarters that transnational democracy is as impracticable as it is undesirable. The usual view of politicians and publics alike is that representative democracy is only practicable in national polities, the historical locus, after all, of the special relationship between citizens and those they elect to serve the public interest. This relationship is historically embedded in the idea of demos, the special sense of political identity and membership rooted exclusively, at least to date, in the 'sovereign' nation-state. The relational view of democracy is both pervasive and persuasive, and it was bound to influence debate in the Convention.

This matter has become more urgent since 1985, with yet more national legislation in the politically sensitive domains of economic and social policy now shaped by European directives, regulations, framework programmes and the like. So much so, that some commentators maintain that firmer democratic control over the Union's governance depends rather less on increasing the European Parliament's powers than on improving the accountability of national ministers to their domestic parliaments for their actions in European Councils. What is often described as the 'Europeanisation' of public policy has seen a significant transfer of national legislative discretion and executive power from the member states to Europe, and with it the Union's encroachment into once exclusively domestic public policy such as policing, judicial and criminal justice policy, macro-economic management and not least foreign and security policy. This development has naturally raised concerns in national parliaments about loss of authority, the diminution of national sovereignty and, at the very least, the lack of effective accountability of the agencies of European governance.

The issue is directly related to the question of EU democracy, and as some see it to a crisis of legitimacy. Few actors in domestic politics demand the wholesale repatriation of powers 'lost' to Brussels, but there are increasingly insistent voices calling for more reliable procedures to scrutinise European legislation, and even for improving the public's access to EU decision-making during its formative stage, well before a policy initiative becomes a firm proposal, let alone a directive or regulation and as such mandatory in national law. Some national parliaments began to address this problem before others, though for the most part in an *ad hoc* fashion, making their own quite separate arrangements for reviewing EU legislation. Denmark and Finland, for instance, have developed more rigorous scrutiny procedures for monitoring EU legislation than most other member states, but this is a matter of concern now to parliaments throughout the Union.[130] The issue of accountability was first raised during the Maastricht IGC, the member states agreeing to append an annexe to the Treaty requiring that more detailed information about impending European policy proposals be made available to national parliaments. A further declaration proposed that national parliaments should play a more active role in the work of the Union.

The Amsterdam Treaty went further, for the first time incorporating a protocol with binding provisions relating to national parliaments, requiring a minimum six-week interlude between the publication of legislative proposals and their formal inclusion on the Council's agenda for adoption, whether as a Council act or as a common position. And a period during which national parliaments could make known their views before the final Council decision. A list of Commission proposals was drawn up that required consultation with national parliaments. None of these measures, however, resolved the issue of what an appropriate role for national parliaments should be in the Union's political and policy processes. The issue was revisited at Nice, but again without resolution and it remained high in the priorities of some political leaders.[131] Tony Blair, Jacques Chirac and José María Aznar, all leaders facing intense domestic criticism of the Union's democracy deficit, had each proposed a greater role for national parliaments in monitoring the Union's affairs, and the issue was discussed at Laeken.[132] The fact that it was says rather more about domestic politics than it does about the commitment to improve European democracy. There was, nevertheless, general agreement about improving linkages between the Union and domestic politics, especially parliaments, despite the limited scope of the EU's rules for determining the functions of what are after all non-EU institutions.

The Convention's working group on national parliaments chaired by Gisela Stuart, the British government representative, took up the challenge, as did the subsidiarity working group. Both working groups reviewed the various national arrangements for scrutinising EU policy, and considered how far the Amsterdam protocol had in fact improved communications between the EU and national levels, as well as the negative impact of opaque Council procedures. One possible 'solution' considered here was whether to add a second chamber to the Strasbourg Parliament, though the legal complexities of making national institutions part of the Union's constitutional order precluded this. The national parliament working group's report lacked bite, in part because the subsidiarity group reported first, stealing its thunder by making similar recommendations. Both reports did advocate a surer role for national parliaments in EU governance, by strengthening the Amsterdam protocol that had recommended national parliaments should be better informed and more involved in EU affairs. This is an advance on past practice, but as one critic has observed a fairly predictable conclusion after all, and as such 'worthy rather than gripping [to the effect that] some of their ideas – such as organising "European weeks" involving national parliaments and European institutions – were thin'.[133]

The Convention made three broad recommendations for bringing national parliaments closer to EU governance, though significantly these were not included in the body of the Constitutional Treaty but appended as separate protocols. The Protocol on the Application of the Principles of Subsidiarity and Proportionality establishes the means for national parliaments to forestall European legislation intruding on the 'proper' domain of national governance. The Protocol on the Role of National Parliaments in the European Union is similarly designed 'to encourage greater involvement of national parliaments in the activities of the European Union and to enhance their ability to express their views on legislative proposals'.[134] By these means, national parliaments are acknowledged as having the right to take part in EU governance, with full rights to information, and for the first time having a direct role in the EU's legislative process and in monitoring subsidiarity. This would be accomplished by exercising a form of veto power, in effect an 'early warning' system, using so-called 'yellow cards' to signal objections to legislative proposals from the Union's executive institutions. These same institutions are included in the Lisbon Treaty. National parliaments will have a six-week period to assess whether proposed legislation accords with EU competencies, conforms to the subsidiarity provisions or otherwise encroaches on national or sub-national competencies. The Commission is required to provide national legislatures with sufficient information, including relevant background documents relating to the proposed legislation. The Council of Ministers for its part is required to permit national parliaments access to its own papers during the six-week interlude between the submission of a proposal and its further enactment by the Council of Ministers, so as to allow for an informed response. The threshold for triggering a review of a Commission proposal is set at one third of national parliaments, though the Commission is not necessarily obliged to rescind the measure in question.

This represents progress, but it still leaves the problem of how to make a response to a significant minority below the threshold who register disapproval of proposed legislative action. Or for that matter, of how to redress the negative impact on the public's attitudes to European integration where such a national 'trigger' evokes no satisfactory response from decision-makers in Brussels. The Protocol also recommends regular meetings between national MPs and MEPs, with a forum of European Affairs Committees of the national parliaments and more specialist committees on matters such as foreign and security policy as the means for institutionalising inter-parliamentary contact. The British government representative, Gisela Stuart, wanted to go even further, proposing a 'red card' system whereby a legislative proposal would be abandoned if two-thirds of national parliaments raised objections. But in the event, this proved to be unworkable because it would, in effect, transform national parliaments into a new EU law-making institution. And for this reason would supposedly compromise the Laeken objective of simplifying the Union's governance, as well as breaching the ever-sensitive matter of demarcating the boundaries between the national and the European domains. A British proposal for a second chamber of the Parliament to consist of representatives from national parliaments was excluded on much the same grounds.

Whether these proposals will markedly improve the Union's democratic life is a matter for conjecture, for there are widely divergent views and competing expectations about the prospects for improving transnational democracy. While the case for increasing the influence of national parliamentarians on policy-making at the European level is now widely accepted as desirable, and one way of reducing democracy deficits, such changes are criticised as merely cosmetic, designed to appease domestic opinion rather than to significantly improve democracy across borders.[135] Strident voices on the opposite side of the argument resist the very idea of European democracy and the federal polity it supposedly betokens, dismissing as fanciful the notion of transnational democracy. These critical voices regard firmer control by national legislatures (in their view the only legitimate locus of representative democracy) over an EU policy process that, as they see it, threatens to undermine the fabric of national democracy as the surest safeguard of national sovereignty, short of withdrawing altogether from the Union. What is clear is that this procedure will certainly remove a convenient alibi sometimes used by national parliaments when confronted by hostile public opinion with regard to EU policy. For national politicians will no longer be able to refute criticism of their own lack of vigilance over impending European policy by resorting to the convenient defence that unpalatable policy proposals come exclusively from Brussels. National parliaments can, if they are so-minded – and as those in Scandinavia, particularly, have shown – do much more to effectively monitor and hold accountable national ministers operating at the European level, and even to bring influence to bear on EU public policy before it becomes binding on national authorities. There are, however, limits to such accountability. The fact is that national parliaments are, by and large, peripheral and even politically impotent in the face of well-marshalled Commission proposals, especially those supported by powerful coalitions of vested interests that coalesce around, and ultimately help to determine Council decisions. Even the co-decision procedure, though a considerable improvement on what preceded it, is not enough to ensure effective countervailing power as MEPs, in much the same way as parliamentarians everywhere, come to terms with the limits on representative democracy, their modest capacity for proposing and shaping public policy where governance at every level, but especially beyond the 'familiar' nation-state, is dominated by powerful, entrenched, well-resourced and mobilised corporate stakeholders. What the new 'veto' procedure does do, however, is to confirm that it is at the very least the responsibility of national parliaments 'to monitor what is going on in Europe'. And this will certainly make it more difficult for them 'to deny knowledge or any responsibility for European laws that eventually come through'.[136]

## The European Court of Justice

Deliberations on the role of the Court of Justice were much less politically charged than those on the political institutions. A discussion circle was convened to review the appointment procedures for Justices, the remit of judicial review, access to EU justice, compliance issues and so on. As things stand, the Court of Justice is, strictly speaking, not the Court of the European Union since it has no effective jurisdiction over the intergovernmental matters in Second Pillar (foreign and security policy) and Third Pillar (home affairs and justice). This continued to be the situation under the Constitutional Treaty, notwithstanding the proposed removal of the pillarised structure.

The most contentious issue was whether the Court should have any legal competence in the field of the Common Foreign and Security Policy. In the end, this innovation was resisted, and the Court's role confined to ruling on the legality of sanctions imposed on third parties. Aware that any proposals to blur the boundary between the Community and national domains would be resisted, not least by some leading member states, the Convention avoided recommending the application of European law to Common Foreign and Security Policy, or to internal matters relating to law and order and domestic security, all of them matters jealously guarded by the member states and subject at the Convention to what Prime Minister Blair insisted were his so-called inviolable 'red lines'. The Convention did, however, recommend stricter penalties and swifter action against any member states reticent about the application of EU legislation.

The Convention adopted most of the discussion circle's uncontroversial and largely procedural recommendations: *inter alia* the establishment of an advisory panel to assist member states with judicial appointments to the European Courts; retitling the Court of Justice of the European Communities as the European Court of Justice; renaming the Court of First Instance as the High Court of the Union; the establishment of more specialised courts; and changes to most of the Court's statutes, to be made the subject of laws passed by QMV instead of by unanimity. The Constitutional Treaty also proposed that the Court be permitted to review the legality of acts undertaken by EU agencies and subsidiary bodies (Article 3-270). In the Articles relating to the operation of the Court of Justice, there is a slight though telling alteration in the wording on the Court's jurisdiction to decide on the legality of an act adopted by the European Council or by the Council. This was now to be 'solely at the request of the member state concerned', a subtle choice of words but nevertheless a significant one in as much as it reaffirms intergovernmental strictures on the procedures of what is a supranational institution, and as such one regarded by governments as having a propensity to expand both its judicial discretion, and by those means even the scope of European integration. By and large, the Court's role remains what it has always been, namely to ensure that actions by any European institution or member state in relation to EU legislation is interpreted and applied strictly in accordance with European law. Though the Court's critics would no doubt point out that this has not prevented it thus far from expanding the reach of 'Europe' into policy areas not remotely anticipated at the outset.

## The other institutions and the regions

The Constitutional Treaty defined the European Central Bank (founded in 1998) as an EU institution (Article 1-30), though it remains outside the main institutional architecture. At the same time, the Convention sought to safeguard the Bank's independence. The Treaty requires the ECB to exercise its supervisory powers over other EU central banks and financial institutions (though not over insurance companies) by QMV, and with Parliament's assent by means of co-decision instead of by unanimity. The Convention also endorsed the Court of Auditor's supervisory role over the EU institutions' financial arrangements, and it proposed an increased membership for both the Economic and Social Committee (established by the Treaty of Rome, 1957) and the Committee of the Regions (established by the Treaty of Maastricht, 1992), so as to ensure that after enlargement these institutions remain representative of the Union's wider social and economic interests.

Regional governance was less a priority for the Convention than it should have been in a transnational polity where multi-level governance means an enhanced role for regions as much as for national states, and where structural policy and regional initiatives are a more reliable route to cohesion and closer integration than they are a direct challenge to territorial states. The multi-levelness of EU polity means that the regional issue invariably raises some critical constitutional issues, including subsidiarity and the problem of the legitimacy deficit, how to connect policy-makers with civil society and, not least, how to encourage wider participation in public affairs, including ways of bringing the Union closer to its citizens.

The regions are important actors in the EU policy process, not least because upwards of 70 per cent of Community programmes are managed by sub-national political authorities. The Maastricht Treaty had acknowledged the role of the regions in EU governance, permitting regional ministers to represent regions in the Council of Ministers, and by establishing a Committee of the Regions to act in an advisory capacity. Nevertheless, the praesidium decided against appointing a dedicated working group to review regional policy, and confined debate here to a special plenary session.[137] In consequence the Convention hardly did justice to one important aspect of the Union's multi-level arrangements, beyond acknowledging the right of regional and local governments to manage their own affairs consistent with the principle of subsidiarity. Sub-national governments are permitted through the medium of the Committee of the Regions to challenge perceived infringements of their right to take decisions appropriate to their level. However, the Committee of the Regions is hardly representative of Europe's many and diverse regions, and despite *conventionnels'* awareness of the significance of regional governance, shortage of time, and no less a lack of both urgency and consensus amongst Europe's principal territorial voices about their own priorities for reform, lessened the impact of the issue.

The reform proposals contained in the Constitutional Treaty were a timely reminder that EU governance faces new challenges and needs to adjust its institutions and procedures accordingly. These reforms were as far-reaching as anything enacted by previous treaties and in some cases more so. But this is of course a relative judgment, for politicians here have long been reticent about bold, let alone imaginative designs for European governance, and no less so about improving the quality of participatory (rather than plebiscitary) democracy in this unique polity. Measured against more radical aspirations, the Constitutional Treaty was hardly a dramatic break with the past, and one can readily concur with the commentator who said of it: 'Clearly, the Constitutional Treaty is an evolutionary step forward rather than an institutional revolution, so that further changes are likely to become necessary in a not too distant future.'[138]

The critical matters of common governance did cause a stir. There was the usual sense on all sides of the constitutional debate that what was at stake here was the meaning and purpose of 'Europe', and accordingly of interests threatened and preferences to be defended. Yet, as on all previous occasions, differences were reconciled if not settled, and agreement eventually reached. This outcome was the sub-optimal bargain that is familiar to students of EU treaty reform. And it raised as many questions as it settled about the purposes of decision-making, not least about the abiding problem of legitimacy and democracy deficits, the continuing lack of connection with citizens in this transnational polity. These are hardly incidental questions, for they are after all the essence of any constitutional endeavour worth the name in every supposedly democratic polity. Yet the governments who steered the process towards this less than satisfactory outcome were as determined as their predecessors not to open the Pandora's box that is democratic reform. The Lisbon Treaty picks up where the Constitutional Treaty left off on this critical matter, concentrating on a slate of procedural and institutional reforms intended to improve the efficiency of decisional outputs, addressing the concerns of those who manage EU affairs, but not remotely addressing those issues that launched the constitutional endeavour in the first place: the lack of connectivity between remote and arcane governance and the citizens, abiding democracy deficits and weak public legitimacy.

In part, the focus on institutions is part of the Union's legacy, a natural reflex learned from the founding fathers. Jean Monnet had acknowledged the critical significance of building effective common institutions, and no less of adapting them to changing circumstances. Looking back on his monumental achievement in putting European integration on the political agenda, he observed that: 'The tragic events we have lived through ... have perhaps made us wiser. But men pass on and others take their place. We will not be able to hand on our personal experience. It will die with us. What we can hand on are institutions. ... Institutions, adequately structured, can accumulate and transmit the wisdom of successive generations.'[139] This may well be true, but institutions on their own cannot carry ordinary people with them, they do not transmit to them a sense of common purpose, the scale of challenges to be confronted, and always tend towards merely narrow bureaucratic preoccupations, unless the institutional process is complemented by more democratic endeavour. And in this respect, Europe's latest founding fathers simply missed the point. We shall return to the consequences of this for both the authority and effectiveness of governance in the European Union in the discussion of establishing a meaningful public space at Chapter 12.

# 7    Simplifying EU governance

## Simplifying governance

The complexity of EU governance as 'described' in the convoluted language of the treaties confirms the citizens' sense of a remote and inaccessible polity.[1] The problem was duly acknowledged at Laeken, but rectifying it was no easy matter for this is a polity caught between quite different, indeed competing ideas about governance. This much is apparent in the Constitutional Treaty's attempt to tidy up an intricate and for most outsiders, and even for some insiders, Byzantine procedures. The Constitutional Treaty set out to condense layers of legal archaeology accumulated from previous treaties into a more cogent structure: Part I outlines the Union's constitutional architecture and was divided into nine separate Titles; Part II incorporates the Charter on Fundamental Rights; Part III refers to the policies and functioning of the Union; and Part IV lists general and final provisions.

Simplifying governance was the objective of some of the most significant reforms in the consolidated Treaty, notably the decision to end the co-operation procedure, replacing it with co-decision, and with the Council and the Parliament operating as joint legislators. With only a very few exceptions, this would become the normal legislative procedure for the enactment of European laws and framework laws (Article 1-33.1), with its application extended to even more policy domains. Most commentators saw this as 'a natural development, building on what has occurred in earlier Treaty reform [that] enhances the legitimacy of Union legislation and its democratic credentials by enabling the European Parliament to have input into the making of legislation in these areas'.[2]

The same can be said for decisional arrangements. The 'ordinary legislative procedure' and QMV in the Council will be the norm when these changes are enacted as they will be by the Lisbon Treaty, but other arcane procedures have survived the drive for simplification. Although the Constitutional Treaty improved clarity with regard to decision-making it did not entirely resolve the problem of multiple procedures. Wessels has estimated that while the ordinary legislative procedure would cover some 34 per cent of all relevant rules, compared with 26 per cent in the Nice arrangements, with regard to reducing procedural complexity 'there will be only a modest reduction from 50 to 48 different types of procedure'.[3] The end of the three-pillar design would shift a number of First Pillar competencies to what amounts to a general constitutional overview (Part I), principles that apply to the entire range of policy Titles covered in Part III of the Constitutional Treaty. However, regardless of a unified legal basis and legal instruments, the Constitutional Treaty still permitted 'specific [decisional] provision relating to the common foreign and security policy' (Article 1-40), the common security and defence policy (Article 1-41) and to the area of freedom, security and justice (Article 1-42).

Extending QMV to more policy domains is another example of the drive to simplify governance, though here, too, multiple voting procedures make for more confusion than clarity. The founding treaties required unanimity in the Council on some 80 occasions. The proposed new arrangements would extend QMV to new areas of policy and remove others from unanimity, affecting some 50 articles in all.[4] However, politics intruded as it was bound to do, and the so-called 'red-line' issues seen by leading member states as essential national interests would remain subject to unanimity. The unanimity procedure was retained for decisions on transferring any competence from member states to the Union, for accession of new member states and for decisions on politically sensitive matters such as defence and for sanctioning common military operations. Some leading member states simply refused to give ground on what they saw as a vital instrument for the defence of the national interest. France, for instance, secured a veto over trade and cultural industries, as did Germany on asylum and immigration, and some other member states signalled their own 'no go' areas for QMV, notably the United Kingdom and Ireland on the controversial issue of tax harmonisation.

Where there was to be an increase in QMV it was not, in most instances, in controversial areas, despite most governments' acknowledging the shortcomings of the unanimity procedure in a much enlarged Union. One might nevertheless anticipate political difficulties with the proposal to make decisions 'binding in their entirety' in the sensitive policy domain of CFSP. And similarly with the provision in Article 1-6, which stated unequivocally that EU law should have primacy over national laws in matters relating to the Treaty. This was a procedural change that 'would appear to introduce the concepts of direct effect and supremacy into the framework governing Union-Member State relations under CFSP [and is] a proposition which, whatever its merits or faults, would surely amount to a significant departure from the current legal position under the Second Pillar'.[5]

These changes were nevertheless progress of sorts, though much less than required to meet Laeken's commitment to procedural clarity, let alone to bring transparency to what many see as arcane governance. There was more to this relative failure to deliver greater clarity than merely lack of political will, though politics was the heart of the matter. Complex governance is of course unavoidable in this uniquely complex polity, the legacy of the founding bargain that established the European Community, the very fact that the political architecture resulting from this bargain is not merely multi-level but, as Wessels sees it, based on the 'fusion' of quite difference ideas about governance, with 'shared, pooled responsibilities between the EU and national levels ... the parallel strengthening and close merging of Community and intergovernmental methods'. The juxtaposition of competing ideas about the power of this governance makes procedural simplification elusive, and for some commentators illusory.[6] Attempting to balance intergovernmental and supranational impulses invariably makes for complicated governance. As one legal expert sees it, even 'the existence of a unitary Union would not *in itself* imply generalisation of the "Community method" currently applicable in the First Pillar'. Accordingly, any European treaty has to 'accommodate the special – essentially intergovernmental – characteristics of the Common Foreign and Security Policy (CFSP) and to a much lesser extent of police and judicial co-operation in criminal matters (PJCCM), as regards matters such as inter-institutional relations, decision-making procedures, and the jurisdiction of the Court of Justice'. Even depillarisation, proposed in the Convention as part of the solution to these inordinately complicated arrangements, 'would not exclude continued differentiation in the legal principles governing separate sectors of Union activity'.[7]

The most that can be said about the procedural reforms proposed by the Constitutional Treaty is that they do at least improve legal clarity. But though legal clarity is essential for any polity committed to constitutional norms, it is not the same thing by any means as making clear where authority actually lies for decisions between competing governance agencies, at least in a way that might legitimise the constitutional order in the eyes of its citizens. And in this important respect the Constitutional Treaty largely failed to deliver. The Convention worked to put in place a uniform treaty base, proposing a single legal personality for the Union, combining the cumulate treaty base into a single treaty and merging the three separate pillars introduced by the Maastricht Treaty (Article 4-437; note also, Article 4-438 on legal continuity in the transition from the extant treaty to the proposed Constitutional Treaty). European directives were duly retitled as EU laws and the number of decision-making instruments was reduced from 15 to 6, with the two principal legal instruments now being described as laws and framework laws. All of these measures, as we shall see, contributed to simplifying EU procedures, 'both in operational terms and for [their] comprehensibility'.[8]

The same could be said for the decision, discussed above at Chapter 5, to abandon the Nice formula on weighted votes in the Council in favour of a simpler double majority voting, though as we have seen there were rather more self-interested motives behind this decision. These changes contributed to tidying inordinately complicated procedures, but if referendum results are any guide they mostly failed to convince citizens that this was governance they could understand, let alone access or influence. The commitment to simplification was well intentioned, but for most citizens it simply failed to assuage growing doubts about the 'the continuing elitist nature of EU construction'.[9]

To win over a sceptical public required something altogether more imaginative and, no less important, inspiring than the encyclopaedic tome written in inaccessible legalese that is the Constitutional Treaty. It requires instead a clearer explanation of how this polity works, and, just as important if the politicians want people to feel commitment to the project, one written in plain language so that citizens and not merely the insiders who run the show can see more clearly who does what and why, and with what consequences for their everyday lives. Simplification requires, then, not only greater transparency, a clearer demarcation of competencies, a plain map of the distribution of power, a more straightforward account of how the polity works, but also an explanation of the political authority that is the essential normative ballast for any democratic polity.

A European constitution worthy of the name must provide clear answers to these fundamental questions that have been more implied than explicit in the development of the European polity from the beginning. What kind of polity is the European Union? How do we describe its unique political architecture in language that permits its stakeholders to compare it with the altogether more familiar nation-state? What are the relations between its constituent member states and the common institutions, and how are these relations legitimised? And just as important, how should relations between the various European institutions be structured? Significant, too, in view of the problem with legitimacy, is to define and to explain the linkages between governors and citizens, just as surely the bedrock of political authority in this non-statal polity as it is in the nation-state. The Constitutional Treaty barely touched on these critical matters, and there was little to suggest from the politics of the exercise that these are matters of much concern to those who negotiated the latest Lisbon Treaty. What follows is a summary of the Convention's contribution to this ongoing and far from straightforward debate about how to simplify EU governance.

## The Union's legal personality

The constituent communities that make up the EU – the EC (Article 281, TEC), the ECSC and EURATOM – each has a separate legal personality in its own domain. The Constitutional Treaty would be subsumed within a singular and overarching legal persona, except for EURATOM (incorporated into the EC in 2002), which would remain as a separate entity because Austrian members of the Convention hostile to nuclear energy had resisted the merger of EURATOM with the EU.[10] These difficulties notwithstanding, the working group on legal personality was unanimous that 'the Union shall have legal personality', and be subject to rights and obligations in international law, a position endorsed by the Convention and included as Article 1-7 of the draft Constitutional Treaty.

The principal effect of this change would be to consolidate the Union's institutions, removing the pillarised structure introduced in the Maastricht Treaty. This would supposedly facilitate what is modishly called 'joined-up' governance, more coherent policy-making, as well as enhancing the Union's status and capacities as an international actor. In effect, the European Community would cease to exist as a distinct legal entity, being fully absorbed into the European Union. This would, in turn, provide it with the legal base to conclude treaties with third countries and international organisations, making the Union subject to international legal proceedings in its own right with regard to EU matters (Articles 1-6 and 3-323), and allowing it to have collective external representation in international institutions.

This is significant as far as it goes. But the question here is how far does it go? A singular EU legal personality is by no means the dramatic step some commentators assume it to be, for the Union is not a state and neither is it remotely on the way to becoming one, let alone 'a country called Europe'. Indeed, some other international organisations already have a similar legal status. Some expert legal opinion even maintained that, 'despite the lack of an explicit provision in the TEU, the Union already enjoys its own legal capacity'. Consequently, the Union's status as a subject under international law 'would not jeopardise the member states' own existence as such'. Nor would this change 'imply any expansion of Union competence in the field of external relations, beyond the limits explicitly laid down in the Constitution', and neither would it 'require a single procedure for the negotiation and conclusion by the Union of agreements with third countries and international organisations'.[11] The most that can be said about those new arrangement in the Lisbon Treaty is that confirming this status 'beyond question would contribute to legal certainty and it could improve transparency in relations with third countries'.[12] If the objective here is simplification, it is not clarity for the benefit of the citizens, but rather for those crucial actors with whom the Union must engage 'at home' and 'abroad'.

## The primacy of EU law

Previous revisions of the founding treaties had avoided incorporating into the treaty base the principle of the primacy of EU law over national law. Abiding sensitivity on this issue is borne out by resistance, or at least the reticence of national legal authorities about the very idea of EU legal supremacy. The draft Constitutional Treaty (Article 1-6) confirmed supremacy as a constitutional norm, categorically affirming that the Constitutional Treaty and the law embraced by the EU's institutions in exercising their respective competencies would have primacy over the law of the member states, thereby disallowing a role for domestic courts and national legal norms in determining the legality of EU acts. Some legal experts saw this as nothing less than a step-change in relations between national courts and the Union's legal order 'excluding any way back', imposing a limit 'on those national constitutions (and on those courts that apply them) whose vocation is to be the ultimate legal authority', to the effect that in the 'well-known formula of the German Constitutional Court, Member Stares will no longer be entitled to present themselves as the masters of the Treaties'.[13]

This is, however, an exaggerated reading of the situation. Things are by no means as clear-cut as either federalists or Eurosceptics, each from entrenched political perspectives, have supposed. Uncertainty remains the way of things here, for as Dougan sees it 'the whole point of the *kompetenz-kompetenz* debate is that the authority of those statements at the national level remains contested by certain domestic courts'.[14] The Constitutional Treaty did not remotely resolve this issue once and for all. Certainly, there was nothing in Articles 1-11/14 to sustain the Union's claim to be the definitive arbiter of the boundary between the domestic and Union legal domains, and academic legal opinion remains divided as to the precise application of the supremacy principle. The reference in the Treaty to this immensely complicated concept is, to say the least, inconclusive because insubstantial, such that it 'would still be possible for the German courts to say that the Constitutional Treaty cannot confer upon the Union powers which contravene certain fundamental requirements contained in the Basic Law; or for British courts to rule that the sovereign Parliament may in the future legislate clearly and expressly in a manner contrary to the United Kingdom's obligations under the Constitutional Treaty'.[15] The question remained – and in the context of constitution-making it was a crucial question – of whether supremacy would apply here to every aspect of national law pertaining to primary and secondary legislation, or whether instead the critical realm of national constitutional law was excluded from EU primacy.

A more nuanced assessment of relations between the national and the Union's legal/constitutional orders had envisaged the continuation of a pluralist legal status quo. An arrangement whereby 'as a matter of EU law, EU law may be the supreme law of the land, but as a matter of national constitutional law … national constitutions provide the ultimate criteria for determining what is the law of the land'. As Kumm and Comella see it, if the member states had intended the Constitutional Treaty to alter this delicate legal balance, then 'a clearer statement along the lines of the Supremacy Clause of the United States' Constitution would have been the approach to take'.[16] The issue is a sensitive one for politicians and for the judicial authorities alike. One can easily foresee circumstances whereby political expediency would give rise to a challenge from national courts and parliaments about where power ultimately resides in the matter of law. But there is no reason to assume that the outcome of any future legal challenge here will be any different from the decisions of national constitutional courts thus far: in effect, that the supremacy of Union law derives solely from the constitutional order of the member states, and on that basis it should be accorded primacy only because the national constitutions of the member states allow it. There is already a strong presumption of this 'fact' in European jurisprudence. In the view of one eminent legal mind: 'The idea that a Union regulatory act, in effect, secondary legislation, should be deemed to have primacy over the law of the Member States might not be readily accepted by some constitutional courts. More especially so if this is taken to include primacy over national constitutional norms as well as national legislation [for] they might rule that their national constitutions do not allow ratification of a Constitution in such terms.'[17] The Constitutional Treaty did little to resolve this problematic issue.

## Legal instruments

One consequence of the incremental development of the EC/EU treaty base is the lack of a uniform legislative procedure over the entire range of EU actions. The treaties do not define legislative power as such but rather the roles and decisional procedures of the various institutions on an iterative and case by case basis. These inchoate arrangements are, to say the least, untidy and have resulted in quite separate legislative procedures involving both the Council and the Parliament, as follows: QMV with co-decision, co-operation or assent; QMV without involvement by the Parliament; unanimity with co-decision, co-operation or assent, with a straight opinion and without Parliament's participation. The praesidium's review of these arrangements identified 22 different procedures in the TEC for adopting legislation, and it duly acknowledged 'the dreadful complexity of the Union's legal instruments'.[18] The most significant legislative instruments are regulations, which must be implemented without procedural discretion, and directives which give discretion to the member states over the means for implementation. However, all manner of additional instruments have accumulated over time, including 'decisions', 'guidelines' and 'framework programmes'. The institutions may 'make regulations and issue directives, take decisions, make recommendations or deliver opinions'.[19] One consequence of this procedural flux, and 'one of the more bizarre qualities of the EU and EU treaties was that policy instruments would share the same name but have different characteristics'.[20]

The pillar system installed by the Treaty of European Union has merely increased this complexity, with Common Security Foreign and Security Policy (CFSP) and Justice and Home Affairs (JHA) each having its own distinctive instruments. The former policy domain has myriad instruments, including 'common strategies', 'joint actions', 'common positions', 'enhanced systematic co-operation', 'principles' and 'guidelines'. The latter, however, utilises 'frame-work decisions', 'decisions', 'common positions' and 'conventions'. These convoluted arrangements were compounded by the fact that 'the treaties made no distinction between legislative and executive acts, leaving the whole area of secondary legislation in limbo'.[21] Of greater concern for a Union facing formidable challenges across the board is the seeming lack of coherence of much EU legislation, with policy outcomes too often the result of sub-optimal bargains, and with side payments disconnected from any overarching strategy, trade-offs made for the short term or merely to appease narrow vested interests. If the gauge for simplification is to improve clarity, and thereby to increase the public's understanding of what the Union is about, then the Convention, for the most part, failed to deliver.

The proposed changes in decisional procedures in the Constitutional Treaty hardly simplify arrangements, nor do they make them more accessible for citizens, as the detailed catalogue of policies in Part III of the Treaty well illustrates. As one critic saw it: 'The layman will not know, from reading the document, where final responsibilities rest, and in which case, for procedures and decision-making powers still vary according to pillar and area.'[22] The commitment to greater simplification notwithstanding, some 48 different decisional procedures remained, a reduction of only two on previous arrangements, and these are scattered throughout the Constitutional Treaty rather than brought together and listed in Part I.[23] The IGC that followed the Convention compounded the problem by 'reintroducing complexities conventioneers had meant to streamline (or added new ones, such as the revised formula for the double majority in the council)'.[24]

The Convention failed, too, in another related task, equally important for meeting the Laeken objective of improving decision-making procedures: namely, that of formalising so-called 'soft policy' instruments, for instance the Open Method of Co-ordination, by making clear how these increasingly important instruments relate to more formal and binding instruments. This issue must be resolved so as to ensure more effective decision-making in an enlarged and a more diverse Union than was the case even with EU15.[25] The Nice Declaration had signalled as a priority the need for greater simplification of these legal instruments, but without really addressing the issue. The Laeken Council endorsed the urgency of reform here, mandating the Convention to review the medley of legal instruments with a view to reducing their number.

The Working Group on Simplification took up the challenge, convinced that a clear framework for making rules was indispensable, not least for instilling greater public confidence. It proposed measures to simplify both legislative procedures and policy instruments, trimming these instruments from the current 15 to 6 and giving them more familiar names so as to facilitate the public's grasp of what the Union actually does.[26] Accordingly, the co-operation procedure – by now confined to only four aspects of economic and monetary policy – was abolished, with co-decision (to be known as the 'ordinary legislative procedure') becoming the general procedure for adopting legislative acts, and extended to all the main areas of EU legislative action, the Council of Ministers and the Parliament acting as co-legislators. And with the Council using QMV, though with unanimity retained for some matters of particular significance to the member states. Some *conventionnels* in plenary discussions questioned whether unanimity – with the prospect of the blocking veto – has any place in the legislative procedure. However, representatives from the United Kingdom, Ireland and Sweden insisted that it be retained for politically sensitive policy domains such as taxation. The assent procedure, which requires Parliament's express approval for any action, is confined in these arrangements to the ratification of international agreements. A clear distinction is also made in these revised arrangements as between legislative and non-legislative acts. The Constitutional Treaty proposes that non-legislative acts would be called 'decisions' and directed to specific addressees. Acts of a non-binding nature would be called either 'recommendations' or 'opinions', as they are in the current provisions of extant Article 249.5, TEC. Two types of binding non-legislative act are European regulations, to be used for implementing legislative acts, or some specific constitutional provisions. The idea here is that it should be made absolutely clear when the Union acts which legislative instrument applies, and in what particular circumstances.

In the meantime, all of these terms would be employed across the range of EU policy-making, though decisions that pertain to CFSP would be prefixed with that acronym. Non-standard acts such as 'declarations', 'resolutions' and 'conclusions' would remain as EU instruments, though non-binding and outside the scope of the Treaty, but important nevertheless as statements of current emphasis or future intent in EU policy. Furthermore, common positions under the Third Pillar and common strategies under the Second Pillar would no longer be separate legal instruments. The Convention settled instead for two principal and binding legislative instruments (Article 1-33/34): European laws, similar to existing regulations (Article 249, TEC) as acts of general application, binding in every sense, and directly applicable in every member state; and EU framework laws, the equivalent of directives (Article 249.3, TEC), which would bind member states only with regard to their desired outcome but not as to their procedures. Laws and framework laws would have the status of legislative acts, adopted by the Council of Ministers and Parliament by co-decision. Delegated acts or regulations would be secondary acts, normally the Commission's prerogative and used to add detail to or otherwise amend legislative acts; whereas 'implementing acts', so-called, that give force to legislative or delegated acts, would remain the prerogative of member states.

These changes were the Convention's response to the Laeken injunction for greater simplification. And though they did propose some useful changes to procedure, they went only some way towards meeting the Union's need for greater clarity about how it goes about its work. In this as in so many other aspects of the Convention's work, the requirement for consensus between quite different preferences, produced a sub-optimal outcome, a less than cogent, let alone a comprehensive arrangement. And one that is much less a blueprint for simplified governance than it is a series of *ad hoc* compromises. This less than satisfactory outcome prompted one observer to wonder whether there is any 'coherent rationale behind some of these relationships enshrined in the new hierarchy of norms (legislative and non-legislative acts, delegated regulations and implementing acts)'.[27] The decision of politicians to play down anything that might hint at statehood or federalism saw them reverse even these modest changes in the latest reforms in the Lisbon Treaty, preferring to retain the technocratic language of directive and the like rather than to use the more political term of 'laws'. Legislative acts are renamed as Ordinary (previously co-decision) and Special (most other forms of Council–Parliamentray interaction) Legislative Procedures.

## Budgetary matters

EU budgetary politics are rather less fraught now than when annual negotiations over money matters raised tensions between the member states over who were net payers and net beneficiaries from common expenditure. Some, but by no means all, of the political heat was taken out of budgetary politics when the Union adopted in the Delors I (1988) and Delors II (1992) packages a longer-term or future financial perspective for ensuring fiscal discipline, by planning expenditure for some years ahead as its preferred budgetary procedure. The Convention undertook to simplify this procedure, to make it both more transparent and democratically accountable. The working group on simplification, for instance, proposed to apply co-decision to budget-setting, once a draft budget has been submitted by the Commission to the Parliament and Council. But there were still contentious issues to be resolved, not least the role of the respective institutional actors in determining the budget.

As things stand, Parliament has no discretion over the significant proportion of the budget allocated to compulsory expenditure (not least here, the controversial matter of expenditure on the Common Agricultural Policy), and it can only propose changes to non-compulsory expenditure. The working group recommended ending this rigid distinction, to bring together within one cogent article various references to the budget scattered throughout the treaties, and likewise to incorporate the multi-annual financial perspective into the Constitutional Treaty

in order to reinforce it. By removing the distinction between the expenditure categories, the Constitutional Treaty intended to enhance the Parliament's budgetary
role and to improve its scope for determining EU public expenditure, though the
proposal raised predictable objections from some national finance ministers.

The Italian presidency in the course of the IGC adjusted the original wording in the
draft treaty pertaining to the EU's multi-annual financial frameworks (Article 1-54),
to the effect that the framework scheduled for 2006 would be adopted by unanimity,
but thereafter by QMV. Anticipating objections from the usual quarters – the United
Kingdom, the Netherlands and Spain – the revised wording did allow for a further,
albeit limited veto, with a majority vote to determine at that stage whether to proceed
to QMV. The Convention's initial proposal, to require that the Parliament approve
the EU's multi-annual spending programmes so as to enhance that institution's input
into the annual adjustments, albeit with the governments retaining overall control of
total revenue, was subsequently challenged in a formal submission to the IGC by the
Council of Finance Ministers during the 2003 Italian presidency, a move determined
to reinforce intergovernmentalism in money matters. Ministers preferred to retain
national vetoes over EU spending programmes, challenging the clause that would
give Parliament the final say on all aspects of agricultural expenditure, in marked
contract with its previous restricted role in deciding non-compulsory expenditure.
In a crucial change to the Convention's draft treaty, the finance ministers proposed
instead that the Parliament could submit amendments on all aspects of expenditure,
but insisted that the member states have the final say, even though the Convention
had agreed to end this veto after 2013.[28]

In the event, the member states moderated their resistance here, but only
during the IGC's final ministerial session, permitting Parliament the last word
on the budget, though only after a rigorous co-decision procedure. Once again,
this tactical compromise made between quite different interests makes for more
confusion than clarity. For instance, no specific time limits are applied to national
vetoes on EU spending programmes. There was no detailed reference in the final
version of the Constitutional Treaty to new rules relating to the multi-annual financial framework, other than to set the term of duration at a minimum of five years,
and widely expected by informed observers to be for a period of seven years.[29]
After intensive lobbying by the United Kingdom, Ireland, Spain and Estonia
during the early part of the IGC, a double veto right was agreed for the Council on
the Parliament's second reading of the annual budget procedure (Article 3-404),
and vice versa, in order to reinforce the need for inter-institutional compromise.
Despite Parliament's objection to this compromise on the grounds that it denied
the Union's only elected institution the final say on the annual budget, the Parliament's president did at least accept that even this 'unsatisfactory' revision is an
improvement on the Economic and Financial Affairs Council's (ECOFIN) preference for retaining ultimate control of budgetary procedure.

The final version of the Constitutional Treaty merely referred to the maintenance of the current rules until the Council adopts a European law to determine a
new financial framework (Article 1-402.4, new), due when the current framework
ended in 2006. It likewise made vague reference to the three principal institutions,

each one being required to 'take any necessary measures to facilitate the successful completion of the procedure'. The rules for setting the financial perspective – yet to be agreed – will be crucial for determining budgetary power, in so far as the annual budget round is now very much constrained by the longer-term financial perspective. Whichever institution secures disproportionate influence over these future financing arrangements is likely to take the lead in shaping the Union's annual budgetary priorities. But one might wonder, nevertheless, why an exercise widely advertised as constitution-making failed to resolve such a critical decision.

On the matter of own resources, the IGC added a line to the initial version of the draft treaty article (Article 1-54.3) to the effect that, notwithstanding the provision that the Council may legislate to 'establish new categories of own resources or abolish an existing category', such a law may 'not enter into force until it is approved by the Member States in accordance with their respective constitutional requirements'. This is a default provision deliberately designed to confirm member states' ultimate control of the Budget's revenue side, a fire-break rooted in the principle of national constitutional discretion. This precaution was the response to pressure anticipated from supranationalists in the institutions who preferred to increase the size of EU own resources, a necessary condition for extending the scope of European integration. In similar vein, the final version of the Constitutional Treaty made the European Council acting unanimously rather than the Council of Ministers the final arbiter of the multi-annual financial framework. Accordingly, a unanimous vote in the European Council was required to adopt the multi-annual framework, a more politically exacting requirement in a Union of 27 member states than it ever was in EU15. Again, this change was intended to reinforce intergovernmentalism, in as much as such compromise will require mutually advantageous trade-offs between governments.

## Economic governance

The EU took a significant step towards closer economic integration with the launch of the single currency in 2002. Despite a decade and more of preparation and planning, monetary union has not been without problems. In the run-up to the Convention the Commission had found it necessary to issue warnings to Germany and Portugal for transgressing the rules of the Eurozone's Stability and Growth Pact that require members to abide by strict fiscal discipline regarding national budget deficits. The problem was resolved, though not to the satisfaction of some governments, and the significance of this issue, a touchstone of 'ever-closer union' but also an indication that some member states could seemingly flout common rules with apparent impunity, ensured that economic governance would figure on the Convention's agenda. The European Central Bank (ECB) and some Eurozone central banks were particularly concerned about the lax fiscal and macro-economic discipline in the draft treaty. Laeken had placed co-ordination of economic policy on the Convention's agenda, and it was discussed during the 'listening phase', the praesidium establishing a working group on economic governance.

The working group on economic governance reviewed a number of important issues here, including the consequences of the single currency for the management of the Union's economic policy, and not least fiscal harmonisation and taxation, whether and how to enhance policy co-ordination and how to represent the euro in the wider international community. But the sheer diversity of views on economic governance, both in EU15 between Eurozone members and euro-agnostics and amongst the accession countries, precluded the working group reaching agreement on any clear proposals. Further differences surfaced during these discussions, not least abiding inter-institutional tension between the Commission on one side, determined to press its claim as the most suitable locus for co-ordinating macro-economic policy, and national finance ministries on the other, the latter supported in this instance by the Central Bank, who preferred the current arrangements.

These differences were considerable, more than incidental for the future of the European project and they figured frequently in the debates on specific issues: for instance, tax harmonisation and whether decisions in this politically sensitive area should be taken by unanimity or QMV; the role of the Commission in policing the broad EU economic policy guidelines; and discussion about the link between the social dimension and economic policy that has long divided Europe's centre-right and centre-left parties.[30] The Franco-German alliance, co-operating as closely on this as on other issues, made a joint recommendation intended to improve co-ordination of economic policy within the Eurogroup, though only after the working group itself had deliberated on the issue.[31] This proposal went further than the working group's more cautious compromise, and included, *inter alia*, a proposal for a Euro-ECOFIN Council, a forum in which Eurogroup members could reach common policy decisions for the entire Eurozone; formal recognition of the Euro-group in the Constitution; QMV to be applied to decisions on taxation pertaining to the single market; and harmonisation of turnover and consumer taxes. The ECB also wanted price stability included as a principal objective in Part I of the Constitutional Treaty. The text of the joint Franco-German initiative, whilst acknowledging the ECB's broad concerns about lax fiscal discipline, was more guarded in its proposals than Europe's bank and merely referred to the preferred objective of 'balanced growth' instead of the more onerous requirement of 'non-inflationary growth' included in the Maastricht Treaty.

Politics was the principal driver here, and recent events influenced the outcome, not least the seemingly cavalier attitude of France and Germany to the rules of the Eurozone. France had resisted mandatory sanctions in 2003 despite breaching the terms of the Stability and Growth Pact on agreed targets for national budget deficits. These two countries demanded weaker Commission enforcement powers, and the issue was bound to be considered because of its centrality to national policy rather more in IGC discussions on economic governance than at the Convention. Some Eurozone countries backed the demand by the Netherlands for stricter enforcement of the rules, exercised by what it saw as double standards, but France and Germany saw off the challenge and in the event no such sanctions were included in the IGC's revised draft of the treaty. Neither were these two member states by any means isolated on this issue, with other governments quite prepared to support their resistance to any increase in supranational powers in this politically sensitive domain.

Some member states, principally the United Kingdom, supported by Spain and Ireland, had opposed inclusion of proposals in the initial version of the Treaty they believed would increase the Commission's competency in what they regarded as a wholly national competence. The British government was particularly concerned about the provision in Part III of the Convention's draft text that referred to the EU competence to co-ordinate the economic and employment policies of the member states, and referring to national economic policy as 'a matter of common concern'.[32] The choice of words here encouraged familiar conspiracy theories in Britain, where the CBI 'saw' nothing less than designs by Brussels to secure control of Britain's North Sea oil, amounting to some 90 per cent of the EU total reserves.[33]

Despite the reluctance of the Italian presidency to reopen the issue the British government, with support from Germany and France though for quite different reasons from those that informed the British position, and having more to do with their recent experience of conflict with the Commission over their failure to conform with the fiscal discipline required by the Stability and Growth Pact, pursued what Prime Minister Blair insisted was a 'red-line' issue. The finance ministers for similar reasons opposed a clause in the Convention's final draft intended to bolster the Commission's powers *vis-à-vis* those member states in breach of agreed rules and protocols. As things currently stand, the Commission may propose what is called an 'excessive deficit procedure' whenever member states are in breach of the Stability and Growth Pact rule of a 3 per cent limit of GDP on budget deficits, although the final decision remains with the Council. The Convention had proposed that the Commission should have the authority to trigger this sanction but the finance ministers blocked any such move, ECOFIN suspending the excessive deficit procedure without reference to the Commission.

The Constitutional Treaty gave formal powers to the Eurogroup (the informal meeting of Eurozone finance ministers), including the exclusive right to vote on issues pertaining solely to the single currency and to enforce the fiscal rules, for instance setting the rules on public expenditure and the long-term sustainability of public finances. These rules presently included in the Stability and Growth Pact would now be incorporated into the Constitutional Treaty, thereby constraining the Commission's role. While the Commission would retain the prerogative for making recommendations, these must be agreed by the Council of Finance Ministers and would remain confidential. At most the Commission would retain a degree of licence in these matters, though hardly the firm sanction it sought, amounting to little more than a right to issue an 'early warning' to those Eurozone countries operating outside the agreed fiscal framework. Any changes in the terms of the Stability Pact would now need unanimous approval, including even those states outside the Eurozone who are, almost by definition, sceptical about supranational fiscal governance. In the circumstances, the best solution seemed to be the one favoured by the Convention: to leave the precise details for monitoring conformity to a policy not subscribed to by every member state only to those states directly affected by it, and this was included in a special protocol (Protocol on the Euro Group) to stand alongside yet formally remaining outside the Constitutional Treaty.

These issues connected with what some member states chose to define, in the terminology adopted by the United Kingdom, as their so-called 'red lines'. The lack of agreement on these matters shows that the Convention achieved little more than to consolidate existing EU powers in this critical policy area, recommending co-ordination rather than harmonisation of economic policies, and leaving the ECB to manage monetary policy relating to the euro, although the working group's report did propose better representation for the Euro-zone in the appropriate international organisations. The member states rather than the Union *per se* would retain control of budgetary, employment and social security policy, despite some insistent federalist voices in the Convention calling for a more supranational approach here. And though this radical idea did appear in the first draft of the treaty, which declared that 'the Union shall co-ordinate the economic policies of the member states', this in turn provoked predictable objections from the British government, concerned lest slack drafting might at this stage be exploited by pro-integration actors so as to increase the Union's competence in economic and labour policies.[34]

The 'offending' Article 13 was subsequently revised at the IGC, the new text confirming that it is the member states rather than the Union, its agents or institutions that are responsible for co-ordinating their own economic policies, albeit subject to the benchmarking provisions of the Lisbon process subscribed to even by staunchly intergovernmental member states, but only within the limited framework enshrined in the Treaty.[35] The section of the revised draft treaty relating to the provision of general application of economic services that promote social and territorial cohesion (Article 3-122) added the all-important proviso that: 'European laws shall establish these principles and set these conditions without prejudice to the competence of Member States, in compliance with the Constitution, to provide, to commission and to fund such services'. This clearly reaffirms national discretion, the right of member states to resist any commitments that might clash with domestic policy.

The benchmarking or 'open co-ordination' rules were also included in the Treaty in order to reinforce 'best practice', an incentive to improve all-round policy performance on measures designed to expand and improve the EU labour market. However, neither the Council nor the Commission acquired any additional powers with regard to member states' employment policies. As in previous treaty provisions, the Constitutional Treaty proscribed either the Union or any member state from redeeming another member state in financial difficulties. Another contentious issue, in view of the pressure from some members of the Eurozone to tighten macro-economic discipline, was whether QMV should be extended to some aspects of taxation policy directly related to competition, notably VAT and corporate tax. This, too, brought predictable reaction from those countries – notably the United Kingdom, Ireland and Sweden – determined to resist what they saw as yet more interference in national economic policy. In the end the national veto was retained here. This was a particularly sensitive issue for the United Kingdom, and this revision accommodated one of Tony Blair's most important 'red lines', though permitting the Council acting unanimously to allow majority voting in enacting measures for combating tax evasion. The final version of the Constitutional Treaty omitted the Convention's controversial proposal for measures to combat tax fraud and tax evasion, and to be enacted by QMV.

Other contentious matters at least found their way on to the agenda. The Convention debated the Union's role in policing the international trade in public services, another matter of acute political sensitivity not least because of some considerable differences of national interest between the member states. The Commission has a mandate from the Council to negotiate in the World Trade Organization on behalf of the EU as a whole, including on services such as communications, telecommunications and transport. Some member states were concerned lest pro-integrationist voices in the Commission with support from elsewhere should try to expand this limited mandate, to include for example public welfare services. This would give the EU (in effect, the Commission) a powerful lever for intruding into national public policy domains such as education, health and social welfare services. The objection from some quarters was political, resistance to intrusion on national sovereignty *per se*, but others were just as concerned about exposing domestic interests (not least, lucrative markets in public-sector purchasing) to greater international competition. The Nice Treaty had already included trade in services in the Common Commercial Policy, and confirmed that trade in some services is not an exclusive EU competence. *Conventionnels* decided nevertheless to revisit this issue on the grounds that services should indeed be an exclusive EU competence. This had provoked resistance from France, who insisted on trade in cultural and audio-visual services remaining a shared rather than becoming an exclusive EU competence. The Nordic countries made the same demand in relation to education, social services and health care. The matter was only settled when the praesidium, mindful of time constraints and seeking consensus as much as trying to establish a clear constitutional principle, intervened at the very end of the Convention's deliberations to impose limits on the Union's role here. The Constitutional Treaty reflected this belated compromise with a restricted list of exclusive EU competencies relating to the trade in services. It likewise confirmed that, unlike the rules pertaining to trade in commercial goods, in this matter the Council must act unanimously. In what is an acutely sensitive area for national policy-makers any Council proposal for a trade agreement would require the approval of national parliaments.

Public services was also controversial territory in as much as public goods and welfare have a special place in relations between national governments and their citizens, underpinning the affective bonds that sustain affiliation and political allegiance between the state and its citizens, the ontological sense of membership of the national polity. The nation-state is still regarded after all as the primary, if no longer the exclusive source of public welfare and personal security, and nothing that has occurred so far in the remarkable process of European integration has undermined this powerful affective as well as functional bond between citizens and the state. For this reason, these policy domains would remain as a national competence 'beyond the scope of harmonisation', and they could not be supplanted by international trade policy agreements, with any so-called 'flanking' actions here requiring a unanimous decision in the Council. This outcome is quite revealing of the constraints on European integration, for regardless of alarmist claims made by Eurosceptical opinion about 'insidious' and exponential integration, the supposedly steady erosion of the fabric of nation-statehood, the member states firmly retain 'the capacity to decide how and on what terms they provide welfare services'.[36]

## Demarcating competences: exclusive and shared powers

The distribution of competences, in effect the authority to perform governance functions and deliver policy outcomes, has always been a contentious matter for the EC/EU, provoking boundary disputes between some governments and the European institutions about 'who does what', or even who *should* do what. This issue is crucial, not only for the distribution of power but in as much as it relates to the continuing debate about the meaning of European integration, the central purposes of and the prospects for transnational governance. For this reason alone it is an issue of considerable constitutional significance.[37] Academics have long debated the relative impact of various agents for transferring power from the member states to the Union. And there are many such agents, from politicians to judges, though one legal expert has maintained that the most vital factor in the expansion of EU competencies has been politics rather than law. As Craig sees it, it is not so much judicial decisions – lacking as these do the approval of democratically elected politicians – that carry most weight, but rather the wilful granting of powers to the Union, 'the result of a conscious decision by the Member States ... reached after extensive discussion within Intergovernmental Conferences'.[38] For Craig and indeed for other commentators this signal fact shows the limitations of using the federal comparator as a gauge for the political dynamics driving European integration.

In the classic federal polity it is constitutional law rather than political expediency that determines the balance of power, the allocation of competencies between the centre and the territorial polities, demarcating 'who does what' and on the basis of what authority. The courts by means of judicial review determine the division of competencies as between the respective tiers of governance, an arrangement 'based on some general constitutional provision', and as such a political decision in the first instance. The courts have a secondary, though no less important role, determining the consequences of this political decision, 'the ramifications of this [constitutional] clause for federal/state relations'.[39] This situation does not pertain in the EU, in as much as the Union lacks any such clear-cut constitutional *modus operandi*. Not only because it has yet to establish a definitive constitutional order, but because it is neither a state nor even a federal polity in the proper meaning of the term.

In these circumstances, the competency issue is bound to be problematic, most especially for those member states whose domestic constitutional order is based on federalism, for their political cultures are shaped by a normative discourse about the allocation of competencies between the respective levels of government, the *sine qua non* of federalism. Prior to Nice the German *Länder*, motivated in part by the usual federalist concerns with 'appropriate boundaries' between levels of governance, but also influenced by raw politics, the concern since Maastricht about the German federal government 'unconstitutionally' ceding powers to Brussels without the proper approval of the Bundesrat as required by the Basic Law, indicated that they might exercise their prerogative under German constitutional law to decline ratification of a future constitutional treaty, should it fail to properly delineate competencies. This was a matter of some considerable delicacy here because of the federal character of the German state, whereby a formal *Kompetenzkatalog* necessarily demarcates respective competencies as between the federal and the territorial or *Länder* levels.[40]

The same issue was also a matter of concern to the EU's unitary states, though for quite different reasons, not least because some of them exhibited concerns about what they saw a remorseless expansion of the Union's policy domains, and seemingly by stealth, whether the result of ECJ decisions, the so-called 'flexibility' procedures in the treaties or as a consequence of cumulate treaty changes. From the outset, the Community has depended on attributed competencies, powers given to it by the member states. This power base has gradually increased by various means, both indirectly through the Court's creative interpretation of the existing treaties, by legislative action or directly by the formal agreement of the member states to revise the Community's legal base so as to enhance the scope and capacity for common action. By no means every member state is sanguine about this incremental ratcheting up of power at the centre, and many are distinctly uneasy about the way power has been transferred to the Community, apparently in zero-sum fashion, and as these critics see it, seemingly at the expense of the member states. Some governments were less resigned to this development than others, and even alarmed by the consequences for national power of the import of the remark of the former German chancellor, Helmut Kohl, that European integration, like the river Rhine, never flows backwards.

For these reasons, the competence issue was bound to loom large in this latest attempt to reform the treaty base. The issue had surfaced in the post-Nice debate, some member states concerned that the Union had acquired competencies in ways unanticipated in the founding treaties, notably as a direct consequence of increasingly detailed primary legislation. Simplification would, or so some commentators maintained, be one feasible solution to what might be called the 'law of unanticipated consequences'. For where decision-making is inordinately complex, its procedures unduly opaque and with actors at various levels of governance pursuing quite different, frequently competing policy preferences as is the case in the EU, it is all too easy to lose sight of subtle shifts in the balance of political advantage between the institutional actors. For this reason, simplification was one solution to preventing unintended slippage of power from governments to the centre.

By the time the Convention met the feeling was widespread amongst the member states that the Union's treaty base was at best untidy, at worse ravelled. Concern, too, in some EU capitals that the member states had lost, or were likely to lose, control of the decisional process determined some governments to stem what they saw as a remorseless seepage of powers to the Union. The Laeken Declaration had put down a marker in this regard, noting the threat from the 'creeping expansion of competences of the Union'. Some wanted to go further, to regain the initiative from Brussels, 'restoring tasks to the member states'.[41] These concerns were signalled at Laeken, with the demand 'that the scope of [EU competence] exclusivity [should be] defined clearly and accurately'.[42] The mandate handed to the Convention was both to clarify and simplify the distribution of competencies as between the member states and the Union.

The secretariat steered this particular debate in the Convention, issuing a background paper that maintained that the current distribution of competencies was indeed too 'complex and impenetrable'.[43] It found evidence, too, of the Union impinging unduly on the powers and prerogatives of the member states.[44] Indeed, the fact that powerful vested interests were perplexed about the competency issue ensured that it received greater coverage in the Convention than either the democracy deficit or citizenship, both issues critical to redressing the abiding problem of the Union's remoteness from its citizens. Representatives of the German *Länder* were particularly active in this debate, concerned that too much power, too many competencies had been divested from member states and located at the EU level, and for this reason demanding action to arrest if not to reverse this trend. The German chancellor, responding to this domestic pressure, had already raised the matter at Nice, where he made the case for 'a more precise delimitation of powers between the European Union and the member states' to better reflect 'the principle of subsidiarity'. Schroeder was supported in this by France and the United Kingdom, albeit for their own particular reasons.[45]

The demand for a stricter cataloguing of competencies from this influential trio raised counter-objections from other member states that to catalogue competencies would be unduly inflexible, and as such likely to curb the very adaptability that has thus far served the EU well, enabling it to adjust to unpredictable events as circumstances permit. Even those states convinced of the need to curb what they saw as the steady shift of power to the centre – a formidable group that included Germany, France and the United Kingdom, and supported by Poland and Ireland – resolved in a joint position paper to resist an overly rigid cataloguing of competencies that might hinder the Union's capacity to respond imaginatively to fast-changing circumstances.[46] In these circumstances, the drive for simplification at all costs was compromised by the usual requirement in this polity to strike manageable bargains between quite different preferences. The British government's representative, Peter Hain, reminded the Convention early on that it was the member states and not some putative constitutional authority that conferred competences on the Union. This resolutely intergovernmental outlook prevailed throughout its proceedings, on this as on many other issues.

On the matter of the demarcation of competencies between the Union and the member states, the first draft of the Treaty combined a general statement on the principle of subsidiarity, with a typology of competencies: Article 1-11.1 of the Constitutional Treaty duly acknowledged that Union competencies are conferred by the member states and that their exercise is subject to the principles of subsidiarity and proportionality. Article 1-11.2 reinforced this position, confirming that the Union may act only within the scope of these conferred competencies, in order to achieve the Treaty's objectives. Competences not conferred on the Union would remain with the member states. There are few policy areas where the EU has exclusive competence: the regulation of competition of the internal market, trade policy and duties and monetary policy for the members of the Eurozone. The Treaty also acknowledged the Union's competence in economic and employment policy co-ordination (Article 1-12.3) and foreign and security policy (Articles 1-11.4 and 5), though tellingly only referring in the vaguest terms to the 'progressive framing' of a common defence policy (Article 1-16.1).

This outcome was significant for settling the long-standing wrangle over competencies, the distribution of institutional power, and was the first time the Treaty had unequivocally confirmed the principle of national sovereignty, acknowledging the member states as the source *de jure* of general competences. Even so, this hardly amounted to a fundamental overhaul of current practice but rather a reworking of Article 5.1, TEC, thus confirming that these designated competencies derive from the member states through the medium of the Constitutional Treaty.[47] Neither did the Convention propose any expansion of Article 5.1, TEC, and though it did widen the legal base of the flexibility clause beyond the scope of extant Article 308 (TEC), 'on balance there are sufficient safeguards in Article 1-18 to ensure that it should not pose any serious threat to a meaningful principle of conferred powers'. The fact that Article 1-18 required unanimity in the Council reduced the scope for expanding competencies by this means, especially so in a Union of 27 member states. For this article ensures 'that the flexibility clause could not be used, either to add new objectives to the Constitution, or to exceed the basic parameters of Union competence established in Part III'.[48] The objection raised in some quarters to any unduly rigid cataloguing of competencies during the early stages of these deliberations was eventually resolved, and a detailed catalogue of exclusive and shared competencies duly appeared in the final draft of the Constitutional Treaty. Accordingly, the principles of subsidiarity and proportionality were confirmed, with more precise rules for determining the remit and to guide the exercise of Union action in a way that answered the concerns of some member states.[49]

The Commission's reaction to this categorical approach was predictable, concerned lest a definitive demarcation of competencies should limit its capacity to encroach extempore on to what have so far been grey areas of policy. This motive explains the recommendation in the Commission president's personal manifesto, the so-called 'Penelope' text, for retaining an altogether vaguer categorising of competencies.[50] The Commission's own official submission to the Convention likewise maintained that rigid competency lists 'would have the disadvantage of artificially strait-jacketing the Union's capacity for action'.[51] The Commission's case here was less about procedure and more about the balance of institutional power, and as such it failed to convince key players at the Convention, whether governments or members of national parliaments. These national, and in some cases sub-national, constituencies were concerned to reduce ambiguity that might give convenient cover to any future unauthorised and no less unintended seepage of power to Brussels. For this reason, the Convention opted for a straightforward categorisation of competencies.[52] The praesidium proposed three broad categories: exclusive and shared competencies and supporting actions, and this formulation found its way into the final draft. Where the Union has exclusive competence, it alone would be empowered to act by adopting legally binding measures (Article 1-12.1). The member states were permitted to act in these matters only where expressly authorised to do so by the Union, or when implementing measures already adopted by the Union.

The Treaty provides a comprehensive list (Article 1-13) of those matters that are exclusively EU competencies. These are matters that, for the most part, relate to the functioning of the internal market, and include monetary policy (for those member states that have adopted the euro), the common commercial policy (notably, competition rules), customs union and the conservation of marine biological resources under the Common Fisheries Policy. The member states would have no autonomous legislative prerogatives in these areas. For this very reason, the four freedoms were omitted from the list of exclusive competencies, since to include them would preclude member states taking action to enhance the single market on their own initiative in advance of collective action by the Union *per se*, a prohibition that would clearly be contrary to the spirit of enhanced co-operation. EU competence was expressly related to the legal bases referred to in Part III of the Constitutional Treaty, defining its scope precisely and indicating in detail its impact on national regulatory discretion.

The Constitutional Treaty identified actions in employment, social and economic policy and in the Common Foreign and Security Policy as special categories of national competence, precluding any EU legislation to harmonise national legislation in these politically sensitive domains. The situation was less straightforward, however, with regard to the Union's external competencies. Article 1-13.2 gave the Union exclusive competence for concluding an international agreement when such an outcome is provided for in a legislative act of the Union, is indispensable for the Union to exercise a designated internal competence or when it otherwise impacts on an internal Union act. However, this provision seemingly conflicts with a previous interpretation of such a competency in a judgement in the European Court, and endorsed in the recommendation of the working group on complementary competencies, to the effect that: 'the Constitutional Treaty should [only] indicate that the Union is competent to conclude agreements dealing with issues falling under its internal competencies; but that this should in no way modify the definition of competences between the Union and Member States'.[53] Again, these arrangements are muddled and hardly accord with the Laeken goal of simplifying EU governance.

The Constitutional Treaty did expand some existing EU competencies: for instance, with regard to (and contravening what was agreed at Nice) the free movement of citizens in relation to passports and social security (Articles 3-133/136); defining the principles/conditions relating to the management of the operation of services of general economic interest (Article 3-6); in matters relating to strengthening the co-ordination of economic policies; and with regard to the external representation of the single currency amongst the members of the monetary union

(Articles 3-144/150). It also proposed that additional competencies should accrue to the Union, amongst which were competencies that relate to the Union's role in external relations, notably in CFSP (Part III, Title V) and in matters relating to freedom, justice and security, notably police and judicial co-operation in civil matters (Part III, Title III, Chapter IV). There is also a new legal base for the Union's role in energy (Article 3-256), intellectual property (Article 3-176), space (Article 3-248), humanitarian aid (Article 3-321), sport (Article 3-282), civil protection (Article 3-284) and administrative co-operation (Article 3-285).

The Constitutional Treaty listed those competences to be shared between the EU and the member states (Article 1-14.1), covering some 80 per cent of EU decision-making, and in key policy areas such as the internal market, consumer protection, agriculture and fisheries, transport and European networks, social and regional policy, environmental and consumer matters. And with more recent additions in energy policy and some aspects of internal and justice affairs, though these are assumed to relate only to matters of secondary legislation. In such cases both parties would have the right to legislate and to adopt legally binding acts, member states exercising that right to the extent that the Union has not exercised its competence. Again, these matters were listed as an aid to clarification. Moreover, the precise configuration of power-sharing differs as between the various categories, a direct consequence of a complicated treaty base and a legacy of incremental accretion of Union interventions in public policy. The detailed rules pertaining to these particular shared competencies were enumerated in Part III of the Treaty. The critical point here is that member states might only act in these shared policy areas where the Union has omitted to act, or ceased to take action (Article 1-12.2). On one reading of this situation, it seems as if the balance had been irrevocably tilted towards the Union and away from national discretion. As Wessels sees it, 'while the degree of EU regulation and intervention differs significantly from one field to another, it is noticeable that the last strongholds of the nation states' exclusive competencies – the *domaines réservés* – are increasingly restricted'.[54]

On the face of it these arrangements seemingly conflict with the political objective of those seeking to contain the Union's steady incursion into domestic policy, those preferring to stand firm on what in the classical federal narrative is known as 'states' rights'. However, the concession to supranationalism here is much less than it might seem. The member states would be deprived of competence in a shared domain only in so far as the Union has exercised its own competence. Furthermore, as one legal expert interprets these arrangements:

> It would be wrong to conclude that the Member States lose their competence even where the EU has exercised its competence [for although] EU legislation may entail complete harmonisation ... it may also be framed so as to constitute minimum harmonisation, with the specific intent of leaving Member States with room for action in the relevant area. There is nothing in the proposed constitution to suggest that this latter option should not be open to them. On the contrary, the thrust of many of the constitutional provisions is to ensure that the EU does legislate where action is better taken at the national level.[55]

On this reading, these arrangements would in fact constrain the Union's intrusion into the domestic domain, though clarity, establishing a firm boundary between the legal prerogatives of the Union and those of the member states, depends rather less on iterating formal norms, even those enshrined in a constitutional treaty, and rather more on political dynamics, the actual working out of relations between the respective levels of governance. This much is hardly new, and is in fact the usual way of things in this uniquely 'mixed' and 'in-between' polity.

The areas of policy where the Union may take supporting actions, or otherwise co-ordinate or supplement the actions of member states without superseding their competencies in these matters (Article 1-12.5), includes the following: industry, health care, education, vocational training, youth and sport, culture and civil protection (Article 1-17). However, the competency boundary between shared and supporting actions was not as clearly defined as it might have been, and for this reason may prove to be problematic should the Union adopt this particular categorisation. For one thing, there is potential for overlap in some policy domains in this category, for instance, aspects of public health are also covered in some degree by shared powers.[56] There is scope, too, for action by the Union to bind member states in areas supposedly within their own legal competence. Dougan has observed that while the dividing line here is 'meant to lie in the capacity of Union action to have (fully or partially) pre-emptive effects upon Member States regulatory power ... the coherence of that distinction is undermined by the Constitution's failure to allocate specific Union activities to the most appropriate category'.[57] In addition, the Constitutional Treaty identified a particular competence for dealing with economic and employment policy (Article 1-12.3), but again at the risk of adding to confusion: notably, measures to co-ordinate the economic policies of the member states by adopting general guidelines (Article 1-15.1), specific commitments entailed by the adoption of the euro (Article 1-15.1) and with regard to employment policy (Article 1-15.2) or initiatives to co-ordinate social policy (Article 1-15.3).

There was lively debate in the Convention about whether these matters would be better subsumed under shared competencies rather than listed as a distinct category. The praesidium took the view that co-ordinating economic and employment policy should be a separate category, a somewhat arbitrary decision and one motivated more by politics than by concern with procedural efficiency.[58] For to include this as a shared competence, with the prospect of the Union pre-empting state action in such sensitive policy areas, would surely have raised objections from the usual intergovernmental quarters. At the same time, there was a widespread feeling in the Convention that to categorise this critical policy domain as merely a supporting or co-ordinating action was an inadequate response. In the event, caution prevailed and the praesidium, notwithstanding a recommendation to the contrary from the working group on defence and related matters to include open co-ordination,[59] omitted a general clause to 'constitutionalise' the open method of co-ordination in these supporting and related areas of competence.[60] The final draft version of the Treaty settled for merely recommending initiatives to establish appropriate guidelines relating to best policy practice, and to monitor and evaluate social policy, research and technology development, public health and industry policy (Article 3-209/210; Article 3-248/255; Article 3-278.2; and Article 3-279).

The matter of allocating competencies, in effect cataloguing 'who does what' in EU governance, is both a complex and a controversial business, as it is bound to be in any multi-level polity lacking a definitive constitutional order. The consensus of experts here is that 'the revised provisions on Union competencies should rightly be regarded as a significant achievement for the Convention in meeting the Laeken objective of clarification'.[61] Despite the difficulties of demarcating, let alone policing precise boundaries between areas of competence, the final outcome did at least improve on the previously imprecise definition of exclusivity. A less complacent evaluation, however, would be that clarification here was designed primarily with insiders in mind, intended to help those who operate the system but hardly simplifying what for the public at large are still immensely complicated, indeed incomprehensible procedures. Nor was every commentator convinced that the crucial *Kompetenz-Kompetenz* issue, the demarcation of powers between the Union and the member states would be settled once and for all by these arrangements.

Whether this matter can ever be categorically resolved in what is complex and multi-level governance is doubtful, Constitution or no. The formula that was eventually adopted in the Constitutional Treaty – to the effect that 'where the powers of the member states are not specified, they are assumed, by default, by the Union' – seems to be less than clear-cut in some important aspects of public policy. Not least in the critical matter of the Union's foreign policy, where, as one critic sees it, 'the draft does not make it unambiguously clear that the ultimate power in this field will, and must, remain with the member states'.[62] What this contributes to simplification is questionable, for the way competences are allocated in these proposed arrangements 'barely leaves one field of action for member states, exclusively'.[63]

This outcome brought an alarmist response from some quarters, seeing in this less than straightforward configuration of competencies proof-positive of deliberate obfuscation designed to hide what might be called the Union's 'mission creep'. For Malcolm, these arrangements would ensure that by degrees 'something that could not legally be considered as a state' has been transformed into 'something that most definitely can'.[64] Critics in similar vein predicted an 'escalator effect', whereby 'the extensive application of "shared competences" – whilst not changing their legal nature – might turn them through use into "exclusive competences"'.[65] The assumption here is that by degrees critical competences that are the very essence of nation-statehood are irrevocably shifting from state to EU level, and that the eventual outcome 'will be a final, self-denying treaty, one that will repeal the treaties of Rome, Maastricht and so on and that will ensure that the authority of the EU will, from that moment onwards, no longer be treaty based', with the result that 'any disputes about [the authority of the EU] will have to be dealt with not under international law, but by the EU's own constitutional court – whose powers will be derived from the EU's own authority'.[66]

This claim is both ideologically driven and exaggerated and even alarmist, at least on the evidence of the Constitutional Treaty. Revealing in this respect was a clause inserted at the request of Peter Hain, the British government's representative, that acknowledges the member states as the EU's ultimate source of authority. It confirms that in those policy areas where it has designated competences, these powers are 'conferred' on the Union by the member states. And, presumably, on that same basis may be rescinded by them should they so wish. As one legal scholar sees it, 'the competence of distributing competencies is still a state competence and this it remains so as long as it is not unanimously transferred to the Union'.[67] Moreover, the IGC underlined the point, confirming in the final version of the Treaty (Article 1-12.5) that: 'Legally binding acts of the Union adopted on the basis of the provisions in Part III (The Policies and Functions of the Union) relating to these areas may not entail harmonisation of Member States' laws or regulations.' Even so and with much at stake, a minority of *conventionnels* from eight countries, including the United Kingdom, Sweden, Denmark, France and Ireland, were sufficiently concerned about the possible implications of the proposed changes to issue a minority report.[68] The issue was bound to be controversial and will continue to be so, for this is an issue that goes to the very heart of the debate about the meaning and dynamics of European integration. One that touches on the fundamental question of whether the object of 'ever-closer union' is to bury the nation state, or merely to enable it to survive and even to flourish in an age of remorseless global change.

Even so, the Convention's debate on the competency issue obscured rather more than it clarified where power actually resides in the EU. Whether this was deliberate, reflecting covert political purposes, or merely the result of genuine confusion about the meaning of European integration is debatable. For whatever reason, the same defensive outlook that sees deliberate conspiracy by federalists as driving change here overlooks the crucial difference between a federal state and a confederal polity. Furthermore, this reading of events misconstrues the significance of subsidiarity (Article 1-II.3), a precept that quite deliberately demarcates and delimits respective spheres of influence in this multi-level polity. And this defensive outlook likewise overlooked again, whether by accident or design, the new provision attached to the Treaty (Protocol 1) that permits national parliaments to block Commission proposals for legislation that compromise the subsidiarity principle attached to the Treaty. Alarmists who choose to see the Union as a state-in-the-making if not yet one in legal or political fact are wrong on two main counts. In the first place, this narrative misreads the significance and no less the meaning of EU 'constitutionalism', overlooks the fact that even contemporary international governmental organisations operate under agreed rules, amounting to an albeit informal constitutional order implied by formal statements about mission, shared values and with an institutional architecture and authoritative decisional procedures to facilitate common business. In short, there is nothing exceptional, let alone sinister about a transnational polity adopting a constitution. The claim frequently made by Eurosceptics that 'in the political realm, only states have constitutions – and the definition of a sovereign state is that its own constitution is not subject to the authority of any higher constitution', is historically inaccurate and plainly wrong.[69]

Another fallacy given wings in this particular narrative is that the absence from the Constitutional Treaty of a definitive list of competences exclusive to the member states was somehow evidence of federalist conspiracy. The fact is that anything not expressly listed as an EU competence, whether exclusive or shared, was to remain *ipso facto* the preserve of the member states.[70] This may be an untidy way of dealing with such a politically sensitive issue, but the fact is that as things currently stand no such clear categorisation of competencies is possible in what is a polity of mixed and competing purposes. This is a polity that resists any straightforward definition of its collective purpose, and for this very reason 'competences cannot be *a priori* rigidly divided and codified', as they might be in a national constitution designed for a hierarchical political architecture whose future status as a polity, its political *finalité*, is already settled.[71] In these circumstances, simplification in the sense anticipated by some reformers may well be beyond the Union's reach, though if so this significant fact might at least have been conveyed to the public at large and in plainer terms. What happened instead was an exclusive conversation about 'who does what' between vested interests, couched in coded language and with no attempt to explain or to translate these admittedly complicated matters into the political vernacular.

The Constitutional Treaty's attempt to resolve the competencies conundrum was much less a lurch towards federalism, a covert move to bring in European statehood by the back door, and rather more an attempt to demarcate appropriate levels of competency that confirm the Union's status as a project that balances competing preferences. In effect, to put in place a unique balance of competencies appropriate to unique multi-level governance. The liberal institutional narrative for instance presents a more measured account of the Constitutional Treaty than the singularly partisan narrative of resolute Eurosceptics, seeing these developments as merely an acknowledgement that intergovernmentalism 'has moved centre-stage in Europe during the past decade', and likewise confirming that 'though the Eurosceptics dare not admit it the Maastricht treaty was the high water mark of Jean Monnet's vision of a federal Europe [and that] overall, the constitutional implications of the new treaty are trivial against those of Maastricht or the Single European Act'.[72] Which of these competing ideological narratives offers the most plausible explanation of these proposals depends on how one chooses to see the broad trajectory of European integration. And this is more a matter of ideology than objective political analysis. What is beyond dispute, however, is the failure of those who engaged on these issues to broaden their self-regarding conversation, to bring these critical issues to a wider audience and in language they can understand.

## Subsidiarity

Subsidiarity was introduced in the Maastricht Treaty, the principle that even in policy domains where the Union has exclusive competence it should act 'only if and in so far as the objectives of the proposed action cannot be sufficiently achieved by the member states and can therefore, by reason of the scale or effects of the proposed action, be better achieved by the Community'.[73] A protocol attached to the Amsterdam Treaty required any proposal for action by a European institution to comply with subsidiarity, for the Commission to consult with all relevant parties before taking any action. The principle was confirmed at Laeken, the declaration agreed there referring somewhat defensively to concerns expressed by some member states about 'undue interference' by the Union in domestic affairs. By now this issue was being seen less as a struggle for power between key players and more as a democratic reflex, expressing widespread concern about 'European institutions inveigling their way into every nook and cranny of life'.[74]

The working group on subsidiarity included *conventionnels* favourably disposed to a federalist design, as well as national parliamentarians concerned about the limited role for domestic actors in the Union's policy processes. In the circumstances, the working group sought balance between the community interest and national discretion. Those who preferred firmer policing of subsidiarity made much of the fact that the Court, responsible as it is for monitoring compliance, had thus far never struck down a single EU measure on the grounds that it infringed subsidiarity. As one legal expert observed in his evidence to the working group, the justification for Community action depends on the 'essentially political and subjective' definition of the word 'better', as that condition applies to the Maastricht definition of subsidiarity.[75] These definitions were discussed, but there was no serious challenge as such to the subsidiarity principle from either side, and common ground of sorts was found in a commitment to at least improve the monitoring of policy. Measures designed to reinforce the subsidiarity protocol were reviewed but discounted, for instance a proposal to appoint an official to oversee the boundaries of subsidiarity, and another from some mainly French *conventionnels* to establish a second legislative chamber consisting of representatives from national parliaments, and charged with the task of monitoring whether proposed EU legislation meets with the criteria of subsidiarity and proportionality.

Despite clear differences on this issue in the working group and in the praesidium a compromise was reached that did not involve any fundamental reallocation of powers, whether to the member states or to national parliaments, but merely reiterated the need for a balance of power between the respective levels of EU governance. Accordingly, the Constitutional Treaty affirmed Article 1-11.3, and the Protocol on the Application of the Principles of Subsidiarity and Proportionality attached as an Annexe to the Treaty states that: 'Under the principle of subsidiarity, in areas that do not fall within its exclusive competence, the Union shall act only if and insofar as the objectives of the intended action cannot be sufficiently achieved by the member states, either at central level or at regional and local level, but can be better achieved at Union level'. Similarly, 'under the principle of proportionality, the content and form of Union action shall not exceed what is necessary to achieve the objectives of the Constitution', or where such actions are better implemented, by reason of scale and effect, at the level of the Union. The only revision to the extant provision on subsidiarity was the reference to action at the 'regional and local level'. The revised Protocol was in fact less detailed than the Amsterdam Protocol. Nor was there any suggestion here of enforcing subsidiarity, a fact that reflects the preference of the working group that monitoring subsidiarity is best left to the common sense of the political and institutional actors rather than being determined by formal legal/judicial procedures.[76] The working group did propose to improve monitoring of the Union's legislative procedures, including a role for national parliaments in policing the boundaries of Union competencies, supposedly as an insurance against undue intrusions into the national legislative domain, and a procedure that it was assumed would counter apathy by increasing public interest in European affairs.[77]

Concern from national politicians and publics alike about undue centralisation, in effect unwonted interference from Brussels in national affairs, was met by a significant concession. National parliaments would have a role in monitoring subsidiarity, by means of an 'early warning' system. The idea of bolstering the role of national parliaments in Union's affairs has long been seen as one way of closing the legitimacy gap between national politics and governance at the EU level, a means of bringing the Union closer to its citizens. The then British commissioner, Sir Leon Brittan, had suggested in the early 1990s establishing a committee of national parliamentarians with the power to request the Court at any stage in the legislative process to rule on whether a proposed EU measure conflicted with the subsidiarity principle. The Union did establish the Conference of Community and European Affairs Committee as a forum for national parliamentarians to review EU developments, though as one contemporary commentator duly observed, this committee 'remains an obscure body, unable to attract the best and the brightest MPs to sit on it, because it has no real power'.[78]

The idea of bringing national parliaments into the EU policy loop was revived during the diplomatic build-up to the Convention, not least by the British prime minister, Tony Blair, in a speech in Warsaw in October 2000.[79] Blair proposed that national parliamentarians should sit in a second chamber of the European Parliament tasked with examining proposed legislation for its compatibility with an agreed charter of EU competencies, as well as monitoring common initiatives in the field of foreign and defence policy. This proposal was resisted, however, both by the European Parliament and by many governments. In part, for political reasons, but also because of the legal complexities that would, in effect, follow from making national parliaments part of the Union's institutional architecture. The Convention settled instead on a compromise for resolving the issue: eschewing the bicameral model that might detract from the European Parliament's emergent role as co-legislator, whilst giving national parliaments an opportunity to veto EU legislation. The revised Protocol requires the Commission to ensure that any proposed legislation accords with the principles of subsidiarity and proportionality. Accordingly, the Commission must inform national parliaments concurrently (and both chambers of bicameral legislatures) about legislative proposals, with parliaments having a six-week interlude during which to communicate any objections as 'reasoned opinions' to the presidents of the Commission, the Parliament and the Council, the so-called 'yellow-card' procedure discussed above. Objections from one third of the EU parliaments (one quarter in police and judicial co-operation matters, pillar three – with unicameral parliaments exercising two votes and bi-cameral parliaments one vote per assembly) would then require the Commission to review the proposal, though not necessarily to revise or rescind it. Should no 'satisfactory action' follow such an intervention, the parliaments could then refer the matter to the Court for adjudication.

An even more stringent procedure proposed by the British government representative, Gisela Stuart, was discussed by the praesidium, a so-called 'red-card' intervention whereby objections by two-thirds of national parliaments would require a legislative proposal to be withdrawn *sine die*. This proposal was blocked, however, largely on the basis of Giscard's somewhat dubious claim that the Commission would automatically withdraw any proposal for action if ever confronted by substantial opposition. The Committee of the Regions, though not the sub-national or territorial polities that this same Committee represents, would also have the right of appeal to the Court in cases where it deemed subsidiarity to have been flouted and its objections duly ignored. Some difficulties remained, nevertheless, over the actual details of this veto power, not least the precise circumstances in which national parliaments might raise such objections. It was far from clear, for instance, whether complaints made by individual parliaments on grounds of subsidiarity would 'have to raise substantially the same issues/ relate to substantially the same provisions within the proposed legislation?' It was unclear, too, what the outcome would be should national parliaments 'misuse their right to make reasoned objections by focusing on other aspects of the proposed legislation – its proportionality, legal basis or substantive policy content – which are then dressed up as subsidiarity points?'[80]

The role of national parliaments in blocking policy proposals is hardly straightforward, and would be affected, too, by the way EU legislation is made. Commission proposals are subject to amendment and revision by both the Council and the European Parliament, especially so under the elaborate conciliation arrangements required by co-decision. And such politically driven inter-institutional bargains, concluded at a very late stage in the legislative process, might well threaten the principle of subsidiarity at a juncture where domestic legislatures are no longer involved in the policy process. In these circumstances, the Court would be the obvious, indeed the only means for redress. The working group on subsidiarity did anticipate this eventuality and called for national parliaments to have an independent right under extant Article 230, TEC to bring legal actions to annul policy, on grounds of subsidiarity. The difficulty with this solution, however, is the perceived conflict between the member state standing as a unitary actor before the Court, and the fact that for political/legislative purposes member states are by no means monolithic but pluralistic actors, and increasingly so these days, when so many EU states have national constitutional arrangements that include devolution, or even fully federal arrangements. What in these circumstances is 'the' putative national interest, and who could speak authoritatively for it at the EU level?

The Convention did propose to allow the Court to hear actions brought by member states for breach of the subsidiarity principle, 'or notified by them in accordance with their legal order on behalf of their national Parliaments or a chamber of it'.[81] What was less clear, however, was which political actor would have authority to make this decision: the national government or the parliament of the member state concerned, or indeed a second chamber representing territorial governments? This muddle was by no means resolved in the Constitution, persuading one observer to note that the proposals on subsidiarity still fail 'to reflect a truly coherent conception of the role national parliaments should play within the Union legislative process'. As Dougan sees it, if the Convention was indeed serious about giving national parliaments a meaningful role in monitoring compliance with the principle of subsidiarity, 'why are there such major gaps in their ability to discharge that function effectively?'[82] Again, the attempt by the Constitutional Treaty to simplify this critical constitutional principle of multi-level governance raised as many questions as it answered.

## Enhanced co-operation

Successive enlargements have made it difficult for the EU to retain the commonality of purpose that was possible between the founder members. One response to this problem has been to permit member states to opt out of some common policy initiatives, for instance Britain's self-exclusion from the Social Chapter and its subsequent opt-out from membership of Economic and Monetary Union (EMU). The corollary of the opt-out is an arrangement that also permits member states to opt in to particular enterprises designed to accelerate closer, or what is sometimes described as 'positive' integration *à la* Monnet. With an unprecedented enlargement in 2004–7 about to significantly increase this differential capacity, and quite possibly diluting in the process the political will for deeper integration, it was inevitable that attention would be given to the idea of enhancing co-operation between some member states in some policy domains. This idea was broached during the Amsterdam IGC and was developed further in the Nice Treaty. The principle was revisited in the Convention. Following the precedents established by the Schengen and Eurozone arrangements the Convention decided to expand enhanced co-operation (Article 1-44), determining that it should be open to every member state, and simplified into a mechanism for better adjusting to the requirements of depillarisation, and for the better management of the Union's affairs in light of the growing diversity that will inevitably follow the latest enlargement.[83]

The Constitutional Treaty made three specific proposals in this regard. First, the number of member states needed for enhanced co-operation was changed from the current fixed number of eight to a variable one third of the current EU membership. Second, enhanced co-operation remained a solution only of last resort, though the Nice rules were altered so that the Council need have no formal or informal role in discussing any policy matter designated as appropriate for such action. Third, the Convention agreed to widen the scope for enhanced co-operation in CFSP. The previous limitation imposed by Article 27(b), TEU, to the effect that any enhancement under Title V cannot include matters relating to military or defence issues was removed. Article 1-44 identified three instances of enhanced co-operation in the framework of common security and defence policy.

These were as follows: Council decisions to assign an agreed task to a sub-group of member states who wish to, and have the capability to undertake it; structured co-operation between those member states with advanced military capabilities, and who have undertaken firmer, binding commitments to each other in relation to missions 'abroad'; and closer co-operation (albeit only when the European Council agrees a common defence policy) in matters of mutual defence in response to armed threats to the territorial integrity of a participating member state. The Constitutional Treaty listed the procedural arrangements for author-ising such co-operation. The Commission would continue to exercise the power of veto, retaining the discretion to decline to submit any proposal to the Council. Member states, in line with the procedural revision in the Nice Treaty, were to be denied any right to object to the launching of enhanced co-operation initiatives by initiating a vote (QMV) in Council. Finally, the Commission and, where appro-priate, the Union minister for foreign affairs would keep the European Parliament 'informed' of developments in enhanced co-operation (Article 3-418.3), thereby increasing, albeit modestly, that institution's previous but conditional right of assent in the enhancement process. With regard to enhanced co-operation within CFSP, the new foreign minister would have the prerogative to issue an opinion on the consistency of any proposed enhanced action with the overall CFSP.

Significantly, the old-style veto power of member states over enhancement in the CFSP context (under extant Article 23.2 and 27 (c), TEU) was to be rescinded, with the Council permitted to give authorisation by means of QMV. The Council might nevertheless impose conditions on would-be participants in such enhanced activities: for instance, one such condition was a clear ability to positively contribute, as too was compliance with all previous acts already covered by the Council's authorisation for the given policy domain (Article 3-420.2). Enhanced co-operation in policy domains other than CFSP would likewise require clear conditions: the Commission must confirm that all prospective participants meet the requirement for the action. Two disqualifying decisions by the Commission (Article 3-420.1) would entitle the member state concerned to the right of appeal in the Council. And the final version of the Constitutional Treaty expressly excluded enactment by qualified majority of any decisions with military or defence implica-tions (Article 3-422.3, new), a clause being inserted at the IGC stage to reinforce what might be called the intergovernmental firewall in this most politically sensi-tive policy domain.

Some commentators saw real potential in these provisions on enhanced co-oper-ation for facilitating closer integration, even in an enlarged and still expanding Union where otherwise increasing diversity might threaten initiatives for greater commonality of purpose or action, amongst those member states willing to do so. It offers, too, an answer of sorts to the Convention's reticence about extending the opportunities for QMV, acutely aware as most *conventionnels* were of pressing political realities. And it is also one way of circumventing the determination of some member states to exercise their veto power in those critical policy domains still subject to unanimity. As Dougan sees it, 'the revamped provisions on enhanced co-operation could help bypass the awkward squad for the purposes not just of adopting a specific act, but also of authorising the principle of differentiated integration, and then transforming the relevant policy field into a system of QMV for the participating countries'.[84]

This might just pass muster in the case of CFSP, assuming that the big three member states are not distracted, as they have been previously and indeed recently by fundamental differences over their respective national policy objectives. But it remains doubtful whether graduated integration through enhancement could so readily be applied to the most critical policy areas (taxation is the obvious example here), still defined and no less defended by most member states behind their so-called 'red lines' as fundamental national interests.

## Voluntary withdrawal from the Union

The Constitutional Treaty acknowledges for the first time (Article 1-60.1) the right of a member state to withdraw from the Union, 'in accordance with its own constitutional requirements'. Of course, the right of exit was always implied, and Greenland, an autonomous territory of Denmark, actually exercised the option to withdraw from the Community following a referendum in 1985. The formal inclusion of this right in the founding Treaty is nevertheless significant in so far as it confirms the Union's status as a voluntary community of member states, and even more the fact that ultimately the member states are sovereign actors in the fullest sense. Consequently, this article both 'resembles and partly replaces the Luxembourg compromise of 1966, whereby a member state can demand a unanimous decision in matters of vital national interest'.[85]

The right to withdraw and no less the threat to exercise it might in some circumstances, and certainly for some key member states, increase their political leverage *vis-à-vis* the EU institutions. Any member state intending to exercise the exit option must first inform the European Council. Thereafter, the Union would open negotiations on an agreement to this effect, in order both to establish satisfactory arrangements for withdrawal and for settling future relations with the Union. The agreement on withdrawal would then be confirmed by the Council using QMV, the departing state being excluded from these deliberations, and by Parliament using the assent procedure.[86] There are some commentators, not least those favourable to deeper integration, who saw this as an untimely concession to Euroscepticism. Or at least, as offering an incentive to member states less convinced about the 'nobler purposes' of European integration, and prepared to use unseemly threats so as to maximise their bargaining power at the expense of the common interest. In fact, this arrangement merely confirms *de jure* what already pertains *de facto*. In any event, this sort of provision should figure in any liberal constitutional order designed for a community composed of sovereign nation states, and significantly it is retained in the Lisbon Treaty. The right to exit is 'the ultimate constraint upon Union competence', in the event that any given member should 'feel that its own national interests have strayed so far from those of the wider Union that secession is the only method of redressing the balance'.[87]

## Amendment procedures

The Constitutional Treaty, like any constitutional arrangement worthy of the name, has its own revision procedures (Articles 4-443/445). There are, nevertheless, some important differences here from revision procedures as these apply in the current treaties (Article 48, TEU). The European Council must consult with both the Commission and the Parliament before deciding (by simple majority) to proceed with even minor constitutional changes. Moreover, the Parliament and not only the member states and the Commission would now submit proposals for amendment to the Council. Otherwise, the convention method was institutionalised as the normal rather than an occasional or *ad hoc* procedure for constitutional review, forwarding its recommendations to an IGC, as was the case with the 2003 Convention. It is interesting to note here that after the rejection of the Constitutional Treaty in two referendums, followed by what amounted to a protracted crisis over what to do next, the governments reverted to type, abandoning at least for the time being the idea of recalling a convention to debate how best to progress with reform. As democrats see it, and no less those concerned about more surely connecting governance with citizens, this is a case of one step forward and two in reverse!

Amendment procedures always give some indication of the balance of political forces, of where power ultimately resides in a polity. Some *conventionnels*, concerned lest treaty amendment might in future be too easily stalled if member states should retain the ultimate veto, wanted amendments to proceed only by means of so-called 'super-qualified majorities' of the member states. Others, however, prepared to concede that the member states should indeed have the decisive say in settling the big institutional issues, preferred a more flexible arrangement, and proposed a differentiated amendment procedure: full approval by every member state for amendments to Parts I and II, but with a more variable procedure for amendments to the policy aspects in Part III. Controversy centred particularly on the so-called *passerelle*, variously described as the enabling, 'escalator', 'overpass' or 'bridging' clause, in effect a procedure for fast-track decision-making. The *passerelle* permits the European Council acting unanimously, to apply QMV to some areas of EU procedure where, to date, the decision rule is unanimity, and without formally changing the Treaty. This amounts in effect to treaty amendment by the back door, in as much as the procedure permits the European Council to make constitutional changes on its own initiative without recourse to national constitutional procedures in cases where the distribution of competences between the member state and the Union is unaffected.

The proposal originated with Jean-Luc Dehaene, instinctively favourable to a federalist design for the EU polity, and recommended, at least as his critics saw it, on the disingenuous grounds of building 'flexibility' into the new constitutional arrangements. What some *conventionnels* saw instead in this proposal as an implied threat to the currently flexible amendment procedure is hardly credible, given that the EU already permits enhanced co-operation, and as its corollary opt-outs by member states even from mainstream policies. Nevertheless, the constitutional implications of this proposal raised objections from those member states concerned by what they saw as insidious or 'creeping' integration. These same voices resisted the Italian presidency's proposal during the IGC, to the effect that future constitutional changes should be enacted by QMV, a move bluntly described by one senior EU diplomat as 'barking mad'.[88] This certainly proved to be a step too far for most governments, with Britain in particular, though by no means on its own, actively resisting the idea, mostly because it seemed to imply a fundamental shift in the Union's *raison d'être*. The British position was unequivocal: in effect, that 'on the day that the power to amend the Constitution is given to EU institutions, the very constitutional nature of the Union will then acquire state-like powers'.[89]

In the event the Convention avoided any such dramatic shift in the balance of power between the Union and its member states, eschewing more radical preferences to fast-track some aspects of treaty revision, notably in Part III of the Constitutional Treaty relating to policies and the functioning of the Union. Problematic here is the fact that Part III contains key policy aspects that affect the national competencies of every member state, just as much as those measures contained in Parts I and II. In the event, this consideration dissuaded the Convention from approving the differentiated route to constitutional amendment by means of the *passerelle*. After much debate, the Convention permitted this procedure in only a few, and even then clearly circumscribed matters: namely, for the allocation of parliamentary seats after 2009; to determine the rules on rotation for both the Council of Ministers and the Commission chairs; changes to Commission organisation and future rotation procedures; and for moving from a special legislative to an ordinary legislative procedure, or moving from unanimity to QMV.

These changes may be few in number but they are hardly insignificant, for the use of such executive discretion does enhance the European Council's powers, not least in the matter of when to move from unanimity to QMV in the technical policy domains in Part III, without having recourse to the cumbrous unanimity procedure for treaty revision. The European Council, acting unanimously, would be able under this revised procedure to apply QMV to those areas where unanimity is the decision rule, though only after securing consensus amongst the member states, by no means an easy task in an EU of 27 member states. This proposed reform may well have expediency on its side, but in view of mounting evidence from opinion surveys signalling public disaffection with a 'remote' political class and rising disquiet about how they exercise power, it might improve simplification though at the expense of public goodwill. This problem is compounded by the fact that the decisions of the European Council, unlike those of the other EU institutions, are beyond judicial review by the Court of Justice.

The amendment procedure for Parts I and II, dealing with the critical aspects of EU governance, remains firmly in the hands of the member states. The European Council may decide by simple majority and with Parliament's approval whether to allow proposals for treaty amendment from a future convention. The member states retain the prerogative to decide such amendments by unanimity. Should any member state delay adopting a constitutional amendment, the European Council would institute a review after two years, a more imprecise procedure than currently prevails in most national constitutional orders. Critics, not least the Commission, have claimed that these procedures would undermine constitutional amendment.[90] As they see it, the retention of the national veto on the 'big' constitutional questions is itself testament to the continuing impact of negative intergovernmentalism.[91] This may well be so on the 'big' issues, but as things currently stand no other outcome is politically feasible. To allow Parliament the exclusive right to amend the Treaty would be to shift authority over constitutional amendment to an EU institution, in effect to acknowledge that the member states would 'no longer be "Masters of the Founding Treaties"'.[92]

## Constitutional revision: IGC or convention?

Significant for future revisions of the treaties is the clause added to the final draft articles on the functioning of the European Court of Justice, to the effect that the 'Member States undertake not to submit a dispute concerning the interpretation or application of the Constitution to any method of settlement', other than a convention followed by an IGC. This is clearly designed to preclude the Court exercising or even attempting to exercise the judicial review that is the constitutional prerogative of supreme courts in federal polities. Whether it would have quite this effect is debatable, however. In the General and Final provisions of the Constitutional Treaty at Part IV relating to the ordinary revision procedure of the Constitution, the clause included in the Treaty's final version (Article 4-443.2 – ex Article 48, TEU) stipulates that, notwithstanding the arrangements for revision recommended by the Convention, whereby the government of any member state, the European Parliament or the Commission may each submit proposals for constitutional amendment, and with the European Council required after consulting the other two institutions to establish a convention, the European Council may, nevertheless, 'decide by a simple majority, after obtaining the consent of the European Parliament, not to convene a convention should this not be justified by the extent of the proposed amendments'. Furthermore, 'in the latter case, the European Council shall define the terms of reference for a conference of representatives of the governments of the Member States'.

What this means in effect is that the member states built into the revision procedure a default mechanism, ensuring that they remain the final arbiters of both the processes for Treaty review and for revising the Treaty *per se*. The decision to proceed with many of these reforms in the Lisbon Treaty, despite widespread public disquiet about changes implied in the Constitution, without reinstating a representative convention, would seem to indicate that the bold experiment in deliberative constitutionalism launched at Laeken is now done with, at least for the time being.

There were more detailed procedures, too, in the final draft of the Treaty which would give the Council the authority to notify national parliaments of any proposed changes (Article 4-444.3, new). Thus, in the event that these same institutions indicate opposition to any proposed constitutional revisions within six months of such notification, they may not be adopted. And in the matter of the revision procedure relating to Union policies (Title III of Part III), either the Parliament or the Commission may submit proposals for revision to the European Council. However, any such revision would only come into force 'after being ratified by all the Member States in accordance with their respective constitutional requirements' (Article 4-443.3, new), another clear indication that the authority for EU constitutional revision ultimately resides with the member states, and will remain so for the foreseeable future.

All of the reform measures discussed above were a response to the Laeken mandate to simplify EU governance, to more clearly demarcate its respective competencies, and to elucidate its procedures with a view to demystifying its operations for citizens. The outcome was by no means what was intended, however, when Laeken embarked on unprecedented constitutional overhaul. As we have seen, simplification in some degree would indeed follow from adopting at least some of these reforms, though hardly the transparent or cogent constitutional design anticipated at Laeken. Some of these changes would certainly contribute to a clearer understanding of how power is exercised in the Union and by whom. However, a dispassionate appraisal of the contribution of these proposed reforms to simplified and no less to pellucid procedures would surely conclude that these remedies hardly amount to much by way of improvement on current governance arrangements, and that in reality EU governance remains as convoluted, as complicated and no less baffling to its citizen as ever it was.

# 8　A people's Europe

## Citizenship, rights and justice

### Defining 'Europeanness': the elusive search for common values

Constitutions for established states have little need to define the polity's present or intended geographical boundaries, for there are already historical borders in place when the authorities embark on the task of designing rules and procedures for governance. The EU is not a fixed geographical entity in this sense. A Community that began with six founder members has expanded its membership on five separate occasions to the present 27, and with more changes likely to follow future enlargement there is no clear idea what its final boundaries will be. Moreover, the European polity is indeterminate in a quite different sense. What the Union stands for, its *raison d'être*, the values and the cultural cement that give any stable polity commonality of purpose remain contested.[1] A constitution provides the normative ballast that holds together otherwise diffuse communities, symbolising their commitment to shared goals by means of a *Grundnorm*. In essence, a constitution is a formal statement of values, and supposedly of common identity that shapes citizens' perceptions about belonging to a political community.[2]

As we have seen, however, the EU is not a polity in the usual sense, and this issue has never been resolved, either by scholars or by politicians. There was bound to be lively debate in the Convention about what it means to be 'European' in this affective sense, whether and how to attribute normative meaning to European citizenship beyond the notion of geographically contiguous peoples with broadly similar cultural roots. The idea of Europe has always been controversial, ever since Aristotle's figurative attempt to distinguish pukka 'Europeans' from so-called 'barbarians'. For this reason, there was as much resistance as support in the Convention for the idea of a Constitution for 'Europe', or at least for one that traded in the currency of unequivocal 'European' values.

Yet belonging to a shared political project is precisely what constitutionalism is all about. Democratic constitutions do more than formulate procedures for governance. They are also concerned with iterating the principles on which the polity is founded and giving it distinctive historical rationale, and likewise locating it within a historically grounded constitutional tradition. The search for collective purpose in this sense is hardly new to Europe. It has figured in both academic narratives and in actual political projects since the Enlightenment, and not least in the endeavour from 1945 to build a European Community.[3] European values were central to discussion in the rights convention, and were bound to figure in the debate on the Constitution. The most controversial issue here was a proposal to include an explicit reference to Europe's Christian heritage in a Preamble to the Constitution. A determined campaign was waged by representatives, mainly from the German CDU and CSU parties supported by an alliance of various Christian churches backed by Pope John Paul II and lobbyists from civil society, to make reference to 'God' a core European value.[4] This provoked a clamour from secularists and others who disputed such a narrow interpretation of 'European values', preferring more secular references to rights, democracy, the Enlightenment legacy and so on.[5] France, a country with a strong secular tradition and a commitment since 1789 to universal values as embodied in that country's strict separation of Church and State, strongly resisted any such narrow definition of European identity. As did Britain and Germany, both countries with multi-cultural or multi-ethnic traditions, and as such concerned not to offend the sensibilities of their own cultural, and especially Islamic minorities.[6] Turkey, the first Islamic country (though a secular state) with a realistic EU membership prospect, voiced its own anxieties on this matter, vigorously objecting to any exclusive reference to European identity that might complicate its accession. Foreign Minister Abdullah Gul, for instance, proposed instead the inclusion in the Preamble to 'other religions', including Islam.

Argument here was both intense and prolonged. Several countries, including Poland, Spain, Italy, Ireland, Slovakia, the Czech Republic, Portugal and Malta, with albeit lukewarm support from Germany and Hungary, all demanded at least a reference in the proposed Preamble to Europe's Christian roots. The Italian presidency under Berlusconi's leadership was supportive, even inserting a reference to Christian heritage into its own working version of the draft treaty for the IGC. Again, secularist voices were raised in protest. Representatives from both government and civil society in France, Belgium, Denmark, Sweden, Finland and Estonia, supported by the Liberal, centre-left and Green parties in those countries, objected to such theocratic connotations. And they found a powerful ally in Giscard, determined as he was to avoid exclusive cultural referents, preferring that Europe's new constitutional order be based on secular and multi-cultural values. The issue became entangled in the bargaining that usually occurs in IGCs, linked in this instance to the deal-making (or deal-breaking) issue of voting weights, not least because Poland and Spain were leading protagonists on both issues. Some government representatives thought these two countries might be persuaded to drop their demand for an explicit reference to the Christian God in return for some limited concessions on voting weights. In the end, however, neither country found sufficient support, nor did it have the political clout to successfully trade one headline issue against another.

In the event, there was no substantial support in the Convention, let alone amongst those member states whose views mattered most, for explicitly linking 'European values' with Christianity. If the idea here was to use this cultural referent as an excuse to exclude Turkey from the Union, that cause was already undermined by the fact that 15 million Muslims are already legally resident there, some of them EU citizens. Accordingly, any reference to God was omitted from an altogether more general statement about a common European heritage. The IGC settled for a broader (critics said 'weaker') and altogether less contentious reference to Europe's cultural legacies from antiquity to the Enlightenment. The Constitutional Treaty avoided making any explicit reference to cultural or ethnic exclusivity, settling instead for those values Europeans supposedly have in common in an otherwise culturally heterogeneous continent. In fact, the Preamble and the general Title referring to 'Definitions and Objectives of the Union' avoids making unduly narrow claims for common values, and settled for the altogether broader observation that the EU and its peoples draw 'inspiration from the cultural, religious and humanist inheritance of Europe from which have developed the universal values of the inalienable and indivisible rights of the human person, freedom, democracy, equality, the rule of law'.[7]

The choice of words here is quite deliberate, and reflects a less than clear-cut view about European identity. The decision, for instance, to excise from the Treaty the often-quoted and by now almost iconic phrase 'ever-closer union' – though it remains in the Charter of Fundamental Rights – and to replace it by the phrase 'the peoples of Europe … united ever more closely', is testament to the lack of conviction about the idea of uniform 'Europeanness' as the basis for a common political project. Even the motto originally adopted from Thucydides for the Constitution's header, about the virtues of democracy as a fundamentally shared political value, and the controversial claim that Europe is 'a continent that brought forth civilization' that featured in an early draft of the Preamble were dropped from the final version of the Constitutional Treaty.[8] This draft settled instead for merely generalised references to values that now have universal appeal. There is, for instance, explicit mention of minorities (Article 1-2), and reference to the equality of the member states (Article 1-5.1).[9] This is a catalogue of values that few contemporary Europeans, or for that matter enlightened people anywhere, would gainsay, though the Vatican continued to press the matter of making Christian values the focal point of European culture rather than the Enlightenment values celebrated by more secularist voices.[10] These values are included though hardly elaborated in a brief statement on the Union's objectives (Article 1-3.4) and the values the EU seeks to promote in its relations with the rest of the international community as the most reliable base for a civilised and peaceful world order.

In the constitutional lexicon words are symbols as much as literal descriptors, and potent symbols, too, that connote both inclusion and exclusion, who belongs to the body politic and who does not. This symbolism is as much in evidence in the Constitutional Treaty as in any national constitution. Title I (Article 1-I.2), for instance, notes that 'the Union shall be open to all European states which represent its values and are committed to promoting them together'. This, too, is coded as much as it is formal language, and represents a compromise on an issue that has divided the Union from the moment Turkey first applied for membership in 1983. After Turkey achieved full candidate status at the Helsinki European Council in

1999 and the prospect of full membership increased, objections were raised in some quarters that its human rights record (itself code for cultural and implicitly ethical difficulties) was enough to deny it accession. Of course, the issue was not debated in explicitly racial terms, but for some objectors it amounted to just that. To date, Turkey has not been permitted to join the Union, nor is its eventual accession a foregone conclusion.

These objections make much of cultural differences, and especially of whether a Muslim state with a below-par human rights record can be expected to meet the democratic norms and other civic standards that are the *sine qua non* of EU membership. This has raised the counter-argument of 'convenient' double standards, some commentators pointing to the equally dismal record on civil and human rights for sexual and ethnic minorities in the Eastern and Central European accession states that have already been allowed to join the Union.[11] That formal objections to Turkish accession make much more of 'cultural incongruence' than they do of Islamophobia, and point to the fact that most of that country's landmass is geographically situated in Asia rather than the European peninsula, may seem to be merely disingenuous. Yet the case against Turkish accession carries some weight even amongst otherwise progressive voices, not least the former Commission president, Romano Prodi, though he insisted that his objections were made on cultural rather than on racial grounds. This may seem a spurious distinction to Turkish minds, but this case does show that what it is to be 'European' is far from being settled, and may never be so. And it shows, too, why the Convention settled in the end for an inclusive definition of Europe, choosing to embrace the convenient notion of 'unity in diversity'. As one *conventionnel* tactfully put it: 'We must be careful not to nurture an insidious Euro-nationalism that relies smugly on European virtues and excluded the rest of the world. A Europe united in diversity is open and pluralist, and cannot erect a wall shutting out "the other side"'.[12]

There was greater recognition, too, in this debate about regional and territorial identities. The Convention came up with a formula that sought to reconcile primordial identity with 'Europeanness', 'convinced that while remaining proud of their own national identities and history, the peoples of Europe are determined to transcend their former differences and, united more closely, to forge a common destiny'.[13] In the end, this squared the circle of cultural diversity on the one hand and commonality of purpose on the other, and accordingly Article 1-3 lists values that few contemporary Europeans would dispute as common aspirations, namely: freedom, democracy, human rights, the rule of law, freedom of movement for people, goods, services and capital and commitment to the promotion of peace and the well-being of its peoples, a wish-list from full employment to gender equality. The IGC's amended version of Article 1-2 added to the list the following common values: respect for human dignity, social peace, tolerance, justice and solidarity. What the debate about values makes clear is that agreeing mutual norms was seemingly a more challenging business than refashioning common institutions and decisional procedures.

History divides as much as it unites Europe, with long centuries of bloody conflict, wars of conquest, internecine feuding, religious schism and revolution, and more recently murderous ethnic strife rooted in persistent primordial rivalries. In some cases this conflict has even been perpetrated on the basis of the utterly perverse claim of furthering European integration. These are baleful legacies, yet they are part of Europe's story. The absence of a common cultural cement and the difficulties of agreeing on incontrovertible 'European' values persuaded the Convention to give the Union some icons or symbols that might, over time, become a cause of affective attachment for citizens, as they are in its nation states. The Constitution accordingly identified some shared 'symbols of the Union' (Article 1-8), a European flag and anthem, passport and driving licence and the like. These are, after a fashion, emblems of common identity, though they hardly resonate emotionally with most EU citizens. To replicate Europe's experience of historic nation-building by utilising emotionally potent symbols of affiliation is in one sense an attempt to foster the sense of belonging, allegiance and political membership that similar icons represent in established nation-states, but thus far hardly an effective one.

Whether this unique and mostly successful historical process can be repeated at the European level is questionable. The concerns expressed by some governments about anything that might indicate putative EU statehood meant that references to these symbols – though not the symbols *per se* – are excised from the Lisbon Treaty, a decision that seems to indicate that for the politicians, notions of civic patriotism are merely a forlorn aspiration for idealists. Of course, political identity is always constructed, and all polities are, in Benedict Anderson's choice phrase, 'imagined communities', though whether the EU can ever aspire to be a community of sentiment in quite this sense is debatable.

Social scientists must of course remain reflexive and open-minded about the prospects for political change, neither ruling anything in nor out until they have examined the evidence. It may well be that in time the EU will exhibit potential for a common identity that corresponds with its increasing commonality of purpose as it faces up to global challenges, such that a sense of political identity will take root in the popular imagination. Even if it does, the process will be inordinately complicated, and will certainly require something altogether more substantial than the token iconography of flags and anthems. The evidence so far of nation-building in Europe indicates that icons are just that, mere ideography, and that the emotional resonance they instil in individuals reflects rather more than it creates that deeper sense of socio-cultural identity required for an ingrained and affective sense of common purpose, the ontological belonging and social solidarity that sustain political identity over time. Myths are a potent source of social solidarity but they cannot be made convincing, nor can they be sustained merely by declamation or for that matter by political elites trying to manipulate popular sentiments. A legally binding constitutional charter with a statement of common values was certainly one historic landmark in building political communities at the national level, but the task is altogether more challenging at the transnational level. Icons are a necessary but hardly a sufficient condition for this process of community-building and for ensuring solidarity, and there is, as Bogdandy has pointed out, every difference between 'a political design for collective identity [and] a socially embedded institution which actually fosters identity'.[14]

More important by far than 'mere' symbols for ensuring political solidarity is purposive engagement between political leaders and citizens, and not merely as top-down and didactic leadership, even less as diktat, that has characterised so much EU governance thus far, but as a democratic conversation about the very purposes of such governance.[15] This is precisely what is missing from Europe's contemporary politics, and no less so from its constitutional project. Of course, this is much easier to prescribe than it is to realise, and especially so in such an inchoate polity lacking what passes for meaningful democratic life of the kind that exists in its separate national communities. So far this democratic conversation has not been remotely attempted at the European level. There is instead a 'deafening silence' about how to connect governors and people beyond the nation-state.

The task here will not be an easy one to accomplish. Politics is everywhere discounted by publics as venal, citizens reacting 'quite sceptically to political rhetoric' almost as a first instinct.[16] So far the political class has avoided engaging directly with citizens on the future of the European polity, about common problems and how public policy might address them, and no less about how governance should be conducted at this level and to what ends. Yet this is precisely what a meaningful post-national constitutional endeavour should be about.[17] These matters hardly figured in the Convention, and even less so at the subsequent IGC. The political class confined their discussion about individual membership of the Union to two issues, both of them concerned with what might broadly be called 'a people's Europe', though 'the people' here are seen as mainly passive recipients of notional and quite limited rights. These issues were as follows: the constitutional status of the Charter of Fundamental Human Rights of the European Union, adopted at the Nice Council in December 2000; and the novel and no less controversial status of EU citizenship. These are crucial matters for addressing democracy and identity deficits in any polity, and issues, too, with potential for giving citizens a sense of empowerment. How the Convention dealt with them was therefore an indication of how seriously it took the issue of a 'people's' Europe.

## The Charter of Fundamental Rights

The history of fundamental rights in the EC/EU confirms its ambiguous status, both as a polity and as a cultural and social space. The legal protection of fundamental rights has been cumulate, with the Court leading the way, establishing an impressive corpus of case law, and with the Parliament and the Commission as its allies in the endeavour to make the Union a rights-based community rather than merely a common market. The rights convention established by the Tampere European Council in 1999 was mandated to address rights as an appropriate matter for the treaties, rather than one reserved exclusively to the Court. The Charter of Fundamental Human Rights that was its outcome went further even than the ECHR in the matter of defining human rights and civil liberties. Consisting of some 54 articles grouped under six titles: Dignity, Freedoms, Equality, Solidarity, Citizens' Rights and Justice, it was unveiled at the informal European Council in Biarritz (October 2000) and subsequently approved by the Nice Council the following

December. However, the Charter had only declaratory status and was not legally binding. Moreover, the question of the Charter's legal status and whether to incorporate it wholesale into the Constitutional Treaty, or instead to 'park' it as a separate document, a protocol annexed to the Constitution and as such merely a benchmark for non-binding rights, proved so controversial that the Nice Council postponed the decision.

The Convention could hardly avoid the issue, not least because constitutional lawyers lent their weight to the view that it was advisable to incorporate a legally binding bill of rights into democratic constitutions as the surest means for informing citizens about their rights entitlement.[18] The Constitutional Treaty is unexceptional in this, and it duly acknowledged the EU as a rights-based polity committed to the formal protection of human rights (Article 1-9) and likewise affirming (Article 1-2) respect for human rights as a core value of the Union. Indeed, Article 1-2 of the Constitutional Treaty recognises fundamental rights as 'general principles' of EU law. After due deliberation, the Convention decided that the best means for citizens to access these rights would be to incorporate the Charter as Part II of the Constitutional Treaty, and furthermore to enable the EU to accede to the European Convention on Human Rights.

The Charter was a 'done deal' even before the Convention met. The working group on the Charter reviewed its constitutional status, though it was reluctant to revisit substantive content.[19] Even so, the Convention could not easily reach agreement about incorporating the Charter into the Treaty, or indeed how to do so, whether 'simply by reference, or perhaps as an annexed protocol, or even by including the full text within Part I'.[20] There was resistance to embedding human rights protection in the Constitution from those concerned about the steady (and for some the insidious) accumulation of powers at the EU level through the seemingly innocuous medium of European law, not least in critical aspects of public policy and in the equally controversial area of civil and social rights. Support for making the Charter legally binding notwithstanding, representatives of some governments (most notably, the United Kingdom, Denmark and Ireland) were far from convinced that this was the best way forward. The British government was particularly opposed to incorporating the Charter into the treaties, at least without firm guarantees of national legal discretion in some key areas covered by the Charter, most especially economic and social rights.[21] This resistance eventually paid off, the final draft treaty text making a clear distinction between rights *per se* and mere 'principles', or guidelines for judicial action. As one expert saw it, the distinction between rights and principles was more than merely notional, and 'presumably … meant to address concerns that purely aspirational values (such as social assistance or legal aid) might be taken up by the Court of Justice and transformed into directly effective rights enforceable as such against the Member States'.[22]

Prime Minister Blair stated his position in a speech in Cardiff in November 2002, and though he endorsed the principle of fundamental rights, he refused to 'support a form of treaty incorporation that would enlarge EU competence over national legislation [for] there cannot be new legal rights given by such means'.[23] Blair was quite aware of the concerns of Britain's business community that the Charter would

open up an entirely new body of justiciable social and labour rights with the prospect, as they saw it, of weakening British competitiveness, persuading the government to demand even firmer guarantees of national discretion. The working group
had to acknowledge these objections, but though it recommended amendments
that clarified the Charter's original design it did not significantly alter its fabric.
Yet the compromise devised by the working group and included as new Article
2-112.5 bears the imprint of British lobbying. Nor did the United Kingdom leave
matters there, securing additional amendments to the draft treaty in the IGC, with
the Charter's legal effects further constrained by some significant caveats. There
is evidence of concessions at Part II, Title VII, General Provisions Governing the
Interpretation and Application of the Charter, Article 2-112.7, where the scope
and interpretation of rights and principles includes a brief but nevertheless telling
paragraph to the effect that: 'The explanations drawn up as a way of providing
guidance in the interpretation of the Charter of Fundamental Rights shall be given
due regard by the courts of the Union and of the Member States'.

The amended preamble to Part II further confirms that future interpretations of
the Charter by the European and the national courts must take account of these
updated explanations circulated widely amongst the EU's legal community.[24] The
praesidium's revisions implied that these 'explanations' would not have the status
of law, and instead are merely intended to facilitate a more precise interpretation
of the Charter.[25] The relevant article states that principles 'may be implemented
by legislative acts', in effect watering down the earlier and firmer commitment
to enlarge upon 'rights'. Political objections are a constraint on the exercise of
fundamental rights, significantly diluting what was intended in the earlier draft
text, the direct consequence of energetic lobbying by governments during the
IGC, concerned lest the Court should assume licence to further encroach on the
national legal domain. These changes confirm – or at least this is how the British
and some other governments preferred to see it – that the European Court, or for
that matter any other supranational actor, may not infer that the Charter creates
wholly new rights, nor even that it enhances extant rights over and above what is
permitted by domestic law and national constitutional procedures.

The decision to incorporate the Charter as a free-standing Part II of the Constitutional Treaty did nevertheless have important consequences. For one thing, it
made the Charter altogether more visible, and the fact that it would be included in
the Treaty proper was bound to enhance its legal and political standing. At the same
time, the decision to incorporate it merely replicated what was already covered
elsewhere, both in the Treaty and in other legal sources. There are references to
rights scattered throughout the Treaty, for instance in the provisions on Union
citizenship, rights relating to the prevention of discrimination, environmental and
consumer protection, rights on free movement and so on. So, though no new rights
are created by the Charter, such 'pointless duplication' hardly makes for clarity
or simplification, with Part II looking as some critics see it 'rather inelegantly
like a treaty within a treaty'.[26] Nor was the outcome here a definitive nucleus of
incontrovertible rights, in effect a bill of rights as in any established constitutional
order. For these rights were confined to the European institutions, obliging the

member states only to abide by agreed norms in those matters pertaining to the application of EU legislation.[27]

Things might have been different had politics not intruded. The Charter does have potential to be a charter for European citizenship, a catalogue of rights available to individual members of the Union, and applicable at both the national and EU levels. But raw politics played its part, ensuring that this was not what the Convention was about. As we shall see, the Convention added little that was positive to existing citizenship rights, other than some limited window-dressing. Rights – and even more, duties – pertaining to citizenship, with the capacity to 'promote the construction of a European political identity and mobilise citizens around it', were barely considered.[28] And one can see why, for allocating and more crucially policing rights is traditionally the preserve of nation-states, inextricably linked to citizenship defined as primary membership of a historically defined national polity. Many of the more controversial economic and social rights listed in the Charter were in reality circumscribed as to their application, and deemed to apply only in accordance with extant national and European law and practice. Indeed, the Treaty expressly precludes the Charter from investing the Union with additional law-making powers. Moreover, the Union does not as such acquire any new judicial competence in the matter of rights. The protection of fundamental rights remains with the member states, as determined by their political/legal (constitutional) authorities. It was only on this limited basis that steadfast opponents of the Charter were prepared to permit its incorporation into the Constitutional Treaty. On any other terms, the Charter might have become a judicial Trojan horse for the European Court intent on expanding its own authority in matters currently the preserve of national courts and governments. The telling phrase here is that applying rights conferred in the Charter must be wholly 'in accordance with Union law and national laws and practices'.[29] And even this limited outcome might yet prove to be problematical, for the boundary between national and European law is always difficult to demarcate to the mutual satisfaction of authorities on either side of that divide.

Some expert opinion sees ambiguity as the inevitable outcome of this uncertain compromise, even in the revised Article 2 that gave licence to judicial activism, permitting the Justices to interpret the general principles that frame the rights catalogue. Certainly, the distinction here between rights and general principles that inform particular rights is less clear than it might be, and may yet prove to be a bone of contention between the Court and some governments now that the Charter has received formal recognition in the Lisbon Treaty. There was no clear definition (Part II, Article 112-7) about which articles of the Charter would 'merely' be principles and which rights *per se*, a sure recipe for future disputation. Governments and many national judicial authorities chose to interpret this as a reliable fire-wall, a guarantee of the discretion of the domestic legal and constitutional order, convinced that there was nothing in Part II of the Constitutional Treaty to 'alter the substance of fundamental rights protection in the Union', but instead merely making 'that protection clearer for European citizens'. Matters are rarely that straightforward where the Court is concerned, and some voices, not least those determined to consolidate a EU rights culture, would be tempted to interpret these arrangements as an opportunity for judicial activism. And as an invitation no less to give 'a strong legal foundation for human rights [that] would make it easier for courts throughout Europe to build a singular framework of human rights law as part of EU and national law'.[30]

If it was the intention of those governments who resisted a clearer definition of EU rights to keep the Court at bay, this compromise may well have quite the opposite effect. As one commentator sees the situation, 'by injecting lots of uncertainty into the operation of the Charter', the Union's would-be founding fathers 'have hurt their own cause [for] they have handed some of the initiative for defining the balance of power between member states and the EU institutions over to the vagaries of litigation in the European Court of Justice'.[31] Whether the decision of the Brussels European Council (June 2007) to deconstitutionalise the Charter, to park it outside the substantive treaty base, will deter the Court from regarding it as a benchmark for future rulings with important constitutional implications remains to be seen, but those Justices who have offered their opinions on this matter show every inclination to interpret even this qualified status as a green light for judicial activism.

Uncertainty over the status of rights may not then be a deterrent to judicial activism, and this recent decision to exclude the Charter from the Treaty proper may actually incite action, prompting the Court to act decisively so as to clarify, and maybe even to expand human rights. Some legal experts see this as a likely outcome, and 'expect the Court to avoid any such detrimental impact upon the legal significance of the basic values contained in the Charter, and [to] insist that those values form part of the policy framework within which the Union institutions exercise every legislative and administrative discretion conferred upon them by the Constitution'.[32] Significant, too, for the Court's mission to expand rights at the European level is the provision (Article 2-112.3) which on the one hand seems to confine the meaning and scope of 'guaranteed rights' to 'those laid down by the Convention', but then notes that 'this provision shall not prevent Union law providing more extensive protection'.

This provision was a direct response to the concerns of some legal commentators that the Charter 'could otherwise have a rigidifying effect on the types of freedom recognised and protected in a socially and politically dynamic Europe'.[33] These arrangements have by no means settled once and for all the constitutional status of EU fundamental rights. Whether the supposedly firm demarcation between rights *per se* and merely indicative principles will hold over time is questionable. As one commentator sees it, human rights are, after all, 'universal by nature', and 'defining fundamental rights is the first step towards creating a common supranational value basis'.[34] Some experts in European jurisprudence doubt that the Court, or for that matter other social agencies with a vested interest in widening the EU's rights base, will resist testing such imprecise boundaries, challenging in the process the received political wisdom about the supposedly limited application of fundamental rights.

The Constitutional Treaty did at least resolve one matter of long-standing concern to legal experts, by specifying that the EU will accede to the European Convention on Human Rights, currently disallowed by the ECJ (Article 2-112.2).[35]

Article 1-9.3 of the Constitutional Treaty did ensure that Charter rights would enjoy the same status as in the ECHR, and permitted EU-based rights to give a level of protection above the ECHR's minimum standard.[36] This was widely regarded as a positive move, not least because it removed an inconsistency in the judicial interpretation of rights as between the legal orders of Luxembourg and Strasbourg. This would rectify the patent legal anomaly of the current arrangements, namely the lack of any means of legal redress when the EU falls short of the rights standards guaranteed by the ECHR. In future, the European Court of Human Rights would be permitted to issue rulings on EU decisions. But this reform, too, has potential for confusion. Some legal experts foresaw difficulties in ensuring a perfect 'fit' between the Charter and the ECHR regimes. Accession to the ECHR binds signatories to its obligations under public international law, but this might conceivably clash with the Charter's rights code. In this event, the challenge that faced the Court of Justice to reconcile two separate but generically related rights regimes would require exceptional judicial ingenuity, though the Luxembourg Court over the duration has shown remarkable aptitude for imaginative judicial action.

With the Constitutional Treaty abandoned, at least in its original format, the Charter seemed set to remain outside the treaty base. The Lisbon Treaty did not reinstate it, adding it as a Protocol to the Treaty, but it is in effect binding on member states, except for those countries (Poland and the United Kingdom) who expressly secured opt-outs at the Brussels Council in June 2007. What are the prospects for the Charter expanding on a rights-based citizenship? And on that same basis, what are the prospects for building on citizenship rights so as to deepen the ontological sense of personal affiliation with the Union, a sense of individual citizens belonging to a European *Rechtsstaat*? In view of growing public vexation with what many citizens see as a project wholly out of touch with popular concerns, a rights-based approach might well contribute to reducing the Union's legitimacy deficit. On the other hand this seems to be unduly optimistic, for the Constitutional Treaty required national courts merely to 'give due regard' to a series of explanations intended to provide 'guidance' when interpreting the Charter. It is difficult nevertheless to imagine that incorporation into the treaty base will not increase the Court's ambition to extend the reach European law in these matters, notwithstanding the British and Polish opt-outs. However, though this self-exclusion hardly proves the Charter is toothless or lacks legal value, it is not quite the firm basis for any effective assault on the legal sovereignty of territorial authorities that a bill of rights would be in a federal polity.

This interpretation will no doubt be challenged as unduly complacent by radical and conservative legal opinion alike. The former remain confident that the Charter, despite its lack of formal constitutional status, will be a touchstone for judicial activism, reassured in this view by a legacy of positive, even creative interpretations by the Court over the duration. As such, those who take this view place considerable faith in the Justices to stretch existing rights provisions, and in ways that will deepen the sense of common purpose of a European *Rechtsstaat* no less. For much the same reasons but from entirely opposite motives, Eurosceptical opinion is chary about any such prospect, wary of reform that might give rise to yet more judicial stealth, concerned lest the Court should be inclined to resort to 'the parts of the explanations [in the Charter] it finds convenient on the grounds that they provide "guidance", while ignoring those sections that purport to limit its power on the grounds that "they do not have the force of law"'.[37] Commentators on both sides of this debate are convinced 'that rights-based claims against the legality of Union and member state action will increase, and that this will lead to the further juridification of political life within the Union [and] this is especially so given the broad list of rights protected by the Charter'.[38]

There is foreboding amongst those who subscribe to the latter opinion about potential 'loopholes', and not least the fact that 'nowhere does it say that the Charter does not have legal status, which would be the only watertight way of preventing judicial meddling by the European courts'.[39] Embedding the Charter within the treaty base might possibly mean that 'the courts will feel free to become more aggressive' in citing it as the basis for rulings. But even though the Charter does not have uniform legal status, there is scope for the Court to act in ways that some governments are bound to resent. Indeed, some members of the Court have already endorsed this positive reading of the Charter, not least Vassilios Skouris, the Court's president, who in an interview published at the time the Constitutional Treaty was formally agreed by the member states claimed that the Charter 'will bring new areas and new subjects under the court's jurisiction'.[40] Another leading Justice, Fidelma Macken of Ireland, has likewise maintained that it would be 'foolish' to assert that the Charter will not alter the balance between national and EU law.

Of course, EU jurisprudence is not bound to be a negative, let alone a pernicious force. Even where conflicting interpretations do arise between the European and the national legal/political orders – an unavoidable consequence of an emergent but inchoate European constitutional order where testing competency boundaries is normal procedure – this may well be creative tension rather than merely confrontational, a stand-off between two intrinsically irreconcilable normative orders. To this extent, the current situation does suggest 'opportunities for the development of a richer, more integrative common European tradition that embraces constitutional diversity'. Experience, as much as merely wishful thinking, would tend to support this constructive interpretation, with national courts operating much less as defenders of 'an idiosyncratic national tradition against the EU', but instead generally seeking to make accommodations and adjustments to changing circumstances, 'to give meaning to the principles of their national Constitutions in light of a common European constitutional practice', and to 'do so in co-operation with EU institutions'.[41]

In these fast-moving times the Charter, applied as it surely will be as a benchmark for European law-making (and regardless of its precise constitutional status), is bound to become an indispensable referent in the perennial contest over where legal authority ultimately should reside for determining citizens' rights.[42] The point is well made by Kuman and Comella that rights are now both 'more visible', and 'they will be invoked more often, probably, and the ECJ cannot be indifferent to their gravitational pull'.[43] Indeed the Charter had already begun to perform this bench-marking function, even when it had only the status of a non-binding protocol. The Charter was cited, for instance, by the national constitutional court of Austria as early as September 2000, and subsequently by the Spanish court. One academic source estimates that even as early as May 2002 the Charter had been cited by both the advocates-general in 19 cases, and in a further 5 cases by the European Court of First Instance. In the meantime, it has become an authoritative benchmark for both national judiciaries and the ECJ, though so far only in 'relatively non-controversial ways'.[44]

Although important, benchmarking is hardly the same thing as the Charter operating as a definitive bill of rights, an authoritative legal and constitutional code for challenging (one might even say in some circumstances, for breaching) the member states' discretion in the most critical and politically sensitive matters of governance and public policy. Disagreements about the authoritative source of legal rulings on the interpretation of rights – in effect who may exercise judicial review – will continue between the European Court of Justice and national constitutional courts. Furthermore, though the distinction is imprecise as between legally enforceable rights and merely benchmarking general principles as indicative guidelines for legislative and executive actions, it remains nevertheless a critical boundary demarcating national sovereignty. As such, it will not be breached lightly, nor will it go unchallenged by national authorities if, as they see it, the European Court of Justice oversteps the mark here, overrunning a boundary clearly marked out in previous jurisprudence. The scope for creative jurisprudence, though tempting no doubt to the Justices in Luxembourg, will continue to be constrained by the exigencies of politics. The Justices' ambitions to expand the Court's discretion in the matter of rights will continue to be defined, and no less constrained, by the ambiguities of Europe's pluralistic constitutional order.

## Citizenship: the contemporary challenge

Constitutions in democratic polities are, in theory at least, contracts made between citizens and the polity, usually a state. In practice, however, the constitutional order is much more the outcome of complex bargains, a process managed for the most part by social and political elites. Citizenship, in its legal or contractual sense – in essence the rules pertaining to political and civic membership of the polity – is nevertheless a significant aspect of contemporary liberal democratic constitutions, and 'citizenship' does figure in the constitutional fabric of even some authoritarian regimes, though hardly on the same basis as in liberal democracies. Citizenship matters precisely because it defines who belongs in a polity, and elucidates the rules of membership. In the real world of politics, membership in this sense is usually the outcome of the trade-off between rulers and ruled, essential for legitimating the exercise of power, for ensuring the legitimacy of public power by guaranteeing participation and deepening the citizens' identification with the polity's underlying goals, norms and values, in essence its historic 'mission'.

Membership of a democratic polity confers rights and imposes duties on citizens, though there is more to this than merely listing formal criteria for political participation, or defining the rules of political engagement in terms of a code of legally enshrined rights and duties. Citizenship has an affective as well as a legal dimension, an ontological sense of belonging that sustains an individual's affiliation to the polity as a primary political community. In this sociological sense citizenship both affirms and reaffirms affective belonging, and as such it is an expression – and a significant one in democratic polities – of meaningful political identity. The affective dimension of citizenship as identity and belonging is traditionally associated in Europe, and in recent times elsewhere in the world, too, with the post-Westphalian nation-state. Whether citizenship in these terms can be extended to encompass membership of and affective belonging to other forms of post-national polities is a matter widely debated by contemporary political science. Though it was not always so.

Affective connection between the people and the polity was hardly essential for consolidating the European Community during its formative years, when it was more an international organisation than it was a polity, a regional regime for market-making and thence for regulating a common market. And though from the outset this regime acquired some of the institutional paraphernalia of governance, its tasks were strictly delimited. It remained an endeavour remote from the concerns, and no less from the affections of 'ordinary' people. As La Palombella has described this situation: 'Europe does not conceive of the single individual as the *cognitive premise* that enables the Union to be comprehended. And the "spirit of the Union is not that of individuals" as it is in the classical statist constitutional tradition, it does not require that their vision of themselves as "Europeans" should assume priority as compared to many other representatives of themselves [and] it is partly for this reason that Europe lacks the driving force a movement towards community republicanism.'[45] As such, the citizen was remote, indeed almost incidental to the European project from the outset. This had important, and it must be said mostly negative, implications for the prospects of turning a common market into a polity, and no less so for installing a legitimate European constitutional order. The Community derived its legitimacy during the foundational period indirectly, from and through the participation of national ministers in the then exclusive legislative body, the Council of Ministers. However, the very success of the EC/EU in widening the scope of its policies, extending its regulatory reach into domestic economic, social, legal, and even into the political life of the member states subsequently raised serious questions about this merely notional legitimacy.

Critics, by no means all of them confirmed federalists, have begun to question what is widely regarded as the nominal, and for some the threadbare legitimation of the Union's intrusion into aspects of socio-economic life once the exclusive preserve of the member states. This critique has grown apace during recent years, with the Union's gradual extension of its powers and competencies.[46] Concern about legitimacy deficits and democracy shortfalls are now reflected in the theoretic disquisition on European integration. Contemporary theorists apply to transnational politics those same normative standards that have shaped democratic discourse in relation to the theory of state-building in Europe over past centuries. These theoretic narratives focus not only on the institutions, on where power actually lies in the Union, but also on normative questions about who should exercise power and on what basis. It is a testament to the gathering pace of the Union's political development that scholars now debate as a matter of course the prospects for realising transnational democracy, and on that basis for initiating a post-national citizenship, for instilling a sense of cosmopolitan identity alongside pre-existent primordial (national and sub-national) identities. And by these same means, for evaluating the potential for meaningful participation by citizens as much as by elites in politics and even in governance above the nation-state.

The debate about EU citizenship is central to this inquiry into the prospects for democracy beyond the nation-state. An emerging discourse on post-national identity and citizenship challenges conventional thinking about the cultural roots of political affiliation. Moreover, it raises some intriguing questions: whether, for instance, political, or for that matter cultural identity can be realised in a non-statal polity. And not least, the agency question, how such new expressions of polit-ical identity might be transmitted, and the consequences of this for politics and governance. Citizenship defined in terms of identity rather than merely as rights is familiar to students of historic nation-states, especially those where successful nation-building has embedded a sense of political community, shared affinities that in turn facilitate a meaningful conversation between citizens as stakeholders and their governors. Moreover, a conversation conducted in a vernacular language and through the medium of established institutions, and all of this supposedly underpinned by a shared history and common values.

This is hardly the experience of community-building in the EU polity, where shared identity is largely absent. European citizenship thus far is a modest and essentially a rights-based endeavour. But conferring rights is only part of the process of 'making' citizens, of imbuing in them a sense of personal membership of a political community. In fact, the legal and cultural dimensions of citizenship are complementary. The one should inform and reinforce the other, or at least it should in any polity that imposes redistributive policy outcomes on its citizens. The notion of identity and the sense of common purpose it brings to the body politic is an essential precondition for stable and legitimate governance, in the EU as in any other polity that lays claim to democratic values. It is a functional as much as a normative requirement for legitimating the intrusive impact of EU policies on citizens. Yet this crucial dimension is missing from the EU polity, and the consequences of this merely deepen the Union's legitimacy deficit. As Maduro sees it, there is a need to develop 'criteria of distributive justice capable of justifying before [the public] the differentiated impact of certain EU policies [for] citizenship of a State which agreed to a certain policy may no longer be sufficient to justify before a citizen the differentiated impact of a certain EU policy'.[47] In essence then, citizenship and legitimacy are inextricably connected, or at least they ought to be in so far as EU governance has direct, and more than a merely incidental impact on its citizens.

The important question for determining whether the Union is a post-national polity rather than merely a sophisticated international regulatory regime is whether 'directly redistributive policies and redistributive impacts in the Union' are 'simply a function of national borders and not of the individual status of European citizens?'[48] In so far as the answer to this question is the latter condition, a case has to be made for basing legitimacy directly on citizens rather than indirectly through the member states. This means citizenship conceived not merely as conferred and so far quite limited rights, but also in terms of individual identity, a sense of belonging, the only sustainable basis for a legitimate and implicitly contractual bond between those who, to use David Easton's much-quoted aphorism, make 'authoritative allocations of values', and those directly affected by these critical decisions.

Of course, this is easier to state as a formal requirement for a transnational polity than it is to put into practice, and at the very least it represents a formidable challenge for any multi-cultural polity where the very idea of commonality of purpose remains contested, a fact well attested elsewhere in the world by the history of failed federalist experiments in polyglot and multi-ethnic societies. How much more difficult then to realise citizenship as shared identity in the inchoate and transnational European polity. Yet this is precisely the challenge the Union's political leaders set themselves during the 1990s after they had initiated the concept of EU citizenship. A progress report on their success or otherwise in responding to this challenge makes for less than encouraging reading, as we shall see below.

## Benchmarking citizenship

It is useful at the outset of this discussion to put the citizenship issue into historical perspective, the better to grasp the scale of the task facing the Union. Most commentaries on citizenship use as their starting point T. H. Marshall's classic exegesis. Marshall took as the historical and cultural gauge for citizenship the experience of the modern European nation-state. The nation-state bestowed citizenship – primarily a legal status at the outset, conferring membership as individual rights and duties – only on full members of the polity community. As Marshall saw it, there 'are no universal principles that determine what those rights and duties shall be', though there is at least the basic assumption of core political rights 'protected by a common law'. This status confirms a sense of primary membership of a polity for all citizens, irrespective of social status. Moreover, it imposes obligations on citizens, and 'by creating a feeling of belonging, citizenship plays an important role in forming national identity. … citizenship, in other words, symbolises the existence of a state'.[49] These rights and duties help in turn to instil 'loyalty to a civilisation which is a common possession', sustaining the political legitimacy which is indispensable to good governance, and defined both in normative terms as morally robust, and empirically as the most effective way of ensuring political stability.[50]

While contemporary commentators acknowledge Marshall's considerable contribution to the scholarship on citizenship, they tend to be critical of his approach, not least his failure to reflect on the altogether more complex and variegated nature of political identity.[51] Marshall's narrative was unduly narrow in its focus, and today looks dated in so far as it fails to reflect the cultural flux of an interdependent, cosmopolitan and globalising world. Contemporary political theorists have responded by broadening the concept of citizenship, reformulating it to take account of current circumstances. Kymlicka, for example, utilises a sociological approach, describing citizenship 'not just [as] a certain status, defined by a set of rights and responsibilities [but[ also an identity, an expression of one's membership in a political community'.[52] By acknowledging the cultural context of political membership Kymlicka and those who share his cosmopolitan outlook allow for the possibility of detaching political membership – as a catalogue of conferred legal rights, but also as affective identity – from its traditional moorings in historical territorial (usually national) polities.

A new citizenship narrative, defined by cultural as much as by legal or political referents, has opened up the prospect of relocating political affiliation in transnational, or even in what some see as post-national polities, with political allegiance shared between several complementary polities. These ideas are novel and as such unfamiliar, even unacceptable to those used to thinking about polities in neo-Hegelian terms as activity confined to national communities. But these ideas have acquired intellectual salience and are no longer confined to the radical academy, contributing nowadays to a lively debate about identity and politics on a much broader front. They have featured, too, in the Union's recent constitutional discourse, and as such raised some interesting questions about the sociological fabric of contemporary European politics that challenge long-established ideas about the sociological and cultural roots of politics. Contemporary discourse on European citizenship, the idea that a sense of personal belonging and affiliation could conceivably exist beyond the nation-state is the first attempt since the high Middle Ages to breathe life into the idea of political community beyond the boundaries of the post-Westphalian nation-state.[53] The critical question here is whether such novel ideas about post-national identity and citizenship are realistic or merely fanciful. And the key to this question, as always is with radical prescriptions, is agency: how far and by what means the EU polity can instil a meaningful sense of affiliation in its citizens.

## EU citizenship: beginnings

The discourse on EU citizenship raises some interesting questions about relations between contemporary 'princes', the Union's political and administrative elites, and the public at large. In times past this was hardly an issue, certainly not a priority during the Community's foundational period. After the launch of the Coal and Steel Community in July 1952, European construction was driven primarily by technocratic actors and policy-orientated elites, built on narrow and often covert bargains made between privileged vested interests. The process was not remotely concerned with democratic approval, other than indirectly, and certainly not with securing public approval at the ballot box. The EC was not at that stage of its development a polity, and if its political development since then has transformed it into one, it is by no means a democratic polity as that concept applies to the liberal nation-state.

At the outset, political union, too, was a secondary concern, overshadowed by the drive for closer economic integration, establishing a viable market for which public support was no more than implied. If the idea of popular approval did occur to the 'princes' who ran the show, it was largely taken as read, a matter of what was euphemistically called 'permissive consensus' rather than something to be tested by the usual means for demonstrating public legitimacy. It was assumed, for instance, that decision-makers could be trusted to 'do the right thing' by the public, indeed that elites always 'know best' what is in the public interest. A patrician instinct revealed in the telling response by Pascal Lamy – later to be an EU commissioner but at the time *chef de cabinet* of the Commission president, Jacques Delors – to a journalist's question, when he observed that 'the people weren't ready for integration so you had to get on without telling them too much about what was happening'.[54]

This was more than a careless *faux pas*; it reflected the mindset in Brussels about European integration. The foundational narratives of integration theory, indeed the very procedures by which the European project was constructed simply took public approval for granted. As intergovernmentalists see it, integration was legitimised at best indirectly through the medium of national democratic politics, in much the same way as foreign policy is assumed to have public support, even if its conduct is highly specialised and altogether remote from everyday politics. According to this complacent narrative, ministers representing democratically elected governments, and as such accountable to their parliaments and publics alike, transact policy in the Council on behalf of their people, mandated as they do so to defend the national interest. Whereas the supranational and predominantly federalist narrative of European integration, though prescribing the virtues of democratic politics at the EU level and even anticipating the gradual shift in popular allegiance from the national to the supranational level, paid as little heed as their ideological opponents to securing public approval for the cumulate transference of powers from the domestic to the European level. They, too, settled for a benign elitism, again something akin to permissive consensus, with the citizens deemed to be willing to accept the judgements on complicated policy issues of supposedly 'better informed' Community-builders acting in the public's 'best interests'.

The Community's founders on both sides of this debate paid little heed to citizenship. The founding treaty did not specify common citizenship as such, though it did include some specific rights for individuals, for instance free movement, as well as proscribing discrimination on grounds of nationality. It also established access to the ECJ in these same matters, though even these modest rights were circumscribed, pertaining only to those economic and commercial matters that were at the heart of the integration project. Over time, ECJ jurisprudence expanded on these rights, as we saw in the discussion at Chapter 2, giving them a substantive significance beyond a narrow economic interpretation. After the landmark *Van Gend en Loos* judgement (1963), for instance, the Court attempted to empower and to more closely involve individuals in Community affairs. A significant consequence of this jurisprudence was the establishment of a rights-based approach to the concept of a European polity, with the Court as its principal agent.

The impact of cumulate jurisprudence on the development of individual rights was part of the Community's agenda from the early 1970s, and the Single Market programme launched in 1985 gave greater prominence to the social consequences of economic integration, leading in turn to the Delors Commission's commitment to building a 'people's Europe'. The intention here was to redress, or at least to ameliorate the impact of powerful market forces on consumers and producers who might otherwise feel detached from, possibly even hostile towards the project, by incorporating a compensatory social policy dimension. For the most part this strategy was about making the public more receptive to free-market principles, though once launched it did acquire its own momentum. This, too, gave greater substance to the debate on citizenship. But precisely what kind of citizenship did the EU's political class have in mind?

The idea of a transnational citizenship has long appealed to idealists, and especially to federalists, and it was debated in the European Parliament long before it found its way onto the Commission's, let alone the Council's agenda. Yet even for the European Parliament, the idea of EU citizenship was confined to notional rights, as for instance in Article 3 of the kite-flying draft European Union Treaty of 1984, which had defined EU citizenship 'as something open only to citizens of member states and involving rights of participation and acceptance of the rule of law'.[55] By degrees, however, citizenship came to figure more in the deliberations on the social chapter, driven by the need as some saw it to balance deeper economic integration with a more uniform rights protection for the individual worker or consumer. This issue was raised, too, and for much the same reasons, by those campaigning for the EU to accede to the Council of Europe's Convention on Human Rights and Fundamental Freedoms (ECHR). This was progress of sorts, but still some considerable way short of endorsing a common European citizenship.

At this juncture, support for the idea was no more than spasmodic. Citizenship was defined as little more than a modest catalogue of rights, certainly not as political membership *per se*, nor as a vehicle for redressing the Union's democracy and legitimacy deficits. Nevertheless, it was a beginning, and it did indicate a subtle shift in official thinking about how to bring the European project closer to the citizen. The report of the Adonnino Committee (1985), for instance, acknowledged the gulf between the EC's institutional actors and the people at large, recommending positive measures to better relate to them, and some of these proposals subsequently found their way into the Maastricht Treaty's citizenship articles. As the optimism of the mid-1980s gave way to the growing challenges of the more turbulent nineties, the imperative to strengthen the Union's legitimacy, to bring it closer to the people, gathered pace. The political difficulties encountered in some member states over securing public approval for the Maastricht Treaty merely confirmed the extent of the problem, with widespread public disquiet about the European project.

Citizenship beyond the nation-state is not exactly unprecedented, as any student of ancient Rome will be aware, but it is problematic because it is difficult to ensure popular allegiance to a polity whose governance is remote and unfamiliar. Squabbling local fiefdoms and more immediate primordial allegiances challenged over time then replaced the overarching *Pax Romana*. As the empire became more polyglot and eventually divided into its eastern and western parts, and in the process became more dependent on the political goodwill of mutually antagonistic cultural and ethnic groups within its porous borders, the more difficult it was for the centre to hold. In the end, the empire fell apart, and since that historic implosion all manner of cultural diversity has given rise to a patchwork of territorial polities in Europe, with exclusive primordial or at best territorial allegiance as the primary focus of allegiance.

The pan-European idea did survive the fall of Rome, though realities on the ground have made it elusive, to say the least. The idea of European society is woolly at best, and tends to imply dense political and social networking between resourceful and usually privileged actors undertaking business, political, technocratic and other boundary-crossing activities, though hardly yet the affective social and cultural linkages that define and give meaning to civil society within the European nation-state. The nebulous concept of European society as La Palombella sees it 'presupposes a fundamentally "passive" citizen', one whose sense of belonging to a social entity beyond the national society is based much less on any sense of shared identity, and rather more on narrowly functional criteria. To this extent, the European citizen is little more than 'the "beneficiary" of "policies"'. For a European society to exist even in this attenuated sense requires something more than 'a series of citizenship rights that are connected to economic activity and to freedom, rights of residence, labour rights'. European society as presently constituted hardly meets such exacting criteria, it barely signifies in terms of mutual belonging or solidarity, let alone as ontological identity, for it is 'a society of *individuals* who are not yet linked by any specifically European social bond [they] appear simply as the *marketburger*, mere citizens of a supranational public space perceived as an extension of the private spheres'.[56]

The challenge for those who prescribe a deeper sense of personal attachment between the Union and the citizen as a firmer basis for political legitimacy is how to develop meaningful civic bonds beyond this functional concept of *marketburger*. How to develop European society as a public sphere based on individual membership, with individuals as members of a political community sharing a sense of common purpose, imbued with feelings of civic attachment, in effect citizenship defined as rights plus affective identity. Those commentators who make the case for European citizenship as affective identity make much of the importance of a civic or public space, a locus for collective endeavour, for facilitating a conversation, and on experience above all beyond the merely functional or material needs of the *marketburger*. This requires means for conducting a conversation between governors and the governed, and no less between representatives of the governed across borders, both about policy choices and fundamental goals. Moreover, a conversation that is two-way, with citizens having capacity both to influence and to constrain decision-makers. Citizenship in this sense is relational, it requires democratic participation and as such it actively rather than merely passively legitimises governance, translating the exercise of raw power into democratic authority.

The European public sphere, such as it is, hardly meets with these exacting standards for political community. The Maastricht Treaty (1992) made a tentative start, introducing the concept of European citizenship, but only as a belated and no less a limited response to the concern in some parts of the political class about low levels of public interest, declining public support for the critical policy responses to the challenges of globalisation. The concept of EU citizenship introduced at Maastricht conferred some notional supranational rights on EU citizens, though by no means all of the rights traditionally conferred by nation-states on their own citizens. Moreover, these limited rights were in essence retrospective, 'largely restricted to setting out what was already being done'. As such, they embodied 'a limited view of what civic rights actually are rather than creating new rights within a separate genus of citizenship'. Above all, these rights, reflected 'the fact that citizens of member states already have rights mainly directly but also through the ECHR'.[57]

In effect, EU citizenship was from the start essentially rights-based, expressly avoiding anything that hinted at diluting the primary bonds of attachment to the nation-state. And though it was intended to foster a notional sense of commonality of purpose amongst EU citizens, this was for the most part tokenism, falling some way short of fostering even the notional sense of identity with the European polity that Habermas has described as 'constitutional patriotism'.[58] More even than that, the citizenship criteria specified in the Maastricht Treaty are not only modest but also discriminatory, or rather they are exclusive to national citizens of the Union's member states. EU citizenship is derivative, not conferred by the Union *per se* but depends instead on prior citizenship of one of the Union's member states, a status that expressly excludes from membership of the Union legally resident nationals of third countries, however long they have resided in the Union and regardless of their positive contribution to the Union's civil society, its public goods and economic prosperity.

After Maastricht, the Union embarked on integrating monetary policy and some aspects of macro-economic policy, and since then it has aspired to play an even greater role in managing regional security, as well as pursuing enhanced co-operation in justice and home affairs policy. These are all policy domains once considered to be the exclusive preserve of the nation-state, and this fact has contributed to deepening the Union's legitimacy deficit. Legitimacy became a critical consideration during the 1990s, how to deepen popular attachment to a Community that, though by no means a state, was clearly something more than an international organisation or transnational regulatory regime.

The responses to this challenge have been varied. They include techniques already familiar in historical nation-building, though building a European state is not what the political class for the most part had in mind. The EC/EU has long utilised icons and symbols, including a European flag, a notional anthem and latterly a common currency, and documentation such as the European driving licence, passport and so on, as mean for reminding its peoples of shared endeavour. But icons are essentially passive, they do not in themselves ensure affective, let alone active linkage between citizens and the European polity. For one thing, they are altogether too vague, lacking emotional resonance for most people, and on their own they are incapable of reimagining the citizen's political identity away from exclusive allegiance to the primary (national or territorial) community. Politicians have gradually assimilated this fact, though mostly with reluctance. Yet by the early 1990s they were at least amenable to finding more reliable ways of fostering popular attachment to the European polity.

A benign interpretation of these modest developments might well attribute such shortcomings – largely unaddressed, it has to be said in subsequent treaty revisions – to politicians' preoccupations with their own narrow priorities, not least a pressing need as they saw it to confront the challenges of globalisation, rising threats from malevolent forces to domestic and not least to international security and closer to home the demands imposed by an unprecedented enlargement. Radical critics are less forgiving. As they see it, these challenges are hardly new, and what events do show is the continuing failure by those who manage Europe's affairs to confront the Union's legitimacy deficit, to find imaginative ways of connecting with citizens.

These same critics – whose voice has grown more insistent – see this failure to respond constructively to the Union's legitimacy crisis as not merely a lack of political imagination but also a cynical refusal to countenance bold measures that would weaken their own power base because undermining citizens' affiliation to the nation-state. Whether this is the case or not, it is clear from what occurred at the Convention and the following IGC that politicians resist doing anything that might promote awareness of multiple identities. It might be argued that this issue is less to do with the fallacy of post-national identity than with the reticence of politicians about anything that might encourage a fundamental reimagination of political identity. A lively debate has been joined on these very issues, and we shall return to it later. In the meantime, we must review the content and assess the significance, as well as the shortcomings of the citizenship articles introduced into the treaty base at Maastricht.

## EU citizenship and the Maastricht Treaty

The European Council in December 1990 endorsed the idea of EU citizenship, although not quite in the form proposed by those who had first raised the issue in the lead-up to the 1991 IGC. The debate was initiated at that time by the French president, François Mitterrand, supported by the Spanish government and with the Commission's approval. The case for including a formal statement of citizens' rights, freedoms and duties as a separate pillar of the European Union was made on pragmatic as much as on idealistic grounds. Citizenship as it was introduced in the Maastricht Treaty of European Union (Article 8) conferred limited rights in matters such as free movement, voting/standing in local/EU elections and consular representation in third countries. Maastricht did not create new rights as such, but rather codified extant rights scattered throughout the Community Treaty and the *acquis*. That citizenship rights were only available on the basis of prior nationality of a member state prompted one observer to comment that 'in practical terms [EU citizenship] is a weak and nebulous concept ... more political rhetoric than legal rights in the strict sense'.[59] Yet the very fact that the Treaty identifies individual citizenship rights (Article 2, TEU) did increase their visibility, a fact that would – or so it was claimed – encourage citizens to actively pursue them. Significant, too, was the fact the new citizenship articles did at least acknowledge the idea of Union citizenship as a status beyond the narrow economic rights attaching to citizens as 'mere' *marketburgers*, whether as consumers, business people concerned with influencing the regulatory regime or as members of the labour force in a common market.

The impact of this innovation was blunted, however, by the decision to include citizenship in the Community Treaty rather than in the new Treaty of European Union. The formal reason given for this decision was as follows: the EU lacks a legal identity and for that reason citizenship rights would not be legally enforceable in the European Court of Justice. In fact, politics as much as legal protocol was the main reason for the decision. To include citizenship rights in the Treaty of European Union, however limited the catalogue, would have enhanced the Union's political profile, and many governments opposed its inclusion in the TEU in case it sent the wrong message, preferring to confine the concept of political membership exclusively to the nation-state. Better then, as these states saw it, to include citizenship rights in the Community Treaty, an altogether more familiar and seemingly less threatening arrangement. For similar reasons, governments resisted the idea of citizenship directly conferred by the Union. The fact that EU citizenship depends on prior national citizenship gives it a derivative, and as many critics see it a secondary status, and reflects the view of most political leaders that only nation-states should have the legal right, and indeed the political authority, to confer citizenship in the usual sense of that term.

These limits were confirmed in the Declaration No. 2 attached by the Maastricht IGC to the Treaty on European Union. The Declaration, though not substantively part of the Treaty, confirms the principle of national sovereignty, to the effect that the member states should retain the exclusive right to determine all matters pertaining to political membership, whether questions of nationality or citizenship. It also made it clear that 'the question whether an individual possesses the nationality of a Member State shall be settled solely by reference to the national law of the Member State concerned'.[60] Moreover, EU citizenship rights are conferred automatically and cannot be rescinded by citizens, other than by revoking their national citizenship. There is no question of the individual opting either in or out of this conferred status as there is with national citizenship, though 'the rights themselves are such that there would be no obligation to actually make use of them [and] many people would not do so anyway'.[61]

The absence of any reference to the duties of citizenship in the Maastricht Treaty, those responsibilities and obligations that as much as rights define citizenship in democratic polities, confirms the idea of an implied contractual relationship between the polity that confers membership status on the recipient. This means in effect that European citizenship lacks the relational quality that is essential for demos. One can quite see why the member states are reluctant to specify citizenship duties. The history of nation-building in Europe shows that reciprocal obligations between citizens and the polity have potential for fostering affective attachment, and were a relational citizenship to develop beyond the nation-state it would weaken the bonds of political obligation and the emotive affiliation between citizens and their national polities. Predictably, Eurosceptical opinion has raised objections even to these limited citizenship provisions. Denmark, for example, sought reassurance that EU citizenship was merely an addition to and not a substitute for national citizenship, and that it should in no way be deemed to threaten replacement of prior allegiance to or membership of the national polity. It duly received this assurance at the Birmingham European Council (October 1992), an arrangement later confirmed by the Edinburgh European Council (December 1992), to the effect that 'every person holding the nationality of a Member State shall be a citizen of the Union', and that furthermore 'citizenship of the Union shall complement and not replace national citizenship'. There were further, though half-hearted attempts after 1992 to expand these limited citizenship rights. The Westendorp Reflection Group, for instance, argued for the inclusion of additional rights, such as greater institutional transparency and access to official Community documents. Citizenship rights were extended in the revisions of the Amsterdam (Article 8), and the Nice Treaties (Articles 17–22), though only to a limited degree.

### Citizenship after Maastricht: limited rights, minimal duties, elusive affinities?

The founding treaties have been revised on three further occasions since Maastricht. The revisions undertaken at Amsterdam added little that was new on citizenship, except to confirm consumer protection, employment and social balance as matters pertaining to citizens. And with some aspirational references to extending civic rights, more transparent decisions taken closer to the citizen (Article 1, TEU) and encouraging voluntary service and sport.[62] Amsterdam also made reference to the importance of politically 'educating' citizens, with better access to data, information and language support. This, too, was hardly much of an advance on the Maastricht citizenship provisions. The second paragraph of Article 17, for instance, reaffirmed European citizenship as derived exclusively from the EC Treaty and not from the Union. Whereas Amsterdam merely hinted at 'future' developments, with the addition (Article 22 – ex 8e) of procedures for enhancing citizenship rights.[63]

The procedure envisaged here is as follows: the Commission, monitoring the working of the citizenship articles, may propose additional rights on the basis of soundings reported in triannual reports to the Parliament, the Council and the Economic and Social Committee. It is left to the Council by unanimous decision and after consulting the Parliament, to decide on any additions to EU citizenship rights. Even then, member states are permitted to adopt any changes in the citizenship articles, 'in accordance with their respective constitutional requirements'. The point being made here is that any future development of citizenship will be determined, not by the usual legislative procedure but instead by treaty amendments, with the prospect of national vetoes should proposals be deemed to be too radical, for this procedure requires both unanimity and formal ratification by every member state.

The Nice Treaty arrangements that apply at the time of writing also added little that was new to the citizenship articles, though it did attempt to strengthen the link between citizenship, passports and social security. The post-Nice citizenship provisions amount to five succinct articles. The status of EU citizenship is referred to in Articles 17–22 (ex 8) and, consonant with Article 2, TEU, it defines citizenship as an objective rather than merely as derivative from the other Treaty articles. The reference to national citizenship here reiterates that European citizenship is derived from nationality rather than being free-standing. The Article is quite explicit about this. European citizenship is automatic for those who qualify and it cannot be rescinded. Telling here is the fact that it is up to the member states and not the Union to decide who shall enjoy this privilege, providing the Council presidency with details of who they consider to be nationals for the purposes of defining eligibility for European citizenship.[64] The Treaty reaffirms the jurisdiction of the member states in matters that define nationality status, such as the rules for conferring citizenship and residency, though the member states singly do not have the right to determine the content of EU citizenship. Free movement remains the essence of EU citizenship, and the core of individual citizenship rights remains linked with the proper functioning of economic relations in a common market, notably the right to reside freely and to move freely within the territory of the member states (Article 18 – ex 8a).

The primacy accorded to economic rights says much about the abiding reservations of most member states over anything that might weaken the affective political bonds between national polities and citizens. The Nice Treaty did anticipate further action under Article 251, should the Union deem it necessary to act further to safeguard the right of free movement. Nice likewise confirmed co-decision and QMV as the procedure for determining the future content of European citizenship, but pointedly resisted extending this decisional procedure to politically sensitive matters such as passports, identity cards, residence permits or to documents relating to social security or social protection. Furthermore, any proposed secondary legislation to improve citizenship rights would have to make a good case in the face of certain resistance from member states determined to keep control of critical matters that, after all, define the bounds of national sovereignty, what it is to be an independent state. Once again, a major treaty revision avoided anything but very limited changes to EU citizenship, more a matter of semantic flourishes than of substantive improvements.

The controversial political aspect of citizenship (Article 19 – ex 8b) was introduced at Maastricht, and though it does go beyond the narrow *marketburger* concept of economic citizenship and includes the right to stand and to vote in some elections beyond national borders, this is more a symbolic than a significant incursion on the powerful affective bonds between governments and national demos. There are, for instance, restrictions on transnational political participation that clearly show the determination of most member states to resist weakening the symbolic political linkage between citizens and their national polities. The right to vote is restricted to second-order (municipal and European) elections. Moreover, in local elections only EU citizens who are residents are entitled to vote, and they do so on the same terms as nationals. The Council again has the right to decide, on advice from the Commission, the terms and conditions of this limited, if symbolic extension of the franchise. The European Parliament's role here is merely consultative. Furthermore, member states were permitted to delay or even to defer this elective right where local circumstances make for difficulties, a concession designed to accommodate the problem raised by Luxembourg, to the effect that in some of its municipalities the native electorate is outnumbered by guest workers from other EU states.

EU citizens also have the right to diplomatic representation by the consular services of member states other than their own (Article 20 – ex 8c). This is a practical as much a symbolic innovation, for when this provision was first introduced in the Maastricht Treaty only 5 non-EU states had consular representation from all EU15 states, and there were another 17 states where only 2 EU15 states had diplomatic representation. The point here, however, is that procedures for consular representation are intergovernmental arrangements, a matter for the member states concerned after due negotiation, rather than the outcome of a formal and uniform treaty-based arrangement. The citizenship articles also give judicial protection or redress for maladministration (Article 21 – ex 8d). EU citizens may petition the European Parliament and present grievances to the EU Ombudsman. The Amsterdam Treaty extended this particular right, entitling any citizen who corresponds with one of the EU institutions to receive a reply in their mother tongue. Declaration 4 in the Treaty of Nice further confirmed that correspondents should receive a reply within 'a reasonable time', though without specifying what is 'a reasonable time' or how this right might be enforced. There is also lack of clarity about precisely which EU institutions are covered by this provision. Clearly, it implies the major institutions identified in Article 1-19 of the Treaty, but with less certainty about whether this includes, for instance, the Committee of the Regions, EcoSoc and so on.

These provisions are all well and good as far as they go, but critics do not see them as going all that far. At best they are a modest advance on previous treaties, but they amount to little more than a limited category of rights.[65] Furthermore, these are political or civic rights rather than redistributive social or economic rights, and rights that signify little for what is nowadays described in advanced democracies as social citizenship. As such, these rights impact much less, are altogether less intrusive on citizens' affective relations with the European polity than are social and civil rights acquired from membership of a national polity. It seems reasonable then to conclude that these notional transnational rights are hardly likely to resonate affectively with citizens as members of the European polity, let alone to undermine their primary allegiance to the national polity. Of course, the member states prefer it that way, and are likely to continue to do so for the foreseeable future. Yet a meaningful sense of civic membership, one that instils a sense of affective membership or affiliation to the EU polity will surely depend on extending rights-based citizenship, to include rights not remotely considered as part and parcel of European citizenship as presently defined. So far, however, progress on this front has been limited, and the question remains whether such 'a gradual and dynamic process' can realistically 'build on the largely symbolic nature of European citizenship in the future'.[66] Few contemporary commentators are optimistic about any such far-reaching prospect.[67]

## EU citizenship and the Constitutional Treaty

The Constitutional Treaty consolidated but hardly extended existing citizenship provision. Citizenship was covered in Part I, Title II, Article 1-10.1 and 2). There was further elaboration on citizenship rights in Part II, The Charter of Fundamental Rights of the Union, at Title V, Article 2 99-106. Whereas Part III, Title II, Non-Discrimination and Citizenship, Articles 3-123/129 refers to European laws and framework laws prohibiting discrimination on the grounds of nationality. The Union was empowered (as it was under the previous treaties – ex Article 13, TEC) to enact legislation within the powers assigned to it 'to combat discrimination based on sex, racial or ethnic origin, religion or belief, disability, age or sexual orientation', the Council acting unanimously after consulting the Parliament. Article 3-125 (ex Article 18, TEC) likewise empowered the Union to act, where necessary, 'to facilitate the exercise of the right ... of every Union citizen to move and reside freely'.

The other Articles under this Title provide for the Council to determine the following: arrangements for exercising citizenship rights referred to in Article 1-10.2 (b) on citizens standing and voting in municipal and European elections, without being a national of that state; for member states to 'adopt the necessary provisions to secure diplomatic and consular protection of citizens in third countries' (Article 3-127 – ex Article 20, TEC); and on the languages in which EU citizens have the right to address the institutions and receive answer (Article 3-128 – ex Article 21, TEC). Article 1-50.3 further provides that: 'Any citizen of the Union, and any natural or legal person residing or having its registered office in a Member State shall have, under the conditions laid down in Part III, a right of access to documents of the Union Institutions, bodies, offices and agencies, whatever their medium'.[68]

There are no significant changes here from provisions already included in the existing treaty base. Citizenship remains what it has been from the outset, 'no more than a very modest enhancement of the rights nationals of member states already enjoy'. Moreover, 'the most important of [these rights], the right to move and reside freely anywhere in the Union is restricted, and quite significantly, by various provisions designed to prevent people of inadequate means becoming a "burden" on the social security system of the member state where they choose to reside'.[69] This much is confirmed in Part I, Title I (Definition and Objectives of the Union, Article 1.5), which refers to the primacy of member states in determining the Union's constitutional order, and notes that: 'The Union shall respect the national identities of the Member States, inherent in their fundamental structures, political and constitutional, inclusive of regional and local self-government.' And furthermore that: 'It shall respect their essential State functions, including those for ensuring the territorial integrity of the State.'

The same Article also includes a reference to the principle of loyal co-operation (Part I, Article 1-5.2), which sets out the principle of 'sincere co-operation' between the member states *vis-à-vis* the Union, including the undertaking that 'Member States shall take any appropriate measure, general or particular, to ensure fulfillment of the obligations arising out of the Constitution or resulting from acts of the institutions of the Union'.[70] This is clearly a reference to the usual formula that balances supranational integration with the intergovernmental preferences of the member states, with all that this implies for the member states' primacy in determining the Union's constitutional order. Furthermore, Article 1-10.1 reaffirms the derivative nature of EU citizenship, that: 'Every national of a member state shall be a citizen of the Union. Citizenship of the Union shall be additional to national citizenship; it shall not replace it.' This, too, confirms the primacy of relations between member states and the EU, discounting direct and unmediated relations between the EU and its citizens that might, over time, facilitate a sense of constitutional patriotism towards the Union. Even the Convention's more radical voices were wary of pushing too hard for directly conferred Union citizenship.[71] In effect, the status quo prevails, except for the inclusion of an explicit reference to the principle of equality of the sexes before the law.[72] The rights included in the revised citizenship Title V, Articles 2-99/106 are just that, rights: important, but not enough to upgrade European citizenship as an expression of affective identity.

These arrangements, then, hardly develop the concept of European citizenship beyond its already modest substance. Citizenship in the full meaning of the concept is more than a merely passive, rights-based status. It is relational, involving reciprocal duties and obligations between the citizen and polity that underpin the individual's sense of personal belonging and emotive attachment to the body politic. This relational aspect is still missing from EU citizenship a decade and more after the concept was first included in the treaty base.[73] The closest the Constitutional Treaty comes to endorsing active membership of a European polity is the principle of participatory democracy (Article 1-47) that permits citizens' initiative, where 'not less than one million citizens coming from a significant number of Member States may take the initiative of inviting the Commission within the framework of its powers, to submit any appropriate proposal on matters where citizens consider that a legal act of the Union is required for the purpose of implementing the Constitution'.[74] But this is as far as it goes, for it omits any precise details. It remains doubtful, too, whether this provision would make that much difference to citizens' sense of personal affiliation to the Union, or bring them closer to what is widely regarded as a remote and inaccessible policy process, let alone to enhance their sense of empowerment. This measure seems more like an afterthought than a considered proposal intended to enhance the citizens' sense of political inclusion. Additional and so far unspecified legislation would be required to clarify, for instance, precisely how many signatures are needed to trigger an initiative, and from how many member states. Nor is there any guarantee that such an outcome would be legally binding on the legislators.

The Convention working party that reviewed citizenship did consider extending citizenship, for instance to those legally resident in the Union for five years, to refugees and to stateless persons. But in the event, even these quite modest extensions did not find their way into the final draft of the Constitutional Treaty, blocked precisely because they risked compromising the member states' monopoly of all matters pertaining to membership, citizenship and nationality.[75] Consequently citizenship remains derivative, it is dependent on already having nationality status in a member state. To this extent, the Constitutional Treaty perpetuates the anomaly whereby citizenship is withheld from some 10 per cent of the Union's population, those non-EU nationals who legally reside, work and otherwise contribute to its economic prosperity and general well-being. This amounts to overt and legally sanctioned discrimination, and confirms the EU as unduly insular, an exclusive 'fortress Europe' rather than an inclusive and outward-looking community, a beacon of tolerance in an otherwise fractured world. A no less anomalous instance of discrimination is that each member state offers economic migrants who are citizens of another EU state quite different social political and civic rights from those available to their own nationals as a consequence of exercising their right of free movement as EU citizens. This anomaly noticeably worsened in 2004 as a consequence of the restrictions imposed by most EU15 states on would-be migrants from the recent accession countries.

One solution proposed by some legal experts to what amounts to double standards here was to detach European citizenship from national membership, to make its conferral the prerogative of the Union *per se*. The obvious difficulty here, however, is the marked reluctance of governments to relinquish control to the Union of any matter connected with political membership. This was after all why Denmark had sought reassurance on this very issue when the Maastricht Treaty first introduced the idea of European citizenship. Reticence about expanding the EU's reach into what is a politically sensitive area is bound to be an obstacle to future reform. Landmark judgments since the 1960s in the *Bundesverfassungsgericht*, Germany's Constitutional Court, have blunted the ECJ's legal claim, and quite possibly its political appetite, too, for intruding into national constitutional affairs, to make rulings on these very delicate matters without reference to the national constitutional authorities.

Notable here is the 1967 ruling referred to in Chapter 2 that objected to the assumed supremacy of EU law in matters pertaining to the national constitutional order. On that occasion the German court ruled that any transfer of powers from the (West) German state to the Community could not deprive German citizens of their right to the protection afforded them under the Basic Law. This set a precedent that all EC law should be examined to determine its compatibility with the national constitution. When the Court of Justice subsequently made another such intervention, referring in one post-Maastricht ruling to the idea of European demos, the *Bundesverfassungsgericht* again firmly rebutted any implications this ruling might have, even if only in the opinion of the European Court itself, for initiating a direct political link between individual citizens and the EU polity, and reiterated that legitimacy accorded to any actor at the EU level derives exclusively from domestic constitutional sources.

In time this situation might change, quite possibly as a consequence of fully incorporating the Charter of Fundamental Rights into the Union's treaty base, thereby adding legal weight to the Court's political aspiration to be the Union's ultimate constitutional arbiter. Then again, the weight of precedent and the logics of EU politics suggest otherwise. On the face of it, the Charter does present an opportunity to expand the scope for a rights-based European citizenship, by including within its list of rights some aspects of social and civil citizenship, those rights that historically have made a signal contribution to deepening citizens' attachment to their national polities during the era of European state-building. The Charter's second chapter, for instance, lists civil and political rights that are closely associated with citizenship, and chapter 3 catalogues social and economic rightss (in the fields of employment, health care, living standards, gender equality and so on) that some legal opinion sees as having potential for enriching both national and EU citizenship. On the other hand, there is simply no consensus amongst the member states about the Charter's constitutional substance, or its significance for expanding those rights associated with citizenship status in contemporary democratic polities.

For this and other reasons most governments preferred the Charter to have merely declaratory status, a useful though non-binding codification of rights to be used as a benchmark by governments enacting legislation, and as a legal referent to guide national courts. And though the decision was taken at the time to incorporate the Charter in the Treaty, safeguards were added to restrict its application in European law. Even that decision has been modified in the Lisbon Treaty. The Charter is included, but as a protocol, and with the right of any member state to opt out, and as such it hardly has the normative force of a bill of rights in the national constitutional order. In these circumstances it is questionable whether this catalogue of rights will give the EU courts greater leverage on the national legal order, let alone encourage the European Court to take the constitutional initiative in conferring social citizenship rights by standing up, for instance, to elected governments concerned about both the budgetary and political implications of more firmly embedding social rights.

The Court's appetite for testing the boundaries of legal convention should never of course be underestimated. Over time the Justices have expanded rights in the workplace, in economic relations, consumer rights and health and safety by means of a series of landmark judgements that extend the reach of EU law into politically sensitive policy areas such as welfare and pension rights, gender, disability and so on. The Court has always had the capacity to surprise, and not least an aptitude for legal novelty and constitutional experimentation. There is no reason to doubt that such judicial innovation will continue. Nevertheless, the Court's members are not lacking in political realism, and though they may well be convinced about the merits of international law they are quite aware of the limits on the Court's authority, not least the constraints imposed by politics. For this reason, they will surely be reluctant to take on national judicial establishments and governments on those highly sensitive constitutional matters that have historically marked out the boundaries between the nation-state and European-level governance. And with good reason, for treaty-based norms do not enjoy the status of higher law.

This fact has deterred the ECJ so far from making judgments in politically contentious areas. Political barriers stand in the way of a directly conferred citizenship. Anything that threatens to weaken the affective bond between the citizen and the nation state is bound to be resisted by national authorities, whether political or judicial. The Court is fully aware of these facts and it has tended to tread carefully; it is on altogether firmer ground when it rules on technical or economic matters related to market-making, but much less so when it strays into the realm of politics. So far, it has deliberately resisted defining European citizenship, understandably so for it cannot confer what it lacks the authority to confer. Telling here is the key judgement in *Cinéthèque SA and others* v. *Fédération nationale des cinémas français*, to the effect that the Court 'has no power to examine the compatibility with its human rights catalogue of laws concerning areas that fall within the jurisdiction of national legislation'.[76]

For all of these reasons, the Constitutional Treaty was a disappointment to those who had anticipated constitutionalism as a process that in part would establish a meaningful 'contract' between citizens and polity. On the critical matter of finding ways to legitimise a polity out of touch with, disconnected and remote from its 'citizens', who are after all its stakeholders, the Convention flattered only to deceive. Much was expected from a deliberative forum whose membership included democratically elected politicians, many of them at least connected with if not actually agencies of civil society. In the event, *conventionnels* were preoccupied with different priorities, not least with the inter-institutional balance of power in which most of them had a vested interest. Even the Commission, for all of its supposed attachment to federalist principles, its concern with building a 'people's Europe' to counter-balance rampant corporatism, failed to promote citizenship.

The running was made here instead by the member states, as it is on most other critical issues. Predictably, the leading governments were simply not convinced about developing what they regarded as an altogether risky concept. Much has been made by critics of the failure of current political leaders, their lack of vision compared with their predecessors during the foundational years, when Robert Schuman, Alcide De Gasperi and Konrad Adenauer led from the front, prepared to take political risks in order to launch the European project. Contemporary politicians on the other hand tend to hide behind public opinion, using the public's natural reticence about visionary politics as an excuse for inaction. But the evidence here is, to say the least, mixed. Although opinion polls and attitude surveys do reveal public indifference and even wariness about some aspects of European integration, this does not necessarily mean outright hostility to the idea of European construction.

What the polling evidence does show is ambivalence about the European project, a response that suggests there is everything still to play for. The response in the *Eurobarometer* survey (November 2002), for instance, to a question about 'feelings' of attachment to the EU indicated that Luxembourgers exhibited the strongest sense of identification with the Union (75 per cent), predictable perhaps from a city-state whose population has a high proportion of immigrants. This was followed on the plus scale by Italians (62 per cent), the French (53 per cent) and the Irish (50 per cent). At the other end of the spectrum a mere 24 per cent of Finns identified with Europe, 27 per cent of the British, and 29 per cent of the Dutch. Surprising perhaps, in light of their resistance to the Maastricht Treaty, the Danes recorded the same level of European identity as the Germans (46 per cent), a country whose post-war governments and public have shown consistently high levels of support for European integration, in marked contrast to the Danes, who have been altogether more lukewarm. The average figure in this survey for the EU as a whole was 45 per cent.[77] What this and other polling evidence does indicate is that public disquiet rather than outright Euroscepticism is citizens' usual response to 'Europe', with widespread wariness about being 'kept in the dark' by political elites seemingly more attentive to the insistent demands from special interests.

This mood of public disquiet has found expression, either as support for anti-EU parties (as in the 2004 European elections) or as voter apathy. As Vernon Bogdanor sees it, though political leaders 'try to lead … the people will no longer follow', a situation that gives rise 'to that most dangerous of cleavages – between the political class and the people'. He continues: 'In almost every member state, governing parties are strongly committed to Europe. Voters, however, are increasingly sceptical [and] Europe's leaders have only themselves to blame for their troubles. Since the Maastricht treaty in 1992, the people have been sending increasingly strong signals, but they have chosen to ignore them. They have failed to explain the purpose of the EU in a post-cold war world and how it can be made more accountable to the people.' The message here is patent for those who conduct the Union's affairs: 'The draft European constitution … ought to have tackled these issues' but failed to do so.[78] The Constitution quite simply failed to respond to citizens' concerns, not only about 'Europe', but also about the consequences and costs of accelerating economic change and related matters. Instead of connecting with citizens, finding ways of deepening public attachment to the Union, the central preoccupations of contemporary leaders were altogether too narrow, seemingly self-indulgent and concerned above all with 'rebalancing the EU's institutions', whilst doing 'almost nothing to alter the balance between the institutions and the citizens'.[79] It is hard to disagree with this forceful but reasoned judgement. It was precisely the perceived remoteness and even the arrogance of the politicians after all that brought about the defeat of the Constitutional Treaty in the French and Dutch referendums.

The public's reaction to what many see as a venal, or at best a remote political elite is only part of the explanation for the negative reaction to the Constitution. Poor or unimaginative political leadership was compounded by cultural resistance to change, particularly but not exclusively amongst the political class. The citizenship question in Europe connects with a long-standing debate about the meaning of political membership and identity.[80] On one side of this discourse are those political theorists and practitioners who subscribe to what amounts to a realist or neo-realist outlook. The view here is that citizenship should be confined to nation-states, that transnational political identity is fanciful in a continent lacking common values and the shared history that binds nation-states through time in common endeavour.[81] In Stanley Hoffmann's memorable phrase, there is simply 'too much history' in this small yet culturally diverse and polyglot continent to be cancelled by mere expressions of good intentions about common purpose or vague allusions to common values.[82]

In this narrative, the very idea of individual membership of a European polity is dismissed as illusory. How, these 'realists' ask, can anything remotely resembling mutual purpose or shared destiny bind together a continent whose history resonates with all manner of conflicts, whether over ethnicity, religion or other potent expressions of primordial allegiance? A continent, moreover, whose peoples continue to manifest acute cultural diversity, with a plurality of languages, a pervasive sense of deep-rooted cognitive boundaries reinforced by long-standing geographic frontiers. In these unpropitious circumstances, the very idea of common identity is, as Hoffmann sees it, purely fallacy, something akin to an hallucination induced, in his memorable phrase, by 'a mind-expanding substance'.[83]

Of course, yet other voices challenge this familiar realist mantra, denouncing it as deliberately reactionary because out of kilter with a modern world undergoing rapid structural and cultural transformation. The debate on the prospects for reimagining the polity, for remaking political identity is now fully engaged in the social sciences as well as on the ground in Europe's political and social institutions. We shall briefly review it here precisely because the issues raised by it go to the heart of the matter about the prospects for post-national European citizenship, but also because it raises important questions about the making of a constitutional polity beyond the nation state.

## Critiquing EU citizenship: competing theoretic narratives

The prospect for EU citizenship based on a shared identity rather than merely defined as a catalogue of notional rights may be intellectually appealing, but it is, to say the least, problematic. As the controversy over the Preamble to the Constitutional Treaty shows, there is simply no consensus on 'core' European values. It is easier by far to prescribe shared 'European' values a priori than it is to show any convincing evidence for them in public attitude surveys, let alone as a reliable basis for a common political project. The discourse on putative 'common' values tends to be conducted in suitably generalised terms, with commentators identifying what they see as shared cultural influences at work in Europe, whether in governance, jurisprudence, the arts, science, popular culture or architecture. Nor, according to this narrative, are these values a recent development, a consequence of post-modernism. On the contrary, they are supposedly rooted in antiquity, subsequently reinforced by the Christian heritage, leaving aside the inconvenient facts of the Great Schism of 1054 that separated the Eastern from the Western Church and of the Protestant Reformation. And they are bolstered in turn by the civilising and modernising legacies of the Renaissance and the Enlightenment, the Copernican scientific revolution, the rise of possessive individualism and the spread of liberal values from the seventeenth century, and followed latterly by the pervasive influence of free-market principles, the rule of law and representative government.

This amounts to an impressive catalogue of enduring 'common' values – or so the advocates of 'Europeanness' claim – that have permeated European thought and society over many centuries, though this legacy has by no means negated the narrow parochialism that has characterised European politics and distorted the continent's international relations since the high Middle Ages.[84] Even if we acknowledge the undoubted impact of these values, it is by no means clear whether the 'idea of Europe' amounts to anything more substantial than a convenient and retrospective intellectual construction, at best an 'imagined community' above the nation-state and national society, though one invented by a cosmopolitan elite for its own political ends and signifying little to the public at large. Critics here disparage what they see as an ideological hybrid, a 'pick and mix' selected from myriad sources and quite different cultural legacies. And one employed, too, by convinced 'Europeans', misguided 'Kantian doctors', as Stanley Hoffmann has mischievously described them, seeking to construct a synthetic cosmopolitan identity as the antidote to 'corrosive tribalism', the wrong solution, as he saw it, to the right problem.[85] For Delanty and other commentators, this influential realist narrative maintains that 'European identity' is pure invention, the political dimension of a fictive idea that only existed as the counterpoint to perceived threats from 'the other', as an antidote to internal divisions'.[86] Understanding the terms of engagement between these competitive claims is essential for evaluating the prospects for meaningful European citizenship. What follows is a review of these competing narratives on identity and citizenship, and some discussion of their relevance for the very idea of a European constitutional tradition.

### The realists' view

In the realist narrative the nation-state is the primary, indeed the only reliable source of political legitimacy, the *locus classicus* of political identity, notwithstanding recent shifts in the organisation and scale of the international community brought about by accelerating interdependence and globalisation. The national polity and society may well be constructed, a historically contingent development, yet the social, cultural and political roots of these communities have become over time embedded in both the individual mindset and the collective historical memory, a consequence of mostly successful nation-building in Europe over long centuries.[87]

One consequence of this is national identities that are enduring yet adaptable. They persist and provide cultural support and political legitimation for Europe's post-Westphalian states, and for that matter for those states further afield.[88] These developments have modified in turn the structure of international society, and likewise impacted on the conduct of international relations, but not in ways that some critics of nationhood had anticipated. Europe's nation-states have adapted to change, and reacted to pre-1945 anarchy and autarchy by building liberal institutions to enhance co-operation and to manage residual conflict. Yet these very structures have consolidated rather than weakened the 'obstinate' and enduring nation-state as the principal actor of international politics.[89] As one notable contributor to this narrative sees it, far from making the nation state obsolescent regional integration in Europe has ensured its survival.[90] The nation-state in this quasi-realist liberal-institutional narrative is the principal interlocutor between still competing preferences, notwithstanding the imperative for near neighbours to make accommodations, those positive sum policy bargains that balance narrow national interests with the common European good.[91]

In this narrative, the nation-state remains as the optimal and even the natural form of governance, still the most significant focus for political affiliation and cultural identity.[92] National affiliation may be constructed identity, but nevertheless it is one that is embedded in shared norms and values instilled and perpetuated by the agencies of political socialisation that operate in contemporary societies. The ingrained sense of belonging is reinforced in turn by legal rights firmly rooted in a constitutional and political order. Constructed it may be, but over time membership of a national polity gives rise to a potent affective bond between citizens and the state at several levels, and in ways that frame political identity. Moreover, this unique relationship has acquired status in international law with the ruling by the International Court of Justice, to the effect that nationality is a legal covenant that binds the individual to his/her polity, a bond that represents 'a social fact of attachment'.[93]

On the other hand, according to this narrative the EU is primarily about the limited functions of market-making.[94] In these circumstances, citizenship is confined to membership of a national polity, is rooted in shared cultural values and the sense of solidarity it implies is, indeed can only be expressed in a common language, a medium for conducting a meaningful conversation about those issues, great and small, that underpin a sense of belonging to a political community.[95] European citizenship in this account is pure artifice, merely notional, is at most about limited economic market-related rights such as free movement of people as labour or service providers.[96]

Whether an affective bond can be constructed between a transnational polity and people who are already members of a nation-state is, to say the least, problematical. This very question is the key to determining the prospects for an identity-based citizenship. The outcome is by no means clear-cut, certainly not as patent as the realists would have it. It depends, to a degree, on how national citizens perceive the EU polity, on whether citizenship at this level is invested with political legitimacy in its own right independent of the member states; or whether the EU is seen by its citizens as merely a second-order, indeed a second-hand polity borrowing its legitimacy indirectly from the component member states. Moreover, legitimacy defined merely in terms of performance or output criteria, rather than as the direct and affective relations that exist between national citizens and their states.

Realist thinkers discount the possibility of building a polity with meaningful identity beyond the nation-state, and they remain sceptical about the prospects for transnational identity. This case is made by David Miller, amongst other contemporary political theorists. Miller sees the nation-state as the most effective agency for maintaining political order in an otherwise turbulent world. Miller conflates functional and normative criteria, both of them essential prerequisites for effective polity-building. The national community is for Miller the most successful example of a stable, functioning polity, in so far as it 'embodies a real continuity between generations', and likewise 'performs a moralising role, by holding up before us the virtues of our ancestors and encouraging us to live up to them [for] people are held together not merely by physical necessity, but by a dense web of customs, practices, implicit understandings, and so forth'. Accordingly, the solidarity that is needed to hold people together in a stable polity owes much to an abiding sense of the familiar, in so far as 'in a national community a case can be made out for unconditional obligations to other members that arise simply by virtue of the fact that one has been born and raised in that particular community'.[97]

The logics of polity-building here are functional as much as they are normative; indeed, the one reinforces the other. Modern governance is in some degree about making significant and not least redistributive resource allocations, principally through taxation and public expenditure. By these means, the polity secures support and even emotional attachment from it members. Redistributive decisions are invariably contentious and frequently contested, and for Miller and those who share his outlook such decisions are only likely to be successfully transacted in a political community capable of ensuring public compliance, deterring so-called 'free riders'. Public trust, or what Putnam calls 'mutual reciprocity', is key to any successful co-operative endeavour, an essential ingredient of the social capital on which political stability and a healthy polity depends. The pervasive sense of common purpose, shared values, general solidarity and no less of meaningful political identity are qualities that reside most securely for Miller only in the nation-state.[98]

Might not these affective qualities, over time and with favourable circumstances also come about in a transnational polity? Realists and neo-realists of every stripe think not. Miller lists five essential elements for political community, all of them present in national politics, but much less in evidence or missing altogether from governance beyond the nation-state. The optimal political community is, as Miller sees it: '(1) constituted by shared belief and mutual commitment, (2) extended in history, (3) active in character, (4) connected to a particular territory, and (5) marked off from other communities by its distinct political culture'. It is also deeply embedded in a distinctive historical experience which can 'serve to distinguish nationality from other collective sources of personal identity'.[99]

These particular qualities sustain a sense of meaningful political identity, the awareness of being 'a people', possessing a common identity, demos, membership – individual as much as collective – of belonging to a territorial polity rooted in time (history) and place (geography). For Miller, 'the guiding ideal here is that of a people reproducing their national identity and settling matters that are collectively important to them through democratic deliberation [and] to achieve that, they need a political unit with the authority of the relevant scope, but what that scope must be will depend on the particular identity of the group in question, and on the aims and goals that they are attempting to pursue'. The 'relevant scope' is confined in this narrative to the nation state, for 'once you combine the principle of national self-determination with the proposition that what counts for the purposes of national identity is what the nation in question takes to be essential to that identity, it follows that nothing in principle goes beyond the scope of sovereignty'.[100]

Political and social institutions perform a vital function here, instilling in members of a body politic a sense of shared political identity and much else, a process akin to what Rawls describes as 'reciprocity'.[101] Institutions, above all familiar institutions that have some affective resonance for the citizen, not only shape the content of values but also determine their authoritative allocation, the 'who gets what, when, and how' question critical for any polity. Political institutions mediate between myriad competing interests in what would otherwise be corrosive competition within the body politic and civil society. Amidst an otherwise potentially destructive competition over always scarce resources, these national agencies foster a sense of common identity and help to sustain shared purposes, socialising citizens in 'appropriate behaviour', educating them about what is possible, and no less to facilitate collective action.[102] Above all, familiar institutions inculcate a sense of trust between citizens without which social and political order would dissipate.[103]

As these realists see it, only long-standing, familiar and above all deep-rooted national institutions can perform these critical functions. One commentary written in this quasi-Burkean vein wonders, for instance, if the EU can ever meet such exacting requirements, 'whether European citizens can act as a people at this moment, in order to be the *subject* that holds the "*pouvoir constituant*" [for] doubts arise with regard to the existence of a European public sphere, the necessary structure of civil society, or a sufficient sense of solidarity created by a sufficiently thick collective identity'.[104] This critique of the prospects for identity-based European citizenship is telling, and it is one that those who postulate a meaningful political identity beyond the nation state must address.

### Radical visions

The realist narrative has been challenged by a radical exegesis of the prospects for identity-based citizenship beyond the national community. There is a burgeoning literature that both reviews and challenges the supposed fixity of the linkages between identity and nation states, raising instead the prospects for citizenship defined as political identity in a post-national polity. This case notably figures in the writings of Jürgen Habermas, Elizabeth Meehan, David Held and Joseph Weiler.[105] The narrative combines a range of theoretic perspectives, some essentially normative-prescriptive, others drawing on empirical research, but all of them in their way convinced of the real potential for transforming political identity, persuaded about the prospects for relocating political membership beyond the territorial-ethnic or national polity.

Some radical theorists who have engaged this issue are influenced by multiculturalism, the idea of coexistent identities, acknowledging the multiple layers of meaning about belonging and identity that are rooted in an individual's manifold attachments: to territory, ethnicity or to cultural referents, not as exclusive affinities but rather as complementary or overlapping layers of meaning and identity. And each of them with potential for connecting people and peoples with significant 'others' beyond the primary community, thereby engendering an inclusive sense of 'we-ness' rooted in a growing perception of universal rights, shared goals and mutual interests.[106] These arrangements, it is claimed, are capable over time of fostering complementary and inclusive regional, national, continental and even global affinities.[107] According to this narrative post-nationalist, and for some post-modern citizenship is essentially 'multilayered'.[108] In the particular context of the debate about EU citizenship, advocates of post-nationalism see no incompatibility between national citizenship and European citizenship, the latter 'nested' in but in no way dependent on primary or territorially-based citizenship. As such, EU citizenship may in the first instance be merely a modest rights-based status, but it has potential nevertheless for inculcating affective political attachment beyond the nation-state.[109]

Another variant of the post-nationalist citizenship narrative focuses on the prospects for cosmopolitan identity. The emphasis here is less on accommodation between diverse sub-identities and more on their replacement over time by an inclusive and overarching identity, a process driven by inexorable social, economic and cultural change.[110] Globalisation in all its forms gives rise to common values, making possible as the writers in this narrative see it a cosmopolitan identity, and with it a transnational citizenship that over time will permeate, even replace narrower primordial affinities, inculcating a sense of belonging to an inclusive political community, and prospectively even to a country called 'Europe'.[111] Commentators here see the EU as a kind of experimental laboratory for reimagining political identity, and they make much of its 'state-like' qualities, citing the recent development of European citizenship as evidence of the prospects for fostering a growing attachment between citizens and the EU polity.[112] The cosmopolitan narrative inverts almost all of the claims made for abiding nationhood in the realist narrative. As such, it challenges conventional assumptions about the nature of the political community and by extension about citizenship too, and this is no easy case to make. For as Jorg Monar points out, 'to be a citizen of something other than a nation-state polity – and the Union is clearly not a nation-state – seems to contradict all inherited notions of political order as it has emerged from the development of political theory over the last few centuries [because] it is precisely in the political thinking which prepared the ground for the modern Western democracies that the most valid reasons for citizenship is to be found'.[113]

The post-national narrative tackles this rooted assumption head-on, refuting the idea that political membership is confined exclusively to the territorial polity. It prescribes instead a citizenship that is directly conferred by a transnational polity. Critics point to the idealised, even visionary tenor of this narrative, maintaining that it requires altogether more convincing evidence than merely vague and prescriptive, if well-meaning rhetoric about universal cultural norms, the *condition humaine* as reflected in Kantian ethics or the humanism manifested in the *oeuvre* of Shakespeare, Beethoven, Raphael and other great European artists and thinkers whose humanism rises above the merely parochial. The cultural legacy of the European Enlightenment gave rise to what might be claimed on the face of it to be common values, and these values do indeed appeal to the sensibilities of the well educated, emotionally secure and comfortably off, in Europe as elsewhere.

But the cosmopolitan narrative requires something more substantial to sustain the case for an inclusive pan-European or even, as some of its exponents anticipate, global citizenship.

This narrative has an essentially, and some would say a necessarily visionary quality, prescribing a world so far not remotely in sight let alone *in situ*, in as much as European demos, a common political identity, a political community and social solidarity beyond the bounds of primordial and parochial nationalism is novel by any historical yardstick, confronting as it does all the accepted dictums of 'normal' politics. This narrative is also of variable quality. Some advocates make the case rather more convincingly than others. One prominent exponent of the prospects for a post-national polity goes beyond merely moral exhortation, and introduces some supposedly empirical evidence, though as things currently stand in European politics this evidence is somewhat thin. For Jürgen Habermas a European 'public space' is not only desirable but feasible, even imminent, a location where in due course citizens as individual stakeholders will interact, participating in its transnational politics, debating and influencing policy agendas as effectively as they do now in national politics. As Habermas sees it, this process is already underway by means of value shifts and value-sharing, giving rise to a meaningful European *Verfassungspatriotismus*, or constitutional patriotism.[114] In time and with political maturity the European polity will develop, he maintains, as a *Bundesstaat*, a European federal state and a clear stage beyond the current political *Staatenbund*, a confederation of sovereign states.[115] There is more wishful thinking here, however, than convincing evidence for such ineluctable change.

The normative and the sociological case for such a transformation of European politics and governance figures, too, in the work of Joseph Weiler, a philosopher of law and constitutionalism who explains the logics of the transformative process as a shift in the psychological or cognitive, as much as the cultural or institutional base of European politics. Weiler questions the persistence of present arrangements, and in one of the more visionary passages in his work conjectures thus:

> Is it mandated that demos in general and the European demos in particular be understood exclusively in organic cultural homogenous terms? Can we break away from that tradition and define membership of a polity in civic, non-organic-cultural terms? Can we imagine a polity whose demos is defined, understood and accepted in civic, non-organic cultural terms, and would have legitimate rule-making democratic authority on that basis? ... a coming together on the basis of shared values, a shared understanding of rights and societal duties and shared rational, intellectual culture which transcend organic-national differences.

For Weiler, this fundamental reconfiguration of European politics depends on social and cultural as much as on political change. The affective roots of political identity that explain the resonance and persistence of exclusive primordial affiliations (nationalism or other forms of 'organic' identity) are not so much replaced as complemented by other expressions of identity, less insular, more inclusive but essentially complementary. As Weiler sees it: 'On this reading, conceptualisation of a European demos should not be based on real or imaginary trans-European cultural affinities or shared histories nor on the construction of a European "national myth" of the type which constitutes the identity of the organic nation. European Citizenship should not be thought of either as intended to create the type of emotional attachments associated with nationality based citizenship.

'The de-coupling of nationality and citizenship opens the possibility, instead, of thinking of co-existing multiple demoi [which] invites individuals to see themselves as belonging simultaneously to two demoi, based critically on different subjective factors of identification.' Decoupling identity from place or territory is the key here, for though 'I may be a German national in the in-reaching strong sense of organic-cultural identification and sense of belongingness [I am] simultaneously a European citizen in terms of my European transnational affinities to shared values which transcend the ethno-national diversity. So much so, that in a range of areas of public life, I am willing to accept the legitimacy and authority of decisions adopted by my fellow European citizens in the realisation that in these areas I have given preference to choices made by my outreaching demos, rather than by my in-reaching demos. ... One nation, Indivisible Under God is not what Europe is about.'[116]

These are fine words, admirable sentiments, and they have some emotional and even intellectual appeal in a world where corrosive nationalism is still the harbinger of the sort of destructive competitiveness that has inflicted untold suffering on excluded minorities, or so called 'lesser' nations over Europe's long centuries. But the critical question here, as it always is for those concerned about practical politics, is agency. How to realise such a radical transformation in politics? To anyone versed in European or for that matter international history, the prospect for reimagining political identity, and on that basis for affecting such a dramatic shift in political allegiance seems far-fetched indeed.

The difficulties here are patent and not merely confined to changing mindsets after some three centuries of bellicose nationalism, replacing an emotionally resonant legacy and one still evident in, for instance, sports rivalry, with an inclusive and overarching political identity based entirely on new values about political identity, entirely different from those that have sustained the national polity. This is the extent of the challenge facing those who make this case, nothing less than a wholly new political culture to which post-nationalists, whether of a multi-cultural or a cosmopolitan outlook both aspire. Yet the Constitutional Treaty did little to realise these ideas, and the Lisbon Treaty that has replaced it even less.[117] The concept of European citizenship included in the final draft of the Constitution did not remotely begin to engage the challenges of connecting citizens in a common endeavour, let alone to instil in them a meaningful sense of common political purpose.

How and by what means might the idea of transnational citizenship be translated into practical politics? As we have seen, for realists this question is redundant, even subversive. Yet post-nationalists regard such a shift as both possible and desirable. Is there anything remotely feasible in what they prescribe? Are they being realistic, or is the very idea merely far-fetched? Certainly, some of those who propose a shift in the fabric of identity politics are by no means completely out of touch with political realities, nor unaware of the difficulties of altering both institutional and individual mindsets. And neither are things quite as static here as Eurosceptics might prefer. There is evidence of cultural shifts underway of the kind the post-national narrative prescribes, though these processes are immensely complicated, and if they occur at all, they will take time to work through human agencies, let alone to fundamentally reshape Europe's social structures and alter prevailing political instincts. Post-national commentaries that make this case are on altogether firmer ground when they propose practical measures designed to at least accelerate social and cultural change.

One such measure is to expand EU-derived rights conferred by the Union *per se* rather than by the member states. Furthermore, it needs to be a catalogue of rights that goes far beyond the limited rights already guaranteed in the Union's citizenship articles, and to include social and cultural rights, educational rights, basic welfare entitlements, access to EU public goods, direct access to justice at the EU level and so on. This, the post-national narrative claims, will not only give citizens greater access to rights *per se*, but crucially to different rights from those they presently enjoy as EU citizens. Moreover, rights that will facilitate the reimagining of political affiliation and allegiance, of who 'citizens' are or who they think they are, thereby enabling them to rethink their political allegiance on the basis of what they see as the principal source of their rights and welfare entitlements.

The assumption here is that change in the locus individual rights, and the personalisable public goods that follow from them, has potential for dramatically altering political allegiance. The rights-based approach is at least a start, plausible precisely because it is tried and tested, a way of changing citizens' perception of themselves and of their relations with the political community. This after all is how allegiance to the national polity was instilled during the state-building era in Western Europe after the French Revolution of 1789. Democratisation in the broadest sense, as gradual empowerment, access to justice and subsequently to public goods, was an important driver of this process, in as much as these public goods develop the citizens' sense of belonging to the national polity. The notion of the citizen as stakeholder did enhance the individual's sense of personal security through the receipt of welfare and by way of redistributive public policy. The resulting improvement in social status in turn underpinned public order and society, embedding the idea of the legitimate polity as the protector of life, liberty and property, with the national polity as the surest guarantor of personal safety and universal welfare.

None of these crucial linkages can be taken for granted even at the national level, for the process worked rather better in some European states than in others, at least in the early stages of the continent's political modernisation.[118] The question here is whether this same process of political socialisation can translate to the European polity *per se*, and if so how it might be realised. The Convention did give some consideration to finding means for reducing the EU's legitimacy deficit in just these terms. The historical linkage between access to justice and democratic rights, and deepening the citizen's sense of political obligation as a way of legitimating governance at the EU level were discussed by the working group on the Charter. In the event, however, caution prevailed, and an opportunity to reinforce the connection between the citizen and the Union in this crucial area was squandered. The Constitutional Treaty's provisions directly relating to citizenship (Part I, Title II, Article 1-10 relating to Union Law, and Part II incorporating into the treaty the Charter on Fundamental Rights, Title VI, Justice), patently failed to clarify the citizens' prospects for proper legal redress at the EU level.

Again, domestic priorities prevailed over other considerations, the political and judicial establishments in the member states having quite different priorities for the management of the Union's justice system. Citizens, too, have different levels of awareness, motivation and knowledge about how best to advance their claims to judicial protection under EU law. For whatever reason, EU law has yet to acquire the same significance as national law as a change agent, a means for reinforcing public allegiance to the European polity, as national agencies have done in Europe's historic nation states. The critical interface between ordinary plaintiffs and the EU justice system remains unduly constrained by 'the use of discretion, a phenomenon which the law is simply unable to monitor let alone track in an adequate and satisfactory manner'.[119]

The Constitutional Treaty did include some useful reforms designed to improve citizens' access to justice, for instance enhancing the rights of accused persons and the better alignment of criminal justice procedures/codes to ensure closer approximation of penalties and tariffs for particular offences throughout the Union. Less helpful in this regard, however, was the maintenance of restrictions on those entitled to 'stand' before the ECJ, restricting this right to litigants with a 'direct and individual concern'. And this despite the notable recommendation by Advocate-General Jacobs, in his evidence to the Convention, who proposed an altogether less restrictive definition of 'direct' and 'individual' concern in determining access to the Court.[120] Critics have pointed out that the present rules are merely self-defeating when measured against the commitment to deepen the sense of citizens' affiliation to the Union, for 'citizens must ultimately go to the courts to enforce their rights [and] if they cannot get timely justice from the court system because it is overloaded then fancy constitutional provisions protecting human rights are pointless'.[121]

The Constitutional Treaty did little overall, then, to improve the individual's access to the European courts, which continues to be determined for the most part by the domestic courts, where very different bureaucratic rules and public policy cultures determine who has access to the judicial system. There was rather less in the Constitutional Treaty, too, about reforming the European courts to enable them to cope better with the anticipated increase in their workload as a consequence of the proposed reforms in the area of fundamental rights. The complexity of these arrangements merely serves to confirm the citizens' sense of remoteness from justice at the EU level. Much the same can be said of the Convention's efforts to enhance the Union's role in citizens' sense of personal security.

## Freedom, justice and security

The Single Market has seen a substantial increase in cross-border movement, both economic activity and social transactions, which in turn has contributed to the harmonisation of national civil law codes. However, an EU 'area of justice' implies even greater harmonisation. The process began in earnest with the Maastricht Treaty, introducing Justice and Home Affairs (JHA) as the 'third pillar' of European Union, albeit a distinctly intergovernmental arrangement that includes policy pertaining to asylum, immigration and borders, judicial co-operation with regard to civil and criminal matters and police co-operation in countering terrorism, fraud, drug trafficking and cross-border crime. These are certainly matters that are central to the very idea of nation-statehood, directly affecting relations between citizens and their governments However, since these are all policy domains that impinge on national sovereignty, the retention of the unanimity procedure here was bound to make for difficulties in increasing the scope for co-operation.

The issue was revisited in the Amsterdam Treaty (1997), with the commitment to establish an area of freedom, security and justice: in effect, communitising what had formerly been exclusively intergovernmental aspects of immigration, asylum, border controls, visa policy and judicial co-operation in civil matters. There were also moves here to establish some common procedures between separate systems of criminal law in the EU, so as to improve the efficiency of the Union's courts, as well as to establish procedures to facilitate national police and public prosecution services to work more effectively together: for instance, setting up a common border guard for the Union to prevent illegal entry and to deter other illegal activities; agreement on common asylum and visa arrangements; and providing surer safeguards for individual rights, and to ensure the accountability of EU agencies.[122]

The heads of government returned to the issue at the Tampere Council (October 1999). The so-called Tampere agenda set deadlines for JHA reform, but by the time the Convention met in 2002 the Union had only partially achieved these targets. A perceptible threat from international terrorism even as they deliberated these issues, persuaded most EU political leaders that combating terrorism does require international as much as merely regional, let alone national action. Even so, words were rather easier to come by than concrete actions. Differences between the various national legal and policing regimes, to say nothing of acute domestic sensibilities about sharing information in an area associated both in the public and political mind with national security, delayed more effective co-operation.

At the Nice Council (2000) the heads of government, or at least most of them, did reaffirm a broad commitment to the Tampere agenda. But again, a sense of common purpose failed to materialise, not least precluded by the fact that for many member states, these issues are politically sensitive, and as part of the intergovernmental JHA pillar subject to unanimity. Another problem was that issues in this policy domain are dispersed across all three pillars, and as such complicated by the existence of quite different decisional procedures. Even when governments came round to accepting the need for greater commonality in a policy domain where nowadays no one government can on its own account ensure its national security, there was reticence about taking action, with a decision to delay the adoption of the unanimity procedure for a further five years, and even then only after unanimous agreement by all the member states.

Events continued to raise the profile of JHA on the Union's agenda. Governments were well aware of the growing threat from terrorism, rogue states and cross-border criminality. The events of September 11 2001 reinforced the message in spectacular fashion, a graphic illustration that even the world's most powerful state was not immune to what Chris Patten, then commissioner for external affairs, described as 'the dark side of globalisation'. The public's mood, too, was changing, *Eurobarometer* surveys showing increased public support for common action in the area of security and public order.[123] With international terrorism ever higher on the European Council's agenda, the justice ministers did find the political will to agree to a European arrest warrant, as well as adopting a firmer framework for dealing with the terrorist threat. Meeting in the aftermath of September 11, the Laeken Council could hardly avoid the issue. The member states were already increasing their own counter-terrorism measures and the Council responded likewise to 'frequent public calls for a greater EU role in justice and security, action against cross-border crime, control of migration flows and reception of asylum seekers and refugees from far-flung war zones'.[124]

A joint paper submitted by France and German (November 2000) had already made some proposals for action, *inter alia*: the abolition of the third pillar; introducing QMV after a transitional period for measures pertaining to police co-operation and to most aspects of judicial co-operation, with both the Commission and the member states having the right of initiative in policing issues; turning Eurojust into a fully-fledged public prosecutors' office; giving Europol a more secure legal treaty base to engage in cross-border investigations; making for easier co-ordination between Eurojust and Europol; agreeing rules to enable national police forces to operate in the territory of other member states, with controls over asylum and immigration imposed at EU external borders; setting a date for establishing a European border police service; and referring to 'harmonising' rather than merely 'approximating' criminal law. These proposals found their way into Convention deliberations on security policy. The idea here was to improve co-ordination of national security regimes throughout the Union. However, if the security agencies are to meet the current level of threat to public security from insidious and malevolent forces they will require even greater powers, for instance measures to ensure cross-border collaboration in the ever-sensitive domain of intelligence-gathering and -dissemination, and for joint-threat assessment, as well as for better co-ordination of national agencies and legal/investigative and intelligence-gathering/security procedure.

Anticipating resistance from countries less disposed to deeper integration in matters closely identified with national sovereignty, France and Germany had proposed a form of flexible integration under the enhanced co-operation procedure introduced in the Amsterdam Treaty. In effect, some member states would be permitted to engage in closer, or enhanced co-operation in these matters when fewer than eight member states had supported a proposed measure in the Council.[125] Some governments nevertheless had deep reservations about even this level of co-operation, and some but by no means all of these proposed measures found their way into the final agreement. The member states opted, for instance, for mutual recognition of each other's judicial decisions in the relevant areas, and similarly for recognition of differences in their respective trial procedures and punishment regimes, with approximation (advocated by the United Kingdom, Ireland and others) preferred to the more rigorous harmonisation of national procedures being proposed by France and Germany, supported by Belgium.

The Convention was bound to revisit these issues and the task fell to the working group on freedom, security and justice chaired by John Bruton, the former Irish *Taoiseach* (prime minister). Bruton saw this issue as going beyond 'merely' governments or professional experts, seeing rising public concern with security as an opportunity to reinforce the citizens' sense of a common predicament, to demonstrate the relevance of the Union to citizens 'in the most visible way'. Accordingly, Bruton informed the December 2002 plenary session that 'we are dealing here with crimes that affect people directly ... issues that need a response at the European level'.[126] Old habits die hard, however, with resistance from the usual quarters as the Convention faced the not inconsiderable challenge of communitising a policy domain still regarded by powerful voices in the Union as the exclusive preserve of the nation-state. The Convention did consider more radical proposals, for instance the prospects for the mutual recognition of criminal and civil judicial decisions, the application of QMV to most aspects of asylum and immigration policy and reinforcing the powers of Europol. What was actually discussed in the working group, and later in the praesidium was constrained, however, by persistent objections from some member states to anything that might undermine their authority in this most symbolic of policy domains.

The working group did, however, take up the Tampere proposal for defining criminal acts and appropriate penalties for such matters as trafficking in drugs or people and the sexual exploitation of minors. It also recommended the adoption of common rules of procedure for JHA, to be included in a single title in the Treaty, and to include: the principle of mutual recognition of judicial decisions, approximating aspects of national criminal law with a cross-border dimension, or for offences against EU policy such as counterfeiting the European currency, as well as common minimum standards to safeguard individual rights. There was broad agreement, too, that unanimity was an inappropriate decisional procedure for JHA policy in the enlarged Union, and accordingly the working group proposed QMV and co-decision for legislation relating to asylum, refugees and displaced persons, common asylum system and common immigration policy, whilst retaining unanimity for decisions on procedures for establishing agencies such as Europol and Eurojust. The group further proposed support measures and incentives (also subject to QMV and co-decision) so as to integrate legally resident third-country nationals. These recommendations were accepted by the praesidium and included in the first draft of JHA articles.

This represented progress, at least when measured against current policy and procedure, but there were those who doubted that even these measures would be enough to match the unprecedented challenge to EU security. Even the proposal to establish an internal security committee under the Council's direction so as to 'facilitate co-ordination of the actions of member states' competent authorities', was described by one source as little more than 'a toothless standing committee staffed by low-ranking ministerial officials'.[127] Some experts maintain that nothing less is required to meet the current threat level than a full-fledged European Security Committee chaired by the Council president, tasked with making thorough-going threat assessments, and with authority to co-ordinate the various national defence, law enforcement and security agencies, and backed up by better-co-ordinated training programmes.[128] There have already been some positive initiatives here, but bilateral and trilateral arrangements between police, customs and immigration authorities to jointly police border areas and arrangements remain for the time being outwith the EU framework. Meanwhile, the German government has taken its own initiative to establish a permanent office in Berlin to improve co-operation between EU land border guards.

These arrangements would be more effective, however, and would certainly signal more purposeful intent, if they had been established under the broad umbrella of the Schengen Accord. For though these *ad hoc* initiatives do represent an advance on what already happens in this policy domain, as Townshend sees it none of what has so far been agreed or delivered in this policy area remotely meets 'the step change that many think necessary'. As things now stand, the Treaty 'in its current form ... would not give the EU enough power to deliver the area of freedom, security and justice [for] Europe needs to do much more to address major cross-border issues such as crime and international terrorism'.[129] For those who take this view, the Constitutional Treaty hardly addressed the mounting challenges facing the Union in this critical policy domain. What is required instead, as they see it, is nothing less than 'to regulate migration and reform its judiciaries to cope with the creation of free movement and the resulting increase in cases with cross-border elements'. For 'these issues are beyond the ability of any individual member state to control', and though many EU leaders have admitted as much, political considerations remain their paramount consideration, with too 'many national governments ... unwilling to accept that addressing this situation will mean pooling more sovereignty at the EU level'.[130]

Even a common approach to the growing problem of immigration was in these proposals little more than an aspiration, notional co-operation compared with what is actually required in light of mounting regional and global population movements. There was, however, rather more progress on asylum policy. The abiding problem here is that the Union lacks effective policing arrangements, although the Schengen agreement is almost two decades old. There are those who claim that the very existence of Schengen has actually made it easier for international crime and terrorist activity to flourish, opening borders whilst border security, police organisation and criminal prosecution arrangements are still confined by national procedures that make for difficulties in the exchange of information and sharing criminal intelligence, or for conducting joint investigations and prosecutions. Again, these are of course highly sensitive matters, with powerful vested interests in the justice and interior ministries 'often amongst the most conservative members of society', and as such resistant to any reduction in national control of these matters.[131]

The changes proposed in the Constitutional Treaty would at least improve the prospects for a cogent and prospectively a more secure area of freedom, security and justice, by permitting only one procedure for JHA policy and with QMV as the norm for deciding matters pertaining to criminal justice and police co-operation. These proposed changes would for instance give the Union a modest capacity for setting minimum standards for court procedures and on the rules on evidence, though again subject to QMV. Yet even these relatively modest concessions to EU-wide legal standards were blocked by some governments, notably the United Kingdom, the Netherlands, Ireland, Denmark and Sweden, who preferred to retain unanimity for all matters pertaining to criminal justice.

Such resistance highlights the difficulties of implementing changes in this policy domain. These issues were sufficiently controversial to be revisited at the IGC, when the Italian presidency, responding to objections from the United Kingdom and Ireland on legal harmonisation, proposed an amendment to draft Article 3-172 permitting these two states to wield what amounts to a veto on any matter pertaining to their national legal systems. Although QMV was retained in principle, any member state that rejected the outcome of such a vote could appeal to the European Council to suspend or rescind the proposed legislation. And since this institution makes decisions on the basis of unanimity, any objection would more than likely be upheld. These obstacles to a common approach to EU security resurfaced in the 2007 IGC and have been carried over to the Lisbon Treaty.

The provision in the final draft of the Constitutional Treaty for facilitating mutual recognition of legal judgements and judicial decisions, for expediting police and judicial co-operation in criminal matters with a cross-border dimension, and likewise for framework laws to establish minimum rules for the definition of criminal offences and sanctions in areas of serious criminality (Article 3 – 271, new, ex Article 31.1, TEU) all touched a sensitive political nerve. Some states were determined to resist what they regarded as unwarranted intrusion into national discretion. So much so, that the final version of the Treaty added the telling phrase to Article 3-270.2, to the effect that: 'such rules shall take into account the differences between the legal traditions and systems of the Member States'. This is a reference to – more than that an accommodation of – concerns expressed by the British and Irish governments in the 2003/4 IGC, both countries with a common law tradition. The Article goes even further in accommodating national concerns, adding an entirely new paragraph (Article 3-270.3), confirming that: 'Where a member of the Council considers that a draft European framework law, as referred to in paragraph 2, would affect fundamental aspects of its criminal justice system, it may request that the draft framework law be referred to the European Council', in which case the co-decision procedure is suspended. An intergovernmental default position then comes into operation whereby, after four months of suspension and following discussions, the European Council may either refer the matter back to the Council of Ministers for consideration under co-decision, or it may otherwise request the Commission to redraft the proposal, thus nullifying the original proposal.

This is clearly a precautionary measure, a recourse for any member state that feels its national interests are threatened by a proposal in this politically sensitive policy domain. To safeguard against any outright stalling of integration, there is at least the provision for enhanced co-operation, enabling states that so wish to further integrate their policy in this area. Accordingly, where no action is taken on a proposed European framework law (Article 3-270.4), either 'by the European Council or if, within 12 months from the submission of a draft under paragraph 3 (b), the European framework law has not been adopted, and at least one third of the Member States wish to establish enhanced co-operation on the basis of the draft framework law concerned', they are authorised 'to proceed with enhanced co-operation'.

Meanwhile, the Convention's decision to simplify the legal basis for Europol would bring that institution within the treaty framework, a move designed to improve monitoring of these procedural innovations, although national parliaments would have the right to monitor its work. The intention here was to improve the co-ordination of the operations of the Union's border guards, essential in view of Eastern enlargement and the new, wholly unpredictable EU neighbourhood this has brought about. There was some progress, too, on common border controls and immigration policy, and on measures to counter serious cross-border crime, matters where the Union would acquire significant new powers from the member states. There would also be enhanced police co-operation, especially through Europol and the establishment of Eurojust, despite serious differences encountered in the Convention. The Treaty likewise permitted the establishment of the office of a European public prosecutor tasked with investigating and prosecuting serious cross-border crime, from terrorist outrages to serious fraud relating to EU expenditure, but only if every member state concurs, and with an open-ended deadline for taking such a step. Many, if not all, of these innovations are accommodated in the Lisbon Treaty.

The IGC revisited these proposals, the Italian presidency recommending that the prosecutor's office should (acting in conjunction with Europol) be confined to investigating and prosecuting only cases of fraud or other felonies relating directly to the Union and its institutions, thereby precluding the rather broader remit of cross-border crimes indicated in the draft treaty. Again there was predictable resistance from some member states, notably United Kingdom, Ireland, Sweden and Denmark, to conferring even limited authority on this office, concerned lest these tasks should grow by degrees to cover criminal law. This is a familiar, indeed a natural reflex by governments, but there were practical reasons for these objections, too, in as much as some EU states have a common law tradition, and for that reason legal harmonisation would impact disproportionately on their legal and criminal justice systems.

The Italian presidency again sought to reassure these particular countries by including in its own working version of the draft treaty a clause requiring EU agreements on criminal law to 'take into account' national differences. A provision added to the initial draft treaty (Article 3-276, new) confirmed the European Council's prerogative to take decisions with regard to enhancing co-operation between national and European agencies in those aspects of serious crime deemed to have a cross-border dimension. The most significant inclusion in the final version, however, was an additional clause confirming that it is the member states in their principal negotiating forum, the European Council, that shall determine the remit of the controversial office of European public prosecutor. Finally, despite agreement on the number and type of work-related visas, the Treaty avoided adopting an EU-wide quota system, with the member states retaining the right to determine access to their own labour markets.

## The glass half-empty or half-full?

The Constitutional Treaty did make some progress in this important policy domain, and one that some commentators see as indispensable for realising the citizen's most fundamental right: to be secure from threats to life, to enjoy security against malevolent forces bent on chaos and threatening Europe's civil order. Yet, despite lengthy deliberation in both the Convention and the IGC, there was no conclusive agreement about where authority should reside for resolving some of these critical issues. And this remains the case some five years later. To this extent the debate continues, with commentators expressing quite different opinions as to whether in this area of European policy the glass is half-full or half-empty.

A positive assessment of these developments would point to measures in the Constitutional Treaty that build on foundations already in place, such as proposals to abolish the pillarised system, to incorporate the Charter of Fundamental Rights, to increase QMV in most aspects of JHA policy – traditionally an intergovernmental domain – and to permit Parliament to take a more active role in legislation relating to JHA policy, thereby improving democratic scrutiny of an increasingly important and politically sensitive policy domain. Legislation here would have greater force, too, because applied by direct effect. All of this amounts to a significant advance in communitising policy, though it has to be said that progress on the ground has been much less than some *conventionnels* anticipated, not least because the member states retain the capacity either to dilute or block policy proposals. The unanimity procedure remains, for instance in agreeing any extension in the definition of border crimes. This is clearly a recipe for any member state so inclined to stall on any measure it deems to be detrimental to the national interest. Furthermore, it is the European Council rather than the Commission that would retain the right to define general legislative policy with regard to freedom, justice and internal security. Nor in these arrangements would the Commission have the exclusive right of initiative in criminal justice and police co-operation. National parliaments, too, would have the right to require the Commission to revisit any proposal deemed to be non-compliant with the subsidiarity principle, yet another constraint on effectively harmonising security and justice policy.

The *passerelle* clause was designed precisely to circumvent obstruction by a persistent minority of member states determined to delay policy changes. However, objections from some member states both to the *passerelle per se* and to the drive, as they saw it, to unduly communitise justice policy made the long-term impact of proposals in the JHA domain less than certain, even before the Constitutional Treaty ran into the sand. The final arbiter in this area is likely to be the ECJ, with its jurisdiction extended in these arrangements to cover justice and home affairs. The decision to incorporate the Charter of Fundamental Rights into the Constitutional Treaty, though qualified in the Lisbon Treaty, and the codification of other rights in EU law will certainly enhance the protection of individual rights and may give greater substance to European citizenship, though two states have negotiated an opt-out on this, and others, too, may well challenge what they or their legal authorities regard as peremptory action by the Court in such delicate matters.

The most pointed objection, however, to any suggestion that these developments imply a pan-European security community, is surely the fact that these matters, important for every EU citizen, were dealt with in the usual way, the customary trade-offs between political elites and vested interests, and with national interest as their paramount concern. Even where these important issues were discussed on the record and in the open, debate was still conducted in a coded and convoluted language, and as such simply passed most citizens by. The benefits of these reforms for the enhancement of individual rights, the protection of freedoms, for improving personal safety through co-ordination of security throughout the Union and better access to justice continue to elude the citizen. This, too, confirms the failure of political leaders, not so much to address citizens' basic concerns in these important matters, but to do so in language they can more readily understand.

## Social Europe and citizenship

Europe's nation-states secured their citizens' allegiance during the era of democratisation and nation-building by providing them with collective public goods: social insurance, welfare, education, public health services and so on.[132] Public goods were important for cementing political allegiance to the state, part of an implied contract between subjects or citizens and the polity, a particularly useful 'instrument of state-craft', and one that has long been 'employed in defining political communities and legitimating the structure of the state'.[133] The Constitutional Treaty hardly ventured into this critical policy domain, doing little to encourage the idea of EU public goods as an agency for social citizenship. Nor is it difficult to see why the idea of social citizenship has lagged behind its civil or political aspects at the European level. To a degree, this tardiness mirrors the sequential lag of social citizenship in Europe's nation-states. Political and civil rights, though momentous for making a liberal democratic political order after long centuries of tyranny and economic exploitation, are much contested, have far-reaching redistributive consequences as between social groups and economic interests, and are by their very nature controversial, even in societies where material resources are not especially scarce. As Klauson points out, social citizenship is more than a matter of rights, important though this is, but rather are 'a particular paradigm of distributional politics in advanced industrial welfare states'.[134]

Moreover, social rights are not equivalent rights, as are political and civil rights, the latter being 'indivisible and non-transferable rights belonging to individuals'.

To use economists' language, political rights are 'non-rival and non-excrudable', in as much as 'one person's civil or political right does not have a significant effect on the value of another's claim'.[135] Social rights are of a quite different order, they tend to be zero-sum not positive-sum, extending or withholding such rights usually implies winners and losers and they are more difficult to implement precisely because they give rise to political controversy, provoking resistance from those who perceive themselves to be net losers from public policy. And not just losers in the obvious sense of reduced social power but also of increased economic costs. Employers and organised business interests, for instance, are certainly more disposed to resist any extension of labour or social rights in the workplace, or enhanced welfare rights paid for from central taxation.

This much is obvious, and a familiar source of political controversy and ideological disputation in contemporary societies. But the right in public law to control one's own body or to exercise sexual freedom may just as readily provoke opposition from faith groups, or the right to enjoy clean air or uncontaminated food or all manner of non-material or post-material rights pursued by those ethical lobbies that trade in moral currency in this post-modern age. For this and for other cultural reasons, obstacles to the development of a transEuropean rights-based distributive polity remain formidable. These are after all acutely sensitive issues that go to the very core of the historical relationship between citizens and the nation-state. As such a viable, and above all an extensive EU welfare system, let alone a European moral order realised in common values, is unlikely for the foreseeable future, notwithstanding the impressive catalogue of social rights included in chapter 3 of the Charter of Fundamental Rights. For all these reasons, the EU does not have what we might call an implied welfare dimension. Rather, what is called 'social Europe' is shaped rather more by neo-liberal than by collectivist values. The intense competitive pressures of globalisation and acute demographic shifts such as ageing populations and increasing expectations about health care and education provision, to give just two notable examples, are factors that are challenging traditional models of social welfare in most EU member states.

Public anxieties about the welfare issue surfaced in the referendum campaigns in France, the Netherlands and elsewhere, and pollsters frequently cite this as a reason why so many EU citizens voted down the Constitutional Treaty.[136] The debate, not least in some leading EU member states, about affordable welfare and the rising costs to taxpayers and to national exchequers alike of 'generous' social provision has undoubtedly spilled over into the debate about EU welfare policy, further reducing the prospects for a comprehensive transnational welfare regime.[137] There is a view widely held by politicians and employers alike, even by politicians once ideologically predisposed to a welfare state fashioned in the conventional social-democratic/Christian democracy mould, that reflects neo-liberal and supply-side preferences rather more than Keynesian assumptions about the role (or as this school of thought once saw it, the 'duty') of government to stimulate demand by using welfare policy. Prohibitive costs and demographic shifts have made this notion of universal 'cradle to grave' provision simply unaffordable. Neo-liberal orthodoxy appeals to a business community exercised by what it sees as a rising tax burden and increased labour costs, damaging as they see it to competitiveness in global markets. Many *conventionnels*, too, saw the EU as, first and foremost, a free trade area, a single market more than a welfare community. The Common Commercial Policy and all that follows from it (the Lisbon process (2000) is the Union's latest response to the challenges of globalisation) has become a priority for many EU leaders in the drive to make Europe more competitive. Redistributive policies are a secondary consideration here, barely an afterthought to what are seen as more pressing concerns, and even then confined to the inadequately resourced structural, regional and cohesion policies.

According to this mindset, it is the member states that remain exclusively responsible for allocating public finances according to what they see as domestic priorities. Any idea of repeating at the EU level the practice of European nation-states a century or more back, of using welfare and other public goods for inculcating political allegiance, to reinforce political belonging, a sense of affective identity or patriotism through social citizenship is, on this reading of events, fanciful to say the least, and for some far-fetched. The most that can be expected of social policy at the EU level are those flanking measures necessary for a more efficient internal market. This limited objective is referred to in the founding treaties, with employment, social protection and cohesion defined as objectives of European construction.[138] By the time of the Amsterdam Treaty social policy had become more important in the Union's policy portfolio, a position confirmed in the Laeken Declarations which noted that 'citizens also want results in the fields of employment and combating poverty and social exclusion'.[139]

But this is as far as it goes. A European social dimension was developed so as to soften the impact of the free market on producers and consumers, but it was never intended even by the Commission who championed it to harmonise, let alone to replace national welfare regimes. Cohesion, reducing the grosser distortions between a wealthy core EU and a less prosperous periphery is fundamental to the Union's commitment to closer integration, but redistributive or social engineering certainly has no part in this policy. There was nothing remotely resembling a Europe-wide welfare state in these notional ideas of social cohesion, no commitment to redistributing scarce resources, and no agreement about universal criteria for 'social justice' or 'need'. The social dimension is intended at most to be limited compensation for the primacy the Union gives to private business and the pursuit of corporate wealth. The single market is still the driving force of the European project, its principal *raison d'être*.[140]

All of this became clear during the Convention. Social policy was not remotely a priority for Giscard, who resisted a call from some *conventionnels* during the 'listening phase' to establish a working group on social issues. His reasoning here was entirely pragmatic, concerned lest the issue should dissipate political energy, dividing the Convention along a left–right fault-line and thus bogging down debate in ideological wrangling, irrelevant as he saw it to the task at hand and squandering scarce time. A coalition of leftist *conventionnels* did launch a petition on the issue, and the praesidium duly relented, belatedly agreeing to set up a working group on social issues.[141] The working group did manage to reach broad agreement on some core social values, even on objectives to be included in the Treaty. However, this was little more than cosmetic, and significantly the draft articles presented after the first stage of deliberations excluded equality from the agreed values listed in Article 2.

The critical fact here is that there was no question of the Constitutional Treaty setting aside the national veto on social issues, though the open method of co-ordination is permitted as one means for more closely aligning the Union's quite different social welfare models, though only on the basis of 'soft' law or benchmarking.[142] The Constitutional Treaty gave the Union no additional powers with regard to social policy. Social security policy and workers' protection decisions would continue to require unanimity. A move to make decisions here subject to QMV was firmly resisted by Britain. And though benchmarking was to be encouraged on pension reform, the member states retained exclusive responsibility for pension policy.[143] There were some other limited policy innovations. Public concern about heath scares did persuade the working group to increase the Union's capacity to act on public health matters relating to cross-border pandemics and the threat of bio-terrorism.[144] Agreement was reached, too, about recognising the contribution of the social partners to the social dialogue. While attention to such worthy matters is long overdue, subsequent action suggests that it was little more than platitudinous, with few concrete policy initiatives. The member states settled instead for the notional benchmarking of minimum national standards in such matters as employment policy, social exclusion policy and macro-economic and fiscal management. Commitment to centrally financed and redistributive EU public goods as a route to a 'people's Europe' was simply not on the agenda, nor is it likely to be for the foreseeable future.

## Envoi

The challenge of reconciling a legal (rights-based) and a cultural- or identity-based EU citizenship was hardly resolved by the Constitutional Treaty. The critical question here is whether post-national citizenship, detaching political membership and identity from its traditional moorings in territorially bounded and historically rooted states, is feasible or fanciful. Political membership and identity continues for the time being to be confined to the national (and in some cases, the sub-national) polity. This much is not in doubt.

Whether this situation will persist is the pertinent question here. Political scientists are not (or should not be) ideologues, they should base their judgements on available evidence, and arrive at conclusions by inductive reasoning rather than abandoning reflexivity to subjective prejudice. On this basis, the prospect for change – even fundamental change – can be ruled neither in nor out, with its prospects at least to be considered as one possible outcome of the massive structural changes and cultural shifts that follow on from globalisation. A glance at any historical atlas shows that the continent's political geography has shifted more than once since the fall of the Roman empire, and it is not unreasonable to expect this map to change again in due course. Of course, a changed political landscape is by no means inevitable, and even if it does happen, its shape and trajectory is far from being predictable or easy to map. But change can never be discounted. What factors, then, might facilitate the remaking of European politics? The answer to that question lies to an extent in recognising that structural processes are what really what count for determining the shape and culture of politics, in Europe as elsewhere.

Political identity was always more constructed and contingent than it was predestined, a conditional outcome of circumstances, subject to cultural shifts, the exigencies of public policy and, not least, of action by determined – and usually self-interested – political elites. This was so during Europe's classic nation-building era from the late eighteenth century, and there is no reason to believe that these same factors have ceased to impact on politics: the pattern cast for perpetuity with the rise of the nation-state, history at an end, the final destination reached, as some commentators predicted at the end of the Cold War. At the same time, established national polities have proved remarkably durable, have survived, though much changed, despite being exposed to massive transformative forces from above and below during the past half-century.[145]

The nation-state does have distinct advantages over as yet untried alternatives, and it will take more than just radical mantras about the 'inevitability' of change, or even bold and imaginative leadership, to bring it about. Of course, political leadership is important for determining the conduct of public affairs, and it has always played a significant part in managing the outcomes and shaping the trajectory of change.[146] And political leadership in the EU in recent times has hardly been inspiring, let alone imaginative, barely concerned to reimagine the European polity in ways that would reduce its multiple democracy, legitimacy and constitutional deficits.

On the contrary, contemporary leaders have mostly failed to confront, never mind to redress citizens' anxieties, even on the more obvious matters, everything from taxation to public policy, and even less for managing security threats and dealing with the immensely disruptive consequences of globalisation. It was belated awareness amongst politicians of rising public anxieties that gave rise to the decision at Laeken to launch the Union on its constitutional trajectory. Yet the Convention and the IGC that followed it merely confirmed the widespread popular perception of remote governance, persistent democracy deficits and, more damaging still, a disconnected political class who prefer as they always have done to pursue their own narrow agenda, dealing with arcane matters of institutional power and the demarcation of competencies than with addressing the public's deeper concerns. Developing EU citizenship is one way of building bridges between politicians and public. But citizenship was simply not on the politicians' agenda, and this was why the Constitution stalled, and in the end failed to pass the democracy test, a crisis that in no small part was one of the politicians' own making.

To connect the EU polity with its citizens will certainly require purposeful and imaginative action by a political class that has so far shown little inclination to improve democracy or to embed legitimacy at the EU level, let alone to rethink the basis of individual membership beyond notional citizenship rights introduced at Maastricht, though barely developed since then.[147] Citizenship as identity rather than as notional rights, a sense of individual membership, is indispensable for legitimising EU governance. Without it the Union will be on altogether weaker ground to meet current challenges, to confront the difficult choices that lie ahead. As Beetham and Lord see this challenge: 'It will be hard to remove the need for some kind of political identity altogether. The Union may need to make substantial allocations of political values if it is to meet the performance requirements of legitimacy. It will often need to override the nation states with all their historically accumulated authority.'[148] Convincing citizens of the need to rethink governance arrangements that have been in place for a century and more will be a difficult task, but by no means an impossible one. Purposive constitutional endeavour has a significant part to play in responding to these challenges, and in the process laying firmer foundations for a European polity than presently exist, for 'the more such a Euroconstitutionalism … comes to shape the rules that govern economy and society, the more the public may learn to differentiate between actions that originate at the two levels of government, so making it more difficult to secure citizen co-operation by disguising Union policies as national policies mediated through domestic institutions. Some may also begin to argue that the Union cannot pretend to draw its legitimacy from the very units that it so frequently overrides.'[149]

Citizenship is critical for this process, for convincing the public that they too are part of the European project, the only acceptable fount of its legitimacy. The Convention's paltry efforts to address this important issue hardly inspires confidence, yet the failure to bring citizens closer to the European polity is by no means the end of the matter. Change is not merely possible, but sooner or later unavoidable. The key here, as it always is at critical historical junctures, is bold and no less courageous leadership. And the matter is altogether more urgent now than it was even when Maastricht first broached the idea of EU citizenship. Time was when the excuse for politicians' disregard for democracy in the EU, that they had more pressing policy priorities to deal with, was just about acceptable as an alibi for complacency or inaction. This convenient excuse is no longer admissible. For what could be a more urgent priority for those who manage the Union's affairs than addressing the shortfall in legitimacy, finding ways of engaging the people with a project that impacts on both their immediate concerns and their longer-term interests across the range of public policy?[150]

The crisis over the European Constitution shows that the EU can no longer rely on benign public indifference, the 'permissive consensus' of the foundational period, that degree of ingrained deference to governors that allowed the founding fathers to simply get on with the task of 'building Europe'.[151] These are more turbulent times, and citizens are less trusting of authority, more cynical about politics; they demand reassurance from politicians about where the European project is heading, how it is being managed and for whose benefit. To ignore the public in these fast-changing times is to risk deeply corrosive cynicism, and no less to put at risk what has been achieved so far.

# 9 The EU and the new international order

## And some have greatness thrust upon them: managing external policy

Constitution-making is primarily about mapping power in a polity and establishing the contractual bonds of mutual obligation between people and government. But constitutional politics is also about promoting the polity's standing and confirming its legal status in the wider world.[1] The EU is no exception, though it has not always been concerned about its international role. The Community's founders were preoccupied far more with laying the foundations of an efficient common market than with its place in international affairs, and in the early years foreign affairs in the usual sense was excluded from its policy remit. Over time, the idea of the EU as an international actor has acquired greater salience. Even 'common markets' trade with third parties, and commercial matters have an international dimension. Trade policy was never confined to just the Common Market, it always had a significant international dimension, and especially so in today's world, and the same can be said of the Union's policy on international development.

Many of the Union's supposedly 'internal' policies, too, whether monetary and fiscal affairs, macro-economic management, labour market regulation or for that matter immigration, asylum policy, the environment, research and development and rules on inward investment, are matters regulated by international protocols and agreements. The impact of international events has accelerated the EU's role as an international actor, not least America's decision in 1971 to abandon the Bretton Woods machinery for managing international macro-economic policy, followed soon after by the diplomatic fall-out from the oil price hike, a consequence of the Arab–Israeli conflict. These events and subsequent global crises have impacted on the Community, and its political leaders were persuaded accordingly to respond by adopting more formal procedures for co-ordinating their external actions, beginning with European Political Co-operation (EPC).[2]

Progress was nevertheless slow in the development of external policy, and the Community struggled to find a balance between feasible co-operation and persistent and quite separate national interests. Even so, in a friable world co-operation has proved advantageous, not least for balancing member states' distinctive national interests. The Single European Act (1986) established a secretariat in Brussels to assist the country currently managing the Council presidency to better co-ordinate EPC. The Maastricht Treaty (1992) finally brought political co-operation within the ambit of the European Union, though keeping it quite separate from the Community's supranational order by locating it as the second (CFSP) pillar of the Union. Consequently, any initiatives or decisions made under these arrangements were wholly intergovernmental, the External Relations Council operating according to the unanimity procedure. The Amsterdam Treaty (1997) went further, appointing a high representative for foreign and security policy, a post occupied since 1999 by Javier Solana, the former Spanish foreign minister and former Secretary-General of NATO. The incumbent of this EU office is designated as Secretary-General of the Council of Ministers and the Secretary-General of the WEU. Yet the sensitivity of foreign policy matters for most member states ensured that this office is located in the Council rather than the Commission, reaffirming the intention of the leading governments to keep supranationalism at bay.

Although the Community was by no means a major player in global politics, EPC did coincide with an increase in its influence in international affairs, for instance through its contribution to the management of some awkward security issues in the 'near abroad' in Macedonia, in Serbia-Montenegro, as well as making a positive contribution to international efforts to stabilise the western Balkans region. The EU has become involved, too, in international efforts further afield, not least persuading Washington and the principal regional actors to embrace the so-called Middle East 'road map' to peace. Over time, the EU has become a significant player in some other important multilateral initiatives, from taking the lead on the Kyoto Treaty and in the World Trade Organization's Doha trade round, to the establishment of an international criminal court.[3]

External policy in the broadest sense of the term was bound to figure in Community politics, notwithstanding the founders' reticence about making foreign policy a matter for the treaties. The very fact that the EC/EU is a major force in world trade has boosted its international standing with other global actors, though this has more to do with commerce than with military prowess or security policy.[4] By any standards, the EU is a major international actor, the world's largest trading regime, with a 20 per cent share of world trade putting it at least on a par with the USA. And it is the pre-eminent force in global financial and related service industries, as well as being the principal source of international development aid, with the Commission playing a central role in managing this significant aspect of international policy. All of this guarantees the Union international standing, though more as a civil or 'soft' power, with its role in world trade not remotely matched by its modest role in global security arrangements. Yet even here things are changing as new and growing threats to international stability, whether from international terrorism or rogue states both within the area and in the near abroad have obliged the EU to respond. Part of that response has been to develop more effective, because better-co-ordinated actions to deal with these immanent challenges to European security.[5]

The Convention duly acknowledged the growing importance of the security issue in the post-Cold War world, one prominent *conventionnel* summarising the imperative for a more convincing response to unprecedented menace as follows:

Today, an effective security policy requires more than just defending the borders of a country against invaders with military force. The true security risks in Europe today are not about invasions threatening the territorial integrity of nations. They are about problems that cannot be solved within the confines of national sovereignty alone. We have seen new types of threats: increasing environmental problems, the dangers of nuclear disasters, the risks involved in decommissioning nuclear weapons, the spread of weapons of mass destruction, organised crime, illicit arms dealing, people smuggling, drug trafficking, genocide, violence spreading from dissolving states, floods of refugees, minority conflicts and the vulnerability of infrastructures and information networks. These problems have no regard for international borders; they are universal. They cannot be combated by military alliances and their security guarantees, and there is no point in declaring oneself neutral with regard to them ... Sustainable security can only be based on close co-operation.[6]

Security policy is hardly a new concern for the EU. It has been there almost from the start, though as an accompaniment, a scherzo to the main symphony, and admittedly played *capriccio*, or on occasions *a capella* by those who intended to make a 'mere' market into a political union, and for some federalists potentially a state *manqué*. The Monnet/Pleven plan for a European Defence Community was introduced even before the founder members had properly come to terms with the impact of the Coal and Steel Community, though it was defeated after four years of discussion, and significantly for the future status of this issue defeated by a member state determined to demarcate the boundary between 'appropriate' supranational co-operation on functional matters and national sovereignty in matters of high politics. The issue faded but never entirely disappeared from the federalist agenda, and it was eventually revived as the Community grappled with new international challenges, finally facing up to the issue raised by the then West German chancellor, Willy Brandt, when he unfavourably compared the Community's position as an economic giant with its negligible status as a political 'pygmy' in world affairs.[7]

The issue has been high on the EC/EU's agenda ever since. And there have been some changes in the Union's capacity for exerting influence beyond its borders since Brandt challenged his contemporaries to confront the discrepancy between the Community's impact on international trade and its relative lack of clout in security politics. The most significant development here came with the sudden end to the Cold War, and the convergence of what is usually described as the new world order, an arrangement that has struggled to fill the vacuum left by the disappearance of familiar certainties represented by ideological polarity between communism and capitalism, or east versus west. Since that historic shift in the balance of international (and no less, of ideological) power, the EU has been obliged to address the security policy as remorseless change has brought new and mostly disruptive forces into play, and forces that pose unprecedented threats to both regional and global security.[8]

The EU can claim some achievements in its conduct of international relations even in these challenging times, though the very fact that it has been required by these events to fashion a role in international politics continues to raise controversy about what is an appropriate role for a non-state actor in a policy domain long regarded as the exclusive preserve of sovereign states. Two issues in particular have featured in this debate. One concerns the broadly normative question of whether an international regime that is clearly not a state has any business intervening in the field of foreign and security policy. The other is essentially practical: how and by what means the EU should conduct itself in international relations. Since the early 1970s there has been general agreement that the EU is indeed an international actor, but this fact in itself has not resolved these issues, and for this reason they were bound to figure in the Convention's deliberations. The practical question has proved no less challenging for the Union than the normative one, and is a more immediate question in so far as there was general acceptance that the Union would by now continue to play a role in the conduct of global affairs, the misgivings of some of its member states notwithstanding.

The fact that the EU is not a state has always been a handicap to the Union in its capacity to operate in the international domain. Measured against the exacting standards that apply to the making and conduct of competent foreign and security policy in modern nation-states, the EU is generally found wanting, unable to exert quite the level of influence 'abroad' commensurate with its economic weight, and certainly less than the sum of its most powerful member states acting on their own initiative. The problem here was aptly summarised in what has become known as the 'Kissinger question', when the then American secretary of state in the Nixon Administration inquired 'who' in the EC a world leader should contact in the event of an international crisis, in effect who could authoritatively speak for 'Europe'. This question has become more urgent, given the novel challenges to the international order that followed the abrupt collapse of the Soviet Union, and with it the end of a predictable world order based on Cold War bipolarity. The EU was suddenly confronted by altogether new threats, but also by new opportunities to shape the emerging international system, the prospect as some saw it for the Union finally to punch its weight in global affairs.

The persistent problem for the EU has been how to co-ordinate its various national responses to an increasingly mutable international system. This was bound to be controversial for a polity consisting of nation-states, each with its own preferences and national interests with regard to foreign and security policy. The member states have resisted harmonising what might be called 'foreign policy', preferring instead to marginalise the role of the supranational institutions (Commission, Parliament and Court), and to keep the management of policy in their own hands, whilst looking for ways to improve co-operation. In matters such as trade policy where the Community does have competence under the treaties, the member states have conceded some discretion to the Commission, though shared competency has made the procedures for managing external affairs complicated, if not confused. The 'solution' to separate the management of external policy – the Council retaining control of conventional diplomacy, whereas the Commission manages external economic and trade relations – was in the circumstances a necessary compromise. But it was hardly one designed to ensure that the Union would pursue cogent external relations or present a consistent face to the world.

Under these arrangements, the Union has a high representative for foreign and security policy who remains accountable to the Council, whereas the commissioner for external affairs reports directly to the Commission. And though the present and recent incumbents of these offices, Javier Solana and Chris Patten and Benita Ferrero-Waldner, the former Austrian foreign minister, have developed good working relations, this bifurcated structure has tended to give the impression to outsiders, as one seasoned commentator sees it, of being 'inherently unstable', with all the attendant risks of 'turf wars and large disparities in culture and financial resources between the low-budget, fast moving operation of the high representative and the very well endowed but lumbering Commission external affairs directorate'.[9]

When the Convention reviewed this issue there was more at stake, however, than merely tidying up muddled procedures. The debate about commonality of approach, or what has been called 'actorness', in this acutely sensitive policy domain touched on a parallel debate, one that goes to the heart of the ideological wrangle over the meaning of European integration. The very idea of establishing formal procedures for managing policy that has long been the exclusive and jealously guarded preserve of the nation-state was bound to provoke objections, a fact acknowledged by the first incumbent of the new foreign policy office.[10] The matter is far from being resolved. Co-operation on external policy as outlined in the Maastricht Treaty was by no means intended to harmonise policy, but amounted merely to agreement to consult before making a response or taking any action. The European Council sets the policy agenda and the Council of Ministers, guided by the presidency, manages day-to-day affairs, with the High Representative employed in the capacity of a plenipotentiary, his actions subject to the usual constraints of balancing the competing and sometimes opposing national interests of the member states. The Commission's role – the one EU institution with a commitment to what at least it sees as a 'European' interest, and with singular capacity for operating in external affairs – was deliberately constrained by governments, some would even say marginalised by them, its role confined for the most part to managing the modest CFSP budget.

By the time the Union's leaders met at Laeken the world was changing and fast, and they responded by acknowledging a need for the Union to play a more energetic international role. The Council mandated the Convention to look at ways to make the Union 'a stabilising factor and a model in the new, multi-polar world … a power resolutely doing battle against all violence, all terror and all fanaticism, but which would not turn a blind eye to the world's heartrending injustices … a power seeking to set globalisation within a moral framework, in other words to anchor it in solidarity and sustainable development'.[11] The Convention chose to interpret this rhetoric as a mandate for increasing the Union's capacity for taking action 'abroad', encouraged in this by a marked shift in public opinion, whereby views on the rising significance of security issues were undoubtedly influenced by the terrible events of 9/11. The *Eurobarometer* 58 survey (autumn 2002) found, for instance, that some 67 per cent of respondents agreed with the view that there should be 'one common foreign policy among member states', with

73 per cent endorsing a common defence and security policy.[12] Of course, support levels varied as between the member states, with higher levels recorded in Italy, Luxembourg and Greece than in Finland, Sweden and Ireland, but only in Britain was a majority of public opinion opposed to the closer integration of external policy.[13] A special poll commissioned by Giscard and published in April 2003 likewise found that some 63 per cent of EU citizens now endorsed a common approach to foreign policy, with 71 per cent backing a common defence policy. The need for a credible European response was merely increased by the spectacle of the leading states falling out over the latest threat to international peace, the crisis over Iraq.

## Fall-out over Iraq

The Iraq crisis (2003) exposed the limitations of the EU as an effective global actor.[14] The gathering crisis overshadowed the Convention from the outset, and despite the best efforts of the foreign ministers to avoid discussing Iraq precisely to minimise Franco-British differences, these grew wider as events unfolded. The Anglo-French fall-out, though disruptive and deeply disappointing to those who preferred the EU to adopt a united front on the issue, was hardly unexpected. More disconcerting than the 'unwillingness, particularly of the larger member states, to discuss and manage their differences or to minimise the damage from following different points of view', was the rift between Paris and those accession countries that supported Washington's position.[15] The rights and wrongs of the conflict were less the issue here than the perception of these accession countries that their voice was discounted, even disparaged by France and the other EU15 states opposed to the war. What seemed to the newcomers barely disguised intolerance became outright hostility when neither France nor Germany saw fit to consult with them, or for that matter with any other EU country, before issuing a stinging public rebuke to American policy. Secretary for Defense Donald Rumsfeld responded in kind, no doubt content to widen the rift in EU ranks when he referred to the fall-out as one between 'old' and 'new' Europe, code for a schism between America's critics and supporters.

Fault here was by no means all on one side. Those EU states that took Washington's part in what was soon a crisis of global proportions also forbore to consult, either with the Greek presidency or with the Union's high representative before – and this only shortly after the General Affairs and External Relations Council had adopted a 'common' EU position on the developing crisis – signing a letter at the instigation of the British and Spanish prime ministers and published in the *Wall Street Journal*. The letter was endorsed by the leaders of five EU15 states (the United Kingdom, Spain, Italy, Portugal and Denmark) and by three candidate countries (Poland, the Czech Republic and Hungary) and endorsed Washington's decision to rid Iraq of what turned out to be fictive 'weapons of mass destruction'.[16] This untimely intervention was followed in turn by a statement from the so-called 'Vilnius Ten', again supporting the Atlanticist position. This too provoked, in what was fast becoming an acrimonious cycle of accusation and counter-accusation, an intemperate reaction by French President Jacques Chirac, a barely concealed threat no less to those candidate states that supported the Anglo-American position on Iraq, and further confirmation of the Union's disarray. More than that, these rifts revealed the Union's diplomatic impotence, a fact underlined by High Representative Solana's studied inaction, the failure of his office to do anything that remotely resembled effective intervention, diplomatic inertia that was echoed from the office of External Commissioner Chris Patten. The Greek presidency did make a token proposal for an emergency EU summit, but in vain. It seemed then that at the first sign of crisis in international affairs old instincts, the familiar reflexes of European statecraft, came to the fore, with 'a complete lack of political interest in either undertaking a basic minimum of communication or co-ordination with European partners'.[17]

The issue was deeply divisive, even corrosive of trust, widening existing fissures and opening new ones, not least between some EU15 states and some newcomers. It confirmed to the world at large the Union's limitations as an international actor, at least in matters of security policy. Iraq was an object lesson to *convention-nels* on the difficulties of realising effective European external policy, yet a stark reminder, too, as if one was needed, of the costs of failing to respond effectively to critical international issues, spurring the Convention to look for ways to improve co-ordination of foreign and security policy. To this extent, though it was inconvenient, the crisis was also timely, highlighting long-standing differences and difficulties, and an incentive to those *conventionnels* determined to raise the EU's international game.[18] As one EU diplomat has observed: 'It is not fashionable to say it but the war in Iraq concentrated our minds. It showed that the EU had zero influence if its member-states do not pull together. It showed too why we had to set our strategic objectives ahead of enlargement.'[19] In one sense the crisis over Iraq was a low point, yet all was far from unremitting gloom. For Iraq served as a wake-up call, a reminder of how much still has to be done if the EU is to stake a claim to be a convincing international actor. As such, these events injected a renewed sense of realism into the debate on foreign policy, bringing to an end any prospect for a pan-European policy, at least for the foreseeable future.[20]

Meanwhile, the Union struggled to cope with the diplomatic fall-out. The second Gulf War revealed abiding divisions, and not only on the substantive issue. As the crisis deepened the French government grew increasingly pessimistic about the prospects for a viable common foreign policy, though President Chirac stayed on-message, maintaining that the very fact of deep differences over Iraq might somehow bring about 'repentance' by those member states supposedly 'out of step' with the majority of European political and public opinion. Chirac was motivated here less by the search for a common denominator between different national preferences on Iraq than he was by an instinct familiar in previous incumbents of his office, the Gaullist ambition to bring Europe behind a policy of greater independence from Washington, an altogether more conditional Atlanticism. Chirac, indeed France's political establishment *per se*, saw the crisis as nothing less than a defining moment, and one that offered France its 'last and best chance to build a European foreign policy construction in which it can expect to predominate, and which would be independent of the USA, and to create structures, whether within the EU or parallel, which would be intergovernmental in nature and limited to like-minded states'.[21]

The German foreign minister, Joschka Fischer, whose ideological disposition was rather closer to Kant than Kaisers, nevertheless endorsed Chirac's position, though for altogether different reasons, convinced that it offered the best prospect for realising a pan-European foreign policy. Fischer was moved here far less by visceral anti-Americanism than by his own principled conviction that the Iraq debacle clearly showed that a common European foreign policy was long overdue. And he certainly had a point. The 1990s had seen some convergence between the member states in their responses to the world's troubled regions, notably the Middle East and after a shaky start even in the western Balkans, as well as progress in co-ordinating EU strategy on international trade policy.[22] Intermittent, not to say tentative movement towards closer co-operation in external affairs was suddenly checked by the fall-out over Iraq.

In the event, the cracks were duly papered over and momentum just about recovered, and the prospects for co-operation were enhanced by the Convention's generally positive review of CFSP. A clause inserted in the Constitutional Treaty committed the Union to developing clearer strategic priorities ahead of enlargement, and Solana was mandated to draft an EU security strategy to include both an updated threat assessment and to recommend appropriate multilateral responses. Solana's office drafted the document, eventually presented to the Union's leaders at the Thessaloniki summit, where it received a mixed press. With some justification, for this was hardly a convincing response to current challenges, notwithstanding action by the European institutions and many of the member states to define some shared strategic objectives.

Critical questions remain unresolved, those very questions that have overshadowed CFSP from the outset: in particular, where authority should reside for drafting external policy, and, not least, how to phrase the key reference in the policy to the 'legitimate use of force' as a credible policy instrument. These critical issues remain as contentious as ever they were. On the one hand, the very fact that the Union could address the issue as part of its constitutional make-over represents a marked advance on what had gone before. The review was certainly welcomed by Europe's foreign policy establishments and by Americans, too, as an expression of a 'new realism', and even as a 'sign of the maturing of the [transAtlantic] relationship'.[23] On the other hand, prioritising foreign policy objectives is as problematic as ever for a union of nation-states, each one with quite different policy preferences. The delicate matter of sovereignty at the centre of this issue remains as the principal bone of contention, compounded in some cases by age-old differences as to national priorities.

The security strategy also figured on the Convention's agenda, unavoidably so as the world grows ever more turbulent and threats to peace proliferate. This was bound to be more controversial even than foreign policy co-ordination. Surprisingly, the Convention made more progress here than might have been anticipated. As one commentator sees it, the strategy document that eventually ensued from

Solana's office struck just about the right balance between a familiar wish-list and practicalities. Above all, it resisted 'the EU's penchant for producing endless shopping lists of "key issues"'. And though 'it rightly mentions global warming, energy security and other regional crises', there was 'a helpful focus on the three main threats to European security: terrorism, WMD proliferation and the nexus of failed states and organised crime'. Furthermore, 'the document goes on to highlight three priorities: extending the zone of peace around Europe; promoting "effective multilateralism"; and countering the new security threats'.[24] The strategy paper was a positive outcome in another sense, too, in as much as its 'most important political message was its repudiation of the traditional view that the EU believes only in deploying "soft power" tools such as economic aid, trade or diplomatic pressure and enticements'.[25]

This is positive as far as it goes, and especially so in view of the ill feeling stirred by the fall-out over Iraq. At the same time, it hardly amounts to a significant shift in the capacity, let alone the capability for delivering a more co-ordinated external policy. The member states remain as the ultimate source of political authority, and not least the principal resource base for the material capability required for policy delivery on the ground. And though the responsibility for the day-to-day management of what passes for EU common external policy would, under these arrangements, pass to an entirely new common actor, the critical issues of policy management and delivery of common EU external policy remain largely unresolved.[26] This much became apparent during Convention deliberations on the management of external policy.

## Managing external policy

The praesidium responded positively if somewhat charily to the prospects for more effective external policy.[27] Caution was understandable in view of the Iraq conflict, and it likewise reflected deep-seated ideological differences between supranationalists and those opposed to integration in a policy domain traditionally the preserve of the nation-state. These differences were bound to surface in the working group on external relations and defence. Integrationists, supported by the Commission, wanted to extend the Community method to common foreign and security policy. A Commission paper submitted in May 2002 proposed that the high representative, accountable exclusively to the Council under current arrangements, should be absorbed into the Commission.

On the other side of the debate, those determined to curb Commission ambitions in this sensitive area preferred merely to improve co-ordination between the external affairs commissioner and the high representative for foreign and security policy. This issue was as ideologically charged as ever, though there was at least acceptance on both sides that compromise was required to avoid deadlock. It was agreed to improve the capacity for co-operation on external policy, prompted in no small measure by a growing realisation that the EU could no longer count on the extent of American security cover available during the Cold War. The passing of the Cold War and with it the end of bipolarity ushered in a new era of hyper-power unilateralism, the reorientation of Washington's strategic priorities. And this in turn required a more nuanced EU response to international relations and no less to security policy. With this realisation came acceptance, albeit more grudging in some quarters than in others, that the EU could no longer opt out of serious policy-planning for regional security, nor avoid its 'share' of the responsibility for managing the new and increasingly turbulent international order.

There was a basis for agreement here, not least because both the current threat assessment and the definition of 'appropriate instruments' for delivering effective security in Europe are now less closely connected with the employment of hard power, particularly the use of weaponry, than was the case during the Cold War. Soft power instruments are widely regarded as more appropriate for pursuing security and foreign policy goals, and their deployment is less controversial. The experience of European integration is itself an object lesson in the successful application of soft power for political ends, 'a highly successful example of conflict resolution through integration', with a capacity for dealing with systemic threats and challenges 'in a transparent and fluid manner, rather than through the familiar "trench warfare" of intergovernmental negotiations and backroom deals'.[28] This fact alone has reduced resistance all round to making a more positive response on this issue.

The working group came up with an agenda consisting of five key points: procedures for defining common interests; the requirement for greater consistency in the management of external policy, in view of the plethora of available policy instruments; more efficient decision-making procedures; assimilating the experience of the high representative's office for policy coherence; and institutional changes to enhance the Union's international standing. The working group's chairman, Jean-Luc Dehaene, capitalised on the widespread realisation even amongst unremitting intergovernmentalists, that the Union should take greater responsibility for the management of post-Cold War international relations. Accordingly, he published a paper that sought to reconcile quite different philosophical positions on this issue. Dehaene's report confirmed on the one hand what every realist knew would be the baseline for common action, that CFSP must remain as an intergovernmental domain, with the European Council as the principal locus for managing external policy. However, the report did acknowledge the need for a Community dimension in external policy, that feasible common policy in any field should be more than merely the sum of different national interests.

The Convention followed Dehaene's lead, focusing as much on means as on ends, ways to improve policy co-ordination by reforming current and rather feeble decision-making procedures, acknowledging that this much at least is the first requirement for making progress. For though the Union has acquired a battery of policy instruments for managing external affairs, so far these have lacked cogency, they are not sufficiently 'joined up' in a way that makes for coherent and thus for convincing policy, for the EU countries themselves and those 'abroad'. With the likely consequence that 'the existing and amended provisions will not create a regime sufficiently strong to induce governments and diplomats to translate the constitutional norms into everyday practice'.[29]

What is missing here are means for better co-ordination of the Union's portfolio of external policies, to ensure proximity or better 'match' between policies on aid, trade, migration and security at the Union's external borders. The particular instruments for delivering these policies are compartmentalised, with decisions 'made in separate fora by different ministers and too often with conflicting objectives'.[30] The preferred solution for improved policy co-ordination and the principal innovation (on CFSP) in the Constitutional Treaty was the decision to merge the separate Council and Commission roles into one European external representative, in effect to install a foreign-policy supremo. This idea is hardly new and has been on the EU's agenda for some time. What was new, however, is that this proposal received strong backing from the working group on external action, supported by other influential voices, Chris Patten, the commissioner for external relations, amongst them, who argued as follows: that for the Union 'to fulfil our common ambitions, we need to show third countries that they are dealing with a single figure better able to muster the backing and resources of member states and the EU as a whole [for] the only credible alternative would be to revert to something like the status quo [and while] that would be no disaster ... it would be a failure of ambition'.[31]

This was in its way a belated answer to the eponymous Kissinger question, promoting the current office of high representative to the Union's foreign minister, charged with managing security policy, utilising both civilian 'soft' and, albeit rarely, 'hard' power and even military capabilities to achieve some common policy goals.[32] The Commission, in what critics saw as a barely disguised bid for greater influence in a policy domain where its role has been resisted by leading member states since the onset of EPC, proposed combining the office of the high representative with the Commission's external role. This provoked predictable opposition from the British Government's representative, Peter Hain, notably at the December 2002 plenary. Hain was unconvinced about so-called 'double-hatting', and wondered how inevitable conflicts of interest – and just as much the differences of organisational ethos – between the Council and Commission might be mediated. He was far from convinced that this solution would improve policy coherence, or indeed how a commissioner could possibly chair discussions on security and defence, matters that are critical for promoting national interests. Similar objections were raised by other representatives of foreign policy establishments, including De Villepin (France), Alfonso Dastis (Spain), and Lena Hejm Wallen (Sweden). The working group proposed, nevertheless, to give this office 'a right of initiative in crisis management matters', and in certain instances, even the capacity to make decisions on his/her own account.[33]

These recommendations were incorporated into the Constitutional Treaty (Article 1-41.1), to the effect that the common security and defence policy 'shall provide the Union with an operational capacity drawing on civil and military assets'. Furthermore, 'the Union may use them on missions outside the Union for peacekeeping, conflict prevention and strengthening international security in accordance with the principles of the United Nations Charter [and] the performance of these tasks shall be undertaken using capabilities provided by the member states'. Significant here is a notable amendment to the Convention's earlier version of the Treaty that made reference to the implementation of the common foreign and security policy, with the omission in the final version of the clause to the effect that 'the Court of Justice shall have jurisdiction to monitor compliance with this Article'. This belated revision certainly removes a potential source of supranational pressure from a policy domain many member states regard unequivocally as a matter for governments rather than for the Union. And it was a compromise indispensable for overcoming rooted objections from some leading governments, including the United Kingdom.

The same intergovernmental preference is apparent in the Treaty's reference to international agreements. Where such agreements relate principally or exclusively to the common foreign and security policy, the Commission or the Union's foreign minister are required to submit recommendations to the Council. The Council would then adopt a European decision 'authorising the opening of negotiations'. The revised version of the Constitution did add the proviso, however, that depending on the subject of the envisaged agreement the Council shall nominate the Union negotiator or leader of the negotiating team (Article 3-325.3 – ex article 300, TEC). This addendum clearly reinforced the Council's control over this delicate and potentially problematic aspect of international negotiations.

## Answering the Kissinger question? A foreign minister for Europe

What is at stake on this issue is more than merely differences over substantive policy, but rather competing ideas about the appropriate locus of political power in the Union, and indeed about the meaning of European integration *per se*. These differences were played out in the manoeuvring over the office of EU foreign minister. The Commission had proposed combining the offices of the high representative with that of the commissioner for external policy, though the British representative, Peter Hain, informed the December 2003 plenary of his government's opposition to 'double-hatting' on the grounds that this would not make for cogent policy. Even France, though committed to closer co-operation in external policy, was reluctant to endorse any changes that might enhance the status of the High Representative in this critical matter at the expense of the member states. The outcome was a compromise, a familiar trade-off between various national bargaining positions, most notably those of the leading member states. There was strong support from Germany for merging the two existing external offices, notably from its radical foreign minister, Joschka Fisher, who favoured communitising foreign and security policy. This, in turn, persuaded France to accept double-hatting for the foreign policy office, but only so long as the Council remained as the policy principal with the minister as its agent. Once this novel idea had found its way into the influential Franco-German position paper on institutional reform it acquired significant political momentum. With the Franco-German alliances fully behind the proposal, it was politic for the United Kingdom to moderate its own opposition, to make a concession here by accepting double-hatting in exchange for a deal on some of its own policy priorities, including reassurance that the new office would, like its predecessor the high representative, be accountable to the European Council for its management of CFSP.

The new 'double-hatted' office was to be 'elected' (in effect, appointed) by the Council by qualified majority, to chair the Foreign Affairs Council, and to be accountable to it for the management of CFSP. But the incumbent was also to be a member (a vice-president, no less) of the Commission, though with special status and without voting rights (Article 1-28).[34] The foreign minister's authority was thus derived and supposedly enhanced by having both a supranational and intergovernmental institutional base, though whether on equal terms or not will only become clear over time. In this particular division of labour the Commission will continue to take the lead in development and trade policy, but with the member states retaining even firmer control of CFSP and security policy. The case for 'double-hatting' here was made principally on grounds of efficiency, an objective no member state can reasonably resist, and a key goal of policy-making after all, identified as such at Laeken. As things stand, there is no connection for instance between the diplomatic functions of the high representative under the current arrangements in the Council and the Union's external spending programmes that are the responsibility of the commissioner for external affairs. Two quite separate bureaucracies deal with the similar, indeed overlapping issues, yet their policy priorities are by no means always closely aligned. Charles Grant has offered a revealing example of this problem as follows: 'The European Commission is negotiating a new trade agreement with China, which is supposed to open up hitherto protected Chinese markets. China will not sign such an agreement unless the EU lifts its arms embargo. Yet the EU officials who deal with the arms embargo, in the Council of Ministers, have no contact with those working on the trade agreement', or at least not officially.[35]

The premise behind the proposed change is that inter-institutional mediation by means of a new office and with one foot in both institutional camps might help resolve policy confusion, avoiding unnecessary duplication and overlap, as well as reducing friction, the rivalry that currently exists between these quite separate external policy offices. It was assumed here that chairing the Foreign Affairs Council will somehow lend the new office much-needed authority, as well as making the conduct of foreign policy more transparent. Yet the combined office will, under these arrangements, remain the creature of the member states, and especially the leading member states. For though the foreign minister has formal authority for taking policy initiatives on all matters falling under the Union's competence in external affairs, this hardly amounts to executive discretion since all decisions in this policy domain ultimately reside with the Council of Ministers for Foreign Affairs, with decisions reached either by unanimity or qualified majority depending on the issue. On this reading, merging the two offices might not resolve the problem of inefficiency, nor improve policy coherence, and may even add to confusion.[36] As Temple Lang sees it, 'the crucial issue is who the Foreign Minister would take his orders from (and who would in theory appoint and dismiss him, or her)', so that 'any arrangement by which the Foreign Minister is half in one institution and half in the other, must necessarily be a compromise which will be difficult to work in practice and confusing in theory'.[37]

One might wonder, as many commentators have done, whether the EU would have dealt better with the Iraq crisis had this office already been in place. On balance this seems unlikely, for as Hughes observes, 'it must be open to considerable doubt whether a more permanent president of the European Council and an EU foreign minister instead of a high representative would have been in any stronger position to prevent or even limit the damage from the EU splits over Iraq. On the contrary, such splits would call into question the value of both roles.'[38] This is not the only, nor even the principal difficulty with this proposed office, for the long-standing tension between the most powerful institutional actors is about politics more than it is about procedure. The question of 'who does what' is, in essence, about where power lies, a long-standing turf war whose roots lie in the unresolved ideological dispute over the meaning of European integration rather more than it is a difference of view over 'appropriate' administrative procedures, or even a clash of institutional cultures. The Commission for its part is unlikely to be reassured by a procedural change that reinforces the Council's primacy in the management of external policy, and not least one likely to impact negatively on its own role in any policy domain with an external aspect, whether it be transport, environment policy, trade, or aid and development.

The same concerns surfaced over the related proposal to establish an EU diplomatic service to assist the foreign minister. Those who supported the idea maintained that a transnational diplomatic service would afford an EU foreign minister greater independence from the Council machinery. Opponents resisted it for the very same reason. The diplomatic service was approved, but only after heated discussion. It is significant in view of these reservations that the service will consist of EU officials from the Council, the Commission, but also some representatives, no doubt high-level functionaries, from national diplomatic corps. Furthermore, the service is justified in practical terms as contributing to better co-ordination of distinct national policies, as 'an integrated set of officials, coming from the relevant centres of power ... to promote joined-up policies for EU external action', and not as a means for realising the Commission's ambition for a singular EU foreign policy managed from Brussels.[39]

The issue of 'who does what' in external policy cannot be separated from the parallel debate about the full-time council presidency discussed above at Chapter 6. Brussels-watchers have sought to dampen any unduly optimistic expectations about commonality in external policy resulting from the new office, for as Hughes sees it 'as long as the presidents and prime ministers from the member states, particularly the larger ones, continue to insist on their own independent roles and voices on the world stage, then a new President of the European Council will not be able to fulfil the role of representing the EU internationally'. In other words, merely to introduce new offices and titles will not in itself change the principal locus of policy-making in this politically sensitive domain. Nor will it 'make it easier to forge consensus among the member states, or to go further than Solana has been able to go so far in his role as High Representative'.[40] The title of the office as amended in the Lisbon Treaty – the High Representative of the Union for Foreign Affairs and Security Policy – downplays any suggestion that the incumbent has plenipotentiary powers, let alone ministerial status.

The new office and its supporting diplomatic service – designated as the European External Affairs Service –is intended to improve co-ordination of the member states' respective positions on current international issues, to overcome those impasses that arise from frequently divergent and entrenched positions, by mediating between the Council and the other EU institutions. Both sides of a familiar argument about where power should reside settled for compromise: for federalists, better co-ordination is at least a start, and for intergovernmentalists it is as much as they are prepared to concede. Both sides saw these new offices as a useful resource, enhancing the EU's international presence, especially so with the Iraq imbroglio clearly demonstrating that the Union is 'in need of an inter-institutional and inter-member state mediator and communicator in order to increase its effectiveness on the international stage'.[41] The fall-out over Iraq was timely, at least in so far as it reaffirmed the need for greater mediation. Yet considerable obstacles remain, not least abiding differences amongst the member states, and between them and the supranational institutions about both the procedures and strategy for a more co-ordinated external policy. There is no reason to believe that these differences will not hamper the work of the new office when it eventually begins its work, as it will, albeit under a revised nomenclature, according to the terms of the Lisbon Treaty, and as such hinder its capacity for better co-ordination of external policy.

A critical test of the extent of common purpose and shared endeavour was the procedural as much as the strategic issue of whether to extend QMV to CFSP. A Franco-German proposal had endorsed QMV, except for decisions on defence and security issues. And though a majority of EU states prefer QMV for foreign policy matters, the Iraq crisis rekindled doubts in Paris about making this radical change. In the event, France and the United Kingdom had second thoughts and blocked the change, though Germany remained committed in principle. After discreet but no less insistent French lobbying, Germany accepted a more modest praesidium proposal to restrict QMV to joint proposals from the new EU foreign minister and the Commission. Even this compromise was further diluted in the final version of the Constitutional Treaty. Concerned that excessive use of blocking by smaller member states might impede negotiations over common positions on the big international issues, Britain resisted even a modest increase in QMV, prepared to accept some changes in CFSP management, but 'not in ways that will constrain its national freedom of manoeuvre'.[42] The Convention could hardly ignore objections about such a significant change from these important players, and accordingly unanimity remains the procedure. The Constitutional Treaty gave the Union no significant new competencies in this important policy domain, and confirms the right of member states to exercise a veto.

The plain fact is that the new office notwithstanding, it is the member states and especially the big three, each of them significant international actors in their own right, who retain the initiative on external policy, resisting the Commission's more radical ambition to set the agenda for external policy as it does for first-pillar policy. The way the new office was to be organised confirmed this fact. For though the new office will sit on and report to the Commission College, this office in effect represents 'one more effort to reduce the influence of the Commission, and [is] another part of the contest between intergovernmentalism (and the three large states) and the Community method, which safeguards the small states'.[43] And though member states could request the foreign minister to give an account of the EU's position on current issues/problems to the UN Security Council – assuming that consensus does exist – there is little evidence so far of any significant co-ordination of outlook in those issues that the respective foreign policy establishments regard as their core national and security interests. The point is well made by Kirsty Hughes, that a common EU security policy depends in the end on agreeing a common foreign policy, and despite much discussion and even firm proposals to this end in the Constitutional Treaty and its successor, the Lisbon Treaty, what remains, plainly visible to the world, is 'the [lack of] political will and commitment of the member states to build a genuine foreign policy'. Moreover, though 'common policies and actions may develop over less controversial and lower-level issues', as she sees it the member states will continue to 'emphasise their national sovereignty and freedom of action on major strategic areas and issues'.[44] As John McCormick has put it, a common policy is very much on the Union's agenda now, though this is hardly the same thing as a single policy, and precisely where the line is drawn between these two positions is by no means resolved by these latest reforms. In the circumstances it almost certainly cannot be resolved to the mutual satisfaction of those of a supranational or an intergovernmental disposition.[45]

## European defence: responding to a new security agenda

Defence and security policy has been another contentious issue for the EU, ever since Monnet, responding to international events at the time of the Korean crisis in 1950, attempted to accelerate functional integration by proposing a European Defence Community organised on similarly supranational lines to the Coal and Steel Community. The project failed to take off after four years of political manoeuvring, largely as a result of French opposition to the idea of West German rearmament required by the project. Thereafter a policy domain claimed by nation-states as central to their historic purpose, a symbol of their 'inalienable' sovereignty was relegated down the order of Europe's priorities. Relegated maybe, though by no means entirely removed from the wish-list of those committed to the idea of Europe as a serious political project destined, at least as federalists saw it, to replace the nation-state as the principal actor in international politics. The idea of closer defence co-operation was eventually revived in the Maastricht Treaty (1992), reflecting the aspiration of those for whom a common external policy should 'include all questions related to the security of the Union, including the eventual framing of a common defence policy, which might lead in time to a common defence'.[46]

Maastricht approached the issue with due caution, reviving the Western European Union (WEU), an early arrangement for mutual European security that was a direct consequence of Monnet's failure to carry the idea of a defence community in the face of stiff opposition, and the means designed by the Atlantic powers for reintegrating the German Federal Republic into the West's security architecture.[47]

There was steady though by no means spectacular progress towards a notional common security policy, as for instance when the revived WEU launched the concept of a European Security and Defence Policy (ESDP).[48] The first significant development here followed a meeting at Petersberg Castle in Germany in 1992, where the so-called 'Petersberg tasks' were agreed as area and out-of area 'humanitarian and rescue tasks, peacekeeping tasks and tasks of combat forces in crisis management, including peacekeeping', and eventually incorporated into the Amsterdam Treaty (Article 17.2) in 1997.

The accession of three non-aligned former Eftan states in 1995 was bound to be problematic for a policy that countenanced even limited intervention 'abroad'. The solution was to reinforce the notion of conditionality, confirming that any collective military action must always be reactive rather than pre-emptive, multilateral and above all non-aggressive. Political constraints would seem to indicate that there is little prospect of the EU going further than this limited notion of mutual action to ensure regional security. Nor are the Union's non-aligned states the main problem here, because, for the most part, they are peripheral actors, and for them this policy is simply not a priority. More problematic by far are those member states that have no principled objection as such to collective military action, yet have fundamental differences over how to activate it and for what ends. The critical determinant of whether common security policy will acquire substance much beyond well-meaning rhetoric are the fundamental differences over the precise objectives and the means for a common security policy between the only two EU member states with enough military clout, the requisite levels of manpower and *matériel* needed for delivering a credible common EU security policy.

The problem here is much the same as it has been since Churchill turned down de Gaulle's proposal, made during a train journey to the Alsace front in November 1944, for Britain and France post-war to jointly lead the other European nations as a third force entirely separate from the two emergent superpowers.[49] Churchill declined the offer, preferring, as his successors in Downing Street have ever since, to cash in on a 'special relationship' and the political capital supposedly accruing from it so as to exert influence over Washington in its leadership of the Western powers, maintaining that 'it is better to persuade the stronger than to go against them. That is what I am trying to do. I am trying to enlighten them.'[50] Atlanticism became the defining principle of the United Kingdom's foreign and security policy thereafter, whereas France has resolutely resisted what its leaders see as American hegemony, Washington's unilateral assumption of leadership of the 'free world' under cover of acting as Western Europe's security guarantor of last resort.[51]

Meanwhile, the Amsterdam Treaty (1997) incorporated WEU into EU structures, notably its instruments such as the Institute for Security Studies (Paris) and the Satellite Centre (Torrejon, Spain), other than the security guarantees in Article 5 of the WEU Charter. And with good reason, because for the time being a mutual and unconditional defence obligation was simply unfeasible. The most practical solution was the usual one where member states could not agree a way forward on integrating controversial policies: those states willing to co-ordinate security policy would be permitted to do so under the enhanced co-operation procedure.

There have been remarkable, and for some observers unexpected, initiatives even in this controversial area. None more so than the tentative, yet for all that the patent progress in Anglo-French collaboration that followed the signing of the St Malo Agreement (December 1998), with the incoming Labour government still seemingly committed to its promise made in opposition to 'put Britain at the heart of Europe'. Events, both regional and further afield, contributed to this development. However, relations between these two countries are never easy, mistrust always lurking beneath surface *politesse*. Despite mostly superficial *bonhomie*, the encouraging rhetoric that accompanied the St Malo accord, what transpired was less a historic reconciliation between quite different views of the world, and instead a pragmatic trade-off between competing Anglo-French preferences. Much less a breakthrough on issues that have divided London and Paris since the onset of the Atlantic order in the late 1940s, let alone a new beginning, than a timely compromise between very different official mindsets about European security.

The St Malo agreement was a modest pay-off, then, but it did nevertheless commit the signatories to at least make a positive contribution to managing affairs in an increasingly capricious world through the medium of the EU. The CFSP was the principal policy instrument here, with the European Council building on existing machinery so as to enhance capacity for common security; for instance, by improving the institutional means for undertaking policy analysis, risk-assessment, shared intelligence, collective procurement and research, strategic planning and no less controversially for ensuring greater capability for collective action. Measured against previous inactivity and long-standing mutual suspicions, this was certainly progress.[52] But this was also a classic EU fudge, the usual trade-off between quite different and indeed competing national preferences. The United Kingdom, reticent about anything that threatened NATO's primacy, finally came to accept that 'the Union must have the capacity for autonomous action, backed up by credible military forces, the means to decide to use them and a readiness to do so, in order to respond to international crises'. This implied that the EU should have its own military capability to enable 'autonomous action', and the capacity 'to take decisions and approve military action where the Alliance as a whole is not engaged', all of which would require 'appropriate structures and a capacity for analysis of situations, sources of intelligence and a capability for relevant strategic planning, without unnecessary duplication, taking account of the existing assets of the WEU and the evolution of its relations with the EU'. Whereas France, for its part, acknowledged 'our respective obligations in NATO', and accepted that 'strengthening the solidarity between the member states of the European Union, in order that Europe can make its voice heard in world affairs', would contribute 'to the vitality of a modernised Atlantic Alliance which is the foundation of the collective defence of its members'.[53]

By the twentieth century's end and with the world a much less predictable place, security policy has acquired greater salience for the Union. The European Councils at Cologne (June 1999) and Helsinki (December 1999) responded positively to the challenge, integrating ESDP into EU external policy, and establishing an EU rapid-reaction force. But, again, progress was patchy at best, mostly confined to less controversial logistical questions, for instance finally putting in place the means for carrying out the Petersberg tasks. The Helsinki summit also agreed detailed rules for crisis management, the common accord described as the Helsinki Headline Goal that agreed to a task force of some 50–60,000 personnel by 2003, to be supported by 400 aircraft and 100 navy ships, and deployable within 60 days. A rapid-response force would also be established for civilian evacuation and other support measures. The Nice European Council (December 2000) finally confirmed decision-making arrangements for the Petersberg tasks: the Political and Security Committee (COPS) to manage operations, providing the political steer and strategic direction, with committees of experts to supervise military activities and direct staff, namely, the Political and Security Committee, the European Union Military Committee (EUMC) and the European Union Military Staff (EUMS).

This was steady, if tentative progress, and it certainly put in place procedures for realising the Laeken objective that the Union should be in the position to be 'able to conduct some crisis management operations', and to further develop its security policy capabilities. Confidence was boosted here by the fact that the EU had already undertaken a number of successful crisis management initiatives. The first such operation was in Macedonia (March 2003), to which every EU state apart from Denmark made a contribution. In response to the request from the UN secretary-general, Kofi Anan, the EU also despatched a peacekeeping force to the Democratic Republic of the Congo in May 2003 under French command, the first time the EU has undertaken a military operation outside Europe. Significantly for those who want the EU to develop a distinctive and even a free-standing European security role, this venture took place without any consultation with NATO. The Convention responded to this challenge, attempting to build on these foundations, not least because the present treaty base for common security policy is wholly inadequate, by merely referring to 'the *eventual* framing of a common defence policy, which might *in time* lead to a common defence'.[54] Even so, all was by no means plain sailing. There were predictable objections from some governments even to these modest developments, not least from the United Kingdom but supported by the EU's other Atlanticists, concerned lest a free-standing and pan-EU security dimension might send the 'wrong signals' to Washington. There was, after a fashion, a reprise of the British preference to avoid unduly antagonising its closest alliance partner and certainly to avoid doing anything that remotely looked like a challenge to NATO.

The time was when Germany and some other Western European states would have backed London in this endeavour, but Atlanticism has become *démodé* in some EU countries when it was once *de rigueur*. Times are changing and Germany has moved with them, now more concerned to accommodate its closest regional ally than it is about offending Washington. Both of these countries, yoked together in a powerful regional alliance as much by self-interest as by principle, now concur that the Union must adjust to new post-Cold War realities if Europe is to respond effectively to the challenges of a fast-changing international order. For this reason, Berlin and Paris have brought pressure to bear in EU councils for a wider-ranging review of Europe's strategic priorities. In these circumstances, the Convention was bound to reflect on the policy priorities of these principal actors, contributing to the review of available options for European security. Determined to lead this debate, these close allies published (November 2002) a joint proposal on European defence and security policy in advance of the working group meeting, advocating a European defence and security union (EDSU) and emphasising a pan-European rather than a NATO perspective.

Anticipating resistance from some member states, the Franco-German proposal made the case for flexibility, in effect to permit smaller groups of member states to move ahead on integrating their national security policies in the absence of unanimity, by inserting a solidarity or mutual assistance clause into the Constitutional Treaty.[55] The solidarity clause hardly breaks new ground, for the requirement that 'member states shall support the Union's common foreign and security policy actively and unreservedly' was already included in the Maastricht Treaty. As such, solidarity in the face of adversity is already implied by the very fact EU membership. What the proposed arrangement does entail is solidarity without mandating the member states to take any action that compromises their right to opt in to, or for that matter to opt out of, military action as their national interests dictate. A member state finding itself under external threat can request assistance (including military aid) from other member states. This does commit the EU to adopt a common position on terrorism and similar threats to regional security brought on either by unprovoked attack or by natural disaster.[56]

What is altogether more problematic is when and how to implement collective security measures in the event of so-called 'hot threats' from third parties, possibly rogue states in the EU's new and turbulent neighbourhood, or even more awkward, hostile actions perpetrated by a powerful neighbour. Russian pressure on Poland or the Baltic states would, for instance, present a threat of a wholly different order, and presumably involve responses of an entirely different kind from the symbolic solidarity extended by EU member states to Spain or the United Kingdom in the aftermath of terrorist outrages in both countries in 2004 and 2005 respectively. This would be a real test of commonality of purpose, reflecting both the scale of the security challenge currently facing the EU and its member states, and the problems in the way of making an effective common response. Some commentators quite rightly see a concomitant danger here, of 'raising expectations [the EU] cannot yet meet [for] to fulfil such a commitment, at a minimum the EU would need to be able to co-ordinate soldiers, policemen and emergency response services across borders and create a high-level intelligence body'.[57] And things currently stand, this is a remote prospect indeed.

The Constitutional Treaty settled then for easy rhetoric over concrete action, listing broad policy objectives for external policy that would be readily subscribed to by any liberal democratic state committed to maximising both the national and regional interest in a volatile international order. These general objectives were listed as follows:

(a) To safeguard the common values, fundamental interests, security, independence and integrity of the European Union.

(b) To consolidate and support democracy, the rule of law, human rights and international law.
(c) To preserve peace, prevent conflicts and strengthen international security, in conformity with the principles of the United Nations Charter.
(d) To foster sustainable economic, social and environmental reforms within developing countries with the primary aim of eradicating poverty.
(e) To encourage the integration of all countries into the world economy, including the progressive abolition of restrictions on international trade.
(f) To help develop international measures to preserve and to improve the quality of the environment and the sustainable management of global natural resources, in order to ensure sustainable development.
(g) To assist populations countries and regions that face natural or man-made disasters.
(h) To promote an international system based on stronger multilateral co-operation and good global governance.

Words, however, are rather easier to come by than the deeds they refer to are to perform, and in truth good intentions do not in themselves mean the EU is closer to realising a cogent or feasible security policy. As always with wish-lists the devil is in the detail, and the detail here, or rather the lack of it, confirms the persistent difficulties with a controversial policy. The Union's crisis-management capability has previously been utilised only for external or 'out of area' actions, expressly excluding actions on EU territory. The inclusion of the solidarity clause in Part I of the Treaty (Article 1-43) does represent willingness to commit to collective security guarantee, Article 3-329.1 stating: 'should a member state be the object of a terrorist attack ... the other member states shall assist it at the request of its political authorities', with every available means except military capability. However, the definition of 'attack' here is confined only to actions to counter terrorism, and 'crisis' is broadly defined so as to include natural disasters and other forms of catastrophe. In the event of other forms of threat, the Constitutional Treaty leaves the decision on 'appropriate action' to the discretion of the European Council (Article 329.3)

There is deliberate ambiguity about these arrangements that confirms abiding political problems with common security policy. And logistical problems, too, that invariably accompany any attempt by the national political and military establishment to co-ordinate external policy. That the solidarity clause is a compromise between quite different aspirations for common security policy is plain to see from the way the details are fudged in the Treaty. On the one hand, the Constitutional Treaty acknowledged the principle (Article 1-16) that 'the progressive framing of a common defence policy ... might lead to a common defence'. In which case, 'member states could also choose (but would not be obliged) to sign up to a defence clause, which would allow an EU country that comes under external attack to ask for military help from other members'. This echoes the pledge in the NATO Treaty (Article 5), and likewise a similar arrangement included in the 1948 Brussels Treaty. On the other hand, Article 1-41.2 enters the important caveat that such actions 'will lead to a common defence' only 'when the European Council, acting unanimously, so decides'. And the Treaty introduces a further caveat, to the effect that 'the policy of the Union in accordance with this Article shall not prejudice the specific character of the security and defence policy of certain member states'.[58]

The final version of the Treaty made specific arrangements for the implementation of the solidarity clause, by means of a European decision adopted by the Council acting unanimously, and, where this decision has defence implications, through a joint proposal by the Commission and the Union foreign minister (Article 3-329.2, new), thus confirming the intergovernmental tenor of the arrangement. Although the very idea of the EU as a community based on solidarity is a clear advance on previous arrangements for European collective security, the problem of how to ensure effective leadership remains to be resolved, in as much as 'a technocratic head of the capabilities agency is unlikely to command the respect of EU defence ministers'.[59]

The Convention considered setting up an equivalent office in the defence field to that of EU foreign minister, but this proved too controversial and was blocked by the United Kingdom and some other governments, concerned lest this, too, send Washington the 'wrong message'. These governments refused to countenance a separate EU defence identity, a free-standing regional defence system operating outside NATO. At one level this amounts to a reaffirmation of Atlanticism, resistance to weakening a tried and tested formula for regional security. But there were practical objections, too, not least the Union's shortfall in the military hardware and force deployments required for a credible independent capability. As the Atlanticists saw it, reliance on NATO's *matériel* and manpower means complementarity between regional and out-of-area security policy. The Constitutional Treaty tried to balance, if not exactly to reconcile these policy preferences. On the one hand, the Treaty acknowledged the fact of current commitments, whether to alliances such as NATO, or for some member states their preference to remain non-aligned. At the same time, the Treaty permits member states to engage in purposeful if reactive regional security and peacekeeping initiatives, as was the case with the EU's role in Macedonia.

This is collective security in only the most limited sense, and it acknowledges abiding differences of national interest. So much so, that the flexibility criterion is applied to crisis management/collective defence, a procedure designed to enable small groups of like-minded member states to undertake joint actions. The EU's recent failure to co-ordinate its response to the Balkans crisis following the breakup of the former Yugoslavia was an object lesson if ever there was one of the limits of commonality of purpose, and flexibility in these circumstances is the best that can be hoped for as a way of co-ordinating policy in this controversial domain. Certainly, the EU has some considerable way to go before it can claim anything remotely resembling common purpose with regard to security policy. Questions remain, both about the political will to implement a specifically European security policy, and no less the strategic capability for delivering it. The Thessaloniki summit that formally received the Constitutional Treaty from Giscard considered a proposal to give priority to a multilateral pan-European strategy for dealing with terrorism, and the threat, actual or implied, from rogue or failed states.[60] The EU foreign ministers meeting in the same month agreed a more proactive European approach to combat the proliferation of biological, chemical and nuclear weapons.[61]

This was progress of sorts, but though well-meaning it was nevertheless more rhetoric than substance. Whether there is consensus on even the least contentious matters such as specific threat analysis, let alone the political will for dealing with localised, to say nothing of rising global threats to European security remains a matter for conjecture both for media commentators and scholars or for the principal actors. In these circumstance it is difficult to avoid the pessimistic, or as some would have it the realistic conclusion of many experts in the security field, to the effect that 'until a focused, co-ordinated approach is built up and demonstrated over time, many doubts will remain over the success of a credible European foreign and defence policy'. A by no means inconsiderable problem here is that, regardless of good intentions and even some residual goodwill, in an ever more dangerous world 'France, Germany and the United Kingdom will continue to adopt somewhat different views on these key questions'. This means, in effect, settling for an agreement to differ, so that 'for the foreseeable future, a degree of flexibility and ambiguity will probably remain necessary and visible in these fields, limiting the advance of a strong European voice in the world'.[62]

As so often in the past, Franco-German co-operation was the key to setting the parameters of debate, in this critical policy domain as in so many others. These two countries had joined forces in the teeth of British opposition at the time of the Amsterdam Treaty to advocate a more effective response in the matter of common defence. The language used for announcing this latest joint proposal confirms Franco-German determination to be the main axis for EU security. Yet things are not quite what they once were, even for this alliance, its political stock having fallen somewhat with successive enlargements, and its ambition to give leadership diminished accordingly. There are also some differences between their respective positions, or at least a perceptible gap between commitment and delivery. Commentators have noted, for instance, the patent mismatch between Germany's warm words about security co-operation on the one hand, and the decision to cut its military budget on the other, a response to growing budgetary constraints, and likewise the marked lack of enthusiasm in Berlin about participating in joint Euro-programmes related to security policy, notably the Airbus A400 heavy-duty transport plane project.

The impact of such inconsistency has not been lost on Paris, and this merely adds to uncertainty about security policy. Both the working group and the praesidium discussed the strategic and resource implications for a credible European security policy. Debate at every level of the Convention highlighted these differences between the member states. On one side, those who preferred a more independent and pan-European approach. And on the other, the Atlanticists (the United Kingdom, the Netherlands and some of the accession countries) opposed to an exclusively or even a predominantly European security model, on the usual grounds that political differences would compromise commonality, and not least weaken both Europe and the West in the face of a growing threat level. In any event, those who argued thus maintained that a specifically EU-centric security policy was simply redundant in view of NATO. Though the secretariat under Giscard's aegis was at least amenable to the Franco-German position and directed the working group to consider how the EU might usefully contribute to collective security beyond the present Petersberg tasks, it was constrained nevertheless by the need to steer a middle course, or else invite failure on the issue. Accordingly it proposed a twin-track approach somewhere between traditional unilateralism, where member states follow their own policy, and a more co-ordinated regional security with appropriate policy instruments and resources, expanding the Petersberg peacekeeping tasks on crisis management and conflict resolution both in and out of area. Events outside Europe influenced these deliberations. The turbulent aftermath of 9/11, the rising threat from global terrorism, the capriciousness of so-called 'rogue states', all served to reinforce the case that 'a purely national framework is no longer enough [that] the public is calling out more than ever for security and protection and appears to be very much in favour of European defence'.[63] The principle of co-operation was established, but other questions remained.

There was no consensus, for instance, on rules of engagement, how the EU should operate as an actor in security matters. The working group decided that the only feasible solution was to endorse the Franco-German proposal for extending 'enhanced co-operation' to security policy, a procedure introduced in the Amsterdam Treaty and subsequently endorsed at Nice. This arrangement was intended to appeal to both sides of the argument, in as much as it permits likeminded member states to extend the principle of European co-operation, whilst permitting 'constructive abstention' for those unable or unwilling for reasons of national policy to commit to joint action. A group of member states, for instance, might agree to undertake closer integration in security matters, much as in any other policy domain, and utilise the Union's institutions for the purpose, though it would require that at least one third (eight) of the member states must participate in any common action.[64] However, this procedure merely highlights the difficulties of realising effective collective action in this politically contentious policy domain.

The new concept of flexible co-operation was soon put to the test, utilised by a group of member states that included France, Germany, Belgium and Luxembourg, who wanted to show their opposition to what they saw as illegal military action in Iraq by some other member states. To that end, they held a mini-summit in Brussels in April 2003 to explore closer European security co-operation. The summit considered a Schengen-type arrangement for mutual assistance in defence and crisis management, and for taking decisions about capabilities. As some *conventionnels* saw it, 'structured co-operation' was the best solution to persistent EU differences here, a way of facilitating closer defence for those member states prepared to commit to it in much the same way as the Eurozone permits co-operation in monetary and related policy, and in this case with crisis management tasks allocated, and capabilities shared, between the participants.

Closer co-operation would require formal adherence to agreed convergence criteria by all participants in a European defence zone, for instance the proportion of GDP allocated to defence, force deployment capabilities, and so on. This was easier, however, to prescribe than to deliver. There were problems with this proposal from the outset. Patent disparities in material capabilities, the wherewithal for any feasible security policy, raised questions for some potential participants about differential capacity for influence as between the larger states and smaller states, and not least between EU15 and the accession countries. The Franco-German bid to realise closer security co-operation seemed to hint at a hierarchy of influence, similar to how some see the politics of the Eurozone. In this instance a bid for dominance by those member states with substantial military capabilities, and with ambitions for global influence to match. The Brussels summiteers could not resolve these difficulties, and retreated, rather than risk diluting their already fragile consensus over Iraq. The most they managed was a joint communiqué, a form of words that proposed closer co-operation, yet sufficiently anodyne to secure the endorsement of the Atlanticists.

The Convention took a similar line and settled for a rather bland endorsement of defence co-operation, proposing that the 'member states shall undertake progressively to improve their military capabilities'. This is hardly different from the enhanced co-operation in security and defence policy envisaged in previous treaties. The Constitutional Treaty's security guarantee or 'solidarity' clause is much less than the collective security preferred by more radical *conventionnels*. But in view of the abiding differences between Atlanticists and those who want a pan-European security framework, it was the best that was on offer. By no means the common security policy preferred by committed integrationists, though a modest advance on the previously limited doctrine of 'crisis management'.[65]

The solidarity clause is a guarantee of common action, but less than collective security in the full sense. Nor does it preclude any state calling on additional support from other quarters, the obvious candidate being NATO. The various tasks related to this commitment were elaborated in Article 3-309, and these include: 'joint disarmament operations, humanitarian and rescue tasks, military advice and assistance tasks, conflict prevention and peacekeeping tasks, tasks of combat forces in crisis management including peacemaking and post-conflict stabilisation'. More radical ideas by far circulated in the Convention, but in the end caution prevailed in the proposals from the working group, for it was recognised that any European security strategy without Britain is simply doomed to fail, and London would never agree to anything that was remotely likely to downgrade the central role of NATO in Europe's security arrangements.[66]

On a more positive note, there is less uncertainty now about Britain's commitment to European collective security than there used to be. That commitment was underlined at the St Malo summit (1998), which launched a nascent European defence initiative with the Union's two dominant military powers acting in partnership, and confirmed that 'Britain's military capabilities are, beside those of France, the most significant ones in Europe'. Even so, conditional bilateralism is not quite what France and some other EU partners mean by European security policy. Whereas for London, contributing to European security is no more than a facet, if an increasingly important one, of its role in NATO, as it has been since the end of the Second World War, when the British government persuaded the USA to commit to European security, with London operating as the regional interlocutor between its Western European and American partners.[67]

The defence issue was revisited at the IGC. The 2003 proposal that France, Germany, Belgium and Luxembourg should co-operate more closely on security matters had excluded Britain, but by the end of that year and notwithstanding tensions generated by Iraq, both France and German acknowledged that any credible European defence initiative required British involvement. For its part, Britain responded positively, softening its resistance to any form of military operational planning for the Europe region outside of the NATO framework. One moderately encouraging sign of progress here was the agreement between Chirac and Blair at their bilateral Le Touquet summit (February 2003) that the EU should, in principle, have the capacity to deploy forces within 5 to 10 days in order to meet agreed commitments, a considerable improvement on the present target of a 60-day deployment for the EU 'rapid' reaction force. There are also moves afoot to facilitate joint intelligence-gathering.[68] And likewise an admittedly tentative initiative to pool internal security intelligence assessments through the medium of Europol.[69] Patience is of the essence, however, in these matters, and slow rather than spectacular progress will be the most likely outcome.

The IGC made progress, too, on the equally thorny issue of defence co-operation, with agreement between the big three, a direct response to the widespread perception of the damage to the Union's self-image as a community of nations capable of exerting influence over international affairs wrought by the fall-out from Iraq. Britain, Germany and France agreed (November 2003) to institutional changes designed to improve defence co-operation, including an EU military planning unit to be part of the secretariat of the Council of Ministers, though this was rather less than the earlier and more ambitious plan to establish a new military headquarters at Tervuren in Belgium. This agreement required changes in the Treaty articles on mutual military assistance, the deletion of the defence clause in the original version of Part III, and a dilution of the general article in Part I which referred to member states assisting each other 'in accordance with Article 51 of the UN Charter'. It likewise refers to NATO as 'the foundation of members' collective defence and the forum for its implementation'.

The change of emphasis, for this is what it amounts to, required minor redrafting of Part III of the original version of the draft Constitutional Treaty. The original wording relating to structured co-operation was amended so that the rationale for an avant-garde group now referred to 'enhanced military capabilities'. A separate protocol was added to the Treaty defining the extent of structured co-operation, and decisions would now be made by QMV, though the requirements for participants were deliberately imprecise so as to maximise participation by member states. The revised wording implies a more onerous commitment than is required in practice. There was certainly nothing here to challenge NATO's role as the principal vehicle for European security.

Any positive developments that might follow from this agreement will certainly not be realised until the political wounds inflicted by the Iraq War have faded from official minds. And it will require considerable political will, to say nothing of skill, resolving highly contentious matters of strategy and resource allocations to make such co-operation work, including agreement to enhance EU military capability and to pool resources, in the first instance with small groups of member states leading the way.[70] The EU military mission to Macedonia in March 2003 was the first such initiative, followed by the deployment of EU forces in the Congo at the behest of the UN, and the decision to replace the American peacekeepers in Bosnia in 2004. An initiative by France and Germany to establish a joint school for attack-helicopter training and maintenance, though a necessary precursor for the Union's designated task of taking over NATO's peacekeeping role in Bosnia, was an attempt, albeit modest, to enhance policy credibility. Further progress on improving regional security co-operation is likely to follow this pattern, but is no more than modest and incremental steps rather than any major breakthrough. To date, developments here have been more symbolic than substantial, but even tentative progress is an advance on previous inaction or, worse, fall-outs over broad policy objectives. What this development does point to is a discernable, if cautious response to new and much increased security challenges, a determination to perform positively at this level, and to contribute to peace-keeping both in Europe and out of area.[71] Though, it has to be said, as a complement to rather than in competition with the USA.[72]

The scale of the task in ensuring greater commonality in EU foreign and security policy is illustrated not merely by the Iraq conflict, but how the Union tried to mend its broken fences when the clash of competing national preferences threatened to paralyse a cogent response to international issues. EU leaders instructed Solana to undertake a detailed review of the common security strategy in the aftermath of the Iraq imbroglio, to be presented to the December 2003 European Council. This was in part a belated attempt to respond to the Union's patent shortcomings in the run-up to the outbreak of hostilities. What this outcome did reveal is how much still needs to be done if the EU is to overcome its present difficulties, to accommodate even modest objectives of a common approach to regional security. Two expert witnesses to these events see this daunting task as follows:

> The EU needs to overcome its habit of reacting to crises with glorified ad hocery. Too often the EU can only agree for ministers to monitor the situation while it remains split on what substantive actions to take. Instead, the EU needs to set out in advance how it might respond to certain types of behaviour and agree to give a mandate to Javier Solana to implement pre-identified responses. A more fleshed-out security strategy would identify what kinds of developments would trigger what sort of responses. Secondly, the EU must come up with more precise formulations on the principles governing the use of force. ... Those pressing for a more interventionist approach have to show they accept a crucial role for international law, and in particular the UN, in legitimising the use of force prior to military interventions. By the same token, the 'pacifist' camp in the EU must accept that, in tightly prescribed circumstances, military force is called for – and in extreme cases even of the pre-emptive variety.[73]

This is a sober, and even a pessimistic assessment of achievements in this policy domain so far, though it accords with Solana's own evaluation and is entirely realistic about the need to balance quite different national preferences. Whether the EU is ready to embark on a common security policy worth the name remains to be seen. For there is still widespread reticence amongst member states about making even a notional commitment to collective security, and at the very least residual doubts and in some cases rooted objections to the idea of pro-active collective military action, notwithstanding the fact of the serious and growing threat to regional security.[74] The Brussels summit (December 2004) did agree a new EU security strategy, to include an operational military headquarters. Controversy remains, however, about any expansion of the EU's role in security policy beyond 'mere' peacekeeping and crisis management operations, and not least where there appears to be any hint of overlap with NATO. For this reason, the European intelligence committee to be attached to Solana's office and tasked with making common intelligence assessments, both for the foreign ministers' council and for the EU foreign minister, though broadly endorsed by academic specialists and security practitioners alike, remains a distant prospect.[75] There are nevertheless some positive signs of agreement at least in principle to put in place the foundations for a more cogent EU security system when circumstances allow, though any tentative consensus on this is motivated more by practical considerations than by visionary notions for the supranational management of European security. This is hardly surprising, for the pursuit of self-interest as much as any idealistic idea about 'Europe' *per se* has been the surest driver of 'ever-closer union' from the outset.

### Defence industry, *matériel* supplies and the European Armaments Agency

The Convention found it rather easier to reach agreement on the less controversial issue of defence industry co-operation, prompted not least by the extra incentive of economic benefits. Each of the major EU countries has its own national arrangements for the production and contract tendering for defence *matériel*. The Constitutional Treaty provided (Article 3-311) for co-ordination of the production and supply of armaments through a European armaments and research agency organised on an intergovernmental basis. The objective here was to reduce the significant gap in military-related R&D between the EU and the USA, the latter spending some 53 billion euros per year while the EU allocates a mere 10 billion. But this, too, is an area where past-performance, including some joint initiatives, has delivered little by way of policy streamlining either in research or procurement.

The European Armaments Agency is intended to redress these shortcomings, to co-ordinate research in defence technology, to facilitate joint arms procurement and to facilitate compatibility of defence equipment throughout the Union and essential for effective and concerted operations. The functions of the Agency as defined in Article 3-311.1) are as follows:

(a)  To contribute to identifying the member states' military capability objectives, and to evaluating the observance of the commitments with regard to capability made by member states.

(b)  To promote harmonisation of operational needs and the adoption of effective, compatible procurement methods.

(c)  To propose multilateral projects to fulfil the objectives in terms of military capabilities, and to ensure the programmes implemented by the member states.

(d)  To support defence technology research and plan joint research.

(e)  To strengthen the industrial and technological base of the defence sector, and to improve the effectiveness of military expenditure.

The agency will utilise the experience of existing institutions such as the four-country Organisation conjointe de coopération en matière d'armament (OCCAR), and the work already undertaken by the six EU arms-producing countries who are signatories of the Letter of Intent of 1998, and already working to improve the management of multinational armaments programmes.[76] The agency is designated to go beyond co-operation on research and procurement, however, and to facilitate co-operation in 'the military capabilities directly in the command of the sovereign state' including harmonising operational needs and military capabilities, and likewise to promote 'multilateral projects to fulfil these objectives', such that 'the creation of an autonomous European military capability is a major step … a step towards a common defence for the EU'.[77]

This may well be one prospective outcome of collaboration on research, material and procurement over the long term, but as we have seen above this remains a distant prospect. As European security is currently arranged, an even more concerted approach to the development and procurement in world markets of military hardware will hardly be enough to realise the elusive pan-European security architecture prescribed by some voices as the best solution to meet the EU's current situation.

## Overview

These developments amount to an improvement on present arrangements in this important policy domain, though they hardly match the expectations of those who continue to advocate a cogent and co-ordinated EU external policy. They neither match the ambitions of federalists and others who see the future in terms of a pan-European security framework, nor do they meet with the threat assessment of pragmatists more concerned about securing Europe in an unstable world. At most, these latest proposals for common action refine the response to the growing security challenges that confront Europe, and improve the Union's intergovernmental procedures for managing external policy, amounting to 'some limited steps towards pooling and merging national and supranational resources', though without in any way resolving the 'tension and conflicts' that have attended CFSP from the outset.[78]

The trade-off between improved efficiency in the planning, conduct and delivery of external policy and accommodating quite distinct and enduring national interests is a familiar one to any close observer of EU politics, and it figured in this latest as it did in previous versions of the EC/EU treaties. What these proposed reforms amount to, in effect, is less unremitting spill-over predicted by classic neo-functionalist theorists, a significant upgrading of the common interest, than modest, incremental but above all tentative adjustments between still-contested ideas about the meaning of and prospects for European integration.[79] Wessels has described this situation as follows: 'All in all, the gap between ambitious goals and allocated capabilities remains wide', and accordingly 'the efficiency and effectiveness of the CFSP will only be improved within day to day diplomacy, but not in crises of high politics'.[80]

The evidence from the deliberations in the Convention and further afield about the reformulation of CFSP and CSDP confirms this patent truth about the European project. The fact that while, on the one hand, the EU member states are prepared to revise their rules of engagement, to refine intergovernmental procedures so as to facilitate closer co-operation in external policy as in any other area of common concern and mutual interest, at the same time they continue to resist transferring even a modest slice of their sovereignty in this critical policy domain that for most governments continues to confirm their survival *ultima maximus* as sovereign states. This policy domain remains firmly rooted, then, in what Wessels describes as 'the intergovernmental trap'.[81]

# Part 3

# The politics of ratification

# 10   The politics of ratification

## Referendum or parliamentary procedure?

The Union's political leaders met in Rome to initial the Constitutional Treaty on 29 October 2004 in the Sala Degli Orazi e Curazi, where the original Treaty of Rome was signed almost a half century previously. The Constitutional Treaty was a landmark for the EU but ratification was far from straightforward, and made more difficult by the widespread perception that the Constitution was a step into the political unknown, a 'milestone that marks the fork in the European road', a significant step-change from previous European treaties.[1] One seasoned observer even compared the EU to the Holy Roman Empire, with the Constitution a 'high watermark of European unification – never again to be reached'.[2] This almost certainly exaggerates the significance of the event, for the Constitutional Treaty did not significantly extend the Union's remit into new policy areas though it did appear to supporters and opponents alike to be an important step and in its way a kind of Rubicon.[3] Commentators on both sides of the debate saw ratification as a litmus test of the public's commitment to the European project, 'Europe's way of asking: are you with us or are you against us?'[4]

The crisis that overtook ratification can be explained to an extent by expectations raised at Laeken about a more transparent, even a democratic process. There is a marked difference between an IGC, where political elites make narrow bargains, the usual trade-offs between privileged insiders, and a Convention, a deliberative forum if not quite the democratic conversation some participants might prefer. Treaty reform had so far been barely concerned with public consultation and was much more a top-down bargain made by politicians. This was not the first occasion treaty reform was put to the people in a referendum – the constitutional arrangements of some member states require referendums for EU treaty changes as a matter of course – but the first occasion on which so many were to be conducted for treaty ratification. In the event, the public's response showed that they were less than convinced about what their leaders had agreed, seeing the Constitution as something more than 'merely' procedural change, and many took fright and voted accordingly.

Of course, referendums lend themselves to unpredictable outcomes, an opportunity to register protest, to send a message to governments, though by no means a message always related to the particular question being asked of voters.[5]

Referendums depend, too, on politicians making a plausible case for or against a proposed change in policy or constitutional procedure, but much depends on how they go about this. For all these reasons the outcome of a referendum is often unpredictable, even when politicians give a firm steer. The public is fickle, frequently obdurate and increasingly disposed to rebel against their leaders. This may be no bad thing in a democratic polity, but electorates tend to be information-poor, and this makes it more likely than not that they will misunderstand the question(s) being asked or be misled about them, one reason why this plebiscitary form of democracy is regarded by politicians as unreliable for deciding complicated issues.[6] The polling evidence in this case bears this out, indicating a public hardly well informed about the Constitution. A *Eurobarometer* 'flash' survey found, for instance, that 'only a minority of citizens (some 45 per cent) across Europe had even heard about the Convention', let alone understood its complexities.[7] The Constitution became, then, a lightning-conductor for all manner of popular concerns. This fact was patently clear in the referendum campaigns on the Constitutional Treaty, as we shall see in what follows.[8]

There was a widespread feeling throughout the Union that the Constitution was significant, with much at stake, though the lack of accurate information meant that voters were too easily deflected by other concerns, many of them only remotely connected with the substance of the Constitution, with too many governments reluctant to explain the issues in plain language, let alone to confront public concerns head-on. As Leduc sees it, the politicians were especially culpable here, too often leaving 'the public ... unaware of the complicated background from which the draft constitutional treaty ... is emerging'.[9] Some observers felt, too, that politicians were less than candid about what was at stake, and for that reason were disinclined to believe their assurances that the Constitution amounted to little more than tidying the treaties. The feeling became widespread that this was anything but 'business as usual', that voters were being asked to approve something 'wholly new and not merely re-styling of what is already happening'. For all of these reasons, many governments faced 'a real challenge' to convince their publics to endorse the Constitution.[10] If governments were complacent about ratification it was mainly because few of them had anticipated that the Constitution would meet serious opposition, whether in referendums or parliamentary votes.

There was of course always the chance of a set-back in a Eurosceptical country, with the United Kingdom the likeliest candidate, but even this was not regarded as a serious stumbling-block to eventual ratification. In fact, this possibility had been factored into the political equation. Article 4-443 had made provision that in the event that the Constitutional Treaty was approved by four-fifths of the member states within two years of signature by the European Council, but was prevented from being implemented by political difficulties in some other member states, the matter would be referred back to the European Council, presumably to exert pressure on the laggards. And should a state fail to ratify thereafter, it seemed inconceivable that the situation would revert to the status quo ante, in effect the original treaties, but instead that any member state in this untenable position would be required to negotiate what would amount to second-class membership, probably associate membership, or even be required to withdraw from the Union altogether. This view, it has to be said, was more enthusiastically supported by France than by most other member states, and was based on its long-standing *Angst* about what is seen in Paris as less than whole-hearted British commitment to 'Europe'. But at this stage French *Schadenfreude* at London's expense seemed to accord with the political facts and not remotely to be tempting fate.

This likely outcome was not without historical precedent, albeit in quite different circumstances, where continental state-building was actually in prospect. The consequences of the non-ratification of a constitutional settlement were duly considered by the Philadelphia Constitutional Convention of 1787. The prospect there of a few tardy state legislatures holding up the 'great Continental project', thwarting the will of the great majority of American states and people, persuaded the founding fathers to rescind the provision of the original Articles of Confederation (1777) requiring unanimity, the approval for constitutional amendment by every state. The Philadelphia Convention decided instead to permit the new United States Constitution to come into force once two-thirds of the states had ratified, leaving the others either to catch up in their own good time or to remain outside the Union. This convenient option was not considered to be feasible by EU leaders. The situation here was not remotely comparable to that in former British colonies in eighteenth-century America, for the EU is not engaged in state-building or anything like. And despite its name, the Constitutional Treaty remained in essence an intergovernmental treaty, a bargain made between independent states, and as such one that required for its enactment quite different arrangements from those pertaining to classical nation-building. But in the event of non-ratification, the political fall-out was likely to be at least serious, and a situation perhaps even more difficult to resolve precisely because sovereign states are involved.

At the outset few commentators seriously contemplated that a founder member would fail to ratify, let alone two of them. On the contrary, the prevailing assumption was that the Community's founders were bound to endorse a Constitution 'written for countries seeing themselves as being at the heart of the EU', and that only those 'governments whose commitment to further integration is in doubt or which pretend the EU is fundamentally about economic benefits and free trade' would face difficulties over ratification.[11] In these circumstances, the prospect of non-ratification was more potential irritant than crisis. There were some early signs that the British government was facing difficulties, as when it distanced itself from the comments made by the German chancellor that the Constitution was 'the latest step in the onward march of pan-European politics'.[12] Anticipating that trouble, even in a notoriously Eurosceptical member state, would be problematic for the Constitution, the Commission suggested ratification by stages.[13] The Convention, however, had already ruled out any such arrangement as compromising the very idea of a uniform 'one size fits all' European Constitution applicable to every member state and in every respect.[14] Constitutions by definition enact uniform rules and common procedures, and as such cannot countenance selective application, the sort of derogations or delays in application that might exceptionally be allowed in particular policy domains. For that very reason a founding treaty requires contemporaneous implementation by all contracting parties. The Constitutional Treaty had said as much in the provisions for ratification by the 'high contracting parties' (Article 4-447), though each new state would ratify according to its respective national constitutional procedures. In some cases this required a mandatory referendum, a constitutional obligation in Ireland, Denmark, Luxembourg and Portugal. However, in view of the 'historic' nature of the Constitutional Treaty some other states not constitutionally required to seek public approval decided that it would be politic to do so. The reason these governments gave for their decision was precisely the historic nature of the Constitutional Treaty, the very fact that the EU and EC treaties, and all related acts and treaties, would be rescinded once the Constitutional Treaty came into force, thereby strengthening the argument for a referendum to ensure due legitimacy.

While there was no sense of impending crisis at the beginning of the ratification phase, there was palpable public disquiet. Public approbation was crucial for the Constitution, even where the decision was reserved to parliaments. Some *conventionnels* had recommended holding a Europe-wide referendum in every member states on the same day, alongside European elections scheduled for June 2004.[15] The idea here was to foster latent enthusiasm for Europe, to encourage 'a feeling of solidarity' within 'a common political space ... a means of bringing the peoples of Europe closer politically',[16] so that the people 'were more engaged with, had a greater knowledge of the project'.[17] A proposal to this effect was submitted to the secretariat (March 2003) by a group of *conventionnels* and alternates, and subsequently endorsed by the European Parliament.[18] A European referendum campaign was duly launched, but the idea never took hold in the public's imagination. Most politicians, not least those favourable to the Constitution, saw such an event only as an opportunity for giving vent to populist prejudices, a touchstone of public disquiet over the political establishment's handling – or mishandling – of all manner of parochial issues, and not merely over the Constitution.

The case for a European referendum might have fared better had the stakes been higher, if the Constitution had presaged, for instance, a fundamental shift in the balance of legal and political power between the member states and the Union. But its title notwithstanding, the Constitutional Treaty was not a constitution in the historic sense, let alone the founding charter for a European state. This much at least was understood by governments. As one *conventionnel* observed: 'I would like nothing more than to eulogise the historical importance of the Constitution in relation to its subject, the European Union [however] the Union will not in fact be changed fundamentally by the Constitution, and no substantial new competences will be transferred to it by the member states'. In these circumstances, an EU-wide referendum might actually do more harm than good by seeming 'to exaggerate the significance of the Convention's achievement', and as such provide an opportunity for making political mischief.[19]

The Convention, following the praesidium's lead on ratification, confirmed that the European treaties are a matter for international law and cannot be altered without the unanimous agreement of all the parties to them, with 'parties' here unequivocally defined as the member states.[20] For that very reason, how and for that matter when to ratify the Constitution was left to each member state, in

accordance with national constitutional procedures, some states opting for referendums, others for the more predictable parliamentary route. Some governments
not required by law to hold a referendum on the Constitution nevertheless opted
to do so, constrained by intense media and political pressure to put the matter
to the popular vote. Belgium and the Netherlands decided to hold indicative or
non-binding referendums for the first time on the European treaties, though in the
event the Belgian government reversed that decision. Of the newcomers, Poland
and the Czech Republic decided to hold referendums because the issue threatened
to destabilise already fragile governing coalitions. Even the British government
decided it could not avoid a referendum, though it would have much preferred to
do so, a decision that in turn put pressure on France to follow suit, and one as it
turned out with dramatic consequences.[21] In the event nine of the EU25 countries
decided on referendums, by no means a majority but including some states where
the outcome would determine the Constitution's fate.

  Referendums were bound to be politically risky.[22] Federalists saw referendums as
useful in the '"deeper and wider debate on the future of the European Union" with
an increasingly disenchanted public', one way of countering the familiar complaint
of Eurosceptics that 'the EU is inherently undemocratic'.[23] But this was expecting
rather too much of electorates lacking either the information or the motivation to
engage objectively with the 'debate' on Europe.[24] Eurosceptics on the other hand
saw plebiscites as the surest way of halting the Constitution in its tracks, and one can
see why, for referendums tend to present simple if not simplistic choices on otherwise complicated issues, and are as much about political manipulation as they are a
vehicle for informed democratic voice. In the circumstances these EU referendums
were, as Keohane saw it, hardly likely to be 'the cusp of a direct democracy revolution'.[25] This much was already apparent from past experience. To say the least, referendums on European issues have a mixed record: more successful for the authorities
who put the questions on the 15 occasions they have been used to decide accession,
with only Norway so far rejecting membership; but less so when the issue has been
the more complex matter of treaty reform. Denmark, France and Ireland had previously held referendums on treaty revision, but with unpredictable consequences.
The Danes voted 'no' in the first Maastricht referendum (1992), the Irish rejected the
Nice Treaty (both verdicts subsequently reversed) and there was only a bare majority
for ratification in France (51 per cent) in the 1992 Maastricht referendum.

  The fact is that referendums are a political lottery, their outcomes unpredictable. Public deliberation about complex matters requires reliable information, yet
opinion surveys show that barely 30 per cent of EU voters felt 'well informed'
about the issues. This was due in part to the fact that despite the Convention's
deliberations being on the record, the issues seemed remote from most people's
experience of politics.[26] Moreover, the Constitution was not about making a
choice on a singular issue, as was the case with accession or the adoption of a
particular common policy. The Constitution was a complex matter, its text an
inordinately lengthy document, for the most part unreadable by the layperson,
several hundred pages of incomprehensible text, with additional protocols and
annexes, and written in arcane 'Euro-speak' and impenetrable legalese, and as

such hardly user friendly for the citizen. One diplomat made the telling point that 'direct democracy is an inadequate instrument for dealing with international issues such as the compromise hammered out between 25 sovereign nations on a constitutional treaty consisting of several hundred pages of complex legal and political content'.[27] Most insiders were not much concerned about how they might translate these complicated issues into plainer language, but instead how to stake their own claim to institutional power. Even where referendums took place, the issues remained obscure and mostly passed people by. Much of the blame here lies with political leaders for failing to make the case for a Constitution they had spent the two years and more negotiating at the Convention and the IGC.

Research by the European Policy Institute Network (EPIN) bears this out, showing how the politicians simply failed to take the issues to the public, to explain what was at stake, and in a clear and accessible language.[28] National debates did occur but for the most part they were ill-informed, often intemperate affairs, unduly parochial and suffused with partisan clamour, more often than not wrangles for party or personal advantage than anything resembling an informed public conversation. These domestic fault-lines were apparent from the outset, and they were mostly predictable. The centre-left/centre-right parties by and large backed the Constitution, though with some notable exceptions. At the European level, the Party of European Socialists (PES) was generally favourable to the Treaty, whereas some of the 36 centre-right parties that belong to the European People's Party's (EPP–ED) criticised it, making their respective cases on grounds of national interest, including the British Conservative Party, the Czech ODS, the Finnish Christian Democrats, the Estonian Fatherland's Union, the Polish Citizens' Platform and the People's Party, with a further four conservative parties (in Denmark, Estonia, Poland and Slovakia) undecided.[29]

The relatively low profile taken by the European parties is remarkable on an issue central to the very idea of political union. For whatever reason, these transnational party families left the field mostly to national parties, so that debate tended to be conducted in the narrow currency of domestic preferences, and no less national prejudices. Only very occasionally did a political party attempt to widen the national debate, to connect with ratification campaigns elsewhere. Spain's governing PSOE, for instance, invited EU leaders from both the centre-left (Schroeder) and centre-right (Chirac and Berlusconi) to participate in its rallies prior to that country's referendum. Predictably, support for the Constitutional Treaty was strongest amongst governing parties whether of the left or the right that had negotiated it, though some junior coalition partners did express reservations, as did some factions of governing parties such as *Debout la République*, a movement within France's governing UMP, the Christian Democratic Movement (Slovakia), and elements in Austria's FPO and Italy's Lega Nord. The British Labour Party, despite a minority of vocal Eurosceptics on its parliamentary benches, maintained party unity on the issue, unusually for a governing British party where Europe is the issue of the moment.

In the Czech Republic, too, the principal governing party, the CSSD, was broadly supportive of the Constitution, whereas the main opposition ODS party was opposed, with most of the smaller parties and potential coalition partners divided or otherwise undecided. Opposition parties tended to be more divided on the Constitution, again predictably, for these parties are unencumbered by the responsibilities of office and less likely than governing parties to be preoccupied by party discipline. The opposition French centre-left PS, for instance, formally endorsed the Constitution but failed to convince its own grassroots. The principal opposition parties in Poland (Citizens Platform and PSL) were mostly sceptical about the Constitution, and some of the smaller parties (Law and Justice, Self-Defence and the League of Polish Families) staunchly opposed it.

## The transnational dimension

The national ratification campaigns hardly amounted to a pan-European conversation. There was little by way of transnational campaigning. Research conducted by a leading European think-tank shows instead disjointed national campaigns, each focused on domestic issues rather than on the 'Europe' dimension, on the national interest, rather than how the Constitution might improve Europe's standing in the world.[30] Even the few occasions where campaigning actually crossed borders hardly amounted to the European conversation anticipated by federalists, 'a European debate across national, linguistic and cultural boundaries of the member states'.[31] The most that could be said was that these national campaigns raised similar issues, the salience of the issues varying between countries. The debate about 'social Europe', for instance, engaged by the French left did raise an echo in the Belgian francophone Parti Socialiste, and to a lesser extent amongst the German social-democrats. There was, however, little actual contact between national campaigners, whether on the pro- or anti-side, and where there was it was mostly confined to neighbouring member states: for instance, between France and Germany, Sweden and Denmark, Austria and Germany, Poland and the Czech Republic and even the campaigns in the United Kingdom and Ireland.[32]

But this was only an occasional and always low-key activity. Some of these exchanges were motivated by circumstances. As a French '*non*' became a distinct possibility, campaigners from elsewhere and on both sides of the question factored the prospect into their own strategies.[33] President Carlo Ciampi of Italy, for example, was so exercised by the prospect of defeat for the Constitution in France that he wrote to the heads of government of the Community's founder states urging them to publicly renew their countries' commitment to the founding ideals [34] Less helpful though no less significant for the eventual outcome was a confidential memo from Britain's former Europe minister, Denis MacShane, criticising what he saw as Chirac's political 'ineptness' in failing to make the case for the Constitution that was leaked to the media at a sensitive moment in the French campaign.[35] This was a notable intervention precisely because it was exceptional activity. The more usual response was governments' reticence about interfering in what they regarded as other people's politics.[36]

The European institutions were likewise reluctant to intrude in to other people's affairs. The Commission was especially wary about giving ammunition to Eurosceptics.[37] When it did allocate funds to pro-Constitution campaigners for public information, protests predictably followed from opponents.[38] With opinion polls registering rising support for anti-Constitution campaigns in France and the Netherlands, the Commission did become more directly involved in the campaign.[39] The Justice commissioner and Commission vice-president, Franco Frattini, broke cover, warning that victory for Euroscepticism in two key states, both founder members of the Community, would be a 'much more serious' matter than even a British 'no', which had already been factored into Commission's calculus.[40] The former competition commissioner, Mario Monti, who had often clashed with the French government over state aid, likewise cautioned French voters that defeat for the Constitution risked provoking a crisis of confidence among investors, and might even turn Europe into a 'suburb of Shanghai'.[41] In the penultimate week of the French campaign, the situation was serious enough for Commission president, José Barroso, finally to go on the record and 'advise' voters that to sink the Constitution would be 'very bad news for the economy in France and Europe', because 'there was no Plan B, no re-negotiation option'.[42] The Council, for its part, played no direct part in campaigning, nor was it inclined to do so. After all, this is an institution with an intergovernmental outlook, and as such circumspect about intruding on domestic politics. The General Affairs Council confined its role merely to discussing timetables for ratification, and though it wanted to see a concerted push for ratification, affirmed nevertheless that 'this remains a national process'.[43]

The Parliament was rather less circumspect about campaigning for the Constitution, though divided about how best to make the case for it. In the debate on the Constitution (September 2004) initiated by Jo Leinen (PES), president of the Constitutional Affairs Committee, there was no agreement amongst MEPs on overall strategy for ratification. Leinen urged the Council and the Commission 'not to remain inactive', to ensure that the 'flame of the Constitution ... be maintained'.[44] A draft resolution from the same committee (May 2005) intended to commemorate the fifty-fifth anniversary of the Schuman Declaration proposed both a joint inter-institutional strategy and concurrent ratification, though it was light on substance. And though in January 2005 the European Parliament approved the Constitutional Treaty (500 votes in favour, 137 against and 40 abstentions), and with all of the principal groups (EPP–ED, PES, ALDE and the Greens) voting for it, Parliament, too, decided that it was better not to be seen meddling in domestic politics. To do so might just make life more difficult for the pro-Constitution camps in countries where the 'no' side was making the running. Although Parliament did go further than the Commission, encouraging pro-Constitution campaigners and even making some 8 million euros available to them, their role was deliberately kept low-key.[45] The nearest thing to serious controversy was when Leinen and the European Parliament's vice–president, Alejo Vidal-Quadras, took exception to the vitriolic anti-Constitution rhetoric of the Czech president, Vaclav Havel, though they insisted their censure of Havel was made strictly in a personal capacity rather than as senior representatives of their institution.[46] Even the Committee of the Regions, though it supported the Constitution at its plenary meeting in November 2004, gave little overt help to pro-Constitution campaigners.[47]

# Campaign issues

## *Institutional matters*

Institutional questions, the meat of the Constitutional Treaty when all is said and done, were bound to figure and prominently in national campaigns, though not in quite the same way as they did at the Convention, for these are highly technical issues, more important by far to those directly affected by them but much less so to the public at large. Where these issues did feature in national campaigns they were mostly translated into the familiar currency of national interests, in essence who benefited most from the proposed new arrangements. The compromise on Council voting weights, for instance, negotiated during the Irish presidency, figured in the ratification campaigns in Poland and Spain, the principal losers from the compromise. The same thing happened in France, too, which lost the parity with Germany secured at Nice, and likewise in the Czech Republic, where anti-Constitution opinion raised the issue in order to censure the government for its failure to show solidarity with neighbouring Poland.[48]

The proposal for a full-time Council presidency featured in several national campaigns. Supporters of the Constitution claimed it would improve institutional efficiency, whereas opponents saw it as evidence of insidious federalism. Debate in the smaller member states made much of loss of prestige from abandoning rotation. The inclusion of the Charter of Fundamental Rights in the Treaty figured in campaigns in 15 countries, for the most part favourably for those who supported ratification, though some complained that the Charter was too weak. On the other hand, 'no' campaigners in Belgium and Slovakia, and predictably in the United Kingdom, objected that the Charter was too intrusive and compromised national legal discretion.[49]

## *Democracy and efficient governance*

The Laeken Council had raised the matter of democracy deficits and the need to improve decisional procedures. Both issues figured in the campaigns of pro-Constitution movements in several member states. More efficient decision-making was a prominent theme in the 'yes' campaigns in Sweden and the United Kingdom, where pro-EU opinion was defensive in the face of voluble criticism from political and media sources of the Constitution. The Constitution's supporters in these two countries took the view that an appeal to efficiency would be more effective than one based on idealism, the nebulous appeal of the European idea, and as such would be more likely to win over those voters not yet committed either way. But their task was hardly made easier by the fact that the Constitution did so little to advance EU democracy, whether by improving institutional access or by increasing accountability and transparency. Nor did the Constitution do much to improve opportunities for direct participation by citizens in politics at the European level. These shortcomings were readily seized on by 'no' campaigners in the United Kingdom, Sweden, Estonia and Denmark as evidence of a remote project managed by a narrowly based elite. And though the EPIN survey does shows that improved access to rights by means of the Charter featured in the pro-Constitution campaigns in France, Denmark, Ireland, Germany, Slovakia and the Czech Republic, it was just as readily dismissed by opponents as an unwarranted intrusion into the national affairs.[50]

### EU membership

The issue of more or less 'Europe' has acquired increased political salience, but is hardly yet a major issue in domestic politics, and even less is it a major cleavage demarcating party competition compared with either territorial identity or social class.[51] Whether EU membership has positive value barely featured in the ratification campaigns, not even in the more markedly Eurosceptical countries. Even where the issue was raised, there was broad agreement about the advantages overall from EU membership. A *Eurobarometer* survey actually showed support for EU membership rising by 8 percentage points to 56 per cent between April and October 2004, even though support for the Constitution was by then less than firm.[52] Only opinion polling in Poland and the United Kingdom registered more negative than positive ratings for EU membership. Poland, a newcomer concerned to preserve its independence, was much exercised by the withdrawal of what its politicians and media regarded as a better deal on voting weights secured at the Nice Council. Whereas public opinion in the United Kingdom is primed by a virulently Eurosceptical print media, and for that reason is predisposed to see the EU in an unfavourable light, come what may.

The membership issue figured, too, in an increasingly fractious campaign in France, a founder member and supposedly the linchpin of European integration, where the electorate, following the lead of the mainstream parties, did manage to make the crucial distinction between the European Constitution (negative) and EU membership *per se* (positive).[53] The inclusion of an exit clause in the Constitutional Treaty permitting any state to negotiate withdrawal from the Union figured in campaigns in only six countries, most prominently in Denmark and Austria. Though surprisingly not in the United Kingdom, where pro-EU opinion wanted to avoid raising that 'unpalatable prospect' and Europhobes were uninterested in anything that lessened the apparent 'threat' of a supposed 'super-state'. Where this issue was raised elsewhere by the Constitution's supporters, it was cited as proof positive of inalienable sovereignty, the ultimate right of every member state to exercise national self-determination.

### European identity

European identity hardly figured as a critical issue anywhere. In part, this is because the issue is more a preoccupation of scholars than it is a matter for the ordinary citizen. The formal status of EU citizenship notwithstanding, there is little affective identity between EU citizens, let alone a pervasive sense of political affiliation, of belonging to a political community with shared values and a common identity. This is hardly surprising, for the new constitutional arrangements were negotiated at a remove from the people and primarily by elites more concerned to improve decisional efficiency and reforming institutional procedures than with bringing 'the people' closer to the project.

The identity question is closely linked to the Union's demonstrable legitimacy shortfall, and it did figure in the campaign in France, though marginally and only in a negative sense, part of the case made by opponents of Turkish accession. The EPIN survey that tracked public attitudes on the Constitution found that the references to identity in the Constitution's Preamble, though hardly a critical issue anywhere, did feature in campaigns in 15 member states, and with more negative than positive value.[54]

### Material benefits

The economic benefits accruing from European integration featured almost everywhere as an argument for ratification, and most prominently in those states (Spain, Portugal, Greece and Ireland) that since their accession have been the principal recipients of EU structural and cohesion funding. This issue figured, and for similar reasons, in campaigns in the new member states, who 'are in principle going to be the main beneficiaries of EU funding in the coming years'. The material benefits of EU membership are important for accession countries coming to terms with the twin shocks of transition and acquiring the infrastructure that will reduce the costs and increase the benefits of the Single Market for less competitive economies. One commentator has concluded that 'ultimately, east Europeans will judge the success or failure of EU membership largely by its impact on their pockets [and] with unemployment in these countries averaging 14 per cent, living standards well below the EU average, and budget deficits threatening economic stability – particularly in Hungary, where a foreign exchange crisis in 2004 ensued after currency traders became alarmed at a rising fiscal and current account deficit, the Czech Republic and Poland – the benefits of economic integration seem rather more problematic than they do further west'.[55]

Pro-Constitution campaigners in the accession countries made much of unprecedented levels of economic growth, and attributed this to the gravitational 'pull' of imminent EU membership. GDP was set to rise by 5 per cent in 2005, an increase of 1.3 per cent on 2003, with the World Bank forecasting even higher growth of twice the annual rate of the former EU15 states. The prospect of accession has encouraged large-scale inward investment, especially in portfolio capital, with stock markets rising markedly, in Slovakia for instance by an impressive 84 per cent, admittedly from a historically low base. Exports, too, had grown by some 20 per cent, with notably strong performances from Poland and the Czech Republic, particularly in agricultural produce. Farmers in the accession countries received their first agricultural payments under CAP in 2004, capped by EU15 but nevertheless with a minimum of 500 euros for even the smallest farmers. The Commission estimated that in 2004 farmers' incomes had risen by 50 per cent in the new member states, with a rise of 108 per cent in the Czech Republic and 73 per cent in Poland.[56]

By any previous measure this is an impressive economic performance, with supposedly better to follow, and this helped offset understandable concern in the accession states about receiving what they saw as a less than inequitable share of structural assistance in the 2007–13 financial perspective. The present beneficiaries, particularly Spain and the other Mediterranean states, had resisted a significant redistribution of these resources, giving rise to resentment in the accession countries that found expression during the ratification campaigns. Even so, perceptions of deprivation were relative rather than absolute, and though one *Eurobarometer* poll did record levels of satisfaction with the EU generally lower in Eastern than in Western Europe, this was offset by a pervasive sense of realism there, with generally low dissatisfaction ratings for the EU.

Pro-Constitution campaigners in the accession states used the material benefits of membership against opponents, notably in Poland.[57] As Stephen Wagstyl explains the situation, 'a large number of voters in the middle are waiting to see how membership will turn out for their countries. For eastern Europe's supporters and critics of EU integration there is everything to play for [and] the first few months of membership have done more to emphasise the advantages than the disadvantages of the Union.'[58] One issue that Eurosceptics in these countries did raise was the unseemly wrangle over Council voting weights, the concern of some smaller member states especially in the accession countries about the undue influence of the 'big three'.

### Global standing

Neither the pro- nor anti-Constitution campaigns made much of the Laeken objective to improve the Union's global standing. This was hardly surprising, in as much as opinion everywhere, other than in the most Eurosceptical countries, was far more concerned about material matters. After all, citizens look to national governments to guarantee their security, and this issue for most of them is regarded as primarily a national rather than an EU matter. An enhanced role for CFSP, and particularly for the full-time EU foreign minister, featured in pro-Constitution campaigns in 10 countries, with opponents countering that the proposed extension of QMV *per se* to cover some aspects of external policy threatened an independent foreign and security policy. QMV was better received in countries historically favourable to deeper integration (France, Germany, Italy and the Netherlands) than in the traditionally Eurosceptical countries (the United Kingdom, Sweden, Denmark), or in those that might be called Euro-pragmatic countries (Austria, Slovakia, the Czech Republic), where there was also some public concern about loss of sovereignty.[59]

## Critical national debates: the big three

### Britain – managing domestic expectations

Euroscepticism is widespread in the United Kingdom, and it was bound to feature in the debate on the Constitution, with the familiar mantra from some political and media sources that the Constitution was merely the latest chapter in the long-running conspiracy to deprive the nation of historic sovereignty, yet another political betrayal by a 'misguided' liberal establishment.[60] True to form, the media highlighted alleged 'conspiracy'. One prominent journalist, for instance, described the choice facing voters in a referendum in neo-apocalyptic terms, as nothing less than a defining moment in national history, 'the biggest political decision for British voters since 1945', and one that 'would change everything', warning that: 'If you believe in the European ideal which is to create a United States of Europe, you should vote for the constitution in the referendum and a pro-constitution party in the General Election [but] if you are opposed to the US of E, and believe in British independence and democracy, you should vote No in the referendum and for an anti-constitution party in the General Election.'[61]

The timing of ratification was critical, not so much for the outcome, which was never really in doubt, but to the government's choice of tactics for ensuring damage limitation. With the media in full cry against the Constitution from the start, and the government facing a collapse in public trust after damaging revelations about the veracity of the intelligence used to take the country to war against Iraq, Prime Minister Blair gave way to the clamour for a referendum. As he saw it, it was the least worse option in the circumstances, though a decision driven primarily by political calculus and damage limitation, not by constitutional propriety, and even less by principle.[62] The decision brought, nevertheless, its own complications. With a general election imminent and with it the tantalising prospect of Blair becoming the first Labour leader to win three successive general elections and thereby securing his place in history, the prime minister needed to neutralise the Constitution issue as a likely vote loser. This meant postponing the issue and thus the ignominy of almost certain defeat, delaying this particular showdown with the electorate until the general election was safely out of the way.[63]

Referendums are far from being customary procedure, and even less so for enacting what passes for constitutional change in Britain. They have generally been opposed by the mainstream parties as an affront to Blackstone's classic defence of parliamentary sovereignty. This historical predilection was confirmed by the politically neutral Electoral Commission (the public body charged with ensuring fair practice in elections), who saw only danger in politicising constitutional issues, and even offered the opinion 'that referendums on fundamental issues of national importance should be considered in isolation [for] cross-party campaigning on a fundamental referendum could cause significant confusion amongst the electorate if combined with normal party election campaigning'.[64] The Conservative opposition had no such doubts. For them, the Constitution was political or it was nothing, and they condemned what they saw as government prevarication over holding the referendum.[65] Though this was mostly disingenuous, for delay suited their interests, too, concerned as they were lest a 'flawed' and 'unnecessary' treaty should pass in Parliament by means of a government majority larger than that predicted by pundits for the government after the general election. Delay suited both main parties, and in fact it took some of the heat out of the issue, until the results of votes in France and the Netherlands relegated the issue down the nation's political priorities, at least for the time being.[66]

There was little to cheer the pro-Constitution campaign, though some early polls briefly indicated that public opinion was viscous, fairly evenly divided on the issue. A *Eurobarometer* poll conducted immediately after the IGC had concluded its business actually found a slight majority (51 per cent) of British respondents in favour of the idea of at least a European constitution, with 52 per cent of respondents prepared to accept the Constitution with some changes, but this finding was reversed in all subsequent polls. The important statistic here is the 71 per cent of respondents who admitted to being 'ill-informed' about either the Constitution's implications or content. The media's role was critical here for changing minds, and it did what the British media tends to do where the EU is concerned, framing the agenda for the most part in negative terms, informing – critics would say 'misinforming' – the public about the Constitution in a way that reinforced endemic hostility to all things 'European'.

It is hardly surprising, then, even at this early stage, that the levels of support recorded by pollsters as favourable to a European Constitution were amongst the lowest in any EU member state, vying for 'least popular' with the Scandinavians.[67] Government strategists tried to make the best of a poor hand by characterising the anti-Constitution campaign, and especially its opponents in the Conservative Party, as unremitting 'reactionaries' whose visceral Europhobia was nothing less than a threat to the national interest.[68] Government spokespersons duly dismissed the Conservatives' ritualistic call for renegotiation of Britain's EU membership as merely fantasy politics, and a folly that would marginalise Britain.[69] And a disingenuous ploy no less that supposedly disguised the Opposition's 'true' intentions, to take Britain out of the Union altogether.[70]

The prime minister made much of an otherwise difficult situation by ridiculing the Conservatives' 'unrelenting' propagation of 'myths' about the Constitution. The decision was timely as Blair saw it, for it would 'resolve once and for all whether this country, Britain, wants to be at the centre and heart of European decision-making or not', it was 'time to decide whether our destiny lies as a leading partner and ally of Europe or at its margins'. Warming to his theme, he added: 'Let the Eurosceptics, whose true agenda we will expose, make their case. Let those of us who believe in Britain in Europe not because of Europe alone but because we believe in Britain and our national interests lying in Europe – let us make our case too. Let the issue be put and let the battle be joined.'[71] The Conservative Party refuted these charges, but it proposed nevertheless opting out of some aspects of the current treaties, whilst 'magnanimously' offering not to stand in the way of member states that wanted to integrate further. But this objective was, to say the least, problematical, for it was far from clear what was optional about a Constitutional Treaty that covered every aspect of EU membership.[72]

The government tried to make the most of this apparent inconsistency, presenting the Constitution not so much on its procedural merits but rather as a stark choice between 'staying in' or 'quitting' the Union.[73] It gambled here on what it took to be British pragmatism, that while the electorate routinely complains about 'Brussels' they would vote nevertheless for 'Europe', if only on the basis of material self-interest.[74] In fact, the choice facing Britain was nothing like as stark, in spite of being put to the public in a single referendum question.[75] The long-promised and equally long-postponed referendum on Eurozone membership was a quite different matter. This was a straightforward choice in the same way as Britain's previous European referendum in 1975, the question then being whether to remain as a member or quit the Community. The Constitutional Treaty presented no such clear-cut options. It was instead an inordinately complicated document with myriad articles, clauses and protocols, some that would empower the Union and others the member states. A singular question could hardly do justice to such complexities, or indeed to those ambiguities implicit in this choice. Nor was it apparent what the consequences of a 'no' vote would be.

This issue was as much a predicament for the pro-Constitution camp as it was for the Conservative Party, for whom the issue was a straightforward 'no' to 'more Europe. Those who favoured the Constitution were vulnerable to the argument that a 'yes' vote amounted to a blank cheque or blind bargain. The government preferred in the circumstances to say as little as possible about the Constitution. The task of making the case for it was left to a small group of pro-Europeans. What they lacked in numbers they made up for in zeal, convinced that the case 'for' Europe could be made and with advantage, persuaded, too, that the more people learned about the Constitution the more easily would be dispelled the baleful myths being peddled by its opponents. But only if the government would take the initiative and confront the Eurosceptics head-on.[76] The extent of public ignorance on the Constitution was plain to see. A report published by the EU Commission and based on a sample of 25,000 EU citizens showed British respondents to be the least informed about the EU, only 11 per cent of respondents claiming to know anything of the Constitution's content.[77] It is notable, too, that knowledge levels about the EU were marginally lower in countries holding referendums, 65 per cent compared to 67 per cent for those opting for parliamentary ratification. One third of all respondents had not even heard of the Treaty, and of the 58 per cent who had most knew little of its substance. Of a generally poorly informed public opinion throughout the Union, British respondents reported having least knowledge of the Constitution.

The 'yes' campaign roundly criticised the government for its reluctance to dispel public ignorance.[78] One of Blair's former policy advisers, Roger Liddle, now a cabinet member of the new British commissioner, Peter Mandelson, advised the government to explain the Constitution's merits, to make the case for Europe as a bastion of stability and free trade, a worthy partner rather than a mere supplicant of American hyper-power, and the best way for Britain and its continental partners to respond to the daunting challenges of globalisation.[79] The government, however, abjured any such boldness and preferred to be reticent in the face of growing opposition. Once the decision to hold a referendum had been taken, the view from Downing Street seemed to be that the less said about the Constitution the better, except for the occasional official homily.[80] The government preferred to react to rather than to lead the debate.[81] When official voices did refer to the issue, they traded in generalities, avoiding any concerted effort to sell a Constitutional Treaty the government had already signed up to.[82] The prime minister in a parliamentary statement made much of the Union's limited incursion on national sovereignty, and recommended even this as a fair trade for participation in a project that is 'the most successful way anyone has yet devised of managing relations between European countries whose national rivalries had, until sixty years ago, only ever been settled in a series of bloody conflicts'.[83]

This pragmatic case for the Constitution was a principal theme in the government's White Paper on the Constitution, published in September 2004. In the foreword, the prime minister wrote: 'I have no hesitation in commending [The Constitutional Treaty] to the country as a success and as a significant step forward in creating the kind of Europe that the British people want: a flexible Europe in which Britain remains a strong and influential power; a wider, peaceful and free Europe to which we can be proud to belong; and an effective Europe which benefits all our lives.'[84]

The official case maintained that the Constitutional Treaty was in the national interest and in no way extended the Union's powers over its member states, but was merely a way to better secure the national interest in Europe. This was precisely what the foreign secretary, Jack Straw, meant when he asserted that the objective of the European project is not to surrender sovereignty to a super-state but instead to 'reclaim the flag', and that 'the real patriotic case' is for 'Britain's engagement in the European Union'.[85] But the government knew it was on shaky ground. The case for the Constitution was made, where it was made at all, *sotto voce*. Despite hiring a public relations firm to advise on how to better get the message across, the government throughout followed rather more than it led public opinion.[86] Some pro-Constitution campaigners, perplexed by the government's limited engagement with the public on the issue, made an unflattering comparison with the more upbeat campaign in neighbouring Ireland, where the government had launched a National Forum to explain the reasons for adopting the Constitution.[87]

As always where 'Europe' is the issue, political divisions were by no means exclusively along party lines. European integration has always been divisive for both of the main British parties, though since the Thatcher years the Conservative Party, and core Tory voters generally, are more hostile to the EU than either Labour or Liberal Democrat supporters.[88] An alliance of political convenience between business and organised labour had delivered victory for the pro-European side in the 1975 referendum, when even Mrs Thatcher, then a government minister and before her subsequent political metamorphosis into a janissary of Europhobia, had campaigned for Britain to stay in the EC. But things had changed since then, and markedly, with the business community more divided now about the benefits of Europe when making the familiar calculus between market opportunities versus the costs to business of over-regulation.[89]

The trades unions, too, were by now less enthusiastic about a project many of their members regard as a bastion of neo-liberalism and a stalking horse for remorseless globalisation, one with an adverse impact on labour conditions, employment levels and pay. The Trades Union Congress, representing some 6 million workers, refused to endorse the Constitution, and some trade union leaders echoed the case being made by the French left against a Constitution designed, or so they claimed, to 'institutionalise privatisation and the neo-liberal economics that have helped wreck industries in Britain and turned the EU into one of the world's low growth regions'.[90] A group of Labour backbench MPs formed Labour against a European super-state, some of them hostile, as many on the left always have been, to this supposedly 'capitalist club', though others amongst them were less exercised by ideology *per se* and plainly concerned lest this deeply unpopular project should damage the party's prospects – and with it their parliamentary seats – in the forthcoming general election.[91]

The anti-Constitution lobby had no such reservations about a political project they saw as wholly inappropriate for what should be 'merely' an international organisation of independent states. Some commentators went even further in their critique, castigating a metropolitan elite 'utterly out of touch', as they saw it, with the public's instinctive patriotism, and as such lacking its 'innate common sense'. Simon Wolfson, for example, a board member of the 'Vote No' campaign, described the White Paper as 'like the ramblings of a slightly pompous megalo-maniac', not least the fanciful claim in the Constitution's original Preamble 'that the people of Europe are determined to transcend their ancient divisions and, united ever more closely, forge a common destiny'. As Wolfson saw it, Europe's political class is patently wrong in 'this entirely unjustified conviction', for 'how can they be so sure of what the people of Europe think, let alone that we want to forge a common destiny?'.[92]

The anti-Constitution campaigners certainly reflected the public's mood more accurately than their opponents did. Polling data showed the extent of the government's predicament. The 'no' side held a clear lead from the outset. The only comfort for the pro-Constitution side was the large number of voters (65 per cent according to a MORI poll conducted for the Foreign Policy Centre) who had yet to make up their minds, and with a further 20 per cent who registered a 'don't know' response. This same poll found that only 31 per cent, however, were 'strongly in favour' or 'in favour' of the Treaty, with 50 per cent 'strongly opposed' or 'opposed'.[93] Another survey identified a mere 8 per cent of these undecided respondents as 'persuadable sceptics', that is almost certain to vote in a referendum, but more inclined to say 'no' to the Constitution.[94]

Public opposition to the Constitution grew as the campaign gathered pace. The more the British were reminded about the Constitution, the less they seemed to like it. Opposition grew markedly after the government published the referendum enabling Bill on 26 January 2005.[95] One poll conducted in late January 2005 registered almost 70 per cent against the Treaty, compared with just 45 per cent in a poll by the same organisation in July 2003.[96] Public antipathy was in inverse proportion to knowledge of the issues, with only half the electorate in another poll reporting that they had even heard of the Constitution and 94 per cent of those admitting to knowing little or nothing about it, only 6 per cent broadly claiming to know anything of its contents.[97] The dearth of public knowledge was not of course confined to the British, but with support for the Constitution generally higher else-where (at around 50 per cent), this was less a handicap for 'yes' campaigners.[98] This knowledge gap did nevertheless prompt Commission vice-president, Margot Wallström, to warn governments that 'the process of ratification of the Constitution will only succeed if governments and all other relevant actors mobilise to provide information to citizens, to ensure a truly informed debate'.[99] The European Parliament was similarly concerned that a lack of information would reinforce public apathy, or even make it easier for Eurosceptics to perpetuate their 'falsehoods'. MEPs called on governments, NGOs and other political institutions 'to mount an information campaign', with the vice-chairman of the Parliament's Socialist group claiming that the 'better-informed people are, the more likely they are to form a positive assessment of the Constitution'.[100]

The British parties wrangled over the referendum question, and though it eventually approved the actual wording of the question the Conservative Opposition demanded an amendment to separate from the Bill the enabling legislation for implementing the Treaty, claiming that by rolling two bills into one the government was trying covertly to bring the Treaty into law even before a referendum.[101] The supposedly neutral wording of the referendum question, 'Should the United Kingdom approve the treaty establishing a constitution for the European Union?', persuaded anti-Constitution campaigners of the government's duplicity, maintaining that the word 'approve' breached the Electoral Commission's own guidelines on neutrality, by putting a positive spin on the proposal. The government was accused in effect of loading the question. Even the Electoral Commission was indicted for failing to stand up to the government on this issue. These same critics argued that the official question did not 'make clear that the treaty which the United Kingdom is invited to approve doesn't just apply to the distant EU but will affect Britain, indeed fundamentally change our laws and constitution'.[102]

The Electoral Commission had already suggested a model question in October 2004 which used the official name, *Constitution for Europe*. The Commission took the view that while the government's preferred wording did not diminish the significance of the issue, nor devalue what was at stake, it agreed nevertheless with the government's critics that the choice of question was strictly speaking inaccurate, in so far as it modified rather than used the exact Treaty title, namely a *Treaty Establishing a Constitution for Europe*. The Electoral Commission stated that its own preference was for a direct reference in the referendum question to the actual name of the Treaty. Opinion poll data added to the controversy. An ICM poll using the government's preferred wording reported that support and opposition for ratification was tied at 39 per cent. Whereas a second poll conducted concurrently by the same organisation found that a slightly modified wording produced a clear 54 per cent to 26 per cent margin against ratification.[103]

Whatever the form of words used, the public was broadly hostile to the Constitution. The *Eurobarometer* poll (conducted in October/November 2004, published in May 2005) confirmed a broad trend in national polling showing support for the Constitution throughout the Union was well below 50 per cent. This was not the first *Eurobarometer* survey to inquire about the idea of a European constitution, but the first one to gauge the state of public opinion about the actual Constitutional Treaty, and it found that Britons were the least likely EU electorate after Denmark to endorse this, with 49 per cent against, 29 in favour and 22 per cent undecided.[104]

On the eve of the French referendum there seemed to be little prospect of the British electorate supporting this Constitution, whenever the referendum was held. By now the abiding impression was of a government lamely trying to talk up a Constitution certain to be rejected, waiting on events rather than managing them. Even after Blair secured his historic third term – albeit with a much-reduced majority – the government simply failed to make the case for the Constitution, let alone to actively campaign for it. The Constitution had barely figured in the election campaign. Neither of the two main parties, for their own quite different reasons, wanted to discuss Europe. An anti-Constitution alliance, a curious mix of socialists and right-wing Eurosceptics, business representatives and Greens tried to make the Constitution an election issue, to copy the successful French populist alliance that had done so much to deliver the 'no' vote in France, but in vain.[105]

This much is familiar to close observers of British policy towards the EU over the past decade and more. And something of an embarrassment, too, for those who had bought into Blair's boast early in his premiership about putting the country 'at the heart of Europe' rather than settling for a semi-detached role on the margins.[106] Events elsewhere, however, came as welcome relief to the government. The result of the French referendum, a decisive '*non*' and this from a country that was not only a founder member but a self-appointed engine of the European project, threw the ratification process into disarray, rescuing a government already well adrift of the electorate on an issue for which it had showed little enthusiasm, and given even less by way of firm leadership.

### France – snatching defeat from the jaws of victory

The French constitution requires that treaties be ratified, either by a two-thirds vote of both chambers of parliament or by means of a referendum. The decision to hold a referendum on this occasion was entirely determined by politics. Chirac's preference for parliamentary ratification was nullified, in no small part by the British government's decision to defer to public opinion on a measure generally regarded by supporters and opponents alike to be historic, and in the process making it difficult for Chirac to deny his electorate the same opportunity. Referendums had previously been used in France to decide European issues, though only occasionally, and their outcome had always turned on the state of domestic politics, as much as on the issue in question.

This latest referendum was no exception, with leading politicians using the issue to position themselves in advance of the 2007 presidential elections. Aware of his government's poor opinion poll ratings and concerned by factionalism within his own party, Chirac tried to outmanoeuvre those seeking to prevent his renomination for the presidency.[107] Pressure grew inside the ruling UMP for a referendum as rivals manoeuvred on the succession. The then finance minister and party president, Nicolas Sarkozy, Chirac's leading challenger for the party's 2007 presidential nomination, called for a referendum, part of a strategy to bolster support for his own candidature.[108] Unable to avoid a referendum, Chirac's tried to turn it to his advantage, both to outflank Sarkozy and to highlight an even deeper split over Europe in the opposition Socialist Party.[109]

The left was the easier target here, fatally divided on the Constitution, itself a symbol of deeper ideological differences over an appropriate social and economic response to globalisation. One faction led by Françoise Hollande saw the Constitution as a historic opportunity for closer integration, as did another presidential contender and former finance minister, Dominique Strauss-Kahn.[110] But another party faction grouped around the former prime minister and deputy leader, Laurent Fabius, an enthusiast for a quite different model of European integration, opposed the Constitution as too 'Anglo-Saxon' in its preoccupation with 'markets' and 'competition', and for that very reason a threat to French jobs and to the welfare state.[111] Fabius and those who shared his concern to protect 'social Europe' were particularly exercised by Part III of the Constitution, criticising this for being 'a list of policies, rather than principles, [that] has no place in a constitution', and moreover policies that threatened to impose unpalatable neo-liberal reforms.[112] The Constitution was proxy, then, in an ideological struggle between modernisers and revanchists for the soul of the French left.[113] The Socialists tried to head off what threatened to be a corrosive dispute by holding an intra-party referendum in November 2004.[114] And despite a clear victory for those in the party who favoured the Constitution, internecine warfare continued, with devastating consequences for the party's electoral credibility, and no less for the Constitution at the ballot box.

When the ratification campaign began this catastrophe was not remotely visible on the political radar. Early polling evidence showed a commanding lead for the Constitution, well up in the comfort zone of the mid-60 per cents.[115] Referendums are frequently determined by issues that have little or nothing to do with the substantive issue, and there was certainly much in this campaign for a disquieted electorate to use against the incumbents. Chirac's government was deeply unpopular on a range of issues wholly unrelated to the Constitution: the notorious financial scandal that enveloped finance minister Hervé Gaymard;[116] controversial welfare reforms;[117] and widespread concern about an anticipated increase in immigration following Eastern enlargement. The referendum became a convenient political lightning-conductor for these and for other issues, an opportunity for a protest vote.[118] The opinion polls showed as much, recording a steady loss of support for the Constitutional Treaty during the campaign.[119] There was a notable precedent, too, for in the campaign on the Maastricht Treaty in September 1992 a supposedly unassailable lead for ratification fell away during the course of the campaign to a majority of barely 2 per cent, the so-called '*petit oui*'. There were undoubtedly substantive grievances over the Constitution, but for many voters the Constitution became confused with their broader concerns about European policy, whether opposition to the highly unpopular services directive concerned by 'the question of how to keep some social solidarity within the framework of market economy',[120] or to Turkish accession.[121]

It has become fashionable to discount the role of ideology in contemporary politics. Whether this is so or how far it is so elsewhere in Europe in what some now describe as 'post-modern' politics, it hardly applies to France, where ideas continue to have both emotional and cultural, as much as intellectual resonance for politics. The debate here was grounded in fundamental differences over the meaning of 'Europe'. As Tim King has observed, those who campaigned in France against the European Constitution did so 'for precisely the opposite reason to that of Britain's Eurosceptics [for] the French are fervent Europeans, who believe that the EU is becoming too "Anglo-Saxon"'.[122] The 'no' camp was not so much against Europe as concerned that a familiar Europe should not be swamped by an alien political economy, and for many swamped by aliens *per se*!

There was circumstantial evidence to justify some of these concerns. The proposed services directive, for instance, designed as many saw it precisely to facilitate American-dominated globalisation by establishing a single European market for services, seemed to threaten both jobs and wage levels. Impending enlargement and an accompanying influx of cheaper labour threatened the domestic labour market. The Constitution became a lightning-rod for these and other concerns, and more than that a harbinger for a model of public policy alien to traditional social values, a Trojan horse as some saw it for rapacious Anglo-Saxon rather than the more humane home-grown Rhenish capitalism.[123] The alternative, as opponents of the Constitutional Treaty saw it, was to hold out for a more familiar Europe, to 'rebuild [the EU] as a more integrated – and inward-looking – political grouping with France and Germany at its centre'.[124]

This defiant mood hardly appealed to so-called modernisers, whether on left or right, who saw instead 'the need to embrace change'. For them, resisting a liberalising EU was misplaced sentiment and they duly served warning that 'France's battle against Brussels [over the services directive] is in need of a reappraisal … as indeed are many of the arguments of the [French] opponents of the European Constitution'.[125] The principal fault-line in this debate was not between left and right, for the issue divided the mainstream parties, as it did those in the Netherlands, where there was a similar debate about social priorities. The debate was grounded instead in fundamental differences over the logics and direction of global change.[126] Some politicians, notably Sarkozy on the centre-right, served warning that France could not opt out of the emergent global order, nor avoid facing up to the challenges that confront every advanced country in the new century, facts that demanded a revision of old shibboleths. For Sarkozy and other modernisers: 'The best social model is the one which gives everyone a job [and] alas, that is no longer ours, with three million out of work. It is ideological blindness to reject for our country what is happening elsewhere.'[127] This message was hardly likely to resonate with an electorate rooted in a collectivist tradition. Chirac's government had simply failed 'to prepare domestic public opinion for the way the EU is changing', preferring short-term fixes and rhetoric to decisive action and tough talking, though polling data did show rising public anxiety about how the EU might cope with global pressures. There was concern about a Europe that 'is very much about open markets and competitiveness', and whose citizens are 'struggling to accept that an enlarged and fast-changing EU resembles British ideas more closely than the old Gallic vision'.[128]

Yet the government seemed content merely to wait on events, hardly bothering to make the case for the Constitution, let alone for the 'new' Europe. Even when official spokesmen mentioned the Constitution they mostly concentrated on technicalities, failing to confront the potent arguments levelled against it by energetic '*non*' campaigners. Public unease with 'Europe' barely seemed to signify with the government. Prime Minister Raffarin, for instance, tried to take the politics out of the issue, by claiming that 'this *rendez-vous* with history is not a partisan *rendez-vous*. Europe is not of the right. Europe is not of the left. Europe is our future. It is our destiny.'[129] But such rhetoric did little to assuage growing doubts about a Constitution its opponents claimed reflected everything that was wrong with France, with Europe and with a rapacious global order. When Chirac was eventually shaken from torpor late in the day, his response was typically jejune, less statesmanlike than that of a gambler backing a long shot. He decided to bring the referendum forward to May 2005, a full month earlier than planned, a vain attempt to deny the opposition momentum. Accordingly, he convened a joint session of both houses of parliament to meet the constitutional requirement for a referendum. But it was too late to affect the outcome, for events had already moved beyond his capacity to influence them. What had seemed at the outset to be a fairly straightforward ratification became more problematic by the week.[130]

By spring 2005 opinion polls predicted a close-run outcome, then the '*non*' camp moved into a firm lead that they maintained for the duration.[131] Every published opinion poll showed a strong tide running against the Constitution, with the government and its allies in the business community seemingly paralysed, unable or unwilling to make a convincing case for ratification.[132] Chirac was especially culpable here, entering the fray in earnest only during the latter stages, and even then without conviction, let alone impact. His one presidential broadcast to the nation, an opportunity to show statesmanship, to win over waverers, simply lacked conviction. He preferred instead to be defensive about the Constitution, vaguely alluding to a loss of international prestige in the event of a defeat, hinting, too, at a threat to CAP funding. But this was the negative tenor of the government's campaign, reasons not to vote against the Constitution rather than a convincing case to vote for it.[133] It was a lacklustre performance, even by Chirac's usual standards, and by no means enough to turn the tide of public opinion already strongly running against the Constitution. The business community tried to do the government's job, issuing a manifesto signed by prominent business leaders that warned of the dangers of retreating into 'Fortress France', claiming that the labour market reforms outlined in the Constitution and making for a more flexible Europe would be no bad thing, equipping the continent for confronting the challenges of globalisation, by facilitating competitiveness and without undermining the French social model.[134] But this was too little and too late, with the 'no' campaign well ahead and winning the arguments that mattered.

The result of the referendum, a clear defeat for the Constitution, was a foregone conclusion before a single vote was cast. Of the 28,985,293 votes cast (69.34 per cent), the 'no' campaign won by a comfortable margin, 15,450,279 (54.68 per cent) to 12,806,394 (45.32 per cent), with 12,814,573 abstentions (30.66 per cent of the total electorate), and with 728,620 (2.51 per cent) blank or invalid votes. Even these figures do not tell the whole story. The turnout of almost 70 per cent is an indication of the level of public interest, higher than for the Maastricht referendum of 1992, and much higher than the 42.8 per cent recorded for the June 2004 European elections, the lowest turn-out figure ever recorded in France for a European election. This was by no means victory by default. The breakdown of these voting figures gives some indication of the public's mood, and reveals much about the shift in French attitudes on Europe. Those who voted '*oui*' did so, as we might expect, primarily because they were generally content with the project. Whereas '*non*' voters were more ambivalent, many expressing not so much anti-EU sentiments as dissatisfaction with their material prospects and life-chances, concerns that were by no means entirely attributed to the current trajectory of European integration. But for some voters a decline in their sense of personal security and employment prospects was attributed to Europe, and the Constitution as they saw it would merely make things worse. The policy proposals outlined in Part III, for example, were a case in point, adding to regulations and threatening to diminish further Europe's social model.

But this was by no means the whole picture. The reasons for the '*non*' vote are many and disparate, reflecting both national and/or social concerns, rather than being directly related to European integration. For some voters the negative effects of the Constitution on employment (31 per cent) was the clinching argument, for others it was France's poor economic situation (26 per cent), or the perception of the Constitution as being too liberal from an economic perspective (19 per cent). Yet others voted 'no' as a protest against Chirac/the government (18 per cent). The *Eurobarometer* poll conducted immediately after the referendum bears out these findings, concluding that 'generally, the key element which motivated the majority of the "yes" supporters is their general view of the European Union, while the majority of those who voted '*non*' were guided by their views of France's economic and social situation'.[135]

An unholy alliance of traditional left and the far right joined forces to defeat the Constitution, a revolt from below, and if not quite revenge visited on Europe's political establishment by latter-day sansculottes, at least a populist protest against *les métropolitains* who run the show, always have run things and seemingly in their own narrow interests. As one commentator saw it: 'The right wants to recover lost sovereignty, the left to preserve the old social state, regardless of expense. The grassroots are about to have their revenge on the establishment. … The EU has become the surrogate target for that revolt.'[136] The situation on the '*oui*' side was almost a mirror-image of this, decisions determined less by domestic concerns than support for European integration. The polling data shows that '*oui*' voters saw the Constitution as indispensable for consolidating European construction (39 per cent), some respondents even expressing enthusiastic support for yet deeper integration (16 per cent), but others voting 'yes' in what they saw as the national interest, to strengthen France's role in the EU (12 per cent), or to improve EU–USA relations (11 per cent), and some because the Constitution was seen as a means for consolidating Europe's social dimension (8 per cent).

The breakdown of polling data shows a marked contrast between support for the idea of Europe and support for the Constitution, which for many voters was by no means the same thing. Europe as an idea or even as an ideal, fared far better with voters than the Constitution did *per se*. For the size of the '*non*' vote notwithstanding, the special *Eurobarometer* survey concluded that 'the French people do not call into question their country's membership of the European Union and 88 per cent of all respondents consider that EU membership of the EU is a good thing'. Moreover, 'this positive opinion is shared not only by all the 'yes' supporters (99 per cent) but also by the vast majority of the supporters of the 'no' vote (83 per cent)'.[137] A majority of respondents on both sides of the question continued to have a positive image of the European institutions (53 per cent), especially amongst the 18–24 cohort (62 per cent), though paradoxically this group was strongly resistant to the Constitution. Urban voters, too, were generally more receptive to EU institutions (58 per cent) compared with rural voters.

There were also some significant demographic and geographical disparities between opponents and supporters of the Constitution. Opposition was greater amongst the 40–55 age cohort (63 per cent) and the 18–24 cohort (59 per cent), and amongst those not living in big cities (61 per cent) and those in smaller urban centres (61 per cent), but above all manual workers (76 per cent). The abstention rate was markedly higher for voters under 40 years of age, although only 14 per cent of abstainers cited opposition to the Constitution as their principal reason for abstention, with more respondents citing material factors (66 per cent), the complexity of the issue (60 per cent) or a lack of information (49 per cent).[138] Although this was by no means an exclusively partisan affair, domestic political allegiances, too, influenced popular attitudes, with supporters of the governing UMP/UDF parties more inclined to view European institutions favourably (69 per cent) compared with extreme right (FN/MNR) supporters (19 per cent) or the Communist Party (34 per cent).[139]

The data confirm an electorate altogether less hostile to European integration than to the Constitution, and less opposed to the idea of a European constitution *per se* than to this particular Constitution. Significantly, some three quarters of all voters accepted that a constitution is indispensable for consolidating European construction (75 per cent), even including 66 per cent of '*non*' voters.[140] This paradox is explained by comparing present concerns with future aspirations. The same survey showed that more than 6 out of 10 respondents believed that a '*non*' vote would somehow ensure renegotiation of the Constitutional Treaty, replacing it with a version more favourable to the national interest (59 per cent), or for some others a constitution altogether more favourable to the social dimension (62 per cent), far less conducive to 'predatory' Anglo-Saxon-style globalisation. This response was especially favoured by respondents in the age cohort 40–54 (67 per cent) and as such nearer to retirement, and by manual workers (71 per cent), a group traditionally receptive to a strong welfare state.[141]

These findings by no means bode ill for future constitutional endeavour in the EU. Declaration 30 attached by EU political leaders to the draft Constitutional Treaty had prescribed that if, two years after signature by the heads of state and government, four-fifths of member states had ratified, but one or more had not done so, the matter should be referred to the European Council. In that eventuality, this survey showed that only 36 per cent of French voters actually preferred to see the Constitution abandoned, a further 35 per cent opting for another referendum or parliamentary vote in those countries that had not yet ratified: by no means a majority, but indicative nevertheless of the fact that a significant part of public opinion is not intrinsically opposed to the idea of a European constitution. The idea of holding another referendum, presumably to ask much the same question, invariably appealed more to those who had voted yes (54 per cent), as well as to government party supporters (45 per cent).[142] Nevertheless, only 48 per cent of '*non*' voters wanted the complete abandonment of the constitutional endeavour. As one French commentator saw the situation, 'very few No-voters are against the EU. They do not want to leave the Union; rather, they aspire, in a revolutionary spirit, to change it. After a No vote, everything will be better. Even the supporters of national sovereignty do not dare to reject Europe.'[143] But what they did do on this occasion was to reject the Constitution, an outcome that brought the EU closer to 'crisis' than at any previous time in its history.

### *Germany*

Germany has an aversion to referendums, a direct consequence of its pre-war political history. Constitutional matters are not entrusted directly to the people but instead are dealt with by parliament and the courts. The fashion for referendums elsewhere did win some support for the idea even in the ranks of the governing parties, fuelled in part by lingering public resentment at least in some quarters that Germans had been denied any say in replacing their trusty D-mark with the euro.[144] To hold a referendum, however, would have required a revision of the Basic Law, a time-consuming process and one with an uncertain outcome. Some elements in both major parties and in the minor opposition parties did propose draft legislation to this end, a response in part to the opinion of some eminent legal theorists that a referendum on the Constitution would serve as retrospective legitimation denied to citizens on both the historic decisions on reunification and on the adoption of the common currency. But it proved impossible to effect change of such constitutional magnitude without all-party support.[145]

The two mainstream or 'catch-all' parties endorsed the Constitution as both good for Germany and indispensable for Europe. Chancellor Schroeder and foreign minister Fischer wanted a speedy rather than a long-drawn-out ratification. Opinion polls were favourable to this, showing a significant majority – in some polls up to 70 per cent – supported the Constitution.[146] Even so, there was some public disaffection, for instance a tendency for some to link the Constitution with the anticipated adverse consequences of Eastern enlargement such as illegal immigration, social dumping and undercutting labour costs, and no less the relocation of jobs to low-cost labour markets in the accession countries.[147] There was also public concern over the EU's new seven-year financial perspective announced in July 2004 which doubled Germany's fiscal contribution to the Union budget.[148]

Opposition to the Constitution here as elsewhere was not strictly confined to European issues. There was some concern, too, in this federal polity about excessive centralisation and whether the Constitutional Treaty would disturb a delicately wrought constitutional balance, strengthening power in Berlin, and no less in Brussels, at the expense of territorial autonomy and national sovereignty. One CSU Bundestag member was moved, for instance, to file a lawsuit with the Federal Constitutional Court to prevent parliamentary ratification expressly on grounds that 'this Constitutional Treaty is incompatible with the [German] Constitution', in so far as it transfers powers upwards to the EU level. Another member sought an injunction to prevent a parliamentary vote pending a ruling on this matter by the Constitutional Court, though the Justices refused the petition on grounds that no one can challenge a Bundestag decision on a law not yet in existence, such a challenge only being permissible with the express approval of both houses of parliament. In the event, the Constitutional Treaty had an uneventful passage, clearing the Bundestag (12 May 2005) by 569 to 23 with 2 abstentions and to loud applause after barely four hours of discussion, a majority well above the two-thirds threshold required by the Basic Law.[149] The handful of dissidents were mostly CDU members concerned by the Bundestag's putative loss of power. Meanwhile, the public at large were for the most part either seemingly indifferent to or accepting of the outcome.

The ratification process was one of the very few where domestic campaigning did, if notionally, connect with events elsewhere in Europe. In view of Chirac's political difficulties on the issue, France's closest EU partner deliberately timed its own parliamentary ratification to try to help him. Schroeder used his own comfortable ratification in an attempt to bolster the flagging '*oui*' campaign 'next door', making much in his public utterances of the signal contribution of the historic Franco-German alliance, the mainstay of post-war prosperity and peace in the continent, without which 'reconciliation and partnership, a European Union would not have been possible'.[150] This was a proud boast, but one that had on this occasion greater resonance with the German public than it did with their French neighbours.

## The other EU15 member states

### Spain

The first referendum on the Constitution took place in Spain, though referendum results here are not constitutionally binding, the final decision remaining with the Cortes. The major political parties endorsed the Constitution, described by Prime Minister Zapatero as an 'enormous, qualitative step forward in the process of European integration'. The moderate territorial parties, the Basque Nationalist Party (PNV) and the main Catalan party, the Convergence and Unity party (CiU), followed suit.[151] Opposition was confined to the political margins, including the United Left Green/communist coalition, the Basque and Catalan nationalists – the Esquerra republica de Catalunya (ERC), and the left-environmentalist Catalunya-Els Verds (ICV) – who all opposed the Constitution on grounds that it failed to recognise stateless nations or their right to self-determination. The United Left criticised the Constitutional Treaty as undemocratic and because it failed to commit the EU to international peace. Opponents on the far right for their part objected that the Constitution would facilitate Turkish accession.

The outcome was never in doubt, despite opposition from the Catholic hierarchy, disconcerted by the new socialist government's liberal social policies, who instructed their communicants to abstain in protest.[152] Public opinion, already overwhelmingly favourable to the EU, followed the lead of the mainstream parties, though for pragmatic more than idealistic reasons. The benefits of EU membership were indisputable. Between 1987 and 2004 Spain had received some 81 billion euros from various EU structural assistance programmes, far more than any other member state.[153] At the time of accession in 1986 Spanish per capita GDP was only 68 per cent of the EU average, a figure that had subsequently risen to 95 per cent. Economic growth outperformed the EU average between 1994 and 2004, with unemployment falling from 20.6 per cent of the working population at the time of accession to 10.38 per cent over the same period, a remarkable performance by any standard. EU membership likewise brought inward investment, creating some 300,000 new jobs and a surge in infra-structural development, for instance 8,000 kilometres of motorway, with 40 per cent of the cost funded by the EU.[154] In the circumstances, it was simply inconceivable that the public would reject what was recommended to it as the latest stage of a wholly advantageous project. The government was on firm ground, making the case for ratification less on the Constitution's merits than on the need to avoid anything that might jeopardise such material benefits

The 2005 referendum was the fourth since Franco's death in 1975 ushered in democracy. Even so, this referendum produced, and by some way, the lowest turn-out so far, well below the 76 per cent recorded at the 2004 general election. No one could accuse the government of not trying to win minds, if not hearts, on the issue, but the problem was less antipathy to the EU than apathy. Even those who turned out to vote for the Constitution did so without any real knowledge of its content or significance, whether for Spain or for Europe. Voters were unmoved for the most part by the government's efforts to promote public education on the issue, a campaign that included issuing a free summary of the Constitutional Treaty with the Sunday newspapers, broadcast readings of its contents by celebrities, a special issue of postage stamps and even football stars flaunting copies of the Constitution. The government tried to impress on voters what was at stake, even inviting some EU leaders to address pre-referendum rallies, though only Jacques Chirac took up the invitation, surprisingly perhaps in view of his inactivity at home in the same cause.[155] Two weeks before the referendum some 50 per cent of voters had still not heard of the Constitution, a higher figure than even in the supposedly 'semi-detached' United Kingdom, although 49 per cent of respondents did indicate that they would nevertheless support ratification, with only 20 per cent opposed. As one prominent '*si*' campaigner observed: 'People don't know what we are talking about. People have the feeling that Europe is there as the Mediterranean is there. It's like voting whether we want to sit at the Mediterranean or not. It is very difficult to explain to citizens to what extent the European Constitution affects their lives.'[156]

This paradox of high levels of public ignorance/apathy alongside firm support for ratification persisted until polling day, producing a result that Prime Minister Zapatero described as 'without ambiguity' but also 'without enthusiasm'.[157] The turn-out was low, only 42.32 per cent of an eligible 35 million voters casting a vote, a sure sign of popular disengagement. Of those who did vote, 76.73 per cent backed the Constitution, 17.4 per cent rejected it, with 6 per cent spoiled ballots. Abstention rates were highest amongst the opposition centre-right voters and in the Basque and Catalan regions. Turn-out in previous referendums on political reform (1976), on the adoption of a democratic constitution (1978) and on whether to remain in NATO (1986) were all markedly higher, varying between 60 and 78 per cent. The lower house of parliament (the Congress of Deputies) voted to formally ratify the Constitutional Treaty on 28 April, by 331 votes to only 19 against, and the upper house (Senate) followed suit on 18 May, by 225 votes to 6, with one abstention.

### The Netherlands

A founder member of the Community with consistently high levels of public support for European integration, the Netherlands has recently experienced a marked shift in public attitudes on the EU. This is a response to concern over immigration, the problem as some saw it of failing multi-culturalism, but also to what others see as the country's disproportionately high contribution to the EU budget.[158] A change in attitudes towards Europe had begun to stir in Dutch politics before the European Constitution became an issue, making the government cautious about putting the case for the Constitution. The politicians were mostly favourable to the Constitution, and at the outset there seemed little to cause them concern about the outcome. And though referendums here are merely consultative and not constitutionally binding on governments, the parties agreed to accept the result so long as turn-out reached a 30 per cent threshold. The timing of the referendum was designed to take advantage of what was widely seen, both at home and abroad, as a successful Dutch EU presidency. A deliberately low-key government campaign tried to counter strident populist opposition from far-right and nationalist movements, not least the Lijst Pim Fontuyn.[159]

At the outset of the campaign there was no sign of the shock to come, opinion polls showing a clear majority for ratification. The *Eurobarometer* survey conducted in late 2004, for instance, registered 58 per cent support for the Constitution, with only 38 per cent opposed and 8 per cent undecided.[160] This was confirmed in a rash of national polls.[161] This early lead seemed merely to reinforce official complacency, confirming the government in its reticence about making a positive case for the Constitution, a fact underlined by the decision to delay the referendum. This move backfired, for it allowed the '*nee*' camp to regroup, giving it time to reinvigorate a flagging campaign, and to turn the referendum into a plebiscite on what they claimed was government 'mishandling' of several controversial policies, some only remotely and others not at all connected with the Constitution.

These flanking issues, the introduction of the euro, immigration, the role of the monarchy, euthanasia, the rise of militant Islam, the official policy of multi-culturalism, Turkish accession and 'excessive' bureaucracy, were all quite separate from the referendum question but all issues that contributed to public disquiet.[162] And as the campaign gathered momentum support for the Constitution dipped, and markedly, as opponents of ratification played successfully on widespread public disaffection with the political class, a cumulate sense of policy failure that gave oxygen to familiar populist obsessions with conspiracy, supposedly 'hidden agendas', and all compounded by growing unease about perceived 'threats' to the Dutch way of life that seriously undermined the government's position.[163] This sour public mood surfaced in opinion surveys, showing a clear correlation between the '*nee*' vote and the pervasive sense of a nation no longer at ease with itself. The polls did not so much show endemic Euroscepticism as palpable if muddled public unease about a 'rag-bag of conflicting grievances'.[164] The '*nee*' campaign did strike a chord with the public mood, though rather more as a reflection of the country's identity crisis than as an expression of unalloyed Euroscepticism, although that, too, was on the rise in this once liberal and outward-looking country. Cosmopolitanism and the European idea have gone hand in hand here for a clear half-century, but both are now tarnished, as some see it, in this once progressive country unsure of its political bearings in a fast-changing world, a country 'emerging disillusioned and with a renewed sense of national identity from a failed 40-year experiment in multiculturalism and "open door" immigration'.[165]

The referendum result was an overwhelming rejection of the Constitution.[166] This outcome could not be attributed to abstentions, a triumph for mere apathy. As in France, the turn-out (62.8 per cent) was significantly higher than for the recent European elections, an indication of a public mobilised on an issue that its opponents managed successfully to link with a plethora of domestic grievances. But again, as in France, the actual figures do not tell the entire story, for despite a convincing victory for the '*nee*' campaign (with 61.6 per cent rejecting the Constitution) the result itself, what it signifies, is open to interpretation. One post-referendum survey indicated, as a similar survey did in France, several by no means consistent reasons for the outcome, including anti-government protest (14 per cent), concern over loss of sovereignty (19 per cent) and the perceived burden of EU membership on taxpayers (13 per cent). Yet some 82 per cent of voters continued to see EU membership in a positive light, and even 78 per cent of '*nee*' voters registered a positive image of Union's institutions.[167]

'Europe' was less the issue here than the kind of Europe represented by the Constitution. While more than half the Dutch electorate, for instance, rejected the very idea of a European Constitution as necessary for European construction, others who voted '*nee*' did so, as did some voters in France, because they saw this as the surest way of getting rid of a problematic Constitution.[168] But these same respondents did not rule out the possibility of a more 'appropriate' constitutional arrangement at some future time, one with, for instance, a greater social dimension (66 per cent), and with surer safeguards for national interests.[169]

Pro-Constitution voters, on the other hand, saw the Constitution as indispensable for closer European integration (24 per cent of the 'yes' vote), with many referring in their responses to pollsters to the Constitution's importance for reinforcing 'the feeling of a European identity', or to enhancing 'the role of the Netherlands within the Union and the world' (13 per cent of 'yes' votes).[170] What is clear from these survey findings is that the rejection of the Constitution did not equate with unalloyed

Euroscepticism, any more than the same outcome did in France. As *Eurobarometer* concludes: 'Regardless of whether or not citizens voted and whether or not they expressed their support or rejection of the Constitution, their country's membership of the European Union is far from being questioned: 82 per cent consider EU membership as being a good thing.'[171] The national interest was of paramount concern, as it was with many voters elsewhere. Two-thirds of those who voted '*nee*' did not subscribe to the official line, that to do so would reduce their country's influence in the EU. In fact, some 62 per cent of respondents believed that a '*nee*' vote, following close on the same outcome in France, would actually persuade voters elsewhere to follow this lead, thereby forcing an out-of-touch political class to rethink the entire project, and to come up with a better constitution.[172] As in France, the general outlook of Dutch voters was rather more anti-this Constitution than it was anti-EU.

### *Italy, Belgium and Luxembourg*

The Italian national constitution proscribes the use of referendums for ratifying international treaties, although the Northern League, a member of the governing coalition and a movement with reservations about the EU, did propose a referendum on the Constitution. However, widespread public support for the EU *per se* and to a lesser extent for the Constitutional Treaty permitted the government to ignore the League's demand. The Constitution barely registered on the public's radar. In fact, it was the government as much as their opponents that voiced criticism of the Constitutional Treaty, for being too cautious about European integration. The foreign minister, Franco Frattini, preferred even more QMV, not least for managing the common foreign policy, and he claimed that the Constitution was only the beginning of yet deeper integration.[173] The Chamber of Deputies voted for ratification (25 January 2005) by a large majority (436 in favour and 28 against – mostly Northern League deputies, with 5 abstentions), and the Senate followed suit on 6 April 2005, making Italy the first founder member to ratify.[174]

The situation was much the same in Belgium, where the prime minister, Guy Verhofstadt, acted as cheer-leader for the Constitution in the country's three autonomous and federalised language communities. A referendum is optional under the terms of the revised Belgian constitution, but Verhofstadt orchestrated what he hoped would be a national consensus across the communal divide, negotiating a timetable for ratification with the parliaments of the three language communities.[175] Ratification proceeded smoothly, though concern was expressed by some socialist deputies that such a historic measure should be decided without any direct public involvement. This prompted a proposal for biannual consultations between parliamentarians and representative organisations from civil society to deliberate on the state of the EU, a move that was rejected by the national parliament.[176] The Senate approved the Constitutional Treaty on 28 April, but there was delay in its passage through the lower house because of sensibilities about communal politics, though the national parliament eventually approved ratification (19 May 2005), and by a substantial majority. The matter was then passed to the regional assemblies.

The Constitution had widespread support from both politicians and the public in Luxembourg, the Union's smallest member state, where the mainstream parties have traditionally been enthusiastic about European integration. *Eurobarometer* surveys and national polls conducted by RTL/ILRES showed consistently high levels of support for the Constitution, in the range of 77/62 per cent in favour to 14/24 opposed, with 9/14 per cent 'undecided'. Luxembourg occupied the EU presidency at the very moment when the two referendums brought a halt to the Constitution. The prime minster, Jean Claude Junker, had used his occupancy of that office to warn other member states about the costs of non-ratification, with Luxembourg setting what he hoped would be an example to others, ratifying the Constitution by a parliamentary vote in June 2005 followed by a referendum in July that recorded a comfortable though by no means an overwhelming majority in favour (56.5 per cent in favour to 43.48 per cent against).

## *Ireland*

Ireland has held six referendums on European issues over the past two decades or so, and the Ahern government, though winning plaudits at home and abroad for its painstaking work in securing the final version of the Constitutional Treaty, was nevertheless concerned to avoid a repetition of the failure in 2001 to secure ratification of the Nice Treaty at the first attempt.[177] The three principal parties broadly endorsed the European Constitution, with only the Green Party and Sinn Fein opposed to it on the grounds that it was an elite-driven federalist project, and as such not in Ireland's national interest.[178] Concern amongst the political parties and the legal establishment that the European Constitution might override national constitutional authority was resolved when the government, after consulting the other parties, agreed to reword the referendum question so as to exclude the enabling or *passerelle* clause that would permit the member states in Council to sign up to EU policy changes without further referendums. This confirmed that any future changes in the EU's Constitution would require the express approval of the Irish electorate.[179]

The other sensitive issue raised by critics and supporters alike of the Constitution was Irish neutrality, a status recognised in the Seville Declaration and reaffirmed in the government's official guide to the EU Constitution that explained those parts of the text concerning the Union's role as an international actor. There was some public concern, too, about the acceleration of integration and about the consequences for employment of increased immigration, a hot issue now that Ireland has reversed its historical role as a country of net emigration, and one ironically that is a direct consequence of remarkable economic growth and inward investment after accession in 1973.

Linked to this was the diminution, as some saw it, of cultural identity, and, not least, the consequences for the smaller member states of being overborne, not to say overridden by the leading states in the proposed new institutional arrangements. The public overall was more indifferent to than it was alarmed about the Constitution, a fact confirmed in opinion polls that showed widespread lack of knowledge about the issues, though these same polls revealed little evidence of outright Euroscepticism. The *Eurobarometer* surveys, for instance, indicated a marked lack of public awareness about the key issues, and though some 77 per cent of voters in one poll signalled approval of EU membership, and 87 per cent identified clear benefits thereof, the electorate was nevertheless far from convinced about the actual merits of the Constitution, which here as in most other countries were denominated principally in the currency of the national interest.[180]

A mood of public uncertainty persuaded the government to delay announcing a date for the referendum until they could mount an effective publicity campaign.[181] Meanwhile, the ground for the campaign was prepared by the publication of a White Paper on the Constitution, and by enacting the legislation required for holding a referendum.[182] The main opposition party, Fine Gael, preferred an early referendum, concerned lest a widely predicted 'no' in the British referendum, and the back-wash from a virulent Eurosceptic press there, should spill back across the Irish Sea, making life difficult for the Republic's pro-Constitution lobby. The *Taoiseach*, Bertie Ahern, resisted these pressures, keeping to his own timetable, launching the official ratification campaign just as the shock of the 'no' votes in France and the Netherlands brought the entire process to a halt.

### *Austria and the Scandinavian countries*

The Austrian Nationalrat voted unanimously for ratification (182 votes in favour, and with only one MP from the extreme right opposing it) on 11 May 2005. The Upper House endorsed that decision by 59 votes to 3. Chancellor Wolfgang Schussel had already canvassed the idea of a Europe-wide referendum, proposing that a double majority of states and people should decide future EU constitutional reform. This was wishful thinking, and in part little more than gesture politics, for it was never a realistic prospect and designed merely to boost Austria's credibility during its presidency term.[183] Only the far-right Freedom Party led by Jorg Haider, a politician whose extreme nationalism was hardly favourable to the European idea, broke ranks and opposed the Constitution. Haider was adept at populist posturing, and on this occasion he invoked the idea of the 'people' against a liberal establishment, as he had done previously over Austria's accession to the EU in 1985, also decided by a referendum. Haider's party again threatened to challenge the decision in the constitutional court, on the grounds that the proposed Constitutional Treaty would have precedence over the national constitution, but to no avail.[184]

Denmark has a history of Euro-scepticism, as demonstrated by its previous referendums on European issues, beginning with the resounding 'no' recorded in the first Maastricht referendum that resulted in its government negotiating significant opt-outs from the Eurozone and the Schengen agreement. Public opinion is now less endemically Eurosceptical than it is pragmatic about European integration, and as one commentator sees it: 'The EU is no longer simply regarded as a question of "pork prices" but is seen as a political project, and the proportion of Danes who see themselves to be as much European as Danish has doubled in the past ten years.'[185]

The case against the Constitution was made from the usual quarter, notably the anti-immigration Danish People's Party, which depicted the Constitution as merely the latest stage in the development of a familiar elitist project to impose a United States of Europe, a populist critique endorsed by the Red–Green Alliance of environmentalists and former communists. One prominent member of the People's Movement against the EU, Ole Krarup MEP, described the Constitution with typically Eurosceptical hyperbole as 'the final step to a militarised superstate aiming to control Denmark down to the tiniest detail'.[186]

Timing was critical here as elsewhere, and the government set the referendum date for 27 September 2005 in order, as Prime Minister Anders Fogh Rasmussen explained, to allow sufficient time for an informed national debate, but no doubt, too, to avoid giving the anti-Constitution forces enough time to make mischief, to wobble the public with their usual scare-mongering tactics.[187] There was every prospect that Denmark would vote in favour of the Constitution until things went awry in France, a view corroborated to an extent by the victory, and by the comfortable margin of two to one, for the pro-Constitution campaign in an internal plebiscite conducted by the formerly Eurosceptic People's Socialist Party.[188] Anti-EU sentiments are much less rooted here now than they once were, with opinion polls showing that more than four-fifths of parliamentarians supported the Constitution, and with a *Eurobarometer* poll (December 2004) indicating that some 44 per cent of the public endorsed it, with only 26 per cent opposed and 30 per cent undecided.[189]

Though referendums are not unknown in Sweden, as with the 2003 vote not to join the Eurozone, the government opted for ratification by a parliamentary vote scheduled for December 2005. The polling data did indicate strong support amongst the electorate for a referendum, itself a reflection of public concern about the Constitution. The 'no' votes in France and the Netherlands brought the whole process to a halt, providing the government with a convenient excuse not to take things further. Finland, too, has previously held referendums but there is no constitutional requirement to do so, and Prime Minister Vanhanen resisted holding one on this occasion on grounds that the issue was too complicated to be so decided. Undoubtedly, this decision was influenced by national polls that predicted defeat for the Constitution, with a clear majority opposed to ratification and only one third in favour, though a *Eurobarometer* survey (January 2005) did reverse these earlier findings. The government prevaricated on the issue, but Finland's assumption of the EU presidency during the second half of 2006 persuaded the government to underline its pro-EU credentials by ratifying the Constitution by parliamentary vote (5 December 2006), the sixteenth member state to do so. Meanwhile, the Finnish presidency launched a series of consultations with other member states on whether and how to revive the stalled Constitution, but without success.

### Greece and Portugal

Domestic politics was as much the determinant of the public's view of the European Constitution as it was in every other member state. Political expediency persuaded PASOK, the main opposition party that in government had actively supported the idea of a European Constitution and continued to do so, to back the call for a referendum from more marginal parties – the Coalition of the Left, Movements and Ecology (SYN) – that opposed the Constitution in principle. The PASOK leader, George Papandreou, justified what seemed to be merely political opportunism by claiming that the Constitution was a momentous step 'concerning Europe's and our country's future as an EU member', and that as such it 'requires a wider consensus which can only be achieved through a popular mandate'.[190] The opposition parties mustered some 133 votes in parliament for a motion demanding a referendum, but this was some way short of the 180 votes required by the national constitution to formally approve a referendum.[191] The public were, for the most part, indifferent to the issue and rallies organised against the Constitution by the KKE (Communist Party) in Salonika and in Athens were sparsely attended

The issue became a bone of contention between the party elites, with opposition parties accusing the New Democracy government of withholding from the public information on the implications of the Constitution so as to curtail public debate.[192] The government responded by setting up a committee to review the Constitution,[193] to be followed by an intensive plenary debate.[194] The final decision on ratification, however, was reserved to parliament. Prime Minister Costas Karamanlis heralded the Constitution as a 'milestone' in European integration, despite acknowledging that it was for all that a compromise, 'not the best, but ... the best out of the worst'.[195] Parliament overwhelmingly approved the Constitution (268 deputies in favour to 17 against), and Greece became the fifth country to ratify, though the opposition parties – including PASOK, who voted with the government – continued to demand a referendum. Parliament rejected a follow-up motion to this end, though only by 151 votes to 123, but again some way short of the required three-fifth of votes threshold required by law.

Both of Portugal's mainstream political parties, the PS and the PSD, approved of the Constitution, but less in terms of principle than for what President de Sousa described as the necessary price for ensuring Portugal remains 'at the heart of Europe'.[196] Opinion polls showed a public badly informed about the substantive issues. A *Eurobarometer* survey confirmed as much, prompting the government to fund a promotional campaign in support of ratification.[197] The issue was overshadowed, however, by a growing domestic political crisis that culminated in a defeat for the governing party in the 2005 general election. The incoming socialist prime minister, José Sócrates, proposed to hold a referendum at the same time as the October municipal elections, though referendums here are binding only if there is a minimum 50 per cent turn-out. Again, events elsewhere in the Union led to the indefinite postponement of this referendum.

## The newcomers

The ratification of the Constitutional Treaty took place in the new accession countries of central and eastern Europe against a background of rising concern about the impact of membership on economy and society. The transition from collectivist to market economies – steered for the most part by modernising governments headed by social-democratic parties – gave rise to considerable public disquiet, and boosted support for populist parties highly critical of European integration as a threat to national independence.

A mood of political crisis accompanied the ratification campaigns in Poland, the Czech Republic and Hungary. In Poland, Prime Minister Belka was forced to resign as support for the governing social democrats fell below the threshold required for parliamentary representation. The Czech Republic also experienced crisis politics, with three different prime ministers during the post-accession year. The ruling Hungarian social-democrats faced similar problems. This situation was a reflection of the dilemma facing governments in the transition countries, committed on the one hand to social reform to 'ease the pain of the economic transition', but 'on the other hand obliged to impose stringent fiscal and other supply-side discipline in order to accommodate daunting accession conditions and indeed to better cope with the rigours of globalisation'. These circumstances brought about drastic retrenchment, budget reductions, welfare cuts and labour market reforms, all of which hit hard their main constituency amongst the less well-off, leaving them politically 'outflanked by right-wing parties that play on the disappointment of [EU] membership and promise to champion national interests more aggressively'.[198]

The Hungarian parliament did nevertheless ratify the Constitution (20 December 2004), only the second member state to do so, and with little fuss in a country where EU membership was regarded as a major reason for accelerating growth and rising prosperity.[199] Meanwhile, Slovenia became the third country to ratify during an extraordinary session of parliament in February 2005, by a majority of 79 to 4,[200] notwithstanding concern expressed by the Slovenian National Party about what it regarded as 'wilful ignorance' of the Treaty's consequences for national independence.[201] Opinion polls indicated general, though hardly overwhelming public approval for the Constitution.[202]

Poland was more divided over the Constitution. The ruling Democratic Left Alliance (SLD) wanted to ratify before the parliamentary elections scheduled for June 2005, anticipating gains for nationalist parties opposed to European integration in the aftermath of corruption scandals and a severe economic downturn.[203] The government tried to broaden support for the Constitution beyond narrow partisan allegiances, to reach out to the public by making connections with civil society, NGOs and the media. The social democrats (SdPl) also supported early ratification, arguing that delay would marginalise the country in Europe.[204] The leftist parties resisted this course, and demanded a referendum – not a constitutional requirement in Poland – as the only sure means for giving the public a voice.[205] The rightist and nationalist parties, too, were sceptical about the Constitution, as they were about the EU *per se*. The League of Polish Families (LPR), for example, regarded it as a betrayal of a hard-won national independence and tried to indict the government before the Tribunal of State for signing the Constitutional Treaty.[206] The conservative Civic Platform party group, on the other hand, was more concerned about the lack of any reference to God in the outline reference to common European values, and like these other critics castigated the government's surrender on voting weights, a fact that seemingly confirmed the dominance of the 'big three'.[207]

Public opinion did move slowly behind the Constitution, however, especially in the rural regions that had begun to experience financial benefits from the Common Agricultural Policy. A CBOS poll conducted in November 2004 found that 68 per cent favoured the Constitutional Treaty, with only 11 per cent opposed and 21 per cent undecided. This turnaround was significant, for as recently as June 2004 a national poll showed 21 per cent opposed to the Constitution.[208] Opposition parties (PiS, the PO and the Polish Peasant Party, the PSL, and the LPR) continued to demand a referendum, but wanted it delayed for tactical reasons calculating, perceptively as things turned out, that a widely anticipated 'no' vote in Britain's referendum, or for that matter anywhere else would surely derail the project.

A similar argument over the procedure for ratification ensued in the Czech Republic, though both pro- and anti-Constitution opinion favoured a referendum. Anti-Constitution campaigners demanded a public voice on what they saw as an essentially elite-driven project and one detrimental to national autonomy and even to civil liberties. The government and other pro-Constitution groups preferred a referendum precisely because the issue was so divisive in parliament that there was no guarantee of securing a majority there for ratification. The governing parties (the Social Democrats – CSSD, the Christian Democrats – ODS and the Freedom Union) endorsed the Constitution, but powerful political forces on both right and left opposed it.

A particular problem was the fact that the anti-Constitution forces were led by the charismatic Czech President, Vaclav Klaus, and though his conservative ODS party was generally in favour of European integration he claimed that the Constitution would lead in time to a European state, a 'superior entity which will take us to abandon our national democracy, sovereignty and political independence'.[209] Klaus derided the constitutional project as a political fantasy concocted by idealists, and as such entirely remote from the aspirations and indeed the needs of 'normal people from the non-political sphere'.[210] As he saw it, it was the result of 'wishful thinking of European centralists and federalists [and] not a feasible project', because it 'separates Europe from democracy and freedom' in a way that threatens independent statehood.[211] There was the same basic concern here as in many of the new accession states that the proposed Constitution would make second-class Europeans of the newcomers. The government presented a general referendum bill to parliament that included a question on the Constitution, a move opposed by the principal opposition party, the Civic Democrats (ODS), who demanded a referendum exclusively on the Constitution, and as soon as possible.[212]

Public apathy was as much a problem here as it was elsewhere. Opinion polls indicated that over 70 per cent of respondents had no interest in the Constitution as it stood, though *Eurobarometer* recorded 63 per cent support for the idea of a European constitution (more or less in line with the EU average of 68 per cent), with only 18 per cent opposed and 19 per cent undecided.[213] There was evidence of a gradual shift of opinion in favour of the Constitutional Treaty, as there was in neighbouring Poland. This movement showed the effect of concerted government publicity campaigns pointing out the material benefits of EU membership, an important factor in political cultures still disposed to follow cues from political leaders.[214] A wafer-thin majority in favour of the Constitution at the outset increased over time.[215] If a referendum had taken place ratification would undoubtedly have been its outcome, but intense debate between the parties about how to proceed was never resolved and the issue was parked after the referendums in France and the Netherlands.

In Slovakia, as in some other accession countries, the Constitution was rather less controversial than was the procedure for ratification. Most of the parties, including those in opposition (the Movement for a Democratic Slovakia (HZDS), Smer and Free Forum), endorsed the Constitutional Treaty, despite the concern expressed by President Gašparovič that it was unclear whether the outcome would merely be a union of independent states or a European super-state.[216] The government preferred parliamentary ratification, maintaining that the constitutional requirement of a three-fifths majority of the Slovakian parliament (90 of 150 votes) would be sufficient for due legitimacy. However, the junior coalition partner, the Christian Democrat Party (KDH), opposed the Constitution on the grounds that it compromised national democracy, demanding a referendum to ensure that such an important matter receive public approval. In support of their position they cited an article in the national constitution which, as they interpreted it, required a referendum.[217] The Communist Party (KSS) also opposed the Constitution on the predictable grounds that it was a neo-liberal charter that threatened to create a militarised super-state, and was bound to impoverish the country.[218] Public opinion was overwhelmingly in favour of the Constitution, opinion polls showing well over 80 per cent support for ratification, and the country's unicameral parliament voted to ratify (11 May 2005) by a large majority (116 to 27, with 4 abstentions), comfortably reaching the 60 per cent threshold required by the national constitution.[219]

The Baltic States opted for speedy ratification by parliamentary vote, the best way as their governments saw it of confirming support for the EU. In what Giscard described as 'a courageous step', Lithuania was the first member state to ratify, and by a large majority in the parliament (the Sejmas), 84 in favour, 4 against and with 3 abstentions.[220] This despite some members of the opposition Liberal and Centre Union criticising an 'over-hasty' ratification, and calling for wider public discussion.[221] Immediately after ratification, the government announced its intention of applying to join both the Schengen accord and the Eurozone.[222] In fact, there was little serious effort to engage the public.

The Estonian government saw speedy ratification as the most effective way to underline the country's European credentials, though critics also complained of undue haste, especially as polling data indicated that some 39 per cent of citizens had not even heard of the EU Constitution.[223] As critics saw it, this fact alone required the government to do more to explain the Constitution's merits.[224] The government pressed on regardless, sending the Constitutional Treaty to parliament for ratification on 9 May 2006, where it was passed by 73 votes with only 1 vote against.[225]

The Latvian government passed the Treaty to parliament for ratification in January 2005, but had to withdraw it because of some 500 errors in the translation of the text, which the government conveniently blamed on a shortage of Latvian translators in Brussels! The government sent it back to the parliament where it was duly ratified by an overwhelming majority (71 in favour, 5 against, with 6 abstentions) on 2 June 2005.[226]

## So what went wrong?

The Constitutional Treaty was a lightning-conductor for other and diverse public concerns, some of them purely national but others Europe-wide or even global in their focus and few of them actually related to the Constitution. Referendums as we have seen are an opportunity to vent all manner of public discontents, many of them only remotely related to the specific referendum question, if at all. After referendum defeats in France and the Netherlands had scuppered the Constitution, some Brussels 'insiders' maintained that it was a tactical error to put to the popular vote what was after all an immensely complicated document, and one that raised all manner of issues about EU power and decision-making. One former senior Commission figure stated this objection thus:

> In my view, it was a fundamental mistake to submit a document of this kind to a referendum. Arguably a referendum would be appropriate for decisions to join or leave an international organisation or for genuinely radical changes such as the introduction of a single currency. The EU Constitution is however an incremental, rather than radical step forward. It is a legalistic more than a political text.[227]

Of course, wisdom after the event is a familiar reflex of politicians. And it is debatable whether the Constitutional Treaty was merely an arcane legal text, let alone one with only limited political consequences for people at large. In any case, this claim to technocratic complexity is all too familiar, and no less politically expedient in a Union built largely without the public's involvement, or even its express approval. As such, it is a convenient foil to be used against the demand for public voice, and shows the condescension of the Brussels insider, however well-meaning and supposedly calibrated to serve the public interest. By any yardstick the Constitutional Treaty was a signal moment in the development of the European polity. And whether it is a constitution in the proper meaning of that term or 'merely' the latest version of a rolling international treaty, it did have far-reaching constitutional implications, for the member states and for the common institutions alike. No less significant, it had important consequences for citizens. Why then in these circumstances should the public not be consulted, and in the process be entitled to a full and candid account of what is at stake in this attempt to constitutionalise the Union?

More pertinent as an explanation for the crisis that engulfed the Constitution is the timing of the exercise. The Constitutional Treaty may be merely the latest in a series of incremental revisions of the founding treaty, an attempt to simplify complex governance and to improve decision-making arrangements prior to a

Table 10.1 Ratification timetable

| Member state | Procedure | Date | Result | Previous European referendums |
|---|---|---|---|---|
| Austria | Parliamentary (Nationalrat and Bundesrat) | Approval by the Nationalrat: 11 May 2005<br>Approval by Bundesrat: 25 May 2005 | 182 Yes, 1 No<br>59 Yes, 3 No | 1994: accession |
| Belgium | Parliamentary (Chamber and Senate plus Assemblies of Communities and Regions). Indicative referendum ruled out | Approval by the Senate: 28 April 2005<br>Approval by the Chamber: 19 May 2005<br>Approval by the Brussels regional parliament: 17 June 2005<br>Approval by the German community parliament of Belgium: 20 June 2005<br>Approval by the Walloon regional parliament: 29 June 2005<br>Approval by the French community parliament: 19 July 2005<br>Approval by the Flemish regional parliament: 8 February 2006 | 54 Yes, 9 No, 1 abstention<br>118 Yes, 18 No, 1 abstention | No |
| Bulgaria | Parliamentary | Approval by parliament (11 May 2005), as part of preparations to join the EU on 1 January 2007 | – | No |
| Cyprus | Parliamentary | Approval by the House: 30 June 2005 | 30 Yes, 19 No, 1 abstention | No |
| Czech Republic | Referendum | Referendum postponed | * | 2003: accession |

*Continued*

| Member state | Procedure | Date | Result | Previous European referendums |
|---|---|---|---|---|
| Denmark | Referendum | Referendum postponed (no new date set) | * | 1972: accession; 1986: Single European Act; 1992: Maastricht Treaty (twice); 1998: Amsterdam Treaty; 2000: euro |
| Estonia | Parliamentary | Approval by parliament: 9 May 2006 | 73 Yes, 1 No | 2003: accession |
| Finland | Parliamentary | Presentation by the government of a report to the parliament on 25 November 2005 Ratification by parliamentary vote on 5 December 2006 | 125 Yes, 39 No, 4 abstentions, 3 absent | 1994: Consultative referendum, accession |
| France | Referendum | Referendum: 29 May 2005 | Negative results: 45.13% Yes, 54.87% No; turn-out: 69.34% | 1972: enlargement EEC; 1992: Maastricht Treaty |
| Germany | Parliamentary (Bundestag and Bundesrat) | Approval by Bundestag: 12 May 2005 Adoption by Bundesrat: 27 May 2005 | 568 Yes, 23 No, 2 abstentions 66 Yes, 3 abstentions | No |
| Greece | Parliamentary | The left parties submitted a joint proposal for a referendum. Approval by Parliament: 19 April 2005 | 268 Yes, 17 No | No |
| Hungary | Parliamentary | Approval by parliament: 5 December 2004 | 322 Yes, 12 No, 8 abstentions | 2003: accession |

| Member state | Procedure | Date | Result | Previous European referendums |
|---|---|---|---|---|
| Ireland | Parliamentary plus referendum | Referendum postponed (no date set). White Paper presented to parliament on 13 October 2005 | * | 1972: accession; 1987: Single European Act; 1992: Maastricht Treaty; 1998: Amsterdam Treaty; 2001 and 2002: Nice Treaty |
| Italy | Parliamentary (Chamber and Senate) | Approval by the Chamber: 25 January 2005<br>Approval by the Senate: 6 April 2005 authorising the President of the Republic to ratify the Constitutional Treaty | 436 Yes, 28 No, 5 abstentions<br>217 Yes, 16 No | 1989: Consultative referendum, possible draft Constitution |
| Latvia | Parliamentary | Approval by the Chamber: 2 June 2005 | 71 Yes, 5 No, 6 abstentions | 2003: accession |
| Lithuania | Parliamentary | Approval by Parliament: 11 November 2004 | 84 Yes, 4 No, 3 abstentions | 2003: accession |
| Luxembourg | Parliamentary (two votes) plus consultative referendum | Approval by the Chamber (first reading): 28 June 2005.<br>Positive referendum on 10 July 2005<br>Final approval by the Chamber: 25 October 2005. | —<br>56.52% Yes, 43.48% No<br>57 Yes, 1 No | No |
| Malta | Parliamentary | Approval by parliament: 6 July 2005 | 65 Yes | 2003: accession |
| Netherlands | Parliamentary (First and Second Chambers) plus consultative referendum | Referendum: 1 June 2005 | Negative results:<br>38.4% Yes; 61.6% No; turn-out: 62.8% | No |

*Continued*

| Member state | Procedure | Date | Result | Previous European referendums |
|---|---|---|---|---|
| Poland | No decision so far | The parliament failed on 5 July 2005 to vote on the ratification procedure. | * | 2003: accession |
| Portugal | Referendum | Referendum postponed | * | No |
| Romania | Parliamentary | Approval by parliament 17 May 2005, as part of preparations to join the EU on 1 January 2007: | – | No |
| Slovakia | Parliamentary | Approval by parliament: 11 May 2005 | 116 Yes, 27 No, 4 abstentions | 2003: accession |
| Slovenia | Parliamentary | Approval by parliament: 1 February 2005 | 79 Yes, 4 No, 7 abstentions | 2003: accession |
| Spain | Parliamentary (Congress and Senate) plus consultative referendum | Referendum: 20 February 2005<br>Approval of the Congress: 28 April 2005<br>Approval of the Senate: 18 May 2005 | 76.73% Yes, 17.24% No; turn-out: 42.32%<br>Yes 311, No 19<br>Yes 225, No 6 | No |
| Sweden | Parliamentary No referendum envisaged | Ratification postponed | * | Consultative referendums: 1994: accession 2003: euro |
| United Kingdom | Parliamentary (House of Commons and House of Lords) plus referendum | Parliamentary ratification process suspended by UK government on 6 June 2005 | * | 1975: continued membership of the EC |

Sources: Based on http://europa.eu.int/constitution/ratification_en.htm; http://www.unizar.es/euroconstitucion/Treaties/Treaty_Const_Rat.htm.

Note  * denotes no outcome by either designated procedure

historic enlargement. But it was heralded as something more significant when Laeken launched the constitutional venture. At the very least, this latest attempt to overhaul the Union's governance was an opportunity to take stock after more than a decade of accelerated integration that began with the Single European Act and the launch of the Single Market. The Union's current problems stem, in no small measure, from the very success of this relaunch of the European project. The Single Market politicised the EC/EU to an unprecedented degree, changing its institutional arrangements, extending the reach of its governance and range of its activities by adding policy domains such as social policy, monetary and macro-economic policy and security and home affairs, all issues once the exclusive preserve of the member states.

The successive revisions of the treaties since 1986 have significantly enhanced both the role of the Union's institutions, and their scope for intruding into domestic policy domains, and in ways that significantly impinge on the citizen. The expansion in the scope of EU policy has likewise raised concerns about democratic and legitimacy deficits, institutional efficiency and accountability, and not least the role of the citizen, matters that were described in Chapter 1 as being the root of the Union's polity problem. These are important matters, not merely for the efficiency of governance but also for its legitimacy. Any polity that claims as the EU does to conform with and to embody democratic norms sooner or later has to address the matter of its constitutional status. The EU almost had its 'constitutional moment' during the Convention, until narrower concerns about power overtook principle and the moment passed. The political class that dominated affairs both in the Convention and in the IGC rather missed the point, embarking not on a democratic conversation but instead on a process of reforming the institutions to better suit their own interests. This reform is a necessary but hardly a sufficient condition for public credibility, a requirement in every polity for political legitimacy, in as much as it overlooks the equally important need to connect with and respond to popular concerns, those issues raised everywhere in the ratification debates.

The outcome of these deliberations was much the same as previous bouts of treaty reform, an unwieldy hybrid, and something closer to a European treaty than a constitution, a text of inordinate detail couched in the arcane legalese of treaty-making. The Constitutional Treaty is a cluttered text lacking the brevity of a framework constitution, much too technically intricate, far too complex for most citizens to grasp. It is at most a map of power, a manual for bureaucrats, a charter for lawyers, and above all a compendium for professional functionaries, those 'insiders' who have always run the show. Opinion polling conducted throughout the EU after the referendums in France and the Netherlands showed that had the Convention produced a framework document akin to the leaner American Constitution it might have met with greater enthusiasm. Instead, ambition overtook common sense, and self-interest took precedence over the wider public interest, with the result that the Constitution became 'overloaded … with all the accumulated detail on EU policies and exceptions agreed in previous treaties'. Furthermore, 'quite apart from being impossibly dense', the Constitution became a hostage to political misfortune, in effect giving 'everyone something to dislike'.[228]

A Constitution that leaves so little to chance, covering every eventuality, is in itself a symptom of a deeper problem that faces the European polity. It is altogether easier to write a parsimonious constitution for a polity with abiding consensus as to its central purposes, where the basic norms and fundamental ends of the polity are uncontested, where there is broad agreement about underlying principles, the values that give democratic constitutions their normative ballast. The EU quite simply lacks these constitutional virtues, and it remains a problematical polity in every sense. It has neither political finality nor geographical fixity, and there is no agreement amongst its principals about the ultimate political destination, and instead deep uncertainty about both its form and future that is reflected in a complex and still-contested political architecture. Abiding ambiguity about the European polity was quite apparent during the Convention, its mandate to review the options for constitutionalising its governance made altogether more difficult because of abiding differences over the very purpose of the project. This much is hardly new. Conflict over the meaning of the European project has never been resolved, and, as some commentators maintain, cannot, or indeed should not be if the EU is to survive. Those who argue thus regard ambiguity as the Union's claim to uniqueness as a polity in a fluxional world, *un objet politique non identifié*, as it has been described, one that balances quite different ideas about and aspirations for transnational governance.

The debate about how or indeed whether to formally constitutionalise the European Union will certainly continue into an uncertain future. A European Constitution that balances even if it does not reconcile competing ideas about governance, and within a cogent and cognate political architecture, is a formidable task to carry off, difficult yet necessary as the 1990s brought new challenges. Whether the Constitutional Treaty made any significant progress in resolving these matters is debatable, though there are some encouraging signs from these events. As one *conventionnel* saw it, the founding treaties were always more 'than standard international treaties' in so far as 'they have a direct impact on matters covered by the constitutions of member states, unlike the regulations of international organisations as a rule'. And though it is by no means a state and even less a 'country', the EU is nevertheless much more than merely an international organisation, more even than a sophisticated international regime, and its constitutional arrangements must take full account of its unique political status. To that extent, 'the EU's founding treaties are [already] constitutional in nature. They define the Union's basic values and competences, its decision-making system, the relationship between its institutions and the division of competences between the member states and the Union. These are all matters typically enacted in constitutions.'[229]

These are promising developments as far as they go, but something more is required to persuade citizens to embrace far-reaching reform of EU governance. Political leadership is of the essence here, and in this regard the Union's 'princes' were found wanting. Those who assumed the responsibility for writing a European Constitution rather lost sight of the challenge, of the need to bring the people with them, preferring instead to resort to prolix language and technical jargon wholly unfamiliar to citizens. The idea of governance and even more of politics beyond national boundaries is by no means easy for citizens to grasp, used as they are to thinking about political allegiance, membership of a polity in rooted in historical nationality.

The debate about an appropriate terminology to describe this latest endeavour to constitutionalise the Union reflects the ambiguous quality of European governance from the outset. The matter was resolved at the beginning of the Convention by a judicious compromise, as these matters so often are in the EU, though one designed to appeal more to insiders, those who know how things actually work, used as they are in their everyday dealings to transacting governance and conducting politics beyond the bounds of the nation-state. Accordingly, the praesidium chose to describe the objective as a 'Constitutional Treaty'. The emphasis was quite deliberately placed on the noun 'treaty' rather than on the adjective 'constitutional', a telling distinction.[230] In the event, the Convention decided 'to call the end result what it actually is, both *de jure* under international law and *de facto*: a Treaty on Constitution'. In this nomenclature both the key words 'treaty' and 'constitution' 'are on an equal footing, both being nouns'. This was widely regarded as an 'excellent solution', appealing to *conventionnels* on all sides of the debate on Europe's purposes as a polity, what it is actually about, for 'this is an international treaty as far as the member states are concerned, but for the EU it is a constitution. It fits the special nature of the Union as something between a state and an international organisation. A federal state has a constitution and international organisations conclude treaties between states. A supranational Union, therefore, has *a Treaty on Constitution*.'[231] The critical fact here, as Kiljunen points out, is that 'the nature of the EU is determined by its content, not its title', in that 'to be governed by a constitution per se does not ensure that a polity is a state [so that] legally speaking [the Constitution] is an international treaty, and calling it a constitution will not turn it into the constitution of a state, because the Union it governs is not a state'.[232]

So far, so good! For pragmatists, harbingers of common sense governance, there is nothing here to alarm anyone, or so one might think. The fundaments of statehood under international law were formally defined by the Montevideo Convention (1933), with the outcome that a state as a legal personality should have certain properties: a permanent population, a defined territory, sovereign government and a capacity to enter into relations with other states in the international community. It is clear that, regardless of the growing momentum and expansive reach of European integration, and with collective action now extended into aspects of domestic policy once regarded as the exclusive preserve of the nation-state, the EU does not manifest these elemental attributes of statehood, and that these continue to reside with the member states. The very first Article of the draft constitutional treaty makes clear where the locus of political authority resides in the Union, noting that 'this Constitution establishes the European Union, on which the member states confer competences to attain objectives they have in common'.[233]

The emphasis here is on the continuing authority of the nation-state, at least for determining the big, 'historic' questions. This much was obvious to those who drafted the Constitution. But this is not the point. Somehow these crucial distinctions got lost in translation, at least as far as most citizens were concerned. The significance of the Constitution for demarcating the crucial balance of power between the Union and the member states was much less clear to those not closely involved with, or apprised of, its day-to-day workings. There was much uncertainty then about the meaning of the European Constitution, what it was about or why it was needed at this juncture, and who benefited most by it. This, in turn, raised doubts in the public's mind about the very idea of a European Constitution. The seeds of the rebellion that downed the Constitution lie in this uncertainty, giving rise to an insurgent mood that caught the politicians largely unawares, although anyone with half an ear tuned to the popular clamour as Europeans face up to remorseless change, challenges to their customary prosperity, employment prospects and security in a febrile world could hardly fail to register it. Even so, these early signals were largely ignored as politicians celebrated their historic achievement at the signing ceremony in Rome.

The problem of legitimacy, for this is what is the root of the Union's constitutional crisis, cannot be resolved merely by ignoring the public's concerns, and certainly not by avoiding, as most EU leaders still seem intent on doing, proper engagement with the public, settling instead for bringing in as many of the substantive reforms written into the Constitution by the back door, to be ratified by parliaments on the grounds that this is a 'mere' reform treaty. Setting aside democratic constitutionalism as 'unmanageable', or for some irrelevant, is a short-term fix, but it is not one that will resolve the serious matter of disengagement between politicians and people. The decision of the present crop of leaders to avoid public censure by bringing in under the cover of 'mere' treaty revision much of what was rejected in the 2005 referendums on the rather specious grounds that a revising treaty is a technical matter best left to experts will do little to convince the public that their concerns are being addressed, their anxieties taken seriously, and will just as surely reinforce negative public attitudes about how Europe is governed. There is conceit here, but, worse, also contempt, as if these matters are of no concern to citizens. And no less, a cynical refusal to engage the public in a mature conversation about what is, after all, 'their' governance.

# 11 Crisis or 'normal' politics?

## The Constitution fails the democracy test

The failure of the EU Constitution to gain public approval was inconvenient for EU governments but hardly surprising.[1] The history of European integration has been uneven from the start, with forward momentum followed by periodic stasis. Some of the foundational thinkers who attempted to explain the dynamics of European integration saw a process driven by almost irresistible teleological forces, even predestined, 'a series of advances and retreats along a defined road' whose 'general route, as well as the final goal, is assumed to be known'.[2] But the process that some writers now refer to as 'Europeanisation' is by no means straightforward, and this latest episode is hardly exceptional. To acknowledge this, however, does not say a great deal about the particularities of the Union's recent efforts to embrace a formal constitutional order, or for that matter about why the public resisted the recommendations of their political leaders.

Why then did the European Constitution fail the democracy test? No singular reason can explain the crisis that overtook ratification. Some commentators attribute the failure of the Constitution to the usual contingencies that shape politics everywhere, and not least to poor timing, the plain fact that the moment chosen by political leaders for undertaking a major reform of EU governance 'was simply *unripe* for such an audacious experiment'.[3] Others go further, blaming the Union's leaders for failing to prepare the ground, for ignoring public sensibilities, the failure to engage the citizens in a debate about European futures and instead simply assuming consensus. And for disregarding popular concerns about, for instance, the negative impact of the Eurozone on labour markets and price inflation, or how the impending enlargement and accelerated migration has threatened welfare benefits and undermined job security. As Walker sees it, EU leaders failed to counter the widespread public perception of the EU as remote, its procedures as arcane and its 'princes' as patronising, overly reliant on glib claims of 'past achievement and realising immanent possibilities over the development of a more open long-term vision'.[4] Dominique Moisi goes even further, laying the blame squarely on inept leadership for not helping the public to 'transcend their fear', to 'understand that the EU is their destiny'.[5]

Complacency has certainly played its part in these events. The defence of the Constitution launched to coincide with the Dutch EU presidency of 2004 was widely derided by the media 'as high-brow and philosophical, further evidence of the gulf between politics and people'.[6] The response of Dutch politicians who supported the Constitution was symptomatic of a self-satisfied political class throughout the Union, seeing no good reason even to make the case for the Constitution. When a rash of opinion polls revealed the extent of public hostility or indifference to the Constitution, all they could muster by way of an answer was a belated, mostly inept attempt to declaim the Constitution, though without seriously trying to sell the idea to their electorates. The official case made for the Constitution simply lacked conviction, let alone a 'killer argument'. There was no persuasive personality, whether from government or from the mainstream pro-Constitution parties, capable of taking on a mobilised opposition, or even willing to do so, nor able to win over those perplexed voters yet to make up their minds about the issue.

The campaigns that derailed ratification by no means focused exclusively on the Constitution, even in those countries holding referendums. Referendums are an opportunity for venting all manner of public discontents. As Dominique Moisi has observed, few French voters deliberated on the particular merits of what was, after all, an immensely complex and highly technical document. Many who voted 'no' did so in order to register a protest vote against a government unable to provide enough jobs, or against a Union seemingly incapable of protecting Europe's national labour markets and welfare systems from the depredations of globalisation.[7] Some other voters concluded that this was simply the wrong constitution, a misconceived project concerned with issues almost exclusively the province of the political class, a project 'hardly driven by politicians' dedication to promoting European grandeur and unity, nor by member states' commitment to a progressive agenda for democracy, power-sharing, social justice, or universal rights', values usually associated with liberal constitutionalism.[8] Critics saw a Constitution neither radical nor democratic, but instead a form of 'hegemonic preservation', by 'risk-averse' elements 'to cut a deal' that maintains their 'own privileges, world views and policy preferences through constitutionalisation', and then 'trying to foist it on the public'.[9] For too many ordinary voters the would-be founding fathers were either 'fixated by the traditional federalist agenda' or by 'the power struggle between the EU institutions', both giving too little attention to those who advocated a 'social Europe'.[10]

The Convention certainly paid too little heed to the public's concerns, barely advancing the concept of EU citizenship introduced in the Maastricht Treaty. Giscard had tried to avoid setting up a working group on social issues, and even when such a group was established it had little impact on the outcome, though an intervention by the Belgian government during the IGC did lead to the inclusion of the provision (Article 3-117) that member states should conduct their economic policies so as to enhance social cohesion and economic harmonisation.[11] But even this did little to reassure publics anxious about social dumping, external pressures on national labour markets to drive down costs, the impact of globalisation on social protection, a looming pensions' crisis and so on.

The constitutional process was driven much less by concern for resolving social issues or developing a 'people's Europe' than by the need, as the principal actors saw it, to adapt the institutions and decisional procedures to imminent enlargement that would add a further 80 million new citizens, increasing the Union's total population by some 20 per cent.[12] In place of serious debate about constitutional principles, or even any 'clarification of the political characterisation of the Union' the Constitution was, as Maduro saw it, the usual 'piecemeal intergovernmental bargain whose impact on the constitutional principles legitimating and organising power will largely be a product of unintended consequences'.[13] There is of course nothing unusual or necessarily ill-conceived about a constitution that maps the distribution of power and defines the competencies of a polity, 'on the contrary, that is a key concern of Constitutions'.[14]Yet the debate, both in the Convention and the IGC, on the institutions hardly touched on those important normative questions that should inform democratic constitutionalism. There was nothing in the Constitutional Treaty that could be reasonably described as constitutional philosophy, too little deliberation about first principles that balances the exercise of raw power in any polity with an appropriate discourse about democracy, legitimacy and citizenship.

A constitutional project, even one devised for a non-statal polity, should be concerned to legitimise the exercise of institutional power, connecting governance with first principles and no less with the citizen, so as to foster a sense of common endeavour and shared purpose, and even political identity, all qualities so far missing from the EU polity. Any constitution worth the name must address the citizen, after all the fount of political legitimacy in a democratic polity. Constitutions should express, and in symbolic language, the normative alchemy that transforms 'mere' power into authority, affirming some sense of personal attachment to a political community, 'the catalyst of a common identity', that is 'the product, not the precondition, of the exercise of constitution-making power'.[15] After all, a democratic constitution is more than merely 'a body of laws and norms,' but is rather a compact, or in the classical liberal narrative a contract made between polity and public, and one with its sociological and cultural roots in 'a pre-political community of values and a common identity ... the legal embodiment of a community of values where Europeans address and see themselves as fellow compatriots'.[16] The EU Constitution does not remotely meet these exacting normative standards for democratic, accountable and legitimate governance.

The Constitution's principal architects did too little to address these shortcomings, either at the Convention or in the subsequent IGC. And they did even less during the national ratification campaigns to make the positive case for a European constitution, and little more for this particular Constitution. Opinion poll data from both EU15 and the accession countries gathered throughout 2004 show consistently low levels of public information about the Constitution. Instead, politicians tried to play down its significance, claiming that this was no more than the streamlining of decision-making procedures, incorporating *de jure* into the treaty base changes already operating *de facto*, in effect simplifying and 'tidying' the existing treaties. The politicians for the most part avoided the symbolic nature of the exercise.[17] While the formal language of constitutionalism was not disavowed, neither was it celebrated.[18] As Pfersmann observed, 'although the term

'Constitution' passes easily into common parlance, it is absolutely not clear in which respect it would be different from just another treaty'. What was clearly missing here was what this same author has described as 'a mission of clarification, unification and common acceptability'. There is much more to a constitutional conversation than 'princes' offering the people a take-it-or-leave-it 'change in constitutional competence'.[19] In fact, there was nothing here that could remotely be described as a constitutional conversation, little attempt by the political class to 'enter into a direct relationship with its own social constituency'.[20] For Imig and Tarrow it is an indictment to say that 'we know much more about participation in consultative committees in the five square kilometres of Euro-land in Brussels than we do about contention over the effects of their decisions among the 375 million people who have to live with their consequences'.[21]

There was nothing by way of convincing initiatives to explain to citizens (and in plain language) what was actually happening; no attempt to make the case for the Constitution in accessible language. The Constitution was promoted instead merely in practical terms, as 'tidying up' ramshackle governance.[22] For this was how most governments saw the endeavour, a treaty more than a constitution, and with good reason, for the European Constitution was 'much less ambitious than its proud wording would have it'. It was seen in these terms, little more than 'a revision of an old Constitution, Nice-II if one likes to start with the last step, Maastricht-IV, if one prefers to date things with the introduction of the European Union'. Whatever federalist miasma Eurosceptics might choose to see in this Constitution hardly accorded with the facts, did not 'pertain to its legal nature or substance, but to wishful thinking or frightened ideology'.[23] But perception matters in politics, and the failure of the Constitution to explain what was at stake enabled opponents, and for that matter some supporters, too, to portray it as something it clearly was not, a quasi-federalist charter confronting national sovereignty, and for some even a threat to national identity.

This mismatch between facts and fantasy goes some way to explaining why the Constitution fared badly during ratification. The Constitution did not fail to resonate positively with the public because it was too radical. On the contrary, it barely addressed the most controversial questions of democracy, identity and citizenship, paid little heed to the politically sensitive matter of how to foster the affective cement that binds citizens in shared political endeavour across borders, the solidarity indispensable for legitimacy, for sustaining public support when the things go awry as they do sooner or later in any polity.[24] More is required to instil in the public a sense of being part of a common endeavour, let alone anything remotely approaching European identity, the so-called *affectio societatis* that Giscard had anticipated, than concocting a formal legal bargain between the principal political actors that allocates power between common, but for all that essentially elite institutions.[25]

This was always going to be a tall order, even with a fair wind and favourable circumstances. The Convention was not a constituent assembly, nor in any way one mandated by 'the people' to write a constitution, but instead a preparatory body consisting in the main of self-selected insiders. For that reason, it lacked authority to deliver a definitive constitutional outcome, even though it acted throughout as if it had such a democratic mandate.[26] This was more than merely wilful neglect on the part of politicians. The undertaking was daunting in any event, made even more difficult by the Convention's very remoteness from the general public and the fact that it was largely out of touch with their concerns. Moreover, academic commentators, who might reasonably be expected to objectively articulate 'the idea of Europe, and the notion of a Europe of values' from the ground up and in something like plain language, and by this means to better connect politicians with public opinion, fared little better.[27] Academic commentaries on the European Constitution for the most part were written in abstruse language, debate confined mostly to scholarly journals and other specialised academic outlets far removed from the prosaic concerns of ordinary people.[28]

What was missing from this constitutional endeavour was the connection, and more than this the sense of trust (*fides*) between the politicians who steer the project and the citizens in whose name they act. Without public trust there can be no constitutional bargain worth the name, certainly not one that is durable. For trust is 'an essential condition for deep and binding co-operation and for the settlement of conflicts by neutral procedures', which 'can help foster allegiance and respect for law'.[29] Trust is essential underpinning for those trade-offs between vested interests that sustain the constitutional bargain in any democratic polity, and an even more critical resource in the EU multi-level polity with its competing claims to authority, its complicated procedures and its lack of transparency in crucial decision-making arenas. As Follesdal has observed: 'The need for trust and trustworthiness arises under circumstances of complex mutual dependence. The regular co-operation by each depends on their conscious or habitual expectation of the regular co-operation of others.' Accordingly, 'trust in future compliance by others is central for the long-term stability of a just political order. The "truster" must believe that it is in the interest of the trusted to act according to the shared expectations'. For this reason, 'it is important for the long term support for institutions that they develop and maintain a sufficiently large group of citizens and politicians who are contingent compliers', who comply on the basis of reciprocity and a faith that the rules are fair 'as long as they believe that others do so as well, for instance out of a sense of justice'.[30]

Trust in this ontological sense is more discernable in national democratic systems than it is in the EU. Nevertheless, it is not impossible to foster a degree of trust amongst the citizens of a non-statal polity, if they can be convinced that the authorities make decisions without fear or favour, by fair means and as transparently as possible. Especially so on those critical decisions with significant consequences for resource allocation, when it can reasonably be expected that other parties will comply with decisions even if they do not serve their immediate interests. For the EU polity the key to trust in this sense depends in part on reforming institutions and decision-making procedures so as to reduce democracy deficits, improving accountability and transparency, but no less increasing the opportunities for citizens and representatives of civil society to participate in and to influence decisions.[31] The European Constitution did propose some improvements in these matters, but not enough was made of this by governments and their official spokespersons during the ratification campaigns.

The sheer extent of disconnection between politicians and people was plain to see once the Constitution became public property in these national campaigns. Of course, this problem is by no means confined to EU politics, for despite technological advances such as the growth of electronic media and the internet, there is a pervasive sense of popular alienation from politics everywhere. Improvements in literacy and the expansion of public education have brought about unprecedented access to information, though paradoxically the surfeit of information has merely increased the public's sense of disengagement from formal politics.[32] People may be less tribal nowadays in their political affiliations, but by the same token their electoral preferences are more volatile, many content now, to use the modish phrase, to 'bowl alone'. Less deferential, cut loose from tribalism, they are also more likely than their forebears to hold negative opinions about political leaders, to regard them as motivated more by narrow self-interest than by principled concern for the public good.[33] This makes governance at any level a difficult art to practice, and this growing sense of public alienation undoubtedly contributed to the Union's recent 'crisis' over the Constitution.

### Responding to constitutional impasse

Crisis is an overused word in the lexicon of contemporary politics, though even 'crises' can have positive outcomes, facilitating compromises that resolve current difficulties and in due course restoring normalcy. Indeed, 'crisis' politics in the EU has been normal politics throughout, integral to problem-solving and as such part of the dynamics of constructing the European project. The impasse that followed the abortive European Defence Community eventually led to the Messina conference that launched the European Economic Community. The *chaise vide* crisis following De Gaulle's rebuttal of Hallstein's proposals for deeper integration produced the Luxembourg Compromise that set the Community on the road to the confederalist phase during the 1970s and beyond. Likewise Margaret Thatcher's persistent objections to the budgetary implications of the CAP that plunged the Community into prolonged deadlock culminated in the Fontainebleau deal on a British budget rebate that kick-started the Single Market project.

More recently, the problematic ratifications of the Maastricht and Nice treaties after Danish and Irish referendums had stalled them were resolved by negotiated deals on opt-outs and clarifications that removed ambiguities. In every case, 'crisis' was a prelude to pragmatic adjustment, the resolution of temporary difficulties that brought renewed momentum to the European project. The EU was on familiar ground, then, as the outcome of the referendums in France and the Netherlands plunged it into renewed crisis, though the scale of this latest impasse, and maybe its significance, too, for the future of the European project, was of a different magnitude.

The Constitution was undoubtedly a touchstone for widespread public unease about European integration. To an extent, this was to be expected in as much as the Union is a victim of its own success. Over time it has responded to all manner of challenges, coming through periodic crises, and in ways that have inflated public expectations whilst simultaneously raising concerns about still remote and undemocratic governance. There is little in recent events to suggest that these problems will be easily resolved. The Union continues to face formidable policy challenges. The reunification of Europe after the 1989 revolutions in the former communist East, the challenges of accelerating globalisation bringing cultural shifts and socio-economic changes, continue to pose daunting problems for an arcane institutional architecture. There is confusion, too, over the Union's purpose, not least about its international role, whether it should remain firmly Atlanticist or instead embrace a pan-European orientation, and all manner of related questions about its international role. The 2004 enlargement has compounded such problems. For one thing, an increase in size was bound to add to institutional strain, but it has also brought in states with very different experiences, problems and expectations for the European project from those of the founder members. And this has serious implications for what the EU does, for its governance and no less for its future direction.

The Union's governance was designed at a time when policy demands and pressures from without were both fewer and less complicated, and when the public was more disposed to leave matters to the politicians. An institutional design for a Community of six founder members and thereafter occasional accession states much like them, and one with a manageable policy portfolio, is now experiencing unprecedented pressures. In these circumstances, the political class has had to rethink the Union's role, to review priorities and not least to reform the institutions and decision-making procedures. And this is not all that the politicians have had to confront. There are problems, too, with public perceptions, rising disquiet, new anxieties, even distrust about what seem to many citizens to be remote politicians out of touch with popular concerns, a clash 'between overly distant elites and underprivileged classes struggling with the difficulties of unemployment and stagnation'.[34] This captious mood has grown, and the Union's present difficulties are its direct consequence. The sense of crisis now is no longer confined to privileged insiders or vested interests, but affects the wider public, who barely seemed to notice previous crises. This much became clear during ratification campaigns everywhere, and not only in the two countries where the Constitution was rejected at the ballot box.

The present situation hardly bears comparison with previous 'crises', for the most part wrangles between insiders and brought about by tensions over competing preferences. For one thing, the latest impasse was not a fall-out between governments as in times past. These earlier 'crises' were typically resolved by governments settling their differences, making bargains well within the capacity of politicians and their advisers to deliver, and mostly without reference to public opinion. This was hardly the situation that faced the Union in the aftermath of the 2004 referendums. The fall-out over the Constitution was not a spat between privileged insiders but something altogether more serious, a challenge from below that called into question both the authority and the competence of the political class.

This grassroots 'revolt' has important consequences for relations between politicians and people, for in some degree it is a crisis of confidence between those who manage affairs and those on whose behalf they do so, a crisis of legitimacy whose resolution will require something more convincing as a response to public disquiet than the trade-offs between elites that resolved previous crises. Yet it is for this very reason that the latest attempt to find a way forward, the deal made in Brussels in June 2007 to bring in reforms by the back door, simply misses the point, as we shall see when we discuss the outcome of the German presidency.

Yet seemingly things had begun on a more positive footing. Political leaders signalled willingness to confront some of the problems facing the Union when they agreed to launch a constitutional review at Laeken. Even then, this had about it an air of make believe, with most leaders quite oblivious to the public's concerns. The Convention flattered to deceive, promised more than it delivered on democracy and citizenship. After two years and more of deliberation and negotiations the public remained largely unconvinced about the outcome, hardly persuaded that this supposedly constitutional make-over in any significant way addressed their own broad concerns. After the referendum defeats the critical question was how EU leaders would respond to public rebuff, and the early signs were far from encouraging. Some political leaders at least seemed to grasp the fact if not quite the extent of public disquiet. Chancellor Schroeder, for example, served warning that if the constitutional crisis was not speedily resolved it might further deteriorate into 'Europe's general crisis'.[35] But this was far from being the typical response of the political class, a mix of disbelief and even disdain, altogether less humility, let alone willingness to face up to the consequences of the public's verdict, and for some even impatience with a public that had clearly given 'the wrong answer' to the constitutional question.

Some politicians were in outright denial, whereas others were prepared to wait, to take time out to 'reflect', a sure sign in the EU of being wrong-footed by events. It seems at the time of writing that the lessons of 2005 have not been learned. Reflection was a breathing space for politicians with little clear idea about what to do next, and it brought belated recriminations, even a tendency on the part of some member states to settle political scores. The fact that 'reflection' took so long and in the event resulted in more of the same, albeit repackaged and in a way that permits politicians to disallow public voice on what was touted not as a Constitution but 'merely' a reform treaty, shows how unreceptive are these leaders to anything remotely democratic at the European level. Reflection did take place and options were reviewed, but seemingly with every intention of bringing in 'necessary' reforms come what may. Cynics had predicted as much, forecasting that the politicians would lie low, stay relatively quiet, and after what seemed like a decent interlude had elapsed restore the Constitutional Treaty, or at least those significant aspects of it dealing with procedural and institutional reforms. This is exactly what they did do, under the anodyne name of a reform treaty, thereby avoiding yet more politically risky referendums. On the face of it this seems complacency at best, and in a less benign interpretation even contempt for public anxiety about reforms already voted down in referendums.

What the post-referendum events do show is that the politicians can no longer rely on permissive consensus to push through their narrowly contrived bargains. For permissive consensus assumes at least latent public confidence in 'princes', allowing them to press on regardless, to concoct their deals and make their trade-offs amongst themselves as they see fit, as they once did. There is little in the latest attempt to resurrect key aspects of a failed Constitution to indicate that the politicians have remotely begun to assimilate these lessons, and this can only bring more problems. To avoid further breakdown of trust, and more than that to carry the public with them on these important and timely matters, the Union's political leaders must at the very least show some humility, cultivate the habit of listening and, just as much, explain what these reforms mean and why they are needed. Above all they must have 'the courage to make the case' for Europe, something few of the present generation of leaders with short-term electoral considerations in mind can be bothered to do.[36] The point was well made by one commentator, who wryly observed:

> I struggle to recall anything quite so absurd as the images this week of Jean-Claude Junker ... and José Manuel Barroso ... asserting that the ratification process must continue as if nothing had happened. What is needed now is a change of mindset. There are much bigger challenges to the cohesion of Europe than rescuing the treaty. Institutional fixes can no longer be offered as a substitute for political imagination ... Nationalism is filling the vacuum left by national leadership. Europeans should know all too well the dangers that lie ahead when chauvinism feeds on the fears and frustrations of the unemployed.[37]

It is patent, or at least it should be to any contemporary European statesman even remotely in tune with the febrile public mood, that these matters cannot possibly be addressed by such complacency. But more of this below, for we are getting ahead of events.

## Time for reflection

The referendums in France and the Netherlands ensured that what was always likely to be a difficult ratification campaign would now be a momentous one. Difficulties had been anticipated from the outset, with the signatories to the Treaty appending the requirement (Article 4-447) that the Treaty would 'enter into force on 1 November 2006, but only providing that all the instruments of ratification have been deposited, or, failing that, on the first day of the second month following the deposit of the instrument of ratification by the last signatory State to take this step'. The signatories in fact hedged their bets, prompted by France's decision (ironically as things turned out) to add a Declaration – not legally binding, but with some considerable political weight behind it – giving the European Council leverage over any laggards holding up the Constitution. The Declaration served due warning that 'if, two years after the signature of the Treaty establishing a

Constitution for Europe, four fifths of the Member States have ratified it and one third or more Member States have encountered difficulties in proceeding with ratification, the matter will be referred to the European Council'. President Chirac, who was behind this implied sanction, did not remotely imagine that it might apply to his own country, expecting any difficulties here to be caused by the usual Eurosceptical states, with the United Kingdom as the most likely culprit.

But things did not go according to plan. When voters in France and the Netherlands delivered their negative verdicts some politicians reacted with a mix of incredulity and defiance. Chancellor Schroeder, for instance, consulted the Council president, Jean-Claude Juncker, and they both insisted that ratification should go ahead regardless, with the Union making a decision about what to do next only after the conclusion of the ratification process elsewhere.[38] The Spanish foreign minister, Miguel Moratinos, was similarly complacent, and together with pro-Constitution politicians from Belgium to the Czech Republic made the absurd claim that these 'no' votes were much less an outright rejection of the Constitution than untimely protest by a disgruntled but above all a misinformed public answering altogether different – and by implication, irrelevant – questions from those being asked of them.[39] Even Joschka Fischer, the German foreign minister who with his Humboldt speech had launched the constitutional episode as an exercise in democratic constitutionalism, and a statesman with impeccably progressive credentials, was unfazed by the public's negative verdict, quite convinced that 'this is not the end of the process for the constitution and not the end of European integration'.[40]

The presidents of Germany, Austria, Italy, Finland, Poland, Portugal and Latvia all rallied to the Constitution, calling for its continuation after time out for reflection, though they at least paid lip-service to the idea of 'a more democratic, more transparent and more efficient EU'. Moreover, one with 'procedures to involve citizens more in the European project and make them part of its implementation and further development'.[41] Other national leaders drew rather different conclusions about the governments' room for manoeuvre, amongst them the Dutch prime minister, Jan Peter Balkenende, who informed his national parliament that he would carry the referendum's clear 'message' to Brussels. He called on his fellow national leaders to be suitably chastened, to accept that the challenge now is 'not always more and always further' integration, but instead 'how can we bring Europe closer to the people'.[42] Such realism, however, was by no means the first reflex of many of Europe's leaders.

What the politicians did at least agree about was the need to respond to the challenge from below. But there was less agreement about how to do so. The leading member states, predictably enough, preferred damage limitation. The Franco-German alliance, a key driver of the constitutional bargain, called for an emergency summit of the six founder members to find a way forward.[43] The usual response of the more enthusiastic Europhiles, however, when this project hits turbulent waters, to retreat into a laager of old and trusted allies, was no longer feasible, as unacceptable to the accession countries as it was to the United Kingdom and other member states who had not been in the club from the start.[44] It soon became apparent to Berlin that any resolution of the present crisis must involve the United Kingdom. The plain fact is that the Franco-German alliance, once the engine of European integration, has lost much of its diplomatic leverage in an enlarged Union, some member states even seeing this close alliance as more problem than solution. Recent events served to reinforce this impression. A cavalier disregard for the rules of the Eurozone's stability pact by these two countries, and latterly the disdain with which Chirac had dismissed the decision of some of the new accession countries to embrace Atlanticism rather than back a pan-European approach to regional security under Franco-German direction, had hardly endeared this bilateral axis to many of the newcomers and even some of the established members. In the end, Germany, with the support of France and Spain, decided to launch a broader diplomatic initiative in an attempt to keep the Constitution on track, though not at this stage with support from London.

The British government's reaction to these events was, as it usually is where Europe is the issue, pragmatic, motivated less by concern about public disaffection than by self-interest. There was even some relief in government circles about shelving what had promised to be almost certainly an unwinnable referendum. And though Blair feigned hesitancy about suspending the enabling bill for the British referendum, he soon enough endorsed the judgement of his foreign secretary, Jack Straw, that the enabling bill was now simply unsustainable. Blair readily fell in behind the idea, by now widespread amongst EU leaders, that what was needed was reflection and debate.[45] The withdrawal of this legislation sent a clear signal, not just to the British public and to a generally Eurosceptical media but to other member states, too, that as far as Britain was concerned the Constitution, at least in present form, was effectively dead.[46] Even the Foreign Office, a long-time subscriber to Britain's European 'destiny', took the realistic view that to press ahead with the Constitution, as the Commission was at this stage still insisting, would merely inflict greater damage on the constitutional project, and indeed on European integration *per se* over the medium to long term. As one senior government source saw it, to hold further referendums in the current climate would be to invite rebuttal, starting 'a domino effect, with "No" after "No" vote [that] will send a disastrous signal'.[47]

By no means all governments were so persuaded, however, of the need to abandon the Constitution, and to go back to the drawing-board. Some of the member states who had already ratified the Constitution wanted to press on regardless, even referring to 'double standards' in a Union of 25 supposedly equal member states. They queried why a 'no' vote that would have provoked little more than admonishment for its lack of 'commitment' to the Union had it occurred in most of the non-founder states, should now require the suspension of ratification where two founder members were involved. A Finnish MEP, for instance, indignantly demanded that 'we should go on with the ratification [for] this is like a snooker game with 25 frames – if we reach 22 frames won out of 25 we are doing quite well. Perhaps the countries that have voted against will have to reassess.'[48] The Greek and Maltese governments echoed the call for 'business as usual'. The Irish government, too, announced that it would press on with its own referendum.[49] And Luxembourg, the smallest member state, did actually proceed with ratification and in July 2005 became the first country in the aftermath of the failed referendums to ratify the Constitution. This was sincere enough, but it nevertheless ignored political realities. For these are relatively small member states, and the EU is not a 'game' where there is parity between players. The very fact that the two lost 'frames' had occurred in historically (and, in France's case, politically) significant member states was bound to make a difference to the outcome of the game. How could it not do so?

The Commission, too, was in denial, refusing as always to countenance anything that slowed the pace or otherwise arrested the momentum of 'ever-closer union'. Some in the Brussels establishment, displaying political logic reminiscent of Soviet *nomenklatura*, maintained that the 'no' votes were actually a protest against the tardiness of political leaders, in fact a vote in favour of even more radical changes.[50] Commission President Barroso did not strain political credulity quite that far, though his mood was more complacent than it was chastened by the outcomes of the referendums. He counselled those member states yet to ratify to hold their nerve, asserting that 'we have a serious problem but we must continue our work'.[51] As Barroso saw it, Britain's response to the impasse was crucial to its eventual resolution, and he wrote to Prime Minister Blair to remind him of his government's formal undertaking to allow the British people a say on the Constitution. The line from Brussels was mostly 'business as usual', albeit business delayed temporarily by 'local' difficulties. The Commission insisted that every member state should continue with ratification as agreed, though some commissioners better atuned to the rhythm of national politics, not least the British trade commissioner, Peter Mandelson, warned that simply pushing on with ratification regardless risked inflicting on the Union 'creeping paralysis', [52] and strongly recommended 'hitting the pause button'.[53]

Another influential Commission voice, Margot Wallström, the commissioner for communications, showed at least a glimmer of understanding about what had overtaken the Constitution. She readily acknowledged the need to respond to palpable public disquiet, to make a greater effort to convince the people of the EU's virtues. To this end she announced a so-called 'Plan D', promising more democracy, and to 'listen' to people.[54] Yet this initiative was less radical than it sounded; an acknowledgement of public consternation, but for all that little more than tokenism.[55] The European Parliament followed much the same incredulous line, its president, Josep Borrell, and the leader of the EPP-ED, Hans-Gert Pöttering, both calling for ratification to continue. The leader of the Alliance of Liberals and Democrats (ALDE), echoing a view expressed by Austrian Chancellor Schuessel, even proposed holding a super- or pan-European referendum, to be preceded by governments patiently explaining the meaning of Europe to their presumably uninformed electorates, sparking 'a truly European debate', the key as he saw it to bringing public opinion firmly behind the Constitution.[56] Belgium's foreign minister, Karel de Gucht, likewise criticised those of his colleagues who had failed to firmly endorse the Constitution, though his own government's position was somewhat undermined here by the fact that it had yet to complete ratification.[57]

Much was made at this stage of the ratification arithmetic in those member states that wanted to press ahead with the Constitution. A year after the 'no' votes the number of countries approving or about to approve the Constitution had risen to 16: Lithuania; Latvia; Estonia; Hungary; Slovenia; Italy; Slovakia; Spain; Austria; Germany; Greece; Cyprus; Malta; Luxembourg; Finland; and it was endorsed by Belgium's national parliament, though a dispute there over how far the draft Constitution conforms with the subsidiarity principle had delayed formal ratification. There was undue optimism at this stage that an additional five countries might somehow be found to trigger the formal review procedure in the Declaration appended to the Constitutional Treaty. But this was not how most governments saw the situation. The critical issue here was not so much numbers as politics. Ratification had indeed continued, but not in those countries that mattered if the Constitution was to be revived. Caution soon replaced complacency in Europe's chancelleries, and though Latvia became the tenth member state to ratify the Treaty by a parliamentary vote (2 June 2005), and with Malta and Luxembourg both deciding to press on with ratification despite opinion polls showing a fall in public support for the Constitution, some more significant member states including the United Kingdom, Denmark, Portugal and by now Ireland suspended their referendums. As the dust began to settle so the politicians came to acknowledge an entirely new political landscape, and no less the constraints this imposed on them.

The problem of Euroscepticism did not apply to merely a handful of member states, the 'usual suspects', though polling data in the United Kingdom, the Czech Republic and Denmark showed a marked shift against the Constitution. The crisis over the Constitution had an impact on public opinion, even where there had been high levels of support for, or at least limited opposition to it.[58] One opinion poll, for instance, showed that had German voters been given the opportunity to vote, a clear majority of them would have rejected the Constitution.[59] In these unpropitious circumstances, 'reflection' seemed the only option available, though it meant different things to different actors.

The EU is no stranger to 'reflection', after all a familiar response to political crisis over the duration. European construction has been anything but straightforward, a process punctuated by periodic setbacks that have given rise to pauses so as to review available options, though to date these 'pauses' have usually been of fairly limited duration. This latest impasse was altogether more serious, not just a spat between insiders otherwise disposed to make a bargain, but evidence of widespread public disquiet.[60] In the circumstances, reflection on its own was not enough to resolve matters, or at least not unless it 'directly addresses the larger malaise that characterises the attitude of a growing part of the population towards the EU'.[61] Commentators on these events saw a situation redolent with danger, precisely because it goes beyond the reform of the institutions, to the very idea of a European polity. As one contemporary observer has predicted: 'For the next few years, because the great integration projects have largely been completed, EU politics will be less about building institutions, and more about ensuring that existing policies are delivered.' As such, the public can no longer be excluded from the reform process, for as Mark Leonard sees it: 'In these arguments over policy, political differences will need to be aired. If elites avoid frank discussions, genuine differences do not go away – they simply provide a rallying ground for populism. Politicians and commentators should therefore see conflict within the EU as normal, and avoid the over-blown talk of profound crisis that followed the French and Dutch "No"s.'[62]

This was not quite what most EU leaders had in mind, though they did recover sufficiently from the initial shock to review their options at a European Summit in mid-June 2005. Chirac, for instance, desperately seeking to restore his political reputation, aimed to reconnect with a disaffected domestic electorate by harnessing the grievances of French voters about further enlargement, and especially Turkish accession, an issue the United Kingdom had signalled would be a central plank of its forthcoming presidency. Still angry with Blair for placing him (as Chirac saw it) in the invidious position of having to match the prime minister's offer of a referendum to placate Britain's Eurosceptical public – the result of which had finished off any prospect of him running for a third term in 2007 – Chirac opened a new front, challenging the 'ethics' of Britain's budget rebate agreed at the 1984 Fontainebleau European Council as discussions commenced on the Union's new financial perspective.[63] This may have been good domestic politics, but it was hardly the sort of statesmanship needed to repair the damage inflicted on the European project by the referendums.

Most other leaders could at least see that much, and at the June summit the realisation began to dawn that this was no ordinary 'crisis', that the Constitution was in serious trouble, and with it maybe even 'Europe'. Some EU foreign ministers warned of the danger of the reflection period becoming merely a prolonged siesta, an excuse for inaction.[64] Yet the response of political leaders hardly corresponded to this assessment, most of them being content merely to tread water by extending reflection until mid-2007. For the most part, they seemed paralysed by the public's negative reaction to the Constitution, and no less wary about provoking even greater opposition that might spill back into domestic politics. Of course, rhetoric is easier than action, a substitute for decisiveness, as when the politicians at their 2006 spring summit issued a political declaration on common EU values to commemorate the fiftieth anniversary of the Union's founding treaty in 2007.[65]

Meanwhile, the leading member states, including the United Kingdom, the Netherlands, Denmark and the Villepin government in France, all gave their support to a Commission proposal for greater transparency, and to include national parliaments in future constitutional deliberations. There were by now tentative moves afoot to resurrect the constitutional project, albeit in modified form. The Dutch foreign minister, Bernard Bot, presciently pointed to a solution that eventually found its way on to the agenda of the German presidency, when he proposed that deadlock could only be broken by scaling down the endeavour, presenting the 'Constitution' to the public as 'merely' a treaty. And if a treaty, he reasoned, it could be passed by parliaments, neatly avoiding the political risk involved in holding further referendums.[66] By now only a handful of countries, mostly those with federalist inclinations and including Belgium, Italy and, not surprisingly in view of its early ratification, Spain, indicated they would resist a dilution of the Constitution, or even cherry-picking selected parts. But these states found little support amongst the member states at large. Few political leaders of any weight agreed with them that the Constitution could still be salvaged and largely intact, merely by making modest adjustments to meet public concerns.[67] The view that began to emerge was to find ways of repackaging the Constitution's essential procedural and institutional reforms to enable the enlarged Union to function much as before. But this solution did not come easily, and only in due course, after a number of possible scenarios for resolving the political impasse had been considered by governments.

## Scenarios and solutions

For two years after the 2005 referendums the Constitutional Treaty remained stalled, though it was not formally abandoned. Governments seem paralysed by events, engaged in reviewing various 'solutions', but lacking the political will to give any clear sense of direction. Certainly there was nothing like the leadership given by an earlier generation of political leaders, when François Mitterrand and Helmut Kohl, ably abetted by Jacques Delors, the last politically astute Commission president, had ushered in the Single European Market, with all that this entailed for deeper political and monetary union. The present crop of EU leaders was caught unawares, seemingly content to follow events rather than to direct them. Disconnection between the political class and the people was a root cause of this latest crisis, widespread mistrust of politicians that went beyond the public's immediate or particular concerns about the Constitution.

In part, this reflects growing anxiety with the EU's overall performance as globalisation has raised the stakes. The perception is widespread that the Union's governance is colonised by privileged insiders. There is concern, too, about the perceived failure to protect people at large from negative externalities, especially the adverse consequences of global competitiveness, social dumping, changes in labour market practices and ultimately threats to the European social model. One commentator has summarised the problem here as follows: 'Despite the creation of a single market and the euro, the EU has not fulfilled its economic promise, even though economics is its undisputed domain, and the growing differences among its increasingly numerous members have tarnished the dream of its political unity.'[68]

The Constitution became the convenient scapegoat for these concerns. The incipient threat to economic security, after all the bedrock of political stability in Europe since 1945, has wider ramifications: it gives rise to insecurities over political and cultural identity, concerns deepened by enlargement, with new external borders facilitating population movements, bringing even closer unstable and impoverished neighbours, and with that increased risks of cross-border criminality, terrorism and all manner of illicit trafficking that threaten public order. These are indeed formidable problems, though things do not have to turn out badly; something might still be salvaged. The public was wary about a European Constitution that seemed to be the harbinger of those very problems that concern citizens, yet they might at the same time be open to persuasion should the politicians for once decide to listen, to engage in democratic conversation about these matters. Polling evidence from *Eurobarometer* showed, for instance, that a clear majority of public opinion, and not least in France and the Netherlands, was quite receptive to the case that the Union does need more efficient decision-making.[69]

The key to managing these important issues is political leadership, and as the constitutional crisis unfolded there was much talk of leadership, or more to the point the lack of it. Energetic and no less imaginative leadership was certainly needed if the EU was to recover its sense of direction, to navigate a way out of the crisis, and to do so without losing international credibility. More than that, leadership from one or more of the 'big three', and not merely leadership *à la mode*, the usual trade-offs made behind closed doors and subsequently announced to the press and the public as *fait accompli*, but an altogether new approach that takes greater account of the public's concerns. This is what Commission vice-president Margot Wallström seemed to be saying when she announced the Commission's so-called 'Plan D', an interlude of 'explanation' and 'dialogue'. What Wallström proposed here was significant investment in programmes to facilitate participatory democracy, not just a vertical conversation between 'princes' and people but horizontal cross-border contacts at the level of civil society.[70] Yet even as this idea was announced it looked less than convincing, dismissed by one critic as merely 'a cheap slogan', rather than facilitating genuine dialogue or discussion, let alone democracy, and in reality offering 'nothing of substance'.[71]

Of those leading EU states that might have realistically been expected to give the Union direction at this critical time, all except Germany had governments in what might be called reduced circumstances, whether down in the polls or with leaders about to retire, treading political water and with little incentive to revive the constitutional project. Chirac's miscalculation, his patent mishandling of the French referendum, fatally damaged his authority, and for the rest of his term he presided over a discredited government seemingly incapable of resolving even domestic challenges, lacking political capital either at home or abroad to give any credible lead on the stalled Constitution. Those who were manoeuvring to succeed him, whether on the centre-right or the centre-left, were hardly better placed, either incapacitated by intra-party machinations over the succession or hemmed in by a public that is now unreceptive to bold initiatives on Europe. As François Heisbourg, special adviser to the Paris-based Foundation for Strategic Studies, observed, 'no freshly elected president is going to undermine his or her legitimacy by bringing up the issue of Europe too quickly'.[72] Nicolas Sarkozy, minister of the interior and once the hope of the governing party's would-be modernisers, who subsequently became president of the Republic in May 2007, had to curb his radical instincts in order to capture the ultimate prize of the Elysée. Though his ideological preference was for an internationally competitive Europe, one less ravelled by regulations and protectionism, better equipped to meet the challenges of an information-rich global economy, he was constrained, as all French politicians are, by a political culture deeply attached to the post-1945 social model, and tied no less to an unreformed CAP that serves narrow national interest rather better than the European interest. With the constitutional issue back on the agenda, the newly elected Sarkozy chose not to lead his people on Europe but instead to follow them.

When the German government did eventually return to constitutional matters on the occasion of its presidency in June 2007, albeit in the guise of a treaty rather than a constitution, in effect a 'cut and paste', slimmed down version of the Constitutional Treaty, Sarkozy made sure in the ensuing negotiations that whatever this reform treaty might include it must dilute the neo-liberalism of its predecessor that had so alienated French voters in the 2005 referendum. In the event, Sarkozy pulled off what many bystanders in Brussels saw as a minor coup, persuading the assembled heads of government and state to excise any references to competitiveness from the framework document. A move that bespeaks national interests far more than what used to be called 'the vision thing' for Europe. And by this stage, France was by no means the only government mobilising in defence of its own interests.

The United Kingdom was hardly more inclined and certainly no better placed to offer leadership on the issue, for it too faced an imminent change of government. Whoever succeeded Blair would be constrained by that country's preoccupation with sovereignty. The fall-out from Iraq, problems of reforming, managing and financing the public services and the unfinished business of national constitutional reform are all more pressing matters here than 'Europe'. In any event, Blair had secured, more or less, the deal he wanted on the Constitutional Treaty and was loath to unpick if for fear of losing ground won on his so-called 'red lines'. After Blair departed the scene in June 2007 his successor, Gordon Brown, more Euro-sceptical by far and committed to rebuilding trust in politics, would hardly risk disaster at the polls in 2009 by recklessness over Europe.

Meanwhile, Italy was threatened with familiar political paralysis following the virtual dead heat in the 2006 general election. Romano Prodi's fragile hold on office precluded him giving a positive steer on European affairs, and in any event his reputation for muddle and vacillation from his days as Commission president precedes him. The new member states from eastern and central Europe are more pragmatic than idealistic about the EU, and as such perplexed that some established member states simply failed to grasp reality, some of them clinging vainly to the wreckage of the Constitution instead of concentrating their energies on practical matters such as economic reform and other policy areas where the EU is facing stiff global challenges.[73] In the past whenever Europe has faced periodic crises salvation usually comes in the shape of a 'big' project – the Single Market or monetary union are obvious examples. But there are no big projects to hand now to kick-start Europe. The Constitution *is* the big project, and now that this had faltered few amongst the Union's current crop of leaders, whether in the member states or in the common institutions, seemed to have any clear sense of where to go next

Where then might the bold, and indeed imaginative leadership required for tackling the stalled Constitution come from, if not from the leading member states? The Commission might have played a more decisive role than it has done over recent years, but seemed to see the current impasse merely as the opportunity to recover some lost prestige. However, the Commission is nothing if not cautious and it has well-honed political instincts, remaining wary of damaging its fragile reputation yet further by precipitate action. The Barroso Commission, though it did seem to have shaken off the torpor that afflicted its predecessors, and exhibiting a refreshing sense of renewed purpose, was constrained by its lack of a mandate, and even more by its limited authority. At best, this institution's legitimacy is indirect if not second-hand because acquired from formal legal process rather than popular consent.

This much is hardly new, but it mattered less when the EC was more a regulatory regime, much less the polity it has become over recent decades. As with all post-Delors Commissions, this unelected institution lacks serious political capital, as was plain to see from its reticence about giving a lead on the headline issues compared with its predecessors of the 1980s and early 1990s. The Commission was simply in no position to resolve the deadlock, resigned as it now is to playing its part in framing policy, operating as a focal point, the *interlocuteur valable* for the multiple actors, those agencies, lobbyists and policy networks that gravitate towards this uniquely multi-level governance. The Barroso presidency has at least come to terms with these constraints, and has shown commendable forbearance, a marked reluctance to pontificate, quite aware that political leadership, at least on the 'big' questions, is a matter for governments. Of course, Barroso wanted to resurrect the Constitution and said so, convinced that 'Nice simply cannot be enough'. He regarded far-reaching institutional reform as indispensable for meeting the challenges ahead, but circumstances obliged him to adopt Fabian tactics, putting whatever political weight Brussels can now muster behind the efforts of those member states opposed to what he saw as the folly of a two-tier EU. And in the meantime vainly hoping that a new generation of political leaders in the key member states might somehow reinvigorate the constitutional project.[74] For in the end, these big questions always come down to the politicians, and not least to those from the leading member states.

Politicians come and go, and a new generation of leaders unencumbered by inconvenient ideological baggage might just approach the present impasse with greater vigour and determination, bringing fresh thinking to persistent problems. One leader who did show refreshing candour on the problem of the stalled Constitution was Angela Merkel, the incoming German chancellor. She had the considerable advantage as a newcomer of not being encumbered, unlike her predecessor, by personal loyalty to Chirac, and so was free to construct an alternative alliance of member states to get things moving again. Her early actions showed her to be a realist about the EU, fully aware of what is at stake, not least apprised of the damage to the Union's reputation in Germany and abroad if the deadlock should persist. Moreover, Merkel was committed to rescuing the Constitutional Treaty, or at least the substance of it, promising that her country's upcoming presidency would report on 'the state of discussion' on the Treaty, and 'explore possible future developments'. But at this stage, new to government and still finding her bearings on the international stage, even Merkel preferred caution to boldness, opting to retain only as much of the original text as was politically feasible. And though she was determined to use her presidency to secure a deal on a new Treaty, this was hardly the same thing as restoring the Constitutional Treaty, let alone reforming governance so as to meet the usual benchmarks of democracy or even to ensure greater public voice. Above all, she was concerned to rehabilitate the EU's reputation abroad. But Merkel, too, faced political constraints, not least her fragile domestic power base. After an almost dead-heat general election she headed a brittle 'grand coalition', and had to contend with a fickle and divided electorate that now gave greater priority to remedying domestic problems than to European issues.

The Declaration appended to the Constitutional Treaty by the heads of government provided for a review of the situation with regard to ratification by the European Council, if four-fifths of the 25 member states have ratified by October 2006. The failure of two founder member states to ratify ensured that this convenient fall-back position no longer applied and the Constitution was in effect suspended *sine die*. The longer the impasse over the Constitution lasted, the more likely it was that political leaders would accept the inevitable and abandon the Treaty, at least in its present form. This did not mean, however, the end of the Union's constitutional endeavour, for the very same problems identified at Laeken still had to be addressed. Whatever the fate of the Constitutional Treaty, the EU was bound to revisit the issue. The question was when and, just as important, how to do it. The principal actors accepted as much, though with little agreement about either timing or procedure. A number of scenarios were considered during the interlude for reflection, each one an attempt to answer this perplexing question.

### The Lazarus option

In the aftermath of the referendums the idea of carrying on with the Constitution as it stood was strongly supported by some governments, by leading figures in the European Commission and by the European Parliament. Those who took this view were encouraged by the Union's capacity for recovery, a phenomenon first witnessed at the Messina conference when enlightened politicians had rescued the Community from the blow dealt by the failure of the EDC to overcome all-party opposition in France's National Assembly. This scenario made rather much of the Declaration appended to the Constitutional Treaty that permitted the Council to review the situation, should 80 per cent of the member states ratify. There was insufficient evidence, however, to support such an optimistic prognosis. Ratification had occurred in 10 member states before the first real tests of public opinion in the French and Dutch referendums, but occasional ratification thereafter hardly suggested onward momentum, and the total fell some way short of this critical threshold even with Finland bringing the tally to 15 in December 2006.

It was difficult to see where further ratification might come from, especially in a key member state, and there was no firm evidence of the breakthrough required to trigger Council action under the Declaration. A majority of countries had in fact ratified the Constitution before the problematic referendums, rising to 18 out of 27 member states, with Ireland and Portugal yet to ratify but committed to do so, and with Denmark and Sweden rather more conditionally supportive. A group, Les amis de la Constitution, convened in Madrid in January 2007 and recommended changes to address the concerns of the public and governments alike, such as improving mechanisms for controlling subsidiarity, but also proposing more integration in critical policy areas, for instance immigration policy, economic policy and the development of a European social area.[75]

A similar proposal for resurrecting the Constitution came from the so-called Amato Group of independent experts set up by the former vice-president of the Convention, now Italian minister for the interior. This lobby included some influential figures who had served on the Convention, such as Michel Barnier and Jean-Luc Dehaene, and Commissioner Margot Wallström. They proposed in June 2007 a new version of the Constitutional Treaty that recycled Parts I and IV, with Part II to be clarified 'by appending additional declarations and protocols', with modest changes such as removing the Preamble and those symbols that had conjured images of statehood. Two further protocols were added, one on the 'functioning of the Union' reviewing legal and institutional consequences of a new treaty for the extant treaties, and another on 'the development of European policies to meet the challenges of the 21st century'.[76] The Charter would remain legally binding, with new policy competencies in, for instance, energy and the environment.[77] Not to be outdone Giscard, naturally reluctant to abandon his own creation, and a group of former European leaders signed a text in Florence in November 2006, *The Appeal from Florence*, calling for a 'political wake-up' on constitutional matters.

These proposals maintained that the Constitution was not moribund, that it should and indeed could be revived, a view supported by, amongst others, Joschka Fischer, the former Italian president, Carlo Azeglio Campi, and former Portuguese president, Jorge Sampaio.[78] The idea of pressing on regardless certainly appealed to many MEPs, for whom the Constitution was symbolic, something more than a mere treaty, confirmed by their call to rename the treaties as 'the' European Constitution.[79] In the meantime, the Parliament's constitutional affairs committee approved the Constitution, and MEPs passed a resolution (by 385 to 125) during the January 2006 plenary session, a good six months after the fateful referendums, calling on the member states to ratify the Constitution as it stood by 2009 at the outside. MEPs tended to blame governments for the current inertia and suspected them of wanting to 'cherry-pick' only those parts designed to improve executive functioning and decision-making, whilst jettisoning more controversial proposals for strengthening democratic culture, or reinforcing European identity by giving greater substance to a European rights culture and to common citizenship. While Parliament did support reflection, it refused to see it as an excuse for inaction, a convenient alibi for prevarication, but rather as a prelude to a thoroughgoing review of options designed to win over the public.[80] Accordingly, MEPs called on the Commission to undertake a study of the costs of delaying the reforms proposed in the Constitutional Treaty.

The Parliament expended considerable energy and no less political imagination on finding ways to revive the Constitution, supported in this by some national parliaments. The presidents of the Finish, German and Austrian parliaments, for instance, in a letter to the president of the European Parliament called for 'a joint strategy on how to engage in lasting debate', intended to bridge the wide differences between national parties and citizens on the Constitution.[81] A British Liberal Democrat MEP, Andrew Duff, was the author of a notable attempt to breathe life into the stalled Constitution, his *Plan B: How to Rescue the European Constitution* (October 2006) proposing to utilise the so-called 'constitutional articles' in Part I of the draft, annexing the Charter of Fundamental Rights without altering its legal status, and making Part III that deals with policies (and as such more controversial in some of the national ratification campaigns) subordinate to Part I. Duff likewise advocated strengthening the Union's role in some policy domains in Part III, including economic governance and energy security, where Duff considered the original draft Constitution too weak.

Proposed reforms here included an extension of the Lisbon agenda and Eurozone autonomy; reforming the European social model so as to bridge the seemingly irreconcilable objectives of competitiveness and social solidarity; ecological measures and CAP reform; budget reform and greater transparency about 'where the money goes'; and finally, clarifying asylum and immigration policy to reassure citizens concerned about being out-priced in the labour market, or the pressures on social welfare. These changes would, he believed, address issues of real concern to the general public, not least: the underlying purposes of integration; Europe's role in the world; the future of the economic and social model; and how to enhance freedom, justice and security across borders. As he saw it, an IGC but one with participation from the Parliament would renegotiate Parts III and IV. In a subsequent pamphlet, *Constitution Plus: Renegotiating the Treaty* (February 2007), Duff elaborated on these proposed changes, above all urging fellow MEPs to take the case to the people, to inform citizens about the Constitution's many 'virtues'.

A suitable mechanism here was parliamentary and citizens' forums proposed by Duff and Austrian Green MEP, Johannes Voggenhuber, in an earlier intervention that likewise argued for taking the case out to the public, adjusting the Constitutional Treaty so as to take greater account of concerns expressed by voters in France and the Netherlands, not least by adding further protocols or declarations to safeguard the Union's social model. These same authors proposed making the Constitution easier to understand by restructuring it, creating 'a proper hierarchy between the different parts, so that Part III – mainly the common policies of the Union – becomes distinctly subsidiary to Part I'.[82] Whether this would amount to a democratic conversation, genuine public discourse, or whether it was merely a familiar top-down constitutional fix, an 'enlightened' elite explaining the benefits or otherwise dispelling inconvenient myths about Europe, a version of what some political theorists have aptly described as democratic elitism, is debatable.[83] Voggenhuber, for instance, criticised the Austrian presidency's conference on subsidiarity (itself a response to concerns of national politicians and public opinion about encroaching EU power) as a retrograde step, a move to repatriate EU competencies instead of pressing on with a federalist agenda, and proposing 'a concerted and stronger marketing campaign' to sell the Constitution to the public.[84]

When the Parliament's Constitutional Affairs Committee did launch a Civil Society Forum in April 2006 the preference for proselytising and propaganda rather than for civic conversation was quite apparent, with a familiar mantra from

Strasbourg that the stalled Constitution, whatever its shortcomings, was a marked improvement on the Nice Treaty. And though this civic forum did include representatives of TEAN network which brings together civic and other organisations that network within the Union's policy framework, participants were predominantly Brussels-based 'insiders' from organised networks and groups in civil society – education and the churches, civic movements and NGOs. This prompted one participant, Simon Stocker, speaking on behalf of the confederation of aid and development NGOs, to protest that the Union's stage-managed deliberations 'still appear to be confined to the same players'.

There were yet other attempts by MEPs to revive the Constitution. A French Green MEP, Gerard Onesta, proposed a *Plan A-Plus*, a proposal in effect to keep the Constitution, after all a sensible compromise as he saw it between competing preferences, but to simplify it into two parts: one bringing together the 'constitutional' elements (in essence, principles, decisional procedures, institutional reforms and a binding rights Charter); and a second part dealing with 'ordinary' treaty matters, in the main policies. To ensure that this would not be merely another deal concocted by political leaders, Onesta proposed that the revised Constitution be subject to a transEuropean referendum after formal parliamentary ratification. One can only speculate what the political outcome would be if a member state, either its electorate or elected representatives, had rejected this revised Treaty, or for that matter if the people gave one verdict and the parliamentarians a different one.

Another proposal came from Jo Leinen, the German SPD Member and president of the Parliament's Constitutional Affairs Committee. In *The Cost of Not Having a Constitution* (September 2006) he, too, proposed simplifying the Constitution, dividing it into two parts: Part One to consist of a 'Fundamental Treaty' of some 70 articles, the equivalent of Part I of the draft Constitution, and related clauses from Part IV concerned with the application duration and procedures for revising the treaties. The Charter (Part II) would become a protocol, though remaining legally binding by means of a reference article in the Fundamental Treaty. Whereas a new Part Two would contain a 325-article 'Policies Treaty', to include all the aspects of former and new policies negotiated in the Convention and IGC. Two further protocols would be included as annexes; one on climate change, the other on social policy. Ratification would be left to the discretion of the member states.[85]

A final and more official proposal from the Parliament was that of Elmar Brok, an EPP–ED member from Germany, and Enrique Baron Crespo, a PES member from Spain, co-rapporteurs of the Constitutional Treaty text. The so-called 'B-B' report was submitted as the Parliament's formal contribution to the June 2007 summit convened by Germany to review the state of play on the Constitution. This was adopted by the plenary session (21 May 2007) and endorsed the Constitutional Treaty as it stood, making clear the necessity of keeping the existing treaty base and consolidating it in a single treaty, the abolition of the pillar system, the primacy of EU law and not least the retention of Parts I, II and IV of the draft Treaty text, with Part III amended and possibly absorbed into Part I. The Report identified seven key aspects of a 'Treaty Plus', including the European Social Model, the co-ordination of economic policies within the Eurozone, and the consolidation of the enlargement criteria.[86]

Without discounting the enthusiasm of those who advocated resurrecting the Constitutional Treaty, their various efforts reviewed here had rather less impact on governments. Closer to events on the ground and with rather more to lose should they be seen to ignore public concerns, governments were reluctant to revive a discredited Constitution, at least in name. The public was as wary about the Constitution as it had been from the beginning of the ratification process. Opinion poll data indicated as much, though surprisingly perhaps in light of what had happened in the referendums, the *Eurobarometer* surveys conducted on behalf of the Commission continued to show support at least for the idea of a European constitution in many member states, these surveys recording an EU average of 60 per cent in favour. Not, however, in the two countries where referendums had rejected the Constitutional Treaty, or in more persistently Eurosceptical countries, a disparity that raises questions about method-ology but even more about how situational factors affect responses to pollsters.[87]

It was clear, then, and long before the German presidency revisited the issue, that the Constitution in its present form was beyond saving. In the aftermath of the referendums, none of the countries occupying the presidency had much room for manoeuvre. The British presidency, whose term began immediately after the fateful referendums, least of all, and it made no attempt to rescue the Constitu-tional Treaty. And though the Austrian presidency that followed it did allude to reviving the project, in the event it took no steps to do so.[88] Even when Chancellor Merkel, anticipating the German presidency in 2007, showed initial distaste for the so-called 'cherry-picking' option being proposed by some governments, whereby significant parts of the Constitutional Treaty might be incorporated into the Nice Treaty by various legal procedures, claiming that she wanted to keep as much of the original Constitution as was politically feasible because the Treaty was already a carefully constructed compromise between various national and institutional preferences and would surely unravel unless adopted as it stood, she was merely saying what post-war German chancellors are supposed to say about European construction. When the time came for her to act, she put pragmatism before prin-ciple, opting for the very 'cut and paste' solution she had previously disavowed.

### *The fresh-start option*

Another response to the crisis over ratification crisis was to accept the public's verdict and begin the process anew by negotiating an entirely new Constitution from scratch. Those who argued for this 'solution' opted for simplification, seeing the original text as unduly convoluted and for that reason beyond the public's comprehension. Securing public support for a European constitution required, as they saw it, clarity of purpose, brevity, replacing an encyclopaedic text with one that is simpler, altogether less cluttered and as such both more accessible to the citizen and clearly demarcating the boundaries between the respective tiers of European governance, mapping institutional power and defining the central purposes of the European project in a way the citizen can understand.

Advocates of an entirely new constitution were to be found on both sides of the 'Europe' debate. Some of a more radical disposition blamed the failure to win public approval for the Constitution on its essentially conservative, to say nothing of its convoluted format. Those on the other side of the same argument for starting the process anew were residual Europhobes for whom the post-referendum crisis had been merely an opportunity to bury once and for all what they saw as a quasi-federal project, replacing it with a 'constitution' that better reflected the Union's essentially intergovernmental *raison d'être*. The presidents of the Czech Republic and Poland, Vaclav Klaus and Lech Kaczyński, both strong critics of what they saw as the erosion of national sovereignty implied in the Constitutional Treaty, not least for smaller states, proposed an entirely new design to arrest, and even to reverse this 'pernicious' trend.[89]

The fresh-start approach particularly appealed to those, not least in France, who felt that many voters in the referendums had objected much less to the idea of a constitution than to this particular Constitution. Objections were levelled in particular at Part III of the Constitutional Treaty containing the corpus of EU treaty law, which for many critics, and not merely those on the left, made too much of Anglo-Saxon 'market-economy principles implicit in the European Community's competition policy and its single market'.[90] For these critics, neo-liberal principles have 'acquired negative meaning for social interests in France once they gained enhanced legitimacy as part of the Constitution'. The referendum had given French voters their first opportunity since the closely fought Maastricht referendum to formally challenge the direction of the European project. The 'no' campaign seized the opportunity to send a clear message, both to the Elysée and to Brussels, that it was not minded to support anything that undermined the state's control of domestic economic and social policy. Accordingly, 'by simultaneously undermining Part I and demonising Part III no-campaigners gave [French] voters ample reason to mistrust the treaty and no reason to fear the consequences of rejecting it [and] given the French public's traditional distrust of the market and its lack of familiarity with the complexities of Euro-politics, the strategy worked'.[91] The Constitution simply could not be revived, however long the reflection period. Advocates of a fresh start maintained that something entirely new was needed, the only sure way out of impasse.

The critical question here was what a revised and supposedly streamlined Constitution might look like? Nicolas Sarkozy, the principal contender for the governing UMP's presidential nomination, proposed salvaging Part I (the Preamble and statement of EU goals), Part II (the Fundamental Rights Charter) and some limited policy aspects from the policy articles in Part III, and repackaging this as a new simplified Constitution. Sarkozy went even further in a speech in September 2006 where he proposed abandoning the Constitutional Treaty altogether, claiming that the approach of the founders whereby all member states move ahead together and at the same pace is now obsolete, 'no longer adapted to the world of today'. He advocated instead a new mini-treaty designed to incorporate necessary institutional and procedural reforms, dropping the Charter as legally binding, but permitting some policies to be adopted by 'super-qualified majority voting', with guaranteed opt-outs but without the capacity to prevent those who want to move ahead more quickly from doing so.[92] But even this supposedly common-sense approach ignored political constraints, not least the groundswell of opposition generated during the ratification campaigns – and markedly in some key member states – to the very idea of a European Constitution. The times were hardly favourable, to say the least, to anything that resembled a European Constitution in whatever form. In these circumstances, a clear majority of EU leaders meeting in their first summit since the referendums had responded to events by opting for reflection over action, the least divisive option, and in the meantime continuing to deal piecemeal with immediate problems.

The problem with making a fresh start, negotiating an entirely new constitution, was not merely one of timing but also of strategy. There was too little public support for such a bold initiative, and hardly more enthusiasm for it amongst the principal players. Neither governing nor opposition parties had too much to say about European issues after the referendums, apart from talking about the unavoidable headline issues such as the new financial perspective or Turkish accession. Politicians were quite aware that there were few votes to be won, indeed votes to be lost on the issue of Europe. As such, a new constitutional endeavour would almost certainly be doomed from the start, more closely scrutinised now by a public primed by a censorious media and mobilised to stop it in its tracks. And the principal players in any such drama, government representatives operating in the full glare of publicity, would be tempted no doubt to play to the gallery, to grandstand in defence of the putative 'national interest'.

### The 'business as usual' option

Another scenario that emerged during 'reflection' follows what might be called the Helmut Kohl school of thought, who had once likened European integration to a bicycle that keeps moving only as long as velocity is applied. Those who took this line preferred to keep the political process running come what may, and in present circumstances to focus on what the Union could achieve on the policy front instead of publicly agonising over the Constitution. This meant carrying on as if nothing untoward had happened, concentrating on deliverable issues: for instance, addressing the problems arising from the expansion of the Union's borders to new and potentially difficult neighbours, or focusing on policy issues that deal with voters' material and a post-material concerns, from the environment to tackling structural unemployment.

After the shock of the referendum defeats had been absorbed, it was clear that whatever the Constitution's fate the EU would not fall apart, that it would continue to function under the existing treaty base as revised at Nice. In fact, every side of the debate on EU futures at least agreed on this incontrovertible fact. Commission president Barroso, for example, took a line that was broadly accepted by the institutional actors and the majority of member states alike: the need to make virtue out of necessity, not to panic or act with undue haste, because for the time being at least the Union was functioning well enough without the Constitution. As Barroso saw it, in the absence of 'any magic formulas that would bring [the Constitution] back to life [and] instead of never-ending debates about institutions, let's work with what we've got [for] political will and leadership are more important than institutions'.[93] The Dutch interior minister, Johan Remkes, took a similarly pragmatic line, maintaining that 'Europe can continue to go along with its existing treaties'. And Chris Patten, the recently retired British commissioner, similarly observed that 'we have made considerable progress in the last few years', without necessarily altering the treaties.[94] Few commentators, however, and even fewer practitioners saw this approach as being feasible over the medium term. The governance problems that had prompted the Laeken Council to undertake a constitutional overhaul in the first place, to improve decision-making and institutional efficiency, simplify procedures, address the problem of democracy deficits and to increase transparency, and not least to take notice of what voters in these referendums were actually trying to tell their leaders, all conspired to make constitutional reform in some sense unavoidable, if not quite yet.

There were variations of this 'back to what we do best' approach, though none of them offered convincing solutions to the current predicament. While not denying the need for future reform of the institutions and procedures, some preferred to deal with the stalled Constitution simply by avoiding it, striking out in a different direction, or merely by harking back to better days, invoking the dependable alliance of the founders, those who had shared the same *communautaire* vision from the outset. The idea of a 'core Europe' was central to this essentially complacent outlook. This response was hardly novel. The so-called EU 'core' solution tends to surface whenever the Union finds itself in difficulties, a reflex that makes much of the firm foundations laid by the founder members, those who were there from the beginning, supposedly deeply committed rather than merely pragmatic or 'fair weather' Europeans. The provisions in the Amsterdam and Nice Treaties that permit 'closer co-operation' gave some encouragement to this approach, and on this occasion it prompted consideration in some quarters about going ahead, not so much with the Constitution as with deeper integration.

This idea of a core has always appealed to the member states who had been there from the start, and its appeal grew as impending enlargement threatened to complicate decision-making, to hinder the effective operation of the European institutions, with renewed talk in some quarters of 'variable geometry', Europe *à la carte* and other variants of EU fast and slow tracks, supposedly to make 'enlargement less threatening to the Union's political leaders and electorates'.[95] Those who saw this as the solution to the constitutional crisis proposed, for instance, that the Eurozone might be the base-camp for member states prepared to commit to deeper integration, uninhibited about tackling big projects. Needless to say, narrowly partisan motives also played a part in defining who is 'in' and who is 'outside' the core, a settling of old scores that predates the quarrel over the Constitution, though undoubtedly intensified by it. France, whose political class tends to see itself as being at the heart of the European project and in some versions of this 'destiny' narrative even as its primary driver, has long been receptive to the idea that some EC/EU member states are more 'genuinely' European than are others.

Deep-seated Anglophobia certainly plays a part in this outlook, abiding antipathy to 'perfidious Albion', the *agent provocateur* for a wrecking Euroscepticism to those so disposed to see British policy in a negative light. Though behind this approach is also the abiding preference of most occupants of the Elysée and the policy-makers in the Quai d'Orsay to play the 'Europe' card as a way of reinforcing France's claim to 'natural' leadership of the continent. The Belgians, too, are receptive to the idea of a core, after all Brussels is the home of the European institutions, but in their case more with a view to reinforcing European integration than merely pursuing their national interests, except in so far as the two coincide. Prime Minister Guy Verhofstadt published his *Manifesto on the United States of Europe* in the aftermath of the referendums, advocating fast-track integration as one way forward out of deadlock. Nevertheless, this idea has struggled to make headway, even amongst member states who were likely candidates for core status, concerned lest a divisive strategy should make matters worse, driving wedges between member states by underlining different classes of membership. The proposal was particularly unappealing to the new member states, hostile to any suggestion of second-class membership, and concerned, too, about a proposal that would, as they saw it, compromise their security, exposing them to malign Russian influence should the EU be weakened by internal divisions that would undermine both its capacity and no less its will to resist pressure brought to bear by Moscow on neighbouring countries it still regards as within its own historical sphere of influence.

A core of European states, detached in some important respects from a peripheral group, might just be workable, but only if restricted to specific policy domains as it presently is, with opt-outs and derogations from some common policies. Selective participation in projects designed to deepen integration has been possible ever since some member states secured opt-outs from collective commitments entered into by the others. But optionality can work to only a limited extent; it certainly cannot be applied to the basic rules of governance, to those institutions and procedures that apply to every member state, regardless of whether they opt into or remain outside particular policy domains. What does bind the member states together in all their diversity is the fact that every member state is party to the treaties, embraces the *acquis* in its entirety and accepts the rules and procedures for common governance. The very idea of a core of member state using different rules is simply unthinkable and unworkable, indeed is plainly absurd. More than this, it is inimical to commonality of purpose, immensely damaging to the Union's cohesion and not least harmful to its international credibility.

Diversity is certainly a virtue in any plural polity, and flexibility in the application of some aspects of EU policy is unavoidable in a polity that is not a state. But should this principle ever be applied to governance, however, the cement binding these states together would be irrevocably weakened. This after all is precisely the intention of Europhobes who blithely demand the right to opt out of common policies, or even to resign from institutions such as the European Parliament or the European Court, and who loudly protest against imposing 'a centralising, "one rule fits all" regime upon an enormous and exceptionally diverse EU'.[96] The idea of a core EU may well be a rational strategy for those who would derail the European Union by weakening its sense of common purpose. But for those who are serious about strengthening the Union, it seems to be merely playing into their opponents' hands, leading to chaotic governance or worse, the paralysis that would surely follow from this supposed 'solution' to merely temporary difficulties, and as such serving the malign intentions of the enemies of the European project, because more likely to weaken the Union than to reinforce it.

### The cherry-picking option

The most widely supported response to the Union's constitutional impasse, and the one always likely to be pursued, proposed to salvage those parts of the Constitution that might be implemented by executive action: either by means of an addendum to the existing Treaty or by an additional revising Treaty to update Nice. This seemed feasible, a practical and above all a politically manageable solution to some of the problems with EU governance post-enlargement that had prompted governments to set up the Convention. Those who took this line maintained that a selective revision of the existing Treaty would avoid the pitfalls of the options discussed above. This view starts from the premise that neither the resurrection of the failed Constitution nor an entirely new version of it was politically feasible.[97]

Contemporary commentaries cited 'appropriate' reforms that might be incorporated into the extant treaty base, many of them included in the Constitutional Treaty but no less essential for effective governance. This 'list' includes reforms that persuaded governments to embark on constitutional reform in the first place: for instance, removing the rotation principle and establishing a full-time Council presidency; further refinements and additions to QMV and co-decision; simplified 'double majority' voting in the Council; the appointment of an EU foreign minister and diplomatic service to better co-ordinate EU foreign and even security policy, sharpening the Union's responses to external problems; the adoption of a legal personality for the Union to enhance its international credibility; incorporating the Charter of Fundamental Rights: better co-ordination of policing and criminal justice policy; the abolition of pillarisation and the extension of ECJ competence to the 'third pillar' issues; an increased role in EU decision-making for national parliaments; and a greater say for the European Parliament in 'electing' the Commission president.

Some of these reforms appealed rather more to some actors than to others, with no consensus over which measures might be incorporated into the existing Treaty base. The point, however, was that those reforms deemed to be essential for making EU governance work better could be adopted without any need to go back to the drawing-board. And, more to the point as far as the politicians were concerned, without any need to take further political risks with unpredictable referendums. Accordingly, Werner Weidenfeld, director of the Centre for Applied Policy Research in Munich, referred to the need 'to identify those parts of the constitution that increase institutional efficiency and were largely without controversy in the referendum debates', by no means an easy task.[98]

As with any EU bargain, the problem here is how to secure political agreement on a package of broadly acceptable reforms, striking the usual delicate balance between competing preferences that was required for negotiating the Constitutional Treaty in the first place. The situation after the referendum was hardly what it had been at the conclusion of the Convention, with the referendum campaigns complicating matters, raising the political stakes by bringing to the surface latent public disquiet about 'Europe'. And this was bound to constrain the member states, making for greater difficulties even than those that arose in the IGC. In this febrile political atmosphere negotiating a reform package would be difficult, though by no means impossible, for most of the principal actors were at least in agreement that something needed to be done. The critical task was how any deal made between politicians in the usual way of things could be sold to the public, especially in those countries that had rejected the Constitution, or would have done had they been given the opportunity. The public was bound to be suspicious of politicians trying to bring in by the back door even some aspects of the 'failed' Constitution.[99] In these circumstances the management of public expectations, in effect how to explain a revision of the extant treaty base, similar in many respects to the failed Constitutional Treaty, would be crucial for the legitimacy of the exercise.

Clearly, some issues were more problematic than others. For instance, many of the smaller countries were unconvinced about the changes to the Nice formula on voting weights, and accepted them only as part of a package deal; or in the case of Spain and Poland after considerable pressure, and only then as a last resort. Predictably, the issue was raised again at the European Council of June 2007 that took the decision to amend the existing treaties, with Poland's prime minister, Jarosław Kaczyński, almost derailing the exercise on just this issue, and in the process insulting his hosts by references to his country's war dead. In the event, Poland agreed to let the matter rest for the time being, but few imagine that this country, and maybe some others, will not revisit it at some future time. There are doubts, too, about the proposed EU diplomatic service, not least over who will actually control the service. EU legal experts had already ruled – and a Council declaration subsequently confirmed – that despite work to establish the service being fairly advanced it will not happen *ad hoc* and will require a formal amendment to the Treaty.[100] It was clear then that even such *ad hoc* reforms would require some renegotiation, invariably a messy business and one with no certain outcome.[101] After all, what one commentator aptly described as 'the accidental constitution' was 'the fruit of years of negotiations and trade offs. Everything in it pleases somebody and offends somebody else. It comes as a package; any attempt at cherry picking will be doomed.'[102]

Yet the political leaders were by now coming round to just such a scenario, and to implement even some aspects of the Constitutional Treaty would require another IGC to negotiate the details, making the sort of bargains and trade offs between competing preferences that found their way into the Constitution in the first place. As the crisis showed no signs of abating, there seemed to be no other way forward, and this strategy had influential backing from the leading member states. Both France and the United Kingdom fell in behind the German presidency to this end. Chirac had already signalled support for what he trailed as a 'recovery plan' for Europe when he designated 2006 as 'the year of a new start for the European Union', proposing to use the Constitution as a framework for institutional reforms to refresh the existing treaty base, to be enacted by means of the bridging or *passerelle* procedure.

But it was not to be, and even as he set out to salvage something of his reputation as a smart political operator he squandered the opportunity to give convincing leadership. By now hopelessly out of touch with his electorate, Chirac rather lost the plot, even going so far as to claim that to hold a second French referendum might somehow get things moving again, proclaiming in his usual imperious fashion that after all, 'it is not France that has said no. It is 55 per cent of the French people – 45 per cent of the French people said yes.' Even more provocatively he declared that 'people have the right to change their opinion [and they] might consider they had made a mistake'.[103] In the circumstances this was amazing logic, and it found little favour either at home or abroad. Aware of polling figures showing that opposition to the idea of a Constitution was some 6 per cent higher now than the 62 per cent who voted 'no' in the original referendum,[104] Ben Bot, the Dutch foreign minister, brought some realism to the discussion by steadfastly refusing to even consider a rerun of the Dutch referendum.[105] Tony Blair, too, spoke for most of his fellow leaders, observing that the Constitution in its present form was effectively dead if not quite buried, though Blair did lend his political weight to those seeking to salvage some of its main proposals, notably those to improve decision-making, including the proposal for a full-time presidency, a foreign minister and a reformed Council voting system.[106]

This 'pick and mix' approach was certainly gaining favour amongst the leading governments, and it was just what Merkel had in mind as she assumed the presidency, though even this was hardly a trouble-free option. Tensions between the larger and smaller states that surfaced at the Convention, and later in the IGC squabble over voting weights, were just as likely to resurface in another IGC. And there was some evidence for this in the Council of June 2007, as leaders negotiated on what to include and what to exclude as they manoeuvred on a mandate for the IGC. It would require considerable diplomatic skill, both to secure a balanced reform package and, not least, to sell these purportedly 'indispensable' reforms to a public deeply cynical about politicians' motives and in many cases hostile to anything that smacks of constitutionalism at the European level. The problem here, as it always is in democratic polities, is one of perception. There is general acceptance, not least amongst the political class, that the very use of the term 'constitution' has both inflated public expectations and raised disquiet about ulterior motives in equal measure. For this very reason, most politicians concluded that any future reform of governance would have to revert to the familiar language of treaty-making, avoiding the contentious 'C' word that provoked the ratification crisis in the first place. A former senior British diplomat has put it more pithily, observing that 'it was never a constitution and I kick myself, as an adviser to Tony Blair ... for not realising that that piece of hubris would be the treaty's undoing'.[107]

This may well be so, but it does not absolve politicians from the responsibility of keeping citizens informed about what they are doing in their name, and, just as important, why. It would be unwise to say the least to revert to a process that excludes the public from the business of reforming governance, by assuming that matters are too complicated to be understood by them. Public confidence and transparency are indispensable if people are to be persuaded of the need for reform, with some attempt made to engage them in a democratic conversation, both about the purpose of reforms and the benefits accruing from them. Nothing that has happened since the decision at Laeken to open the reform process to a deliberative Convention has changed that. Laeken raised expectations on this score that the Convention for the most part failed to realise.

What followed was certainly novel, but hardly an accessible or an open or noticeably more representative approach to how the Union goes about the business of treaty-making. In the event, the Convention, and even more the IGC that followed it and clinched the final deal, was rather more business as usual. The eventual outcome was not remotely a two-way conversation between politicians and people, and this sense of exclusion goes some way to explaining the crisis in public confidence during ratification and afterwards. Whatever reforms would eventually be adopted in a further treaty – and the perception was widespread amongst those outside the privileged circle of EU leaders that this outcome was in effect most of the 'failed' Constitution minus the name – had to be accompanied by an effort to explain, to reassure, to educate the public as to their meaning, purpose and significance.

This much is common sense, at least for those who would see the EU survive and prosper. The narrow bargain that resulted from the Convention/IGC process only made it easier for forces hostile to the Constitution and to the EU *per se* to use the referendum campaigns to paint a grossly distorted picture of the Constitution, exaggerating the threats it posed to domestic interests, to primordial identity and even to national sovereignty. In truth, no such threats exist, but in politics perception is what matters. The Constitution, on one level, did improve and simplify EU governance, though it did not remotely shift the tectonic plates of governance, moving power irrevocably from the member states and towards Brussels. As Mark Leonard saw the outcome of the Convention:

> After 16 months of deliberations, the Convention … decisively rejected key federalist demands, such as a directly elected president of the Commission, and a European Parliament with the power to initiate legislation … With the EU enlarging to 25 the cause of federalism has weakened. And the huge diversity of the member-states means that even if there was a will to move towards federalism, it would be impossible to agree on a common structure.[108]

Yet these facts about where power actually resides in the EU somehow got lost in a welter of hysteria conjured by forces hostile, not just to the Constitution but to the very idea of European integration. If a reformed treaty is to avoid the same fate, the public must be more fully engaged, have the facts explained to them and the facile myth of a super-state *manqué* debunked. Above all, they should be treated as partners, as stakeholders and not merely as bystanders incidental to what is, regardless of the preferred nomenclature, a constitutional project unfolding 'above' them, and as they see it beyond their capacity to influence.

## Three presidencies but no funeral

It fell to the British presidency in the second half of 2005 to deal with the fall-out from the French and Dutch referendums. This was not the moment for decisive action, nor was this remotely likely, given Britain's track record on Europe. Having avoided almost certain defeat by postponing its own referendum, the Blair government had no wish to invite greater trouble by reviving an issue that could only play badly for it at home. Comfortable with the preachy mode that was his political trademark, Blair took every opportunity to deflect the sort of criticism of the Constitution familiar in most other member states. He acclaimed the virtues of the Anglo-Saxon economic model derided by anti-Constitution campaigners in France, emphasising the need to concentrate on reforming what he saw as Europe's outmoded economic and welfare systems, to make labour markets more flexible and to improve business culture and competitiveness. In his speech to the European Parliament that launched the British presidency, Blair gave priority to economic growth, to be enhanced by flanking measures such as reforming higher education and improving R&D. In short, anything but the relaunch of the Constitution.[109]

The Constitution was peripheral to the priorities of the British presidency, which soon became bogged down in a fresh wrangle over the new financial perspective, in effect a proxy for mutual Anglo-French recriminations over the Constitution. Chirac, looking to settle scores over what he saw as British perfidy in opting for a referendum on the Constitution in the first place, a decision that had obliged him to follow suit, attacked Britain's annual budgetary rebate, secured at a time when that country had a rather better claim to it than it does today. Blair retaliated in kind, linking the budgetary issue to the reform of the Common Agricultural Policy, whose fiscal allocations markedly favour France, but more than that, for the liberally inclined Blair, distorted the free market in foodstuffs. Chirac's insistence that every member state had undertaken a commitment to ratify the Treaty regardless of the outcome elsewhere – in effect implying that if he was in political trouble at home, then so too should Blair be – brought from the prime minister the riposte that the French and Dutch governments should state publicly after their referendum defeats whether they now saw any way forward for the Constitution.[110]

These exchanges and the ill feeling incurred by them were hardly conducive to resolving the impasse, though conspiracy theorists might be forgiven for thinking that this was precisely their purpose. Politics abhors a vacuum, and the EU filled the present void with new issues to fall out over. Tension between two competing visions for Europe highlighted during the ratification campaigns – on the one hand a neo-liberal model, and on the other of a more protectionist or *dirigiste* design – was an ideological stand-off that had played during the Prodi Commission, and it was set to continue under his successor in the squabble over the services directive. There was tension, too, over security policy and enlargement, with France and some other EU15 countries seeking to impose so-called 'absorption tests' before permitting any further enlargement. In a way these fall-outs were reassuring, indicating normality of sorts, evidence of an organisation getting on with its usual business.

The Austrian presidency in the first half of 2006 fared little better in moving things forward, and in the end failed even 'to prepare a cogent response to the [Union's] problems'.[111] The presidency was launched with the usual positive fanfare, Chancellor Schuessel promising the 'revival of Europe', and Foreign Minister Plassnik offering both 'energy and confidence', though deeds hardly matched the rhetoric.[112] By late spring 2006 reality had settled on the presidency and it was pursuing a more prosaic agenda, one that reflected its own national preferences, including a revised version of the Bolkestein directive to reform the EU's services sector and working hours, and settling differences between the Parliament and the European Council on the 2007–13 financial perspective begun under the British presidency. Again, the agreement on the delayed services directive was some evidence at least that the EU can confront and resolve difficult issues, so long as it can summon the collective will and engender a sense of common interest amongst the member states.[113]

There was also a symbolic initiative to establish a European Human Rights Agency in Vienna, and greater effort to stabilise the EU's (and perhaps more to the point, Austria's) volatile neighbourhood in the Balkans, in the shape of a Stabilisation and Association Agreement with Bosnia-Hercegovina, and the speeding up of Croatian and Macedonian accession negotiations, measures designed to steady a region that has been critical for Austria's national interest ever since Metternich famously announced that the Balkans begin outside the southern gates of Vienna.[114] But of Chancellor Schuessel's bold promise 'to bring Europe closer to its citizens and increase confidence in the European project' there was little of substance to report.[115] At a conference on European identity in January 2005 Schuessel did vaguely promise an initiative to draft a new constitution, and one no less that would avoid a 'top-down' approach, beginning with a Europe-wide debate and with a timetable to relaunch a revised version of the Constitutional Treaty. In the event all that happened was more of the same, continued reflection and a vague recommendation that the EU 'shouldn't wait too long to revive the debate on the European future'. The Austrian presidency ended as it began, with gestures rather than action, this time a nebulous call for a pan-European referendum to bring the public closer to the project.[116]

The Finnish presidency during the second half of 2006 followed much the same pattern as its predecessors: bold words at the outset followed by inertia on the Constitution. Foreign Minister Tuomioja promised a 'pragmatic approach' to the Constitution, proposing to work with future presidency countries 'in the hope of ushering in a new treaty by 2008', though with few concrete initiatives to follow.[117] Finland did nevertheless ratify the Constitution, a symbolic act of European solidarity during its presidency term, but significantly without testing the decision in a referendum. Even this gesture proved problematic after a campaign orchestrated by Eurosceptics collected over 50,000 signatures – no small feat in a country that is generally pro-EU – demanding a referendum rather than leaving ratification to the Eduskuntala, the national parliament.[118]

By now the deadlock over the Constitution was proving inconvenient, but it was by no means catastrophic. It had not resulted in the political meltdown anticipated by some commentators. No one in Brussels or in any of the national capitals remotely contemplated rolling back 60 years of 'ever-closer union'. Indeed, as one insider saw it, 'it would be even more difficult to negotiate some kind of disintegration of the Union today than it has been to agree on further integration', for 'there is quite simply no alternative to international co-operation in many areas currently covered by EU law and policy in political, economic and social life today [and] unravelling the massive *acquis* accumulated over 55 years would also be a political and technical impossibility'.[119]

The EU continued to go about its business much as before, despite the institutional 'stretch' that was bound to come with the absorption of 10 new member states. Indeed, the British presidency's Hampton Court summit had secured agreement for renewed common action in several important policy domains, not least in energy policy, but also on migration, R&D and security issues. The fact that closer co-operation, and in some significant aspects of public policy, continued apace despite the deadlock on the Constitution is some indication of the value of the Union to its member states, and explains why they persevere regardless of occasional difficulties. And why, too, there are still European states waiting in the queue to join. Indeed, getting on with functional and technocratic matters is how the EU operates to best effect, working below the radar of public opinion, making deals on matters of mutual national interest. To say this is not to diminish the difficulties, for the impasse over the constitution was proving to be far harder to resolve than any previous crisis.

Few commentators would dispute that the current predicament was significantly different from earlier crises in 1955, 1965 or during the early 1980s. For this was more than a fall-out between insiders, but instead an unprecedented breakdown of trust between people and politicians. Nor is there any iron law that says the EU must always recover from the periodic crises that have marked its development, and neither would it do so on this occasion unless the politicians addressed the problem of public indifference or, worse, of disaffection with the Union and its arrangements. There were few signs amidst much that was uncertain that they were remotely facing up to this challenge. The Lisbon Treaty's jettisoning of the word 'constitution', and with it any legal or ethical obligation to consult the people about prospective treaty changes, in effect to pretend that the situation is merely 'business as usual', may be a short-term fix that will bring much-needed reforms identified at Laeken and reviewed at the Convention. Whether it will answer the serious questions raised by the public during the ratification campaigns is quite another matter, and for some critics it smacks of familiar complacency, the vague notion that somehow the Union will muddle through, making the usual trade-offs, accommodations and sub-optimal bargains between competing preferences, with politicians navigating through periodic turbulence towards the usual self-regarding bargain.

The politicians for their part are wary nowadays about provoking a negative public reaction, not least on an issue that has potential to become a significant, and even an ideological fault-line in domestic politics, threatening a haemorrhaging of votes from any party that handles it badly.[120] Governments had initially responded to the expressions of public mistrust in the referendums by drawing back from an issue with the power to hurt them at the ballot box, concentrating instead on more immediate matters such as the new financial perspective or the emerging neighbourhood policy. The official communiqué issued by the June 2006 European Council had referred disarmingly to a 'double-track' approach, continuing with reflection on constitutional futures whilst improving on policy delivery in matters that opinion surveys show are important to the citizen, such as immigration controls, the environment, security, employment and energy policy.

The foreign ministers at their unofficial Gymnich meeting at Klosterneuburg in Vienna confirmed official reticence on the Constitution, endorsing extended reflection as the only option, not least with general elections imminent in France and the Netherlands.[121] There was, however, growing acceptance amongst the member states of the desirability of having new governance procedures in place before the next European elections, scheduled for June 2009.[122] It fell to the German presidency of 2007 to take the initiative here, to move things beyond reflection and to get on with reforming what most member states now regard as cumbrous governance for a much-enlarged Union.

## Merkel seizes the initiative

As Germany prepared to assume the presidency in January 2007, Chancellor Merkel saw the revival of the Constitution as the best way of rekindling the Union's dynamism, as well as restoring its international credibility. To this end she contacted every EU head of government and listened to their various concerns, but she also advocated a mini-treaty to implement the main reforms in the Constitutional Treaty, changes widely supported in states where ratification has already been accomplished. The situation was quite different in those states where the Constitution had either been rejected, or risked being rejected in a referendum. Politics, as we have seen, usually trumps principle where European matters are concerned, contingency outstripping idealism when it comes to determining the pace and trajectory of European integration, and Merkel's ambitions here were as constrained as those of the preceding presidencies. But she was convinced that something had to be done to end the present impasse. She explored various options, and decided that with new leaders or prospectively new leaders in office in the principal countries, the time was ripe to grasp the nettle, to at least revise the existing treaty base. This was projected not as a Constitution or even as a Constitutional Treaty, but merely as reform of the treaties, the cherry-picking option by any other name. Assured of support from both the Commission and the Parliament, Germany's foreign minister, Frank-Walter Steinmeier, revealed that preliminary consultations with member states showed a broad consensus for making the EU 'more effective and more dynamic', and that this required at the very least reform of decision-making procedures.[123]

Whether procedural reform on its own is sufficient to address the public's concerns is debatable. Political elites are rather more disposed to deal with immediate difficulties than they are to think in abstract terms about politics. This much is apparent, for instance, in the latest utterances of someone who, in the immediate aftermath of the referendums, had talked much about responding to public disquiet by introducing more democratic procedures. Commission vice-president Wallström seemed by now content to claim that the Union had rediscovered its sense of common purpose on the back of some important policy bargains, for instance the new financial perspective and an energy policy. Wallström settled conveniently, then, for a definition of democracy couched in familiar terms in a Union whose governance is dominated by technocrats and specialists, and defined as performance legitimacy rather than as public participation. She duly informed the Parliament that governance was primarily about responding 'to the needs of its citizens, to realise policy goals and to deliver results', and that while 'democracy, transparency and accountability' are important, 'we can't implement agreed policies with one hand tied behind our back'.[124] The most she seemed prepared to concede to the idea of public voice was to acknowledge that the Union does require 'a new narrative', but one to be defined in top-down terms, with elites explaining to citizens why a new treaty was necessary, but with no convincing proposals about how their voice might be better heard.

A similar response to the problem of public scepticism about 'Europe' came from foreign minister Frank-Walter Steinmeier, who promised that any new treaty reform proposals would be made public, but again a promise that hardly meets the minimum conditions for a democratic conversation, and one out of kilter with the spirit of the Laeken commitment to open up the constitutional process to the general public. What this meant in effect was that governments would once again resume their lead role as 'masters of the treaties'. Realpolitik, or at the very least realism, seemed to be back in vogue, with even a majority of MEPs now accepting that any movement to break the deadlock on the reform issue, however modest, was better than nothing. The challenges facing the Union had not subsided, and would have to be confronted. There was nevertheless a broad consensus of political opinion that reforming governance *per se* was essential, and with new leaders in place in the leading member states the time was opportune for revisiting the treaties, though politicians were careful to make clear that governance *per se* and constitutionalism are quite separate matters.

Whether this gamble to revisit constitutional politics on this pragmatic basis will pay off over the longer term, once the amended Treaty is presented for parliamentary ratification in those countries where the mood was distinctly unfavourable, especially as Eurosceptics and federalists alike begin to debate its implications for 'their' vision of Europe, remains to be seen. Bringing in reforms and passing them off as merely 'modest' changes that had only recently been trailed by governments as part and parcel of a wholesale constitutional refit is misleading to say the least, and may even prove politically risky if the public refuse to accept the politicians' convenient distinction.

Parliament, too, seemed more concerned with salvaging some key aspects of the now defunct Constitution than with addressing concerns raised by their constituents during the ratification campaigns. In the weeks leading up to the 2007 Brussels Council, Parliament debated the report mentioned above, a so-called road map for the European constitutional process drafted by two senior MEPs, Enrique Baron Crespo (PES) and Elmar Brok (EPP-ED), a member and substitute member respectively of the Committee on Constitutional Affairs, and known as the 'B-B' report. The report strongly endorsed Merkel's plan for treaty reform. And though the Parliament's views as expressed in its plenary debate were by no means uniform, there was a clear majority in favour of moving forward, even if politics dictated the need to replace formal constitutional terminology with the more familiar language of treaty-making. Another MEP, Jo Leinen (PES), called for something more than a mere mini-treaty, with 'all sorts of important limbs hacked off', and demanded nothing less than 'a constitutional treaty "plus" rather than a constitutional treaty "minus"', as preferred by influential political leaders such Sarkozy and Zapatero.[125]

Federalists, too, were alerted, seizing as they tend to do, on any sign of forward momentum in the EU as cause for optimism, convinced on this occasion that the public would broadly support a 'repackaging' rather than abandoning the Constitution. Andrew Duff (ALDE), for instance, referred to 'a growing realisation' in France and the Netherlands 'that it is not in the interest of those countries to be inside a Union that is too feeble to act'.[126] Yet he remained unconvinced, as did other federalists and quasi-federalists, about diluting the essence of the Constitution, warning against 'this latest craze for the simplified Treaty', on the grounds that 'in trying to simplify we end up by being simplistic, and in seeking to define an amending treaty – rather than a consolidating treaty – we are in the realm purely of semantics, and changing terminology and in suppressing the symbols we risk turning Euro-scepticism to Euro-cynicism'.[127]

The reasoning here was sound enough, though based on an aspiration for European integration beyond anything that appealed to most governments, and certainly to those that mattered. However, the majority of MEPs were realistic, accepting that any movement, however limited, was better than nothing, Duff's warning notwithstanding. As such, they were broadly supportive of the German presidency's plans to revise the treaty. It was left to the Parliament's small but vocal Eurosceptical minority to challenge the consensus between the three main political groupings, seeing in the presidency's plans not merely renewed energy for necessary reforms but subterfuge, and for some on the far fringes of ultra nationalism nothing less than conspiracy to bring the Constitution in by the back door, with governments pretending that what was afoot was merely an amendment of the existing EC/EU treaty base.[128] The United Kingdom Independence Party MEP, Nigel Farage, for instance, referred to the 'downright dishonesty with which this whole process is being pursued'. Merkel's actions hardly helped to defuse the row, for though she used quite different terminology from that of the Constitutional Treaty her clear intention was to salvage at least 90 per cent of its content, including all of the major reform proposals. Overt reference to the idea of a constitution (and not least the word itself) was dropped, as were the more elegiac connotations of the Constitution's Preamble, the references to, though not the actual usage of, common European icons and symbols such as the flag, anthem and the motto *In varietate concordia* – united in diversity.[129]

Merkel's intention, broadly endorsed by other government leaders, of bringing in what she called 'a reduced treaty' was one thing. But her letter to the other heads of government and state, leaked to the British *Daily Telegraph* newspaper, suggested something more, indeed nothing less than outright deception to those primed to find conspiracy. The controversial letter could easily be represented as duplicity in as much as it proposed keeping the substance of the failed Constitution, whilst utilising 'necessary presentational changes' to persuade the public that all that was at stake was 'merely' revision of the existing treaties, thereby avoiding the need for risky referendums. In the circumstances, Merkel's description of her intention 'to use different terminology without changing the legal substance' of the final text was, to say the least, unfortunate.[130]

## Constitutional end-game: a 'mandate' for reform

The European Council organised by the German presidency met in Brussels on 21–22 June 2007 with the purpose of negotiating a draft mandate for a new IGC to replace the Treaty establishing a Constitution for Europe with reforms to the existing treaties which 'will not have a constitutional character', the process to be concluded by the end of 2007 and ratified in all member states according to national procedures before the European elections scheduled for June 2009.[131] The Reform Treaty, as it was originally designated, introduces changes to the treaty base agreed by the IGC, a process that eventually resulted in the Lisbon Treaty (December 2007) incorporating these amendments into the existing Treaty on the European Union and the Treaty establishing the European Community. The principal difference with the Constitutional Treaty is that the Lisbon Treaty amends the extant treaties rather than replacing them outright, both the Treaty on European Union (which retains its title) and the Treaty establishing the European Community, which is retitled as the Treaty on the Functioning of the Union.

Although the new Treaty replaces the European Constitution, it nevertheless includes most of that Treaty's proposed institutional and procedural reforms as reviewed above (Chapters 6–9). The task of organising these negotiations and turning a brief 16-page mandate agreed at Brussels in June 2007 into a detailed treaty text fell to Portugal, which assumed the Council presidency on 1 July 2007, a somewhat ironic outcome of the rotation principle that means the delicate business of securing agreement resided with a member state that did not get around to ratifying the Constitutional Treaty because of domestic differences on the issue. The IGC commenced its work on 23 July 2007.[132]

The Lisbon Treaty that is the result of these diplomatic negotiations includes reference to the Charter of Fundamental Rights of the European Union, as a protocol to the Treaty proper, making it legally binding, except for the United Kingdom, which secured an opt-out on this provision at the Brussels European Council (June 2007). This was a response to France's preference for developing a 'justice, liberty and security space', by enhancing judicial co-operation in civil but also in criminal matters, and deepening police co-operation in combating cross-border crime. The German presidency had proposed inclusion of a reference to the Charter in an article to be included in the new Treaty, insisting on it being legally binding though with some additional safeguards to prevent the Court interpreting the Charter as a licence to enforce changes in national laws, a long-standing German concern in light of previous tussles between the *Bundes-verfassungsgericht* and the European Court. France also signalled a preference to improve co-operation in foreign and security policy beyond what had been agreed in the Constitutional Treaty. The British government however returned to its 'red lines' it had resolutely defended against encroachment during the Convention and the IGC, predictably resisting QMV in judicial and police matters, as it did, too, for foreign policy and taxation and social payments.

In order to expedite progress on the IGC mandate, Merkel had no alternative but to concede to Blair on matters seen by him as benchmarks of national sovereignty. The United Kingdom insisted, for instance, on the inclusion of references in the Council's Conclusions to the fact that the new draft Treaty would state explicitly that the Charter shall not create new rights for the Union, nor will it encroach on United Kingdom law, to the effect that:

> Article 1 (1) The Charter does not extend the ability of the Court of Justice, or any court or tribunal of the United Kingdom, to find that the laws, regulations or administrative provisions, practices or action of the United Kingdom are inconsistent with the fundamental rights, freedoms and principles that it reaffirms; and (2) In particular, and for the avoidance of doubt, nothing in [Title IV] of the Charter creates justiciable rights applicable to the United Kingdom except in so far as the United Kingdom has provided for such rights in its national law.

In addition, Article 2 states that: 'To the extent that a provision of the Charter refers to national laws and practices, it shall only apply in the United Kingdom to the extent that the rights or principles that it contains are recognised in the law or practices of the United Kingdom.'[133]

Doubts remain nevertheless as to whether the British opt-out on the Charter will prove legally watertight in the event of a challenge in the Court. The argument that has been joined here between Europhobes and Europhiles is driven by ideological predilections rather than by objective legal analysis, but its outcome will surely be important for determining the future trajectory of European integration. Only time will clarify the situation, and more to the point the actions of the Court itself. Already, the decision to adopt the Charter as legally binding has encouraged one Justice to boldly announce that it will be 'a basis for challenging national law'.[134]

This view has been expounded, though rather more tentatively, by some academic experts, with Jacques Ziller, a professor at the European University Institute in Florence, asserting that in these circumstances the British opt-out would be unsustainable.[135] At the very least we can expect some controversial judgements and some equally critical legal tussles between the European and domestic legal and political authorities. But history shows that on the big questions pertaining to legal and no less to political sovereignty, whenever the Court confronts national authorities the latter tend to prevail. This is not so very different from the status quo ante, the arrangements that pertained in the Constitutional Treaty, where Blair had negotiated hard to avoid measures that would compromise the United Kingdom's capacity to make its own laws. Sarkozy, for his part, was quite relaxed about Britain opting out of the Charter, seemingly the price for Blair's acquiescence, a concession necessary for securing the omission from the Reform Treaty of politically sensitive references to greater competition and global markets.

Poland, too, secured its own politically motivated opt-out on the Charter, with the unilateral inclusion of a footnote to the IGC draft mandate that satisfied that country's obscurantist mindset, to the effect that the Charter cannot affect national governments' power to legislate in the sphere of 'public morality [and] family law'.[136] This is clearly a concession to Poland's determination to abide by a moral code influenced by its powerful Catholic hierarchy, one that proscribes personalisable rights and freedoms that apply everywhere else in the EU, for instance the right to abortion and the recognition of alternative lifestyles and sexual preferences. But that country was less successful with its demand to reopen the voting weights issue that had delayed agreement on the Constitutional Treaty in the 2004 IGC. Polish negotiators tried to use the issue to prevent agreement on the mandate, but without success. Poland had proposed a 'square root' system that would narrow the weighting of votes between the largest and smallest countries in terms of population, but more to the point would almost give it voting parity with Germany, despite having barely half that country's population.[137] There was little support for this, only the Czech Republic endorsing it in principle, though not to the point of holding up agreement on an IGC mandate.[138] With Merkel and Sarkozy playing a calculated 'hard cop–soft cop' routine, the former expressing 'understanding' of Warsaw's objections, the latter demanding the Poles fall in line, a modest compromise was agreed, helped in no small part by the inclusion of a clause on energy solidarity designed to ensure collective support for any member state held hostage on its energy supplies, with Poland's tricky dependence on Russia for energy supplies as a clear case in point.[139]

In the event, there was simply too much at stake for the big member states to allow one awkward newcomer to hold up, let alone to unravel this hard-wrought deal. After a series of exhaustive bilaterals on June 22, and even an oblique threat from the presidency to launch an IGC without Poland, Warsaw accepted a facesaving compromise. The QMV formula included in the Constitution – a double majority of 55 per cent of member states representing 65 per cent of EU citizens, to better reflect the true size of populations, whilst taking account of the concern of the smaller member states about being overruled by the larger countries – would remain, though the current voting rules will apply until 2014. Thereafter, a transitional phase (2014–17) will see the implementation of the new QMV rules, although the Nice voting weights may be applied when a member state so wishes, and who can see Poland and possibly some other states such as Spain not being tempted to exercise that option? Furthermore, from 2014 a new version of the 1994 Ioannina Compromise will take effect, which permits small minorities of EU states to call for the re-examination of any EU decisions they do not like.[140]

The latest Treaty retains most of the important institutional innovations in the Constitutional Treaty, including the permanent president, a foreign minister (though, to assuage British sensibilities, now designated the 'High Representative of the Union for Foreign Affairs and Security Policy'), with the same distribution of parliamentary seats, the reduced number of commissioners, the exit clause on withdrawal from the EU and the adoption of a full legal personality (a status currently assumed only by the European Community), which will allow it to sign international agreements. This latter change has naturally attracted much criticism from the usual quarters. The Union's uneven – some would say untidy – development has meant that 'the member states still sign international economic agreements as the "European Union" [and] often the EU's international agreements contain both economic and foreign policy or justice aspects, which makes their negotiation extremely complex'. The revised Treaty will permit member states to sign international treaties as 'the EU', making things altogether less confusing for would-be international partners to such agreements, as well as making it easier for the Union to operate in those international bodies – the World Bank, for example – that permit participation by non-state actors.[141] This is no different from the situation that pertains in international organisations such as UNESCO, the IMF and the WHO, and no one would claim that these bodies remotely aspire to sovereign statehood. Even so, critics maintain that change here amounts to the Union having unprecedented powers that will facilitate its eventual emergence as a fully-fledged state, and will even permit it to declare war on a third party.

There is nothing in either the defunct Constitution or in the new reformed treaties that remotely indicates anything so far-fetched. As Brady sees it, this change 'would allow the EU no new powers [for it] could not sign an international agreement without the unanimous approval of the member states. Thus the single legal personality gives the EU more capability, without giving it more power.'[142] Moreover, the exit option included in the Constitution remains. Omitted from the reformed treaties, however, are references to those iconic symbols that for some connote statehood, or at least an aspiration to it, not least the very title of 'constitution', as well as references to common values and symbols such as the EU flag, anthem and motto, though most objective observers always saw these referents to common identity as notional at best.[143] Also left out of the new arrangements will be the reference to the primacy of EU law and new names for various types of EU legislation, not least the description in the Constitutional Treaty of all such measures as EU 'laws'. Instead the current terms 'regulations' and 'directives' will remain in use.[144] The intention here, clearly, is to confirm that these latest reforms are not intended as constitutional endeavour, substituting in their stead the altogether more familiar idea of a treaty-based order.

The Constitutional Treaty had also abolished the pillar structure and, as we saw in Chapter 9, enhanced the Union's competencies in foreign and security policy, and likewise in justice and home affairs. France and Spain in a joint position paper to the 2007 European Council proposed the extension of QMV to 51 areas, more than the 39 areas agreed by the previous IGC, and to include criminal law, all aspects of immigration policy and foreign policy. These proposals were supported by both the Commission and the Parliament, a move that alerted London to a development that could only increase the demands from domestic Eurosceptics for holding an almost certainly unwinnable referendum.[145] For this reason, Blair secured a deal that allows any member state so inclined to opt out of EU policies in the area of police and criminal law, already one of his so-called 'red lines'. The national veto is also retained for foreign policy and defence, with the draft mandate acknowledging unanimity as the decisional procedure here, and expressly stating (indeed underlining in the text) that: 'In particular, national security remains the sole responsibility of each Member State.'[146] The IGC mandate reaffirmed, too, that the division of power between member states and the Union is a two-way arrangement, implying that powers can be taken back from the Union, another British demand and one that was supported by the Czech Republic.[147]

In the usual way of European Councils the member states nuanced their way to a compromise deal that balanced competing national preferences. And as they did so, they kept a weather eye on the critical audience back home. President Sarkozy, for instance, fresh from two convincing election victories and facing a demoralised and divided socialist opposition, felt able to confront his own Eurosceptics, safe in the knowledge that even French '*non*' voters in the referendum had been altogether more hostile to what they saw at the Constitution's neo-liberal sub-plot than they were to reforms of EU governance.[148] By skilful manoeuvring he secured the omission from the IGC mandate of the troublesome reference in the draft Constitutional Treaty to 'free and undistorted competition', and the cause of so much angst to voters in the 2005 referendum. This omission would give him considerable room for manoeuvre when it came to securing domestic approval for the new Treaty, notwithstanding the insertion of a special protocol in the mandate to assuage British concerns about EU competitiveness that reaffirms those very same principles, a deal that one observer has referred to as 'a classic piece of euro-fudge'.[149]

The outcome of these negotiations follows closely the proposals from the Amato Group discussed above, and seemingly confirm a trajectory of differential integration, if not quite the core–periphery Europe proposed by some member states disconcerted by what they regard as foot-dragging by more Eurosceptical countries.[150] The provision for opt-outs, for instance, in the area of police and criminal law, included at the express request of the United Kingdom and supported by the Czech Republic, are cases in point.[151] Telling here was the reaction to these events of someone who more than anyone had launched the Union on its constitutional Odyssey with his Humboldt speech in 2000. Joschka Fischer, erstwhile German foreign minister, saw these proposed arrangements as an improvement on Nice, but hardly fulfilling the project outlined at Laeken for democratising as much as for simplifying EU governance. As Fischer saw it, derogations permitted in response to national sensibilities merely consolidate a two-tier and top-down Union.[152] What the outcome of the Brussels summit did confirm is that in spite of, or perhaps as a consequence of, enlargement to 27 the EU agenda is now dominated by the big three, with a stronger showing, too, from the medium-sized member states, though these countries are far more effective as allies of the key players (Spain being the principal case in point) than when standing out (as Poland did) against their preferences.[153]

The Brussels mandate nevertheless did the trick, putting reform back on track, though it had little to say about the principal concerns expressed either at Laeken or in the Convention for improving democratic life in the Union. The closest the political leaders came at Brussels to acknowledging concerns of democrats and Eurosceptics alike about an imposed constitutional settlement was to reaffirm the commitment to subsidiarity and proportionality, and likewise the proposal in the original protocol on national parliaments in the Constitutional Treaty that gives elected national representatives a brief time-window to study European Commission proposals for law before their enactment, though Germany and some other member states had wanted to extend this review period from six to eight weeks.[154] Each national parliament will be allocated two votes (some parliaments are bicameral): a simple majority (28 votes minimum) will trigger the review and explanation procedure. The German presidency also recommended that if a third of national parliaments should object to a proposal, the Commission must submit a 'reasoned opinion' as to why it seeks to bring in the law, with the Council and the Parliament jointly deciding whether the Commission's explanation is convincing. The Commission will not, however, be automatically obliged to withdraw a legislative proposal.

In light of the public's hostile reaction to the Constitutional Treaty, however, the question that remains is whether or how far the politicians have remotely addressed their concerns. What is there for citizens in these reforms? Some commentators maintain the decision to make the Charter legally binding is a step towards entrenching citizens' rights at the EU level, not least Commission president Barroso, who regards such rights as a safeguard 'against any power that could limit those rights', and as such 'central to the system of checks and balances in our Union law'.[155] There is still, however, no equivalent charter of explicit duties to stand alongside individual rights, other than the implied duty to obey EU law.

Other initiatives were discussed in Brussels, and designed to reassure a public seemingly concerned about EU encroachment on domestic policy. Both the Netherlands and the Czech Republic sought a clearer demarcation of competencies as between the EU and the member states, and an enhanced role for national parliaments in the Union's policy process. Both countries wanted to go further than the two protocols on these matters attached to the Constitutional Treaty, presumably to convince their domestic Eurosceptics that the principle of subsidiarity was being effectively policed. The Netherlands proposed the so-called red-card system first considered in the Convention, to supplement the yellow-card mechanism for national parliaments that requires the Commission to take account of national objections to proposed legislation. However, this proposal was not included in the IGC mandate as such, with both the Commission and some member states seeing this as unduly hampering the former's right of initiative, as well as compromising the Council's legislative prerogative and the role in co-decision of a democratically elected European Parliament. The Czech government even wanted to restore some powers to the domestic level, but this, too, is unlikely to happen.

## A Constitution in all but name?

The decision to move on from reflection, to try to secure long-overdue reforms in the Union's governance came as no real surprise, either to participants or to the caravan of camp-followers who pitch up at every summit. The real debate was not whether reform would occur but how much, and what it will actually mean for the Union, whether or how far it will change 'the nature of the beast'. The critical issue here, and one much debated outside the Council enclave, is whether this latest Treaty is merely the Constitution in all but name, and brought in by the back door. Or whether, instead, it is merely an agreement *ad minima*, a timely revision of the Nice and Maastricht Treaties, cherry-picking by any other name and as such something less than the Constitutional Treaty. It was left to Giscard, who steered the constitutional endeavour to its conclusion, to ask the pertinent question: 'Does the sought-after "simplification" aim to facilitate ratification by the few states which still hesitate, or does it in fact hide the goal of reversing certain advances in the Constitutional Treaty?'[156] Merkel's controversial letter to the Union's political leaders proposing an exercise in renaming, but in effect keeping the substance of the Constitutional Treaty, has brought predictable vitriol from Eurosceptics. Yet other commentators see this as less a plot to subvert the nation-states than political pragmatism, the realisation that something needed to be done, and quickly, to reform institutions threatened with paralysis after the recent enlargement, with Turkey and Croatia already in the queue and the rest of the western Balkans possibly to follow.

The broad consensus of opinion, amongst governments and the supranational institutions alike, is to make the case that the newly amended treaties are something quite different from the abandoned Constitution, to seek to convince the public at large that this is not covert constitutionalism without the name or anything like it, but 'merely' familiar treaty revision, in effect *restitutores orbis*. In part, this message is conveyed by the omission of the word 'constitution' as an adjective, let alone as a noun. Even more than that, by leaving out any mention of the more emotive, and for some controversial, references to common European values included in the Constitutional Treaty's Preamble, the normative ballast of any constitution worth the name, though the general references already included in the EU Treaty that refer to the Union 'drawing inspiration from the cultural, religious and humanist inheritance of Europe' do remain.[157] The heavy symbolism that figured in Part IV of the Constitutional Treaty is abandoned, as is the title of 'foreign minister', with the office renamed as 'merely' the permanent high representative, though performing the same role, no more or no less, as that described in the Constitutional Treaty.

Will these cosmetic changes be enough to reassure critics who fear a plot by politicians to impose their Constitution in all but name, or in this case by leaving out any mention of the name? There is, of course, a more prosaic explanation. One cannot but wonder what the point is of this default position, if not to persuade the public that the constitutional phase as such is indeed over, to reassure them that the EU does not have latent ambitions to become a state or anything like one.

Reassuring the public is indeed the object of the exercise, though this in itself does not answer the really critical question about where the Union is headed. For Luxembourg's prime minister, Jean-Claude Juncker, merely to drop these symbolic titles 'is completely ridiculous because they will always exist anyway', as they did before they were formally recognised in Constitutional Treaty.[158]

Some other commentators see in this latest endeavour by the politicians not subterfuge but merely weakness, needless retreat, populist posturing that merely plays into the hands of Europhobes, with the Italian prime minister, Romano Prodi, referring disparagingly to an 'empty gesture', lamenting what he calls a lost opportunity to give the Union some affective resonance with its citizens. As Prodi sees it: 'The way [United Kingdom, Poland and other governments] insisted in denying every emotional aspect of Europe (flag, anthem, motto) hurt me [for] it is those same governments who complain that the idea of Europe is distant from the people. But how can you involve citizens without involving their emotions?'[159] The more Eurosceptical Danish prime minister, Anders Fogh Rasmussen, however, takes the contrary position, observing that 'the good thing is that all the symbolic elements are gone, and that which really matters – the core – is left'.[160]

Whatever the motives behind this latest response to the governance question, the reaction of Eurosceptics has been entirely predictable. As they see it, a plot is afoot to impose the Constitution come what may and in defiance of public opinion. In the view of maverick British Conservative MEP, Daniel Hannan: 'The corpse of the old constitution will be stretched out on the laboratory table and jolted back to life. Only this time there will be no more referendums. ... In order to pretend that it's a different text, though, the leaders of the EU have to go through the charade of negotiations. ... we shall be treated to some asinine play-acting.'[161] The question that remains then is how far is this talk of reform is indeed play acting, more conspiracy than a pragmatic attempt to at least adjust the Union's governance to the demands on decision-making and policy management post-enlargement? If as Eurosceptics maintain it is merely subterfuge it is hardly convincing, with governments as divided over many of these issues as they were in the Convention and the subsequent IGC. Whether the Lisbon Treaty does amount to the 'failed' Constitution in all but name is no easy matter to resolve.

The issue continues to be debated, but positions vary according to ideological preferences or ingrained political prejudices as much as objective analysis of legal facts. Even then, any objective answer must be mixed, rather than conclusive either way. The proposed reforms are 'constitutional' in the sense that significant amendments and omissions notwithstanding, they incorporate into the treaty base much of the procedural and institutional changes from the Constitution, and discussed at Chapters 6 and 7. To this extent, the latest Treaty is as much a constitutional outcome as the abandoned Constitution.

The former British government representative in the praesidium, Gisella Stuart, has said as much, criticising as 'patently dishonest' the official line from Downing Street that the new Treaty is quite different from the Constitution.[162] But if we apply the usual benchmarks of classical constitutional endeavour to these outcomes, then neither the Constitutional Treaty nor its successor remotely meets the minimum requirements for a democratic conversation about the distribution and use of public power. Nor do they have as their normative basis the sort of constitutional philosophy that confers democratic legitimacy on governance. In this sense, the struggle for the European Constitution is unfinished business, though it has to be said on present evidence this is hardly a matter of urgency for the majority of citizens. Yet as the Union faces up to the daunting challenges ahead, and as decisions made in part at the level of the Union loom larger in the lives of ordinary Europeans, as producers, consumers of goods and services and so on, it may well become so, and sooner rather than later.

Events determine how governments see things, and in the course of the two years or so since the referendums both events and leaders had moved on. This was the challenge that confronted the German presidency, the need to respond to events as they are now, not those pertaining in 2004. The IGC mandate reflected this fact, though clearly most of the important institutional reforms in the Constitution remain, even if the spirit of the exercise has been altered by developments since spring 2005. Some things, however, never change, or do so only imperceptibly. The most contentious procedural issue facing the 2003/4 IGC was voting weights, and this issue resurfaced in the Brussels Council of 2007, with Poland still demanding something akin to the Nice formula. Poland, even though the Kaczyński twins who ran its government when the mandate was being negotiated have now departed the scene, will surely return to this issue in due course. But whatever that country's future demands on this matter, the outcome will not go beyond the limited concession to postpone the new arrangement until 2014.[163]

The new Treaty holds few surprises, then, for those well versed in the Union's procedures for revising the treaties. The Constitutional Treaty was barely readable, a cumbrous text of several hundred pages. This latest attempt to simply matters will hardly reassure citizens on that score, with its still arcane treaty arrangements. The *Draft Treaty amending the Treaty on European Union and the Treaty establishing the European Community* published by the presidency of the IGC in July 2007 and approved by the heads of state and government and at the special Lisbon Council on 18–19 October 2007 is not more readable as a constitutional narrative, but consists of some 65,000 words of detailed inserts written in the usual dense and utterly impenetrable legalese of treaty-lingo, and to be appended to the extant treaties. As George Monbiot saw it at the time, 'the new document is an incomprehensible mess of insertions and amendments, but as far as I can tell it proposes or refers to 448 articles, each of them [with] several clauses. Many of them are contradictory', in effect 'a dreadful tangle.'[164]

As one commentator interpreted the situation even before this latest development, anyone who would understand the implications of the Lisbon Treaty will need to lay this catalogue of badly written legal hieroglyphs over the other treaties to see who gains and who loses by these changes. For in order 'to assess the impact of the IGC, the reader will need a version of the EC and EU Treaties, set beside the articles introduced in those two texts by the draft Constitutional Treaty', and then to insert the new amendments into the extant treaty base. The whole document 'must then be read scrupulously, down to the smallest [foot-] note, to see whether the modification in question is not in turn modifiable by the 2007 IGC. In other words, it will not be easy, at first, to identify which provisions represent progress and which are backward steps.'[165] This is certainly not a task for the fainthearted, and it will appeal far more to lawyers than to citizens. It should be noted, too, in this context that terms like 'advances' or 'backward', 'gains' or 'loss' are no whit objective, but must be calibrated in terms of the ideological preferences of those making such judgements. In these circumstances, legal archaeology is still the appropriate metaphor for working out what the European Treaty base implies for all concerned, and at every level of the game.

The task of making sense of the incomprehensible, of reading this almost unreadable text would defy the fabled wisdom of a Solomon and the patience of Job combined. This latest Treaty really is business as usual, a case of back to the future, with the Union's elite actors now firmly back in charge and determined to impose the changes they see fit, paying no heed to any of the concerns or anxieties voiced by the public during the ratification campaigns. This could be said to amount to collective amnesia, though there are those who see instead wilful arrogance, determination by those actors who have monopolised the process from the outset to regain the initiative for designing EU governance.

This outcome is simply light-years away from what the Laeken Council and certainly more radical *conventionnels* had hoped for from a uniquely deliberative forum intended to give a voice to non-governmental actors in designing their common governance. Rather, the member states have reclaimed the business of treaty-making. Governments seem to be done now with this brief and unconvincing flirtation with democracy, with opening up treaty reform to a broader constituency. Some of them were never remotely comfortable with that wholly unpredictable experiment, and even if the uncertainties of the Convention process did not cure them of an enlightened outlook on the matter of reforming EU governance, then the vagaries of popular ratification, asking the public to approve what the politicians had decided in their name has certainly done so. More to the point, what do these latest arrangements mean for democratic constitutionalism? To some observers they suggest that the 'princes' are now back in sole charge, able to secure the limited procedural and institutional reforms that were always their principal concern, freeing them from the obligation to submit these reforms to the unpredictable test of democracy.

Critics of these developments are by no means confined to the radical fringes of politics. Even Giscard, hardly an instinctive democrat, thought he saw duplicity at work here, observing that the decision to divide the original Constitutional Treaty into separate parts, burying the most controversial proposals as merely amendments to the Treaties of Maastricht and Nice, and presenting the merely technical or procedural changes in 'a colourless, harmless treaty', had about it the whiff of deception. As he saw the situation: 'The [separate] texts would be sent to national parliaments, which would vote separately. Thus, public opinion would be led to adopt, without knowing it, the provisions that we dare not present directly. This process of "dividing to ratify" is obviously unworthy of the challenge at stake. It may be a good magician's act. But it will confirm citizens in the idea that the construction of Europe is organised behind their back by lawyers and diplomats.'[166]

Another seasoned commentator, Jean Qautremer, is just as critical, caustically observing: 'In a word, the elites decided to take matters back in hand. ... the EU is returning to its worst failings – secret diplomacy, last minute negotiations, covert deals, and shady compromises.'[167] Though for Qautremer and for others of a pragmatic disposition this is not an entirely negative outcome, for as he sees it progress where Europe is concerned is defined by its own peculiar logics, and should be judged less by the nature of the procedures and more by outcomes. This reasoning is of course familiar, it amounts to what used to be called 'permissive consensus', justifying the usual covert deals between insiders, the way the project has always been run. But for Giscard, and one suspects for many who shared the novel experience of sitting in the Convention, procedure does matter, and these days procedure that is open, transparent and preferably democratic rather than the usual insider-dealing. And democratic not as a matter of principle, but because the public expect to be at least informed about how their governance works at whatever level, alerted – and increasingly cynical – as they now are about deals done above their heads and behind closed doors. For this very reason, Giscard called on the 2007 IGC to follow the transparency procedures adopted by the Convention, and declaimed: 'Why shouldn't they be public? Since you are going to debate the fate of Europeans, do it publicly: let them hear, themselves, all the arguments.'[168] Anyone who understands how these insiders operate will not wait with bated breath for an honest answer to that entirely reasonable question.

## History repeats: Irish postscript June 2008

The struggle to implement the Lisbon Treaty took what is by now a predictable turn in this seemingly never-ending story with the ratification referendum in Ireland in June 2008, a mandatory requirement of the national constitution. The result was a resounding victory for those opposed to the new Treaty, by 53.4 per cent to 46.6 per cent – 862,415 votes to 752,451 on a turn-out of 53.1 per cent. A variety of reasons have been cited by pundits (and no less by the voters) for this outcome. But the constant refrain, amidst the cacophony of principled objections, thinly veiled self-interest and the merely eccentric is of pervasive pique, a protest aimed at an elite seemingly seeking to impose fundamental constitutional change on a reluctant electorate without making a convincing case, explaining in plain language why the proposed Treaty changes are necessary. The pattern of the earlier referendums was repeated here: a strong lead in favour of ratification being overhauled during the course of the campaign as the electorate grew nervous, resentful and plainly sceptical about what they were being asked to endorse. This was yet another example of a European political class utterly out of touch with the popular mood, complacent, incapable of responding to the public's concerns, mostly taking the electorate for granted, ignoring its concerns in a lacklustre 'yes' campaign. And a case, too, of the politicians being confronted by an unlikely coalition ranged against the Treaty, one composed of groups with little in common except for shared antipathy to the Lisbon Treaty; an inchoate movement, but one that managed in spite of considerable differences to run an effective campaign, notwithstanding the fact that the establishment, the mainstream parties, the trade unions and much of the business community came out in support of the proposed Treaty. The politicians were simply unable to get their message across, or at least a message that voters could grasp or subscribe to with any confidence. As Hugo Brady of the Centre for European Reform observed, 'you don't say yes to something you don't understand'.

The 'no' campaign was similar to those in the earlier referendums, the usual mix of disinformation, misrepresentation and naked self-interest masquerading as 'the' national interest: whether prominent business interests perturbed that favourable corporate taxation rates might be eroded by the provisions in the new Treaty on competitiveness; farmers worried that the generous agricultural subsidies would disappear; a religious lobby likewise alarmed that the proposed Charter of Fundamental Rights would facilitate gay marriage or abortion; and the wider public concerned that the largesse of EU subsidies that had contributed much to Ireland's growing prosperity might be redirected elsewhere in the newly enlarged EU. All of this is understandable enough, indeed it is normal politics in a Europe built from the outset, as even Monnet understood, much less on unalloyed ideals than by pragmatism, the need to reconcile or at least to balance diverse and competing interests. Yet amidst familiar concern about national advantage there are patent signs nowadays of popular disenchantment, already signalled in the Irish referendum that failed at the first attempt to ratify the Nice Treaty. A sense of disconnection with what the 'princes' are doing in their name, replicated throughout the continent as its peoples confront perturbing and seemingly remorseless change, a reflex expressed as hostility on all sides to the incomprehensible, top-down drive to reconfigure the Union's governance.

Mistrust of politicians both at the national and EU levels surfaced in this latest *vox pop*, and was given full voice in radio phone-ins, opinion surveys, and in the populist clamour of the 'no' campaign that looked like a revolt from 'below', even if financed by some wealthy business interests. This clamour outdid the ineffectual efforts of the establishment to emoliate it, those habitués of editorial suites, corporate board rooms, broadcasting studios and smart Dublin salons, frequenters of the distant bubble that the Dublin–Brussels circuit is perceived to be. This repeated the failure of the great and the good in the first referendum on the Nice Treaty to reassure the 'little people' that all is well with the Irish nation in Europe. In fact, where the case for Lisbon was made at all it was made half-heartedly and without much conviction, replicating the failure of the political classes of France and the Netherlands to put across the case for constitutional change in plain language, substituting a democratic conversation for the more familiar instinct of Europe's politicians simply to expect the public to do their bidding, to trust them at a time in the continent's history when trust is a discounted commodity. The message that 'all was well' with the Treaty, or for that matter with Europe *per se*, simply did not register with most voters, though this unease had several root causes. What the voting figures do indicate, as they did in those earlier referendums, is a pervasive sense of disconnection, a shortfall in confidence between government and people on the question of Europe. Could there be any clearer evidence than this latest in a series of grass-root rebellions that Europe's political class is out of touch with those whom it claims to represent, evidence, if more proof was needed, of the end of that compliance on matters European that was once called 'permissive consensus'?

And so at the time this book goes to print, despatched to the technicians who will manage its lengthy production process, Europe's constitutional 'crisis' – for what other word better describes this catalogue of public knock-backs? – continues unabated, despite efforts by political leaders to steady the ship and press on with reforms. Once again ordinary voters have resisted the solicitations of politicians, defied the bidding of the 'princes'. What had briefly seemed to be a deal done in Brussels and signed up to in Lisbon is once again overtaken by uncertainty. Of course, it is not beyond the wiles of politicians to hold out for the reforms they seem determined to have, adopting the usual strategy of delay but not of surrender, embarking on yet another period of reflection, code in the EU for sitting tight and doing little until the storm has quietened, perhaps hoping to bore the public into submission.

This is hardly new territory for the EU. Indeed, since the Danish 'no' vote on the Maastricht Treaty this version of scorched-earth diplomacy has become quite normal when the European projects hits a difficult patch. The future scenario might well be as follows: after some modest cosmetic changes the Treaty will be put again to the Irish people, its government pressured by the Union's 'bigger beasts' abetted by Brussels to ensure the electorate gives the 'right' answer in a second referendum. After all, Ireland is familiar with this scenario. The odds on this happening are quite favourable, though it is by no means a sure bet. Some pundits express doubt that any cynical attempt to ride roughshod over the democratic will of 'the people' freely expressed might not work a second time in one country. The very idea of asking a question and then ignoring the answer if it does not accord with what the 'princes' want to hear betrays an arrogance, indeed reveals an authoritarian instinct not remotely in accordance with the democratic culture on which the Union is supposedly founded. Nor do the circumstances of this latest referendum match those that pertained when this 'solution' was used in 2002 to reverse the 'no' vote on the Nice Treaty a year earlier. On that occasion the turn-out in the first referendum was sufficiently low as to reasonably dispute its legitimacy, whereas the figure for the Lisbon referendum was higher by some way. There are other differences between 2002 and the current situation that suggest that going back to the voters in expectation of a different answer might not resolve the matter. For on the former occasion, too, there was greater unanimity within the 'no' vote about the problematic issue, the sticking-point then being perceived concern about an implied threat to Irish neutrality. The issues underlying the rebuttal of Lisbon are broader, the public's concerns deeper, opposition more entrenched. As such, any attempt to reverse the decision may well confirm the widespread impression that featured in the recent campaign, one of politicians' indifference to popular concerns, and no less of a culture of 'bullying' by Brussels.

This may be so, but the arithmetic of ratification suggests that this may well be the most likely outcome, regardless of potential pitfalls. By now many countries (22 so far, accounting for 367.8 million Europeans, or some 74 per cent of the total EU population of 495.1 million) have already ratified Lisbon, with others well on the way to doing so. Ratification elsewhere is almost a foregone conclusion, only Ireland being constrained by the requirement to hold a referendum. In these circumstances the case made by governments and Brussels alike for Ireland to fall in line with ratification decisions stage-managed by governments without subjecting them to a popular vote is a curious inversion – or worse as some see it – of democratic procedure. In this convenient interpretation of the democratic will, the Treaty is being blocked by a 'mere' 0.00175 per cent of the Union's population of 495 million citizens, though Eurosceptics surely have a point when they claim that had popular votes been held elsewhere some at least would likely have delivered a similar outcome to that in Ireland. Far from being an aberration this latest 'no' vote is symptomatic of the Union's endemic legitimacy crisis. The argument used by those who demand a public voice in what are, in effect, major changes in how Europe is governed, claims that referendums manifest the popular will, and their outcomes should be respected accordingly.

While this may well be the case, the politics of the situation will as always be key in determining the outcome. Ireland is a small country, hardly a central player in the Union, and a country that owes much of its current prosperity to EU membership, a fact not remotely challenged even by the 'no' campaign. The fact that a 'mere' 752,451 Irish voters stand between the 'princes' and their new Treaty suggests how things might be concluded. Considerable pressure will be exerted on them to reverse their decision, a process that was already evident when, after the political leaders had absorbed the initial shock of the vote, they met in Brussels in June 2008 to review the situation. There they politely but firmly made it clear to the new *Taoiseach* Brian Cowen that they expect his government, after a decent interval, to deliver the 'appropriate result' in a second referendum. This at least is the plan; whether it will quite work out that way is by no means certain. Meanwhile, there will be the usual mix of inducements, blandishments and pressure, both on government and people from without will be considerable.

Who can predict the outcome with any degree of certainty? There is much at stake for Europe, and we should not underestimate either the determination of its politicians to have their reforms or their guile, notwithstanding bold talk by sceptics everywhere about 'ordinary people' standing up to bullying and resisting blackmail. It is hard to imagine that in due course most if not quite all of the major reforms enshrined in the Lisbon Treaty will not find their way into the Union's rule book. Yet this outcome will not in itself resolve the abiding problem with legitimacy so starkly revealed by this latest rebellion against what many see as top-down treaty reform. In this sense, the struggle for a European constitutional order that reassures rather more than it alienates citizens, that is inclusive rather than the monopoly of a privileged and unresponsive clique, remains the single most important political challenge facing the European Union.

## As for 'the people' …

One might reasonably conclude that if the EU's leaders are atuned to the public mood after the failed referendums, the people can no longer be excluded from the process of reforming their common governance, not least at the European level. What is in effect the Union's constitutional order should be no longer entirely in the gift of politicians as it was in times past, the outcome of cosy bargains made between privileged insiders. The recent decision to reform the treaties in the time-honoured fashion, and as some see it to smuggle in the Constitutional Treaty or at least a significant part of it by describing it as 'merely' reform of the existing treaty base, may or may not be a deliberate attempt to impose what could not be secured openly and fairly at the ballot box. Yet the fact of conspiracy or otherwise is hardly the point here, though the manner of the process for reforming the treaty base does little to appease those citizens who sent a direct message to their leaders in the fateful referendums. What is at least as worrying about the current situation, is that the politicians have seemingly learned so little from events. They have tried vestigial democracy and do not like it, and seemingly do not trust it because its outcomes are so unpredictable!

The good intentions expressed at Laeken have been set aside, replaced by more familiar reflexes. The Union's attempts so far at what by any other name is constitutional endeavour show the limits of conventional diplomacy for framing the rules and procedures of transnational governance, even in this non-statal and confederal polity. The conclusion of citizens, and not just those in France or the Netherlands, who had an opportunity to give their verdict on the Constitution at the ballot box shows that the public are certainly concerned about the impact of governance beyond the nation-state, though their concerns are rather different from those of their leaders. And one can quite see why, as they come to assimilate, whether as consumers or producers, traders or service providers, the impact of externalities for their welfare, security, health, jobs and overall prosperity. As the once-impervious boundaries between domestic politics and 'foreign policy' are eroded by the tractable quality of globalisation, propelled not least by the multi-level decision-making of this most advanced example of a post-national polity, so its citizens have begun to assimilate that the once-firm demarcation between government 'at home' and diplomacy 'abroad' no longer applies.

Governance is no longer confined within national bounds, it occurs in some degree at every level of the global order. Redistributive allocations of values, both material and post-material, as well as their consequences for citizens' welfare, and no less for their perceptions of governance *per se*, are now increasingly made beyond the boundaries of nation-states. And in the process, are 'spilling over' and 'spilling back', to use concepts devised by neo-functionalist theorists, in ways that impact significantly on the domestic domain, on what is traded by politicians nowadays as the public interest.[169] This has resulted in value shifts unforeseen barely a generation ago, and once described by one theorist of international change as 'cascading interdependence', or more prosaically in recent narratives of international change as 'Europeanisation'.[170] Whatever political scientists might make of these developments, they do amount to a shift in the continent's govern-ance. It can no longer be said of 'Europe' what Metternich once contemptuously said of 'Italy', that it is nothing more than *ein geographischer Begriff*, a mere geographical expression. It is something more than this, but how much more is still a matter of intense debate, and no less of ideological contestation.

The impact of this cumulate change is cultural as much as it is structural, though there is a lively debate about what is cause and what effect.[171] There is growing awareness that Europeans are governed nowadays from 'abroad' as much as from 'home', and with that realisation comes the need to make decision-makers at whatever level of governance demonstrably accountable for their actions. The public seem to sense this ineluctable shift in the balance of political forces, and many are discomfited by it. And from this disquiet comes the sort of nervous reaction displayed by voters during the course of the ratification referendums in France, the Netherlands, but also in countries where politicians decided for what-ever reason to reserve for themselves the historic ratification decision.

For all of these reasons, the EU's governance, how it reaches decisions and in whose interests, remains a matter of critical concern for its citizens, and one that can no longer be left to the 'princes' who have determined Europe's affairs from the Union's beginnings as the European Coal and Steel Community. This is why constitutionalism by default, bargains made between unelected Justices, diplo-mats, officials and ministers operating below the public's radar will no longer suffice. Constitutionalism in any polity committed to democratic norms requires public voice, a democratic *pouvoir constituant*. Only by engaging the public in a conversation about European governance, the meaning and purposes of the project, its future trajectory, can the political class hope to counter widespread public cynicism and indifference, the perception of a polity remote from and, worse, out of touch with its citizens, disconnected from their concerns, arcane governance beyond public accountability, lacking the transparency that is the *sine qua non* of a legitimate political order.

What is needed to overcome mistrust between these latter-day 'princes' and citizens is for politicians to acknowledge the public's concerns, to find ways of deepening attachment that embeds an idea of individual membership, a shared sense of identity that is the essential ballast for every stable and democratic regime. Even those who are not usually to be found in the Eurosceptical camp are disconcerted by the spectacle of these latter-day European politicians, who, after summoning the political energy to revisit the issues raised by the stalled Constitution, seemingly reverted to type, behaving in their usual imperious way by imposing what even by their own admission is a far-reaching reform of the treaty base that contains much that was central to a Constitution that twice failed the democracy test.

In these circumstances it is not difficult to agree with one Brussels watcher who wrote: 'You don't have to be anti-European to believe that the Eurosceptics are right to demand that any mini-treaty … should be put to a referendum. Indeed, you can argue that anyone who really cares about Europe and its future should be calling for just such a plebiscite.' This same writer sees nothing less than calculated 'deceit in arguing for a treaty that you say is essential to get Europe on the road again after the period of stagnation following the rejection of the Constitutional Treaty'. There are, he maintains, two basic flaws in this approach, not least the fact that 'a mini-treaty is the symbolic gesture for a new start [though] if the objective is a demonstrative one, why are they excluding the public? The one thing that the French and Dutch "no" votes showed two years ago was that the EU lacked democratic legitimacy. It was not a case of the public necessarily turning against the European ideal or even the Union. It was that the public no longer had confidence that the institutions were serving and responding to their needs. ... For all the talk, the new generation of European leaders is as cautious and as fearful as the old. But until they grasp the democratic nettle, the whole enterprise will lack legitimacy'.[172] It is difficult not to concur with this damning judgement.

Democracy is indeed central to the constitutional enterprise, or it should be at this stage of the Union's political development. Yet the word itself is contested, elastic and defined differently depending on one's point of view. For Giscard, the principal architect of the Constitution, 'democracy' is defined both narrowly as mere numbers, but also in a broader sense as the means for giving voice to public concerns. In the first instance, he expressed doubts about abandoning the existing Constitution and bringing in its successor seemingly covertly, as if pretending that by making merely 'cosmetic' changes to the Constitutional Treaty 'public opinion will be led to adopt, without knowing it, the proposals that we dare not present to them directly'. To follow this strategy, he acknowledges, is merely to confirm the public's perception of a Union 'organised behind their backs by jurists and diplomats'. Radical democrats who set great store by constitutional propriety and for that matter Eurosceptics, too, who resist the very idea of a clique of cosmopolitans imposing their narrow preferences on ancient polities would, for their own quite different reasons, concur with Giscard's critique. The dissimulation voiced by Luxembourg's Jean-Claude Juncker, to the effect that 'of course there will be transfers of sovereignty [but] would I be intelligent to draw the attention of public opinion to this fact?', simply reinforces this sense of subterfuge, of a deal being done above the people's heads and without their express consent.[173]

In order to avoid this unsatisfactory outcome Giscard called on the Union's political leaders to ensure greater transparency, and more than that to facilitate ongoing public consultation, arguing that 'if governments agree on a simplified treaty preserving the essential institutional advances, they should not be afraid to say so and write so'.[174] These are matters of real concern for anyone interested in making a democratic and legitimate European polity that is in touch with its citizens. But at this point Giscard rather spoiled his case, turning his own argument on its head, settling for a definition of democracy altogether narrower than the one he seemed to be recommending at the beginning of his critique. Reminding those leaders determined to reform the Treaty that a majority of states have already ratified the Constitution, he chose to define 'democracy' not as the meaningful expression of the citizen's voice but merely as formal procedure, and unduly narrow procedure at that. Governments, it seems, have already decided the next stage of the ongoing process that is treaty reform, though he has little to say about how they so decided. According to this narrow intergovernmental formula that fact seems to be enough to satisfy Giscard's requirement for 'democratic voice'.

Governments in this plebiscitary model of liberal democracy are elected, and as such *are* tribunes of the people regardless of how little consultation there is between leaders and people on these momentous matters. And so he concludes that 'in a Europe that professes its desire for more democracy, this fact must not be underestimated. The ratification procedure carried out by two-thirds of member states including the vast majority of new members deserve equal consideration with the two states which rejected the treaty ... and the three who still question it. We must reflect at length before asking them to adopt a text different from the one they already voted for.'[175] In truth Giscard's real concern here was the survival of the Constitution, largely his own creation, and not least his own claim to a place in history. Whether the people are consulted about it or what will replace it was for Giscard a secondary consideration.

In this narrow account of democratic procedure, numbers do count, but not counted as votes in the ballot box so much as at the despatch box, those battalions of tame or ambitious and usually career-minded parliamentarians corralled through the division lobbies by government whips at the behest of executives, so as to ensure that their latest deal on the treaties becomes law. There is no concern here with public voice, or even with opening a meaningful democratic conversation between politicians and people about such matters. Of course, this is indirect and representative democracy, at least as it has been practiced in Europe's liberal states this past century or so, and democracy of a kind the EU is quite familiar with, its leaders altogether more comfortable with than its more radical deliberative or republican variants. But, it should be said, not the sort of democracy that will win citizens' hearts and minds on the big issues.

For one thing, it ignores the democratic quality of 'due process'. Whether the reliance on guaranteed parliamentary majorities and the (often deliberate) avoidance of referendums in these countries that successfully ratified the Constitutional Treaty – frequently in the face of publics demanding a direct say – does satisfy even the minimal conditions for public voice is, to say the least, questionable. The fact that one recent *Eurobarometer* poll indicated that some 66 per cent of respondents (a sample of 444,406 drawn from all 27 member states) did support the ratification of the Constitutional Treaty, neither endorses nor disproves Giscard's argument, as even he has acknowledged with his call for the public to be given a more direct say in determining their own future in Europe.[176] Those who refute the clarion call for meaningful public voice, as did the decent if hopelessly out of touch German president, Horst Kohler, when he disparaged 'populistic, demagogic campaigning', are simply missing the point.[177]

To allow the people voice in determining their own governance is radical but hardly dangerous politics, and to do so is not to abandon common sense for sentimentality, though no one should underestimate the procedural difficulties. At the same time, engaging the public in a meaningful democratic conversation is no easy matter. It is time-consuming, procedurally complicated and sociologically problematic, for politics is hardly a glamorous activity, nor one for which many have either appetite or aptitude. It requires, too, an investment of what are usually scarce resources, not least of citizens' time and energy, and depends no less on access to reliable and comprehensible information. 'Conversation' is shorthand here for public engagement, citizens as partners in a civic endeavour that responds to their concerns and aspirations. A process whereby stakeholders at every level have the opportunity to debate futures, whether they take that opportunity or not, and in the process to become better apprised of the merits and defects of all the available options, to have policy matters explained to them, a process akin to what are now fashionably described as 'citizens' juries'.

Only when these arrangements are fully in place will the EU remotely become a democratic polity, with its citizens as full partners, its governance both transparent and accountable to all of its stakeholders. This is no easy task to accomplish, but it is an essential one, the true gauge of a mature civic polity, a *status civitatus*. By way of conclusion, we shall review in Chapter 12 both the obstacles to and the prospects for such civic engagement, and discuss how the future constitutional history of the European Union might move beyond the narrow bargains that have characterised the struggle for a European Constitution thus far. If, as Jean Monnet once maintained, 'crises are opportunities' the Union's recent constitutional crisis was an opportunity squandered to redress the legitimacy deficit that lies at the very centre of the European project.[178]

# 12  Towards a constitutional conversation

## The disconnection problem

The resounding 'no' votes in the 2005 referendums do not in themselves indicate visceral Euroscepticism, or not entirely so. The rejection of the Constitutional Treaty by a majority of the electorates of France and the Netherlands shows instead widespread public concern about the state of the European project, much of it reflecting contrary views over the pace and direction of European integration. Behind this reaction is rising public anxiety about the remoteness of the political class, disquiet about the top-down manner in which the European project has been constructed and managed. There is little dispute about the fact of disconnection, but rather less concern amongst Europe's political leaders than there ought to be about either its causes or consequences. There are, however, differences of opinion with the commentariat about whether disconnection really matters, its impact on stable governance in the inchoate polity that is the European Union.

Opinion here tends to follow ideological preferences. Those whose views are informed by the realist narrative of European construction, for instance, are mostly unconcerned about the peripheral role of the public or the Union's democratic shortcomings, believing that little is lost by the lack of input legitimacy, what classical political theorists define as popular consent expressed through the various agencies for political participation. The lack of public input is seen as problematic, however, by those commentators who regard the EU as a polity whose governance claims to be based on democratic norms. This, after all, is how politics works or is supposed to work in modern democracies. Political leaders, latter day 'princes', more pragmatists than principled philosophers, make decisions, and citizens have the ultimate sanction of the ballot box, or as Schumpeter saw it the option of 'throwing the rascals out' should they feel after a reasonable interlude that the management of public affairs has gone awry. But though a polity, the EU is not a state and so even this tenuous legitimacy, periodic granting or withdrawal of a mandate to govern, the requisite for democratic governance in modern mass societies, is thought by other commentators not to be applicable. As they see it, the EU lacks demos, and for that reason normal democratic procedures simply do not apply.

In recent times, concern about the Union's democracy deficit has overtaken complacent 'realism' in the debate about the state of the European polity. As the

Union has acquired new competencies and extended its common power over matters once the sole preserve of national governments, a trenchant critique has emerged. According to one such account: 'The EU has always been an elite project with little if any democratic support [and] to a shameful extent, it has been imposed on national electorates by stealth and outright lies, for instance, the assertion that membership [of the Community] would involve no major loss of national sovereignty.'[1] The case that is made here is that the EU political order is rife with deception and dissimulation, giving rise to an anti-democratic political culture that 'has succeeded only because until 15 years ago voters had been sedated by prosperity and asked to make no sacrifices for "the European idea"'. But things are changing and fast under growing pressure from globalising forces, of which European integration is but a regional exemplar. Consequently, 'the cumulative effects of Europe's economic centralisation are being felt', as are 'the political intrusions on [citizens'] liberty and independence'.[2] With the result that the old order – one is almost tempted to describe it an *ancien régime* of at best indirectly unelected 'princes' relying almost exclusively on permissive consensus, though this would surely be stretching the point – has been challenged by the upsurge of popular discontents, giving rise in turn to pervasive mistrust by citizens of what these 'princes' do in their name.

This critique of the Union's democracy and legitimacy deficits is normatively compelling, at least it is for anyone versed in the liberal tradition, but it is also flawed. It misses much of the subtlety, indeed the ambiguous and even contradictory quality of public concern about the European project. The evidence from numerous opinion surveys shows nothing remotely equivalent to incipient rebellion by latter-day *sans culottes*, public rejection of these 'princes' claim to exercise public power *per se*, but rather widespread misgivings about how they use power, in whose interests and for whose benefit. Many voters, certainly those who participated in the referendum in France, were less concerned about excessive regulation from Brussels than by the impact on national economies, labour markets and welfare systems of the neo-liberal forces blowing from across the Atlantic. Many voters read into the small print of the Constitutional Treaty an insidious threat to the European social welfare model that had accompanied the Common Market and latterly the Single European Market.

For some voters, though by no means all, this translates into concern about democracy, at least the perceptible disconnection between people and 'princes' who have acquired – and under the Constitution would have increased – their capacity to influence many aspects of Europe's social life and economic affairs. The fear of being overgoverned or just badly governed is compounded by a growing perception at the grassroots that politicians are plainly out of touch with, or else largely indifferent to popular concerns, the things that really matter to ordinary people. Public cynicism about politics has begun to find a voice, though this *vox populi* is too often perceived by those who composed the otherwise diffuse 'no' constituency in the referendums as *vox clamantis in deserto*. What this mood-change does herald is concern about how the EU goes about governance, a change of emphasis with considerable significance for its future arrangements. At the very least this shift in public attitudes marks the end of permissive consensus, and an end, too, to almost half a century of mostly unreflective public acquiescence in the European project.[3]

Since the Constitutional Treaty stalled there has certainly been reflection and much cause for reflection about how this breach of trust between 'princes' and people might be redressed. Or at least, about how to give citizens greater voice at the EU level, better access to the institutions, what might be done to improve consultation over European public policy, and even how to deepen the sense of personal attachment, individual affiliation and belonging to a common project, notwithstanding the patent fact that primary political membership still resides in the nation-state. These are perplexing but important questions, and they are no less ambitious objectives for a polity where decisions are, by their nature, highly technical and for the most part monopolised by vested interests. The solution to public disconnection here, as in any democratic polity, is engagement.

Of course, this is altogether easier to affirm than it is to realise, to find appropriate means for conducting a meaningful conversation, a two-way exchange between citizens and politicians. And this is an even greater challenge in a polity that lacks a shared sense of identity, one that has neither the tradition nor procedures for conducting democratic transnational politics. The comparison with democratic politics in established national states confirms the extent of this problem. Something approximating a continuous conversation between government and people does occur in national (and in sub-national or territorial) polities, encounters that are facilitated not only by the existence of legitimate institutions and an authoritative government exercising a democratic mandate, but underpinned, too, by the cultural and sociological fabric in which national politics is embedded: in essence, mutual values and common experiences, a shared history, a public discourse about 'futures' conducted in a common language, a lingua franca; and all of this mediated by long-established and legitimate political institutions.

None of these agencies or cultural resources for facilitating a political conversation between governors and governed, and no less for mobilising collective action at the grassroots, exists at the European level. How then to conduct democratic politics in a polity lacking the agency for such a structured encounter between governors and governed? And how, too, to expedite at a level above the nation-state those exchanges, trade-offs and bargains made between elites and people that are the fabric of democratic politics in nation-states, those processes whereby ordinary citizens rather than the usual coterie of insiders, lobbyists and government agencies acquire the resources, knowledge and experience, the political capital, for effective collective action beyond the nation-state?[4] Some commentators see the solution to these dilemmas to be a transnational 'public space'.

Those who advocate a European public space as the solution to disconnection put the blame for shortcomings in democracy squarely on 'princes'. They complain that the Union's political class is hardly concerned – apart from the usual rhetoric, those blandishments necessary for attracting votes and to keep the masses relatively content – with engaging the public, let alone for fostering a sense of empowerment in a Europe-wide body politic. And even then they confine their attempts to relate to 'the people' merely to national audiences, after all their principal electoral base and ultimately the source of their political authority. The issue of civic engagement at the European level figured nevertheless in the debate about how to salvage the European Constitution, though it should be said more in the academy than amongst politicians. In one noteworthy example, a consortium of 13 EU think-tanks, all members of the European Policy Institutes Network (EPIN), proposed a 'citizens' compact' to launch 'an effective "European Democratic and Civic Space"', building on the Convention's legacy of deliberation to foster 'a European dimension in the public debate on the Constitution, by improving the "vertical" links between the national (regional, local) level and the European level as well as the "horizontal" links among the different national forums'.[5] Politicians have hardly matched academic endeavour in this regard. Other than the usual sophistries from shell-shocked politicians, and the Commission's belated and somewhat equivocal attempt to improve communications, how it gets its message over to the public, there has been little effort so far to encourage let alone to facilitate public empowerment. The response has mostly been confined to predictable manoeuvrings between elite actors to buy time as they review their limited options. Yet the 'crisis' over the Constitution, if such it was, did show a failure on the part of the 'princes' to engage citizens in a mature debate about European futures.

This conversation must occur, and sooner rather than later, but it cannot take place in a vacuum. Those national conversations that occur in every democratic state are but a beginning to more meaningful public engagement, indeed a necessary precursor to an altogether wider involvement by citizens in politics beyond national boundaries. This is to say the least no easy task, but it does suggest a way forward. The challenge here is to facilitate informed discussion about EU-related policy issues in national parliaments, an essential precondition for improving public knowledge of European affairs. The national, or for that matter sub-national civic space is important, not least because 'the primary attention in public debate continues to be generated by national politics'.[6] It is the starting-point, an indispensable base for working outwards and upwards to the EU level in what is a multi-level polity, connecting domestic and EU governance in the public's mind in the same way as people and their governments are connected in the national polity. As one commentator sees it: 'European actors could use national debates to give the broad public a better idea about the nature of their work and the functioning and actual competences of the EU', so that it becomes 'clearer to the people what the EU can actually do and also what it *cannot* do under the current conditions. Otherwise the danger persists that expectations are created which the EU ultimately cannot fulfil.'[7]

The public should certainly be better informed by politicians about how the EU actually works, how decisions are made and why and in whose interest, a long-overdue explanation of how the exercise of public power is irrevocably changed in the global age. This requires action at both the national and EU levels: on the one hand 'educating' the public about the changing realities of power, and on the other communicating grassroots concerns and preferences 'upwards' to those responsible for framing European public policy. Some feasible measures here might include communicating details of national parliamentary debates/committee reports to the Commission and to the European Parliament, thereby facilitating dialogue between the principal EU institutions and the national polities. Heads of government could likewise communicate their preferences for EU policy more effectively to national parliaments, or by holding more regular meetings between European and national parliamentarians. More important even than this, politicians should educate the public in the realities of contemporary post-national governance by bringing 'the European agenda to the attention of the citizens'.[8]

These are all procedures that would increase public awareness and stimulate media interest in EU policy.[9] Emphasis here, in the first instance anyway, should be on improving communications, more and better quality information about what the EU is doing on the citizens' behalf, rather than on facilitating public participation. Clearly, this is part of the answer to the problem of disconnection. Improving the public's knowledge of how EU governance works is indispensable for ensuring the accountability of decision-makers, but there is also a need to improve public access to the EU policy-process, to open up what is presently a hermetic system of Byzantine complexity, not just to public scrutiny but to participation from representatives of civil society, who are largely excluded from its decision-making processes.

Only such measures can over time deepen the individual's sense of affiliation, a precondition for legitimising governance, at the European as at any other level. Of the principal agenda-setting and policy-making institutions the Commission alone seems to have registered the importance of connecting with citizens, explaining what the European project is all about, though for the most part only on its own limited terms. Accordingly, it has made some modest proposals for improving communications with citizens, but so far there has been little by way of real reform. The Commission's communications and information initiatives are rather more about improving its own relations with the other institutional actors, the European Parliament and the Council, and with the member states, facilitating a more strategic or 'joined up' approach, effecting best practice on policy implementation, evaluation, and above all with an eye to improving its somewhat battered image. But this process is only tangentially concerned to address citizens' concerns, let alone to facilitate a meaningful dialogue with civil society.[10] The Spokesperson's Service, for instance, a consequence of these initiatives, performs primarily a news management function, assuming responsibility under the president's direct supervision for communicating the Commission's political priorities to the media, with a view to setting the news agenda for the Brussels media pack and beyond.

A more recent Commission initiative, the Action Plan to Improve Communicating Europe, has sought to address the disconnect problem more directly, by engaging citizens and 'setting out the policy vision and the initiatives to be undertaken in co-operation with the other institutions and civil society stakeholders'. This has the longer-term objective of developing 'a European Public Sphere particularly through audio-visual media as well as a European narrative'.[11] The rhetoric here is suitably radical, referring to 'initiating dialogue' with citizens, listening to and connecting with 'the people', avoiding merely didactic communication, the one-way and top-down transmission of elite preferences. The reality, however, is somewhat different, with the principal intention seemingly to improve the Commission's defective public image, to enhance its profile in the member states, and to ensure better communication from the centre about European policy. The rationale here is primarily 'top-down', more didactic than it is interactive or deliberative. It is intended to bring about a more professional approach to managing public (in effect, media) relations across all departments, sharpening the Commission's impact from the centre outwards by improving the drafting of policy proposals, enhancing staff training in communications skills to get across positive messages about policy delivery, providing short and simple summaries of policy, for instance on the Commission's home page on the Europa website and other internet and audio-visual publicity tools.[12]

The emphasis on communicating policy and in an accessible manner, addressing 'target audiences' in everyday language is commendable as far as it goes. But how far in fact does it go? There is, too, some modest provision for consultation, using designated citizen contact centres to obtain feedback, and providing the Commission's policy wonks with detailed and accurate information from beyond the Brussels *route de ceinture*, taking greater account of the public's concerns in order to meet the objectives of the European Transparency Initiative and Better Regulation action plan.[13] Again the principal intention here is less to listen than to inform, to educate 'outsiders' about the 'realities' and complexities of the Brussels policy milieu, using communication initiatives at national level to provide governments, national stakeholders and regional and local media 'with timely and relevant information about developments within the Commission'.[14] This, too, is classic 'top-down' and essentially one way communication, rather than a democratic conversation, as theorists of deliberative and republican forms of democracy understand the term. It is a strategy more concerned with explaining what Brussels is doing, 'presenting a single face' for the broad sweep of EU public policy so as to avoid confusion, using simple and repetitive 'slogans and symbols' to get the message over to the wider public, than with facilitating dialogue, let alone public access.

Of course, educating the public in the realities of European public policy, the available options, is part of the solution to disconnection, but only a part. There is complacency here and even denial that implies in large measure the problem is much less about disconnection defined as the remoteness of elites from the public, but rather the public's inability, or as some see it its unwillingness, to invest appropriate time and energy in order to comprehend policy, and a propensity for citizens to misunderstand what elites are doing 'for' the people. Looked at from this perspective the problem is more one of misconception than wilful misinformation. It amounts neither to deception by politicians nor conspiracy to deny the public proper information. And it is a problem best remedied according to this account by providing more and better-quality information. Of course, information is a critical resource for encouraging informed debate in any democratic polity, a necessary though hardly a sufficient condition for public engagement. For without the means for ensuring transparency and the accountability of those who govern

– public oversight (and a measure of democratic control) over what 'princes' do, opportunities for exercising real influence over policy at the framing stage – even these long-overdue reforms will hardly make possible a genuinely democratic encounter, a meaningful conversation between those who direct public policy and those who must live with the consequences of that policy.

The Commission nevertheless responded to the crisis over the Constitution with its usual reticence. In autumn 2005 it launched a new initiative, *Plan D for Democracy, Dialogue and Debate*, consisting of measures supposedly designed in response to public disquiet, including more frequent visits by commissioners to member states and parliaments, and a system of 'goodwill' ambassadors to promote the Union, much as the United Nations does. A similar initiative was its launch of a website to facilitate a transEU 'debate' in some 20 languages about the future of the Union. For the most part, however, these are cosmetic measures, and in their way just as patronising as the anodyne appeal to the public that 'we want to know what your hopes for Europe are and what worries you as a European?'[15] These belated attempts to fill the communications void over European public policy are better than nothing, but they do not remotely amount to a democratic conversation.[16] Propaganda or even artful political persuasion is no substitute for a significant effort to bring the public closer to a policy process that currently happens without their participation.

How, then, might the EU political class meaningfully engage with citizens? How can it foster effective linkages with civil society? And how to find ways of 'bringing society back in' to the Union's political process?[17] Some commentators see the answer to this democratic predicament in conventional modes of political participation, notably through the familiar agency of political parties, the vehicle supposedly best suited for involving the public in transnational politics, the most reliable medium for holding the agencies of governance above and beyond the nation-state publicly accountable. The problem with this 'solution', however, is that political parties designed to operate as two-way transmission belts in national polities with a hierarchic and legitimate political order do not easily translate to the heterarchical and multi-level EU polity, lacking either demos or common political identity. EU-level parties do exist, but they are pale shadows of the mobilised, structured and active organisations that presided over the democratisation and modernisation of Europe's nation-states. They are at best nascent organisations and intrinsically elitist, lacking grassroots organisation. European party politics as such is non-existent on the ground, and there is little to indicate that the European party families that inhabit the Parliament can remotely perform the functions of parties at the national level, recruiting activists, transmitting popular sentiments upwards into party counsels, debating policy options, connecting the 'merely' parochial with wider concerns and not least citizens with government. This fact is graphically illustrated by persistently low turn-out at European elections, an indication of how little store voters place on EU-level parties.[18]

There are other constraints, too, on transnational politics, for whatever its normative rationale, liberal democratic politics is in practice dominated by elites. The more resourceful, better-educated members of civil society have greater political resources, more reliable means of accessing decision-making, and as such they contribute more to deliberations on public policy, exert greater influence over outcomes and in ways that the generality of citizens simply cannot do. This unsatisfactory outcome is not the result of deliberate conspiracy to deny democratic rights, but it does reflect the fact that political influence requires a sense of purpose and commitment, and no less a level of resources that most citizens simply do not have. This is as true at the EU level as it is in domestic politics. Indeed, the problem of differential access to influence is that much greater at the European level in view of the very remoteness, the unfamiliarity of EU governance for citizens, a fact that as one commentator sees it consolidates 'a new class bias between an elitist highly educated, mobile (or cosmopolitan) new bourgeoisie as the included voice and a localised, immobile and traditional proletariat with a low educational profile as the excluded silence of the EU's social constituency'.[19] To remedy this situation requires much more than merely improved communications or better public information. The problem is in essence one of an endemic legitimacy deficit, a shortcoming that needs to be addressed if the Union is to begin to engage – and meaningfully – with its citizens.

## Legitimacy deficit

Few commentators would deny that the EU has a legitimacy deficit, and though this problem is hardly exclusive to the European Union, the unique design of this polity does accentuate it.[20] Citizens everywhere have lost much of the respect they once had for political elites. This is the case at every level of contemporary governance, but the situation is made worse in the EU because its governance lacks meaningful democratic input. The remoteness of the European institutions, even the Parliament, from the citizens precludes effective transparency and accountability of what is, in essence, technocratic governance dominated by the insiders who monopolise the policy agenda.[21] Permissive consensus, citizens' perception of national elites operating in defence of national interests in these distant institutions – in effect, legitimacy based on effective performance, the delivery of policy outcomes – is no longer sufficient for ensuring the public's compliance, let alone their enthusiastic support for the project.[22] The referendums on the treaty changes conducted in some EU15 states throughout the 1990s, the Swedish referendum on the euro (September 2003) and even the accession referendums in the new member states, together with declining turn-out in European elections and rising support for Eurosceptical parties, all serve to confirm this trend.[23]

The European Union's multi-levelness and the lack of channels for effective democratic input, whether from national and sub-national governance or directly by the citizen, deepens the legitimacy deficit, and with adverse consequences for how citizens perceive the Union. As one contemporary commentator sees it: 'The notion that European citizens are prepared to defer to technocratic wisdom for the sake of the benefits of European integration is less sustainable now than during the previous phases in the integration process.'[24] This may well be so; times have certainly changed and the forces that drive the global economy seem to defy the constraints imposed by national authorities. Globalisation is a hard task-master and throws up prodigious challenges. Connecting with the public was never more necessary for making people aware of the formidable challenges that confront Europe. What nation-states acting on their own initiative cannot hope to achieve by way of curbing these forces, transnational actors such as the EU with a regional reach and pooled resources beyond the scope of any national polity might yet succeed in doing, imposing more effective regulatory, and no less political constraints on otherwise unfettered global forces. This may be the best, indeed the only prospect for taming those powerful agencies that are propelling globalisation. Yet, this is not how the public sees the Union. On the contrary, its governance is perceived by many citizens to be 'backward, lagging, threatening, or merely self-serving ... a technocratic, output-orientated version of European democracy [that] looks increasingly out of step, not only with the shift to a more participatory democracy, but also with the consumer-driven market economies with which European citizens are now familiar'.[25]

This is one prevailing image of the European Union, but it is not the only one. Perceptions of the Union are mixed, and public opinion is by no means uniformly hostile. And in this lies the prospect of turning things around, notwithstanding immense difficulties in the way of change. The polling data are to say the least ambiguous. On the one hand, there is widespread unease about the impact, indeed the growing incursion of the EU into domestic affairs. Yet experience of what is generally described as the 'Europeanisation' of public policy has, nevertheless, begun to alert the public to the realities of a changing political order, not least the fact that there is nowadays a blurring of the once-pristine boundaries between the domestic and the European levels. As Kleinman sees it, political integration for many Europeans is 'no longer a far-off aspiration, an ideal to which nominal assent could be given in the sure knowledge that no action was necessary, but increasingly it is a live political issue throughout the member states [such that] political integration became an issue of greater salience, not only to European elites, but increasingly to citizens too [for] the economic reality of the euro and the legal reality of citizenship of the Union both imply a European government.'[26]

This may be going too far, at least for the time being, but people do at least have a sense that changes are underway in the conduct and procedures of public affairs. There is a realisation, if hardly yet much enthusiasm, for the fact that governance at the European level is increasingly intruding into and impacting on their lives, and in ways not anticipated even a short while ago. It was certainly no idle boast, nor was it mere wishful thinking, when Jacques Delors predicted a decade or so ago that before long the EU would 'soon' be responsible for the bulk of decisions on economic policy, even if that bold prediction has yet to be fully realised.[27] However, public acceptance of these new realities is hardly the same thing as approval. Many citizens remain unconvinced, and some of them are perturbed by the prospect of even 'more Europe'. The 'no' votes in the referendums are but one expression of growing popular disquiet reported in public opinion surveys throughout the Union, concern about perceived neglect of citizens' interests, resentment, too, that public opinion is taken for granted and irritation about being patronised by politicians.

The referendum campaigns on ratification seemed to confirm public perceptions of such remoteness, wariness about an elite regarded by many as out of touch with grassroots opinion, a political class seeking public endorsement of a constitutional bargain made without any serious attempt to engage the wider public, let alone to acknowledge their concerns or indeed aspirations for the European project. A bargain that was briefly described as a constitution, but one that nevertheless seemed to critics to be little more than a deal negotiated by the same privileged insiders who have always run the show.[28] One commentator sees in this public reaction 'a growing demand on the part of the European electorates to comment on the parameters of European integration' and 'further evidence that the days of "permissive consensus" are now long gone'.[29] And if there are some admittedly nominal signs that the political class is responding now to public vexation, even this appears to be less a principled response to the legitimacy deficit, a Damascene conversion to democratic principles, and much more about safeguarding their own power base. A case 'of the political elite in Europe increasingly recognising a growing political danger to their own fortunes if they continue to ignore public frustration and dissatisfaction with parts of EU evolution'.[30]

The evidence for public disquiet is apparent in the findings of countless polls and opinion surveys, but again this is only part of an altogether more complex picture. A sense of ambiguity prevails, as it always does where 'Europe' is the issue. The same polling data that indicate unease about political leaders also show consistently high levels of support, both for the Union's principal institutions and even for the idea of closer integration, widespread recognition that the European project has contributed both to increasing prosperity and to regional peace and security after centuries of bloody warfare. The European project is at least accorded some credit amongst the wider public for this remarkable achievement, though the overall picture remains mixed, doubts persisting in the public's mind about how the politicians manage EU affairs.[31] There is a marked discrepancy, for instance, between the general acceptance of the idea of European co-operation in marked contrast with the near-anarchy that prevailed before 1945, and legitimacy in the full and proper sense. This can be seen as the difference between input legitimacy measured as public support for the way the Union manages its affairs, its institutions and decision-making procedures; and output or performance legitimacy, in effect how far the Union accommodates citizens' aspirations and preferences, addresses their basic concerns, and contributes to their overall welfare. Both aspects of legitimacy are complementary, essential for stable governance and for determining how far citizens feel that public institutions and public policy are responsive to, reflect and represent their own concerns and accommodate their preferences.

The EU has relied much more on performance legitimacy, but now seems to be failing to meet citizens' expectations even on this count. Many citizens seem distinctly underwhelmed, both by the Union's modest capacity for democratic input and with output measured as policy performance and institutional efficiency. To date, the principal focus of treaty reform has been improving procedural and institutional performance. The constitutional process launched at Laeken, despite promising much by way of 'improving democratic life' in the Union, gave far greater emphasis to performance or output capacity, concerned as it was with enhancing institutional efficiency rather than improving the Union's credentials as a *status civitatus* in the classical sense of a community-based polity.[32] In these circumstances, it seems reasonable to assume that engaging the public in an informed conversation about the benefits of European integration, the challenges facing European society, will more likely confirm a sense of common purpose, and perhaps even evoke in Europeans some sense of 'their shared past, their collective destiny and their future collective projects', a propensity 'to recognise one another as relevant to each other in daily practice ... as belonging to a particular group sharing a particular history, enduring a shared destiny and starting off towards a common future'.[33]

Concern with 'merely' institutional performance was understandable enough while the EC/EU's work was largely confined to the technocratic and regulatory aspects of market-making. It was quite appropriate for an organisation defined as more international regime than polity, and moreover a regime whose outputs were principally addressed to functional actors and vested interests rather than to the public at large. Things have changed, however, over recent decades, and markedly so since the launch of the Single Market. The Union has acquired significant competencies, a capacity for intruding directly on citizens' lives on a wide range of public policy. In these circumstances, the lack of democratic input was bound to become critical, both for political legitimacy *vis-à-vis* the citizen, and no less for the Union's credibility as an international actor.[34]

In spite of these shortcomings as a polity – and not least one based on democratic norms – both the Convention and the IGC that followed it had a narrow agenda, notwithstanding the commitment of the Laeken mandate to improving democratic life. Neither forum addressed much political energy to measures for increasing citizens' voice, nor to widening participation in decision-making. In part, this reflects a familiar preoccupation, at least amongst the governments of the member states and certainly of the 'big three', that democracy as public participation is not what the EU is about in what is after all a non-statal polity whose primary actors are nation-states, each with its own established democratic procedures. According to this confederal narrative, the EU is not a polity that operates according to normal elective procedures, whereby electors choose prospective governors from lists of candidates put up by competing parties, a procedure that results in a mandate to govern for the majority party or a coalition of winning parties.

The closest the EU comes to democratic (defined as participatory or representative) politics is the Parliament, and even this institution lacks an elective function worth the name, and has only recently acquired even the legislative (indeed, little more than a co-legislative) function that is the defining characteristic of democratic national parliaments everywhere. As such, the Parliament is removed from those executive actors who undertake the agenda-setting and policy-framing functions that pass for governance in the European Union. Indeed, for part of its work it even sits in a different country from these executive institutions. On the contrary, much authoritative decision-making is undertaken by unelected technocrats (the Commission, but also the plethora of experts who contribute to the comitology process, Council working groups and the influential nexus of Commission advisory and policy management groups, and influenced by powerful lobbies), or at best by indirectly elected politicians, the members of the Council and the European Council. These decision-makers tend to assume legitimacy, but it is legitimacy based not on a popular mandate conferred by means of direct election, or some other procedure that gives the public a voice in affairs. As such, it amounts to something less than public approval tested at the ballot box. In effect, these credentials and the legitimacy they purportedly bestow are assumed more than they are earned, taken as read if not exactly taken for granted.

This procedure worked after a fashion as long as the public was content to be 'governed' at the European level by politicians feigning legitimacy, relying on the convenient notion of permissive consensus. Over time it has become clear that this situation no longer serves to validate EU governance. Political legitimacy can no longer be simply assumed a priori, in the EU as in any other polity that is founded on democratic principles. There is also the not insignificant matter of double standards, for after all democratic legitimacy is the commitment a priori the Union requires from every member state as a condition of membership.[35] For this very reason, performance legitimacy on its own is insufficient normative ballast for governance that is increasingly intrusive on people's lives and life chances. This is precisely where the recent constitutional endeavour has been found wanting, concentrating as it has tended to on the usual elite preoccupation with institutional reform, concerned to improve output or policy performance, whilst mostly overlooking input legitimacy, measures for effecting public voice, for citizens' participation in, or at the very least enhancing their capacity collectively if not singly to influence, the policy process.[36] In spite of some important input-related reforms, for instance extending co-decision, and with additional measures to connect national parliaments more closely with the EU policy process, closing the Union's legitimacy and democracy deficits was hardly a priority for governments who negotiated the final draft of the Constitutional Treaty.

This outcome was a disappointment for those who seek to improve the Union's democratic life, and it was undoubtedly an opportunity squandered. As one critic sees it, the Constitutional Treaty ensured that 'the complicated nature of Union powers and Union decision-making will be no more intelligible to the general public than it was before [for] the constitutional features most generally contributing to the legitimacy of a polity are the checks on powers', prescribing ways 'to hold them responsible and accountable to citizens'. Accordingly, closing the legitimacy deficit was, in effect, a secondary consideration as the principal players confined their best efforts 'to the consolidation of Treaty provisions'.[37] The EU polity remains, then, much as it was before the Convention, inaccessible and incomprehensible to its citizens, with little in an overlong and convoluted Constitutional text to help them comprehend, let alone to better relate to its 'various bits nor [to] understand the meaning and relevance of each nor the way they interconnect'.[38] Matters here are hardly improved by the new but equally convoluted Reform Treaty. These objectives would have been better served by delivering on the undertaking made at Laeken to simplify the Union's political order. But the Convention and what followed it simply lost sight of that laudable intention.

Political legitimacy has both an abstract quality and a practical aspect, it is both constructed and relational. On one level it is about defining appropriate normative standards for the rightful exercise of power in a political community, standards that determine who governs and how, and for whose benefit. At another level, however, it defines membership, who belongs and who is excluded from the political community, and what binds citizens together in common endeavour, how they manage their differences and so on. A viable constitutional order, for the EU as for any polity, depends not just on normative abstractions, important though these are, but also on how the citizens actually experience membership and belonging, the extent to which they share a meaningful sense of identity, citizenship and allegiance to a polity. The solution to the EU's legitimacy deficit, at least in part, one way of bringing people together in a shared endeavour, connecting them to what many still regard as a remote and tenuous project lies here as in any democratic polity in the idea of citizenship. And citizenship defined not merely as abstract rights but as belonging experienced ontologically, a sense of identity and solidarity with others as members of a political community.

## Towards European solidarity? Transforming identity, reimagining citizenship

Belonging defined as individual membership and personal affiliation was a vital aspect of successful nation-building in European states in the post-Westphalian era, a process accelerated by the cultural impact of the French Revolution of 1789 and no less by the economic consequences of industrialisation elsewhere in Europe after the eighteenth century. Citizenship is, after all, not only contractual in the formal or legalistic sense but also relational, constructed in part on the basis of an implied bargain, or rather a series of interlocking or complementary bargains, underpinned by what John Locke described as tacit consent. This amounts, in essence, to an exchange of mutual benefits between those who govern and those over whom they exercise lawful power. This bargain was consolidated, and in the process competing ideas about political identity as exclusive claims to nationhood were constructed, during the age of democratisation, the modernisation of Europe's social, economic and political order in what Berend has described as 'the long nineteenth century'.[39]

These historic bargains made between key social forces were both constructed and contingent, put in place over time. And with the intervention of cultural agencies they acquired their own potent foundational myths: patriotism in exchange for public goods and personal well-being defined as security against 'malevolent' outsiders, public order, the rule of law, welfare and economic opportunities. This 'bargain' on which the modern nation-state is based resulted in benefits all round that helped to cement in turn the political and social bonds of nationhood, fostering affective loyalty to the idea of the national political community. But it was underpinned in part by more mundane bargains, political allegiance in exchange for material pay-offs and other benefits for individual members. In Europe's economically developed societies the political community acquired legitimacy rooted in broadly similar norms, though with some variability depending on the particularities of national history and culture, and it included the idea of an overarching constitutional and legal order – what Hans Kelsen famously called the *Grundnorm* – from which derive individual, civil and eventually social rights, freedom of the person and of speech and thought, universal suffrage, civil liberties and access to social benefits and welfare. All of which helped to transform the 'mere' subject into a citizen with affective loyalty to the polity, and contributing over time both to social cohesion and to political stability.[40]

As T. H. Marshall observed in his seminal study, citizenship as it developed in the context of the national community has defined the boundaries of belonging to a democratic polity. And though 'originally denoting residence within the protective walls of cities', in its modern expression it 'defines a community by establishing who may reside within the boundaries and who may not'.[41] Whether this historic pattern can, or for that matter should, be replicated beyond the nation-state, by detaching citizenship as affiliation, an ontological sense of belonging, from its exclusive location in the nation-state and investing it with civic patriotism towards a transnational polity, thereby widening the very meaning of political identity as it has been understood in Europe over recent centuries, has provoked lively debate amongst contemporary political scientists. Some scholars regard this novel prospect as more fanciful than feasible, seeing the very idea of meaningful political identity, an affective sense of belonging, membership and emotional attachment to a political community beyond the nation-state as merely idealistic, essentially unrealisable. In effect, a fallacy rooted in 'naive positivism', a reflection of the implicit teleology of thinkers cast in the Kantian mould, and convinced a priori 'that each stage of citizenship development is superior to the previous one'.[42]

The case that is made against the idea of transnational membership, for ontological affinities beyond the national polity, draws on ideas about the dynamics of politics and power that figure in the realist narrative of international relations. Realist, and latterly neo-realist, thinkers make much of the 'contrived' nature of political identity, the fact that even during 'the age of nationalism' citizenship as an expression of political identity and belonging, of political affiliation, affinity with a historical political community was constructed, for the most part by those agencies that control cultural transmission, from education authorities to the print media. According to this narrative, political identity is a culturally diverse process, its outcome altogether more contingent than the advocates of putative transnational identity contend. The construction of political identity is problematic even in stable and historically rooted national communities, as the recent constitutional history of Canada, Belgium, Italy, Spain and the United Kingdom well illustrates.[43] How much more difficult then, they maintain, is it to construct and sustain a meaningful sense of socio-cultural solidarity and political membership in a confederation of such culturally diverse nation-states as EU27, a continent after all whose history is redolent with communal strife, and whose politics still manifests competition over national interests. Moreover, a polity lacking any clear idea of its ultimate political destination, its final geographic and cultural boundaries, let alone one that is sure of its 'destiny'.[44]

As the realist narrative sees it, political affiliation depends on instilling in citizens a sense of personal security, yet the provision of public order and personalised welfare in the traditional sense of redistributive social policy and public goods remains very much the preserve of the nation-state, and staunchly defended as such in the Convention, where Prime Minister Blair's representatives – expressing only what many other political leaders were thinking – invested much political capital in what Blair chose to describe as his government's non-negotiable 'redlines' issues in these same policy areas. Those who argue from this perspective dismiss as illusory the prospect of transnational citizenship based either on shared cultural values, or the provision of public goods beyond the nation-state. This in essence is what Raymond Aron meant when he famously wrote that 'there are no such animals as European citizens'.[45] Political identity, the sense of solidarity and membership of a political community remains in this theoretic narrative firmly located in the nation-state, acknowledging the fact that 'citizenship has been linked inextricably with nationality and with the nation state'.[46]

However, this is by no means the end of the debate. For the very fact that identity is constructed does offer encouragement to those, theorists and political activists alike, who challenge what they see as non-reflexive and ahistorical conjecture, the cold rationalism and narrow functionalism of this increasingly 'outmoded' narrative. More progressive thinkers point out that over long centuries of political organisation, the locus of power and authority, the dynamics of real politics and the architecture of governance have shifted in response to the structural and cultural forces that continue to shape and remake human societies. Of course, even those who are disposed to the idea of change in the way mankind conducts its governance and organises its politics concede that the idea of political affiliation is more likely to resonate with citizens in a polity whose public policy outputs have immediacy for the individual, and its affective quality is more likely to be emotionally potent in so far as it impacts directly on their life chances. History would seem to bear this out, for far-flung empires whose governance is remote have proved to be unstable, their subject peoples preferring, as Aristotle caustically observed, to be governed by those closer to them, more like them in culture, speaking the same language than by strangers. But 'remoteness' and even 'difference' is no longer quite what it was, its meaning is open to question as never before because of the cultural and technological shifts that are a direct consequence of accelerating globalisation. It may be a cliché, but it is valid nevertheless, that the world is shrinking, diachronically as well as geographically. What may once have been seen as alien and remote may come to be seen as familiar and proximate. Although to allow this is by no means to underestimate the extent of the challenges facing those who advocate transnational identity.

A sense of solidarity between people beyond the historical (the sociologically, geographically and culturally defined) boundaries of the nation-state is difficult to imagine and even more difficult to realise. It certainly requires more to bring it about than merely idealism or wishful thinking. There has been little by way of cultural integration in the EU to match the progress made in commerce, or for that matter in political co-operation, and this may be one of principal weaknesses of the European project. Jean Monnet seemed to admit as much when he acknowledged the critical role of culture for cementing solidarity, ruefully observing that 'if I were to begin [the process of European construction] again, I would begin with culture'.[47] Of course, whether Europe's political establishment would have permitted any such intrusion into the cultural fabric of national political life, or what that might have amounted to had they done so is a matter for conjecture. Monnet did at least realise that promoting a sense of solidarity between Europe's diverse peoples requires something more than functional co-operation, or even common political institutions. For empathy does not come naturally to people even in established political communities, as the history of statehood well illustrates.

Despite some imaginative initiatives in the field of cultural policy and higher education Monnet's successors have made as little headway in this highly sensitive matter as he did. The European Constitution hardly takes us much further. As we have seen in the discussion at Chapter 8, conferring EU citizenship based on a limited catalogue of rights barely begins to inculcate a sense of individual affiliation to 'Europe', let alone feelings of collective solidarity across borders. Citizenship that confers rights but imposes no duties or obligations that might deepen the citizens' sense of personal obligation is as challenging a prospect now, intellectually as well as practically, as it was when neo-functional theorists and federalist activists alike were making confident yet for all that somewhat ingenuous predictions during the Community's foundational period about eventual 'cultural spill-over'.[48]

The evidence for popular sentiments about 'Europe', for a broad sense of transnational solidarity is scant, notwithstanding the findings of *Eurobarometer* surveys that show a degree of familiarity in public opinion at large with the idea of 'Europe'. Whenever the issue of 'Europeanness' is raised with the public, their response indicates widespread ambivalence, and in some cases outright resistance. The experience of 'Europeanisation' at the affective level, the process of value-change and normative shift as this affects individuals, other than those insiders who colonise the European institutions and in effect run the show is, to say the least, equivocal. And it confirms just how much continues to divide Europeans from one another, precluding any easy sense of solidarity, or even feelings of common endeavour.[49] The extent of this identity problem, what Europeans actually share by way of common values and aspirations, and perhaps more to the point what they think they have in common, was clear to see in the wrangle over the wording of the Preamble to the Constitutional Treaty.[50]

Yet for all that, there are some grounds for optimism about the prospects for refashioning political identity, for realising a degree of European identity to complement rather than to replace pre-existent identities rooted in national or ethnic affinities. One *Eurobarometer* survey showed that 48 per cent of respondents admitted to a composite, part-national, part-European identity, though only 4 per cent of this opinion sample identified themselves as being exclusively European, with some 48 per cent preferring to define themselves primarily or in some case exclusively in terms of nationality. The degree of perceived 'Europeanness' varies as between countries: for instance, in France, Spain, Italy and Luxembourg less than 40 per cent of respondents chose to define themselves as solely 'nationals', whereas more than 50 per cent of respondents did so in Greece, Finland, the United Kingdom and Sweden.[51]

The same polling organisation in an earlier survey found no convincing evidence of a trend in any particular direction, noting that 'the public generally does not become more likely to feel more European and less likely to identify with its own nation (or vice versa) from one measurement to the next'.[52] Concern about the lack of democracy in the EU, the problem of input legitimacy, does, however, trouble a growing number of Europe's citizens, with adverse consequences for a sense of transnational identity. The same survey found that while there is a rise in public mistrust of politics, 56 per cent remain content with democratic procedures in their national democracies, with the highest levels of dissatisfaction with EU govern-ance recorded in Sweden, Denmark and the United Kingdom, whereas a mix of motives (mistrust, lack of knowledge of issues, dissatisfaction with the Parlia-ment's role) contributes to consistently low turn-out in European elections.[53]

There is telling evidence, too, of declining support for the European project, though the figures fluctuate according to circumstances. Approval of EU member-ship reached 72 per cent across the Union in spring 1991, only to decline there-after by some 20 per cent, though things may be improving here, with the level recorded in the autumn 2000 survey higher than the 46 per cent recorded in the survey of spring 1997. Again, there is no clear trend across the continent, with support levels higher in some countries – notably, in Luxembourg, the Nether-lands and Ireland – than in others such as Sweden, Austria, Finland and the United Kingdom. Nevertheless, reassuring is the fact that rising public uncertainty about European construction is not reflected in any widespread decline in respondents' trust with regard to the Union's institutions.[54] The survey findings indicate that respondents do have a generally positive orientation towards the institutions: the Parliament, for instance, achieved a trust rating of plus-26 per cent in the 1999 *Eurobarometer* survey, the European Court of Justice of plus-21 per cent and the Commission of plus-5 per cent, though again these aggregate figures show national disparities. For example, trust in the Parliament and the Commission is lowest in the United Kingdom, followed by Germany, Sweden and Denmark, with the highest trust ratings recorded in Italy, Ireland and Portugal. A recent *Euroba-rometer* survey provides telling evidence of the gap between the Union and its citizens, with 59 per cent – a rising trend – indicating that they do not feel their voice 'counts', and less than 25 per cent feeling involved (and 72 per cent unin-volved) in EU affairs.[55]

The recent rise in Euroscepticism evident during the ratification campaigns, and not least in countries once very supportive of European integration, does require some explanation. One interpretation of ambivalence about the European project is simply the sheer pace of cultural and social change, and in particular a marked shift from materialism to post-material values.[56] Cultural change impacts on poli-tics, affecting both political allegiances and attitudes to politics. The familiar, largely unreflective tribalism of traditional party politics that sustained permissive consensus at every level of European politics throughout long decades of mass politics is gradually being eroded by the effects of accelerating social and cultural change. The characteristic hierarchical style of EU politics has by no means disappeared, but it is being challenged by altogether new public attitudes and aspirations for politics and governance.[57] Survey data indicate, for instance, that generational change and rising social mobility, growing prosperity and increasing educational opportunities have weakened the tribal base of party politics.[58] The public's growing indifference to, its impatience with the EU's political class vented during the ratification campaigns is but one manifestation of increasing iconoclasm in contemporary politics. Changes in political culture have made their mark, contributing to the present crisis over the European Constitution, not least the fact that many are reluctant now to take on trust a constitutional bargain made without public consultation, or even much by way of informed debate.

The impact of social change on contemporary political values is reviewed in research by Michalski and Tallberg, who make some important claims about the significance of what they describe as post-modernisation – in effect, post-material rather than materialist values and public policy preferences – on the general public's receptivity to the idea of what it means now to be 'European'.[59] Modernisation is defined here as material preferences, the public's long-standing preoccupation with redistributive issues, employment, taxation and welfare benefits. Of course, these things still matter – and greatly – to contemporary Europeans, but in line with the post-materialist thesis developed by Inglehart and others these two writers maintain that at this advanced stage of modernisation citizens are now making 'other demands on the European Union compared with those of earlier generations'. Citizens are now in the process of acquiring post-modern and post-materialist values that amount to 'a shift from scarcity values to security values; a diminishing effectiveness and acceptability of bureaucratic authority; a rejection of the West as a model, and the collapse of the socialist alternative; a growing emphasis on individual freedom and emotional experience, and rejection of all forms of authority; and a diminishing prestige of science, technology and rationality'.[60] Something of this is apparent in contemporary popular protests, the activities of new social movements and other citizens' initiatives, and it was plain to see, too, in the public's responses to what many saw as an imposed and 'top-down' European Constitution. Moreover, a constitution that simply failed to address their most pressing concerns for security, protection from the vagaries of globalisation, climate change, arbitrary terrorism, health scares and so on.

The shift from material to post-material values has particular salience for contemporary politics, and it is confirmed by the growing alienation of citizens from politicians as revealed in decreasing turn-out figures in elections at every level. Post-modern values question familiar nostrums, not least 'respect for established authorities, a hierarchical picture of society, and subordination of the individual to the group', those very values that had sustained permissive consensus and permitted the EU political elite to make bargains between themselves without reference to the citizens. Society now gives greater primacy to democratic values and individual freedom, not least the 'rejection of traditional, bureaucratic, and hierarchical authorities'.[61] As such, Michalski and Tallberg conclude that 'to a higher degree than before, European citizens subscribe to values such as the primacy of the needs, desires, wills of individuals', and by the same token they are more inclined now to question the 'traditional centres of power and authority'.[62]

This by no means anti-politics, but in its many contemporary expressions public scepticism or indifference to 'Europe' does represent an unprecedented challenge to those privileged insiders who have run things thus far. And this, in turn, gives rise to a politics without deference to those 'experts' who for so long have claimed to 'know best', replacing it with a kind of populist politics characterised by grass-roots activism, popular initiatives and populist causes, 'active and direct political participation through, for example, petitions and manifestations, instead of traditional and institutionalised forms of political participation, such as elections, parties and trade unions'.[63]

This phenomenon may well seem threatening, and it is undoubtedly irksome for mainstream politicians more used to public acquiescence, preferring to draw on a deep reservoir of authority rooted in the public's almost instinctual respect for their status and power. Yet this challenge does not necessarily bode ill for the development over time of new expressions of solidarity between citizens. The decline of tribalism, those familiar arrangements whereby politics and public policy are filtered or refracted through the powerful lens of elite preferences, and over time the emergence of a new politics rooted in more diverse and popular causes might help connect grassroots movements and citizen-led initiatives across borders, with potential for embedding a sense of solidarity beyond the narrow bounds imposed by historical nationhood. Of course, this outcome is far from being certain, but linkages between European social movements and other civil society actors have just such potential. This has important implications, too, for how Europeans see themselves, and over time for reimagining political identity. The critical issue here, however, is agency, as it always is where change is concerned. In this case, how European solidarity beyond historic boundaries perpetuated by long-standing cultural affinities rooted in ethnicity and with separate and often competing histories, all sustained by protracted separation, might take root and in time even flourish.

## The view from below: challenging political authority or rejecting Europe?

Europe is being transformed at every level by new social, cultural and political forces, such that 'value change is becoming part of the European citizens' daily lives'.[64] This is far from being a uniform process, nor does it necessarily presage a transformation in political allegiance from the national to the European polity. The evidence from opinion surveys shows rising popular concern about all sorts of issues, from employment and social dumping, to the environment and the looming pensions crisis, all of which fuels public disquiet not only about the way the EU works but for whom it works. Public opinion is far less convinced than it once was about 'the Union's capacity to provide the prosperity that has been its hallmark for much of the past fifty years [for] in a climate of sluggish economic growth, persistent high unemployment and deteriorating public services many continental Europeans fear that the pro-market solutions coming from Brussels could make their lives even more insecure'.[65]

A cross-national attitude survey for the European Commission's Forward Planning Unit designed to measure support for the various indices of European integration has acknowledged a growing disparity between politicians and people, and concludes that: 'The time of the European population's permissive consensus to European integration is most likely over.'[66] This same survey shows 'a quite generalised dissatisfaction with the way in which the democratic system works, both on the national and European level. Demands for amending the "democratic deficit" of the Union have been heard since some time. Popular demands for more participation in the European system are likely to grow louder – a challenge to which the Union will have to respond or else a deeper degree of detachment between the EU and the European citizen is likely to be the result'.[67] Yet the same survey found evidence of ambiguity in public attitudes towards the EU, and residual uncertainty has undoubtedly contributed to the public's anxieties about the European project.

At the same time the challenge to political authority such as occurred during the ratification campaign is hardly the same as outright hostility to the idea of Europe. What public anxiety about the European Constitution does reveal is that citizens expect more rather than less from the EU, though this does not in itself mean support for closer political union. Indeed, there is widespread suspicion of supranationalism, what Lee Miles has described as 'Federo-scepticism', the very idea of being locked irrevocably 'into an integrative and constitutional pathway leading to a "federal Europe"'.[68] This may well be so, but it is not necessarily the same thing as endemic Euroscepticism. By and large, the general public remains rather more receptive than hostile to the European institutions, even accepting of the necessity of governance at the European level. By the same token, they acknowledge that in a globalising world 'many of our contemporary problems know no frontiers', with 'the national debate in many EU member states ... conducted on a basis which recognises the incapacity of individual countries to deal effectively with contemporary problems'.[69]

What, then, is the public so concerned about? The same polling data show endemic anxiety about governance that, on the one hand, is exerting greater influence on the people, yet is widely perceived to be remote, barely democratic and unduly complicated. Moreover, governance that privileges insiders and special interests, to the exclusion of the wider public interest. The findings of a recent Commission-sponsored *Eurobarometer* survey (July 2006, from a sample of 29,230 people interviewed in late March and April 2006) were not entirely pessimistic about prospects for a positive outcome from the imbroglio over the Constitutional Treaty. For this survey shows that although a majority of citizens want substantial revisions to the Constitution, almost half of the sample (47 per cent) preferred to see some form of renegotiation, with only a small number (13 per cent) who wanted it set aside *sine die*, with a further 23 per cent in favour of the Constitution as it stood. These findings are similar to those reported in the previous *Eurobarometer* survey (autumn 2005), which again showed support for the general idea of a European constitution as fairly constant: 61 per cent of those respondents favoured a European constitution, only 22 per cent were opposed to it, with the remainder recorded as 'don't knows'.

Opinion on the subject is as variable as it ever was, however, within the various member states, with 70 per cent-plus support recorded in Hungary, Belgium, Germany and Italy, but less than 45 per cent in favour in Denmark, Finland, Austria, the United Kingdom and Sweden. A significant finding in terms of the Constitutional Treaty's then indeterminate status was the fact that a majority of both French and Dutch opinion was broadly favourable to the idea of a European constitution: 62 per cent in France and 59 per cent in the Netherlands. So far, so good for those who support a European constitution. However, neither of these Commission-sponsored surveys asked the key question: namely, what do respondents think about the Constitution already agreed by EU leaders? A Commission official explained this omission by conveniently claiming that Brussels did not seek to intrude into the debate on the Constitution in the member states, and that publishing a 'political opinion poll' on the delicate matter of the Constitution would be deemed by governments to be gratuitous interference.[70]

What is clear from the polling data is that the public throughout the Union is by no means entirely hostile to the idea of future constitutional progress, a fact that suggests that constitutionalism here may well have a future, the reticence of present leaders notwithstanding. Indeed, the public at large seems to be both receptive to new ideas about third-level governance (albeit on the basis of realism, a way of improving life chances and enhancing personal security, rather than idealistic notions of internationalism), and seemingly amenable to bold but at the same time imaginative leadership from their politicians. Where does this leave matters now? Recent events by no means represent an abrupt end to the process of building a European polity, and certainly do not indicate any widespread appetite for rolling back the clock *ex post facto* to a time of unalloyed nationalism, other than in a handful of countries where there is visceral Euroscepticism. What these events do seem to show is a temporary hiatus rather than an abrupt halt to constitutionalism, predictable turbulence as citizens confronted by all manner of uncertainties and facing formidable challenges to their sense of security and well-being look, so far in vain, for inspiring or at least imaginative leadership, whether at the domestic or at the EU level, or both. These surveys also reveal that the public at large is not instinctively anti-EU, but rather is 'far less sure about what the Union may become', a mood of uncertainty about constitutional futures and a public mindset that may well 'restrict its future growth'.[71]

There is no singular view about the prospects for closer political union in Europe. The data show instead discrepant support for the European project depending on the respondent's socio-economic status. Differences in receptivity to Europe measured vertically by social status are at least as significant for determining the extent of popular support for the European Union as horizontal differences between the various member states defined in terms of competing national interests. This much was clear from any objective analysis of public opinion during the referendum campaigns. Revealing here is an in-depth study of changes in Danish attitudes to the EU that illustrates the variability of public opinion, and helps explain its dynamics. Denmark is an interesting case study precisely because it is a country with a reputation for Euroscepticism, though opinion there is now more fluid on the issue of European integration.[72] In fact, recent polling data reveal a complex and changing picture, indicating wide variations in receptiveness to Europeanisation. On the one hand, some socio-economic groups (notably the more prosperous, the better educated and professionals) exhibit more favourable attitudes to the EU, and are more inclined to adapt their definition of the national interest to accommodate European integration compared with the early 1990s. Whereas farmers fishermen, blue-collar and public-sector workers, pensioners, youth and the socially excluded remain cautious to say the least, with some respondents continuing to express unremitting hostility to 'Europe'.[73]

Changes in public attitudes and values with regard to European integration are by no means confined to one or even to a handful of countries, but reflect a general picture throughout the Union. The more socially advantaged groups tend for the most part to be better disposed towards the Constitutional Treaty, not out of idealism but for entirely pragmatic reasons.[74] They see the European Union as quite simply the best means for addressing current problems and for meeting future challenges.[75] This empirical work confirms that 'the most significant determinant of attitudes towards the EU specifically, and Europe more generally, is the level of education, and social class determined by employment position'.[76] Flockhart's study concludes that long-standing differences in the attitudes of elite and 'ordinary' respondents have widened in Denmark over time, especially so since the end of the Cold War, with the better-off/better-educated respondents generally revising their formerly instrumentalist view of the EC/EU as little more than a common market. Whereas this narrow instrumental view is still widely subscribed to by Danes who lack these same social resources.

How to explain, then, such discrepancies in public attitudes? Elite respondents in Denmark as elsewhere have been exposed to what theorists in the social constructivist narrative see as normative conditioning, a process more broadly alluded to by some academic commentators as 'Europeanisation'. What this means is that cultural referents, as reflected in a general shift in values, norms and attitudes – in its turn, a response to changing experiences and life chances – in time overlay mere functionality, so that the better-informed and usually more socially advantaged and economically privileged citizens are more inclined to see the European Union in political terms, 'as a project for peace and stability'. Non-elite respondents on the other hand continue to 'view the EU in purely pragmatic terms, and as primarily an economic actor, with membership of the EU primarily an economic necessity'.[77]

This research shows the extent of the challenge facing those who hope for more favourable public attitudes to the EU, and also gives some clues to the prospects for bringing that situation about. These findings suggest, for instance, that indifference or hostility to a European constitution is not necessarily a permanent feature of the political landscape, that it might be overcome by more assured leadership if the politicians, who after all frame the political agenda, give the public positive cues on the big policy issues, make the case for Europe in practical terms that resonate with the public. This is not something that many of them have been wont to do, at least thus far, or anyway not with much conviction. And to do so not by trading in banalities or nebulous idealism, but by promoting the EU in terms of enlightened self-interest. Flockhart does suggest that there is still everything to play for here, indicating that immutable Euroscepticism is not the public's primary political instinct, its natural reflex to the prospect of closer European integration. What this study does show instead is an altogether more fluid situation, whereby public opinion might be influenced, indeed persuaded about the benefits of more rather than less Europe, even in a traditionally Eurosceptical country.[78] There are degrees of resistance to Europeanisation, wide variation in public attitudes, but the plain fact is that few citizens are irrevocably hostile to the project.

Opinion surveys everywhere show considerable variability in public attitudes towards Europe. On the one hand a natural reticence about change, but on the other acceptance of at least some tangible benefits accruing from European integration, though here, too, elite respondents are better disposed to 'Europe' because better informed and more likely to perceive themselves as gaining from the project.[79] Events, too, play a part, impacting on and changing public attitudes. Cathartic experiences, climactic shocks, 'critical junctures' caused by momentous events that do not conform to conventional expectations or paradigmatic predictions about how the world 'works' have the capacity for altering both the individual and collective mindset.[80] Change thus may bring about an 'ideational vacuum' whereby previous norms and policy models no longer offer any clear guidance as to future direction, during which time 'several competing idea-sets will be promoted through a number of different diffusion mechanisms known as coercive, mimetic and normative' forces for change. Pressure to adapt to novel circumstances, to meet new, externally imposed policy challenges gives rise to such disjunctions with 'normality', thereby bringing about culture shifts that hasten new expectations about how the world works, not least its governance.[81]

The process of change that is described here is both viscous and inordinately complex, but opinion leaders do have political capital and other resources, and as such the capacity to be key agents for managing structural change and the cultural shifts that follow it, those processes that give rise to new values and validate norms more appropriate for dealing with changing and challenging times.[82] The EU may not be quite at this critical juncture yet, and even if it is, its political leaders, both in the member states and in the European institutions, have hardly risen to the occasion. Even so, the imbroglio over the Constitution has at least raised a debate about the meaning and direction of European integration, and not least about its appropriate constitutional order. What has become clear – and the crisis over the Constitution confirms the fact – is that the public can no longer be excluded from this conversation. The fact that this debate on European 'futures' is no longer confined exclusively to the privileged insiders who have so far driven the EU project merely adds to the urgency of the situation.

The challenge for Europe's politicians is to respond to these pressures, as well as to realistically review the prospects that face Europe as globalisation accelerates, with who knows what consequences for governance, the labour market, the environment, commercial competitiveness, personal lifestyles and collective welfare systems. This in turn requires nothing less than a wholesale review of those abiding values by which the continent's centre-right/centre-left political establishment has charted the territory of party politics and competed for domestic electoral support during the half century and more since the end of the Second World War. The familiar consensus between the mainstream parties that has prevailed in Western Europe since 1945 no longer provides a reliable compass for mapping, let alone for responding to these incipient challenges. Politicians need to rethink familiar shibboleths, and this requires greater openness about what is a stake, altogether more honesty and less hubris than we are used to from politicians, a degree of humility, too, about the capacity of conventional economic and political models for addressing contemporary problems.

The debate on the European Constitution is central to this conversation, for it goes to the heart of the problem of public trust, the need to engage minds about how this remote governance works, what are its benefits for 'ordinary' people, why reform of institutions and decisional procedures is needed, and, no less, the need to rethink the objectives of the European project. One thing is clear from the recent struggle over the European Constitution: a new constitutional order can no longer simply be imposed from above, public consent assumed as it has been in times past. Public support and more important public involvement is now a minimum requirement for carrying the people, for securing their consent to be governed by authorities located beyond the national polity. The decision of the European Council at its meeting in Brussels in June 2007 to carry on as if the public's rejection of the Constitutional Treaty matters naught, a minor inconvenience to be overcome by reverting to familiar bargaining between insiders, simply misses the point.

This much at least is apparent from the wreckage of the Constitutional Treaty. Public resentment about the Union's remote governance is hardly new. There had been for some time 'a general dissatisfaction with the way in which the democratic system works both on the national and European level'.[83] What these latest events do signal, however, is growing concern with legitimacy, prompting one commentator to predict that 'popular demands for more participation in the European political system are likely to grow louder – a challenge to which the Union will have to respond', or risk further disappointing its citizens.[84] Political leaders cannot ignore, they must respond to this insistent clamour, and be bold as they contemplate a major overhaul of EU governance. The latest attempt to shirk the challenge, to feign normality, pretending that all that is needed is a tidying of the extant treaty base simply will not do. As Jean Monnet candidly observed in his *Mémoires*, great statesmanship is all about working 'for long term goals which eventually suit situations as yet unforeseen'. Another European statesman who practised decisive leadership, Napoléon Bonaparte, put the test of leadership in somewhat blunter terms, with his proposition: '*On s'engage et puis on voit.*' So far, the Union's political class has failed this critical test of statecraft and by some margin, neglecting to win minds, let alone hearts on the issue of 'Europe'. An abiding sense of disengagement exists between the political class and those whose interests they are supposed to serve, a lacuna of trust and credibility that is tellingly acknowledged in the reminiscences of a former Commission official written after the Constitutional Treaty suffered the ignominy of a double rejection in spring 2005. This 'insider's view' is both forthright and unvarnished, and as such is worth quoting at length. Alastair Sutton has observed that:

> Since my arrival in Brussels 32 year ago (but especially since my departure from the Commission 16 years ago …), I have been acutely aware of an 'insider/outsider' mentality in Brussels and in the EU generally. In my view, this phenomenon can be attributed in part to the unique supranational nature of the EU and its institutions. Historically, civil servants coming to Brussels from a Member State felt (quite rightly) that they were engaged in an unprecedented historical venture. I myself felt this in 1973 working with German and British officials who had been fighting on opposite sides (sometimes fighting each other!) … only a few years before. A certain European camaraderie and 'elitism' developed as a result of this. The Commission fought to establish and expand its role as the exclusive initiator of law and policy, the 'guardian of the treaties', the community's external negotiator in international economic affairs and as the European civil service. Although it took much longer, the European Parliament – at least since 1986 – has become a major player both formally and informally, as co-legislator with the Council and as 'watchdog' in terms of financial and political propriety over the other institutions, in particular the Commission. It, too, has been fighting to strengthen its institutional position … I think that national interests (in the wider sense of this term) and certainly the ordinary citizens of the Member States were perceived as being of secondary importance by 'insiders' in the European project. The situation has changed dramatically since 1992 (with the crisis over the ratification of the Maastricht Treaty), with far greater attention being given to transparency, subsidiarity, devolution, 'repatriation' of policies such as competition policy etc. This seems to have gone unnoticed by public opinion however. As the 'European project' has widened and deepened, so (somewhat ironically) it has moved further away from national public consciousness … It is clear (at least to me) that the Constitution is a symptom (and not the latest one) of a wider malaise about the content, direction and democratic underpinning of European integration. It is ironical that, given the role of European integration in restoring political stability and economic prosperity in Western Europe to unprecedented levels … and in contributing to the collapse of the Soviet empire with subsequent reunification of the European Continent … the EU should be facing its present crisis … Strong and charismatic political leadership is more necessary (but less in evidence) than ever.[85]

The Union's present leaders would do well to heed this timely warning. For in spite of launching a Convention, supposedly to widen debate on European governance, the process has barely touched the public. A *Eurobarometer* poll conducted after the Convention had completed its work found little evidence of public knowledge about what had actually occurred there, despite showing underlying public support for the general idea of a Constitution.[86] There was no discernible sense of the public being engaged in the constitutional process, and the outcome – in effect, a new treaty between the member states – can hardly be said to constitutionalise what passes for politics in the EU. More than that, the unduly elitist legacy of EU constitutionalism (discussed in Chapter 2), a mainly covert procedure where influence is monopolised by elite actors, deprives the process of what Sajo calls 'constitutional enthusiasm', whereby 'emotionally grounded identification with the constitution' ensures 'unconditional bindingness' and emotional support for the process from the wider body politic.[87]

The fact is that the EU's constitutional process continues to lack the popular support essential for what should be a democratic endeavour. This is because, as Weiler sees it, unlike constitutionalism as practised in democratic nation-states it 'has never been validated by a process of constitutional adoption by a European constitutional demos, and hence, as a matter of both normative political principles and empirical social observation, the European constitutional discipline does not enjoy the same kind of authority that may be found in federal states where their federalism is rooted in a classic constitutional order'.[88] What Weiler means by this is that the all-important 'who decides, who decides' question that determines the outcome of any constitutional endeavour is still a matter that in the EU is confined to the few, not the many.[89] For though the Convention on the Future of Europe did broaden the constituency that reviewed these constitutional arrangements, at least compared with preceding IGCs, the *pouvoir* or authority driving the process remained to all intents the prerogative of a narrow group of stakeholders, and lacked any direct involvement from European civil society. The recent attempt in Brussels to move the process forward, issuing a mandate for yet another IGC to reform the treaties, confirms that even a new generation of political leaders sees the only feasible solution to constitutional impasse as 'business as usual'. One is reminded here of Talleyrand's rebuke to the vapid Bourbons, that they had neither learned, nor had they forgotten anything from their eventful past!

The abiding impression from these recent events is that constitution-making in the European Union, even if it is now more firmly in the hands of politicians than of unelected Justices, is still essentially a matter for insiders. A direct consequence of this is that the case that needs to be made for giving the EU proper constitutional ballast has largely been overlooked. To close the Union's legitimacy deficit requires giving substance to those democratic norms and procedures that are elemental for any contemporary constitutional order. Of course, this is by no means easy to realise in a polity lacking demos, one without a clear sense of political identity. The absence of affective identification between citizens *per se*, and between them and the European polity was plain to see once the fate of the Constitution passed from the privileged insiders who negotiated it to those voters who gave their verdict in the referendums. At the outset the Convention was proclaimed as an unprecedented exercise in open, democratic and even deliberative constitutionalism, but in truth it was far from being that. Commentators who had acknowledged the Union's constitutional shortcomings, and who saw the Convention's potential as a 'community-mobilising moment', one that should it become a regular feature of European constitutional politics would institutionalise a democratic conversation between 'princes' and people that might over time facilitate 'the bonding of political community' throughout the Union, were in the end disappointed, altogether less convinced about its capacity for bringing the people closer to the constitutional process. The eventual decision to revert to an IGC to resolve outstanding institutional questions, to side-track the problematic issues raised in referendums on reforming the treaties merely serves to confirm their disappointment.

In the circumstances, the very idea of democratic constitutionalism seems to be at best remote, 'a long term gambit'.[90] Not that the public are crying out for their own version of Philadelphia. They naturally remain cautious about the constitutional project. But how could it be otherwise, unused as they are to being consulted, wary of what many see as populist gimmickry from above, and deprived of an imaginative steer on the big issues at stake in the endeavour to give the Union firm normative foundations. In these circumstances, they are likely to regard any invitation from 'above' to engage in a constitutional endeavour with either indifference or suspicion. It will take time, but more than that careful handling by the politicians and a more plausible agency for ensuring widespread public consultation than the Convention proved to be, to convince the public that a European constitution resembles a democratic contract made between 'princes' and people.

To date this has hardly been the priority for the Union's political class, or at least not on the available evidence. After some four years of intensive constitutional activity at every level, much of it in public and on the record, the results of a flash *Eurobarometer* survey published to coincide with the presentation of the final draft of the Constitutional Treaty to the European Council at Thessaloniki (June 2003) make for sober reading. These survey findings show that some 55 per cent of respondents had still not even heard of the Convention, and only 32 per cent knew that its objective was to produce a constitutional treaty.[91] At most, popular support for the current constitutional endeavour has been no more than second-hand, sold by politicians to the public for their own convenience, and much less a bold enterprise in constitutional reform than merely 'tidying up' the Union's ramshackle governance.

The failure of the Constitutional Treaty to positively appeal to the citizens is a stark reminder that future constitutional endeavour must engage with the wider public, not least because constitutional politics at this level lacks the emotional resonance it has in national polities, a fact plainly seen in the intense constitutional deliberations in, for instance, Belgium, Canada and South Africa, and in many other countries where constitution-making is central to the very idea of defining and of belonging to a political community. Recent experience suggests that an altogether different approach to constitutional politics is called for in the EU.[92] Few would demur at Sajo's observation that 'no constitution can be legitimate in the free world if it does not serve democracy', and that furthermore 'constitutional regimes will suffer a legitimacy deficit if not operated according to the Community's expectations of democracy'.[93]

The key here is how to engage the public, a challenge to the ingenuity as much as to the integrity of politicians. A daunting but by no means a hopeless task even at the European level, where democratic input into the constitutional process is, to say the least, a novel and untried idea. The public's exclusion from constitutional politics at the EU level, as Sajo and other close observers of these events point out, 'does not mean that there is no interest in the *common European future*'.[94] Certainly, there is no easy solution to the abiding lack of solidarity between the people and 'princes', or between Europe's peoples themselves across historical national boundaries. There are, however, some possible ways forward. One indispensable requirement is for politicians to explain at the very least the nature and purposes of the European Union, outlining its benefits to citizens in those aspects of public policy and security they clearly value. And likewise to be candid about the challenges Europeans will face in the coming century. What, then, are the prospects for Europe's political leaders engaging these public concerns, and how best to make the case for 'Europe'?

## Engaging with the public and making the case for 'Europe'

Recent events make it clear that the political class can no longer take for granted public support for their conduct of European affairs. Citizens are increasingly aware of the impact of European governance on their interests, as workers and consumers, as rights-bearing citizens and so on. This situation is hardly novel. The appeal to self-interest rather than to ideals has been essential from the outset for making the political case for 'Europe' prior to every country's accession and indeed thereafter. Community membership has long been promoted in terms of 'practical economic and political welfare benefits', with politicians dwelling only incidentally on 'the supplementary dimensions of "governance" and "polity"'. Selling European integration to the public at large has, as Miles points out, been primarily about pragmatism rather than principles, and to date has deliberately avoided 'the language of constitutions'.[95] The governance question was peripheral, a matter for intergovernmental treaty-making rather than polity-building, and as such it was much more about 'the construction of a constitutional self-mandate' than it was about conducting a public conversation on the design pace and direction of the European project.[96] This was less a conspiracy by self-interested politicians than it was a convenient way for them to retain a relatively free hand in the management of Europe's affairs in what domestic electorates saw and many still do as 'abroad', dealing with the 'significant other' and not as such about 'us'.

Over time much has changed, though there is still a discernible lag between events on the ground and how the public perceives them. People are no longer quite so detached from EU governance, nor indifferent to the considerable autonomy permitted to politicians under the present rules for conducting affairs. Concern about the way the Union is managed, the impact of its common policies on people's lives and life chances is clear to see in opinion surveys, as it was during the ratification campaigns. To a degree, this reflects generational change, in as much as 'a new generation takes peace in Europe for granted', and therefore has quite different expectations of the Union from their forebears. In part, too, this situation also reflects a growing sense amongst the public at large of failing, or at least flawed political leadership, the fact that those who steer the project in ever more uncertain times have simply 'not articulated a convincing answer to the question of what the EU's purpose is in a globalised world'.[97]

Some contemporary observers explain the problem here as follows: 'The EU has a serious existential question when its citizens cannot remember why it was created, they do not appear to like what it has become and they are frightened of what it will be in the future. It used to be simple. ... The European political and economic integration process launched with the Treaty of Rome in 1957 was barely questioned, as it created the prosperity and trust needed to raise western Europe from the rubble of the second world war.' This somewhat providential view no longer applies, for the EU has become 'a victim of its own success [as] war receded into the distant memory'. Meanwhile, citizens' expectations are enhanced as basic material security needs are taken for granted, in as much as 'the economic prosperity and comfortable lifestyles of Europe's social model, underpinned by the EU's single market, have already been banked by Europe's citizens [and] as the Union's original emotional power over its citizens – its ability to deliver post-war security and prosperity – has waned, they started to see the EU more as a bureaucratic machine'. And 'on to this faceless machine [were] projected many of the fears and suspicions of the Dutch and French electorates', and indeed those of European citizens elsewhere.[98]

What is clear from this situation is that the case for Europe, and no less the case for a European constitution, can no longer be made by default, relying on public indifference, or at most on benign approval for something that generally seems to work, at least on the functional level. Instead, this case has to be made directly, for people are wary of, more than they are overtly hostile to, the EU. No one in authority should underestimate the difficulties of making a positive case for Europe. Explaining the tangible benefits from, for instance, monetary union, the Single Market, common foreign policy and security co-operation, or for that matter any other common policy, is only a part of the challenge here. All of these are important issues, and they do figure on the public's radar. At the same time, they are not discrete issues disconnected from more fundamental questions. On the contrary, they relate to normative and intrinsically constitutional questions, not least the issue of values that must figure a priori in any constitutional endeavour, namely the ethical rationale for the exercise of public power. In this case, the elemental question of how, and indeed why, public power should be exercised beyond the nation-state, and the practical challenges associated with it. There is a pressing need now to respond to public anxiety about the direction of the European project. This in turn requires that politicians face up to critical issues concerning democracy deficits, institutional efficiency, the allocation of competencies between the Union's centre and the member states and no less about citizenship and identity. All of them issues that are central to the project of constitutionalising the European polity. A difficult task for sure, but not an impossible one so long as political leaders confront the challenge head-on. Yet this is precisely where the current crop of EU leaders has been found wanting.

The failure to engage in plain speaking about European futures is, in no small measure, a direct consequence of timid or ineffectual, and occasionally of venal leadership. Reticence about taking on and challenging the Europhobic doom-sayers, those who in resisting 'more Europe' paint a far-fetched scenario of a European super-state, who trade in simplistic conspiracy theories, objecting to the slippage of yet more power to 'Brussels', the supposed surrender of sovereignty defined as national birthright. The former Irish prime minister, John Bruton, now EU ambassador in Washington, identified one significant cause of the Constitution's defeat as 'overblown' Eurosceptical rhetoric, populist bombast that has taken a greater toll of public tolerance of European integration than it might have done, precisely because it has met little more than casual rebuttal from complacent politicians. The perception amongst some of the EU's public of the Constitution as a more radical project than it really is, in fact one that threatens nothing less dramatic than relinquishing national sovereignty, should have been addressed directly by the politicians. Having made their own bargain on the issues that mattered most to them, they displayed familiar insouciance, complacently assuming that the public would follow their lead as in times past. Once this extravagant interpretation of the European Constitution gained credence with the public it has proved difficult to dispel. Indeed, some of the Union's key actors, notably the Commission and federalists in the European Parliament, seem to prefer the myth to mundane reality, perhaps hoping that by talking up progress towards 'ever-closer' regional integration they might somehow breathe life into a flagging federalist project, exaggerating for their own purposes the drive towards supranationalism. Indeed, some of them even seem to believe their own rhetoric.

Meanwhile, Eurosceptical voices, doom-mongers from the very opposite viewpoint, have contributed to the welter of misinformation by making the case, as they do after every revision of the treaties, for what they choose to see as insidious supranationalism ratcheting up centralised power. For neither federalists nor Eurosceptics gain much for their respective ideological positions from telling it as it is, trading in qualified constitutional baggage or talking in conditional rather than extreme terms. And certainly not for admitting, as one leading European newspaper sees it, that the use of 'the term "constitution" for what is essentially a consolidation of the treaties is in reality a misnomer'. Or by acknowledging that 'titles like European president or European foreign minister scarcely disguise the fact that they are only mandated delegates of the collective decisions of member states, with whom power still essentially resides'.[99]

Neither side of this ideological divide sees any mileage to be gained by conceding the merely pragmatic case for European integration. Yet the plain fact is that 'the EU is a hugely helpful, part-integrated, partly co-operative framework, but with minimal public funding compared to any member state, limited foreign policy co-ordination, and no EU common defence worth talking about'. Nor do these politicians on either side of this ideological fault-line gain anything from confirming what most EU insiders already know, that 'the indictment of the EU as a fledgling super-state, and presaging a militarised Europe, a new imperialism even, is way off the mark, and is the product of the overheated imagination of ideologues and small parties trying to attract support by appealing to anti-European prejudice, fuelled by some imported newspapers'.[100]

The task of explaining complicated realities in plain language, of justifying to a fickle electorate worried about the apparent seepage of political authority from the nation-state – still after all widely regarded as the *locus classicus* of political authority – to a distant, inaccessible and mostly remote level of governance 'abroad' is daunting enough. How then to explain to publics so far removed from transnational governance the benefits that accrue from pooling rather than merely surrendering aspects of national power? More to the point here is how this more complicated reality might be explained, and in plain political language quite different from the specialised parlance of the technocratic insider or policy wonk; and likewise how to vindicate this situation to electorates wary about, or at best indifferent to European integration? No less challenging here is how to debate these politically sensitive issues without raising the spectre of relinquishing democratic power over public policy to mostly invisible and non-accountable forces, and not just on 'marginal' technocratic or regulatory issues but increasingly in aspects of public policy that matter greatly to citizens as rights-bearing stakeholders, whether as workers, employers, consumers, welfare recipients and so on. This, then, is the extent of the challenge that faces the EU political class.

These are hardly trivial questions. Debating the appropriate locus for governance for exercising public power touches on the critical issue of the scope and quality of democratic life in a fast-changing international order. These issues are challenging for contemporary governance everywhere. There is the need to reassure publics concerned about the delegation of critical decisions to international regimes, where outcomes that favour special interests are negotiated and policies designed largely out of sight of effective public scrutiny, beyond the democratic controls that apply in the national polity. At the same time, there needs to be acknowledgement that insidious globalising forces are here to stay, and require for their effective management governance beyond the nation-state. As Lee Miles sees the dilemma facing the EU here, the politicians must 'appease a largely "federo-sceptic" electorate', whilst simultaneously pursuing 'ambitious European integration that brings the EU "closer to its citizens"'.[101] This is no easy task, and the Convention was just such an opportunity to engage the public in a democratic conversation about these very issues, though in the end it failed to rise to the occasion, settling instead for a more familiar outcome, a negotiated trade-off between national and institutional actors, the usual bargain concocted between vested interests, and with the big three member states dominating proceedings.

The need to address the challenges facing governance in the global order through closer co-operation between neighbouring states that, after all, have many interests in common is something few EU governments, or for that matter most citizens would deny. To acknowledge the fact of unprecedented regional co-operation is one thing, but to accept that this must somehow lead to a fully-fledged federal polity is something else entirely. Many EU citizens who accept the necessity for European institutions and acknowledge the need for common policies draw the line at the idea of European statehood as the ultimate destination of European integration, yet for many the very word 'constitution' implies just such an end-state. As Miles sees it, although citizens 'often feel happy with an evolving supranational EU with blurry edges, one that is supposedly distinct from a "federal Europe" that has overtly constitutional implications', in many EU countries, 'EU constitutionalism in the public domain is equated with a "process of becoming", leading precisely to a "federal Europe" [and] because of this, the language of EU constitution-building is sometimes regarded largely in negative terms by both EU governments and electorates alike'.[102] This fear of the political unknown goes some way to explaining public antipathy towards the European Constitution.

The public's negative reaction to the Constitution reflects widespread concern about how that historic bargain was concluded, as much as the actual details, not least the lack of consultation, the failure to comply with those norms and procedures that are the benchmarks for democratic governance everywhere. Opinion surveys confirm that though the public generally prefers a more 'democratic Europe', a significant majority of citizens did not regard the European Constitution as improving the Union's democratic life.[103] These findings ought to make uncomfortable reading for politicians. At the practical level, the public's verdict in the two key referendums was to say the least inconvenient for the politicians, in so far as it prevented straightforward ratification of their narrow bargain. But if we take the long view, this is not necessarily a bad thing. For one thing, the crisis over the Constitution showed that how the EU is governed does matter for many citizens, and that the public is no longer indifferent to it and will have their say. If the politicians are to remotely succeed in convincing the public about the need for change in European governance they must learn to listen and respond to these concerns. Consultation, and more than that a democratic conversation on matters that affect citizens' life chances and general well-being, is indispensable for carrying the public with them on the formidable challenges that lie ahead.

This conversation has to take place sooner or later, and better sooner. It will be a more convincing encounter if it is institutionalised in what some commentators describe as a European public space. On the face of it this may seem a fanciful prospect, even far-fetched as things stand. Yet legitimacy, the fundament of 'good' governance, requires opportunities for public voice at every level, providing ways for citizens to express debate and reconcile their competing preferences. The normative, but equally the practical case for stable governance applies as much to the conduct of governance beyond the nation-state as it does to government within its bounds. Indeed, the legitimacy question is even more critical for transnational governance precisely because decision-making and the allocation of values beyond the boundaries of the nation-state is so far removed from the people, both spatially and in terms of their everyday experience of 'normal' politics, and for that very reason it lacks the familiarity that sustains national government.

The case for a transnational democratic order, a European public space, has to be made in just these terms. It follows *ipso facto* from the growing impact of transnational governance on European public policy. The problem here is how to realise meaningful political participation beyond the nation-state. The agency question is central to this matter: whether and how democratic politics can operate outside the familiar institutional nexus of the nation-state. There have been no plausible initiatives so far for establishing such a transnational public space.[104] In fact, at the level of everyday politics 'the nation state has remained the primary focus for collective identities', the principal locus for popular participation in politics, the arena for 'public debates ... and notions of citizenship'.[105] This situation is regarded as 'normal', yet is increasingly out of kilter with the times; it hardly corresponds to current realities. As Koopmans sees it, there is a growing 'discrepancy between Europe's institutional development, its increasing competencies and influence on Europeans' condition of life'.[106] It is undoubtedly the case that social and cultural change brought about by accelerating globalisation has altered the rules of the political game, but crucially public perceptions lag behind these realities. What then are the prospects for a genuinely European public space to better reflect these novel circumstances?

## Towards a European public space

European integration has enhanced the transnational dimension of public policy-making, but the relocation of some competencies away from the nation-state has not been accompanied by any significant development of a common European identity, let alone a sense of continental solidarity. If European identity does exist, it is confined for the most part to a vague sense of common endeavour amongst those actors most directly engaged with the EU policy process. Some commentators see this lack of a transnational identity as problematic for political legitimacy, because how citizens define themselves no longer corresponds with the location of public power, the fact that many critical policy decisions that impact directly on the public are now shared between governments at the European level. This is as much a problem for political theorists as it is for practitioners, for as Held (and others) observes, conventional social scientific thinking 'too often privileges the territorial and the national over the super-territorial and the trans-national'.[107] But actual governance no longer corresponds to this theoretic narrative, and the fact that important policy issues are not exclusively the responsibility of governments has significant consequences for the legitimacy of EU governance. Good governance rather than merely efficient governance depends, or should depend, 'on active engagement, acceptance, and legitimacy amongst the citizenry'.[108] This situation hardly applies to the governance of the EU.

One solution to this problem is to establish more effective means for giving the citizens voice. A European public space may be too ambitious a prospect in present circumstances, nevertheless some means for facilitating an exchange of views, for deliberation about current issues by representatives of European civil society, the principal stakeholders after all in an already expansive EU governance, is essential for ensuring the public has a voice. How might such a public sphere be defined? Most commentaries here tend to focus on principle more than on procedure, on theory rather than practice, but at the very least we must take due account of the fact that policy-making is no longer confined within national boundaries. As one contemporary commentator sees it: 'We can speak of a Europeanised public sphere to the extent that a substantial – and over time increasing – part of public contestation neither stays confined to the national political space (the European public sphere's inner boundary), nor extends beyond Europe without referring to it (the outer boundary of the European public sphere).'[109] Prescribing the necessity for a European public sphere is one thing, but this hardly begins to address the question of agency, of ways for bringing it about. How then might such an ambitious project be realised?

The concept of a European public space has featured increasingly in recent debates about democratising the EU polity.[110] There is no simple formula for making such transnational linkages. For one thing, this is unknown territory in terms of how we have come to understand democratic politics in the post-Westphalian state system. Borders are increasingly porous, penetrated by all manner of transnational networks, border-crossing and transactions.[111] The consequence is that many, and some important, governance functions are now transferred to international agencies, as Beck sees it 'operationalised as interconnectedness'.[112] The outcome is a transnational system linking once quite distinct and separate national spaces.[113] Social change, technological innovation and cultural shifts have contributed to freeing contemporary society 'from its national moorings', though precisely what form the new politics will take 'and what holds it together or regulates it is increasingly at issue'.[114] One thing is patent amongst much that is uncertain: that finding ways for giving effect to public voice beyond the nation-state is a challenge to the political imagination, for it requires agency beyond the normal procedures and conventional arrangements of mass democratic politics. Moreover, to establish a form of civil society, to institutionalise political deliberation, to conduct a conversation between politicians and citizens beyond the national space requires something more than making spatial connections across physical borders, for 'trans-national space is not necessarily bounded, cohesive or geographically contiguous'.[115]

Those who have contemplated the prospects for democratic transnational politics make much of historical (and especially national) barriers to effective European-wide discourse, and even more to collective action beyond the nation-state. The plurality of languages, entrenched cultural differences, the persistence of primordial identities and the lack of a shared history are all seemingly insurmountable obstacles to inclusive and democratic engagement between peoples, and no less between peoples and 'princes' beyond the national polity. There is, nevertheless, some evidence that things may be changing. Some commentators see the widespread use of the English language as a potential European, and even a global lingua franca.[116] Even so, there is predictable resistance to the very idea of a lingua franca from those elements in contemporary societies who resist the centrifugal pull of cultural homogenisation, or who otherwise regard vernacular language as a distinctive badge of identity. These critics are quick to point out that most people prefer to converse in their mother tongue. Moreover, cultural agencies as well as political movements readily mobilise in defence of linguistic heritage, seeing it as a symbol of singular identity, and even progressive voices are sometimes raised in defence of cultural exclusivity, a gesture of defiance to the stultifying 'sameness' of globalisation as they see it in an otherwise turbulent and incomprehensible world.

The tribunes of post-nationalism may well celebrate the virtues of diversity, whether of language or any other aspect of culture alongside much that is 'common to all', but this in itself does not overcome the problems, and in fact highlights an abiding difficulty with this progressive narrative. For some post-nationalists simply assume 'a degree of linguistic and cultural homogeneity and political centralisation that cannot be found in many well-functioning democratic nation states', let alone at the European level.[117] In fact, such a medium for common discourse, the means for a transnational conversation if not yet for collective political action at this level remains elusive. And without such a medium for the exchange of views and the circulation of ideas how can transnational discourse occur, let alone the inception of a political space beyond the nation-state? This question is especially pertinent in view of the recent clamour over the European Constitution, and not least public disquiet about the citizens' exclusion from this project. On practical grounds alone, it would seem that the idea of a European public space is far-fetched because in practical terms at least the public sphere continues to 'coincide with territorial borders in Europe – and that, in the absence of a European demos held together by a common European identity, no European public sphere can exist'.[118]

This has been the situation thus far, and for the most part it still is, though things may yet change. Social and cultural shifts do impact on how people see governance, and with this comes the revision of former certainties, the *idées fixes* of politics. To allow this possibility is one thing, but there are certainly more questions here than answers. What is required, for instance, to reimagine political identity in Europe? And for that matter, what passes nowadays for European identity? Whatever it might be, it seems that it is something less like demos.[119] European nationhood or *ethnie* is not remotely possible given the legacies of its recent history, and it certainly goes against the grain of the European project as it has developed since the Second World War. The absence of 'normal' democratic politics at the EU level, governance that lacks the customary procedures for adversarial government and opposition, or the competitive dynamic of party politics as practised in democratic states, and the lack, too, of democratic agencies at the European level to connect the public with their governance through the medium of a functioning party politics, all serve to undermine the prospects for democratic politics beyond the nation-state.

One obstacle to establishing participatory democracy at the European level is the patent fact that the EU is simply not this type of polity. In so far as European issues impact on the public, they do so for the most part indirectly, and even then in ways mediated by governments and national political parties, or by the national media. As such, they are translated into the altogether more familiar currency of domestic politics. Transnational political parties would be one vehicle for bringing about a Europe-wide debate on public policy, and for institutionalising a conversation between politicians and people, and between peoples across the continent about European futures, at a level beyond the nation-state. So far, however, though the Union's party families aspire to a transnational status they operate only at the level of the European Parliament, and even there political activity is influenced at least as much by a calculus of national interests as by transnational preferences.[120] The European parties have little impact and even less affective resonance with citizens, and for that reason they represent no significant constituency amongst the public at large.[121]

In these circumstances, party politics clearly has only a limited role to play in involving the wider public in a conversation across borders. In fact, some political scientists are much less convinced nowadays that this traditional agency is any longer suitable for engaging with the public, even in the national domain. Manin, for instance, unfavourably compares the party agency with the development of what he calls 'audience democracy',[122] a condition akin to what Peter Mair describes as 'populist democracy'.[123] These concepts refer to the relative decline in mediated public engagement with politics, a condition accelerated by the decline in public deference, and if not quite marking the demise of collectivist ideology then at least emphasising the greater individuation of contemporary socio-economic life, the growing inclination to 'bowl alone', the rise of 'me-tooism', each of them a facet of contemporary political culture that marks a decline in civic culture even in well-established democratic polities.

These are cultural reflexes that help account for the growing instrumentalism of public attitudes to, in turn shaping expectations about, politics. The public's rising impatience with politics and those who practise it, an increasingly volatile mood that lends itself to populist instincts or otherwise to disengagement from politics, clearly does not bode well for deliberative democracy, or for the prospects for realising a European public space.[124] In this narrative, political parties are by no means redundant as agencies for public engagement. They still have capacity for mobilising community interests, but these once powerful agencies that presided over Europe's great structural and cultural transformations of modernisation and democratisation are themselves being transformed in turn, as Kreisi sees it, by post-modern forces: from hierarchical organisations anchored in a durable ideological base, into 'a new type of party which, less dependent on traditional party bureaucracies and activists, establishes a direct link between the party leaders and their electorates'.[125]

This may be an unduly optimistic assessment, and even if it is accurate is by no means a uniform development, for it is more applicable to some parties than others and especially so to single-issue parties such as the Greens and populist parties of right and left, than it is to the mainstream 'catch-all' parties. What is clear is that citizens are much less dependent now on political parties for their information about policy and for their cues about politics generally, and they rely instead far more on independent media sources.[126] Detachment thus from traditional hierarchic parties, organisations ironically described by Robert Michels in his classic monograph as 'quasi-authoritarian agencies for democratic participation', is, in its way, a liberating experience. And it is one with potential for transforming the citizen from a mere partisan, a foot soldier for an ideological cause, into an altogether more demanding and increasingly discerning consumer of politics.[127] The case here can be overstated, however, and it frequently is.

Some contemporary commentators have made a more measured assessment of these developments, preferring to see this process as a shift in contemporary politics away from partisanship and towards rational choice, a situation where 'the citizen public no longer manifests itself during elections only, but [by having] a say every day between elections – in the form of opinion surveys, focus groups or all sorts of protest events'.[128] Elections and referendums, opinion polling and other forums for political consumers to exercise voice, those media forums that track the subtle shifts in public preferences, enhance the citizens' capacity to express voice, both individually and as a member of multiple and overlapping constituencies of interests: by such means do the public exerts influence on public policy, an ongoing and cumulate process that impacts on agenda setting in the public domain beyond the occasional exercise of the franchise. This form of political participation was hardly possible even a short time ago, and it empowers citizens even as it constrains the power and diminishes the authority of politicians. These same processes contribute to the commodification of politics, making its practitioners look less like statesmen and more like salesmen glibly marketing merchandise increasingly seen as devalued; not so much trading in noble ideas as seeking to maximise returns in an increasingly volatile market for votes, as tribal politics is replaced by the electorate's increasing instrumentalism. A direct consequence of this cultural shift has been to reinforce the notion of politics as short-term business, and by the same token to weaken longstanding loyalties to parties and ingrained belief systems, the ideological solidarity and electoral tribalism that has characterised party politics throughout the modern era, and to promote in its stead the idea of the elector as political consumer.

Of course, 'me-tooism' and 'me-firstism' are by no means the only instincts that motivate today's voters. As in any market-place, some consumers are more discerning, harder to please than others, some are more loyal to familiar brands, and some still motivated by ideals as much as by self interest, the sense of being part of a wider community of interests bound by shared values rather than mere 'possessive individualism'. And with these changes has come a shift in both the practice and the purpose of politics. The impact of cultural change on the conduct of democratic politics in Europe is apparent in increasing electoral volatility, a shrinking of the core electoral base of established parties, a marked decrease in political tribalism. In the process, the voter exhibits an unprecedented degree of autonomy from party allegiances, and this in turn has increased his political clout. By degrees the voter is becoming aware of that signal fact, but to date this sense of empowerment barely applies to politics beyond the nation-state.[129]

How then might the citizens become properly informed about public policy at the European level, if neither European nor national political parties any longer effectively perform the interlocutory function between governance actors and public? There are some signs of stirrings of a transnational politics at the grassroots level. One recent study of political mobilisation in contemporary Europe identifies a tentative trend towards the blurring of domestic and EU-level politics at the level of civil society, and observes that 'the action repertoire of the national actors in the EU member states has to a considerable extent become Europeanised' in ways that reflect the increasing importance of EU-level decision-making.[130] This may be a portent of incipient transnational politics, but it is one nevertheless that is confined, for the time being at least, to the practice of lobbying rather more than it is to political participation in any broader or more inclusive sense, at least as this is generally understood in today's mass politics.[131] It is certainly the case that many NGOs formerly active only in domestic politics 'have become multi-levelled in their activities', and that as such they 'bridge the different political levels within the EU polity, including those within the nation-state (national, regional and local) as well as trans-national and supranational European levels', and accordingly they 'co-operate strongly across the sector'.[132]

This is indeed transnational activity, but it is hardly widespread and remains limited as to its reach and impact. Moreover, it says much less about the emergence of an EU-wide, Brussels-based, trans- or supranational lobby than it does about the Europeanisation of specific sectoral lobbies representing national and sub-national constituencies, with organised interest groups rather than individual citizens 'providing a more likely avenue for public engagement in [EU] policy deliberation'.[133] At best, this development is moderately encouraging for those who advocate a European public space, but it is activity confined to committed activists who are already politically mobilised, and as such it hardly impinges on the wider public. The challenge, then, is how to reach out beyond the committed actor, how to engage the generality of citizens beyond their occasional participation in European elections, an activity that is anyway essentially passive even for those citizens who bother to vote.

What political opportunity structures might offer suitable opportunities for involving citizens in the critical debates about European futures? Some recent research suggests a critical role here for the mass media. The public have come to rely increasingly for their political information on that agency, albeit one with its own agenda. And one that though independent of party machines, is too often inclined to trivialise complex issues, and to stir up populism in pursuit of bold headlines and increased sales. The media certainly has the technological capacity for facilitating a conversation of sorts with and between the public on national issues, and 'under certain conditions [these] public debates can shape the timing and outcomes of policy decisions'.[134] However, these 'conditions' too often mean that the medium itself becomes the message, setting the public's agenda for its own narrow interests. The mass media through its direct linkages with the public is nevertheless a virtual public space, though undeniably one confined for the time being to the national community.

The media supplements but also challenges the claim of political parties to be the principal medium linking the political domain and the public at large.[135] In so far as politicians in mass democracy engage with the electorate they do so only indirectly, for instance in public meetings, at election rallies, on 'the stump' or at the hustings, and even then party functionaries are the principal conduit for such activities. These exchanges notably occur during general election campaigns, but they are only occasional exchanges and of brief duration, so that linkages between politicians and public, though not entirely displaced, are supplemented by the print and broadcast media. The media has become an important channel for mediating relations between politicians and people, framing issues, priming the 'consumer' of politics and public policy to consider the issues, setting agendas, critically reviewing leadership capabilities and so on. The media interrogates politicians on the electorate's behalf as never before, operating as a self-appointed yet none the less potent agency for public accountability as parliaments, faced by growing executive power, find it increasingly difficult to hold governments properly to account.

The media provides a critical lens on government. It is a powerful medium for public scrutiny, and even prospectively for public voice. The means it employs are varied, and includes investigative in-depth analysis that exposes politicians to closer scrutiny than they have ever before had to endure, by means of interactive on-air debates, organising petitions of listeners, readers and viewers on current issues, or vox pop phone-ins and text messages as part of prime-time rolling radio news programmes, and it leads the way in the latest fashion for 'blogging'. All of this activity highlights current concerns and amplifies citizens' voice. Moreover, framing public issues in this way is active rather than passive engagement in the political process, and it is a public service in as much as it primes citizens to 'identify problems and specify and prioritise their interests and goals'. And it is influential on outcomes because it directs public opinion 'towards causal and normative judgements about effective and appropriate policies in ways that tend to propel policy down a particular path and to reinforce it once on that path'. Furthermore, the media's assertion of non-partisanship – though highly dubious in some instances, risible in others – does help to legitimise not only its own political interventions, but also the activities of those 'actors deemed to have moral authority or expert status', reinforcing their claim to act in the policy field.[136]

In all of these ways the contemporary media adds to the capacity for public voice, even as it sometimes manipulates or distorts that voice for its own narrow commercial or political ends. Of course, politicians have adapted, learning quickly to respond to this challenge, many of them becoming media savvy, adept at the black arts of spinning issues to suit their own purposes, using publicity as a means for controlling the news agenda and as such retaining some leverage on public opinion. News management is a matter of concern for any political party seeking to modify the impact of such a powerful medium, with the resources to offer a fickle public either negative or positive cues on particular issues, and by these means significantly influencing political preferences.[137] Clearly, the media is no passive agency, content merely to report events, but one that engages directly with government and the public alike, determined to hold politicians to account, to challenge the official version of events, to scrutinise and even to oppose government as self-appointed tribunes of the public interest. This, too, enhances the media's potential to be an agency that facilitates wider debate about public policy, and it is a necessary, though by no means a sufficient condition for a public space.[138]

The media can thus enable the citizen to participate indirectly in politics, without either committing the time or expending the energy or other resources required for party political activism or lobbying, and indeed without even having to leave home. As such, it contributes to interactive politics, an essential precondition for a public space, though so far one confined to national polities. The reasons for this are patent: the lack of a Europe-wide print or broadcast media to facilitate a transnational conversation, commercial obstacles to launching a Europe-wide media, the plurality of languages, and not least the lack so far of any demand for such a media, other than from those insiders who study the EU or manage European institutions, and from some parts of the business community and the European policy lobby.

The media's role as a vehicle for public voice is limited even at the national level. For one thing the public's grasp of what are immensely complicated issues is limited, as is their attention span. The low boredom threshold of most citizens allows professional politicians and their *spinmeisters* considerable scope for managing public expectations, by manipulating information and selectively interpreting the policy agenda.[139] As we have seen above, declining partisan allegiance deepens mistrust, gives rise to cynicism about what parties say and how they present public policy. The relationship between politicians and public is altogether less predictable nowadays, in part because it is no longer mediated by powerful party machines that drill down into the community. This much is true at the national level, and is even more so at the European level, where political parties are but pale shadows of their national counterparts. Much the same can be said about European civil society, a nascent formation that offers at best only limited possibilities for political activity across borders.

Whether the media has potential for facilitating a conversation beyond the national community – a Europe-wide conversation no less – is the critical issue here, and one that has begun to attract the attention of academic researchers in several branches of the social sciences. Some who make the case for greater democracy at the EU level maintain that a European public space could, over time, become an arena for more effectively connecting remote elites and citizens as it does in national politics, a means for fostering transnational debate and on that basis for ensuring greater solidarity, or at least promoting greater commonality of purpose across national boundaries. The case being made here is that in the absence of effective pan-European political organisations worth the name, a Europe-wide media offers the best means for constructing a community of interests beyond the privileged circle of insiders and vested interests who presently run things. This in turn would furnish means for framing a common public policy, and likewise be a way of fostering a sense of shared interests across borders, in effect facilitating a Europe-wide conversation.[140]

As things stand, however, the case is less than convincing. The most that can be said here is that this medium has potential for crossing borders. The lack of any direct linkages between the Union's principal policy actors and the public, not least the absence of effective transnational parties, does enhance the media's potential as a purveyor of public information about European issues, information that is indispensable for turning passive and so far barely mobilised European citizens into more discerning and active EU stakeholders. A transnational media, or at the very least the national media operating more effectively than it presently does as a vehicle for raising public awareness of the Union's policy agenda, could, so those who make this case maintain, inform politicians about the state of public opinion. This would be a way to identify public concerns and preferences, and also a means for challenging those same politicians, holding them to account for their stewardship of the Union's affairs in much the same way as the mass media does at the national level. This activity would at least make the Union's policy-making process more transparent, informing the public about otherwise arcane procedures, and opening up covert decision-making in otherwise remote institutions that barely connect with citizens' everyday experiences.

This seems plausible enough, though it is an ambitious prospectus and by no means easy to realise. The media may well offer the best opportunity for informing the public about otherwise inaccessible governance, and it does exert influence over those 'insiders' who manage the Union's affairs. But the limits to this as an instrument for political mobilisation are clear to see. As Koopmans sees it, 'although a small number of resourceful and well-organised actors may gain access to European policy-makers directly (e.g. in the context of the Brussels lobbying circuit), most forms of citizens' participation through NGOs, civic initiatives, and social movements can only influence policy-makers by way of visibility, resonance, and legitimacy they may mobilise in the mass media'.[141] This may be so, but there are formidable obstacles in the way of effectively scrutinising those who hold power, monitoring how they use it and in whose interest, for turning the media into a viable, and for the citizen an accessible, European public space. Professional media-watchers have found little convincing evidence so far for a media-led conversation beyond the national political community, referring at most to the coexistence of separate, albeit complementary domestic spaces, a 'parallelisation of national public spheres in the sense that increasingly the same themes are discussed at the same time under similar criteria of relevance'.[142]

On the face of it, this may seem fairly unpromising, but it is at least a start. An examination of media content reveals that some issues are extensively reported by national media throughout the Union, and within broadly similar reference points and meaning structures, regardless of language and cultural differences. In the recent past, asylum/immigration, the impact of the euro on domestic living standards/prices, terrorism and security risks, demographic shifts and the consequences for welfare and pensions. Eastern enlargement and the prospect of Turkish accession and, not least, the European Constitution have all featured in national conversations throughout the Union. There is growing public recognition, too, of the interdependence of the domestic and foreign policy spheres.[143] As there is widespread anxiety, too, about the negative consequences of globalisation for the European social model.[144] This in itself might be encouraging for those who advocate transnational politics as a response to globalisation, the rise of powerful economic and political forces that are transforming national political economies, which the public are seemingly helpless to influence or control by normal democratic processes. The emergence of a European agenda of shared public concerns might be a portent of things to come, were it not for the fact that this same research also shows that the European media devotes far more column inches and broadcast time to national issues and events than it does to in-depth reporting of Europe-wide matters.[145]

The debate on the future of the social model currently taking place in almost every EU country illustrates this preference for compartmentalisation, with far greater emphasis given in national media coverage either to the defence of the national welfare state or alternatively to prescribing the virtues of labour-market flexibility and the neo-liberal values associated with it. These are issues that certainly relate to the wider debate about an emergent European, and for that matter a global social and economic order. Yet the media is reticent about broadening the scope of the national debate, or locating these issues in a transnational context, a fact that illustrates a general reluctance about encouraging in domestic audiences any sense of common purpose across Europe's historical frontiers, whether geographic, cultural or linguistic. To an extent this reticence reflects resistance by national elites to anything that they feel might weaken the primordial bonds of nationhood and with it their hold on power. At a more mundane level, it simply shows the narrow preoccupation of EU governments with market-making, after all one of the principal reasons these nation-states came together in the first place, but nevertheless one that remains for most governments a limited and for some even a conservative objective that resists a more socially progressive, let alone a redistributive agenda. As Rumford has observed, it is difficult to engender a meaningful sense of transnational solidarity around values that extol competition, and the Union's policy-makers – and most governments, too – set greater store by market-making and competitiveness in the global economic order than they do on social values.[146]

This much is undeniable, but it does have potential for a positive pay-off as far as European integration is concerned. The very fact that the Union's separate national conversations touch on the same broad concerns, the fact, too, that there are parallel policy agendas in the member states does suggest scope for connecting these national yet complementary conversations, and, as such, for launching a transnational conversation on the policy choices that confront all Europeans. Of course, there is and there will continue to be resistance to this prospect, and practical obstacles stand in the way of linking separate national debates, not least from the one agency that has capacity for overcoming parochialism. Certainly, much more is required for translating notional potential into a feasible transnational public space. Technology is a vital resource here, but it is only part of the answer. Technical know-how does make it possible to connect geographically dispersed audiences, linking national audiences in real time through the medium of broadcasting, as it does in the fields of sport or entertainment, from live European Champions League football, the Eurovision Song Contest or festivals of popular music, such as the events organised by the Make Poverty History campaign and staged concurrently in many countries to raise funds for charitable causes, with the electronic and print media covering these events simultaneously. Yet complementariness of this order hardly ever occurs in the coverage of politics.[147] The fact of increasing coverage of Europe-wide issues does not in itself make for a 'Europeanised' media, let alone a 'Europeanised' audience.[148]

The problems here are easy to see, much less easy to resolve. The plurality of languages is clearly a formidable obstacle to a common conversation, ensuring that even as the national media addresses the national public, priming them on the critical public policy issues, they do so largely in parallel, without connecting in a transnational discourse, a shared experience of politics across borders. Research findings show that the respective national media inhabit parallel universes, never quite connecting with an audience beyond the national community, even on issues that have political salience throughout the continent or beyond, issues that might otherwise reasonably be presented as part of a common narrative, indeed of a European conversation. Language obviously remains a barrier to transnational discourse: neither football nor popular entertainment requires vernacular language to communicate its message, for visible action, 'the event' itself, is its own lingua franca.

There are other difficulties that stand in the way of the media giving a transnational flavour to debates on public policy, and they are no less easy to overcome. The media is after all a business more than it is an educational agency motivated by a public service ethic. Above all it is market-driven, and for this reason sensitive to popular prejudices, which tend to be national or even regional in tone. Moreover, owners, shareholders and senior managers who between them determine editorial policy have their own agendas, preferring not to alienate paying audiences in the fierce competition for viewers, listeners or readers that determines profitability derived from lucrative advertising revenue. For all of these reasons the media are reluctant to confront public expectations about how politics is conducted, diffident about challenging the customary boundaries of the public space as their audiences understand it, loath to go against the grain of public prejudices because they are quite aware of the business costs of declining audience ratings should they sponsor causes or ideas the public are indifferent to or hostile towards.

The evidence for this is clear to see in the way the media handles these issues. Framing public issues continues to occur almost exclusively at the national, or even at the sub-national (regional or local) level, and hardly at all in terms of transnational frameworks.[149] A recent study of television news reportage confirms as much, noting that 'the number of news stories from other European countries lags far behind that of domestic and non-European new items [and] editors do not regard the EU area as a space that deserves more attention in coverage terms than the world beyond Europe'. This has consequences for defining target audiences, 'who' or what is 'European', for 'if the formation of a European "we" is regarded as desirable, it is not helped by the lack of attention other Europeans are given in domestic news bulletins'.[150] At best, then, national media coverage of politics is more inclined to report issues by giving primacy to what they choose to see as national interests.[151] One development that might mitigate parochialism is greater and more constructive media coverage of what are defined as European issues, reporting public issues of mutual interest across borders.[152] But seemingly not yet, for to date both the reportage and the public consumption of information about politics and public policy is framed primarily in terms of national debates. In the process, putative connections across national borders are diminished or lost entirely because they mostly go unreported. In these circumstances it is difficult not to concur with Koopmans view that 'as long as the European dimension remains hidden from the public's view, one cannot remotely call such debates "Europeanised"'.[153]

Facilitating simultaneous media debate across borders on issues of mutual concern is only part of the solution to opening a European public space. Another essential requirement here is what media theorists define as 'the similarity of meaning structures'. In effect, putting in place 'a trans-national community of communication' in which both those who voice opinions and those who receive them acknowledge one another as legitimate participants in a shared discourse about matters of mutual concern.[154] This, too, is a challenging requirement for transnational discourse, and one that is difficult to realise. The growth in political communication, the increasing availability of public information about issues with political salience across European borders is not in question here. Yet the fact of a community of interests across historical borders barely registers at the grassroots of politics, and it has resulted in neither increased support for the idea of Europe or for the European institutions. On the contrary, the acceleration of European integration and the fact that it attracts public attention at all has made the issue of closer Union, of 'more' Europe even more controversial. The French referendum is a case in point. Several hundred books and pamphlets about the Constitution were published and many were sold. There was regular and detailed media coverage of issues. Yet none of this served to reassure the public that the EU was on the right course, nor did it persuade voters to back the Constitution. The European dimension of public policy remains similarly discounted amongst the wider public, notwithstanding the fact, noted in the foregoing discussion, of marked similarities across EU borders as to which social groups and age cohorts are more and which less inclined to support European integration.[155]

The quickening pace of regional integration should at least increase the prospects for a Europe-wide conversation, attracting both advocates and opponents of the trend towards greater Europeanisation of public policy. But things are never quite that straightforward, and the facts paint a variable picture. Support for European integration is greater among party/state actors than it is among civil society actors such as NGOs and the traditional social partners, including economic interest groups and the media, the very agency that according to this narrative is supposedly to be the conduit for a Europeanised public discourse. Even within the party/state category, support is highest amongst the most powerful governmental actors and lowest amongst those most directly in touch with the public such as parliamentarians, local elected representatives and the grassroots members of political parties.[156] As Koopmans sees it: 'For all the idealist talk in certain pro-European circles about the EU as a protector of the weak against the encroachment of the evil nation-state, the [research] results indicate that the more weakly institutionalised civil society actors, as well as those actors within the core of the political system that depend more closely on a mandate of the populace tend to be much more sceptical about European integration than the "powers that be" from which Europe is supposed to protect them.'[157] Yet this is precisely the target audience for a media-generated Europe-wide public space. It should come as no surprise to close observers of EU affairs that the debate about Europe is dominated by party/state actors, as indeed was the situation in the Convention or in the IGC that modified and then adopted that Constitutional Treaty.[158] This is precisely where the media could make a difference, opening up these important issues to a wider audience, providing citizens with better and detailed information than it presently does. Yet the European media hardly seems disposed to play that role, or at least not quite yet.

The media's wholly inadequate coverage so far of the European policy agenda or of the admittedly complex workings of EU governance is hardly surprising in view of its general preoccupation with national issues. This is only a part of the explanation, however, for the lack of a public conversation at the transnational level. The public itself is increasingly reluctant to be led on the issue of Europe, understandably cautious about making connections across borders because unused to looking at politics or policy issues from a transnational perspective. The resources issue is compounded, then, by what we might call cultural resistance. The public lacks the political resources, the wherewithal to engage across borders, and it is disinclined even to think about public issues from a European perspective.[159] Whether this reticence is cause or effect is the critical issue here, and undoubtedly the lack of developed structures for involving the public in a conversation across borders on issues of concern to every European, regardless of their national location, is a major constraint that inhibits commonality of concern. It is likewise a considerable procedural obstacle in the way of building a public space beyond the nation-state.[160]

Research by professional media-watchers lends support to this pessimistic conclusion, confirming the lack of engagement between politically mobilised civil society actors and EU-level political opportunity structures, and especially the isolation of those who represent the most socially disadvantaged groups in European civil society. In so far as the media does address both the broader question of European futures and particular policy issues of concern to publics throughout Europe, they tend to do so either by using inaccessible language, codes that 'turn out to be highly elitist' and calibrated for insiders. Or else they simplify issues to the point of banality. This much was apparent in the media's coverage of the Convention. Reliable information is indispensable for public reflection, yet the public was poorly served by the European media during the Convention and afterwards.[161] By and large, press coverage was limited, dull, overly simplistic and frequently biased. This merely served to confirm the public's bewilderment, their detachment from the Convention, and it contributed over the duration to rising public disquiet with the constitutional project that peaked during the ratification campaigns. The British tabloid press, in particular, excelled at its usual rough trade of peddling myths, alarums and pure invention, serving up a familiar diet of conspiracy theory and supposed national betrayal, portraying the constitutional endeavour as a thinly veiled plot by closet federalists determined to impose a European super-state. And one supposedly bent on depriving national citizens, especially those in 'these islands', of their ancient liberties, with some fantasists even predicting the abolition of the monarchy! Even the 'quality' press, so-called, though offering more balanced and detailed reportage, tended to dwell on the national implications of particular issues rather than on the broader implications of the various proposals for reforming EU governance.

Another informative survey in this same research programme has examined the impact of public claims-making in relation to the EU constitutional endeavour.[162] In this case the research team looked for evidence that might confirm the existence of a public constituency on European issues, by using the Constitution as a test case. Their conclusions point to a familiar paradox: that although 'Europe' is increasingly visible in everyday life, the very fact that it appears to ordinary citizens as remote, beyond their reach or influence, detracts from any sense of public empowerment. This much was apparent during the ratification debates, and it undoubtedly contributed to the mood of rebellion that resulted in the 'no' verdicts. Though as we have seen, the public's rejection of the Constitution by no means signalled renunciation of the European Union, let alone of the 'European idea'. The problem here was not so much a shortage of public information, for the media did after a fashion report the issues. Rather, there was and there remains a palpable sense amongst the public at large of a lack of voice, of strictly limited opportunities for influencing those elites who manage affairs and determine outcomes, a dearth of political agencies for public engagement. And a sense, too, that those agencies that do exist for such purposes are monopolised by powerful, well-resourced insiders, those vested interests that have always colonised EC/EU political opportunity structures and dominated its policy networks.

In these circumstances, the public do not feel empowered by incipient Europeanisation, for they are hardly consulted about available options and their concerns for the most part are taken for granted even as the EU polity is actively engaged in shaping ever more aspects of public policy, with important decisions taken in Brussels that affect citizens' quality of life and life chances. The public's concerns here are not so much confined to fears about 'Brussels' or a European super-state – though media priming has raised these particular spectres in the public's mind – but rather about the role of politicians *per se*. European-level governance appears to many citizens to strengthen the hand of the nation-state as much as that of other privileged institutional actors, especially those executive actors who almost exclusively manage EU policy at a level beyond the reach of national representative institutions such as parliaments, NGOs and civil society actors. Whereas for their part, civil society actors who engage with the public policy process are confined, and even then only notionally, to the national political arena, where many important policies are now ratified rather than actually decided.[163] This same research concludes that the process of 'Europeanisation tends to make public debates less inclusive and less egalitarian', and in fact contributes to the citizens' sense of a democracy deficit at the EU level. The media is culpable here for it might play a more positive role, starting with its critical functions of framing the debate on the public policy agenda and priming the public in the national domains by providing more and better information on issues of common concern to national audiences and European neighbours alike. By this means the media could contribute significantly to a Europe-wide public space, facilitating a conversation without borders on those issues that matter to all Europeans.

As things currently stand, the media does contribute to the Europeanisation of the public debate about the present and future challenges facing the continent, but only marginally. In the meantime, 'the true nature of the democratic deficit of Europeanised political communication seems to lie in who gets access to this emerging Europeanised public arena'.[164] If the EU political class is to even remotely begin to engage the public in some sense of a transnational conversation about common futures, their future governance, including the options for a future constitutionalising of European governance, whatever form this might take, this information deficit must needs be addressed and urgently. The media does have the capacity for contributing to a European public space of sorts, but whether and indeed how that public space might develop as a medium for conducting a transnational conversation seems for the time being at least to be a remote prospect. Structural constraints and not least cultural resistance continue to stand in the way of pan-European solidarity.

## Constitutional futures?

We are left with more questions than answers concerning the prospects for Europe's constitutional project. The immediate issue of reforming the Union's institutions to better cope with unprecedented enlargement was resolved with the agreement of the June 2007 European Council in Brussels to launch a new IGC mandated to amend the extant treaties. But it is clear that the reversion to familiar top-down solutions indicates a retreat from the transparent and deliberative constitutional process launched at the Laeken Council in December 2001, and as such hardly begins to address the problems discussed above, especially the gulf that exists between politicians and people. After the shock of the referendum votes had been absorbed, a new cohort of political leaders in the principal member states rallied as it always seemed likely that they would do, summoning sufficient political will to revisit reform, though only as familiar and covert bargaining between elites, activity not remotely resembling democratic constitutionalism. Normal service of sorts was resumed as far as the political class was concerned once the realisation took hold that the constitutional crisis, though troublesome and unprecedented as far as EU 'crises' go, had not entirely derailed the reform project. Even during the dog days of 2005–6, when the referendums had seemingly brought the Union to an unprecedented low in its fortunes, there was clear evidence that it was functioning much as before.

At the height of the crisis, one eminent historian of European integration observed that the EU was hardly 'in danger of falling apart without [the Constitutional Treaty]', and confidently predicted that 'failure to implement the Constitutional Treaty … would not be disastrous for the EU [for] the Constitutional Treaty is desirable but not essential; the EU would be poorer, but not unworkable, without it'.[165] Of course this same argument might be reversed, for even if the Constitutional Treaty had survived the ratification process intact and unscathed, the crisis averted, the Union's endemic polity problems, those particular yet connected issues of governance we have reviewed above would have remained. For this is, above all, a polity that lacks popular legitimacy, and one that is perceived by most of its citizens to be remote and out of touch with their own concerns.

The issue of legitimacy has been there from the start, though much less problematic while the Community was concerned more about market-making than with governance, the 'authoritative allocation of values' within 'the black box' as David Easton famously described it. Even as the Community embarked on 'ever-closer' political union in the aftermath of the Single European Act and the Maastricht Treaty, and the administration of things became by degrees the governance of people, endemic democracy and legitimacy deficits were not seriously addressed by the politicians. These same issues were certainly not high in the priorities of those who negotiated the Constitutional Treaty, nor are they for their immediate successors, who, after waiting out the aftershock of the post-referendum 'crisis', have seemingly reverted to type, setting aside democratic constitutional endeavour and replacing it with the sort of covert trading over narrow insider preferences that has thus far characterised EU polity-making. Improving decisional procedures and institutional efficiency, reviewing the allocation of competencies between member states and the Union, sharpening the Union's capacity as an international actor, are all critical matters for accommodating the demands of enlargement and responding to the challenges of globalisation.

No informed observer of EU affairs would dispute that these are important matters, or that they require urgent attention. But so do those normative issues that go to the core of any polity that claims to rest on democratic principles: democracy and legitimacy deficits, subsidiarity and citizenship. The ratification crisis may be over, but the issues that came to the fore then, and not least the sheer sense of disconnection between politicians and people already acknowledged at Laeken and yet barely addressed during the Convention or at the following IGC, remain as urgent concerns. These same issues will surely return to the fore at some future time, and with who knows what adverse consequences for the progress and stability of the European project as the public come to terms with the decision of the European Council to set aside concerns raised in the referendum campaigns everywhere in the Union, and instead to bring in much of the 'failed' Constitution by the back door and without public consultation.

Doing nothing about these issues is simply not an option, or at least not if the Union's political class wants to carry the people with them as they navigate some tricky waters ahead. Even as these same politicians continue to resist what they see as dangerous and populist experiments, a reform prospectus that in their view is wholly inappropriate for meeting current global challenges, and anyway one that is not feasible in Europe's contemporary political culture, they must acknowledge the need for change, the flexibility that Talleyrand had found wanting in his Bourbon monarchs. What might be called the 'Lampedusa principle' applies here, the position of the instinctual conservative who is also a realist, and thus obliged, however reluctantly, to come to terms with ineluctable change: that 'if we want things to stay as they are, things will have to change'. As this precept applies to the EU, it suggests a pressing need to restore credibility to common governance, the politicians responding to public anxieties the better to ensure the popular legitimacy that is essential for any democratic polity to function with due authority. Jean Monnet understood the importance of connecting the project with the pressing concerns of ordinary people. As his biographer observes: 'His civilian approach was much closer to the outlook of the citizen than that of the servant of the state, bureaucratic or otherwise. ... His insistence on treating as a source of wisdom what he had just been told by the postman, the labourer or the hotel doorman ... arose from the feeling that the final yardstick was the "individual", whom he appears to have associated with the upright citizen of Cognac', Monnet's birthplace. As Monnet himself said 'we are uniting people, not forming coalitions of states'. Those who succeeded Monnet in building Europe have entirely missed the point of that prescient utterance.[166]

The ratification campaigns served due warning on the Union's political class that a political order that assumes a compliant and complaisant public, the persistence of permissive consensus, tacit consent accorded to leaders long used to operating out of sight of and largely unaccountable to the public, is nowadays a regime without due legitimacy. A polity demonstrably lacking public support, that denies its stakeholders 'voice' cannot expect to acquire the legitimacy indispensable for stable and efficient governance 'at home', or for endorsement of its claim to represent its 460 million citizens in those international forums which now take many of the critical decisions that shape the global order.

What is required from the Union's political leaders in troubled and changing times is less complacency and greater engagement with citizens about the regional and global challenges ahead. Constitutionalism by default, the way the EC/EU has previously changed its rules, can neither reassure a restive public nor legitimise the actions of politicians. What is missing here is a constitutional procedure that both speaks to and represents a wider range of interests, responds to the public by listening to them. Public unease about yet another 'top-down' political bargain was apparent from their reaction to what politicians assumed would be straightforward ratification of the Constitution. The Brussels European Council that set the course for the latest Lisbon Treaty has not altered this fact in any significant degree. This is why a constitution, a contract between governors and people that maps powers and allocates competencies, the 'who does what and with what effect' questions that every democratic polity has to confront, is the only convincing way to restore public confidence in the Union.

The need for a constitutional settlement that engages with the wider public, rather than simply taking it for granted as it presently does, is as necessary now as it was when Laeken first broached the prospect, even though the current leaders are mostly in denial about this fact. However, it has to be a constitutional outcome that, unlike the enterprise launched at Laeken, actually relates to the citizens, addresses their concerns and responds to their anxieties, involving them by way of proper representation from civil society. Above all, it must be a democratic process that ensures the public's voice is heard more clearly than in times past. The point is well made by Maduro that every political community, whether a state or a non-statal polity, 'needs a permanent public and reflexive discourse on its political values [and] constitutional texts normally provide the basis for that discourse [for] they provide a common platform of agreement on the basis of which political conflicts assume the nature of competing rational arguments on the interpretation of shared values and not the character of power conflicts without mutually accepted solutions'.[167]

This 'common platform of agreement' is precisely what was missing from the EU's recent attempt to reform its governance. Or at least, a platform that reflects public concerns as much as those of privileged insiders, the vested interests who have steered the project from the start. At best, the Union offers its citizens a modern variant of benevolent despotism, a philosophy and procedure of governance aptly captured in the terse epithet of Charles III, king of the Two Sicilies (and later king of Spain), who boasted: 'Everything for the people, but nothing by them.' Clearly, this is no way to manage affairs in a democratic age. Constitutionalism in any polity that claims to adhere to democratic norms must take due account of popular preferences, as well as merely accommodating vested interests. This requires in turn a constitutional design, and no less a constitutional strategy that includes, but also goes beyond merely institutional reform. Reform of governance is of course essential for any constitutional project and no less so for the EU if it is to meet imminent policy challenges. But more is required here than merely tinkering with institutions and decisional procedures, for instance by introducing a full-time presidency and foreign minister, rebalancing Council voting weights or extending the duration of presidency terms, important though these matters are for more efficient governance. Citizens have to be reached, too, and in ways similar to those utilised by domestic governance, with connectivity, to use the word now in vogue, properly established. These same citizens may not love the EU and may never grow to love it, but they should be given better reasons to respect it, be better informed about what it contributes to their individual and general well-being than is presently the case, made more aware of its contribution to regional peace and security, of its positive role in resolving a host of current problems shared by all Europeans.

One positive outcome from the constitutional 'crisis', if indeed crisis it was, is that this lesson is at least gaining wider currency, though rather more amongst academics and professional commentators in the serious media who monitor the Union's affairs than with those who actually run the show. A manifesto issued by the influential London-based Centre for European Reform and the Institut Montaigne in France, for instance, acknowledges the EU's 'lost sense of purpose', and sees in this one cause of its lack of popularity with citizens. These pundits argue that though the Union 'has helped to bring peace across the continent and wealth for most of its inhabitants [its] citizens are hardly aware of these benefits. Most EU policies directly benefit only a small number of people [but] for many others, the EU has become a problem, rather than a solution: it appears cumbersome and opaque; it adds layers of bureaucracy; it seems to make competition for jobs fiercer by embracing low-cost countries.' This failure is due in part to ineffective, and in some cases to poor, political leadership and requires, as these authors see it, 'a new motor for integration to replace the insular and unimaginative Franco-German "engine"'.[168]

Among the reform proposals listed in this manifesto is the recommendation that political leaders should listen more to citizens than they have done thus far, responding to the issues raised by the public, and with greater transparency in decision-making. For instance, public meetings of the Council when it is operating in its legislative capacity, and greater involvement by national parliaments in decisions, including a blocking mechanism similar to the one included in the Constitution. Reform of this order would, these authors maintain, markedly improve EU governance by democratising it. But at the very least, political leaders must engage citizens in a meaningful conversation about 'futures', by making 'a bigger effort to "sell" the benefits of EU integration'.[169]

The critical issue here, as for any polity that claims democratic credentials, is to enhance the Union's legitimacy with its citizens. This, as we have seen above, is not an issue with which the EU is overly familiar, for even the Convention was more concerned with functional and institutional matters than with improving democratic credibility. Functional or performance legitimacy was once regarded as sufficient constitutional ballast by those who managed the European project, the only mandate required as a *raison d'être* for collective decision-making in an economic community that was not at that stage in its development a polity. Even when the economic community was transformed by degrees into a polity in the successive treaty reforms that followed the Single European Act, any notion of 'the common good was either a product of an agreement between states or conceived as the protection of private autonomy and freedom enshrined in the logic of market integration and efficiency enhancing policies'.[170]

This was a convenient excuse for ignoring public concerns, for denying citizens their rightful place as full and active stakeholders, rather than merely as passive rights-bearing citizens. Times, however, have changed. The Union may be a contested polity, lacking consensus about its central purpose, to say nothing of its ultimate destination or even destiny, but it is a polity none the less. As such, its policy agenda touches the interests of ordinary citizens in ever more critical matters, from monetary policy and macro-economic management, to security policy and social and home affairs, all of them policy domains once the exclusive preserve of the nation-state. It follows from this that the constitutional design for a polity that now shares policy competencies with the member states in these politically sensitive policy domains, a polity that wields considerable political as well as merely administrative power and one that allocates resources and makes important distributive decisions, can no longer be the exclusive preserve of privileged insiders. To conform to those same exacting standards for democracy that it imposes on would-be applicants and member states alike, this Union must now engage with its citizens, after all its principal stakeholders. Constitutionalism appropriate to this uniquely multi-level polity must be 'increasingly the product of a European political process determined not only by the will of a majority of states but of a majority of Europeans'.[171]

To say this is by no means to make a case for a European super-state, to justify over-weaning and centralising governance by 'harmonis[ing] away the political philosophies, economic preferences, and social traditions developed in different nations over hundreds of years'.[172] What this endeavour requires instead and in true Lampedusan fashion is due balance between quite different political instincts. On the one hand the intergovernmental or confederal and the supranational or federal aspects of EU governance, each in their way elite-driven arrangements. And on the other hand, to make a meaningful response to public concerns, some acknowledgement by Europe's latter day 'princes' (whether those residing in the Brussels- based institutions or in governments) of the public's anxieties about particular policies and the general prospects for European integration. This requires nothing less than a new constitutional order, and not a top-down design, as even the Convention saw its task, but an altogether more democratic and open endeavour, one that reaches out to and engages with civil society and citizens as never before, connecting governors and governed.

This is no easy feat, and it requires something more than the limited rights-based citizenship introduced by the Maastricht Treaty, but instead a novel form of post-national citizenship that deepens the sense of personal attachment, fosters common sentiment, even solidarity, across historical borders. This does not mean replicating the rooted primordial cultural identity of classic nationalism that still shapes Europe's political culture, but instead using this form of identity to reassure citizens that they are not being overwhelmed by remorseless change that threatens their sense of who they are, where they belong, their cultural, linguistic and ethnic roots. This new solidarity does not have to be exclusive and inward reaching as in primordial affiliations to region or nation, as Joseph Weiler made clear in the discussion of these matters in Chapter 8. Historical attachment and primary identity can be supplemented by other forms of political belonging and even by affective attachment, both below the level of the national state and above it. A sense of common interests and mutual endeavour in a turbulent world may instil some sense of transnational membership, feelings of rootedness and solidarity with the 'other', of belonging to a Europe-wide political community as well as to national or sub-national politics. But this is hardly likely to be spontaneous, and citizens still take their cues at least on the 'big' questions from their political leaders. And thus far in these matters, assured leadership has been notably absent.

The challenge here is to accommodate the nascent idea of European citizenship to a reviving identity politics that in response to seemingly remorseless change is reawakening in some of Europe's historical nation-states narrow, exclusive, even xenophobic primordial attachments, a process that has been described as 'enclave democracy'. Many Europeans have reacted to the accelerating pace of change, to the sense of bewilderment or helplessness it induces – what sociologists call anomie, a sense of disorientation, a perceived threat to once sure political and cultural bearings, loss of control over their lives as community power gravitates upwards to remote and faceless officials, unelected bureaucrats and special interests – by embracing narrower attachments to nation, region or to the primary linguistic or ethnic group. European integration, a process that to an earlier generation was a positive expression of co-operation, an alternative to the corrosive xenophobia and no less the autarchy that more than once in times past had wrecked the continent on the rocks of war, is seen rather less positively nowadays as an expression of insidious forces imposed from 'above'. The growing subordination of the national polity to a remote and mostly invisible level of governance, one that is as incomprehensible as it is inaccessible, has caused many to retreat into a reassuring, because familiar parochialism. But this brings with it the danger of intolerance, the sort of base instincts and negative reactions to near neighbours the European project was expressly designed to tame after long decades of bellicose patriotism, culminating in the rise of fascism. What is needed now as popular uncertainties impact on the debate on futures, is for those who manage the continent's affairs to remind contemporary Europeans of the moral enormity, the incalculable and indefensible human costs of what Hannah Arendt poignantly described as 'men in dark times'.[173]

To reconcile the instinctive reassurance of the local with the nebulous appeal of the universal is no simple feat to carry off. Yet it is precisely this balance between the common and territorial interests that has been the principal achievement of the European project thus far, and this is exactly what a European constitutional endeavour ought to be about. As Simon Jenkins sees it: 'The new [European constitutional] narrative must run with, not against, the grain of Europe's national groups. It must lie in the cantons of Switzerland, the *mairies* of France, the "free communes" of Sweden, the *rathausen* of Bavaria and the parish halls of England. There must be a new treaty to guide European trade, but it must respect subsidiarity, not just the lip service paid in the doomed constitution. It must grow from the bottom up and cannot be fashioned in a French chateau amid champagne and caviar.'[174] As we saw in the discussion of citizenship at Chapter 8, to strike a balance between primary identity and yet to simultaneously encourage a sense amongst EU citizens of being part of a continental community of common interests is easier by far to prescribe than it is to realise. Academic commentaries on the sociological preconditions for instilling a sense of civic patriotism beyond the familiar national community reveal wide variations in receptiveness to what is usually called cosmopolitan identity, in this case to the idea of 'Europe'. But this same research also shows how much easier is the task of engendering a sense of civic pride and shared identity in smaller-scale communities.[175] By the same token, how much more difficult is it to cultivate a civic tradition in a polity as inchoate, culturally diverse and spatially remote, as affectively distant from its citizens as is the European Union.

A meaningful sense of attachment and belonging may well be difficult to instil at this level, though it is by no means impossible as citizens become more amenable to the idea of global norms, conditioned as they are in these somewhat less 'dark times' to shared notions about 'good' governance, in everything from managing the global commons to protecting human rights, punishing illegality in the practice of warfare to resisting the use of terror as a means for advancing political objectives. Historically human solidarity emerged in small-scale communities, city states and territorial republics, but what is feasible in terms of cultivating a sense of political belonging reflects changing circumstances. The emergence of global society and with it the development of new technologies does provide means for discourse and even for interaction beyond the territorially based polity, and likewise for diffusing empathy beyond the national community. There is evidence of the albeit slow spread of a sense of shared moral purpose, common concern and even a sense of mutual interests on the questions that preoccupy people everywhere, from climate change to human rights and beyond, amounting to a cultural and normative shift that is contributing to the spread of civilised values about the appropriate conduct for organising, and no less for defining the ends of governance.

This is promising as far as it goes, though no one should underestimate the scale of the challenge to embed a meaningful sense of civic patriotism in a polity that is still seen by its citizens as remote from their experience of politics, and which to date has confined notions of membership, identity and belonging to the primary political community that is the nation-state. Europe's political class has barely acknowledged the extent of the challenge here, the need to win hearts and minds for the idea of

'Europe', let alone begun to respond positively to it. Few observers of recent events would demur from Dinan's caustic observation that 'the EU needs better leadership and a more congenial political and economic environment, not simply the palliative of a Constitutional Treaty, to restore its lustre and sense of purpose'.[176]

Even this will not be enough to imbue citizens with a sense of belonging to a shared endeavour beyond the boundaries of their nation-states. All identities are in some degree constructed, even those primary national affiliations many simply take for granted as natural, the result not of 'destiny' but of elite agencies working to inculcate the idea of, and to sustain a historical national project. The task here is altogether more complicated when the community in question is geographically larger than the nation-state, indeed one constructed from several polyglot and historically and culturally distinct nation-states. But it is not an impossible task, so long as the objective is not to replace primordial identity with a singular or cosmopolitan outlook, but rather to reconcile pre-existent identities, and in the process to inculcate at the grassroots a sense of a multiple or multi-layered rather than exclusive identities.

There is little reason thus far to be confident on this score, and even less to indicate that the present generation of leaders has either the imagination or the political will to tackle the problem of disconnection, to respond with empathy to what is a pervasive crisis of legitimacy with regard to EU governance. Not even by the relatively modest step of taking the argument for 'Europe' to the citizens. As Maduro sees it, meeting the legitimacy test is a cultural as well as merely a political challenge, it requires some effort at identity-building, at least to inculcate a sense of belonging in a shared endeavour as much as institutional reform. Above all it needs action, not merely the sort of platitudes that come easily to politicians, and it 'depends much more on tackling the issues … as a necessary pre-condition for a constitutional project [that] both assumes and promotes a political community'. As such, the Union's 'constitutional project must fulfil two polity building conditions: first, it must generate the right incentive to embark on such a constitutional project; second, it must provide an adequate framework for European citizens to engage in the construction of a common political identity. In other words, it must secure the political loyalty necessary to the subsistence of a political community. … And it must guarantee to all members of that political community that they are treated as equal citizens and not as members of insulated and discrete groups'.[177] Just so! Not that this is a simple endeavour to carry off successfully. Neither does it mean that the EU must follow a federal let alone a statist trajectory, but instead one that brings the people more directly into the constitutional process, putting procedures in place for a democratic *pouvoir constituant* so as to legitimate the 'low intensity form of constitutionalism' required for this unique polity.[178]

Critics will surely claim that as things stand this objective is more visionary than it is practicable. Of course, if a European polity is to consolidate, to make its mark in a mutable international order, those who manage its affairs must trade in realities rather than perpetuate idealised foundation myths about a supposedly predestined union, the convenient teleology preferred by some federalists as a substitute for constructive thinking and purposive action, with time *per se* the only requirement for bringing about 'ineluctable' federal union. European identity may well be the key to elusive solidarity in this turbulent continent, but whatever that means – and as the debate on the Preamble to the Constitution revealed, it is hardly a settled issue 'who' or what is 'European' – this putative idea of common identity must accommodate abiding cultural diversity, persistent and deep-rooted national and sub-national primordial identities. David Mitrany, widely regarded in his day as a voice in the wilderness, an eccentric purveyor of outmoded Kantian idealism, long ago warned those who would reimagine Europe, rebuilding its political architecture as part of a progressive, outward-looking and peaceful international order of the folly of relying solely on 'the pagan worship of borders as the source of our public morals'.[179] Little has changed since he issued that timely warning just before the cataclysm of total war in 1939.

During the recent crisis over the European Constitution, the Swiss finance minister, Hans-Rudolf Merz, echoed these same cautious sentiments when he observed that 'European integration that goes beyond economy and security always stumbles at borders'.[180] No one should be surprised by this fact, but things have moved on since David Mitrany disparaged the 'tyranny' of national frontiers. Boundaries do still exist, in the mind as much as on the ground, but this should not preclude contemporary political leaders from exercising greater imagination, trying to reconcile the reality of borders with the potential that exists in an increasingly interdependent world for reducing their leaden impact, concentrating instead on what might be achieved by greater goodwill, better information. And not least, by showing bold leadership, telling things as they are, not as they were even in times past. Europe's politicians could, and just as important for those who want to build on the success so far of European co-operation should, engage citizens in a frank conversation about their common predicament in the new century.

More to the point, they must avoid framing this conversation in arcane 'Euro-speak', the tedious and heavily coded babble of the privileged insider, but rather engage in an inclusive and frank exchange of views, promoting an open conversation amongst 'Europeans' who also happen to be members of thriving national or sub-national communities. The fact that multiple identities and overlapping citizenships are in no way mutually exclusive is only political heresy to xenophobes, those purblind to the benefits accruing from co-operation across borders, who refuse to contemplate what it is to be a 'citizen' in the global age.

To offer such criticism is to highlight the limitations of the Convention on the Future of Europe, and what has followed from it. But at the same time it in no way diminishes the achievements of the Union's brief constitutional moment. The Convention was undoubtedly an improvement on the customary procedure for reforming the treaty base, those essentially narrow and secretive intergovernmental bargains made by successive IGCs, supplemented by judgments made in camera by the European Court's unelected Justices acting without a democratic mandate. The Convention was at the very least more representative of the Union's body politic, detaching even the principal actors from their institutional bases by permitting them 'to take an overall long term perspective … more conducive to the universal rules typical of a Constitution'.[181]

This mandate to 'speak for Europe' rather than for any particular or national institutional allegiance did help to promote 'higher mutual trust, stronger involvement and a more rational engagement between the participants'.[182] It did ensure likewise a degree of reflexivity, an independence of mind amongst many participants, but, as we have seen from the discussion of its proceedings, only to a degree. Yet, measured against the Union's usual 'constitutional' benchmarks, this novel procedure does represent progress of sorts. These improvements in the way the EU conducts its constitutional affairs notwithstanding, the residual impression is nevertheless of 'business as usual', a process still dominated by insiders, by powerful vested interests, and as the 2007 Brussels reform mandate confirmed, one whose outcome remains the usual trade-offs between a privileged few, and with too little heed paid to the concerns of people at large.

The issues raised during the EU's recent constitutional phase cannot be resolved by this latest decision to bring in some of the procedural and institutional changes proposed in the Constitutional Treaty by the usual IGC method. These changes will certainly resolve some institutional blockages and procedural problems identified by successive IGCs throughout the 1990s, making decision-making easier, tackling problems of managing the policy agenda made more complicated by a historic enlargement. But these reforms on their own will not answer deeper questions about democracy deficits, thin legitimacy, the minimal sense of attachment by citizens that weaken the Union's democratic credentials to be a 'people's Europe'. Questions that are hardly incidental for a polity that places great store in its democratic roots and that sooner or later will have to be revisited because the evidence of countless opinion polls and surveys shows that they do matter to citizens, and increasingly so.

To this extent, the EU is not done with what lawyers and political scientists define as formal constitutional matters. For this very reason, the Union will have a future constitutional history, whatever face-saving arrangements the politicians have concocted so as to postpone this outcome. And when these momentous questions are eventually confronted, those who tackle them must avoid the mistakes that brought on the recent crisis. Europe's politicians must learn to listen, to pay far greater heed to the public's abiding concerns by initiating a meaningful democratic conversation about European futures. It was that shrewd observer of democracy, Alexis de Tocqueville, who wisely cautioned 'princes' about their responsibilities for providing citizens with the basic tools for practising informed citizenship, by noting that though it may be 'difficult to induce the people to take part in [democratic] government; it is still more difficult to supply them with experience and beliefs which they lack, but need in order to govern well'. This is the essence of the requisite democratic bargain between those who govern and those on whose behalf they do so, the acid test no less for a workable, fair, durable and, above all, a democratic constitutional order, the very basis of a stable and effective, because a legitimate polity. The EU polity has no less need of such political capital than any other democratic political community, though we should never underestimate the challenge of meeting these exacting standards for a democratic political and civil order in this unique, yet still deeply contested polity.[183]

# Notes

## Chapter 1

1   A. Sbragia (ed.), *Euro-politics: Institutions and Policy-making in the 'New' European Community* (Washington DC, 1992), p. 262.

2   A. Milward, *The European Rescue of the Nation State* (London, 1992).

3   S. Kramer, Approaches to the State: Alternative Conceptions and Historical Dynamics, *Comparative Politics* 16 (1984).

4   R. D. Putnam, Diplomacy and Domestic Politics: The Logic of Two-level Games, *International Organization* 42 (1988); A. Moravcsik, Preferences and Power in the European Community: A Liberal Intergovernmentalist Approach, *Journal of Common Market Studies* 31 (1993).

5   W. C. Muller and V. Wright, Reshaping the Nation State in Western Europe: The Limits of Retreat, *West European Politics* 17 (1994).

6   S. Bulmer and W. Wessels, *The European Council: Decision-making in European Politics* (London, 1987), p. 10.

7   R. A. W. Rhodes, The Hollowing Out of the State, *Political Quarterly* 65 (1994).

8   A. Wiener, Assessing the Constructive Potential of EU Citizenship – A Socio-historical Perspective in the EU. European Integration online Papers (EIoP) 1(117) (1997), available at http://eiop.or.at/eiop/texte/1997-017.htm.

9   N. Fligstein and J. McNichol, The Institutional Terrain of the European Union, in W. Sandholtz and A. Stone (eds), *Supranational Governance: The Institutionalization of the EU* (Oxford, 1998); For a review of the influential concept of multi-level governance see G. Marks, Structural Policy and Multilevel Governance in the European Community, in A. Calfruny and G. Rosenthal (eds), *The State of the European Community: The Maastricht Debates and Beyond* (Boulder CO, 1993); and G. Marks, G. Hooghe and K. Blank, European Integration in the 1980s: State-centric v. Multilevel Governance, *Journal of Common Market Studies* 34 (1996); G. Marks, An Actor-centred Approach to Multi-level Governance, *Journal of Regional and Federal Studies* 6 (1996); T. Risse-Kappen, Exploring the Nature of the Beast: International Relations Theory and Comparative Policy Analysis Meet European Union, *Journal of Common Market Studies* 34 (1996).

10  R. Rose, Is Europe a Community? *Public Opinion* 12 (1989), p. 43.

11  See, for instance, R. O. Keohane and S. Hoffmann, *Institutional Change in Europe in the 1980s* (Boulder CO, 1991); G. Marks, Structural Policy and Multilevel Governance in the EU, in A. Calfruny and G. Rosenthal (eds), *The State of the European Community: The Maastricht Debates and Beyond* (1993). See also, for instance, S. Hix, *The Political System of the European Union* (Basingstoke, 1999).

12  A. Sbragia, Thinking about the European Future: The Uses of Comparison, in Sbragia, *Euro-politics*, p. 262. For a discussion of the concept of a post-national polity as this applies to the EU see B. Axford and R. Huggins, Towards a Post-national Polity: The

Emergence of the Network Society in Europe, in D. Smith and S. Wright, *Whose Europe?* (Oxford, 1999), at p. 181; J. Rosenau and E. Czempiel, *Governance without Government: Order and Change in World Politics* (Cambridge, 1992); M. Jachtenfuchs, Theoretical Perspectives on European Governance, *European Law Journal* 1 (1995); M. Jachtenfuchs, Conceptualizing European Governance, in Knud-Erik Jorgensen (ed.), *Reflective Approaches to European Governance* (Basingstoke, 1997).

13  B. Kohler-Koch, Catching Up with Change: The Transformation of Governance in the EU, *Journal of European Public Policy* 3 (1996).

14  R. Bellamy and D. Castiglione, Democracy, Sovereignty and the Constitution of the European Union: The Republican Alternative to Liberalism, in Z. Bankowski and A. Scott (eds), *The European Union and Its Order: The Legal Theory of European Integration* (Oxford, 2000), p. 169.

15  R. Dahl, A Democratic Dilemma: System Effectiveness versus Citizen Participation, *Political Science Quarterly* 109 (1994), p. 28.

16  Bulmer and Wessels, *The European Council*, p. 10.

17  J. Peterson, Decision-making in the European Union: Towards a Framework for Analysis, *Journal of European Public Policy* 2 (1995); for a more conditional account see H. Kassim, Policy Networks, Networks and European Union Policy-making: A Sceptical View, *West European Politics* 17 (1994).

18  F. W. Scharpf, The Joint Decision Trap: Lessons from German Federalism and European Integration, *Public Administration* 66 (1993); F. W. Scharpf, *Optionen des Föderalismus in Deutschland und Europa* (Frankfurt, 1994); P. Guy Peters, Escaping the Joint Decision Trap: Repetition and Sectoral Politics in the European Union, *West European Politics* 20 (1997).

19  Peterson, Decision-making in the European Union, p. 88.

20  On the theme of overlapping institutional competencies and policy fragmentation, and a policy-making model described as 'big sloppy hexagons', see B. Guy Peters, Bureaucratic Politics and the Institutions of the European Community, in Sbragia, *Euro-politics*.

21  G. de Burca, The Quest for Legitimacy in the European Union, *Modern Law Review* 59 (1996); D. Beetham and C. Lord, *Legitimacy and the EU* (London, 1998).

22  de Burca, The Quest for Legitimacy.

23  K. Neunreither, The Democratic Deficit of the European Union: Towards Closer Cooperation between the European Parliament and the National Parliaments, *Government and Opposition* 29 (1994).

24  A. Heritier, C. Knill and S. Mingers, *Ringing the Changes in Europe: Regulatory Competition and Redefinition of the State* (New York, 1996).

25  *The European Council: Conclusions of the Presidency 1987–1994* (Luxembourg 1995), p. 25.

26  D. Castiglione, Contracts and Constitutions, in R. Bellamy, V. Buffachi and D. Castiglione (eds), *Democracy and Constitutional Culture in the Union of Europe* (London, 1995).

27  T. Pogge, How to Create Supra-national Institutions Democratically. Some Reflections on the European Union's 'Democratic Deficit', in A. Follesdal and P. Kolowski (eds), *Democracy and the European Union* (Berlin, 1997).

28  R. Bellamy and D. Castiglione, Democracy, Sovereignty and the Constitution of the Europe Union: The Republican Alternative to Liberalism, in Bankowski and Scott, *The European Union and Its Order*, p. 170.

29  P. Norris, Representation and the Democratic Deficit, *European Journal of Political Research* 32 (1997).

30  S. Williams, Sovereignty and Accountability in the European Union, *Political Quarterly* 61 (1990).

31  S. Mazey and J. Richardson, Promiscuous Policymaking: The European Policy Style?, in C. Rhodes and S. Mazey (eds), *The State of the European Union: Building a European Polity?* (Harlow, 1995), p. 356.

32 L. Dobson, Constitutionalism and Citizenship in the European Union: A Normative Theoretical Approach. Constitutionalism Web-Papers no. 1 (2000), p. 17, available at http://les1.man.ac.uk/conweb; see also S. Andersen and K. Eliassen (eds), *The European Union: How Democratic Is It?* (London, 1996); F. Scharpf, *Governing in Europe. Effective and Democratic?* (Oxford, 1999); A. Weale and M. Nentwich (eds), *Political Theory and the European Union. Legitimacy, Constitutional Choice and Citizenship* (London, 1999); S. Williams, Sovereignty and Accountability in the European Community, in R. Keohane and S. Hoffmann (eds), *The New European Community: Decision Making and Institutional Change* (Boulder CO, 1991)

33 Ad Hoc Committee for Institutional Affairs, *Report to the European Council* (Brussels, March 1985).

34 For a thorough discussion of this, see M. Newman, *Democracy, Sovereignty and the European Union* (London, 1996), at Chapter 7.

35 K. Neunreither, The European Parliament and Enlargement, 1973–2000, in J. Redmond and G. Rosenthal (eds), *The Expanding European Union* (London, 1998), p. 80.

36 R. Sinnott, Bringing Public Opinion Back In, in O. Niedermayer and R. Sinnott (eds), *Public Opinion and International Governance* (Oxford, 1995).

37 M. Cini, *The European Commission. Leadership, Organization and Culture in the EU Administration* (Manchester, 1996), p. 191.

38 Pascal Lamy, quoted in G. Ross, *Jacques Delors and European Integration* (Cambridge, 1995), p. 194.

39 Peterson, Decision-making in the European Union, p. 72.

40 R. Pryce and W. Wessels, The Search for an Ever Closer Union: A Framework for Analysis, in R. Pryce (ed.), *The Dynamics of European Union* (London, 1987), p. 16.

41 Peterson, Decision-making in the European Union, p. 74.

42 D. Spence, The role of National Civil Servants in European Lobbying: The British Case, in S. Mazey and J. Richardson (eds), *Lobbying in the European Community* (Oxford, 1993).

43 Cini, *The European Commission*, pp. 222–3.

44 D. Dinan, The Commission and Enlargement, in J. Redmond and G. Rosenthal (eds), *The Expanding European Union* (Boulder CO, 1998), p. 26.

45 R. Hull, Lobbying Brussels: A View from Within, in Mazey and Richardson, *Lobbying in the European Community*.

46 B. Guy Peters, in Sbragia, *Euro-politics*.

47 See Ross, *Jacques Delors*.

48 M. Shackleton, The European Community between Three Ways of Life: A Cultural Analysis, *Journal of Common Market Studies* 29 (1991).

49 P. Hirst, *Associative Democracy: New Forms of Economic and Social Governance* (Cambridge, 1994).

50 L. Cram, The European Commission as a Multi-organization: Social Policy and IT Skills in the EU, *Journal of European Public Policy* 2 (1994), p. 199.

51 E. J. Kirchner, *Decision-making in the European Community: The Council Presidency and European Integration* (Manchester, 1992).

52 F. Hayes-Renshaw and H. Wallace, *The Council of Ministers* (Basingstoke, 1997), p. 279.

53 Ibid.

54 H. Wallace, Making Negotiations Work, in W. Wallace (ed.), *The Dynamics of European Integration* (London, 1991), p. 225.

55 M. Troy Johnson, *The European Council: Gatekeeper of the European Community* (Boulder CO, 1994).

56 Bulmer and Wessels, *The European Council*.

57 D. Dinan, *Ever Closer Union* (Basingstoke, 1994), p. 280.

58 J. Pinder, *The Building of the European Union* (Oxford, 1998), p. 50.

59 G. Tsebelis, The Power of the European Parliament as a Conditional Agenda Setter, *American Political Science Review* 88 (1994).

60  M. Franklin, M. Marsh and L. McLaren, Uncorking the Bottle: Popular Opposition to European Integration in the Wake of Maastricht, *Journal of Common Market Studies* 32 (1994).

61  Hayes-Renshaw and Wallace, *The Council of Ministers*, p. 284.

62  See W. Sandholtz and A. Stone Sweet (eds), *European Integration and Supranational Governance* (Oxford, 1998) for some indicative policy case studies.

63  S. Hix, The Study of the European Community: The Challenge of Comparative Politics, *West European Politics* 17 (1994).

64  There is a growing literature on this subject. See, for instance, C. Radaelli, The Europeanization of Public Policy, and T. Borzel and T. Risse, Conceptualizing the Domestic Impact of Europe, both in K. Featherstone and C. Radaelli (eds), *The Politics of Europeanization* (Oxford, 2003); and D. Marquand, The Irresistible Tide of Europeanization, in S. Hall and M. Jacques (eds), *New Times* (London, 1991).

65  W. Wallace and J. Smith, Democracy or Technocracy? European Integration and the Problem of Popular Consent, in J. Hayward (ed.), *The Crisis of Representation in Europe* (London, 1995).

66  B. Constant, *Political Writings*, ed. Biancamaria Fontana (Cambridge, 1988), p. 292.

67  Case 166/73 *Rheinmuhlen-Dusseldorf* v. *Einfuhr- und Vorratstelle für Getreide und Futtermittel* [1974] ECR 33.

68  Case 48/71 *Commission* v. *Italy (Art Treasures 11)* [1972] ECR 527.

69  A. M. Burley and W. Matti, Europe before the Court: A Political Theory of Legal Integration, *International Organization* 47 (1993).

70  J. H. Weiler, The Transformation of Europe, *Yale Law Review* 100 (1991), p. 2413.

71  K. Alter, The European Court's Political Power: The Emergence of an Authoritative International Court in the European Union, *West European Politics* 19 (1996).

72  J. H. Weiler, Journey to an Unknown Destination: A Retrospective and Prospective of the European Court in the Area of Political Integration, *Journal of Common Market Studies* 31 (1993).

73  I. Pernice, Multi-level Constitutionalism and the Treaty of Amsterdam: European Constitution-making Revisited?, *Common Market Law Review* 4 (1999).

74  A. Dashwood, States in the European Union, *European Law Review* 23 (1998).

75  Protocol (no. 30) on the Application of the Principles of Subsidiarity and Proportionality (Amsterdam, 20 October 1997), *Official Journal of the European Communities* (*OJEC*), 10.11.1997, no. C 340, p. 105.

76  S. Weatherill, Is Constitutional Finality Feasible or Desirable? On the Cases for European Constitutionalism and a European Constitution. Constitutionalism Web-Papers no. 7 (2002), p. 24, available at http://www.bath.ac.uk/esme/conWEB %20papers-filestore/conweb7-2002.pdf.

77  K. Lenaerts, Constitutionalism and the Many Faces of Federalism, *American Journal of Comparative Law* 38 (1990), p. 200.

78  Ibid., p. 201.

79  J. Wouters, Institutional and Constitutional Challenges for the European Union – Some Reflections in the Light of the Treaty of Nice, *European Law Review* 6 (1999); and J. Shaw, Postnational Constitutionalism in the European Union, *Journal of European Public Policy* 6 (1999).

80  G. de Burca and J. Scott (eds), *Constitutional Change in the EU: From Uniformity to Flexibility?* (Oxford, 2000).

81  D. Hodson and I. Mather, The Open Method as a New Mode of Governance, *Journal of Common Market Studies* 39 (2001).

82  S. Weatherill, op cit (2002), p. 24, available at http://www.bath.ac.uk/esme/conWEB%20 papers-filestore/conweb7-2002.pdf.

83  Ibid.

84  J. Shaw, Constitutionalism and Flexibility in the EU: Developing a Relational Approach, in de Burca and Scott, *Constitutional Change in the EU*, Chapter 15; and G. de Burca,

Differentiation within the 'Core'? The Case of the Internal Market, in de Burca and Scott, *Constitutional Change in the* EU, Chapter 7.

85 For a discussion of these issues, see A. Rodriguez-Pose, *The European Union. Economy, Society and Polity* (Oxford, 2002), especially at pp. 1–4.

86 T. M. Wilson and M. Estellie Smith, *Cultural Changes and the New Europe: Perspectives on the European Community* (Boulder Co, 1993); A. Smith, The Nations of Europe after the Cold War, in J. Hayward (ed.), *Governing the New Europe* (Cambridge, 1995).

87 C. M. Radaelli, Fiscal Federalism as a Catalyst for Policy Development? In Search of a Framework for European Direct Tax Harmonization, *Journal of European Public Policy* 3 (1996).

88 A. Moravcsik, Preferences and Power in the EC. A Liberal Intergovernmentalist Approach, *Journal of Common Market Studies* 34 (1996); J. Weiler, The Reform of European Constitutionalism, *Journal of Common Market Studies* 35 (1998).

89 Dinan, The Commission and Enlargement, p. 36.

90 Ibid.

91 D. Curtin, The Constitutional Structure of the Union: A Europe of Bits and Pieces, *Common Market Law Review* 30 (1993).

92 See A. Gamble, Economic Recession and Disenchantment with Europe, in J. Hayward (ed.), *The Crisis of Representation in Europe* (London, 1995).

93 P. Schmitter, *How to Democratize the European Union ... And Why Bother?* (Boulder Co, 2000).

94 U. Preuss, Prospects of a Constitution for Europe, *Constellations* 3 (1996).

95 C. Hoskyns, Democratizing the EU: Evidence and Argument, in C. Hoskyns and M. Newman (eds), *Democratizing the European Union* (Manchester, 2000), p. 183.

96 D. Beetham and C. Lord, *Legitimacy and the European Union* (London, 1998).

97 Jonathan Freedland, The Institution Has Failed. For We, the People, Have Not Spoken Yet, *Guardian*, 17 March 1999.

98 J. Habermas, Reply to Grimm: 'Does Europe Need a Constitution', in P. Gowan and P. Anderson (eds), *The Question of Europe* (London, 1997) – this exchange was originally published in the *European Law Journal* 1 (1995).

99 D. Grimm, Does Europe Need a Constitution?, in Gowan and Anderson, *The Question of Europe*, pp. 251–2.

100 Ibid., p. 248.

101 K. Armstrong and J. Shaw, Legal Integration: Theorizing the Legal Dimension of European Integration, *Journal of Common Market Studies* 36 (1998).

102 Hoskyns, Democratizing the EU, p. 184.

103 M. Herdegen, Maastricht and the German Constitutional Court. Constitutional Restraints for an 'Ever Closer Union', *Common Market Law Review* 31 (1994).

104 R. Kuper, Democratization: A Constitutionalizing Process, in Hoskyns and Newman, *Democratizing the European Union*, pp. 159–60.

105 Constitutional scepticism is a familiar refrain of those theorists who see the Union as merely a sophisticated international regulatory regime. See, for instance, F. Scharpf, *Governing in Europe: Effective and Democratic?* (Oxford, 1999); and P. Schmitter, G. Majone and A. Moravcsik, Democracy and Constitutionalism in the European Union, *ECSA Review* 13(2), (2000).

106 N. MacCormick, Democracy, Subsidiarity, and Citizenship in the European Commonwealth, *Law and Philosophy* 16 (1997).

107 See the argument in M. Maduro, How Constitutional Can the European Union Be? The Tension Between Intergovernmentalism and Constitutionalism in the European Union. Jean Monnet Working Paper 5/04, New York University School of Law (2004).

108 D. Beetham and C. Lord, Legitimacy and the European Union, in A. Weale and M. Nentwich, *Political Theory and the European Union: Legitimacy, Constitutionalism and Citizenship* (London, 1998), p. 32.

109 R. Bellamy and D. Castiglione, Normative Theory and the European Union: Legitimising the Euro-polity and Its Regime, in L. Tragardth (ed.), *After National Democracy: Rights, Law and Power in the New Europe* (Oxford, 2005).

110 Dobson, Constitutionalism and Citizenship, pp. 9–10.

111 R. Hirschl, Hegemonic Preservation in Action? Assessing the Political Origins of the EU Constitution. Jean Monnet Working Paper 5/04, New York University School of Law (2004), p. 8.

112 C. Skach, We the Peoples? Constitutionalizing the European Union, *Journal of Common Market Studies* 43 (2005), p. 157.

113 I Pernice, Multilevel Constitutionalism in the European Union, *European Law Review* (2002); I. Pernice and R. Kanitz, Fundamental Rights and Multilevel Constitutionalism in Europe. Walter Hallstein Institut Paper 7/04, March 2004.

114 Skach, We the Peoples, p. 157.

115 N. MacCormick, *Questioning Sovereignty* (Oxford, 1999).

116 R. Schuman, quoted in Kimmo Kiljunen, *The European Constitution in the Making* (Brussels: Centre for European Policy Studies, 2004), p. 20.

117 Tony Blair, Speech to the Warsaw Stock Exchange, 6 October 2000, see http://www.europaworld.org/speeches/tonyblairpoland61000.htm.

118 M. Everson, Beyond the *Bundverfassungsgericht*: On the Necessary Cunning of Constitutional Reasoning, in Bankowski and Scott, *The European Union and Its Order*, p. 111.

119 V. Giscard d'Estaing, Henry Kissinger Lecture at the Library of Congress, Washington DC, 11 February 2003, available at http://european-convention.eu.int/docs/speeches/7072.pdf.

120 P. Craig, Constitutions, Constitutionalism, and the European Union, *European Law Journal* 7 (2001).

121 I. Pernice, Multi-level Constitutionalism and the Treaty of Amsterdam: European Constitution-making Revisited, *Common Market Law Review* 36 (1999); I. Pernice, Multi-level constitutionalism in the European Union, *European Law Review* 27 (2002).

122 Weatherill, Is Constitutional Finality Feasible or Desirable, pp. 25–6.

123 Simon Hix, The Study of the European Community: The Challenge of Comparative Politics, *West European Politics* 17 (1994); the rejoinder by A. Hurrell and Anand Menon, Politics like Any Other? Comparative Politics, International Relations and the Study of the EU, *West European Politics* 19 (1996); and Hix's response in turn to their critique, Simon Hix, CP, IR and the EU! A Rejoinder to Hurrell and Menon, *West European Politics* 19 (1996); for an earlier contribution see P. Gourevitch, The Second Image Reversed: The International Sources of Domestic Politics, *International Organization* 32 (1978).

124 Kiljunen, *The European Constitution in the Making*, pp. 24–5.

## Chapter 2

1 R. Hirschl, Hegemonic Preservation in Action? Assessing the Political Origins of the EU Constitution. Jean Monnet Working Paper 5/04, New York University School of Law (2004), p. 3.

2 See R. Dworkin, *Taking Rights Seriously* (Cambridge MA, 1978), pp. 147–9. Constitutions in democratic polities also list the citizens' fundamental rights and duties, the obligations of membership in the body politic.

3 L. Dobson, Constitutionalism and Citizenship in the European Union: A Normative Theoretical Approach. Constitutionalism Web-Papers no. 1 (2000), p. 4, available at http://les1.man.ac.uk/conweb.

4 O. Pfersmann, The New Revision of the Old Constitution. Jean Monnet Working Paper 5/04, New York University School of Law (2004), p. 5.

5  J. McHugh, *Comparative Constitutional Traditions* (New York, 2002).
6  See F. Scharpf, *Governing in Europe: Effective and Democratic?* (Oxford, 1999); for a discussion of these terms in relation to the EU see S. Andersen and K. Eliassen (eds), *The European Union: How Democratic Is It?* (London, 1996).
7  D. Elazar, *Exploring Federalism* (Alabama, 1987), p. 157.
8  Dobson, Constitutionalism and Citizenship, p. 18.
9  Ibid.
10  Ibid.
11  F. Llorente, Constitutionalism in the 'Integrated' States of Europe. Harvard Law School Jean Monnet Papers (1998), p. 7, available at http://www.jeanmonnet program.org/papers/98/98-5-html.
12  R. Dahl, A Democratic Dilemma: System Effectiveness versus Citizen Participation, *Political Science Quarterly* 109 (1994).
13  F. Palermo, Integration of Constitutional Values in the EU – An Epilogue, in F. Palermo and G. Toggenburg (eds), *European Constitutional Values and Diversity*, EURAC Research, Bolzano (2003), p. 108.
14  Ibid.
15  J. Elster, Forces and Mechanics in the Constitution-making Process, *Duke Law Journal* 45 (1995).
16  Llorente, Constitutionalism in the 'Integrated' States of Europe, p. 7.
17  B. Ackerman, *We the People*, vol. I, *Foundations* (Cambridge MA,1992).
18  Dobson, Constitutionalism and Citizenship, p. 18.
19  One significant account of these developments is J. H. Weiler, The Transformation of Europe, *Yale Law Review* 100 (1991), at p. 2430.
20  M. Maduro, How Constitutional Can the European Union Be? The Tension Between Intergovernmentalism and Constitutionalism in the European Union. Jean Monnet Working Paper 5/04, New York University School of Law (2004), p. 14.
21  G. Sartori, *Comparative Constitutional Engineering* (London, 1994), p. 199.
22  Quoted in Oscar Jaszi, *The Dissolution of the Habsburg Monarchy* (Chicago, 1929), p. 81.
23  See, for instance, M. Cappelletti, M. Seccombe and J. Weiler (eds), *Integration through Law – Europe and the American Federal Experience* (New York, 1986); K. Laenaerts (ed.), *Two Hundred Years of US Constitution and Thirty Years of EEC Treaty* (Brussels, 1988); and A. Stuttaford, Constitutionally Indisposed, *National Review*, 22 February 2005.
24  Llorente, Constitutionalism in the 'Integrated' States of Europe, p. 7.
25  Ibid.
26  See E. Stein, Lawyers, Judges and the Making of a Trans-national Constitution, *American Journal of International Law* 75(1) (1981).
27  B. Guy Peters, Politics and Institutions of the EU, in A. Sbragia, *Euro-politics: Institutions and Policy-making in the 'New' European Community* (Washington DC, 1992), p. 100.
28  P. King and A. Bosco (eds), *A Constitution for Europe* (Lothian Foundation, London, 1991); A. Petroni, A Liberal View on a European Constitution, in P. Lehning and A. Weale (eds), *Citizenship, Democracy and Justice in the New Europe* (London, 1997); G. Schuppert, On the Evolution of a European State: Reflections on the Conditions of and the Prospects for a European Constitution, in J. Hess and N. Johnson (eds), *Constitutional Policy and Change in Europe* (Oxford, 1995); A. Stone Sweet, Constitutional Dialogues in the European Community. EUI Working Paper RSC 95/38, European University Institute (1995); A. Weale, Between Representation and Constitutionalism in the European Union, in A. Weale and M. Nentwich (eds), *Political Theory and the European Union: Legitimacy, Constitutional Choice and Citizenship* (London, 1998); J. Weiler, European Neo-constitutionalism: in Search of Foundations for the European Constitutional Order, in R. Bellamy and D. Castiglione (eds), *Constitutionalism*

*in Transformation: European and Theoretical Perspectives* (Oxford, 1996); J. Weiler, The Reformation of European Constitutionalism, *Journal of Common Market Studies* 35 (1998); J. Shaw and A. Wiener, The Paradox of the 'European Polity'. Jean Monnet Working Paper 10/99, New York University School of Law (1999), available at http://www.jeanmonnetprogram.org/papers/99/991001.html; I Pernice, Multilevel Constitutionalism and the Treaty of Amsterdam: European Constitution-making Revisited?, *Common Market Law Review* 36 (1999).

29 Quoted in M. Mazower, *Dark Continent. Europe's Twentieth Century* (London, 1998), pp. 111–12.

30 F. Duchêne, *Jean Monnet: The First Statesman of Interdependence* (New York, 1994), p. 234.

31 J. Shaw, Constitutional Settlements and the Citizens after the Treaty of Amsterdam. Harvard Law School Jean Monnet Papers, no. 7 (1998), p. 10, available at http://www.jeanmonnetprogram.org/papers/98/98-7-.html.

32 B. de Witte, Direct Effect, Supremacy and the Nature of the Legal Order, in P. Craig and G. de Burca (eds), *The Evolution of EU Law* (Oxford, 1999).

33 See Stein, Lawyers, Judges; K. Laenarts, Constitutionalism and the Many Faces of Federalism, *American Journal of Comparative Law* 38 (1990); G. Mancini, The Making of a Constitution for Europe, *Common Market Law Review* 26 (1989).

34 J. H. Weiler, The Reformation of European Constitutionalism, *Journal of Common Market Studies* 35 (1998), p. 98.

35 Article 6 (ex Article F), paragraph 2 of the Treaty on European Union.

36 Certainly novel but not entirely unique. For what Wiener has described as 'emerging processes of constitutionalisation beyond the state' are emerging in other transnational regimes, including the International Criminal Court, the United Nations, the North American Free Trade Agreement, the World Trade Organization and the like. See A. Wiener, Evolving Norms of Constitutionalism in Europe: From 'Treaty Language' to 'Constitution'. Jean Monnet Working Paper 5/04, New York University School of Law (2004); N. Walker, The Idea of Constitutional Pluralism, *Modern Law Review* 65 (2002), p. 322; and J. Shaw and A. Wiener, The Paradox of the European Polity, in M. Cowles and M. Smith (eds), *The State of the European Union V: Risks, Reform and Revival* (Oxford, 2000), note 13.

37 Stein, Lawyers, Judges.

38 Llorente, Constitutionalism in the 'Integrated' States of Europe, p. 14.

39 See P. Pescatore, The Doctrine of Direct Effect: An Infant Disease of Community Law, *European Law Review* 8 (1983); and Mancini, The Making of a Constitution.

40 Case 26/62 [1963] ECR 1.

41 Case 106/77 [1978] ECR 629.

42 Case C-213/89 [1990] ECR I-2433.

43 Case 11/70 [1970] ECR 1125.

44 Llorente, Constitutionalism in the 'Integrated' States of Europe, p. 15.

45 J. Weiler, *The Constitution of Europe* (Cambridge, 1999); R. Dehousse, *The European Court of Justice* (Basingstoke, 1998).

46 See T. Tridimas, *The General Principles of EC Law* (Oxford, 1999); and U. Bernitz and J. Nergelius, *General Principles of European Community Law* (London, 2000).

47 S. Weatherill, Is Constitutional Finality Feasible or Desirable? On the Cases for European Constitutionalism and a European Constitution. Constitutionalism Web-Papers no. 7 (2002), p. 8, available at http://www.bath.ac.uk/esme/conWEB %20papers-filestore/conweb7-2002.pdf.

48 Case 294/83 [1986] ECR1339.

49 See B. de Witte, Direct Effect, Supremacy and the Nature of the Legal Order, in P. Craig and G. de Burca (eds), *The Evolution of EU Law* (Oxford, 1999).

50 D. Wyatt, New Legal Order, or Old? *European Law Review* 7 (1982); O. Spiermann, The Other Side of the Story: An Unpopular Essay on the Making of the EC Legal Order, *European Journal of International Law* 10 (1999); F. Berman, Community Law

and International Law: How Far Does Either Belong to the Other?, in B. Markesinis (ed.), *Bridging the Channel: The Clifford Chance Lectures* (Oxford, 1996).

51 H. Rasmussen, *On Law and Policy in the European Court of Justice: A Comparative Study in Judicial Policymaking* (The Hague, 1986); T. Hartley, *Constitutional Problems of the European Union* (Hart Publishing, 1999); and C. Bengoetxea, N. McCormick and L. Moral Soriano, Integration and Integrity in the Legal Reasoning of the European Court of Justice, in G. de Burca and J. H. Weiler (eds), *The European Court of Justice* (Oxford, 2001).

52 Weatherill, Is Constitutional Finality Feasible, pp. 9–10..

53 Llorente, Constitutionalism in the 'Integrated' States of Europe, p. 16.

54 For a review of the Parliament's various contribution here, see R. Bieber and P. Widmer (eds), *L'espace constitutionnel européen* (Zurich, 1995).

55 Llorente, Constitutionalism in the 'Integrated' States of Europe, p. 19.

56 Ibid.

57 J. Weiler, Does Europe Need a Constitution, *European Law Journal* 1 (1995).

58 J. H. Weiler, The Community System: The Dual Character of Supranationalism, *Yearbook of European Law* 1 (1981).

59 Case 26/62 *Van Gend en Loos* v. *Nederlandse Administratie der Belastingen* [1963] ECR 1 and Case 294/83 *Parti Ecologiste 'Les Verts'* v. *European Parliament* (1986) ECR 1339.

60 K. Alter, *Establishing the Supremacy of European Law* (Oxford, 2001), Chapter 5.

61 See A. Stone Sweet and J. Caporaso, From Free Trade to Supranational Polity: The European Court and Integration, in W. Sandholtz and A. Stone Sweet (eds), *European Integration and Supranational Governance* (Oxford, 1998); D. Wincott, A Community of Law? European Law and Judicial Politics: The Court of Justice and Beyond, *Government and Opposition* 35 (2000).

62 S. Weatherill and P. Beaumont, *European Law*, third edition (London, 1999), Chapter 12; T. Hartley, *The Foundations of European Community Law* (Oxford, 1999).

63 Case 6/64 *Costa/ENEL* (1964) ECR 1251.

64 A-M. Slaughter, A. Stone Sweet and J. H. Weiler (eds), *The European Court and National Courts: Doctrine and Jurisprudence* (Oxford, 1998); J. Schwartze (ed.), *The Birth of a European Constitutional Order: The Interaction of National and Constitutional Law* (Baden-Baden, 2000).

65 See M. Herdegen, Maastricht and the German Constitutional Court, *Common Market Law Review* 32 (1994); M. Zuleeg, The European Constitution under Constitutional Constraints: The German Scenario, *European Law Review* 22 (1997); and *Sovereignty, Citizenship and the European Constitution*, special issue of the *European Law Journal* 1(3) (1995).

66 J. H. Weiler and N. Lockhart, Taking Rights Seriously: The European Court and Its Fundamental Rights Jurisprudence, *Common Market Law Review* 32 (1995).

67 P. Alston (ed.), *The EU and Human Rights* (Oxford, 1999); and K. Lenaerts, Respect for Fundamental Rights as a Constitutional Principle of the European Union, *Columbia Journal of European Law* 6 (2000).

68 D. Chalmers, Food for Thought: European Risks and National Ways of Life, *Modern Law Review* 66 (2003).

69 M. Everson, Beyond the *Bundverfassungsgericht*: On the Necessary Cunning of Constitutional Reasoning, in Z. Bankowski and A. Scott (eds), *The European Union and Its Legal Order: The Legal Theory of European Integration* (Oxford, 2000).

70 *Internationale Handelsgesellschaft* v. *Einfuhr und Vorratsstelle für Getreide und Futtermittel* [1974] 2 CMLR 540.

71 *Manfred Brunner et al.* v. *The European Union Treaty* [1994] 1 CMLR 57.

72 Schwartze, *The Birth of a European Constitutional Order*, pp. 496–501.

73 H. Rasmussen, Confrontation or Peaceful Co-existence?, in D. O'Keefe (ed.), *Judicial Review in European Union Law: Liber Amoricum in honour of Gordon Slynn* (The Hague, 2000).

74  J. Kokott, Report on Germany, in Slaughter *et al.*, *The European Court.*
75  Dehousse, *The European Court of Justice*, pp. 62–6.
76  Weatherill, Is Constitutional Finality Feasible, pp. 12 and 14.
77  C. Richmond, Preserving the Identity Crisis: Autonomy, System and Sovereignty in European Law, *Philosophy and Law* 16 (1997); M. Kumm, Who Is the Final Arbiter of Constitutionality in Europe?, *Common Market Law Review* 36 (1999).
78  G. Garrett, The Politics of Legal Integration in the European Union, *International Organization* 49 (1995); G. Garrett, The European Court of Justice, National Governments and Legal Integration in the European Union, *International Organization* 52 (1998).
79  Weatherill, Is Constitutional Finality Feasible, p. 15.
80  Ibid.
81  Ibid.
82  Ibid.
83  Palermo, Integration of Constitutional Values in the EU, p. 111.
84  T. Hartley, *Constitutional Problems of the European Union* (Hart Publishing, 1999), Chapter 2.
85  *Brunner* [1994] 1 CMLR 57.
86  See, for instance, the position of the German Federal Constitutional Court, *Internationale Handelsgesellschaft* [1974] 2 CMLR 549.
87  R. Bellamy and D. Castiglione, Democracy, Sovereignty and the Constitution of the European Union: The Republican Alternative to Liberalism, in Bankowski and Scott, *The European Union*, p. 177; see also *Internationale Handelsgesellschaft*, Case 4/73 *Nold* v. *Commission* [1974] ECR 503; and Case 374/87 *Orkem* v. *Commission* ECR [1989] ECR 3283.
88  C. Joerges, Taking the Law Seriously: On Political Science and the Role of Law in the Process of European Integration, *European Law Journal* 2 (1996); and C. Joerges and J. Neyer, From Intergovernmental Bargaining to Deliberative Political Processes: The Constitutionalisation of Comitology, *European Law Journal* 3 (1997).
89  P. Eleftheriadis, Begging the Constitutional Question, *Journal of Common Market Studies* 36 (1998).
90  Bellamy and Castiglione, Democracy, Sovereignty and the Constitution, p. 178.
91  Ibid. p. 170.
92  Ibid. p. 176.
93  I. Maher, Community Law in the National Legal Order: A System Analysis, *Journal of Common Market Studies* 36 (1998).
94  K. Armstrong, Legal Integration: Theorizing the Legal Dimension of European Integration, *Journal of Common Market Studies* 36 (1998).
95  Bellamy and Castiglione, Democracy, Sovereignty and the Constitution, p. 177.
96  Ibid.
97  Ibid.
98  M. Covell, European Union Constitution-making in Comparative Perspective. The Federal Trust (London, October 2003); and Llorente, Constitutionalism in the 'Integrated' States of Europe, p. 9.
99  N. MacCormick, Rethinking European Constitutionalism, in J. Weiler and M. Wind (eds), *European Constitutionalism beyond the State* (Cambridge, 2003); P. Craig, The Nature of the Community: Integration, Democracy and Legitimacy, in Craig and de Burca, *The European Court of Justice*; C. Lord, Assessing Democracy in a Contested Polity, *Journal of Common Market Studies* 39 (2001); C. Lord and D. Beetham, Legitimizing the EU: Is There a Post-parliamentary Basis for Its Legitimation? *Journal of Common Market Studies* 39 (2001).
100  R. Hardin, *Liberalism, Constitutionalism and Democracy* (Oxford, 1999).
101  J. Elster, Ways of Constitution-making, in A. Hodenius (ed.), *Democracy's Victory and Crisis* (Cambridge, 1997).
102  Elazar, *Exploring Federalism*, p. 164.

103 S. Tarrow, Center-periphery Alignments and Political Contention in Late Modern Europe, in C. Ansell and P. Guiseppe (eds), *Beyond Center-Periphery* (Cambridge, 2003).

104 John Erik Fossum and E. O. Eriksen, Europe in Search of Legitimacy: Strategies of Legitimation Assessed, *International Political Science Review* 25(4) (2004); John Erik Fossum and Agustín Menéndez (eds), *The Chartering of Europe* (Baden-Baden, 2003); Erik Oddvar Eriksen and John Erik Fossum, Democracy through Strong Publics in the European Union, *Journal of Common Market Studies* 3 (2002); Erik Oddvar Eriksen and John Erik Fossum (eds), *Democracy in the European Union – Integration through Deliberation?* (London, 2000); R. Kuper, Democratization: A Constitutional-izing Process, in C. Hoskyns and M. Newman (eds), *Democratizing the European Union* (Manchester, 2000), p. 156.

105 R. Bellamy and D. Castiglione (eds), *Constitutionalism in Transformation. European Theoretical Perspectives* (special edition of *Political Studies* 44(3) (1996).

106 D. Judge, The Failure of National Parliaments, *West European Politics* 3 (1995).

107 See the critique of American democracy in these terms in M. Sandel, *Democracy's Discontents. America in Search of a Public Philosophy* (Cambridge MA, 1996), pp. 5–6.

108 Kuper, Democratization, p. 159.

109 Ibid., p. 164.

110 Ibid.

111 J. Habermas, Reply to Grimm, in P. Gowan and P. Anderson (eds), *The Question of Europe* (London, 1997), p. 262. This exchange was originally published as Dieter Grimm, Does Europe Need a Constitution?, *European Law Journal* 1 (1995), with the reply by Jürgen Habermas, Remarks on Dieter Grimm's 'Does Europe Need a Constitution?', *European Law Journal* 1 (1995).

112 Habermas, Reply to Grimm, p. 263.

113 D. Held, Democracy and the New International Order, in D. Archibugi and D. Held (eds), *Cosmopolitan Democracy* (Cambridge, 1995), pp. 106 and 109.

114 J. Weiler, Federalism and Constitutionalism: Europe's *Sonderweg*. Harvard Law School Jean Monnet Papers (2000), p. 13, available at http://www.jeanmonnetpro-gram.org/papers/00/001001.

115 G. La Palombella, Whose Europe? After the Constitution: A Goal-based, Reflexive Citizenship. Jean Monnet Working Paper 5/04, New York University School of Law (2004), p. 9.

116 Dobson, Constitutionalism and Citizenship.

117 A. Moravcsik, Integrating International and Domestic Theories of International Bargaining, in P. Evans, H. Jacobson and R. Putnam (eds), *Double Edged Diplomacy, International Bargaining and Domestic Politics* (Berkeley, 1993); A. Moravcsik, Negotiating the Single European Act: National Interests and Conventional Statecraft in the European Community, *International Organization* 45 (1991); A. Moravcsik, Preferences and Power in the European Community: A Liberal Intergovernmen-talist Approach, *Journal of Common Market Studies* 31 (1993), A. Moravcsik with K. Nicolaidis, Explaining the Treaty of Amsterdam: Interests, Influences, Institu-tions, *Journal of Common Market Studies* 37 (1999); A. Moravcsik, *The Choice for Europe. Social Purpose and State Power from Messina to Maastricht* (Ithaca NY, 1998).

118 A. Milward, *The European Rescue of the Nation State* (London, 1992).

119 D. Grimm, Does Europe Need a Constitution?, *European Law Journal* 1 (1995).

120 J. March and J. Olsen, *Democratic Governance* (New York, 1995).

121 Weiler, European Neo-constitutionalism, p. 4.

122 Ibid., pp. 5–6.

123 Ibid., p. 6.

124 See the discussion in Milward, *The European Rescue*; S. Hoffmann, Reflections on the

Nation-state in Europe Today, in L. Tsoukalis (ed.), *The European Community – Past, Present and Future* (Oxford, 1983); and Moravcsik, *The Choice for Europe*.

125 S. Hoffman, Obstinate or Obsolete? The Fate of the Nation-state and the Case of Western Europe, *Daedalus* 95 (1966).

126 John Stuart Mill, *Considerations on Representative Government* (first published 1861), Everyman edition, ed. H. B. Acton (London, 1980), p. 361.

127 Dobson, Constitutionalism and Citizenship, p. 6.

128 Ibid.

129 C. Beitz, Sovereignty and Morality in International Affairs, in D. Held (ed.), *Political Theory Today* (Cambridge, 1991); A. Linklater, *The Transformation of Political Community* (Cambridge, 1998).

130 H. Abromeit and S. Wolf, Will the Constitutional Treaty Contribute to the Legitimacy of the European Union? European Integration online Papers (EIoP) 9(11) (2005), p. 2, available at http://eiop.or.at/eiop/texte/2005-011a.htm.

131 J. Zielonka, Enlargement and the Finality of European Integration, in Harvard Law School Jean Monnet Papers (2000), Symposium: Responses to Joschka Fischer, ed. C. Joerges, Y. Mény and J. H. H. Weiler, pp. 8–9, available at http://www.jeanmonnetprogram.org/papers/00/00f0801.html.

132 J. Habermas, *The Postnational Constellation: Political Essays*, ed. N. Pensky (Cambridge MA, 2000); and J. Habermas, Why Europe Needs a Constitution, *New Left Review*, September–October 2001.

133 N. Walker, Europe's Constitutional Momentum and the Search for Polity Legitimacy. Jean Monnet Working Paper 5/04, New York University School of Law (2004), p. 39.

134 P. Cerny, Globalization and the Changing Logic of Collective Action, *International Organization* 49 (1995); P. Cerny, Globalization and the Erosion of Democracy, *European Journal of Political Research* 36 (1999); F. Scharpf, Negative and Positive Integration in the Political Integration of European Welfare States, in G. Marks *et al.* (eds), *Governance in the European Union* (London, 1996); F. Scharpf, *Governing in Europe: Effective and Democratic?* (Oxford, 1996).

135 Hans Morgenthau, *Politics among Nations: The Struggle for Power and Peace* (New York, 1946); K. Waltz, *Theory of International Politics* (New York, 1979).

136 S. Krasner, Compromising Westphalia, *International Security* 20(3) (1995); Y. Ferguson and R. Mansbach, Political Space and Westphalian States in a World of 'Polities': Beyond Inside/Outside, *Global Governance* 2 (1996).

137 La Palombella, Whose Europe, p. 7.

138 J. Caporaso, The European Union and Forms of State: Westphalian, Regulatory or Post-modern, *Journal of Common Market Studies* 34 (1996).

139 Dobson, Constitutionalism and Citizenship, p. 10.

140 A. Wiener, Making Sense of the New Geography of Citizenship – Fragmented Citizenship in the European Union, *Theory and Society* 26 (1997); see also G. Federico Mancini, Europe: The Case for Statehood, *European Law Journal* 4 (1998); J. Habermas, The European Nation State and the Pressures of Globalization, *New Left Review*, May 1999.

141 J. Weiler's contribution to the debate on the prospects for realising a EU state in Europe in the exchange with G. Mancini, Europe: The Case for Statehood and the Case Against. An Exchange. Harvard Law School Jean Monnet Papers (1998), p. 33, available at http://www.jeanmonnetprogram.org/papers/98/98-Europe_html.

142 La Palombella, Whose Europe, p. 25.

143 Ibid., p. 19.

144 Maduro, How Constitutional Can the European Union Be, p. 38.

145 N. MacCormick, Beyond the Sovereign State, *Modern Law Review* 56 (1993); N. MacCormick, Democracy, Subsidiarity and Citizenship in the European Commonwealth, *Law and Philosophy* 16 (1997); N. MacCormick, Liberalism, Nationalism and the Post-sovereign State, in R. Bellamy and D. Castiglione (eds), *Constitutionalism in Transformation: Europe and Theoretical Perspectives* (Oxford, 1996).

146 See W. Pogge, Cosmopolitanism and Sovereignty, *Ethics* 103 (1992); D. Held, *Democracy and the Global Order. From the Modern State to Cosmopolitan Governance* (Cambridge, 1995); J. Habermas, *The Inclusion of the Other. Studies in Political Theory: Sovereignty and the Design of Democratic Institutions. Working Papers.* Institute of Governmental Studies, University of California at Berkeley, available at http://www._igs.berkeley.edu?publications/working papers/WP2000_12pdf.

147 Dobson, Constitutionalism and Citizenship, p. 22.

148 T. Christiansen, Towards Statehood? The EU's Move towards Constitutionalism and Territorialisation. ARENA Working Paper no. 21, August 2005, p. 26, available at http://www.arena.uio.no.

149 See K. Featherstone and C. Radaelli (eds), *The Politics of Europeanization* (Oxford, 2003).

150 D. Curtin, Betwixt and Between: Democracy and Transparency in the Governance of the European Union, in A. Winter, D. Curtin, A. Kellermann and B. de Witte (eds), *Reforming the Treaty on European Union – The Legal Debate* (The Hague, 1996); D. Curtin and I. Dekker, The EU as a 'Layered' International Organization: Institutional Unity in Disguise, in P. Craig and G. de Burca (eds), *The Evolution of EU Law* (Oxford, 1999).

151 D. Curtin, The Constitutional Structure of the Union: A Europe of Bits and Pieces, *Common Market Law Review* 30 (1993).

152 A. von Bogdandy, Die Europäische Union als supranationale Föderation, *Integration* 22 (1999).

153 J. Shaw and A. Wiener, The Paradox of the 'European Polity'. Harvard Law School Jean Monnet Papers (1999), p. 17, available at http://www.jeanmonnetprogram.org/papers/99/991001.

154 J. Weiler, *The Constitution of Europe: Do the New Clothes Have an Emperor?* (Cambridge, 1999)

155 See G. Mancini's contribution to the debate on the prospects for realising an EU state in Europe, in the exchange with Weiler, Europe: The Case for Statehood and the Case Against. An Exchange; and G. Mancini, Europe: The Case for Statehood, *European Law Journal* 4 (1998); see also N. MacCormick, Sovereignty, Democracy and Subsidiarity, in R. Bellamy *et al.* (eds), *Democracy and Constitutional Culture in the Union of Europe* (Lothian Foundation, London, 1995) and N. MacCormick, Beyond the Sovereign State, *Modern Law Review* 56 (1993).

156 B. Donnelly, The Future is Federal. The Federal Trust (London, April 2003), p. 2.

157 Shaw and Wiener, The Paradox of the 'European Polity', p. 13.

158 Jo Shaw describes post-national constitution-making thus: 'as a vector rather than a point' whereby constitutionalism as a process conceives of 'linear assumptions about progress from a union of states to an integrated polity, and posits a reflexive critique of institutions, legal forms and identity beyond statist limits, in which the nation state is one actor, but not a privileged one'. J. Shaw, Process, Responsibility and Inclusion in EU Constitutionalism, *European Law Journal* 9 (2003), pp. 47–9.

159 In Case C-376/98 *Germany v. Parliament and Council* [2000] ECR I-8419 'Tobacco Advertising'.

160 Weatherill, Is Constitutional Finality Feasible, p. 5.

161 Ibid., p. 40.

162 See F. Snyder, Governing Economic Globalisation: Global Legal Pluralism and European Law, *European Law Journal* 5 (1999); B. Rosamond, Discourses of Globalization and the Social Construction of European Identities, *Journal of European Public Policy* 6 (1999).

163 K. Lenaerts, Constitutionalism and the Many Faces of Federalism, *American Journal of Comparative Law* 38 (1990).

164 Weiler, Federalism and Constitutionalism, pp. 3–4.

165 Joschka Fischer, From Confederacy to Federation: Thoughts on the Finality of Euro-

pean Integration, delivered at the Humboldt University, Berlin, May 2000, reproduced in C. Joerges, Y. Mény and J. Weiler (eds), *What Kind of Constitution for What Kind of Polity?* (Florence, Robert Schuman Centre for Advanced Studies, at the European University Institute, 2000), pp. 19–30.

166  Weiler, Federalism and Constitutionalism, pp. 5–6.

167  Fischer, From Confederacy to Federation.

168  J. Banquero Cruz, Whither Europe ... and When? Citizen Fischer and the European Federation, in Harvard Law School Jean Monnet Papers (2000), Symposium: Responses to Joschka Fischer, p. 8.

169  Weiler, Federalism and Constitutionalism, p. 3.

170  Ibid., pp. 2–3.

171  J. Weiler, Does Europe Need a Constitution? Demos, Telos and the German Maastricht Decision, *European Law Journal* 219 (1995).

172  Weiler, Federalism and Constitutionalism, p. 4; for a discussion of the limits of the classical federal model applied to the 'emergent' EU federation, and the nature of its multi-level governance, see T. Borzel and T. Risse, Who is Afraid of a European Federation? How to Constitutionalise a Multi-level Governance System, in Harvard Law School Jean Monnet Papers (2000), Symposium: Responses to Joschka Fischer; and L. Cata Becker, Forging Federal Systems within a Matrix of Contained Conflict. Harvard Law School Jean Monnet Papers (1998), available at http://www.jeanmonnetprogram.org/papers/98/98-4-html.

173  Zielonka, Enlargement and the Finality of European Integration, p. 10.

174  Weiler, in the exchange with G. Mancini, Europe: The Case for Statehood and the Case Against, p. 46.

175  Ibid., p. 7.

176  Ibid., p. 10; see also J. Weiler, Epilogue: The Fischer Debate – The Darker Side, in Harvard Law School Jean Monnet Papers (2000), Symposium: Responses to Joschka Fischer.

177  See, for instance, the case made in J. Weiler, A. Ballmann, U. Haltern, H. Hoffmann, F. Mayer and S. Screiner-Linford, Certain Rectangular Problems of European Integration, available at http://www.iue.it/AEL/EP/index html.

178  Zielonka, Enlargement and the Finality of European Integration, p. 10.

179  Weiler, in the exchange with G. Mancini, Europe: The Case for Statehood and the Case Against, p. 43.

180  J. Weiler *et al.*, Certain Rectangular Problems.

181  Weiler, in the exchange with G. Mancini, Europe: The Case for Statehood and the Case Against, p. 13.

182  Zielonka, Enlargement and the Finality of European Integration, p. 10; see a similar argument by R. Dehousse, Rediscovering Functionalism, in Harvard Law School Jean Monnet Papers (2000), Symposium: Responses to Joschka Fischer.

183  R. Bellamy and D. Castiglione, The Communitarian Ghost in the Cosmopolitan Machine: Democracy and the Reconfiguration of Politics in the New Europe, in R. Bellamy (ed.), *Constitutionalism, Democracy and Sovereignty: American and European Perspectives* (Aldershot, 1996); R. Bellamy and D. Castiglione, Building the Union: The Nature of Sovereignty in the Political Architecture of Europe, *Law and Philosophy* 16 (1997); P. Howe, A Community of Europeans: The Requisite Underpinnings, *Journal of Common Market Studies* 33 (1995); T. Kostakopolou, European Union Citizenship as a Model of Citizenship beyond the Nation State: Possibilities and Limits, in A. Weale and M. Nentwich (eds), *Political Theory and the European Union* (London, 1998).

184  This issue is discussed by A. Weale, Democratic Legitimacy and the Constitution of Europe, in R. Bellamy, V. Bufacchi and D. Castiglione (eds), *Democracy and Constitutional Culture in the Union of Europe* (London, 1995); C. Lord, Assessing Democracy in a Contested Polity, *Journal of Common Market Studies* 39 (2001); C. Lord and D. Beetham, Legitimizing the EU; T. Zweifel, Who Is without Sin Cast the First Stone:

The EU's Democratic Deficit in Comparison, *Journal of European Public Policy* 9 (2002); A. Menon and S. Weatherill, Legitimacy, Accountability and Delegation in the European Union, in A. Arnull and D. Wincott (eds), *Accountability and Legitimacy in the European Union* (Oxford, 2002).

185 Zielonka, Enlargement and the Finality of European Integration.

186 E. O. Eriksen, Deliberative Supranationalism in the EU, in E.O. Eriksen and J. E. Fossum (eds), *Democracy in the European Union. Integration through Deliberation?* (London, 2003), p. 51.

187 J-E. Lane, *Constitutions and Political Theory* (Manchester, 1996) pp. 19–25; G. Maddox, Constitution, in T. Ball, J. Farr and R. Hanson (eds), *Political Innovations and Conceptual Change* (Cambridge, 1989), p. 51.

188 S. Elkin, Constitutionalism's Successor, in S. Elkin and K. Soltan (eds), *A New Constitutionalism: Designing Political Institutions for a Good Society* (Chicago, 1993).

189 A. von Bogdandy and M. Nettesheim, Ex Pluribus Unum: Fusion of the European Communities into the European Union, *European Law Journal* 2(3) (1996); B. de Witte, The Pillar Structure and the Nature of the European Union: Greek Temple or French Gothic Cathedral, in T. Huekels *et al.* (eds), *The European Union after Amsterdam. A Legal Analysis* (The Hague, 1998),

190 Cata Becker, Forging Federal Systems, p. 2.

191 Kimmo Kiljunen, *The European Constitution in the Making* (Centre for European Policy Studies, Brussels, 2004), p. 9.

192 Ibid.

193 For an unflattering comparison of the two constitutional experiences, see Andrew Stuttaford, Constitutionally Indisposed, *National Review*, 22 February 2005.

194 Kiljunen, *The European Constitution in the Making* , p. 3.

195 *Library of Congress Information Bulletin* 62(3) (March 2003).

196 See P. Norman. *The Accidental Constitution* (Brussels, 2003), p. 192 and pp. 249–50.

197 See R. Bernstein, *Are We to Be a Nation?* (Cambridge MA, 1987).

198 Kiljunen, *The European Constitution in the Making* , p. 4.

199 Ibid., p. 5.

200 Ibid.

201 Treaty Establishing a Constitution for Europe, Title 1, Article 1, *Official Journal of the European Union*, C 310/11, 47(16) (December 2004).

202 Hirschl, Hegemonic Preservation in Action, p. 10.

203 Elazar, *Exploring Federalism*, pp. 158–65.

204 Ibid., p. 159.

205 D. McKay, *Federalism and the European Union. A Political Economy Perspective* (Oxford, 1999), especially at pp. 174–83.

206 There is an extensive and growing literature on the issue of post-national constitutionalism. See, for instance, R. Dahl, Is Post-national Democracy Possible?, in S. Fabbrini (ed.), *Nation, Federalism and Democracy* (Rome, 2000); R. Dehousse, Un Nouveau Constitutionalisme?, in R. Dehousse (ed.), *Une Constitution pour l'Europe?*, (Paris, 2002); A. Stone Sweet, What Is a Supranational Constitution?, *Review of Politics* 56 (1994).

207 Llorente, Constitutionalism in the 'Integrated' States of Europe, p. 2.

208 R. Watts, *Comparing Federal Systems* (Montreal,1999), p. 1.

209 D. Elazar, *Constitutionalizing Globalization: The Postmodern Revival of Confederal Arrangements* (New York, 1998), p. 3.

210 See L. Diez-Picazo, Treaty or Constitution? The Status of the Constitution for Europe. Jean Monnet Working Paper 5/04, New York University School of Law (2004).

211 Covell, European Union Constitution-making, p. 2; see also J. Hesse and V. Wright (eds), *Federalizing Europe? The Costs, Benefits and Preconditions of Federal Political Systems* (Oxford, 1995).

212 Palermo, Integration of Constitutional Values in the EU, p. 112.

213 Elazar, *Exploring Federalism*, p. 165.

## Chapter 3

1 J. Lodge, Intergovernmental Conferences and European Integration: Negotiating the Amsterdam Treaty, *International Negotiations* 3 (1998), p. 347.
2 Ibid., p. 349.
3 L. Hoffmann, The Convention on the Future of Europe – Thoughts on the Convention Model. Jean Monnet Working Paper 11/02, New York University School of Law (2002), p. 6, available at http://www.jeanmonnetprogram.org/papers02.html (2002); subsequently published in J. Shaw, P. Magnette, L. Hoffmann and A. Verges-Bausili, *The Convention on the Future of Europe. Working towards an EU Constitution*. Future of Parliamentary Democracy Series, 6. The Federal Trust (London, 2003).
4 Ibid., p. 5.
5 See the account in G. Ross, *Jacques Delors and European Integration* (New York, 1995).
6 D. Beach, Towards a New Method of Constitutional Bargaining? The Role and Impact of EU Institutions in the IGC and Convention Method of Treaty Reform. The Federal Trust (London, April 2003), pp. 6 and 9.
7 T. Christiansen and K. Jorgensen, Negotiating Treaty Reform in the European Union: The Role of the European Commission, *International Negotiations* (1998), p. 450.
8 X. Yataganas, The Treaty of Nice: The Sharing of Power and the Institutional Balance in the European Union – A Constitutional Perspective. Jean Monnet Working Paper 1/01, New York University School of Law (2001).
9 Ibid., p. 13.
10 L. Dobson, Constitutionalism and Citizenship in the European Union: A Normative Theoretical Approach. Constitutionalism Web-Papers no. 1 (2000), p. 1, available at http://les1.man.ac.uk/conweb.
11 C. Closa, Improving EU Constitutional Politics? A Preliminary Assessment of the Convention. Constitutionalism Web-Papers no. 1 (2003), p. 4, available at http://www.bath.ac.uk/esml/conWEB/Conweb%20papers-filestore/conweb1-2003.pdf.
12 Introductory speech by President Valéry Giscard d'Estaing to the Convention on the Future of Europe, 26 February 2002, SN 1565/02.
13 Hoffman, The Convention on the Future of Europe, p. 3.
14 Lodge, Intergovernmental Conferences, p. 351.
15 Closa, Improving EU Constitutional Politics, p. 4.
16 D. Curtin, The Constitutional Structure of the Union: A Europe of Bits and Pieces, *Common Market Law Review* 30 (1993).
17 W. Wessels, Nice Results: The Millennium IGC in the EU's Evolution, *Journal of Common Market Studies* 39 (2001).
18 J. Weiler, A Constitution for Europe? Some Hard Choices, *Journal of Common Market Studies* 40 (2002), p. 555.
19 Hoffman, The Convention on the Future of Europe, p. 3.
20 See http://www.cec.org.uk/info/pubs/bbriefs/bb/19.htm; and J. Molnar and W. Wessels (eds), *The European Union after the Treaty of Amsterdam* (London, 2001).
21 Yataganas, The Treaty of Nice.
22 Presidency Conclusions, Nice European Council Meeting, 7–9 December 2000, paragraph II. Press release no. 400/100, Brussels (8 December 2000); Presidency Conclusion, Cologne European Council Meeting, 3–4 June 1999, paragraph IV, CFSP Presidency, Cologne (April 1999), press release no:150/99.
23 Hoffmann, The Convention on the Future of Europe, p. 4.
24 G. Parker, Small Nations Square Up to EU Heavyweights over Commissioners, Voting Rights and God, *Financial Times*, 3 October 2003.
25 Hoffmann, The Convention on the Future of Europe, pp. 6–7.
26 Quoted in P. Norman, *The Accidental Constitution* (Brussels, 2003), p. 1.
27 L. Hoffmann and A.Verges-Bausili, The Reform of Treaty Revision Procedures: The

Convention on the Future of Europe, in T. Borzel and R. Cichowski (eds), *The State of the European Union VI: Law, Politics and Society* (Oxford, 2003).

28 The Resolution on the Treaty of Nice and the Future of the European Union, A 5-0168/2001, text published as Annexe 29 in B. de Witte, The Nice Declaration: Time for a Constitutional Treaty of the European Union?, *International Spectator* XXXVI(1) (2001).

29 See the special symposium on Fischer's Berlin speech, in Harvard Law School Jean Monnet Papers (2000), Symposium: Responses to Joschka Fischer, ed. C. Joerges, Y. Mény and J. H. H. Weiler, available at http://www.jeanmonnetprogram.org/papers/00/symp.html.

30 Ibid.

31 For the full text of this speech, see the French president's website at http://www.elysee.fr.

32 For the full text of the speech, see http://www.number10.gov.uk.

33 A. Hurrelmann, European Constitutionalism and Social Integration, *Die Zeit*, 16 April 2003.

34 C. Church, Implementing the New Constitutional Treaty: A Provisional Introduction. The Federal Trust for Education and Research, April 2003, p. 2.

35 Ibid.

36 S. Laitinen-Rawana, Creating a Unified Europe: Maastricht and Beyond, *International Lawyer* 973 (1994), p. 975.

37 P. Magnette, Deliberation vs. Negotiation. A First Analysis of the Convention on the Future of Union. Paper presented to the first pan-European conference of the ECPR Standing Group on the European Union, Bordeaux, 26–28 September 2002.

38 See the keynote speech by the Belgian prime minister, Guy Verhofstadt, advocating greater procedural simplicity and more transparency of the Union's policy instruments, delivered 24 June 2001, available at http://www.premier.fgov.be.

39 Declaration on the Future of the Union, available at http://www.europa.eu.int/futurum.

40 O. De Schutter, Europe in Search of Its Civil Society, in E. Eriksen, J. Fossum and A. Menendez (eds), The Chartering of Europe: The Charter of Fundamental Rights in Context. ARENA Report 8/2001.

41 CONV 9/02.

42 D. Dinan, Governance and Institutions: The Convention and the Intergovernmental Conference, in L. Miles (ed.), *The Journal of Common Market Studies Annual Review of the European Union 2003/2004* (Oxford, 2004), p. 28.

43 See the speech by A. Vitorino, The Convention as a Model for European Constitutionalization, available at http://www.europa.eu.int/futurum/documents/speeches/sp140601_en.htm.

44 P. Ludlow, *The Laeken Council* (EuroComment, Brussels, 2002), p. 73.

45 For a discussion of deliberative democracy and constitution-making, see C. Sustein, Constitutions and Democracy. An Epilogue, in J. Elster and R. Slagstad (eds), *Constitutionalism and Democracy* (Cambridge, 1988).

46 Quoted in Norman, *The Accidental Constitution*, pp. 23–4.

47 Hoffmann and Verges-Bausili, The Reform of Treaty Revision Procedures.

48 See the contribution to this debate made by two of the previous generation's political leaders, Giscard d'Estaing and Helmut Schmidt, *International Herald Tribune*, 11 April 2000.

49 Support for a wide-ranging constitutional review was by no means confined to the EU's leading statesmen. See, for instance, the intervention by the Finnish prime minister, Paavo Lipponen, speaking at the College of Europe in Bruges, calling on the Union to initiate a 'constitutionalising process' for the Union in his speech of 10 November 2000, available at http://www.government.fi; and J. Chirac, Notre Europe, speech delivered to the Bundestag, 27 June 2000, available at http://www.elysee.fr/cgibin/auracom/aurweb/search.

50  P. Magnette, Deliberation or Bargaining? Coping with Constitutional Conflicts in the Convention on the Future of Europe, in Eriksen *et al.*, The Chartering of Europe, p. 210.

51  It was this conference that launched the current constitution debate, by approving a Declaration in favour of an EU Constitution. See Bulletin EC 11-1990, point 1.1.1, p. 10; and the EP Resolution, 12 July 1990, about the preparation for a joint meeting – an assize – with national parliaments to review the EU's constitutional future; see also Second Interim Report (Duverger Report), Doc. A 3-162/90 22.6.90.

52  See the text of Lipponen's speech at the EUI, Florence, 9 April 2001, available at http:// valtioneuvosto.fi/liston/base.1sp?r=5300&k=en&old=1300.

53  Ludlow, The Laeken Council.

54  Closa, Improving EU Constitutional Politics, p. 5.

55  See Convention documents CONV 345/01/02 REV I; CONV 345/02; CONV 277/02; CONV 178/02; CONV 88/02; CONV 66/02 on the official Convention website at http:// european-convention.eu.int/bienvenue.

56  The Resolution on the Constitutional Process and the Future of the Union 2001/280 (INI) Doc. A-50368/2001.

57  Church, Implementing the New Constitutional Treaty, p. 3.

58  The Resolution on the Amsterdam Treaty, 8 December 1997, OJ C 371; and the Resolution on the Constitutionalization of the Treaties, 25 October 2000, A 5-0289/2000.

59  N. Walker, Europe's Constitutional Momentum and the Search for Polity Legitimacy. Jean Monnet Working Paper 5/04, New York University School of Law (2004), p. 35.

60  E. Philippart, The Convention on the Future of the EU. CEPS Policy Brief, no. 11, February 2002; and Declaration on the Future of the Union, nos. 3 and 4, *Official Journal of the European Communities*, C 80/85, 10 March 2001.

61  F. Deloche-Gaudez, The Convention on a Charter of Fundamental Rights: A Method for the Future? Groupement d'Études et de Recherches Notre Europe, Research and Policy Paper no. 15 (2001).

62  Benelux Memorandum on the Future of Europe, 26 June 2001, available at http:// europa.eu.int/futurum/documents/other/oth200601_en.htm.

63  Magnette, Deliberation or Bargaining; Hoffmann, The Convention on the Future of Europe.

64  Ibid.

65  Deloche-Gaudez, The Convention on a Charter, p. 23.

66  Closa, Improving EU Constitutional Politics.

67  Deloche-Gaudez, The Convention on a Charter, p. 12.

68  K. Kiljunen, *The European Constitution in the Making* (Centre for European Policy Studies, Brussels, 2004), p. 25.

69  For a full account of the Laeken Council, see Ludlow, The Laeken Council.

70  Kiljunen, *The European Constitution in the Making*, p. 44.

71  The Laeken Declaration, SN 300/1/01 REV1 Annexe I, II. Convening of a Convention on the Future of Europe.

72  Kiljunen, *The European Constitution in the Making*, p. 25.

73  Dinan, Governance and Institutions, p. 27.

74  See J. Schonlau, Time Was of the Essence: Timing and Framing Europe's Constitutional Convention, in C. Closa and J. Fossum (eds), Deliberative Constitutional Politics in the EU. ARENA Report 5/04 (Oslo, 2004).

75  Philippart, The Convention on the Future of the EU, pp. 2–3.

76  J. E. Fossum, Still a Union of Deep Diversity? The Convention and the Constitution for Europe, in E. O. Eriksen, J. E. Fossum and A. J. Menendez (eds), *Developing a Constitution for Europe* (London, 2004), p. 233.

77  Magnette, Deliberation or Bargaining.

78  Cited by K. Hughes, The Future of Europe Convention: Travelling Hopefully? Joint Working Paper, EPIN (European Policy Studies Network) and CEPS (Centre for European Policy Studies, Brussels), May 2002, p. 4.

79 See http://European-convention.eu.int/docs/speeches/1.pdf.
80 Hoffmann, The Convention on the Future of Europe, p. 18.
81 Giscard, quoted in Norman, *The Accidental Constitution*, p. 47.
82 Giscard, cited in CONV 601/3, Summary Report on the Plenary Session, Brussels, 27 and 28 February 2003 (Brussels, March 2003).
83 Magnette, Deliberation or Bargaining.
84 *More Europe*. The Programme of the Spanish Presidency of the EU, 1-1/30-6-2002, available at http://www.ue2002.es/principal.asp/opcion=3&subsopcion=1&idioma= ingles.
85 Hoffmann, The Convention on the Future of Europe, p. 9; see also How the 15 Agreed on Giscard d'Estaing, *EU Observer*, 17 December 2001.
86 V. Giscard d'Estaing, Briefing Note: Convention Plenary, 24–25 April 2002, available at http://www.epha.org/a/255.
87 M. Covell, European Union Constitution-making in Comparative Perspective. The Federal Trust (London, October 2003), p. 5.
88 Dinan, Governance and Institutions, p. 28.
89 Covell, European Union Constitution-making, p. 4.
90 Closa, Improving EU Constitutional Politics, p. 5.
91 See L. Lindner and B. Rittberger, The Creation, Interpretation, and Contestation of Institutions – Revisiting Historical Institutionalism, *Journal of Common Market Studies* 41 (2003).
92 Giscard d'Estaing, Briefing Note: Convention Plenary.
93 Beach, Towards a New Method of Constitutional Bargaining, p. 2.
94 J. Shaw, Responsibility and Inclusion in EU Constitutionalism: The Challenge for the Convention on the Future of Europe. The Federal Trust for Education and Research, Working Paper, September 2002, p. 18. See http://www.fedtrust.co.uk/EU/constitution.
95 Closa, Improving EU Constitutional Politics, p. 8.
96 Ibid.
97 Ibid., pp. 2, 15 and 16.
98 Ibid.
99 Norman, *The Accidental Constitution*, p. 160.
100 COM (2002) 247 Final.
101 See the Penelope document on the EU's 'Futurum' website at http://europa.eu.int/futurum/index_en.htm.
102 CONV 457/02.
103 COM (2002) 728 Final; see also CONV 448/02.
104 Ibid.
105 Hoffmann, The Convention on the Future of Europe, p. 9.
106 Dinan, Governance and Institutions, p. 31.
107 Closa, The Convention Method and the Transformation of EU Constitutional Politics, in Eriksen *et al.*, The Chartering of Europe, p. 189.
108 Dinan, Governance and Institutions, p. 31.
109 Ibid.
110 Norman, *The Accidental Constitution*, pp. 155–9.
111 Dinan, Governance and Institutions, p. 32.
112 D. Mitrany, *The Progress of International Government* (William E. Dodge Lectures) (New Haven, 1932).
113 The Committee of the Regions, Liège Declaration, November 2001, Resolution on Strengthening the Role of the Regions with Legislative Power in the European Union. Second Conference of the Presidents of Regions with Legislative Power, available at http://www.europa.eu.int/futurum/conoth_en.htm#po.
114 Ludlow, The Laeken Council, pp. 55–69; Magnette, Deliberation or Bargaining.
115 P. Norman, From the Convention to the IGC (Institutions), paper presented at the thirty-third annual PSA conference in Newcastle, 2–4 September 2003, p. 3.

116 See for example, The European Project of the Socialist Party: The New Federalism (CONV 182/02).
117 See http://www.europa.eu.int/futurum.
118 A Constitution for a Strong Europe, CONV 325/02.
119 A Model Constitution for a Federal Union of Europe, CONV 234/02.
120 H. Kitschelt, European Party Systems: Continuity and Change, in M. Rhodes, Paul Heywood and V. Wright (eds), *Developments in West European Politics* (Basingstoke, 1997), especially at pp. 146–9.
121 Ibid., p. 149
122 There is an extensive literature on this matter. See, for example, T. Borzel, Towards Convergence in Europe? Institutional Adaptation to Europeanization in Germany and Spain, *Journal of Common Market Studies* 37 (1999); T. Borzel, Pace-setting, Foot-dragging and Fence-sitting: Member State Responses to Europeanization, *Journal of Common Market Studies* 40 (2002); M. Green Cowles, J. Caporaso, and T. Risse (eds), *Transforming Europe: Europeanization and Domestic Change* (London, 2001); C. Knill, *The Europeanization of National Administrations. Patterns of Institutional Change and Persistence* (Cambridge, 2001).
123 A. J. Menendez, Three Conceptions of the European Constitution. ARENA Working Paper 03/12, p. 18, available at http://www.arena.uio.no/publications/wp03_12.
124 Deloche-Gaudez, The Convention on a Charter, p. 18.
125 Closa, Improving EU Constitutional Politics, p. 15.
126 Ibid., p. 16.
127 Norman, *The Accidental Constitution*, p. 50.
128 Shaw, Responsibility and Inclusion in EU Constitutionalism, p. 25.
129 B. Crum, Laying Building Blocks or Just Window Dressing? The First Half Year of the Convention and the Future of the EU. *CEPS Commentary*, July 2002, p. 2.
130 Follow-up to inaugural session of Convention: 08/03/2002, CONV 8/02, annexe II.
131 Closa, Improving EU Constitutional Politics, p. 16.
132 Ibid.; see also J. Scott, The Culture of Constitution-making? 'Listening' at the Convention on the Future of Europe, *German Law Journal* 3(9) (2002), available at http://www.germanlawjournal.com.
133 Johannes Voggenhuber, an Austrian Green MEP, cited in Norman, *The Accidental Constitution*, p. 51.
134 Scott, The Culture of Constitution-making, pp. 4–6.
135 M. Keating, Regions and the Convention on the Future of Europe, *South European Society and Politics* 9(1) (2003).
136 Crum, Laying Building Blocks, p. 2.
137 See http://www.fedtrust.co.uk; see also interview with Michel Barnier, Choisir une Europe sous influence américaine ou une Europe indépendente, *Le Monde*, 23 May 2002; Giscard d'Estaing, Briefing Note: Convention Plenary.
138 Deloche-Gaudez, The Convention on a Charter, p. 23.
139 Crum, Laying Building Blocks, p. 2.
140 Cited in S. Kurpas, The Convention on the Future of Europe – Complex But Not Unknown. CEPS Commentaries, p. 1, available at http://www.ceps.be/Commentary/Sep03/Kurpas.php.
141 Closa, Improving EU Constitutional Politics, p. 16.
142 See I. Pernice, De la constitution composée de l'Europe, *Revue trimestrielle de droit européen* 36 (2000), pp. 623–4; and *EU Observer*, Non-paper on Basic Treaty, by the convention's secretariat, 15 June 2002: Convention document CONV 250.
143 Scott, The Culture of Constitution-making.
144 *Eurobarometer* 55–8 inclusive, spring 2001/autumn 2002.
145 Closa, Improving EU Constitutional Politics, p. 22.
146 Hughes, The Future of Europe Convention, p. 9.
147 Ibid., p. 1.

148  For details see Note on the Inaugural Meeting, 28 February 2002, Brussels: *11/03/2002*, CONV 7/02; and Requests by the Candidate Countries: *14/03/2002*, CONV 10/02 and CONV 18/02.

149  Closa, Improving EU Constitutional Politics, p. 8.

150  The terms 'president' and 'vice-president' came to replace the terms 'chairman' and 'vice-chairman' used in the English-language version of the Laeken Declaration.

151  Hughes, The Future of Europe Convention.

152  Norman, *The Accidental Constitution*, p. 159.

153  Ibid.

154  Ibid., p. 152.

155  Ludlow, The Laeken Council, pp. 68–70.

156  Dinan, Governance and Institutions, pp. 28–9.

157  See the contribution by the Council president, Aznar, at the opening of the Convention on the Future of the European Union, Brussels, 28 February 2002: 04/07/2002, CONV 97/02, p. 4.

158  Closa, Improving EU Constitutional Politics, p. 13.

159  See, for instance, Giscard's speech at the College of Europe, Bruges, October 2002, cited at http://www.observer.com.

160  Hughes, The Future of Europe Convention.

161  G. Stuart, Caught in the Coils of Giscard's Folly, *Sunday Times Review*, 7 December 2003.

162  There is evidence of his unilateralism in his article in *Le Monde*, 22 July 2002, in various high-profile speeches and in his interview with the *Financial Times*, 7 October 2002.

163  See the Verbatim Report of the session at http://www.europarl.eu.int/europe2004/textes/verbatim_020624.htm.

164  Note on the plenary meeting, Brussels 6 and 7 June 2002: *19/06/2002;* CONV 97/02, p. 4.

165  Ibid., p. 7.

166  Hoffmann and Verges-Bausili, The Reform of Treaty Revision Procedures.

167  Closa, Improving EU Constitutional Politics, p. 12.

168  Interview reported in the *Washington Post*, 2 September 2003.

169  W. Zartman, The Structure of Negotiations, in V. Kremenyuk (ed.), *International Negotiation: Analysis, Approaches, Issues* (San Francisco, 1999); and G. Garrett and G. Tsebelis, An Institutional Critique of Intergovernmentalism, *International Organization* 50 (1996).

170  Closa, Improving EU Constitutional Politics, p. 12.

171  Ibid., p. 13.

172  H. Abromeit and S. Wolf, Will the Constitutional Treaty Contribute to the Legitimacy of the European Union? European Integration online Papers (EIoP), 9(11) (2005), p. 8, available at http://eiop.or.at/eiop/texte/2005-011a.htm.

173  Kiljunen, *The European Constitution in the Making*, p. 37.

174  Gisela Stuart, *The Making of Europe's Constitution* (Fabian Society, London, December 2003); see also her report to a joint standing committee on the Convention of the two Houses of Parliament, 12 February 2003.

175  Dinan, Governance and Institutions, p. 29.

176  Norman, *The Accidental Constitution*, p. 223.

177  Dinan, Governance and Institutions, p. 29.

178  Abromeit and Wolf, Will the Constitutional Treaty, p. 8.

179  Menendez, Three Conceptions of the European Constitution, p. 30.

180  C. Archer, Implementing the New Constitutional Treaty: A Provisional Introduction. The Federal Trust (London, April 2003), p. 3.

181  See Giscard's report to the European Council, 16 April 2003, in the speeches section of the Convention website. For the text of the presidency press conference, 16 April 2003, see http://www.eu2003.gr.

182  Closa, Improving EU Constitutional Politics, p. 14.
183  J. E. Fossum, Contemporary European Constitution-making: Constrained or Reflexive. Centre for European Studies, ARENA Working Paper no. 4 (Oslo, January 2005), p. 13; see also Magnette, Deliberation or Bargaining.
184  Kiljunen, *The European Constitution in the Making*, p. 56.
185  Norman, *The Accidental Constitution*, p. 129.
186  Note on the plenary meeting, Brussels, 6 and 7 June 2002: *19/06/2002* CONV 97/02; Note on the plenary meeting, Brussels, 23 and 24 May 2002: *29/05/2002* CONV 60/02.
187  Closa, Improving EU Constitutional Politics, pp. 14–15.
188  Kiljunen, *The European Constitution in the Making*, p. 56.
189  Beach, Towards a New Method of Constitutional Bargaining, p. 9.
190  T. Christiansen, The Role of Supranational Actors in EU Treaty Reform, *Journal of European Public Policy* 9 (2002), p. 47.
191  Sir John Kerr, cited in the Summary of Conference Proceedings, EU 25: Making It Work, 19–20 February. CEPS Conference Reports, February 2004, p. 9.
192  Norman, *The Accidental Constitution*, p. 37.
193  Ibid., pp. 37–8.
194  Norman, From the Convention to the IGC, p. 3.
195  Beach, Towards a New Method of Constitutional Bargaining, p. 10.
196  Ibid, p. 7.
197  Closa, Improving EU Constitutional Politics, p. 7.
198  Kerr, cited in Summary of Conference Proceedings, p. 8.

**Chapter 4**

1  L. Hoffman, The Convention on the Future of Europe – Thoughts on the Convention Model. Jean Monnet Working Paper 11/02, New York University School of Law (2002), available at http://www.jeanmonnetprogram.org/papers02.html.
2  E. Philippart, The Convention on the Future of the EU. CEPS Policy Brief no. 11 (2002), p. 4.
3  L. Dobson, Constitutionalism and Citizenship in the European Union: A Normative Theoretical Approach. Constitutionalism Web-Papers no. 1 (2000), p. 19, available at http://les1.man.ac.uk/conweb.
4  J. Lodge, Transparency and Democratic Legitimacy, *Journal of Common Market Studies* 32 (1994), p. 361.
5  Dobson, Constitutionalism and Citizenship, p. 19.
6  A. Weale, Democratic Legitimacy and the Constitution of Europe, in R. Bellamy, V. Bufacchi and D. Castiglione (eds), *Democracy, and Constitutional Culture in the Union of Europe* (London, 1995).
7  Dobson, Constitutionalism and Citizenship, p. 19.
8  Ibid.
9  K. Hughes, The Future of Europe's Convention: Travelling Hopefully? Joint Working Paper, EPIN (European Policy Studies Network) and CEPS (Centre for European Policy Studies, Brussels), May 2002, pp. 4 and 11.
10  Ibid., p. 15.
11  Ibid., p. 12.
12  Ibid., p. 9.
13  Ibid.
14  Ibid., p. 14.
15  K. Hughes, State of the Union. There They Go Again, *Wall Street Journal*, 30 May 2002.
16  B. Crum and W. Coussens, Reforming the EU Presidency: The Key to a New Institutional Architecture. CEPS Commentary, January 2003, p. 1, available at http://www.

ceps.be/Commentary/Jan03/Crum.php.

17 K. Hughes, Franco-German Plans for a Dual Presidency – A Short Comment. CEPS Commentary, January 2003, p.1, available at http://www.ceps.be/Commentary/Jan03/Hughes2.php.

18 D. Gross and W. Hager, Reforming the Council Presidency. CEPS Commentary, June 2002, p. 2, available at http://www.ceps.be/Commentary/jun02/gros-hager.php.

19 Foreign secretary's speech, Reforming Europe: New Era, New Questions, The Hague, 21 February 2002, reported at http://fco.gov/uk/servlet.

20 Chirac's speech, 26 February 2002, available at http://www.ambafrance-uk.org/Nice-Treaty-signature-Speech-by-M.html; and interview reported in the *Financial Times*, 6 February 2002.

21 Hughes, State of the Union, p. 20

22 At the May 2002 Convention; see plenary summary CONV 60/02, available at http://register.consilium.eu.int/pdf/en/02/cv00/00060en2.pdf.

23 Crum and Coussens, Reforming the EU Presidency, p. 2.

24 Ibid., p. 2.

25 Hughes, State of the Union, p. 23.

26 K. Hughes, Giving Brussels a Sense of Direction. CEPS Commentary, January 2003, p. 1, available at http://www.ceps.be/Commentary/Jan03/Hughes.php.

27 Ibid., p. 2

28 D. Gross and W. Hager, Reforming the Council Presidency, p. 1; Hughes, State of the Union, p. 19.

29 R. Schub, 'Let's All Talk' – Bringing Brussels' Outsiders into the EU Fold, *European Voice* 30, 10 July 2002.

30 Ibid.

31 K. Hughes, State of the Union, p. 26.

32 K. Hughes, Giving Brussels a Sense of Direction.

33 L. Hoffmann, Linking National Politics to Europe – An Opposing Argument. Federal Trust for Education and Research (London, June 2002), p. 18.

34 S. Hix, Linking National Politics to Europe. Network Europe Policy Brief, available at http://network-europe.net/political-competition test.

35 R. Corbett, F. Jacobs and M. Shackleton, *The European Parliament* (London, 2000), p. 213.

36 See Hoffmann, Linking National Politics to Europe.

37 Ibid., p. 16.

38 K. Hughes, Giving Brussels a Sense of Direction, p. 1._

39 Ibid., p. 2.

40 Hoffmann, Linking National Politics to Europe, p. 9.

41 K. Hughes, State of the Union, p. 23.

42 Hughes, The Future of Europe's Convention, p. 1; Hughes, State of the Union, p. 19.

43 Gross and Hager, Reforming the Council Presidency, p. 3.

44 Hughes, State of the Union, p. 21

45 COM (2002) p. 247.

46 C. Closa, Improving EU Constitutional Politics? A Preliminary Assessment of the Convention? Constitutionalism Web-Papers no. 1 (2003), p. 6, available at http://www.bath.ac.uk/esml/conWEB/Conweb%20papers-filestore/conweb1-2003.pdf; see also F. Deloche-Gaudez, The Convention on a Charter of Fundamental Rights: A Method for the Future? Groupement d'Études et de Recherches Notre Europe, Research and Policy Paper no. 15 (2001).

47 Cited in Hughes, State of the Union, p. 5

48 G. Majone (ed.), *Regulating Europe* (London, 1996); F. Scharpf, *Governing in Europe: Effective and Democratic?* (Oxford, 1999), pp. 7–13.

49 Hughes, State of the Union, p. 25.

50 Gross and Hager, Reforming the Council Presidency, p. 1.

51  Ibid.
52  M. Maduro, How Constitutional Can the European Union Be? The Tension Between Intergovernmentalism and Constitutionalism in the European Union. Jean Monnet Working Paper 5/04, New York University School of Law (2004), p. 19; see also P. Laenarts and de Smijter, The Question of Democratic Representation, in A. Winter, D. Curtin, A. Kellermann and B. de Witte (eds), *Reforming the Treaty on European Union – The Legal Debate* (The Hague, 1996).
53  Hughes, State of the Union, p. 17.
54  Ibid., p. 18.
55  V. Giscard d'Estaing, Briefing Note: Convention Plenary, 24–25 April 2002, available at http://www.epha.org/a/255.
56  Hughes, State of the Union, p. 18.
57  B. de Witte, Simplification and Reorganization of the European Treaties, *Common Market Law Review* 39 (2002).
58  Hughes, State of the Union, p. 28.
59  Ibid., p. 13.
60  Laeken Declaration, December 2001, p. 2, available at http://european-convention.eu.int/pdf/LKNEN.pdf.
61  Hughes, State of the Union, p. 28.
62  COM (2002), 728 Final and CONV 448/02.
63  CONV 47/02, 23 and 24 May meeting that discussed the competencies question.
64  Hughes, State of the Union, p. 29.
65  COM (2002) p. 247; see also R. Prodi, Towards a Closer Union? The Institutional Structure of the EU and the Role of European Citizens, 13 June 2003, available at http://www.cie.gov.pl/futurum.nsf/0/C9EA3494D868281FC1256D490035E302/$File/Prodi1.pdf.
66  D. Gros, The Franco-German Couple in the EU: From Motor to Brake. CEPS Commentary, November 2003, p. 1, available at http://www.ceps.be/Commentary/Nov03/Gros.php.
67  Ibid., p. 2.
68  See the interview by Fischer in the *Frankfurter Allgemeine Zeitung*, 17 January 2003.
69  U. Guerot, K. Hughes, M. Lefebvre and T. Egenhoff, France, Germany and the UK in the Convention. EPIN Working Paper no. 7, July 2003, p. 5.
70  Report to the House of Commons on the Thessaloniki European Council, 18 June 2003, available at http://www.britainusa.com/sections/articles_show_nt1.asp?.
71  Guerot *et al.*, France, Germany and the UK.
72  Ibid.
73  K. Hughes, What Sort of Europe Does Blair Really Want? CEPS Commentary, December 2002, p. 1, available at http://www.ceps.be/Commentary/Dec02/Hughes.php.
74  Guerot *et al.*, France, Germany and the UK, p. 6.
75  CONV 591/03.
76  The best account by far of Britain's problematic relations with Europe is Hugo Young, *This Blessed Plot: Britain and Europe from Churchill to Blair* (London,1999); Philip Stephens of the *Financial Times* delivered the first Hugo Young Memorial Lecture at Chatham House on 20 October 2004, available at http://www.guardian.co.uk/comment/story/0,,1331787,00.html#article_continue.
77  H. Wallace. Possible Futures for the European Union: A British Reaction, in Harvard Law School Jean Monnet Papers (2000), Symposium: Responses to Joschka Fischer, ed. C. Joerges, Y. Mény and J. H. H. Weiler, p. 7, available at http://www.jeanmonnet-program.org/papers/00/00f0801.html.
78  U. Guerot and T. Egenhoff, Nothing But Federalism? The German Position on the Constitutionalization of the European Union, February 2003, available at http://194.78.234.19/europe/strand_one_detail.asp.
79  Guerot *et al.*, France, Germany and the UK, p. 2.

80 Ibid., p. 6.
81 J. Temple Lang, The Convention on the Future of Europe – So Far. The Federal Trust (London, June 2003), p. 9.
82 P. Norman, *The Accidental Constitution* (Brussels, 2003), p. 136.
83 D. Kral, I. Brinar and J. Almer, The Position of the Small Countries towards Institutional Reform: From Tyranny of the Small to Directoire of the Big? EPIN Working Paper no. 6, June 2003, p. 1.
84 CONV 646/03.
85 D. Dinan, Governance and Institutions: The Convention and the Intergovernmental Conference, in L. Miles (ed.), *The Journal of Common Market Studies Annual Review of the European Union 2003/2004* (Oxford, 2004), p. 34.
86 Kral *et al.*, The Position of the Small Countries, p. 2.
87 Ibid., p. 8.
88 Temple Lang, The Convention on the Future of Europe, p. 8.
89 See J. Temple Lang, How Much Do the Smaller Member States Need the European Commission?, *Common Market Law Review* 39 (2002).
90 Temple Lang, The Convention on the Future of Europe, p. 8.
91 F. Cameron and A. Primatarova, Enlargement, CFSP and the Convention: The Role of the Accession States. EPIN Working Paper no. 5, June 2003, p. 11, available at http://www.ceps.be.
92 I. Motoc, Europe and Its Teleology: Is There a Central-Eastern Vision?, in Harvard Law School Jean Monnet Papers (2000), Symposium: Responses to Joschka Fischer, p. 13.
93 Statement on Iraq by eight European leaders, 30 January 2003, available at http://www.acronym.org.uk/docs/0301/doc25.htm.
94 Kral *et al.*, The Position of the Small Countries, p. 8.
95 Ibid., p. 5.
96 Cited in Cameron and Primatarova, Enlargement, CFSP and the Convention, p. 11.

**Chapter 5**

1 Note on the Working Methods, 14 March 2002, CONV 9/02, Brussels; revision of CONV 3/02.
2 Laeken Declaration SN 300/1/01 REV I; see also Note on the Plenary Meeting, Brussels, 21 and 22 March 2002; *25/03/02*; CONV 14/02.
3 C. Closa, Improving EU Constitutional Politics? A Preliminary Assessment of the Convention. Constitutionalism Web-Papers no. 1 (2003), p. 11, available at http://www.bath.ac.uk/esml/conWEB/Conweb%20papers-filestore/conweb1-2003.pdf.
4 Ibid., p. 21.
5 P. Ludlow, *The Laeken Council* (EuroComment, Brussels, 2002), p. 60.
6 K. Hughes, The Battle for Power in Europe. Will the Convention Get It Right? EPIN Working Paper no. 4, February 2003, p. 1, available at http://www.ceps.be.
7 For example, see the discussion in CONV 234/02, CONTRIB 82; CONV 345/1/02, REV 1; and CONV 235/02, CONTRIB 83.
8 P. Norman, From the Convention to the IGC, paper presented at the thirty-third annual PSA conference, Newcastle, 2–4 September 2003, p. 3.
9 Closa, Improving EU Constitutional Politics, p. 18.
10 L. Hoffmann, The Convention on the Future of Europe – Thoughts on the Convention Model. Jean Monnet Working Paper 11/02, New York University School of Law (2002), p. 9, available at http://www.jeanmonnetprogram.org/papers02.html.
11 P. Magnette, Deliberation vs. Negotiation. A First Analysis of the Convention on the Future of Union, paper presented to the first pan-European conference of the ECPR Standing Group on the European Union, Bordeaux, 26–28 September 2002; and E. Philippart, The 'European Convention': Anatomy of the New Approach to Constitution-making in the EU, *EUSA Review* 15(2) (2002).

12 CONV 3/02, 27 February 2002.
13 F. Deloche-Gaudez, The Convention on a Charter of Fundamental Rights: A Method for the Future? Groupement d'Études et de Recherches Notre Europe, Research and Policy Paper no. 15 (2001), p. 36.
14 Magnette, Deliberation vs. Negotiation.
15 Note on the plenary meeting, Brussels, 23 and 24 May 2002; 29/05/2002 CONV 60/02.
16 Requests by the candidate countries, 14/03/2002 CONV 10/02.
17 Interpretation from the languages of applicant countries, 28/03/2002 CONV 18/02.
18 See the discussion of the role of the mass media in the process of instilling political identity at Chapter 12.
20 CONV 97/02.
21 Hoffmann, The Convention on the Future of Europe, p. 10; The Laeken Declaration, SN 300/1/01 REV 1, Annexe I, II. Convening of a Convention on the Future of Europe, Forum, p. 25.
22 H. Abromeit and S. Wolf, Will the Constitutional Treaty Contribute to the Legitimacy of the European Union? European Integration online Papers (EIoP), 9(11) (2005), p. 8, available at http://eiop.or.at/eiop/texte/2005-011a.htm.
23 D. Dinan, Governance and Institutions: The Convention and the Intergovernmental Conference, in L. Miles (ed.), *The Journal of Common Market Studies Annual Review of the European Union 2003/2004* (Oxford, 2004), p. 29.
24 CONV 9/02.
25 D. Spirant, Parliament Wants to Limit Giscard's Influence, *EU Observer*, 30 January 2002.
26 Norman, From the Convention to the IGC.
27 D. Beach, Towards a New Method of Constitutional Bargaining? The Role and Impact of EU Institutions in the IGC and Convention Method Treaty Reform, paper delivered at the Federal Trust Conference on the Future of Europe, 10–11 July 2003; see the Federal Trust for Education and Research website at http://www.fedtrust.co.uk.
28 P. Norman, *The Accidental Constitution* (Brussels, 2003), p. 45.
29 Ibid., pp. 45–6.
30 J. Shaw, P. Magnette, L. Hoffmann and A. Verges-Bausili, *The Convention on the Future of Europe. Working towards an EU Constitution.* Future of Parliamentary Democracy Series, 6. The Federal Trust (London, 2003).
31 See Giscard's speech to the Convention's opening session, 28 February 2002, CONV 04/02.
32 Ibid.; verbatim report available at http://www.europarl.eu.int/europe2004/textes/verbatim_020624.htm.
33 Ibid.
34 See www.EUobserver.com.
35 Note on the plenary meeting, Brussels, 21 and 22 March 2002: 25/03/2002, CONV 14/02.
36 Preliminary draft Constitutional Treaty, CONV 369/02, Brussels, 28 October 2002.
37 See, for instance, House of Commons, Gisela Stuart and David Heathcote-Amery, Convention on the Future of Europe – First Progress Report from the UK National Parliamentary Representatives, 30 April 2002;House of Commons, Convention on the Future of Europe – Second Progress Report from the UK National Parliamentary Representatives, 20 June 2002.
38 J. Shaw, Process, Responsibility and Inclusion in EU Constitutionalism: The Challenge for the Convention on the Future of the Union. The Federal Trust for Education and Research Working Paper, September 2002, p. 25, available at www.fedtrust.co.uk/EU_constitution.
39 Motion for a decision on the preparation of a Constitutional Treaty, 10/07/02; CONV 181/02. The interface of practitioners and academics has long been a feature of constitutional reflection in the EU: for an early example, see A Constitution for the European Union? Proceedings of a Conference, 12–13 May 1994, Organised by the Robert

Schuman Centre with the Patronage of the European Parliament. EUI Working Paper RSC no. 95/9.

40 K. Hughes, The Future of Europe's Convention: Travelling Hopefully? Joint Working Paper, EPIN (European Policy Studies Network) and CEPS (Centre for European Policy Studies, Brussels) May 2002, p. 3.

41 Giscard, speech to the Convention's opening session.

42 K. Kiljunen, *The European Constitution in the Making* (Centre for European Policy Studies, Brussels, 2004), p. 41.

43 Norman, *The Accidental Constitution*, p. 45.

44 Deloche-Gaudez, The Convention on a Charter, p. 25.

45 See Giscard's speech to the Convention's opening session.

46 Hughes, The Future of Europe's Convention, p. 3.

47 B. Crum, Laying Building Blocks or Just Window Dressing? The First Half Year of the Convention and the Future of the EU. *CEPS Commentary*, July 2002, p. 2, available at http://www.ceps.be/Commentary/jul02/crum.php.

48 Norman, From the Convention to the IGC, p. 3.

49 Beach, Towards a New Method of Constitutional Bargaining, p. 11.

50 D. Galloway, *The Treaty of Nice and Beyond – Realities and Illusions of Power in the EU* (Sheffield, 2001).

51 G. de Burca, The Drafting of the European Union Charter of Fundamental Rights, *European Law Review* 26 (2001); and A. Maurer, Less Bargaining – More Deliberation: The Convention Method for Enhancing EU Democracy, *Internationale Politik und Gesellschaft* 1 (2003).

52 D. Dinan, Institutions and Governance 2001–02: Debating the EU's Future, in G. Edwards and G. Wiessala (eds), *The Journal of Common Market Studies Annual Review of the European Union 2000/2001* (Oxford, 2002).

53 D. Metcalfe, Leadership in European Union Negotiations: The Presidency of the Council, *International Negotiation* 3 (1998), p. 425; and A. Moravcsik, A New Statecraft? Supranational Entrepreneurs and International Cooperation, *International Organization* 53 (1999), p. 279.

54 A. Stubb, *Negotiating Flexibility in the European Union* (Basingstoke, 2002), p. 27.

55 D. Beach, Towards a New Method of Constitutional Bargaining, p. 4.

56 Ibid.

57 Norman, From the Convention to the IGC, p. 3.

58 Closa, Improving EU Constitutional Politics, p. 24.

59 6 March 2002, and listed in the speeches section of the website of the French president at http://www.elysee.fr.

60 Cited Norman, *The Accidental Constitution*, p. 159.

61 Crum, Laying Building Blocks or Just Window Dressing, p. 2.

62 K. Kiljunen, *The European Constitution in the Making*, p. 41.

63 Closa, Improving EU Constitutional Politics, p. 24, note 48.

64 Verbatim report available at http://www.europarl.eu.int/europe2004/textes/verbatim_020624.htm.

65 Closa, Improving EU Constitutional Politics.

66 Shaw, *Process, Responsibility and Inclusion*.

67 See J. Lodge, Intergovernmental Conferences and European Integration: Negotiating the Amsterdam Treaty, *International Negotiations* 3 (1998), p. 348.

68 Hoffmann, The Convention on the Future of Europe, p. 15; Norman, *The Accidental Constitution*, p. 79; see also Jean-Claud Piris, Does the European Union Have a Constitution? Does It Need One? Harvard Law School Jean Monnet Papers 5/00, available at http://www.jeanmonnetprogram.org.papers/00/00501.html.

69 C. Archer, Implementing the New Constitutional Treaty: A Provisional Introduction. The Federal Trust (London, April 2003), p. 8.

70 Hughes, The Future of Europe's Convention, p. 7.

71  Ibid., p. 3.
72  G. Grevi, The Europe We Need: An Integrated Presidency for a United Europe. European Policy Centre (Brussels, December 2002).
73  Reports of all the working groups are available at http://european-convention.eu.int.
74  Quoted in Norman, *The Accidental Constitution*, p. 63.
75  K. Hughes, A Dynamic and Democratic EU or Muddling Through Again? Assessing the EU's Draft Constitution. EPIN Working Paper no. 8, July 2003, p. 3.
76  The Future of Europe Convention, Contribution Franco-allemande à la Convention européene sur l'architecture de l'Union, CONV 489/03 (The European Convention 2003).
77  Hughes, A Dynamic and Democratic EU, p. 2.
78  Ibid., p. 4.
79  See report in *Le Monde*, 3 October 2002, of a speech delivered at the College of Europe, Bruges, 2 October 2002; see also the interview with Giscard in the *Financial Times*, 7 October 2002.
80  CONV 369/02.
81  P. Craig, European Governance: Executive and Administrative Powers under the New Constitutional Settlement. Jean Monnet Working Paper 5/04, New York University School of Law (2004), p. 3.
82  Norman, *The Accidental Convention*, p. 80.
83  Ibid., pp. 72 and 79; see also J.-C. Piris, Does the European Union Have a Constitution? Does it Need One?, *European Law Review*, 24 (1999)
84  Norman, *The Accidental Convention*, p. 80.
85  Ibid., p. 84.
86  Ibid., p. 85.
87  Ibid., p. 82.
88  Ibid., p. 320.
89  CONV 766/03.
90  CONV 723/03.
91  CONV 691/03.
92  Norman, *The Accidental Convention*, pp. 323–4.
93  Ibid., p. 322; see also CONV 732/03.
94  CONV 770/03.
95  CONV 685/03.
96  Editorial, The European Convention is a Much Less Threatening Creature Than Its Enemies Would Like It to Be, *Independent*, 28 May 2003.
97  A. Grice and S. Castle, Giscard Offers Blair Concessions – But Disputes Continue, *Financial Times*, 26 May 2003.
98  Norman, *The Accidental Constitution*, p. 263.
99  Ibid., p. 321.
100  Ibid., pp. 282–3.
101  Ibid., p. 337.
102  See Giscard's letter of 8 May 2003 to Convention members, CONV 721/03.
103  The words used by Vice-president Amato, cited in Norman, *The Accidental Constitution*, p. 245.
104  Speech by Romano Prodi, 28 February 2002; CONV 4/02.
105  Norman, *The Accidental Constitution*, p. 263.
106  Ibid., p. 322; see CONV 732/03.
107  CONV 724/03.
108  CONV 725/03; and CONV 726/03.
109  CONV 728/03.
110  CONV 727/03.
111  Joschka Fischer, quoted in Norman, *The Accidental Constitution*, p. 308.
112  Norman, *The Accidental Constitution*, p. 298.

113 CONV 851/03.
114 W. Wessels, An Ever Closer Fusion? A Dynamic Macropolitical View of the Integration Process, *Journal of Common Market Studies* 35 (1997).
115 Kiljunen, *The European Constitution in the Making*, p. 138.
116 Norman, *The Accidental Constitution*, p. 339.
117 A fact that detracts somewhat from the optimism of those commentators who saw the Convention as one more stage in the gradual assimilation of constitutionalisation of the Union. See B. Peters, Public Discourse, Identity and the Problems of Democratic Legitimacy, in E. Eriksen (ed.), *The European Polity: Reflexive Integration in the EU* (London, 2005).
118 Cited by Norman, *The Accidental Constitution*, p. 298.
119 Ibid.
120 Quoted ibid., p. 317.
121 Ibid., p. 299.
122 CONV 850/03.
123 D. Dinan, Governance and Institutions: The Convention and the Intergovernmental Conference (2004), p. 39.
124 Philippart, The Convention on the Future of the EU, p. 5.
125 Archer, Implementing the New Constitutional Treaty, p. 7; see also Piris, Does the European Union Have a Constitution.
126 Archer, Implementing the New Constitutional Treaty, p. 7.

## Chapter 6

1 K. Hughes, The Battle for Power in Europe. Will the Convention Get It Right? EPIN Working Paper no. 4, February 2003, p. 8, available at http://www.ceps.be.
2 See Giscard's comments to the European Parliament's Constitutional Affairs Committee, 10 October 2001, summary available at http://www.europarl.europa.eu/sides/getDoc.do?pubRef=-//EP//TEXT+PRESS+NR; and Valéry Giscard D'Estaing, Henry Kissinger Lecture, Washington DC, 11 February 2003, available at http://european-convention.eu.int/docs/speeches/7072.pdf.
3 K. Hughes, A Dynamic and Democratic EU or Muddling Through Again? Assessing the EU's Draft Constitution. EPIN Working Paper no. 8, July 2003, p. 1.
4 H. Grabbe, Preparing the EU for 2004. Centre for European Reform Policy Brief, 2004, p. 2.
5 G. Grevi and K. Hughes, The Future of the European Convention. What Prospects for Compromise on Institutional Questions in the Convention Endgame? CEPS Commentary, May 2003, available at http://www.ceps.be/Commentary/May03/Hughes.php.
6 Ibid.
7 K. Hughes, The Institutional Debate: Who is Pre-empting the Convention? CEPS Commentary, February 2003, p. 1, available at http://www.ceps.be/Commentary/Feb03/Hughes2/php.
8 Patrick Wintour, Blair Strikes Doubtful Note on European Constitution, *Guardian*, 16 June 2004.
9 J.-C. Piris, Does the European Union Have a Constitution? Does It Need One? *European Law Review* 24 (1999); Y. Devuyst, The European Union's Constitutional Order: Between Community Method and *Ad Hoc* Compromise, *Berkeley Journal of International Law* 18 (1999); P. Craig, Democracy and Rule-making within the EC: An Empirical and Normative Assessment, *European Law Journal* 3 (1997); P. Craig, Constitutions, Constitutionalism and the European Union, *European Law Journal* 7 (2001); *Can Europe Have a Constitution?* Special issue of *Kings College Law Journal* (2001); K. Lenaerts and M. Desomer, Bricks for a Constitutional Treaty of the European Union: Values, Objectives and Means, *European Law Review* 27(4) (2002).

10  C. Church, Implementing the New Constitutional Treaty: A Provisional Introduction. The Federal Trust (London, April 2003), p. 2.

11  Ibid., pp. 8–9.

12  S. Weatherill, Is Constitutional Finality Feasible or Desirable? On the Cases for European Constitutionalism and a European Constitution. Constitutionalism Web-Papers no. 7 (2002), p. 3, available at http://les1.man.ac.uk/conweb/.

13  L. Hoffmann, Leading the Union. An Argument in Favour of a Dual EU Presidency. The Federal Trust (London, April 2003), p. 3.

14  Grabbe, Preparing the EU for 2004, p. 3.

15  Hughes, The Battle for Power in Europe, p. 11.

16  Ibid., p. 14.

17  Memorandum of the Benelux: A Balanced Institutional Framework for an Enlarged, More Effective and More Transparent Union. Brussels, 4 December 2002.

18  P. Craig, European Governance: Executive and Administrative Powers under the New Constitutional Settlement. Jean Monnet Working Paper 5/04, New York University School of Law (2004), p. 16.

19  Speech delivered at The Hague, 21 February 2002, available under 'Speeches' at the British Foreign Office website, http://www.fco.gov.uk.

20  Blair's speech, Cardiff, November 2002, available at http://news.bbc.co.uk/1/low/uk_politics/2522931.stm.

21  G. Grevi, Options for Government of the Union. The Federal Trust (London, March 2003), p. 6.

22  Chirac's speech is available at http://www.elysee.fr.

23  Aznar's speech of 20 May 2002 is available at http://europa.eu.int.futurum.

24  The Future of Europe Convention, Contribution Franco-allemande à la Convention européene sur l'architecture de l'Union, CONV 489/03 (The European Convention 2003).

25  For a review of this debate, see P. Norman, The Franco-German Paper on the Future of Europe: A Convention Postscript. *EuroComment Briefing Note* 1(11) (EuroComment, Brussels, 2003).

26  A. Duff and L. Dini, A Proposal for a Unified Presidency, CONV 524/03, Brussels 20 June 2003.

27  K. Hughes, Europe's Constitution – One Cheer for Democracy. CEPS Commentary, June 2003, pp. 2–3, available at http://www.ceps.be/Commentary/Jun03/Hughes2.php.

28  Hughes, The Battle for Power in Europe, p. iii.

29  See Craig, European Governance, pp. 42–4.

30  K. Kiljunen, *The European Constitution in the Making* (Centre for European Policy Studies, Brussels, 2004), p. 111.

31  Hughes, The Battle for Power in Europe, p. 9.

32  Ibid.

33  Hughes, Europe's Constitution, p. 2.

34  Hughes, The Battle for Power in Europe, p. 13.

35  Ibid., p. 9.

36  The Future of Europe Convention (2003), The Draft Treaty Establishing a Constitution for Europe, CONV820/03, Brussels, 20 June 2003.

37  Ibid.

38  Treaty Establishing a Constitution for Europe, Article 1-21, para. 2 (3).

39  K. Kiljunen, *The European Constitution in the Making*, p. 111.

40  The Future of Europe Convention (2003), The Draft Treaty Establishing a Constitution for Europe.

41  Duff and Dini, A Proposal for a Unified Presidency.

42  Hughes, The Battle for Power in Europe, pp. 10–11.

43  P. Craig, What Constitution Does Europe Need? The House that Giscard Built: Constitutional Rooms with a View. The Federal Trust (London, August 2003), p. 4.

44 J. Temple Lang, The Convention on the Future of Europe – So Far. The Federal Trust (London, June 2003), p. 5.

45 D. Kral, I. Brinar and J. Almer, The Position of the Small Countries towards Institutional Reform: From Tyranny of the Small to Directoire of the Big? EPIN Working Paper no. 6, June 2003, p. 4.

46 H. Abromeit and S. Wolf, Will the Constitutional Treaty Contribute to the Legitimacy of the European Union? European Integration online Papers (EIoP) 9(11) (2005), p. 9, available at http://eiop.or.at/eiop/texte/2005-011a.htm.

47 Craig, What Constitution Does Europe Need, p. 4.

48 J. Tallberg, The Agenda-shaping Powers of the EU Council Presidency, *Journal of European Public Policy* 10 (2003).

49 P. Norman, From the Convention to the IGC (Institutions), paper presented at the thirty-third annual PSA conference in Newcastle, 2–4 September 2003, p. 4.

50 Hughes, The Battle for Power in Europe, p. 4.

51 Ibid., p. 10.

52 Ibid., p. 13.

53 Ibid.

54 Kiljunen, *The European Constitution in the Making*, p. 110.

55 J. Peterson, Decision-making in the European Union: Towards a Framework for Analysis, *Journal of European Public Policy* 2 (1995).

56 Kiljunen, *The European Constitution in the Making*, p. 110.

57 Craig, What Constitution Does Europe Need, p. 2.

58 See P. Ludlow, *The Seville Council* (EuroComment, Brussels, 2002).

59 H. Grabbe, Preparing the EU for 2004, p. 2.

60 W. Wessels, Keynote Article – The Constitutional Treaty: Three Readings from a Fusion Perspective, in L. Miles (ed.), *Journal of Common Market Studies Annual Review of the European Union, 2004/2005* (Oxford, 2005), pp. 20–1; see also P. Ludlow, The European Council and the IGC of December 2003, Why and How? *EuroComment Briefing Note* no. 28 (Brussels, 2004) pp. 329–39.

61 Wessels, Keynote Article – The Constitutional Treaty, p. 21.

62 Ibid.

63 Ibid., p. 22.

64 Ibid.

65 Grevi and Hughes, The Future of the European Convention, p. 4.

66 Norman, From the Convention to the IGC, p. 4.

67 F. Scharpf, The Joint-decision Trap: Lessons from German Federalism and European Integration, *Public Administration* 66 (1988).

68 S. Kurpas and J. Schonlau, Deadlock Avoided, But Sense of Mission Lost? The Enlarged EU and its Uncertain Constitution. CEPS Policy Brief no. 92, February 2006, p. 2,

69 Ibid.

70 See R. Baldwin and M. Widgren, Council Voting in the Constitutional Treaty – Devil in the Details. CEPS Policy Brief no. 53, July 2004, available at http://shop.ceps.be.

71 Wessels, Keynote Article – The Constitutional Treaty, p. 24; see also H. Wallace and F. Hayes-Renshaw, *The Council of Ministers*, second edition (Basingstoke, 2005).

72 Kiljunen, *The European Constitution in the Making*, p. 123.

73 Ibid., p. 127.

74 P. Norman, *The Accidental Constitution* (Brussels, 2003), p. 145.

75 R. Baldwin and M. Widgren, Commentary. Power and the Constitutional Treaty. CEPS Commentary, June 2003, p. 2, available at http://www.ceps.be/Commentary/Jun03/Baldwin.php.

76 See the discussion of this posted at http://heiwww.unige.ch/~baldwin papers/Decision-making.

77 Baldwin and Widgren, Commentary. Power and the Constitutional Treaty, p. 1.

78 Ibid., p. 2.

79  Kurpas and Schonlau, Deadlock Avoided, p. 5.
80  CONV 448/02 and COM (2002) 728 Final, 'Peace, Freedom and Security'.
81  For an overview of this critique of the Commission, see J. Temple Lang, The Convention on the Future of Europe, pp. 3–4.
82  U. Guerot, K. Hughes, M. Lefebvre and T. Egenhoff, France, Germany and the UK in the Convention: Common Interests or Pulling in Different Directions? EPIN Working Paper no. 7 (CEPS, Brussels, 2003).
83  Hughes, A Dynamic and Democratic EU, p. 7.
84  Kiljunen, *The European Constitution in the Making*, p. 115.
85  Kral *et al.*, The Position of the Small Countries, p. 10.
86  Hoffmann, Leading the Union, p. 4.
87  Norman, *The Accidental Constitution*, pp. 147–8.
88  Hughes, The Battle for Power in Europe, p. 16.
89  Hughes, Europe's Constitution, p. 2.
90  Hoffmann, Leading the Union, p. 4.
91  Hughes, The Battle for Power in Europe, p. 16,
92  Craig, What Constitution Does Europe Need, p. 3.
93  COM (2001), 428 Final, European Governance: A White Paper, Brussels, 25 July 2001.
94  Hughes, The Battle for Power in Europe, p. iii.
95  D. Dinan, Governance and Institutions: A New Constitution and a New Commission, in L. Miles (ed.), *Journal of Common Market Studies Annual Review of the European Union, 2004/2005* (Oxford, 2005), p. 34.
96  *Financial Times*, 3 July 2002.
97  Temple Lang, The Convention on the Future of Europe, p. 5.
98  Giscard's views, cited in Norman, From the Convention to the IGC, p. 4.
99  After the Brussels Summit: What Happened Next for the EU? *Centre for European Reform Policy Brief*, 17 December 2003, p. 2.
100 Provisional consolidated version of the draft treaty establishing a Constitution for Europe, Title III, Article 1-25 6 (a) and (b) (Brussels, 25 June 2004, CIG 86/04).
101 CONV 850/03.
102 Provisional consolidated version of the draft treaty establishing a Constitution for Europe, Title III, Article 1-25 6 (a) and (b) (Brussels, 25 June 2004, CIG 86/04).
103 Grevi and Hughes, The Future of the European Convention, p. 2.
104 Kiljunen, *The European Constitution in the Making*, p. 114.
105 Hughes, A Dynamic and Democratic EU, p. 6.
106 Grevi and Hughes, The Future of the European Convention, p. 2.
107 Temple Lang, The Convention on the Future of Europe, p. 4.
108 Y. Mény, De la Démocratie en Europe: Old Concepts and New Challenges, *Journal of Common Market Studies* 41 (2003).
109 Laeken Declaration on the Future of the European Union, December 2001, available at http://european-convention.eu.int/pdf/LKNEN.pdf.
110 Ibid.
111 B. Crum, Convention Must Breathe Life into the EU's Democratic Character. CEPS Commentary, April 2003, available at http://www.ceps.be/Commentary/April03?Crum.php.
112 Wessels, Keynote Article – The Constitutional Treaty, p. 19.
113 Speaking at a Friends of Europe conference: Understanding Europe – The Citizens' Right to Know, Brussels, 3 April 2003.
114 Abromeit and Wolf, Will the Constitutional Treaty, p. 14.
115 Ibid.
116 Hughes, A Dynamic and Democratic EU, p. 8.
117 The European Ombudsman, Annual Report, 2006, at p. 9, available at http://ombudsman.europa.eu/report06/pdf/en/rap06_en.pdf.

118 Crum, Convention Must Breathe Life.
119 Ibid.
120 Ibid.
121 Hughes, A Dynamic and Democratic EU, p. 7.
122 Ibid., p. 8.
123 Hoffmann, Leading the Union, p. 3.
124 Ibid.
125 Ibid.
126 Wessels, Keynote Article – The Constitutional Treaty.
127 *Financial Times*, 18 June 2004.
128 Quoted in Europe Information Service, *European Report* 2827, 6 December 2003.
129 See the table on projected seat allocations in Dinan, Governance and Institutions, p. 45.
130 K. Kiljunen, Cooperation between National Parliaments and the European Parliament. Discussion Paper, COSAC, Athens, May 2003.
131 Declaration annexed to the Nice Treaty; see also M. Agostini, The Role of National Parliaments in the Future EU, *International Spectator* XXXVI(4), October–December 2001; and Herwig C. H. Hofmann, The Changing Role of National Parliaments in EU Affairs. Parliamentary Representation in a System of a Multi-layer Constitutions: Case Study of Germany and the post-Nice Discussion, available at www.icel.ie/ac2_herwig_hof.doc.
132 Blair in his Warsaw speech, available at http://www.number-10.gov.uk; Chirac in a speech in Strasbourg, available at http://www.elysee.fr; and Aznar in a speech at Oxford, available at http://www.europa.eu.int/futurum.
133 Norman, *The Accidental Constitution*, p. 98.
134 Protocol on the Role of National Parliaments in the European Union, Draft Treaty.
135 A.-M. Slaughter, *A New World Order* (Oxford, 2004), p. 122.
136 Hughes, The Battle for Power in Europe, p. 5.
137 CONV 518/03.
138 Kurpas and Schonlau, Deadlock Avoided, p. 3.
139 Quoted in F. Duchêne, *Jean Monnet: The First Statesman of Interdependence* (New York, 1994), pp. 238–9.

## Chapter 7

1 K. Hughes, The Battle for Power in Europe. Will the Convention Get It Right? EPIN Working Paper no. 4, February 2003, p. 4, available at http://www.ceps.be.
2 P. Craig, What Constitution Does Europe Need? The House that Giscard Built: Constitutional Rooms with a View. The Federal Trust (London, August 2003), p. 2.
3 W. Wessels, Keynote Article – The Constitutional Treaty: Three Readings from a Fusion Perspective, in L. Miles (ed.), *Journal of Common Market Studies Annual Review of the European Union, 2004/2005* (Oxford, 2005), pp. 27–8.
4 S. Kurpas and J. Schonlau, Deadlock Avoided, But Sense of Mission Lost? The Enlarged EU and Its Uncertain Constitution. CEPS Policy Brief no. 93, February 2006, p. 2.
5 M. Dougan, The Convention's Draft Constitutional Treaty: A 'Tidying-up Exercise' That Needs Some Tidying-up of Its Own. The Federal Trust (London, August 2003), p. 2.
6 Wessels, Keynote Article – The Constitutional Treaty, p. 32.
7 Dougan, The Convention's Draft Constitutional Treaty, p. 2.
8 Hughes, The Battle for Power in Europe, p. 4.
9 K. Hughes, A Dynamic and Democratic EU or Muddling Through Again? EPIN Working Paper no. 8, July 2003, p. 9.
10 See Protocol 36 amending the Treaty establishing the European Atomic Energy Community, Treaty establishing a Constitution for Europe, available at http://europa.eu.int/eur-lex/lex/JOHtml.do?uri=OJ:C:2004:310:SOM:EN:HTML.

11 Dougan, The Convention's Draft Constitutional Treaty, p. 2; see also CONV 305/02; CONV 331/02; and European Parliament, Report on the Legal Personality of the European Union, A5-0409/2001.
12 Dougan, The Convention's Draft Constitutional Treaty, p. 2.
13 I. Diez-Picazo, Treaty or Constitution? The Status of the Constitution for Europe. Jean Monnet Working Paper 5/04, New York University School of Law (2004), p. 17.
14 Dougan, The Convention's Draft Constitutional Treaty, pp. 7–8.
15 Ibid.
16 M. Kumm and V. Ferreres Comella, The Future of Constitutional Conflict in the European Union: Constitutional Supremacy after the Constitutional Treaty. Jean Monnet Working Paper 5/04, New York University School of Law (2004), p. 12.
17 Craig, What Constitution Does Europe Need, p. 8.
18 CONV 216/02.
19 P. Norman, *The Accidental Constitution* (Brussels, 2003), p. 100; see also CONV 162/02.
20 Norman, *The Accidental Constitution*, p. 100.
21 Ibid.
22 H. Abromeit and S. Wolf, Will the Constitutional Treaty Contribute to the Legitimacy of the European Union? European Integration online Papers (EIoP) 9(11) (2005), p. 11, available at http://eiop.or.at/eiop/texte/2005-011a.htm.
23 W. Wessels, Der Verfassungvertrag in Integrationstrend: Eine Zusammenschlau zentrale Ergebrisse, *Integration* 4 (2003), p. 289.
24 Abromeit and Wolf, Will the Constitutional Treaty, p. 11.
25 B. Crum, Commentary: Giscard Puts the EU on Track. CEPS Commentary, June 2003, p. 3, available at http://www.ceps.be/Commentary/Jun03/Crum.php.
26 CONV 424/02.
27 Dougan, The Convention's Draft Constitutional Treaty, p. 11.
28 *Financial Times*, 27 October 2003.
29 *Financial Times*, 20 June 2004.
30 CONV 357/02.
31 CONV 470/02.
32 Treaty establishing a Constitution for Europe, Part Three, Title I, Article 3-178/179, available at http://europa.eu.int/eur-lex/lex/JOHtml.do?uri=OJ:C:2004:310:SOM:EN:HTML.
33 C. Hope and E. Conway, CBI Protests over 'Threats' to Industry from EU Treaty, *Daily Telegraph*, 1 December 2003.
34 A. Evans-Pritchard, Brussels Planners Back Down over Economic Control, *Daily Telegraph*, 23 May 2003.
35 Ibid.
36 K. Kiljunen, *The European Constitution in the Making* (Centre for European Policy Studies, Brussels, 2004), p. 144.
37 F. Mayer, Competences – Reloaded? The Vertical Division of Powers in the EU after the New European Constitution. Jean Monnet Working Paper 5/04, New York University School of Law (2004), p. 38.
38 Craig, What Constitution Does Europe Need, p. 6.
39 Ibid.
40 M. Zura, The State in the Post-national Constellation. ARENA Working Papers, WP 99/35 (1999).
41 Abromeit and Wolf, Will the Constitutional Treaty, p. 9.
42 Dougan, The Convention's Draft Constitutional Treaty, p. 6.
43 CONV 88/02.
44 CONV 47/02.
45 Norman, *The Accidental Constitution*, p. 90.
46 CONV 88/02.

47  CONV 601/03; CONV 624/03.
48  Dougan, The Convention's Draft Constitutional Treaty, p. 4.
49  For an overview see J. Kokott and A. Rueth, The European Convention and Its Draft Treaty Establishing a Constitution for Europe: Appropriate Answers to the Laeken Questions?, *Common Market Law Review* 40 (2003).
50  See http://europa.eu.int/futurum/comm/documents/penelope_en.htm.
51  COM 2002 247 Final.
52  CONV 375/1/02 REV; 400/02; CONV 528/03; CONV 601/03; CONV 624/03; CONV 724/03; CONV 798/0.3.
53  Dougan, The Convention's Draft Constitutional Treaty, p. 7; see also CONV 459/02.
54  Wessels, Keynote Article – The Constitutional Treaty, p. 17.
55  Craig, What Constitution Does Europe Need, p. 7.
56  CONV 724/03, n. 7, p. 82.
57  Dougan, The Convention's Draft Constitutional Treaty, p. 7; see also CONV 724/03, pp. 68 and 76.
58  CONV 724/03, p. 68.
59  CONV 424/02; CONV 357/02; and CONV 516/03.
60  CONV 677/03, p. 10.
61  Dougan, The Convention's Draft Constitutional Treaty, p. 7.
62  *The Times*, 14 June 2003.
63  Abromeit and Wolf, Will the Constitutional Treaty, p. 10.
64  N. Malcolm, A Federal Constitution with the Heart of a Manifesto, *Daily Telegraph*, 28 July 2003; see also D. Smith, Roll Up, Roll Up for the Giscard Euro Trap, *Sunday Times News Review*, 18 May 2003.
65  Wessels, Keynote Article – The Constitutional Treaty, p. 18.
66  *Daily Telegraph*, 28 July 2003.
67  O. Pfersmann, The New Revision of the Old Constitution. Jean Monnet Working Paper 5/04, New York University School of Law (2004), p. 7.
68  R. Sylvester, Revolt on EU Superstate, *Daily Telegraph*, 10 May 2003; see also the comments in similar vein by David Heathcote-Amery, the Conservative Party's representative in the Convention, quoted in the *Daily Telegraph*, 16 May 2003.
69  Malcolm, A Federal Constitution.
70  P. Riddell, The 'Blueprint for Tyranny' Is a Figment of Febrile Minds, *The Times*, 22 May 2003.
71  M. Maduro, How Constitutional Can the European Union Be? The Tension between Intergovernmentalism and Constitutionalism in the European Union. Jean Monnet Working Paper 5/04, New York University School of Law (2004), p. 46.
72  P. Stephens, Blair's Surrender to the Sceptics, *Financial Times*, 30 March 2004.
73  Introduced in the Maastricht Treaty (February 1992) and entered into force on 1 November 1993. The present formulation is contained in Article 5 of the Treaty Establishing the European Community – consolidated version following the Treaty of Nice.
74  Laeken Declaration on the Future of the European Union, available at http://european-convention.eu.int/pdf/LKNEN.pdf.
75  See the opinion of Jean-Claude Piris, head of the Council's legal service, Working Group Document WD 04 WG 1.
76  See CONV 579/03, p. 9; and CONV 286/02.
77  See CONV 353/02; and also the proposed Protocol on the Role of National Parliaments in the European Union.
78  H. Grabbe, Preparing the EU for 2004. Centre for European Reform Policy Brief, 2004, p. 4.
79  Speech by British prime minister, Tony Blair, to the Polish Stock Exchange, 6 October 2000, available at http://www.europaworld.org/speeches/tonyblairpoland61000.htm.
80  Dougan, The Convention's Draft Constitutional Treaty, p. 5.
81  Ibid.

82 Ibid., p. 6.
83 CONV 723/03; CONV 724/03; CONV 783/03; CONV 847/03; CONV 853/03.
84 Dougan, The Convention's Draft Constitutional Treaty, p. 13.
85 Kiljunen, *The European Constitution in the Making*, p. 153.
86 See CONV 696/03, p. 10.
87 Dougan, The Convention's Draft Constitutional Treaty, p. 8.
88 *Daily Telegraph*, 23 May 2003.
89 Kiljunen, *The European Constitution in the Making*, p. 145.
90 See Commission press release IP/03/836, 13 June 2003.
91 CONV 696/03 p. 12; CONV/03, p. 4.
92 Kiljunen, *The European Cosnstitution in the Making*, p. 148.

**Chapter 8**

1 F. Cerutti, The Political Identity of the Europeans, *Thesis Eleven* 72 (2003).
2 A. von Bogdandy, The European Constitution and European Identity: A Critical Analysis of the Convention's Draft Preamble. Jean Monnet Working Paper 5/04, New York University School of Law (2004), p. 4, available at http://www.jeanmonnetprogram.org/papers/04/04501-7a.html.
3 See the 1973 declaration of the heads of state and government on European identity, Documents on European Identity, Adopted by the Foreign Ministers of Member States of the European Communities, 14 December 1973, Copenhagen, in *Europa-Archiv Folge* 2 (1974, D.50).
4 *Independent*, 30 June 2003; for a discussion of the role of law in identity formation in Europe, see T. Mollers, The Role of Law in European Integration, *AJCL* 48 (2000).
5 A. Evans-Pritchard, God Has No Place in 'Elitist' Giscard Euro Blueprint, *Daily Telegraph*, 30 May 2003.
6 *The Times*, 27 November 2003.
7 Treaty establishing a Constitution for Europe, Preamble, available at http://eur-lex.europa.eu/LexUriServ/site/en/oj/2004/c_310/c_31020041216en00030010.pdf.
8 See the discussion in von Bogdandy, The European Constitution and European Identity.
9 Treaty establishing a Constitution for Europe, Part I, Title I, Article 1-5, available at http://europa.eu.int/eur-lex/lex/JOHtml.do?uri=OJ:C:2004:310:SOM:EN:HTML.
10 Evans-Pritchard, God Has No Place.
11 P. Greenwood, Crucible of Hate. Why Is Eastern Europe So Anti-gay, *Guardian*, 1 June 2007.
12 K. Kiljunen, *The European Constitution in the Making* (Centre for European Policy Studies, Brussels, 2004), p. 49.
13 Ibid.
14 von Bogdandy, The European Constitution and European Identity, p. 15.
15 J. E. Fossum and H.-J. Trenz, The EU's Fledgling Society: From Deafening Silence to Critical Voice in European Constitution Making. ARENA Working Paper no. 19, July 2005.
16 von Bogdandy, The European Constitution and European Identity, p. 15.
17 See the initiative proposed in A Citizens Compact: Reaching Out to the Citizens of Europe. An Initiative Proposed by Members of the European Policy Institutes Network (EPIN). EPIN Working Paper no. 14, September 2005.
18 CONV 354/02.
19 Ibid.
20 See CONV 378/02; CONV 601/03; and CONV 674/03.
21 CONV 811/03.
22 M. Dougan, The Convention's Draft Constitutional Treaty: A 'Tidying-up Exercise' That Needs Some Tidying-up of Its Own. The Federal Trust (London, August 2003), p. 3.
23 A Clear Course for Europe: speech available on the Downing Street website at http://www.number-10.gov.uk.

24 CONV 811/03.
25 CONV 828/1/03 REV 1; see also CONV 814/03, p. 3.
26 Dougan, The Convention's Draft Constitutional Treaty, p. 3.
27 G. Sacerdoti, The European Charter of Fundamental Rights: From a Nation State Europe to a Citizens' Europe, *Columbia Journal of European Law* 8(1) (2002), p. 43.
28 M. Maduro, How Constitutional Can the European Union Be? The Tension between Intergovernmentalism and Constitutionalism in the European Union. Jean Monnet Working Paper 5/04, New York University School of Law (2004), p. 43.
29 Treaty establishing a Constitution for Europe, Part II, The Charter of Fundamental Rights, Preamble, available at http://eur-lex.europa.eu/LexUriServ/site/en/oj/2004/c_310/c_31020041216en00410054.pdf.
30 Maduro, How Constitutional Can the European Union Be, p. 42; see also M. Maduro, The Double Constitutional Life of the Charter of Fundamental Rights, in E. O. Eriksen, J. E. Fossum and A. J. Menéndez (eds), *The Chartering of Europe: The European Charter of Fundamental Rights and Its Constitutional Implications* (Baden-Baden, 2003).
31 A. Townsend, Can the EU Deliver the Area of Freedom, Security and Justice? EPIN Working Paper no. 9, Centre for European Policy Studies, Brussels, September 2003, p. 6
32 Dougan, The Convention's Draft Constitutional Treaty, p. 3.
33 Ibid., p. 4; see also J. Weiler, Does the European Union Truly Need a Charter of Rights? *European Law Journal* 6 (2000).
34 Kiljunen, *The European Constitution in the Making*, p. 60.
35 Opinion 2/94 [1996] ECR 1-1759.
36 CONV 770/02, Final Report of Working Group II, 22 October 2002, p. 7.
37 Allister Heath, Big Brother and the EU Art of Double-speak, *The Business*, 27 June 2004.
38 Ibid.
39 Ibid.
40 Cited ibid.
41 M. Kumm and V. Ferreres Comella, The Future of Constitutional Conflict in the European Union: Constitutional Supremacy after the Constitutional Treaty. Jean Monnet Working Paper 5/04, New York University School of Law (2004), p. 29.
42 See I. Pernice and R. Kanitz, Fundamental Rights and Multilevel Constitutionalism in Europe. Walter Hallstein Institut Paper 7/04, March 2004.
43 Kumm and Ferreres Comella, The Future of Constitutional Conflict, p. 19.
44 Cited by Heath, Big Brother.
45 G. La Palombella, Whose Europe? After the Constitution: A God-based, Reflexive Citizenship. Jean Monnet Working Paper 5/04, New York University School of Law (2004), p. 26.
46 P. Schmitter, Alternatives for the Future European Polity: Is Federalism the Only Answer? in M.Telo (ed.), *Démocratie et la Construction Européenne* (Brussels, 1995); J. Weiler, Legitimacy and Democracy of Union Governance, in G. Edwards and A. Pijpers (eds), *The Politics of EU Treaty Reform* (London, 1997).
47 Maduro, How Constitutional Can the European Union Be, p. 25.
48 Ibid.
49 C. Church and D. Phinnemore, *European Union and European Community. A Handbook and Commentary on the 1992 Maastricht Treaties* (London, 1994), pp. 78–9.
50 T. H. Marshall, *Citizenship and Social Class and Other Essays* (Cambridge, 1950).
51 For a discussion of the genealogy of this concept, see B. Hindess, Citizenship in the Modern West, in B. S. Turner (ed.), *Citizenship and Social Theory* (London, 1994).
52 W. Kymlicka, *Multi-cultural Citizenship: A Liberal Theory of Minority Rights* (Oxford, 1995); W. Kymlicka and W. Norman, Return of the Citizen: A Survey of Recent Work on Citizenship Theory, *Ethics* 104(9) (1994).

53  See R. Falk, The Making of Global Citizenship, in B. van Steenbergen (ed.), *The Condition of Citizenship* (London, 1994); see also R. Baubock, Citizenship and National Identities in the European Union. Harvard Law School Jean Monnet Papers (1997).

54  P. Lamy, quoted in G. Ross, *Jacques Delors and European Integration* (Cambridge, 1995) at p. 194.

55  Church and Phinnemore, *European Union and European Community*, p. 76.

56  La Palombella, Whose Europe, p. 12.

57  Church and Phinnemore, *European Union and European Community*, p. 77.

58  J. Habermas, *The Structural Transformation of the Public Sphere* (Oxford, 1994).

59  M. Kleinman, *A European Welfare State?* (Basingstoke, 2002), p. 201.

60  Final Act attached to the TEU, Declaration No. 2.

61  Church and Phinnemore, *European Union and European Community*, p. 77.

62  Treaty of Amsterdam Amending the Treaty on European Union, The Treaty Establishing the European Communities and Certain Related Acts, Declaration on Sport (29), available at http://europa.eu.int/eur-lex/en/treaties/dat/amsterdam.html#0001010001.

63  Ibid., Part Two, Citizenship and the Union, Articles 17–22.

64  See the commentary on the introduction of EU citizenship by C. Archer and D. Phinnemore, *The Penguin Guide to the European Treaties. From Rome to Maastricht, Amsterdam, Nice and Beyond* (London, 2002), p. 231.

65  S. Garcia, European Union Identity and Citizenship: Some Challenges, in M. Roche and R. van Berkel (eds), *European Citizenship and Social Exclusion* (Aldershot, 1997).

66  Kleinman, *A European Welfare State*, p. 198.

67  M. Vranken, Citizenship and the Law of the European Union, in L. Holmes and P. Murray (eds), *Citizenship and Identity in Europe* (Aldershot, 1999); E. Meehan, Citizenship and Social Exclusion in the European Union, in Roche and van Berkel, *European Citizenship and Social Exclusion*, p. 18.

68  Treaty Establishing a Constitution for Europe, Title VI, The Democratic Life of the Union, Article 1-50.3, available at http://europa.eu.int/eur-lex/lex/JOHtml.do?uri=OJ:C:2004:310:SOM:EN:HTML.

69  T. Bainbridge and Anthony Teasdale, *The Penguin Companion to the European Union*, third edition (London, 2002), p. 53.

70  CONV 369/02.

71  N. Walker, Protection of Fundamental Rights in the European Union: The Charter of Fundamental Rights, in P. Cullen and A. Zervakis (eds), *The Post-Nice Process: Towards a European Constitution* (Baden-Baden, 2001).

72  M. Azaz, Some Comments on the Draft Constitutional Treaty Provisions Concerning Citizenship. Paper to the RSCAS/EUI Convention Working Group, 19 March 2003, p. 2.

73  See, for instance, the claims made for the contribution of political elites and effective public administration to successful 'nation-building' in R. Bendix, *Nation-building and Citizenship* (New York, 1964), especially at Chapter 4.

74  Treaty Establishing a Constitution for Europe, Title VI, The Democratic Life of the Union, Article 1-47 (4).

75  CONV 574/1/02.

76  [1985] EUECJ R-61/84 *Cinéthèque SA and others* v. *Fédération nationale des cinémas français*.

77  *Eurobarometer* 2002.

78  V. Bogdanor, Europe Needs to Connect with Its Electorate, *Financial Times*, 15 June 2004.

79  Ibid.

80  There is a large and burgeoning literature on this subject. For a flavour of the debate, see especially: S. O'Leary, Nationality and Citizenship: A Tale of Two Unhappy Bedfellows, *Yearbook of European Law*, 12 (1984); U. K. Preuss, Problems of a Concept of European Citizenship, *European Law Journal* 12 (1984); J. Habermas, Citizenship and National Identity, *Praxis International*, 12 (1992); E. Meehan, *Citizenship and the*

*European Community* (London, 1993); J. Olivera, European Citizenship: Its Meaning, Its Potential, in J. Monar, W. Ungerer and W. Wessels (eds), *The Maastricht Treaty on European Union* (Brussels, 1993); R. Baubock, *Transnational Citizenship and Rights in International Migration* (Aldershot, 1994); E. Antola and A. Rose (eds), *A Citizens' Europe: In Search of a New Legal Order* (London, 1995); W. Kymlicka, *Multicultural Citizenship*; J. Shaw, Citizenship of the Union – Towards Post-national Membership? Harvard Jean Monnet Working Paper 6/97 (1997), available at http://www.law.harvard. edu/Programs/Jean-Monnet.

81  D. Obradovic, Policy Legitimacy and the European Union, *Journal of Common Market Studies* 34 (1996).

82  S. Hoffmann, Europe's Identity Crisis Revisited, *Daedalus* (spring 1994).

83  Stanley Hoffmann, Reflections on the Nation-state in Western Europe Today, *Journal of Common Market Studies* 21 (1982).

84  For a more detailed discussion of this iterative approach to unity-amidst-diversity, see J. Pieterse Nederven, Unpacking the West: How European is Europe? in A. Rattansi and S. Westwood (eds), *Racism, Modernity, Identity: On the Western Front* (London, 1994); see also P. B. Lehning, European Citizenship: A Mirage? in P. B. Lehning and A. Weale (eds), *Citizenship, Democracy and Justice in the New Europe* (London, 1997); and J. M. Barbalet, *Citizenship* (Milton Keynes, 1988).

85  Hoffmann, Reflections on the Nation-state.

86  G. Delanty, *Inventing Europe. Ideas, Identity, Reality* (Basingstoke, 1995); see also G. Delanty, The Limits and Possibilities of a European Identity. A Critique of Cultural Essentialism, *Philosophy and Social Criticism* 21 (1995).

87  S. Rokkan, Dimensions of State Formation and Nation Building: A Possible Paradigm for Research on Variations within Europe, in C. Tilly (ed.), *The Formation of National States in Western Europe* (Princeton, 1975).

88  D. Archibugi, D. Held and M. Kohler (eds), *Re-imagining Political Community* (Cambridge, 1998).

89  S. Hoffmann, Obstinate or Obsolete? The Fate of the Nation-state and the Case of Western Europe, *Daedalus* 95 1966.

90  A. Milward, *The European Rescue of the Nation State* (London, 1992).

91  A. Moravcsik, Integrating International and Domestic Theories of International Bargaining, in R. Putnam and N. Bayne (eds), *Hanging Together: The Seven Power Summits* (Cambridge MA, 1987); A. Moravcsik, Negotiating the Single European Act: National Interests and Conventional Statecraft in the European Community, *International Organization* 45 (1991); A. Moravcsik, Preferences and Power in the European Community: A Liberal Intergovernmentalist Approach, *Journal of Common Market Studies* 31 (1993); A. Moravcsik with K. Nicolaidis, Explaining the Treaty of Amsterdam: Interests, Influence, Institutions, *Journal of Common Market Studies* 37 (1999); A. Moravcsik, *The Choice for Europe. Social Purpose and State Power from Messina to Maastricht* (Ithaca NY, 1998); R. Keohane and S. Hoffmann, *The New European Community: Decision-making and Institutional Change* (Boulder CO, 1991).

92  J. Hutchinson and A. Smith (eds), *Nationalism* (Oxford, 1994).

93  S. Hall, European Citizenship – Unfinished Business, in L. Holmes and P. Murray (eds), *Citizenship and Identity in Europe* (Aldershot, 1999).

94  K. von Beyme, Citizenship in the European Union, in K. Eder and B. Giesen (eds), *European Citizenship between National Legacies and Postnational Projects* (Oxford, 2001), p. 80.

95  R. Aron, Is Multinational Citizenship Possible? *Social Research* 41 (1974); D. Grimm, Does Europe Need a Constitution? *European Law Journal* 282 (1995); M. Mann, Ruling Class Strategies and Citizenship, *Sociology* 21 (1987); A. D. Smith, National Identity and the Idea of European Unity, *International Affairs* 68 (1992); C. Tilly (ed.), *Citizenship, Identity and Social History*, Supplement 3, *International Review of Social History* (1996); D. Miller, *On Nationality* (Oxford, 1995)

96  See B. Giesen and K. Eder, European Citizenship: An Avenue for the Social Integration of Europe, in K. Eder and B. Giesen (eds), *European Citizenship: An Avenue for the Social Integration of Europe* (London, 1997), pp. 9–11.

97  Miller, *On Nationality*; see also D. Miller, In Defence of Nationality, *Journal of Applied Philosophy* 10 (1993); and D. Miller, The Nation-state: A Modest Defence, in C. Brown (ed.), *Political Restructuring in Europe: Ethical Perspectives* (London, 1994), pp. 36–42.

98  See, for instance, the discussion in R. Putnam, *Making Democracy Work: Civic Traditions in Modern Italy* (Princeton, 1993), pp. 182–3.

99  Miller, *On Nationality*, p. 27; see also A. Smith for an essentialist account of nationhood and identity, particularly A. Smith, National Identity and the Idea of European Unity, *International Affairs* 68 (1992); A. Smith, *Nations and Nationalism in a Global Era* (Cambridge, 1995); and A. Smith, Gastronomy or Geology? The Role of Nationalism in the Reconstruction of Nations, *Nations and Nationalism* 1 (1995).

100  Miller, *On Nationality*, pp. 100–1.

101  J. Rawls, *Political Liberalism* (New York, 1993), p. 168.

102  J. Checkel, Social Construction and Integration, *Journal of European Public Policy* 6 (1999).

103  L. Becker, Trust as Noncognitive Security about Motives, *Ethics* 107 (1996).

104  Kumm and Ferreres Comella, The Future of Constitutional Conflict, pp. 13–14.

105  Some of the most thought-provoking discourse here is to be found in the following literature: E. Meehan, Citizenship in the European Union, *Political Quarterly* 64 (1993); J. Habermas, Citizenship and National identity: Some Reflections on the Future of Europe, *Praxis International* 12 (1992); J. Habermas, Struggles for Recognition in the Democratic Constitutional State, in A. Gutmann and C. Taylor (eds), *Multiculturalism* (Princeton, 1994); J. Habermas, *The Inclusion of the Other: Studies in Political Theory* (Cambridge MA, 1998): J. Habermas, Constitutional Democracy: A Paradoxical Union of Contradictory Principles, *Political Theory* 29(6) (2001); J. Habermas, *The Postnational Constellation* (Cambridge MA, 2001) at p. 64; M. La Torre, Constitution, Citizenship, and the European Union, in M. La Torre (ed.), *European Citizenship: An Institutional Challenge* (The Hague, 1998); D. Held, *Democracy and the Global Order: From the Modern State to Cosmopolitan Governance* (Cambridge, 1995); D. Held, Between State and Civil Society: Citizenship, in G. Andrews (ed.), *Citizenship* (London, 1991); J. Weiler, European Citizenship and Human Rights, in J. Winter, D. Curtin, A. Kellerman and B. de Witte, *Reforming the Treaty of the European Union: The Legal Debate* (The Hague, 1996); J. Weiler, To Be a European Citizen: Eros and Civilization, in J. Weiler, *The Constitution of Europe* (Cambridge, 1999); J. Thompson, Community Identity and World Citizenship, in D. Archibugi, D. Held and M. Kohler (eds), *Re-imagining Political Community* (Cambridge, 1998); A. Wiener, *'European' Citizenship* (Boulder CO, 1998); J. Shaw, The Interpretation of European Citizenship, *Modern Law Review* 62 (1998).

106  Lars-Erik Cederman, Nationalism and Bounded Integration: What It Would Take to Construct a European Demos. Robert Schuman Centre for Advanced Studies, European University Institute, Working Paper no. 2000/34 (Florence, 2000), pp. 4–5; W. Connor, *Ethnonationalism: The Quest for Understanding* (Princeton, 1994); and A. Follesdal, The Future Soul of Europe: Nationalism or Just Patriotism? A Critique of David Miller's Defence of Nationality. ARENA Working PapersWP 007 (2001), available at http://www.arena.uio.no/publications/wp00_7.htm.

107  J. Checkel, Building New Identities? Debating Fundamental Rights in European Institutions. ARENA Working Papers WP 00/12 (2000), p. 2, available at http://www.arena.uio.no/publications/wp00_12.htm; see also the experimental research findings on the promotion of 'we-ness' of R. Dawes, A. Van de Kragy and J. Orbell, Not Me or Thee But We: The Importance of Group Identity in Eliciting Cooperation in Dilemma Situations: Experimental Manipulations, *Acta Psychologica* 68 (1988); R.

Dawes, A. Van de Kragy and J. Orbell, The Limits of Multilateral Promising, *Ethics* 100 (1990); see the ideas circulated through the working groups of the Council of Ministers, European Integration online papers (EioP) 2(9), available at http://eiop.or.at/eiop/texte/1998-009a.htm; L. Hooghe, Supranational Activists or Intergovernmental Agents? Explaining the Orientations of Senior Commission Officials towards European Integration, *Comparative Political Studies* 32(9) (1999); E. Eriksen and J. Fossum, The European Union and Post-national Integration, in E. Eriksen and J. Fossum, *Democracy in the European Union: Integration through Deliberation?* (London, 2000).

108   J. Shaw, Citizenship of the Union: Towards Post-national Membership? Harvard Law School Jean Monnet Papers (1997), p. 35, available at http://www.jeanmonnetprogram.org/papers/97/97-06-html.

109   J. Weiler, Does Europe Need a Constitution? Reflections on Demos, Telos and the German Maastricht Decision, *European Law Journal* 1 (1995) at pp. 243–4; U. K. Preuss, Problems of a Concept of European Citizenship, *European Law Journal* 1 (1995); and J. Weiler, European Citizenship and Human Rights, in J. Winter *et al.*, *Reforming the Treaty on European Union.*

110   J. Fossum, Identity-politics in the European Union. ARENA Working Papers WP 01/17, available at http://www.arena.uio.no/publications/wp01_17.htm.

111   R. De Lange, Paradoxes of European Citizenship, in P. Fitzpatrick (ed.), *Nationalism, Racism and the Rule of Law* (Aldershot, 1995).

112   E. Guild, The Legal Framework of Citizenship of the European Union, in D. Cesarini and M. Fulbrook (eds), *Citizenship, Nationality and Migration in Europe* (London, 1995), p. 33.

113   Jorg Monar, A Dual Citizenship in the Making: The Citizenship of the EU and its Reform, in La Torre, *European Citizenship.*

114   See J. Habermas, *Die Einbeziehung des Anderen* (Frankfurt am Main, 1996); and J. Habermas, Remarks on Dieter Grimm's 'Does Europe Need a Constitution?', *European Law Journal* 3 (1995); see also J. Habermas, Citizenship and National Identity, in van Steenbergen, *The Condition of Citizenship* and Tassin's notion of a European 'public space of fellow-citizenship' in E. Tassin, Europe: A Political Community?, in C. Mouffe (ed.), *Dimensions of Radical Democracy* (London, 1992).

115   See T. Borzel and T. Risse, Who Is Afraid of a European Federation?, in Harvard Law School Jean Monnet Papers (2000), Symposium: Responses to Joschka Fischer, ed. C. Joerges, Y. Mény and J. H. H. Weiler, p. 7, available at http://www.jeanmonnetprogram.org/papers/00/00f0801.html.

116   European Citizenship – Identity and Differentity, in La Torre, *European Citizenship*; see also J. Weiler, To Be a European Citizen, *Journal of European Public Policy* 4 (1997).

117   Kumm and Ferreres Comella, The Future of Constitutional Conflict, p. 21; and A. Peters, European Democracy after the 2003 Convention, *Common Market Law Review* 41 (2004).

118   See, for instance, Charles Tilly (ed.), *The Formation of National States in Western Europe* (Princeton, 1973).

119   Azaz, Some Comments on the Draft Constitutional Treaty Provisions, p. 4.

120   See Jacobs's submission at WDG II-WDO2O.

121   Townsend, Can the EU Deliver, pp. 7–8.

122   CONV 424/02; CONV 449/02; CONV 571/03; CONV 630/03; CONV 724/03.

123   *Eurobarometer*, April 2002, indicated that 9 out of 10 EU citizens polled believed that combating crime and drug-trafficking ought to be the EU policy priorities.

124   Laeken Declaration on the Future of the European Union, available at http://european-convention.eu.int/pdf/LKNEN.pdf.

125   CONV 435/02.

126   CONV 426/02.

127  Townsend, Can the EU Deliver.
128  Ibid., pp. 11–12.
129  Ibid., pp. 1–2.
130  Ibid.
131  Ibid.
132  Kees van Kersbergen, Double Allegiance in European Integration. Publics, Nation-states, and Social Policy. Robert Schuman Centre for Advanced Studies, European University Institute, Working Paper no. 97/15 (Florence, 1997), available at http://www.iue/RSC/WP-Texts/97_15.html.
133  K. Banting, The Welfare State as Statecraft: Territorial Politics and Canadian Social Policy, in S. Liebfried and P. Pierson (eds), *European Social Policy. Between Fragmentation and Integration* (Washington DC, 1995), p. 271.
134  J. Klauson, Social Rights Advocacy and State Building: T. H. Marshall in the Hands of Social Reformers, *World Politics* 47(2) (1995), p. 245.
135  Kleinman, *A European Welfare State*, p. 194.
136  Kirsty Hughes, What 'Non' Means. Analysis, BBC News report, available at http://news.bbc.co.uk/1/hi/world/europe/4552937.stm.
137  M. Ferrera, A New Social Contract? The Four Social Europes: Between Universalism and Selectivity. Robert Schuman Centre for Advanced Studies, European University Institute, Working Paper no. 96/36 (Florence, 1996); M. Rhodes, A New Social Contract: Globalisation and West European Welfare States. Robert Schuman Centre for Advanced Studies, European University Institute, Working Paper no. 96/43 (Florence, 1996); and B. Jordan, A New Social Contract? European Social Citizenship: Why a New Social Contract Will (Probably) Not Happen. Robert Schuman Centre for Advanced Studies, European University Institute, Working Paper no. 96/47 (Florence, 1996).
138  Treaty establishing the European Communities, Article 2, available at http://ec.europa.eu/employment_social/equ_opp/treaty_en.html.
139  Laeken Declaration on the Future of the European Union, available at http://european-convention.eu.int/pdf/LKNEN.pdf.
140  Alex Warleigh, 'Europeanizing' Civil Society: NGOs As Agents of Political Socialization, *Journal of Common Market Studies* 39 (2001).
141  CONV 421/02.
142  CONV 516/03 and CONV 516/1/03 REV 1 COR 1.
143  P. Norman, *The Accidental Constitution* (Brussels, 2003), p. 127.
144  Ibid.
145  See D. Fuchs, J. Gerhards and E. Roller, Nationalism versus Eurocentrism? The Construction of Collective Identities in Western Europe, in M. Martiniello, *Migration, Citizenship and Ethno-national Identities in the European Union* (Aldershot, 1995).
146  For a discussion of the role of enlightened political leadership in changing public perceptions of the political community, see P. Howe, A Community of Europeans. The Requisite Underpinnings, *Journal of Common Market Studies* 33 (1995); see also P. Howe, Insiders and Outsiders in a Community of Europeans: A Reply to Kostakopoulou, *Journal of Common Market Studies* 35 (1997).
147  B. Laffan, The Politics of Identity and Political Order in Europe, *Journal of Common Market Studies* 34 (1996).
148  D. Beetham and C. Lord, *Legitimacy and the European Union* (Harlow, 1998), p. 38.
149  Ibid.
150  U. K. Preuss, Two Challenges to European Citizenship, *Political Studies* 3 (1996); U. K. Preuss, Citizenship in the European Union: A Paradigm for Transnational Democracy, in Archibugi *et al.*, *Re-imagining Political Community*.
151  W. Wallace and J. Smith, Democracy or Technocracy? European Integration and the Problem of Popular Consent, *West European Politics* 13 (1995), p. 139.

## Chapter 9

1 See M. Koenig-Archibugi, Explaining Government Preferences for Institutional Change in EU Foreign and Security Policy, *International Organization* 58 (2004).

2 D. Allen and W. Wallace, European Political Cooperation: The Historical and Contemporary Background, in D. Allen, R. Rummel and W. Wessels (eds), *European Political Cooperation: Towards a Foreign Policy for Western Europe* (London, 1982); S. Nuttall, *European Political Cooperation* (Oxford, 1992).

3 R. Whitman, *From Civilian Power to Superstate? The International Identity of the European Union* (New York, 1999).

4 C. Bretherton and J. Vogler, *The European Union As a Global Actor* (London, 1999).

5 D. Buchan, *Europe: The Strange Superpower* (Aldershot, 1993).

6 K. Kiljunen, *The European Constitution in the Making* (Centre for European Policy Studies, Brussels 2004), p. 75.

7 See L. Gei, *'Empire' by Integration: The United States and European Integration* (Oxford, 1998).

8 See R. Keohane, Ironies of Sovereignty: The European Union and the World Order, *Journal of Common Market Studies* 40 (2002).

9 P. Norman, *The Accidental Constitution* (Brussels, 2003), p. 140.

10 See Solana's speech in Stockholm, 25 April 2002, filed at S0078/02, in the Secretary-General's archived speeches listed on the Council website at http://www.ue.eu.int.

11 Presidency Conclusions, European Council Meeting at Laeken, 14–15 December 2001, SN300/1/01 REV1, p. 20, available at http://ec.europa.eu/governance/impact/docs/key_docs/laeken_concl_en.pdf.

12 *Eurobarometer* 58 (December 2002), p. 9, and Tables 6 and 7, available at http://ec.europa.eu/public_opinion/archives/eb/eb58/eb58_highlights_en.pdf.

13 Ibid.

14 S. Everts and D. Keohane, The European Convention and EU Foreign Policy: Learning from Failure, *Survival* 45 (autumn 2003).

15 K. Hughes, The Battle for Power in Europe. Will the Convention Get It Right? EPIN Working Paper no. 4, February 2003, pp. 9–10, available at http://www.ceps.be.

16 *Wall Street Journal*, 30 January 2003.

17 Hughes, The Battle for Power, p. 12.

18 Everts and Keohane, The European Convention, p. 167.

19 Quoted in EU Set to Back Security Doctrine, *Financial Times*, 18 June 2003.

20 Europe Loses its Innocence over WMD, *Financial Times*, 17 June 2003; and EU Weighs More Activist Foreign Policy, *International Herald Tribune*, 20 June 2003.

21 J. Temple Lang, The Convention on the Future of Europe – So Far. The Federal Trust (London, June 2003), p. 7.

22 See S. Everts, Shaping a Credible EU Foreign Policy. Centre for European Reform, February 2002.

23 US Arms Talk Test 'Realism' in EU Relations, *Financial Times*, 24 June 2003.

24 Everts and Keohane, The European Convention, p. 177.

25 Ibid.

26 See the conclusion of W. Wessels, A 'saut constitutionnel' out of an Intergovernmental Trap? The Provisions of the Constitutional Treaty for the Common Foreign and Defence Policy. Jean Monnet Working Paper 5/04, New York University School of Law (2004).

27 See the background paper, CONV 161/02.

28 Everts and Keohane, The European Convention, pp. 168–9.

29 Wessels, A 'saut constitutionnel', p. 13.

30 H. Grabbe, Preparing the EU for 2004. Centre for European Reform Policy Brief, 2004, p. 3.

31 Chris Patten, Let's Add Political Clout to Economic Might, *Financial Times*, 28 November 2003.

32  A. Moravcsik, The Quiet Superpower, *Newsweek* (Atlantic edition), 17 June 2002.
33  Final Report of Working Group VIII – Defence, 52 (b) CONV 461/02, 16 December 2002, p. 17.
34  CONV 459/02.
35  Charles Grant, State of the Union: The Good Deal, *Wall Street Journal*, 25 June 2007.
36  D. Thym, Reforming Europe's Common Foreign and Security Policy, *European Law Journal* 10 (2004), p. 21.
37  Temple Lang, The Convention on the Future of Europe, p. 6.
38  K. Hughes, A Dynamic and Democratic EU or Muddling Through Again? Assessing the EU's Draft Constitution. EPIN Working Paper no. 8, July 2003, p. 10.
39  Everts and Keohane, The European Convention, p. 173.
40  Hughes, A Dynamic and Democratic EU, p. 12.
41  L. Hoffmann, Leading the Union. An Argument in Favour of a Dual EU Presidency. The Federal Trust (London, April 2003), p. 5.
42  U. Guerot, K. Hughes, M. Lefebvre and T. Egenhoff, France, Germany and the UK in the Convention. EPIN Working Paper no. 7, July 2003, p. 10.
43  Temple Lang, The Convention on the Future of Europe, p. 6.
44  Hughes, A Dynamic and Democratic EU, p. 11.
45  J. McCormick, *The European Superpower* (Basingstoke, 2007), at Chapter 3.
46  Treaty on European Union, 1992, Title V, Article J.4, available at http://europa.eu.int/eur-lex/en/treaties/dat/EU_treaty.html.
47  A. Deighton (ed.), *Western European Union 1954–1997: Defence, Security, Integration* (Oxford, 1997).
48  A. Menon, A. Forster and W. Wallace, A Common European Defence?, *Survival* 34(4) (1992).
49  H. van Cleveland (ed.), *The European Idea and Its Rivals* (New York, 1966).
50  Charles de Gaulle, *Mémoires de guerre* (Paris, 1999), vol. III, pp. 67–70.
51  N. Winn, Towards a Common European Security and Defence Policy? The Debate on NATO, the European Army and Transatlantic Security, *Geopolitics* 8 (2003).
52  E. Regelsberger, P. de. Schoutheete de Tervarent and W. Wessels (eds), *Foreign Policy of the European Union: From EPC to CFSP and Beyond* (Boulder CO, 1997); for a discussion that specifically discusses the 'shift' in Britain's strategic thinking under the Blair governments, see K. Haugevik, Strategic Adaptation or Identity Change? An Analysis of Britain's Approach to ESDP 1998–2004. Norwegian Institute of International Affairs Working Paper no. 688 (Oslo, 2005).
53  Franco-British summit, Joint Declaration on European Defence, St Malo, 4 December 1998, available at http://www.atlanticcommunity.org/Saint-Malo%20Declaration%20Text.html.
54  See the final report of Working Group VIII.
55  U. Diedrichs and M. Jopp, Flexibility in ESDP: From the Convention to the IGC and Beyond, *CFSP Forum* 2(2) (March 2004).
56  CONV 422/02.
57  Everts and Keohane, The European Convention, p. 174.
58  Treaty Establishing a Constitution for Europe, Chapter II, Article 1-41 (2).
59  Everts and Keohane, The European Convention, p. 174.
60  J. Solana, A Secure Europe in a Better World, paper presented to the Thessaloniki European Council, 20 June 2003, available at http://ue.eu.int/pressdata/EN/reports/76255.pdf.
61  See Basic Principles for an EU Strategy against Weapons of Mass Destruction, available at http://ue.int/pressdata/EN/reports/76328.pdf.
62  Guerot *et al.*, France, Germany and the UK, p. 11.
63  CONV 461/02.
64  See *Handelsblatt*, 2 April 2003.
65  R. Kissack, The European Security Strategy: A First Appraisal, *CFSP Forum* 2(1) (2003).
66  Final report of Working Group VIII.

67 Guerot *et al.*, France, Germany and the UK, p. 11.
68 See D. Benjamin and S. Simon, Who's Listening to Whom, and Why?, *Time* (European edition), 14 August 2000.
69 A. Townsend, Guarding Europe. Centre for European Reform, May 2003.
70 See K. Schake, Constructive Duplication: Reducing EU Reliance on US Military Assets. Centre for European Reform, January 2003.
71 G. Adams, Europe Should Learn to Fend for Itself, *Financial Times*, 21 July 2003.
72 L. Freedman, A Future for European Defence, *Financial Times*, 22 April 2003; and K. Schake, Do European Union Defence Initiatives Threaten NATO?, *Strategic Forum* 184 (August 2001).
73 Everts and Keohane, The European Convention, p. 178.
74 See S. Everts, Iran Is a Test Case for European Foreign Policy, *Financial Times*, 2 June 2003.
75 See C. Grant, Intimate Relations. Centre for European Reform, May 2000.
76 See D. Keohane, The EU and Armaments Cooperation. Centre for European Reform, December 2002.
77 Kiljunen, *The European Constitution in the Making*, p. 86.
78 Wessels, A 'saut constitutionnel', p. 28.
79 J. Tranholm-Mikkensen, Neo-functionalism: Obstinate or Obsolete? A Reappraisal in the Light of the New Dynamics of the EC, *Millennium* 20 (1991).
80 Wessels, A 'saut constitutionnel', p. 29.
81 Ibid., pp. 29–31.

**Chapter 10**

1 A. Kaletsky, Let France and Germany Build Their Superstate, *The Times*, 24 June 2004.
2 T. Garton Ash, This Is Our High Noon: By Adopting This Constitution, Europe Will Only Reach the Starting Line for the Big Race, *Guardian*, 24 June 2004.
3 S. Kurpas, M. Incerti and J. Schonlau, What Prospects for the European Constitutional Treaty. Monitoring the Ratification Debates. Results of an EPIN Survey of National Experts. EPIN Working Paper no. 12, January 2005, p. 2.
4 W. Münchau, In or out: Europe's Ditherers Must Now Decide, *Financial Times*, 21 June 2004.
5 M. d'Ancona, Blair Sang 'Three Lines on a Shirt', *Sunday Telegraph*, 20 June 2004.
6 D. Keohane, A Guide to the Referenda on the EU Constitutional Treaty. CER Briefing Note, 27 October 2005.
7 Convention: Unknown by European Citizens, *Eurobarometer*, 25 July 2003.
8 L. Leduc, Opinion Change and Voting Behaviour in Referendums, *European Journal of Political Research* 41 (2002).
9 Ibid.
10 C. Church, Implementing the New Constitutional Treaty: A Provisional Introduction. The Federal Trust (London, April 2003), p. 8.
11 Münchau, In or out.
12 Kaletsky, Let France and Germany.
13 B. Crum, The European Commission and the IGC: A Carefully Argued Middle Course. CEPS Commentary, September 2003, p. 3, available at http://www.ceps.be/Commentary/Sept03/Crum.php.
14 See Commission Feasibility Study, Contribution to a Preliminary Draft Constitution of the European Union, 4 December 2002, the so-called 'Penelope Draft', available at http://europa.eu.int/futurum/documents/offtext/const051202_ent.pdf.
15 See CONV 696/03.
16 J. Temple Lang, The Convention on the Future of Europe – So Far. Federal Trust (London, June 2003), p. 7.

17  CONV 658/03.
18  *Financial Times*, 13 January 2005.
19  K. Kiljunen, *The European Constitution in the Making* (Brussels, 2004), p. 151.
20  CONV 647/03.
21  S. Kurpas, M. Incerti and B. Crum, Preview of the 2004 Parliament Elections – Results of an EPIN Survey of National Experts. EPIN Working Paper no. 11, Centre for European Policy Studies, Brussels, May 2004.
22  S. Everts and D. Keohane, A New Era in European Democracy, *CER Bulletin* 38 (October/November 2004).
23  Ibid.
24  Kurpas *et al.*, What Prospects for the European Constitutional Treaty, p. 1.
25  Keohane, A Guide to the Referenda.
26  C. Closa Montero, The Ratification of the Constitution of the EU: A Minefield. Real Instituto Elcano, Madrid, available at http://www.realinstitutoelcano.org/analisis/570.asp.
27  Dietrich von Kyaw, Europe's Leaders Are Not Doing Their Job, *Financial Times*, 5 January 2005.
28  Kurpas *et al.*, What Prospects for the European Constitutional Treaty.
29  Ibid., p. 10.
30  Ibid., p. 15.
31  Ibid., p. 19.
32  Agence France Presse, 7 March 2005.
33  *Diário de Notícias*, 7 May 2005; and Agence France Presse, 14 April 2005.
34  ANSA English Media Service, 11 May 2005.
35  *Guardian*, 20 May 2005
36  Kurpas *et al.*, What Prospects for the European Constitutional Treaty, p. 12.
37  European Information Service, European Report, 20 November 2004.
38  Ibid.
39  ANSA English Media Service, 22 April 2005.
40  M. Arnold and J. Thornhill, Chirac Urges French Voters to Support Treaty EU Constitution, *Financial Times*, 27 April 2005.
41  Honor Mahony, A French No Would Mean Reopening the European Debate, Says Frattini, *EU Observer*, 28 April 2005.
42  *Financial Times*, 19 May 2005.
43  European Information Report, 18 September 2004.
44  Ibid.
45  *Eurostep* no. 394, 21 March 2005.
46  CTK National News Agency, 28 April 2005.
47  European Information Service, European Report, 20 November 2004.
48  Kurpas *et al.*, What Prospects for the European Constitutional Treaty, p. 17.
49  Ibid., p. 18.
50  Ibid., p. 17.
51  The classic literature – and even revisionists who critique the Rokkan/Lipset cleavage model – tends to downplay the role of the EU if changing the patterning of party politics, though 'Europe' does have salience as an issue within and between parties. See, for instance, N. Conti, Is There Europeanisation of Party Politics? Toward a Theory of the Impact of European Integration on Domestic Parties, online paper available at http://www.essex.ac.uk/ECpR/standinggroups/yen/paper_archive/4th_yen_rm_papers/nicolo_conti.pdf.
52  *Financial Times*, 21 February 2005.
53  Kurpas *et al.*, What Prospects for the European Constitutional Treaty, p. 15.
54  Ibid.
55  *Financial Times*, 21 February 2005.
56  Ibid.
57  Kurpas *et al.*, What Prospects for the European Constitutional Treaty, p. 16.

58 Stephan Wagstyl, Comment and Analysis, *Financial Times*, 21 February 2005.

59 Kurpas *et al.*, What Prospects for the European Constitutional Treaty, p. 17.

60 A. Evans-Pritchard and G. Jones, Europe Sets Out Sweeping New Powers, *Daily Telegraph*, 27 May 2004; see also Daniel Hannan, The Way Ahead for Europe, *The Spectator*, 26 June 2004; Daniel Hannah, They Won't Listen, Even If You Vote against the Constitution, *Sunday Telegraph*, 26 September 2004.

61 William Rees-Mogg, Who'd Vote for This Vomit of a Dog's Breakfast, *Mail on Sunday*, 30 January 2005.

62 *Financial Times*, 25 March 2004.

63 *Guardian*, 15 May 2004.

64 Quoted in the *Guardian*, 27 January 2005.

65 *The Times*, 20 April 2004.

66 P. Bains and M. Gill, The EU Constitution and the British Public: What the Polls Tell Us about the Campaign That Never Was, *International Journal of Public Opinion Research* 18 (2006).

67 Although the *Eurobarometer* findings indicate that British public opinion was rather more favourable to the idea of a Constitution than polls published in the national media. See *Eurobarometer* 59 (spring 2003) (fieldwork conducted March/April 2003), p. 92, available at http://ec.europa.eu/public_opinion/archives/eb/eb59/eb_59_en.pdf. Perhaps more indicative of abiding British attitudes to 'Europe' are the findings of the following *Eurobarometer* 60 (autumn 2003) (fieldwork conducted October/November 2003), p. 27–28. These indicated that the British respondents had the highest level of pride in nationality, the lowest level of identification with being 'European' and the least positive image of the EU. Meanwhile, polls conducted in the week the referendum was announced were more in line with these findings, altogether less favourable, more typical of British reticence on European matters, with between 16 and 25 per cent of those polled in favour of an EU constitution, some 53–5 per cent opposed, and 20 per cent undecided. Pollsters frequently point out the volatility of public opinion over referendum questions, with far greater opinion swings than is the case in general elections. See, for instance, *Financial Times*, 24 April 2004.

68 The pro-EU voice in the party was increasingly marginalised throughout the 1990s. See the comments by the former Conservative cabinet minister Chris Patten cited in the Press Association news report, 24 April 2004.

69 See House of Commons Debates (Hansard), 20 December 2004.

70 See the editorial, Euro Referendum Needs to Be Held Soon, *Daily Telegraph*, 20 April 2004.

71 House of Commons Debates (Hansard), 20 April 2004; similar criticism was made by the foreign secretary, Jack Straw: see House of Commons Debates (Hansard), 9 September 2004 and *Financial Times*, 8 December 2004.

72 See Stephen Wall, A 'No' to Europe Would Endanger Britain, *Financial Times*, 20 January 2005.

73 *Scotsman*, 22 April 2004; W. Münchau, A No Vote Would Put Britain Out of Europe, *Financial Times*, 26 April 2004.

74 *Daily Telegraph* 7 April 2004.

75 P. Riddell, The 'Blueprint for Tyranny' Is a Figment of Febrile Minds, *The Times*, 22 May 2003.

76 Will Hutton, Why Eurosceptics Won't Win: People Will Vote Yes in a Referendum As They Understand That the EU Is Not the Enemy of Liberty, *Observer*, 13 February 2005.

77 European Information Service, European Report, 29 January 2005: 33 per cent of the sample had not heard of the Constitutional Treaty, with the highest levels recorded in Cyprus (65 per cent), 50 per cent (UK), and 49 per cent (Greece); the highest levels of knowledge about the Constitution were recorded in Finland, the Czech Republic and Slovakia (at 67 per cent each).

78  Philip Stephens, The Poll That Really Matters to Blair, *Financial Times*, 1 February 2005.
79  Roger Liddle, Labour Must Prevent the Disaster of a Referendum Defeat, *Independent*, 2 March 2005; see also R. Liddle, The New Case for Europe. Fabian Society, February 2005.
80  M. Kettle, This is a Victory for Murdoch: Referendum on Europe. Is the Prime Minister Finally Challenging the Eurosceptic Press, Or Capitulating to It?, *Guardian*, 20 April 2004.
81  See John Rentoul, Blair Spoke from the Hip. He Was Honest and Open. It Was a Disaster, *Independent on Sunday*, 25 April 2004; see also Dietrich von Kyaw, Europe's Leaders Are Not Doing Their Job, *Financial Times*, 5 January 2005.
82  For instance, the Blairite minister Stephen Byers quoted in the *Financial Times*, 3 July 2004.
83  Blair, speaking in the House of Commons, cited in the *Independent*, 22 June 2004.
84  White Paper Establishing a Constitution for Europe, Cm 6309, pp. 1–2, HMSO, September 2004.
85  Quoted in the *Guardian*, 27 January 2005.
86  *Financial Times*, 20 January 2005.
87  Quentin Peel, End the Conspiracy of Silence over Europe, *Financial Times*, 10 February 2005.
88  *Daily Telegraph*, 29 January 2005.
89  P. Stephens, The Cost of Not Caring about Europe, *Financial Times*, 1 March 2005.
90  Speech by Bob Crowe, the general secretary of the Rail, Maritime and Transport Union, quoted in the *Daily Telegraph*, 16 September 2004.
91  *Financial Times*, 1 February 2005.
92  S. Wolfson, Stronger Partnership Or a Political Blank Cheque? *The Times*, 18 January 2005; see also Blair Has Signed Us Up to the Sharia of Euro-enthusiasts, *Daily Telegraph*, 30 October 2004.
93  See MORI, The Referendum Battle, September 2004, available at http://www.mori.com/polls/2004/fpc.shtml.
94  Mark Leonard, Why Tony Needs Help from a Tory; Observations on European Referendum, *New Statesman*, 13 September 2004.
95  *Sunday Telegraph*, 24 October 2004.
96  *Financial Times*, 24 January 2005.
97  *Guardian*, 29 January 2005.
98  *Financial Times*, 29 January 2005.
99  Quoted ibid., 24 January 2005.
100 European Information Service, European Report, 29 January 2005.
101 *Daily Telegraph*, 27 January 2005.
102 M. Grove, Whatever the Question, the Answer Is That These Watchdogs Are Wrong, *The Times*, 8 February 2005.
103 *Business*, 6 February 2005.
104 *Eurobarometer* 62 (May 2005), p. 150, available at http://ec.europa.eu/public_opinion/archives/eb/eb62/eb_62_en.pdf.
105 *Guardian*, 19 May 2005.
106 Steve Richards, The Vote on Europe is Winnable – But Only If Mr Blair Deploys His Most Potent Weapons, *Independent*, 10 February 2005.
107 *Independent*, 15 July 2004.
108 *Financial Times*, 14 January 2005.
109 *Independent*, 16 July 2004.
110 *Financial Times*, 9 September, 2004; ibid., 26 November 2004.
111 *Independent*, 14 September 2004.
112 Quoted in the *Belfast Telegraph*, 29 November 2004.
113 *Financial Times*, 12 November 2004.

114 *The Times*, 2 December 2004; ibid., 3 December 2004.
115 *Financial Times*, 21 June 2004.
116 Ibid., 28 February 2005.
117 For a review of this debate on the covert Americanisation of Europe, see W. Pfaff, EU's Growth Triggers Identity Crisis, *International Herald Tribune*, 5 April 2005.
118 *Financial Times*, 13 January 2005.
119 P. Le Coeur, Des sontages inquietent les partisans du traité, *Le Monde*, 12 January 2005; and P. Stephens, The Curious Temptation of a French No to Europe, *Financial Times*, 22 April 2005.
120 Sylvie Goulard, France's Malaise Is Teaching Europe a Lesson, *Financial Times*, 18 May 2005.
121 Peter Beaumont, Europe Decides: Yes, It's on a Knife Edge, *Observer*, 15 May 2005.
122 Tim King, Franco-Euro-Flap, *Prospect*, April 2005.
123 See, for instance, Philip Stephens, France Begins to Question the Rationale for Europe, *Financial Times*, 18 March 2005.
124 Wolfgang Münchau, Europe Is Not Ready for a French No, *Financial Times*, 4 April 2005.
125 *Le Monde*, 11 April 2005.
126 Beaumont, Europe Decides.
127 Quoted in David Lawday, The French Keep It in the Family, *New Statesman*, 23 May 2005.
128 A. Wanlin, Will the French Vote 'Non'?, *CER Bulletin* 40 (February/March 2005).
129 Quoted in the *Financial Times*, 1 March 2005.
130 *The Times*, 18 February 2005.
131 *Guardian*, 19 March 2005; see, for instance, the poll published in *Le Figaro*, 28 March 2005; *International Herald Tribune*, 2 April 2005.
132 For a review of these polls, see *World Markets Analysis*, World Markets Research Limited, 28 March 2005.
133 Stephens, The Curious Temptation.
134 *Financial Times*, 19 May 2005.
135 The European Constitution: Post-referendum Survey in France. Flash *Eurobarometer/EOS Gallup Europe* (European Commission, June 2005), p. 30.
136 Quentin Peel, France Cannot Have the Last Word, *Financial Times*, 26 May 2005.
137 The European Constitution: Post-referendum Survey in France, p. 21.
138 Ibid., p. 30.
139 Ibid.
140 Ibid., p. 22.
141 Ibid., p. 25.
142 Ibid., p. 27.
143 Goulard, France's Malaise
144 *The Times*, 3 September 2004.
145 *Independent*, 31 August 2004; *Financial Times*, 31 August 2004.
146 A poll by Infratest dimap found 59 per cent in favour of the Constitution, only 15 per cent opposed and 26 per cent undecided: BBC Monitoring, International Reports, 9 May 2005.
147 G. Harding, Analysis: EU Enlargement One Year On, United Press International, 29 April 2005.
148 *Financial Times*, 16 July 2004.
149 EUObserver.com, 12 May 2005.
150 Schroeder quoted in *International Herald Tribune*, 14 May 2005.
151 *Daily Telegraph*, 11 February 2005.
152 Ibid.
153 BBC Monitoring, International Reports, 2 February 2005.
154 *International Herald Tribune*, 21 February 2005.

155  *Financial Times*, 14 February 2005.
156  Ignaci Guardans MEP, quoted in the *Irish Times*, 19 February 2005.
157  *El País*, 21 February 2005; *Razón*, 21 February 2005.
158  D. Keohane, Don't Forget the Dutch Referendum. CER Briefing Note, May 2005.
159  Q. Peel, A Treaty Held Hostage to Expediency, *Financial Times*, 13 January 2005.
160  *Eurobarometer* 62 (May 2005), p. 150, available at http://ec.europa.eu/public_opinion/archives/eb/eb62/eb_62_en.pdf.
161  September 2003, for *NRC Handelsblad*; similar polling results are reported by the ANSA English Media Service, 26 April 2005.
162  *Irish Times*, 16 April 2005.
163  Quentin Peel, The Folly of Taking Europe for Granted, *Financial Times*, 19 May 2005.
164  Ibid.
165  J. O'Sullivan, Not the Answer They Expected, *National Review*, 20 June 2005.
166  S. Leitner and G. Parker, Political Elite Startled as Dutch Voters Turn against EU, *Financial Times*, 15 May 2005.
167  The European Constitution: Post-referendum Survey in The Netherlands. Flash *Eurobarometer*/EOS Gallup Europe (European Commission, June 2005), p. 20
168  Ibid., p. 22.
169  Ibid., p. 27.
170  Ibid., p. 28.
171  Ibid.
172  Ibid., p. 25.
173  *Financial Times*, 22 June 2004.
174  Agence France, 25 January 2005.
175  BBC Monitoring, International Reports, 1 September 2004.
176  *La Dernière Heure*, 20 May 2005.
177  *Irish Times*, 29 October 2004.
178  Ibid., 19 May 2005.
179  Ibid., 7 May 2005.
180  Ibid., 18 February 2005.
181  Ibid., 5 February 2005.
182  Ibid., 9 March 2005.
183  EUObserver.com, 17 March 2005.
184  Agence France Presse, 9 May 2005.
185  Trine Flockhart, The Gap between Danish Mass and Elite Attitudes to Europeanization, *Journal of Common Market Studies* 43(2) (2005), p. 268.
186  Quoted in the *Financial Times*, 1 March 2005.
187  BBC Worldwide Monitoring, 9 April 2005.
188  *Guardian*, 13 January 2005.
189  *Financial Times*, 1 March 2005.
190  Athens News Agency, 12 April 2005.
191  Ibid., 11 April 2005.
192  Financial Times Information – Global News Wire, 29 October 2004.
193  Athens News Agency, 3 February 2005.
194  Ibid., 15 February 2005.
195  Xinhua General News Agency, 16 April 2005.
196  *Diário de Notícias*, 30 September 2004.
197  Public Opinion in the EU – Portugal, *Eurobarometer* 61 (Spring 2004), pp. 15–20.
198  *Financial Times*, 10 May 2005.
199  MTI-ECONEWS, 20 December 2004.
200  BBC Monitoring, International Reports, 1 February 2005.
201  Ibid., 2 February 2005.
202  Agence France Presse, 1 February 2005.

203 World Markets Analysis, 20 January 2005.
204 *Gazeta Wyborcza*, cited by BBC Monitoring, International Reports, 3 December 2004.
205 *Financial Times*, 3 March 2005.
206 PAP News Agency, Warsaw, 29 October 2004.
207 *Financial Times*, 13 January 2005.
208 For results, see CBOS website at http://cbos.pl/Opinia/2004/11-2004.pdf.
209 *Hospodarske noviny*, 16 November 2004.
210 Quoted by CTK Czech News Agency, 26 February 2005.
211 *Mlada fronta Dnes*, 29 September 2004.
212 CTK Czech News Agency, 5 March 2005.
213 *Financial Times*, 22 February 2005.
214 CTK Czech News Agency, 13 April 2005.
215 CVVM poll reported by CTK Czech News Agency, 16 May 2005.
216 BBC Monitoring, Europe, 24 November 2004.
217 Financial Times Information – Global News Wire, 30 October 2004.
218 CTK Czech News Agency, 11 May 2005.
219 *The Slovak Spectator*, 8 May 2005.
220 European Information Service, 13 November 2004.
221 Baltic News Service, 3 November 2004.
222 Ibid., 11 November 2004.
223 Agence France Presse, 5 May 2005.
224 Baltic News Service, 30 September 2004.
225 Agence France Presse, 5 May 2005.
226 Ibid., 10 May 2005.
227 Alastair Sutton, Treaty Establishing a Constitution for Europe: Impact of Negative Votes in the French and Dutch Referenda. White and Case (Brussels, 3 June 2005), p. 7.
228 Quentin Peel, Europe's Best Hope for Credibility Is to Grow, *Financial Times*, 2 June 2005.
229 Kiljunen, *The European Constitution in the Making*, p. 44.
230 L. Diez-Picazo, Treaty or Constitution? The Status of the Constitution for Europe. Jean Monnet Working Paper 5/04, New York University School of Law (2004).
231 Kiljunen, *The European Constitution in the Making*, p. 45.
232 Ibid., p. 46.
233 Treaty Establishing a Constitution for Europe, Title I, Article 1-I, available at http://eur-lex.europa.eu/LexUriServ/site/en/oj/2004/c_310/c_31020041216en00110040.pdf.

## Chapter 11

1 A. Moravcsik, The 'Unsung Constitution', *Prospect*, March 2004.
2 Mark Kleinman, *A European Welfare State?* (Basingstoke, 2002), p. 209.
3 N. Walker, Europe's Constitutional Momentum and the Search for Polity Legitimacy, in Jean Monnet Working Paper 5/04, Symposium: *Altneuland*: The EU Constitution in a Contextual Perspective, ed. J. Weiler and C. L. Eisgruber (New York University School of Law, 2004), p. 50, available at http://www.jeanmonnetprogram.org/papers/04/040501.html.
4 Ibid., p. 49.
5 Quoted in Peter Ford, European Integration at the Crossroad, *Christian Science Monitor*, 31 May 2005.
6 *Financial Times*, 2 June 2005.
7 Quoted in Ford, European Integration.
8 S. Chambers, Democracy, Popular Sovereignty, and Constitutional Legitimacy, *Constellations* 11 (2004), p. 153.

9  R. Hirschl, Hegemonic Preservation in Action? Assessing the Political Origins of the EU Constitution, in Jean Monnet Working Paper 5/04, Symposium: *Altneuland*, pp. 3 and 5.

10  *The Economist* (US edition), 28 May 2005.

11  Ibid.

12  Hirschl, Hegemonic Preservation in Action, p. 23; G. Amato and J. Batt, Socio-economic Discrepancies in the Enlarged EU. Final Report of the Reflection Group on 'Long-term Implications of EU Enlargement: The Nature of the New Border', European University Institute, RSC Policy Paper no. 99/2 (1999), available at http://www.iue.it/RSC/Amato992-PP.htm; J. Zielonka and P. Mair, Introduction: Diversity and Adaptation in the Enlarged European Union, in J. Zielonka and P. Mair (eds), *The Enlarged European Union: Diversity and Adaptation* (London, 2002).

13  M. Maduro, How Constitutional Can the European Union Be? The Tension between Intergovernmentalism and Constitutionalism in the European Union, in Jean Monnet Working Paper 5/04, Symposium: *Altneuland*, p. 48.

14  Ibid.

15  J. E. Fossum and A. J. Menendez, Democratic Constitution-making. Reflections on the European Experiment. ARENA Centre for European Studies, Oslo, Working Paper no. 18, May 2005, p. 14, available at http://www.arena.uio.no.

16  J. Fossum, Contemporary European Constitution-making: Constrained or Reflexive? ARENA Centre for European Studies, Oslo, Working Paper no. 4 January 2005, p. 16, available at http://www.arena.uio.no.

17  *Guardian*, 17 February 2004, available at http://politics.guardian.co.uk/print/0.3858.4860768-107988.00.html.

18  A. von Bogdandy, The European Constitution and European Identity: A Critical Analysis of the Convention's Draft Preamble, in Jean Monnet Working Paper 5/04, Symposium: *Altneuland*, p. 7.

19  O. Pfersmann, The New Revision of the Old Constitution, in Jean Monnet Working Paper 5/04, Symposium: *Altneuland*, p. 13.

20  J. E. Fossum and H.-J. Trenz, The EU's Fledgling Society: From Deafening Silence to Critical Voice in European Constitution Making. ARENA Centre for European Studies, Oslo, Working Paper no. 19, July 2005, p. 9, available at http://www.arena.uio.no.

21  D. Imig and S. Tarrow, Political Contention in a Europeanising Polity, *West European Politics* 23(4) (2000), p. 7.

22  A. Wiener, Evolving Norms of Constitutionalism in Europe: From 'Treaty Language' to 'Constitution', in Jean Monnet Working Paper 5/04, Symposium: *Altneuland*, p. 6.

23  Pfersmann, The New Revision of the Old Constitution, p. 1.

24  J. Fossum, Still a Union of Deep Diversity? The Convention and the Constitution for Europe, in E. Eriksen, J. Fossum and A. Menendez (eds), *Developing a Constitution for Europe* (London, 2004).

25  European Convention SN 1565/02, Introductory Speech by President V. Giscard d'Estaing to the Convention on the Future of Europe (Brussels, 28 February 2002).

26  Fossum, Contemporary European Constitution-making, p. 27.

27  Ibid., p. 17.

28  P. Magnette, When Does Deliberation Matter? Constitutional Rhetoric in the Convention on the Future of Europe, in C. Closa and J. Fossum (eds), Deliberative Constitutional Politics in the EU. ARENA Report 5/04, Oslo 2004, available at http://www.arena.uio.no.

29  Fossum, Contemporary European Constitution-making, p. 16; see also R. Schalm-Bruns, On the Political Theory of the Euro-polity, in E. Eriksen (ed.), *Making the European Polity: Reflexive Integration in the EU* (London, 2005).

30  A. Follesdal, Legitimacy Theories of the European Union. ARENA Centre for European Studies, Oslo, Working Papers, WP 04/15, p. 15, available at http://www.arena.uio.no.

31  Ibid., p. 18.

32 C. Calhoun, The Democratic Integration of Europe: Interests, Identity, and the Public Sphere, in M. Berezin and M. Schain (eds), *Europe without Borders: Re-mapping Territory, Citizenship and Identity in a Transnational Age* (Baltimore, 2003).

33 R. Dalton, Political Support in Advanced Democracies, in P. Norris (ed.), *Critical Citizens: Global Support for Democratic Government* (Oxford, 1999).

34 *Le Figaro*, 2 June 2005.

35 *Guardian Unlimited*, 2 June 2005.

36 Philip Stephens, Bring Back the Ideals of Messina, *Financial Times*, 3 June 2005.

37 Ibid.

38 *Daily Telegraph*, 3 June 2005; *Guardian*, 2 June 2005.

39 BBC Monitoring, International Reports, 2 June 2005.

40 Associated Press, International News, 1 June 2005.

41 EUobserver.com, 15 July 2005.

42 *Daily Telegraph*, 3 June 2005.

43 *Financial Times*, 3 June 2005.

44 Ibid., 18 June 2005.

45 *Daily Telegraph*, 3 June 2005.

46 *Independent*, 7 June 2005.

47 A 'senior government source' quoted in the *Daily Telegraph*, 2 June 2005.

48 Quoted in the *Guardian*, 2 June 2005.

49 Agence France Presse, 2 June 2005.

50 *Daily Telegraph*, 2 June 2005.

51 Quoted in the *Chicago Tribune*, 2 June 2005.

52 *Financial Times*, 3 June 2005.

53 Ibid.

54 *Daily Telegraph*, 3 June 2005.

55 *Financial Times*, 2 June 2005.

56 European Information Service, European Report, 4 June 2005.

57 *De Standaard*, 29 May 2006.

58 EUobserver.com, 10 June 2005.

59 Ibid.

60 *Financial Times*, 4 June 2005.

61 A Citizens Compact: Reaching Out to the Citizens of Europe. EPIN Working Paper no. 14, September 2005.

62 Mark Leonard, Democracy in Europe: How the EU Can Survive in an Age of Referendums. Centre for European Reform Essays, March 2006.

63 *The Times*, 17 June 2005.

64 Agence France Presse, 15 May 2006.

65 Ibid., 10 May 2006.

66 Deutsche Presse-Agentur, 15 June 2006.

67 *De Standaard*, 13 June 2006.

68 Laurent Cohen-Tanugi, The End of Europe?, *Foreign Affairs*, November/December 2005.

69 Poll, *Eurobaromer 62*, pp. 34–5, available at http://ec.europa.eu/public_opinion/archives/eb/eb62/eb62_en.pdf; and *Eurobaromer 64*, pp. 100–1, available at http://ec.europa.eu/public_opinion/archives/eb/eb64/eb64_en.pdf.

70 BBC Monitoring, International Reports, 10 June 2005.

71 European Information Service, European Report, 18 June 2005.

72 Quoted in *International Herald Tribune*, 10 May 2006.

73 G. Bowley, Dead or Alive? EU Leaders Taking Constitutional Pulse, *International Herald Tribune*, 28 January 2006.

74 BBC Monitoring, Europe, 15 June 2006.

75 European Information Service, European Report, 19 June 2007.

76 Ibid.

77 Ibid.
78 Ibid.
79 Leonard, Democracy in Europe.
80 European Information Service, European Report, 15 June 2006.
81 European Information Service, 21 January 2006.
82 A. Duff, Improve the Product to Save the Constitution, *Financial Times*, 9 June 2006.
83 P. Bachrach, *A Theory of Democratic Elitism* (Boston, 1967); J. Femia, Elites, Participation, and the Democratic Creed, *Political Studies* 27(1) (1979).
84 European Information Service, 27 April 2006.
85 European Information Service, European Report, 19 June 2007.
86 Ibid.
87 *Eurobarometer* 64, pp. 123–33, available at http://ec.europa.eu/public_opinion/
archives/eb/eb64/eb64_en.pdf.
88 European Information Service, 21 January 2006.
89 BBC Monitoring, International Reports, 17 February 2006.
90 Cohen-Tanugi, The End of Europe.
91 Ibid.
92 *Guardian*, 9 September 2006.
93 *The Times*, 2 September 2005.
94 *Independent*, 2 June 2005.
95 Charles Grant, Staring into the Abyss, *E! Sharp*, July/August 2005, p. 22.
96 Hirschl, Hegemonic Preservation in Action, p. 2.
97 Grant, Staring into the Abyss.
98 J. Demsey and K. Bennold, Preparing to Rescue Key Parts of the Charter, *International Herald Tribune*, 19 June 2005.
99 *Financial Times*, 31 May 2005.
100 EUobserver.com, 13 September 2005.
101 European Information Service, 27 April 2006.
102 Editorial, *Guardian*, 1 June 2005.
103 BBC Worldwide Monitoring, 27 April 2006.
104 *Financial Times*, 31 May 2006.
105 Ibid., 23 May 2006.
106 Ibid., 6 June 2005.
107 Sir Stephen Wall, Reform in Europe Can Wait a Bit Longer, *Financial Times*, 14 June
2006.
108 Leonard, Democracy in Europe.
109 *Financial Times*, 24 June 2005.
110 Ibid., 3 June 2005.
111 A. Duff, Improve the Product to Save the Constitution, *Financial Times*, 9 June
2006.
112 Agence France Presse, 28 December 2005.
113 *Independent*, 1 June 2006.
114 *International Herald Tribune*, 1 December 2005.
115 Agence Presse France, 1 January 2006.
116 EUobserver.com, 12 June 2006.
117 European Information Service, European Report, 30 June 2006.
118 Associated Press Worldstream, 9 May 2006.
119 Alastair Sutton, Treaty Establishing a Constitution for Europe: Impact of Negative Votes
in the French and Dutch Referenda. White and Case (Brussels, 3 June 2005), p. 10.
120 As evidenced by the relative success of far-right, xenophobic/nationalist and Eurosceptical parties in the 2004 European elections; see S. Harrison, Un Fauteuil pour
Deux? The Extreme Right and the Extreme Left in the European Parliament Elections 2004, paper presented at the Conference of the AFSP/GSPE European Parliament, Strasbourg, 18–19 November 2004, available at http://209.85.135.104/

search?q=cache:mQbMSV_3tv0J:www.afsp.msh-paris.fr/activite/diversafsp/collg-spegael04/harrison.pdf+The+vote+for+far+right+and+eurosceptic+parties+in+the+2 004+European+parliament+elections&hl=en&ct=clnk&cd=4.

121 *Independent*, 29 May 2006.
122 BBC Worldwide Monitoring, 29 May 2006.
123 US Federal News Agency, 7 June 2007.
124 Ibid.
125 BBC Monitoring Service, 2 June 2007.
126 US Federal News Agency, 6 June 2007.
127 Ibid.
128 D. Hannan, Tap-dancing towards a Euro Constitution, *Daily Telegraph*, 7 June 2007.
129 US Federal News Agency, 7 June 2007.
130 D. Hannan, Merkel's Honesty Is Not the Best Policy, *Daily Telegraph*, 27 April 2007.
131 Council of the European Union, Presidency Conclusions, 11177/07 CONCL 2, Brussels, 23 June 2007, General Observation (3), p. 16.
132 Ibid.
133 Ibid.
134 Quoted in the *Sunday Express*, 24 June 2007.
135 Ibid.
136 Council of the European Union, Presidency Conclusions, 11177/07 CONCL 2, Brussels, 23 June 2007, p. 25, note 18.
137 *Gazeta Wyborcza*, 15 June 2007.
138 Renata Goldirova, Germany Gives Ear to Poland in 'Reform Treaty' Talks, EUobserver.com, 20 June 2007; and Honor Mahony, EU Leaders Scrape Treaty Deal at 11th hour, EUobserver.com, 23 June 2007.
139 K. Barysch, What the Summit Says about the EU. Centre for European Reform, 26 June 2007.
140 Mahony, EU Leaders Scrape Treaty Deal.
141 Hugh Brady, Hurrah for an End to Navel Gazing. Centre for European Reform, June 2007, available at www.cer.org.uk.
142 Ibid.
143 Andrew Rettman, Merkel Gives Up God in EU Treaty, EUobserver.com, 9 July 2007.
144 Council of the European Union, Presidency Conclusions, 11177/07 CONCL 2, Brussels, 23 June 2007, General Observation (3), p. 16.
145 *Independent*, 19 June 2007.
146 Council of the European Union, Presidency Conclusions, 11177/07 CONCL 2, Brussels, 23 June 2007, Title V, Annexe I, p. 27; Ibid., Title I, Annexe 4 (2), p. 25.
147 Honor Mahony, EU Treaty Blueprint Sets Stage for Bitter Negotiations, EUobserver. com, 20 June 2007.
148 Barysch, What the Summit Says.
149 Charles Grant, We Do Not Need a Referendum, *Guardian Unlimited*, 23 June 2007.
150 Mark Tran, How the German EU Proposals Differ from the Constitution, *Guardian*, 21 June 2007.
151 Mahony, EU Treaty Blueprint.
152 Europe Picking Up the Pieces after the 2005 Debacle, *EU Politics Today*, 4 July 2007.
153 Barysch, What the Summit Says.
154 Council of the European Union, Presidency Conclusions, 11177/07 CONCL 2, Brussels, 23 June 2007, Title II, Annexe I, p. 26.
155 Quoted in US Fed News, 27 June 2007.
156 V. Giscard d'Estaing, *Le Monde*, 14 June 2007.
157 Council of the European Union, Presidency Conclusions, 11177/07 CONCL 2, Brussels, 23 June 2007, Amendments to the EU Treaty, Title I – Common Provisions, p. 24.
158 European Information Service, European Report, 19 June 2007.

159  Quoted in Andrea Bonanni, Prodi: Un'Europa senza cuore abbiamo fatto un passo indietro, *La Repubblica*, 24 June 2007.
160  *Morgenavisen Jyllands-Posten*, 25 June 2007.
161  Hannan, Merkel's Honesty.
162  *Guardian*, 16 October 2007.
163  RIA Novosti, 22 June 2007.
164  *Guardian*, 11 September 2007.
165  IGC: A Complicated Mandate for a So-called Simplified Treaty. European Information Service, European Report, 26 June 2007.
166  V. Giscard d'Estaing, *Le Monde*, 14 June 2007.
167  The Europe of the Heads of State, *Libération*, 20 June 2007.
168  V. Giscard d'Estaing, *Le Monde*, 14 June 2007.
169  Leon N. Lindberg, Political Integration: Definitions and Hypotheses, in B. Nelsen and A. Stubb (eds), *The European Union. Readings on the Theory and Practice of European Integration* (Basingstoke, 1994).
170  There is a massive literature on this subject, but one of the pioneering thinkers here was James Rosenau. For a flavour of his ideas on 'cascading interdependence', see his essay, Governance, Order, and Change in World Politics, in James N. Rosenau and Ernst-Otto Czempiel (eds), *Governance without Government: Order and Change in World Politics* (Cambridge, 1992). Similarly there is an expanding literature on Europeanisation, but for an overview see M. Vink, What Is Europeanization? And Other Questions on a New Research Agenda, paper presented at the Second YEN Research Meeting on Europeanization, Milan, 22–23 November 2002, available at http://www.essex.ac.uk/ecpr/standinggroups/yen/paper_archive/2nd_yen_rm_papers/vink2002.pdf.
171  See for instance the discussion in J. Checkel, Norms, Institutions and National Identity in Contemporary Europe. ARENA Working Papers WP 98/16, Oslo 1998, available at http://www.arena.uio.no/publications/wp98_16.htm.
172  Adrian Hamilton, The Voters Should Decide Any New Treaty, *Independent*, 14 June 2007.
173  Jean-Claude Juncker, Succès objectif, déception atmosphérique, *Le Soir*, 2 July 2007, p. 18.
174  V. Giscard d'Estaing, *Le Monde*, 14 June 2007.
175  Ibid.
176  Ibid.
177  Quoted in the *Sunday Express*, 17 June 2007.
178  Quoted in F. Duchêne, *Jean Monnet: The First Statesman of Interdependence* (New York, 1994), p. 23.

**Chapter 12**

1  J. O'Sullivan, *National Review*, 20 June 2005.
2  Ibid.
3  J. E. Fossum and H.-J. Trenz, The EU's Fledgling Society: From Deafening Silence to Critical Voice in European Constitution Making. ARENA Working Paper no. 19, Oslo, July 2005, available at http://www.arena.uio.no.
4  G. Marks and D. McAdam, On the Relationship of Political Opportunities to the Form of Collective Action. The Case of the European Union, in D. Della Porta, H. Kriesi and D. Rucht (eds), *Social Movements in a Globalizing World* (Basingstoke, 1999). For the broader debate about the prospects for realising transnational politics see A. Linklater, *The Transformation of Political Community* (Cambridge, 1998); J. Smith, C. Chatfield and R. Pagnucco (eds), *Transnational Social Movements and Global Politics: Solidarity beyond the State* (Syracuse, NY 1997); M. Keck and K. Sikkink, *Activists beyond Borders. Advocacy Networks in International Politics* (Ithaca NY, 1998); T. Risse, Transnational Actors, Networks and

Global Governance, in W. Carlnaes, T. Risse and B. Simmons (eds), *Handbook of International Relations* (London, 2001).

5 A Citizens Compact: Reaching out to the Citizens of Europe. EPIN Working Paper no. 14, September 2005, pp. 2–3.

6 Ibid.

7 Ibid., p. 4.

8 Ibid., p. 3.

9 Ibid., p. 4.

10 See COM (2001) 354; COM (2002) 350; COM (2004).

11 http://www.europa.eu.int/comm/dgs/press communications/pdf, p. 2.

12 Ibid., pp. 2, 5 and 12.

13 Ibid., p. 6.

14 Ibid., p. 9.

15 Quoted in Associated Press Wordstream, 27 March 2006.

16 *International Herald Tribune*, 13 October 2005.

17 Fossum and Trenz, The EU's Fledgling Society.

18 See H. Schmitt and J. Thomassen, *Political Representation and Legitimacy in the European Union* (Oxford, 1999).

19 Fossum and Trenz, The EU's Fledgling Society, p. 29.

20 T. Banchoff and M. P. Smith (eds), *Legitimacy and the European Union* (London, 1999); C. Karlsson, *Democracy, Legitimacy and the European Union* (Uppsala, 2001).

21 W. Wallace, Rescue or Retreat? The Nation State in Western Europe, in P. Gowan and P. Anderson (eds), *The Question of Europe* (London, 1997).

22 H. Wallace, Deepening and Widening: Problems of Legitimacy for the EC, in S. Garcia (ed.), *European Identity and the Search for Legitimacy* (London, 1993); and F. Scharpf, *Governing in Europe: Effective and Democratic?* (Oxford, 1999).

23 See the discussion in A. Sbragia, Politics in the European Union, in G. Almond, R. Dalton and G. Bingham Powell (eds), *European Politics Today* (New York, 1999).

24 Mark Kleinman, *A European Welfare State?* (Basingstoke, 2002), p. 207.

25 Ibid., p. 209.

26 Ibid., p. 205.

27 See the discussion in A. Weale, Some Principles of Task-assignment in a Multi-level Polity. New Modes of Governance, Integrated Project, Priority 7: Citizens and Governance in a Knowledge-based Society, August 2006, available at http://www.eu-newgov.org/database/DELIV/DDTFD03_Principles_of_Task-Assignment_Multi-Level_Polity.pdf.

28 J. P. Olsen, Political Engineering in the Name of the People?, *Journal of European Public Policy* 7(2) (2000).

29 L. Miles, Editorial: The Paradox of a Popular Europe, in Lee Miles (ed.), *Journal of Common Market Studies Annual Review of the European Union, 2003/2004* (Oxford, 2004), p. 2.

30 Ibid.

31 M. Kohli, The Battleground of European Identity, *European Society* 2(2) (2000).

32 C. Lord and P. Magnette, Notes towards a General Theory of Legitimacy in the European Union. ESRC 'One Europe or Several?', Working Paper 39/02, available at http://www.one-europe.ac.uk/pdf/w39lord.pdf.

33 Fossum and Trenz, The EU's Fledgling Society, pp. 31–2.

34 See, for instance, R. Bellamy, The Constitution of Europe: Rights or Democracy?, in R. Bellamy, V. Bufacchi and D. Castiglione (eds), *Democracy and Constitutional Culture in the Union of Europe* (London, 1995), p. 167; B. Manin, On Legitimacy and Political Deliberation, *Political Theory* 15 (1987), p. 352.

35 C. Karlsson, *Democracy, Legitimacy and the European Union*, p. 273.

36 S. Andersen and T. Burns, The European Union and the Erosion of Parliamentary Democracy, in S. Andersen and K. Eliassen (eds), *The European Union: How Democratic Is It?* (London, 1996); H. Abromeit, *Democracy in Europe: Legitimising Politics in a Non-state Polity* (New York, 1998).

37  H. Abromeit and S. Wolf, Will the Constitutional Treaty Contribute to the Legitimacy of the European Union? European Integration online Papers (EIoP) 9(11) (2005), p. 11, available at http://eiop.or.at/eiop/texte/2005-011a.htm.
38  Ibid., p. 6.
39  I. Berend, *History Derailed: Central and Eastern Europe in the Long Nineteenth Century* (California, 2003).
40  E. Gellner, *Nations and Nationalism* (Oxford, 1983).
41  J. Klausen, Social Rights Advocacy and State Building: T. H. Marshall in the Hands of Social Reformers, *World Politics*, 47(2) (1995), p. 249.
42  Kleinman, *A European Welfare State*, p. 193.
43  M. O'Neill and D. Austin (eds), *Democracy and Cultural Diversity* (Oxford, 2000).
44  M. Mann, Ruling Class Strategies and Citizenship, in M. Bulmer and A. M. Rees (eds), *Citizenship Today: The Contemporary Relevance of T. H. Marshall* (London, 1996).
45  R. Aron, Is Multicultural Citizenship Possible?, *Social Research* 41 (1974).
46  Kleinman, *A European Welfare State*, p. 195.
47  F. Duchêne, *Jean Monnet: The First Statesman of Interdependence* (New York, 1994).
48  M. O'Neill, *The Politics of European Integration* (London, 1996), pp. 31–53.
49  J. P. Olsen, The Many Faces of Europeanization, *Journal of Common Market Studies* 40 (2005).
50  R. Simeon and D.-P. Conway, Federalism and the Management of Conflict in Multinational Societies, in A.-G. Gagnon and J. Tully (eds), *Multinational Democracies* (Cambridge, 2001).
51  *Eurobarometer* 58, March 2003, pp. 27–8, available at http://ec.europa.eu/public_opinion/archives/eb/eb58/eb58_en.pdf. These findings are almost identical to a subsequent survey.
52  *Eurobarometer* 52, April 2000, p. 10, available at http://ec.europa.eu/public_opinion/archives/eb/eb52/eb52_en.pdf.
53  Ibid., pp. 82–9; similar finding in later surveys suggest this trend has not changed.
54  Ibid., p. 36.
55  *Eurobarometer* 64, June 2006, pp. 29–40, available at http://ec.europa.eu/public_opinion/archives/eb/eb64/eb64_en.pdf. The level of trust invested by citizens in the Union has barely risen above 50 per cent, and for most surveys is well below that break-even point for the last four *Eurobarometer* surveys (61–4 inclusive), ibid., p. 29, with over 80 per cent of respondents of the opinion that EU institutions are culpable for not making a greater effort to encourage public involvement: ibid., p. 40.
56  See, for instance, R. Inglehart, Changing Values, Economic Development and Political Change, *Revue internationale des sciences sociales* (English edition), no. 145, September 1995.
57  M. Gabel, Public Support for European Integration: An Empirical Test of Five Theories, *Journal of Politics* 60(2) (1998).
58  J.-E. Lane and S. Ersonn, *Politics and Society in Western Europe*, fourth edition (London, 1999).
59  A. Michalski and J. Tallberg, Project on European Integration Indicators: People's Europe. European Commission Forward Studies Unit, Working Paper, 1999, available at http://ec.europa.eu/comm/cdp/scenario/scenarios_en.pdf.
60  Ibid., p. 11.
61  Ibid., p. 5.
62  Ibid.
63  Ibid., p. 17.
64  Ibid., p. 33.
65  *Irish Times*, 4 June 2005.
66  Michalski and Tallberg, Project on European Integration Indicators, p. 34.
67  Ibid.
68  L. Miles, Sweden in the European Union: Changing Expectations?, *Journal of European Integration* 23(4) 2002.

69 Michalski and Tallberg, Project on European Integration Indicators, p. 35.
70 Mark Beunderman, Nearly Half of Citizens Want New Talks on EU Constitution, EUobserver.com, Brussels, 6 July 2006.
71 Miles, Sweden in the European Union.
72 T. Flockhart, Critical Junctures and Social Identity Theory: Explaining the Gap between Danish Mass and Elite Attitudes to Europeanization, *Journal of Common Market Studies* 43 (2005).
73 U. Hedetoft, The Interplay between Mass and Elite Attitudes to European Integration in Denmark, in H. Branner and M. Kelstrup (eds), *Denmark's Policy towards Europe after 1945* (Odense, 2000).
74 A. Johnston, Treating International Institutions as Social Environments, *International Studies Quarterly* 45 (2001).
75 U. Hedetoft, Cultures of States and Informal Governance in the EU: An Exploratory Study of Elites, Power and Identity. Series of Occasional Papers, European Research Unit, no. 35 (Aalborg, 2003).
76 Flockhart, Critical Juncture, p. 254.
77 Ibid., p. 255.
78 T. Risse-Kappen, Ideas Do Not Float Freely: Transnational Coalitions, Domestic Structures, and the End of the Cold War, *International Organization* 42 (1988).
79 Flockhart, Critical Juncture, pp. 253–5.
80 M. Marcussen, *Ideas and Elites: The Social Construction of Economic and Monetary Union* (Aalborg, 2000).
81 J. Checkel, Social Construction and Integration, *Journal of European Public Policy* 6(4) (1999); J. Checkel, Why Comply? Social Learning and European Identity Change, *International Organization* 55(3) (2001); and J. Checkel, The Europeanization of Citizenship, in J. Caporasa (ed.), *Transforming Europe: Europeanization and Domestic Change* (London, 2001).
82 P. Di Maggio and W. Powell, The Iron Cage Revisited: Institutional Isomorphism and Collective Rationality in Organizational Fields, in P. Di Maggio and W. Powell (eds), *Institutionalism in Organizational Analysis* (Chicago, 1991).
83 Michalski and Tallberg, Project on European Integration Indicators, p. 7.
84 Ibid.
85 Alastair Sutton, Treaty Establishing a Constitution for Europe: Impact of Negative Votes in the French and Dutch Referenda. White and Case (Brussels, 3 June 2005), pp. 3–4.
86 Special *Eurobarometer*: The Future Constitutional Treaty. European Commission, January 2005, available at http://ec.europa.eu/public_opinion/archives/ebs/ebs214_en_first.pdf.
87 A. Sajo, Constitutional Enthusiasm towards the European Constitution?, in Jean Monnet Working Paper 5/04, Symposium: *Altneuland*: The EU Constitution in a Contextual Perspective, ed. J. Weiler and C. L. Eisgruber (New York University School of Law, 2004), pp. 3–4, available at http://www.jeanmonnetprogram.org/papers/04/040501.html.
88 J. Weiler, A Constitution for Europe? Some Hard Choices, *Journal of Common Market Studies* 4 (2002), p. 567.
89 M. Maduro, Where to Look for Legitimacy?, in E. O. Eriksen, J. E. Fossum and A. J. Menendez (eds), Constitution Making and Democracy. ARENA Report no. 5 (Oslo, 2002), pp. 81 and 91.
90 N. Walker, Europe's Constitutional Momentum and the Search for Political Legitimacy, in Jean Monnet Working Paper 5/04, Symposium: *Altneuland*, pp. 52–3.
91 Flash *Eurobarometer* 142: Convention on the Future of Europe (EDS Gallup Europe, 2003).
92 K. Laenarts and M. Desomer, New Models of Constitution-making in Europe: The Quest for Legitimacy, *Common Market Law Review* 39 (2002).
93 Sajo, Constitutional Enthusiasm, p. 12.
94 Ibid., p. 11.

95  Miles, Editorial: The Paradox of a Popular Europe, p. 5.
96  C. Closa, A Polity without a State? European Constitutionalism between Evolution and Revolution, in Eriksen *et al.*, *Developing a Constitution for Europe*, p. 184.
97  Editorial, *Irish Times*, 4 June 2005.
98  G. Parker, D. Dombey and V. Boland, After the Votes: Europe's Leaders Confront the Consequences of 'the Wrong Answer', *Financial Times*, 3 June 2003.
99  Editorial, *Irish Times*, 4 June 2005.
100  Ibid.
101  Miles, Editorial: The Paradox of a Popular Europe, pp. 5–6.
102  Ibid., p. 6.
103  Ibid., pp. 5–6.
104  P. Schlesinger, Changing Spaces of Political Communication: The Case of the European Union, *Political Communication* 16 (1999).
105  R. Koopmans, Analysis of Political Claims in European Print Media. Integrated Report: Cross-national, Cross-issues, Cross-time. The Transformation of Political Mobilisation and Communication in European Public Spheres, April 2004, p. 3 available at http://europub.wz.berlin.de.
106  T. Borzel, Pace-setting, Foot-dragging, and Fence-sitting: Member State Responses to Europeanization, *Journal of Common Market Studies* 40 (2002).
107  D. Held, A. McGrew, D. Goldblatt and J. Perraton, *Global Transformation: Politics, Economics and Culture* (Cambridge, 1996); see also B. Axford and R. Huggins, Towards a Post-national Polity: The Emergence of the Network Society in Europe, in D. Smith and S. Wright (eds), *Whose Europe? The Turn towards Democracy* (Oxford, 1999); C. Johnson, S. Tagil and G. Tornqvist, *Organizing European Space* (London, 2000).
108  Koopmans, Analysis of Political Claims, p. 3.
109  Ibid., p. 10.
110  See, for instance, P. Schlesinger, Europeanisation and the Media: National Identity and the Public Sphere. Working Paper no. 7, The Norwegian Research Council (Oslo, 1995); R. Koopmans and B. Pfetsch, Towards a Europeanised Public Sphere? Comparing Political Actors and the Media in Germany. ARENA Working Paper no. 23, December 2003.
111  M. Albrow, *The Global Age: State and Society beyond Modernity* (Cambridge, 1996).
112  U. Beck, The Cosmopolitan Perspective: Sociology As the Second Age of Modernity, *British Journal of Sociology* 51 (2000).
113  Held *et al.*, *Global Transformation*.
114  C. Rumford, Rethinking the State and Polity-building in the European Union: The Sociology of Globalization and the Rise of Reflexive Government. European Political Communication Working Party series, issue 4/03 (2003), available at http://europub.wz.berlin.de, p. 7; see also Y. Soysal, Changing Boundaries of Participation in European Public Spheres: Reflections on Citizenship and Civil Society, in K. Eder and B. Gierson (eds), *European Citizenship: Between National Legacies and Postnational Projects* (Oxford, 2001); M. Mann, Is There a Society Called Euro?, in R. Axtman (ed.), *Globalization and Europe: Theoretical and Empirical Investigations* (London, 1998); G. Delanty, Social Theory and European Transformation: Is There a European Society?, *Sociological Research Online* 3(1) (1998), available at http://www.socresonline.org.uk.
116  A. de Swaan, The Evolving English Language System: A Theory of Communication Potential and Language Competition, *Political Communication* 16 (1999).
117  Koopmans, Analysis of Political Claims.
118  F. Groothues, Television News and the European Public Sphere: A Preliminary Investigation. European Political Communication Working Party series, issue 6/04 (2004), p. 2, available at http://wwweuropub.wz-berlin.de.

119 T. Risse and M. Van de Steeg, An Emerging European Public Sphere? Empirical Evidence and Theoretical Clarifications. Conference on the Europeanisation of Public Spheres, Political Mobilisation, Public Communication and the European Union, Wissenschaftszentrum, Berlin, June 2003.

120 S. Hix and C. Lord, *Political Parties in the European Union* (London,1997), p. 139.

121 C. van der Eijk and M. Franklin (eds), *Choosing Europe? The European Electorate and National Politics in the Face of Union* (Ann Arbor, 1996).

122 B. Manin, *Principes du gouvernement représentatif* (Paris, 1995).

123 P. Mair, Partyless Democracy. Solving the Paradox of New Labour?, *New Left Review* 2, March/April 2000.

124 D. Aitkenhead, It's All about Me, *Guardian*, 8 July 2006, reports on some recent research that confirms a trend in contemporary politics towards individualist rather than to collectivist preferences.

125 H. Kreisi, Integrated Cross-national Report of Political Mobilization and Communication Strategies of Collective Actors. The Transformation of Political Mobilisation and Communication in European Public Spheres, July 2004, p. 1, available at http://europub.wz-berlin.de.

126 J. Blumer and D. Kavanagh, The Third Age of Political Communication, *Political Communication* 16 (1999)

127 See R. Michels, *Political Parties* (New York, 1962 edition); for a contemporary discussion, see H. Kitschelt, *The Transformation of European Social Democracy* (Cambridge, 1994).

128 Kreisi, Integrated Cross-national Report, p. 1.

129 J. Stimson, B. Michael, R. MacKuen and R. Erikson, Dynamic Representation, *American Political Science Review* 89 (1995).

130 Kreisi, Integrated Cross-national Report, p. 59.

131 M. Thatcher, The Development of Policy Network Analyses, *Journal of Theoretical Politics* 10 (1998).

132 P. Statham, J. Firmstone and E. Gray, The Impact of EU 'Constitutionalisation' on Public Claims-making over Europe: A Research Outline. European Political Communication Working Paper series, issue 10/05 (June 2005), p. 16, available at http://europub.wz.berlin.de.

133 Ibid., p. 17.

134 See, for instance, C. Husbands, Crises of National Identity As the New Moral Panics: A Modern Agenda-setting about Definitions on Nationhood, *New Community* 20(2) (1994).

135 D. Swanson and P. Mancini, Patterns of Modern Electoral Campaigning and Their Consequences, in D. Swanson and P. Mancini (eds), *Politics, Media and Modern Democracy: An International Study of Innovations in Electoral Campaigning and Their Consequences* (Westport CT, 1996).

136 E. Bleich, cited in B. Pfetsch, The Voice of the Media in European Public Sphere: Comparative Analysis of Newspaper Editorials. The Transformation of Political Mobilisation and Communication in European Public Spheres, Integrated Report, 15 July 2004, p. 7, available at http://europub.wz-berlin.de.

137 J. Dearing and E. Rogers, Agenda-setting, *Communication Concepts* 6 (1996).

138 See, for instance, G. Freeman, The Decline of Sovereignty? Politics and Immigration Restriction in Liberal States, in C. Joppke (ed.), *Challenge to the Nation State. Immigration in Western Europe and the United States* (Oxford, 1998).

139 F. Baumgautner and B. Jones, Positive and Negative Feedback in Politics, in F. Baumgautner and B. Jones (eds), *Policy Dynamics* (Chicago, 2002).

140 P. Schlesinger, From Cultural Defence to Political Culture: Media, Politics and Collective Identity in the European Union, *Media, Culture and Society* 19(93) (1997); and P. Schlesinger and D. Kevin, Can the European Union Become a Sphere of Publics?, in E. O. Eriksen and J. E. Fossum (eds), *Democracy in the European Union: Integration through Deliberation?* (London, 2000).

141 Koopmans, Analysis of Political Claims, p. 3.
142 Ibid., p. 5.
143 See T. Risse, How Do We Know a European Public Sphere When We See One? Theoretical Clarifications and Empirical Indicators. Paper for IDNET Workshop, 'Europeanisation' of the Public Sphere, EUI Florence, February 2002, available at http://web.fu-berlin.de/atasp/texte/pi5s1otn.pdf.
144 Risse and Van de Steeg, An Emerging European Public Sphere, p. 22; see also D. Della Porta, M. Caiani, L. Mosca and S. Valenza, Forms of Europeanisation of the Public Sphere in Italy in a Cross-time, Cross-issue and Cross-media Perspective. Conference on the Europeanisation of Public Spheres, Political Mobilisation, Public Communication and the European Union, Wissenschaftszentrum, Berlin, June 2003, available at http://europub.wz-berlin.de/conferences.en.htm.
145 Groothues, Television News and the European Public Sphere, p. 2.
146 See C. Rumford, *European Cohesion? Contradictions in EU Integration* (Basingstoke, 2000); C. Rumford, European Cohesion? Globalization, Autonomization, and the Dynamics of EU Integration, *Innovation: The European Journal of Social Science Research* 13(92) (2000).
147 V. Bornschier, European Processes and the State of the European Union. Paper delivered at the European Sociological Association Conference, University of Essex, 1997, available at http://www.suz.unizh.ch/bornschier/european_processes.pdf.
148 This is useful evidence precisely because so far much of the work on the issue of a European public space has been normative/prescriptive rather than empirical. See, for instance, J. Habermas, Towards a European Political Community, *Society* 39 (2002); J. Habermas, *The Structural Transformation of the Public Sphere* (Cambridge, 1989).
149 See W. Streeck, Competitive Solidarity: Rethinking the 'European Social Policy Regime'?, in G. Marks, F. Scharpf, P. Schmitter and W. Streeck, *Governance in the European Union* (London, 1996); L. Hooghe, EU Cohesion Policy and Competing Models of European Capitalism, *Journal of Common Market Studies* 36(4) (1998).
150 Groothues, Television News and the European Public Sphere, p. 2.
151 D. Kevin, *Europe in the Media: A Comparison of Reporting, Representation, and Rhetoric in National Media Systems in Europe* (London, 2003).
152 Koopmans, Analysis of Political Claims, p. 5.
153 Ibid.
154 Groothues, Television News and the European Public Sphere, p. 4.
155 Koopmans, Analysis of Political Claims, p. 24.
156 Ibid., p. 28.
157 Ibid.
158 Ibid.
159 Ibid., p. 29; see also Koopmans and Pfetsch, Towards a Europeanised Public Sphere.
160 Koopmans, Analysis of Political Claims, pp. 29–30.
161 See Convention: Unknown by European Citizens, *Eurobarometer*, 25 July 2003.
162 Statham *et al.*, The Impact of EU 'Constitutionalisation'.
163 Koopmans, Analysis of Political Claims, p. 30.
164 Ibid.
165 D. Dinan, Governance and Institutions: The Convention and the Intergovernmental Conference in Lee Miles (ed.), *Journal of Common Market Studies Annual Review of the European Union, 2003/2004* (Oxford, 2004), p. 42.
166 Duchêne, *Jean Monnet*, p. 363.
167 M. Maduro, How Constitutional Can the European Union Be? The Tension Between Intergovernmentalism and Constitutionalism in the European Union, in Jean Monnet Working Paper 5/04, Symposium: *Altneuland*, pp. 39–40.
168 Manifesto for Europe: 20 Steps to Relaunch the EU. Centre for European Reform, Institut Montaigne Manifesto, 24 October 2005.

169 Ibid.
170 Maduro, How Constitutional Can the European Union Be, p. 16.
171 Ibid., p. 11.
172 Anatole Keletsky quoted in the *National Review*, 20 June 2005.
173 H. Arendt, *Men in Dark Times* (New York, 1968).
174 Simon Jenkins, The Peasants Revolt, *Sunday Times*, 5 June 2005.
175 R. Putnam, *Making Democracy Work: Civic Traditions in Modern Italy* (Princeton, 1993),
176 Dinan, Governance and Institutions, p. 42.
177 Maduro, How Constitutional Can the European Union Be, pp. 52–3.
178 Ibid., p. 53.
179 D. Mitrany, *The Progress of International Government* (London, 1933), p. 118.
180 Quoted by Jenkins, Peasants Revolt.
181 Maduro, How Constitutional Can the European Union Be, p. 33.
182 Ibid.
183 Ibid., p. 41.

# Index

Notes and tables are indicated immediately after the page number, e.g. Hirschl, R. centralisation 542n96.